Further Praise for

HUNTING IN THE SHADOWS

"Seth Jones is a gifted writer and scholar. His research, attention to detail, and narrative skills make *Hunting in the Shadows* essential reading." —Steve Coll, author of *Ghost Wars: The Secret History of the CIA, Afghanistan, and Bin Laden, from the Soviet Invasion to September 10, 2001*

"Seth Jones was called to the war zones by commanders of special operations forces to advise them on the nuances of the places, people, and events of high importance in our pursuit of terrorists. . . . [A] clear and engaging account that draws on Seth's long experience in the region." —Admiral Eric T. Olson, U.S. Navy (Ret), former commander of United States Special Operations Command

"A well-documented and perceptive look into the shadowy world of al-Qaeda since 9/11, and a clear-headed assessment of how effective the War on Terror has been in containing it. . . . [A]n important contribution to public debate on America's security and how best to achieve it in a changing Muslim world." —Vali Nasr, author of *The Rise of Islamic Capitalism: Why the New Muslim Middle Class Is the Key to Defeating Extremism*

"Jones . . . explores the waxing and waning of al-Qaeda in this sprawling narrative history. . . . [A] timely addition to the debate over the way forward against international terrorism." —*Publishers Weekly*

"The author ably organizes all the pieces of the puzzle. . . . From a knowledgeable g⸺⸺⸺⸺ ⸺⸺htful study of the pattern of violence and response." —*Kirkus Reviews*

HUNTING IN THE SHADOWS

ALSO BY SETH G. JONES

In the Graveyard of Empires: America's War in Afghanistan

HUNTING IN THE SHADOWS

THE PURSUIT OF AL QA'IDA SINCE 9/11

SETH G. JONES

W. W. NORTON & COMPANY · New York · London

For information about permission to reproduce selections from this book,
write to Permissions, W. W. Norton & Company, Inc.,
500 Fifth Avenue, New York, NY 10110

For information about special discounts for bulk purchases, please contact
W. W. Norton Special Sales at specialsales@wwnorton.com or 800-233-4830

Manufacturing by RR Donnelley, Harrisonburg, VA
Book design by Dana Sloan
Production manager: Anna Oler

Library of Congress Cataloging-in-Publication Data

Jones, Seth G., 1972–
 Hunting in the shadows : the pursuit of
Al Qa'ida since 9/11 / Seth G. Jones. — 1st ed.
    p. cm.
Includes bibliographical references and index.
ISBN 978-0-393-08145-9 (hbk.)
1. Qaida (Organization) 2. Terrorism—United States—Prevention.
3. Terrorism—Prevention. 4. Terrorism—Middle East. I. Title.
HV6432.5.Q2J66 2012
363.325'1560973—dc23

                                                            2012000108

ISBN 978-0-393-34547-6 pbk.

W. W. Norton & Company, Inc.
500 Fifth Avenue, New York, N.Y. 10110
www.wwnorton.com

W. W. Norton & Company Ltd.
Castle House, 75/76 Wells Street, London W1T 3QT

1 2 3 4 5 6 7 8 9 0

CONTENTS

PART III: THE THIRD WAVE

PART IV: THE FOURTH WAVE?

LIST OF MAPS AND GRAPHS

HUNTING IN THE SHADOWS

A MODEL INVESTIGATION

SURVEILLANCE TEAMS FROM London's Metropolitan Police and MI5, the United Kingdom's domestic intelligence agency, were staking out a brick house at 386A Forest Road in Walthamstow. It was late July 2006, and the weather was unusually hot in northeast London: 89 degrees Fahrenheit, with blue skies and a gentle breeze out of the southwest. Number 386A was a three-bedroom flat in a block of close-set houses. MI5 and the police were monitoring Abdulla Ahmed Ali and Tanvir Hussain, who had bought the flat on July 20 for about $250,000.[1] Walthamstow is famous for its market, which stretches nearly a mile along High Street. In recent years the city's Muslim population had swelled, and many of the families were of Pakistani descent. Large-scale immigration from Pakistan to Britain began in the 1950s; by 2005, according the British government, nearly 50 percent of Muslims in England were Pakistani.[2]

As Hussain and Ali walked into the flat, they sensed they were being watched.

"How is the skin infection you were telling me about? Has it got worse or is the cream working?" a contact in Pakistan asked Ali, using a Yahoo! e-mail account.[3]

British and American intelligence agents, who were monitoring their communications, believed the e-mail was sent by Rashid

Rauf, referred to by Ali as Paps or Papa. A known al Qa'ida operative, Rauf had once been a member of the Pakistani terrorist group Jaish-e-Mohammad and was married to a relative of the group's founder, Maulana Masood Azhar. Rauf was born in England to Pakistani parents, who brought him up in Birmingham, where his father was a baker. The CIA had been tracking Rauf on suspicion that he was involved in a number of terrorist plots overseas.

"Listen, it's confirmed," replied Ali a few days later. "I have fever. Sometimes when I go out in the sun to meet people, I feel hot. By the way I set up my music shop now. I only need to sort out the opening time. I need stock."[4]

"Do you think you can still open the shop with this skin problem? Is it only minor or can you still sort an opening time without the skin problem worsening?" came the reply from Pakistan the next day.[5]

"I will still open the shop," Ali responded. "I don't think it's so bad that I can't work. But if I feel really ill, I'll let you know. I also have to arrange for the printers to be picked up and stored . . . I have done all my prep, all I have to do is sort out opening timetable and bookings."[6]

British intelligence officials, who had dubbed the investigation Operation Overt, believed that "skin infection" meant surveillance. Abdulla Ahmed Ali's concerns were, of course, justified. British authorities hadn't yet figured out exactly what the cell was planning, but they knew enough to become alarmed, especially on the heels of the successful July 7 terrorist attack in London a year earlier, which had killed fifty-two people and injured more than seven hundred others. In domestic and international intelligence circles, anxiety was growing that Ali, Hussain, and several of their friends were planning a major terrorist operation.

A Flood of Martyr Operations

Abdulla Ahmed Ali and Tanvir Hussain had raised no red flags as students. "They were normal boys," recalled Mark Hough, a teacher at Aveling Park School, a secondary school of six hundred students that Ali had attended ten years before. "Ali was a good sportsman, a nice lad, and a typical fourteen-year-old."[7] Hanif Qadir, who ran a youth center called the Active Change Foundation, came to a similar conclusion: "Abdulla Ahmed Ali was a very upstanding young man."[8] Qadir and several colleagues had established the foundation in 2003 to provide a haven for estranged youth at risk for violent extremism, and Ali and several friends had worked out at its gym.

Ali, whom his friends dubbed "the Emir," was now twenty-five years old, a husband, and the father of a two-year-old son. He was taller than most of his friends and walked with a self-confident swagger. His charismatic personality and candidness attracted friends and frequently placed him at the center of attention. "I would describe [Ali] as a strong character, someone who's upfront, which I liked about him," one of his friends later remarked. "He would speak his mind."[9]

Ali possessed a good education and a degree in computer systems engineering. Born in East London, he was one of eight children from a successful first-generation Pakistani immigrant family. He had been devout since age fifteen, when he had become a follower of the Tablighi Jamaat movement, which had been founded in 1927 in Delhi to encourage Muslims to adhere more closely to the practices of the Prophet Muhammad. Ali had short-cropped hair and brown eyes. He kept his beard neatly trimmed, though it became patchy below his cheekbones, and he had a pockmark just above the bridge of his nose. Ali wore Western clothes and looked like a typical British young man. But privately he had developed a profound rage at the United States and Britain for their military operations in Afghanistan, Iraq, and other Muslim countries.

"Thanks to God, I swear by Allah, I have the desire since the age of fifteen or sixteen to participate in jihad in the path of Allah," he bragged in a video produced in late July 2006, pointing his index finger at the camera. "Stop meddling in our affairs and we will leave you alone. Otherwise expect floods of martyr operations against you, and we will take our revenge and anger, ripping amongst your people and scattering the people and your body parts and your people's body parts responsible for these wars and oppression decorating the streets."[10]

Ali's friend Tanvir Hussain was also twenty-five years old. Born in Blackburn, Lancashire, he had moved with his family when he was a young child to Leyton, a high-density suburban area of East London that boasted sizable numbers of ethnic minorities, including Pakistanis. In previous days the neighborhood had been home to the film director Alfred Hitchcock and the soccer superstar David Beckham. Hussain met Ali in secondary school. He went on to work as a part-time postman and studied business and information systems at Middesex University in northwest London. He was educated, gregarious, and a respectable athlete, excelling at cricket and soccer. He had an olive complexion, a crew cut that gave him a boyish look, dark brown eyes, and a short beard. His nose, which was crooked and jutted to the right, looked like it had been broken in a bar fight.

Hussain had dabbled with drinking, drugs, and girls in college, before finding Islam. He blamed the West for killing Muslims abroad and vowed to commit suicide to kill Westerners. "You know, I only wish I could do this again—you know, come back and do this again," he shrieked into the camera in his own video confessional, "and just do it again and again until people come to their senses and realize, you know, don't mess with the Muslims."[11]

Links to Pakistan

What most alarmed British and American officials, however, were the young men's connections with al Qa'ida operatives. One of the most notable was Rashid Rauf, who was the primary conduit between al Qa'ida in Pakistan and Abdulla Ahmed Ali and his colleagues. In 2003 and 2004, Ali had worked in Pakistan for a charity called Crescent Relief, which was run by Rashid Rauf's family.

He returned to the United Kingdom in January 2005 and then made several trips back to Pakistan in 2005 and 2006.[12] When he returned in June 2006, British police and intelligence officials were sufficiently interested in him to open his luggage. Inside they found a large number of batteries, the powdered soft drink Tang, and other possible components of a homemade bomb.[13]

Ali kept in regular contact with Rashid Rauf and others in Pakistan via e-mail, text messages, and phone calls. The ability of the plotters to visit Pakistan, which many of them did in the years before 2006, and remain in contact with operatives such as Rauf transformed them from novices to professional terrorists. They became knowledgeable about explosives, including the use of hydrogen peroxide as a key component in bombs. Interacting with radicalized al Qa'ida operatives in Pakistan made them more committed to terrorism. They were savvier, utilizing countersurveillance techniques they had learned in training camps in Pakistan. They also had coaching, operational guidance, and encouragement from Pakistan during the planning process. Several of the e-mails, presumably from Rashid Rauf, prodded Ali and his colleagues to move faster. On July 20, 2006, Ali's contact in Pakistan told him, "You need to get a move on. Let me know when you can get it for me."[14]

The most senior al Qa'ida official involved in the plot was Abu Ubaydah al-Masri, al Qa'ida's head of external operations, who had helped plan the operation from Pakistan. He had been an al Qa'ida commander in Konar Province and had worked his way to the top of al Qa'ida's leadership structure. Rauf appeared to be a middleman between Abu Ubaydah al-Masri and the UK plotters. In addition, British intelligence identified one of Abdulla Ahmed Ali's associates as Mohammed Gulzar, a native of Birmingham who had left the United Kingdom in 2002 after being implicated with Rashid Rauf in the murder of Rauf's uncle. Galzar had returned to Britain from South Africa in 2006 under the false name Altaf Ravat.[15]

Another associate was Mohammed al-Ghabra, a twenty-eight-year-old Syrian-born naturalized British citizen who lived with his mother and sister in London. According to U.S. government documents, which were shared with the British, Ghabra had organized travel for several individuals to meet al Qa'ida leaders in Pakistan and Iraq and undertake jihad training.[16] U.S. and UK intelligence agencies suspected that Ghabra was an al Qa'ida facilitator. In fact, the British began Operation Overt because they came across Abdulla Ahmed Ali's cell when they were monitoring the activities of Ghabra and his network of associates.

American Concerns

By 2006 government officials on both sides of the Atlantic Ocean had become increasingly concerned about a terrorist attack against one or more airplanes in Europe or the United States. The FBI had sent MI5 a 2003 bulletin titled "Possible Hijacking Tactic for Using Aircraft as Weapons," which warned that suicide terrorists might be plotting to hijack transatlantic aircraft by smuggling explosives past airport security and assembling the bombs on board. It concluded that "components of improvised explosive devices can be smuggled onto an aircraft, concealed in either clothing or personal carry-on items like shampoo and medicine bottles, and assembled on board. In many cases of suspicious passenger activity, incidents have taken place in the aircraft's forward lavatory."[17]

The CIA and other U.S. intelligence agencies helped track the cell's support network in Pakistan, and the FBI and the Department of Homeland Security focused on links to the United States. Michael Chertoff, secretary of the Department of Homeland Security, chaired a series of meetings on Operation Overt, using the Roosevelt Room in the White House for several of them. Most of the participants, including John Negroponte, the director of national intelligence, were confident that the British had the investigation under control.[18]

At the FBI, director Robert Mueller called a meeting of his senior staff after being briefed on the plot. "Our first question should be, what are the plotters' capabilities?" said Philip Mudd, who was deputy director of the FBI's National Security Branch, which oversaw counterterrorism and counterintelligence investigations. "Is there an imminent threat? Do they have access to weapons and explosives?"

The advisers nodded. The answer appeared to be yes.

"Second," he continued, "what is their intent?"

The available evidence suggested that they were targeting flights.

"Third, what are their overseas connections?"

The answer was disturbing. Ali and Hussain were in touch with al Qa'ida operatives in Pakistan. This connection made it one of the most serious plots—perhaps the *most* serious plot—targeting the United States since September 11, 2001.[19]

Others agreed. "As an operation," remarked Art Cummings, the FBI's special agent in charge of the Counterterrorism Division and Intelligence Branch at the Washington field office, "it did not appear to be just a homegrown plot. There were growing signs that it had al Qa'ida direction."[20]

Cummings was a rising star at the FBI. His father had worked at the U.S. Department of Agriculture and later been assigned to Pakistan and Brazil, where Cummings spent time as a child. He attended high school in Bowie, Maryland, a suburban town 15 miles northeast of Washington, and served in the U.S. military as an elite Navy SEAL. He had also learned Mandarin Chinese, which came in handy when he investigated Chinese espionage cases for the FBI.[21] By the summer of 2006, Cummings had settled into his job in the Washington field office. He hit the gym religiously, often sailed on the weekends, and most days carried a .40-caliber Glock. At forty-eight, he had magnetic blue eyes and a charming personality. But he was not afraid to be blunt, and Director Mueller occasionally chided him for having "sharp elbows." When asked by the head of a prominent Muslim organization why the FBI was so interested in the Muslim community, Cummings was frank. "I can name the homegrown cells, all of whom are Muslim, all of whom were seeking to murder Americans," he replied. "It's not the Irish, it's not the French, it's not the Catholics, it's not the Protestants, it's the Muslims."[22] Cummings was intensely passionate about his job and now devoted his time to focusing on the airlines plot.

Long before September 11, al Qa'ida had considered using airplanes as weapons. Cummings and other FBI and CIA officials remembered Operation Bojinka, a failed plot by al Qa'ida operatives Khalid Sheikh Mohammed and his nephew, Ramzi Yousef, to blow up twelve airliners and their passengers as they flew from Asia to the United States. The plot was uncovered in the Philippines in 1995 after a fire at Yousef's safe house brought him to the attention of local police. Files found on his laptop contained flight data on aircraft, including departure times, flight numbers, flight durations, and aircraft types. Yousef, who had been involved in planning the 1993 World Trade Center attack in New York, was eventually arrested in February 1995 in Islamabad by Pakistani authorities, with assistance from the United States. Abu Ubaydah al-Masri had apparently drawn on lessons from Operation Bojinka when instructing Abdulla Ahmed Ali and his network.[23]

Preparing the Bombs

In July 2006, MI5 and Metropolitan Police kept Ali under close surveillance, even watching him when he played tennis in the local park with Hussain and other friends. British security agents originally calculated that Ali's and Hussain's cell consisted of at least eight members. But they eventually discovered more than fifty potential members who were planning several waves of attacks, forcing MI5 and law enforcement officials to deploy nearly thirty surveillance teams to monitor the suspects. The security agents watched them around the clock, following them on shopping trips to supermarkets, pharmacies, and garden centers. One of their most unusual purchases was a large quantity of Lucozade and Oasis, energy drinks they found in local supermarkets. After a few weeks, there was a major breakthrough. British intelligence used an informant to get bugged phones into the hands of the cell members. This was to have a remarkable impact on better understanding the plot.

One day Ali met a young man in the park, well outside of eavesdropping range. The surveillance team followed the new suspect to High Wycombe, a town of about 100,000 people 30 miles northwest of London. British intelligence identified the individual as twenty-six-year-old Assad Ali Sarwar, who they soon discovered was the principal bomb maker.

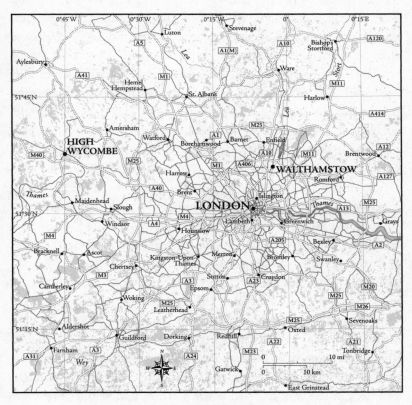

Figure 1: Map of Greater London

Sarwar was heavyset, with dark bushy eyebrows, fleshy cheeks, full lips, and an overgenerous nose. Unlike Ali and Hussain, he didn't grow a beard but sported a thin layer of stubble. Sarwar was an unemployed dropout from Brunel University, a medium-tier British school. At the time he was living with his parents in High Wycombe. Between 2002 and 2005 he held a variety of jobs: postman, shelf-stacker at Asda supermarket, security guard, and information technology worker for British Telecom. He had a reputation for being too direct, sometimes to the point of being boorish. He first traveled to Pakistan in 2003 with the Islamic Medical Association charity and met Ali, and he returned in 2005 when he met a man called Jamil Shah, who taught him how to make bombs. Sarwar's role in buying bomb-making material and mixing ingredients suggests that he received more technical training in Pakistan than other members of the cell.

British intelligence soon discovered that Sarwar was mixing hydrogen peroxide with several other chemicals and storing the mixture in his garage. Hydrogen peroxide is a pale blue liquid, slightly more viscous than water. Most people use it for bleaching hair, cleaning cuts, and other household purposes. But when mixed with certain ingredients, it is highly sensitive to heat, electrical shock, and friction and can be ignited with fire or electrical charges. More important, it is a critical ingredient in such highly explosive compounds as hexamethylene triperoxide diamine (HMTD) and triacetone triperoxide (TATP), which had been used by al Qa'ida and other terrorists in previous attacks.

MI5 and police surveillance teams continued to monitor the brick building on Forest Road, but they needed to get inside to see what the cell was doing. One night when no one was home, a small team broke into the flat with a night-vision camera and videotaped the items Ali and Hussain had bought on their shopping expeditions, including the Lucozade and Oasis bottles. They also installed a camera in the wall to provide live pictures and sound. The position of the camera wasn't ideal, since it showed only a partial view of the flat, but it was good enough to give British authorities a sense of what was going on. MI5 and the police were trying to understand everything about the individuals they were monitoring—they watched the suspects during the day and found out who their friends and associates were, which restaurants and gyms they used, and which Internet sites they surfed. They bugged their flat, tapped their phone lines, tracked their Internet and mobile phone usage, watched their credit card and bank transactions, and covertly monitored their movements, all in an effort to build as complete a picture of the terrorists as possible.[24]

While Ali and Hussain suspected British intelligence might be monitoring their movements, they had no idea that they were being watched on a live video link as they prepared ingredients for the bombs in the flat. Surveillance teams observed them as they drilled small holes in the bottoms of the energy drink bottles and took turns inserting syringes into the holes, extracting the sugary water, and squirting in a mixture of hydrogen peroxide that Sarwar had concocted. They then injected food coloring into each bottle, restoring the appearance of a sports drink, and filled the hole in the bottom so that the seal on the cap remained unbroken.

The homemade bomb was ingenious, though anyone carrying it onto a plane would have to partially assemble it after going through airport security. To set off the bomb, each terrorist was supposed to heat up a low-voltage bulb that was sitting in either HMTD or TATP, using power from a disposable camera. The explosion would then initiate the main charge—the hydrogen peroxide mix—and bring down the airplane. The terrorists also mixed Tang with hydrogen peroxide and other ingredients to color the liquid and create a more powerful explosion. Ali had scribbled notes to help him remember:

> Clean batteries. Perfect disguise. Drink bottles. Lucozade, orange, red. Oasis, orange, red. Mouthwash, blue, red. Calculate exact drops of Tang and colour. Make in HP [hydrogen

peroxide]. Check time to fill each bottle. Check time taken to dilute in HP. Decide on which battery to use for D. Note: small is best.[25]

If they could get the measurements right, a bomb in a Lucozade or Oasis bottle could contain half a kilogram of explosive. A bomb of that size could be catastrophic if placed appropriately on an airplane, especially in a pressurized cabin at 30,000 feet. Surveillance teams overheard the plotters discussing the construction of eighteen bombs for their attack, suggesting that the cell planned to destroy nine passenger flights in midair. Each cell member intended to carry two bottled explosives through security in case one of them was taken away.

In July, with British police and intelligence agents listening, Ali and Hussain discussed potential targets.

"I wanted to find out from the travel agent . . . the ten most popular places that British people holiday," noted Hussain.

"We got six people in it. Me, Omar B., Ibo, Arrow and Waheed," responded Ali, referring to the number of terrorists. "There's another three units, there's another three dudes."

"There's another three more, huh?" Hussain queried. "Seven, eight, nine, ten, eleven, twelve, thirteen—that's 15 . . . 18. Phew! Think of it, yeah."[26]

With the help of colleagues in Pakistan, the British terrorists had learned from past plots and attacks. Their decision to disguise the explosives as sports drinks was calculated to exploit vulnerabilities in airline security, which would enable them to smuggle the bottles through screening. In late July 2006, many cell members had applied for new passports by claiming that their previously issued passports had been lost or stolen. British officials believed that the new passports may have included pictures of the plotters that showed them as Westernized in appearance and would have erased all stamps and visas, especially to countries of concern, such as Pakistan.[27] Moreover, the cell was clearly watching UK and international security agencies and their security practices and probing for weaknesses. The media coverage that had followed many of the previous plots and attacks, including the availability of transcripts from the legal trials of the accused, provided useful information for terrorists on government tactics, techniques, and procedures.

Furthermore, the plotters used coded language in their communications, referring to government surveillance as "skin infection" and "fever," to their bomb factory as the "music shop," to a U.S. airplane carrier as the "bus service," and to a dry run of the attack as "the rapping concert rehearsal."[28] They were also careful to meet in large open areas that were beyond eavesdropping range, in some cases lying facedown to communicate to minimize detection.[29]

Trial Run

In mid-July, Ali's contact in Pakistan, presumably Rashid Rauf, encouraged the cell members to go on a trial run to test airport security.

"Hi gorgeous," he wrote. "Well nice to hear from you . . . Your friend can go for his rapping concert rehearsal . . . But somewhere popular would be good . . . Make sure he goes on the bus service which is most common over there."[30]

British police and intelligence officers followed Ali into an Internet café, where he downloaded transatlantic flight schedules. He appeared to be particularly interested in United and American Airlines, as well as Air Canada. Surveillance teams then heard Ali and Hussain discussing possible destinations, including Washington, D.C., New York, Chicago, San Francisco, Los Angeles, Montreal, and Toronto. British authorities believed that the terrorist cell intended to explode the liquid bombs over the Atlantic.

Throughout their final preparations, the plotters maintained close contact with al Qa'ida operatives in Pakistan, especially Rashid Rauf, who provided operational and tactical guidance. While in

Pakistan in June 2006, Ali had registered two e-mail addresses to communicate with Rauf. For one he claimed to be an American woman called Tippu Khjan from Shepherdstown, West Virginia. In the second address he used the identity Jameel Masood, again filling in "United States" under the location heading. Sarwar also set up e-mail accounts under false names.

Around August 3, British government officials informed their American counterparts that the plotters were probably planning to detonate the bombs on flights to the United States and Canada. This raised the stakes for U.S. officials. Willie Hulon, who headed the FBI's National Security Branch, called Art Cummings at the Washington field office and placed him in charge of the FBI's response. Cummings jumped into his Chrysler 300, switched on the flashing blue and red lights, and raced to the National Counterterrorism Center in McLean, Virginia. After being briefed on the intelligence, he suggested that the FBI begin issuing orders for wiretaps and physical surveillance of people in the United States who were suspected of having connections to the plot.

"Our focus," he said, should be "Is there anything bad that could kill us here?" He told his agents, "Give me everything we've got on these guys. I need to know everybody who's touched any of these guys ever in their lives, from the time they were born. Every person these guys have ever spoken to, paid, run into."

Cummings's list highlighted the complexity of the FBI's response and the quantity of information that the Bureau needed to collect and analyze. He wanted to know "who went to school with them, had any type of contact with them, any type of communication with family members, friends of family, all of them. I want financials, associates, travel. Start giving me numbers that I can start working with." But that wasn't all. "Put on technical surveillance 24/7," he continued, referring to twenty-four-hour wiretaps and electronic bugs. "Wake 'em up, put 'em to bed. Every single piece has to be reviewed and looked at, not just for threats but for opportunity."[31]

By late July 2006, Assad Ali Sarwar had prepared the hydrogen peroxide. Some of it was later recovered from his garage in a boiled-down form, a concentration that could be used for an attack. Sarwar also buried a suitcase that contained bomb components, including thermometers, citric acid, hexamine, hydrogen peroxide, syringes, and glass flasks under the roots of a tree in the High Wycombe woods. In a nearby wooded area, search teams discovered 20 liters of hydrogen peroxide in 5-liter containers hidden in black garbage bags. "We found out we was under surveillance," said Abdulla Ahmed Ali, "so I told [Sarwar] to hide it."[32]

There were other disturbing developments. On July 27 surveillance teams listened to cell members putting together martyrdom videos at 386A Forest Road. Abdulla Ahmed Ali made his video using a Sony Handycam camera and angrily addressed Westerners. "Sheikh Osama [bin Laden] warned you many times to leave our lands or you will be destroyed," he counseled. "And now the time has come for you to be destroyed, and you have nothing but to expect that floods of martyr operations, volcanoes, anger, and revenge are erupting among your capital."[33] The same day Tanvir Hussain produced a similar video warning that "collateral damage is going to be inevitable and people are going to die."[34]

On July 31, British intelligence and police found two plastic bags in East London that contained wires attached to miniature bulbs with exposed filaments designed to spark liquid bombs. The DNA and fingerprints on the bags and material belonged to Tanvir Hussain. On August 7, British home secretary John Reid and MI5, worried that cell members had turned to final preparations and that attacks were imminent, alerted key cabinet members about the plot. On August 8 the secretary of state for transport, Douglas Alexander, was given a full intelligence briefing on Operation Overt while on vacation in the Isle of Man.

The next day Alexander flew back to London in a Ministry of Defense helicopter. The director-general of MI5, Eliza Manningham-Buller, updated him on unfolding events, noting that "there was an alleged plot to bring down a number of aircraft over the Atlantic." She added that "there was surveillance of the suspects under way. And there would be an operational judgment made by the police as to the right time to take action against the individuals who were under surveillance."[35] Manningham-Buller was the daughter of Viscount Dilhorne, who had served as solicitor general, attorney general, and lord chancellor in Conservative governments from 1951 to 1964. Growing up in the company of ministers, she knew how to work with intelligence agents and government officials.[36]

Back in Washington, senior White House, Department of Homeland Security, CIA, and FBI officials were equally alarmed, and they remained in regular contact with the British. Art Cummings observed that U.S. government officials were growing restless because the British had not yet arrested the plotters. Indeed, British officials were willing to let the surveillance efforts continue in order to collect intelligence on the plotters' support network. On Wednesday, August 9, Home Secretary Reid told colleagues that an attack "was not imminent. There was sufficient time left to take any action should it prove necessary."[37]

That day cell member Umar Islam made a martyrdom video in the flat on 386A Forest Road. "If you want to kill our women and children, then the same thing will happen to you," he warned. "This is not a joke. If you think you can go into our land and do what you are doing in Iraq, Afghanistan, and Palestine and keep on supporting those that are fighting against the Muslims and think it will not come back on to your doorstep, then you have another thing coming." Umar Islam then acknowledged that he had been inspired by Osama bin Laden and Taliban leader Mullah Muhammad Omar. "Mullah Omar, Sheikh Osama, keep on going and remain firm. You inspired many of the Muslims and inspired me personally to follow the true path of the Prophet."[38]

Ali directed Umar Islam during the videotaping. "Relax, don't try and speak posh English. Speak normal English that you normally speak. When you mention Allah, do that," Ali continued, extending his index finger upward and then moving it downward violently for emphasis. "When you're making a point, point away, that hand movement, you're warning the *kuffar*. Give a bit of aggression, yeah, a bit loudly. We're higher than everyone else."[39]

Umar Islam had narrowly avoided blowing the operation. A few days before, his wife had stumbled on the script of his suicide video, which had accidentally fallen out of his pocket. "I came in, I saw it on the table," said Islam, referring to the script. His wife picked it up. "Is this what I think it is?" she asked. He retorted, "Don't ask me no questions."[40] Despite his wife's protests, he refused to explain or discuss the matter further.

The Arrests

By August 9, John Reid was still comfortable enough with the pace of the investigation that he attended a soccer game that evening between his beloved Celtic team and Chelsea in London at Stamford Bridge, Chelsea's home stadium. But a development in Pakistan changed the course of the operation. Pakistan's intelligence agency, the Directorate for Inter-Services Intelligence (ISI), arrested Rashid Rauf. British officials believed that once cell members in the UK heard about the arrest, they would stop planning and destroy the evidence.

The British were furious. The CIA, which had been monitoring Rauf in Pakistan, was concerned that he was preparing to go into hiding and had encouraged the arrest. He was believed to be developing several international terrorist plots in addition to the British one, and American and Pakistani intelligence officials wanted to interrogate him. U.S. government officials had reached their risk threshold. It unnerved them that the plotters in the UK were on the verge of launching an attack. As Michael Chertoff acknowledged, "We needed to bring the case to resolution before there was a serious prospect that it might become active."[41] Over at the FBI, Philip Mudd agreed. Rashid Rauf was targeting the United States, and there was a narrowing window of opportunity to capture him. Agents had good intelligence on his current location, but that might change in an instant. American officials were worried that he would go underground in Pakistan's tribal areas, where CIA coverage was spotty. "If we didn't catch him now," Mudd argued, "he would likely disappear." And they might not get another shot at him. "Rauf was a core plotter," emphasized Mudd. "He was a big deal."[42]

For Art Cummings, the capture of Rashid Rauf illustrated a lingering struggle between the CIA and the FBI. Rauf had been seized with his laptop, but the CIA refused to share the laptop—or the information in it—with the FBI. "The irony," said Cummings, "is that we didn't have enough information to prosecute a case against Rashid Rauf in the United States if the Pakistanis extradited him to us, even though they were unlikely to do so."[43]

Senior British officials were stunned that they had not been given adequate warning of Rauf's arrest. They had been caught completely off guard. Even more disturbing, Rauf soon escaped from Pakistani custody. He and his police escort entered a mosque in Rawalpindi to pray; Rauf went to the bathroom, jumped out the window, shaved his beard, and fled to Pakistan's tribal areas. U.S. and British intelligence agents strongly believed that the police officers escorting him facilitated his escape. The United States eventually tracked him down, and two years later he was killed in a drone strike.

On August 9, 2006, however, with Rauf still in Pakistani custody, British police suddenly had to arrest a number of suspects whom they hadn't planned to seize for several more days. "We believed the Americans had demanded the arrest and we were angry we had not been informed. We were being forced to take action, to arrest a number of suspects, which normally would have required days of planning and briefing," remarked Andy Hayman of the Metropolitan Police. "Fearful for the safety of American lives, the U.S. authorities had been getting edgy, seeking reassurance that this was not going to slip through our hands. We moved from having congenial conversations to eyeball-to-eyeball confrontations."[44]

At 9:30 p.m. on August 9, the UK government's crisis committee, referred to as COBRA, held an emergency meeting in Cabinet Office Briefing Room A, which was in a secure cellar in Whitehall between the Houses of Parliament and Trafalgar Square and gave the committee its name. The room is linked to Downing Street, where the British prime minister lives, and other government buildings, such as the Foreign and Commonwealth Office and the Cabinet Office, through a series of corridors. John Reid chaired the meeting wearing sunglasses because of an eye infection.

The meeting included senior officials from MI5, the military, police, and other relevant ministers, such as Douglas Alexander. "There was an air of tension and determination," Reid recalled.[45] In light of Rauf's arrest, the UK government decided to arrest the cell members immediately. The police then moved quickly, with the support of MI5.

That evening, Abdulla Ahmed Ali was saying his prayers outside his car, which was parked at Walthamstow's town hall, when police found him. Assad Ali Sarwar was there as well. Ali's notebook contained a list of ingredients: batteries, drink bottles, and hydrogen peroxide. In his pocket police found the USB memory stick he'd used to download information on transatlantic flights from the Internet café.[46] They also found Umar Islam's martyrdom tape, which had been produced only a few hours earlier.

"What's this?" inquired the police officer who had grabbed Ali.

"A USB stick," he responded.

"Whose is it?" the officer queried.

"Mine," said Ali.

"What's on it?" the officer continued, growing impatient.

"Holiday destinations in America," remarked Ali.[47]

The game was up for Ali and his network. By Friday, August 10, all the main suspects were in custody and had been charged with conspiracy to commit murder.

A Victory

Operation Overt was a model investigation—one of the first major successes against al Qa'ida outside Afghanistan and Pakistan since the September 11 attacks. At the time, skepticism had been growing in the United States about whether al Qa'ida was still a threat. Operation Overt offered a stark reminder that al Qa'ida and its allies posed a serious danger to the United States and other Western countries. Abdulla Ahmed Ali, Tanvir Hussain, and Assad Ali Sarwar were eventually convicted, in 2009, of plotting to use liquid explosives to blow up airplanes, the culmination of an impressive effort by the Crown Prosecution Service, the UK government authority responsible for prosecuting criminal cases investigated by the police. Ali was sentenced to a minimum of forty years in prison, Sarwar to a minimum of thirty-six years, and Hussain to thirty-two years. Umar Islam was convicted of conspiracy to murder and sentenced to a minimum of twenty-two years in prison.

The intelligence collection and analysis displayed in Operation Overt was unparalleled. "We logged every item they bought, we sifted every piece of rubbish they threw away (at their homes or in litterbins)," according to one British police account. "We filmed and listened to them; we broke into their homes and cars to plant bugs and searched their luggage when they passed through airports."[48] The authorities sifted through every piece of intelligence imaginable. As British police later acknowledged, "When a key figure, Abdulla Ahmed Ali, returned from Pakistan in June 2006, we searched his luggage and resealed it without him noticing. Inside . . . were bomb-making components and their discovery led to a step change in the operation." They also blanketed 386A Forest Road: "We were on their tail when Ali bought a flat in Walthamstow for £138,000 cash and we 'burgled' the property to wire it up for covert sound and cameras. We watched as they experimented with turning soft-drinks containers into bottle bombs, listened as they recorded martyrdom videos and heard them discuss '18 or 19.'"[49]

In monitoring the e-mails—and using them as evidence in court—the British reached out to American law enforcement agencies, which contacted Yahoo! headquarters in Silicon Valley, California, to secure the personal correspondence and account information of the suspects.[50] Indeed, following a UK request, a series of court orders in January and February 2009 released the e-mails from a court of law in California. They were used as evidence in the trial.

Even before the investigation began, the UK had devoted a breathtaking amount of time and resources to meld its police and intelligence operations, especially Metropolitan Police and MI5.[51] Peter Clarke, who served as national coordinator of terrorist investigations for Metropolitan Police, noted that "the most important change in counterterrorism in the UK in recent years has been the development of the relationship between the police and the security service . . . It is no exaggeration to say that the joint working between the police and MI5 has become recognized as a beacon of good practice."[52] The British government also adopted a strategy for stopping terrorists, referred to as CONTEST, which was divided into four components: pursue, prevent, protect, and prepare. "Pursue" included intelligence-gathering and other steps to identify terrorist networks and stop attacks; "prevent" involved deterring people from becoming terrorists or supporting terrorism; "protect" focused on hardening targets and strengthening border security; and "prepare" emphasized forward planning and other steps to mitigate the impact of a terrorist attack.[53]

Over the course of the investigation, the police seized a mountain of information contained on 200 mobile phones, 400 computers, and 8,000 CDs, DVDs, and computer disks that contained over 6,000 gigabytes of data. They searched nearly seventy homes, businesses, and areas such as public parks.[54] In addition, the Bank of England ordered banks to freeze the assets of nineteen individuals suspected of participation in terrorist acts.[55] In July 2010 three more individuals were convicted in Woolwich Crown Court of participating in the plot to blow up transatlantic airliners with liquid explosives: Ibrahim Savant, Arafat Waheed Khan, and Waheed Zaman.[56] Several other apparent cell members were found not guilty of conspiring to murder.

It is difficult to overstate the significance of Operation Overt. It was established on the heels of several successful terrorist attacks linked to al Qa'ida: on September 11, 2001, in the United States; on March 11, 2004, in Spain; and on July 7, 2005, in the United Kingdom. In addition, al Qa'ida in Iraq had been conducting a series of attacks against U.S. and Iraqi forces since 2003. The transatlantic plot was a serious effort to kill a large number of American, British, and other civilians. As Michael Chertoff remarked, the 2006 airline bombing plot appeared "to have been well planned and well advanced, with a significant number of operatives."[57] The FBI's Philip Mudd agreed: "It was the most intense plot up to that point after September 11."[58]

Waves and Reverse Waves

Operation Overt proved a harbinger of things to come. Since al Qa'ida was founded in 1988, a series of waves (surges in terrorist violence) and reverse waves (decreases in terrorist activity) have characterized the struggle against the group. As political scientist David Rapoport described, a terrorism wave is a "cycle characterized by expansion and contraction phases."[59] Over time the ability of terrorist groups to conduct attacks in order to achieve their political goals waxes and wanes.

Terrorism waves are examples of a more general phenomenon in international politics: similar events sometimes happen more or less simultaneously within countries or broader geographic regions. Beginning around 1828, for example, democratization spread across the world, a development that political scientist Samuel Huntington dubbed "the first wave" of democratic advancement. This was followed by a second wave from 1943 to 1964, and a third wave beginning in 1974. Each wave saw significant increases in the number of democratic countries worldwide.[60]

Similarly, al Qa'ida–affiliated terrorism has occurred in at least three waves over the decades-long lifespan of the organization. As Ayman al-Zawahiri argued in such books as *Knights Under the Prophet's Banner*, one of al Qa'ida's primary objectives in conducting attacks has been to kill as many enemies as possible.[61] Consequently, the number of fatalities from al Qa'ida attacks provides a useful indicator of the group's activity. Other data, such as the number of attacks, are less useful, since they don't differentiate an operation that fails to kill individuals from one that kills several hundred people. For al Qa'ida leaders, this difference is important. Figure 2 illustrates al Qa'ida's waves using data from the Global Terrorism Database at the University of Maryland. The data include fatalities caused by al Qa'ida and its affiliates in Pakistan, Afghanistan, Iraq, Somalia, the Arabian Peninsula, and North Africa.[62]

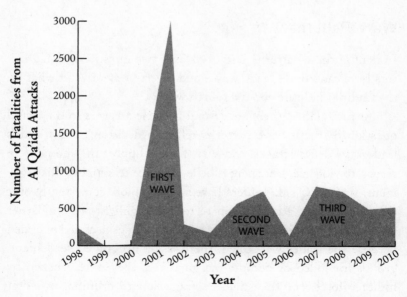

Figure 2: Al Qa'ida Waves

The first wave began with the attacks against the U.S. embassies in Tanzania and Kenya in 1998, followed by the bombing of the USS *Cole* in Yemen in 2000. This wave crested with the September 11 attacks and was followed by a reverse wave as allied forces captured and killed al Qa'ida leaders and operatives in Afghanistan, Pakistan, the United States, and elsewhere. A second wave began in 2003 after the U.S. invasion of Iraq and was characterized by spectacular attacks across Iraq and in Casablanca, Madrid, London, and other cities. A second reverse wave began around 2006, as the Anbar Awakening severely undermined al Qa'ida in Iraq, British and American intelligence agencies foiled numerous plots, and U.S. and Pakistani strikes killed senior al Qa'ida operatives in Pakistan. A third wave surged between 2007 and 2009, following the rise of al Qa'ida in the Arabian Peninsula, and was again followed by a reverse wave as the United States targeted Osama bin Laden and other senior leaders in 2011.

Wave Patterns

In light of these patterns, this book asks two questions: What factors have caused al Qa'ida waves and reverse waves? And what do the findings indicate about a fourth wave?

At first glance, there are several possible answers to the initial question. Perhaps wave patterns reflect a decision by al Qa'ida's leaders to delay attacks and wait for an opportune moment to return to violence. But there is little evidence to support this argument, since al Qa'ida leaders have pursued plots consistently over the past decade. Research on terrorism highlights several other possibilities: terrorist campaigns have sometimes declined or ended because the leader was killed, there was a negotiated settlement, groups imploded or became marginalized, they were crushed by military forces, or they made a transition to criminal or other activities.[63] But these explanations fall short. Al Qa'ida became increasingly decentralized over time, ensuring that the killing of its leader—Osama bin Laden—would not destroy the group. There have also been no settlements with any of al Qa'ida's affiliates, the group has not imploded, the use of conventional military forces has actually strengthened al Qa'ida, and the group has not transitioned to other activities.

Instead, three factors help explain wave patterns: the counterterrorism strategy of America and its allies, al Qa'ida's own strategy, and the competence of local governments where al Qa'ida has tried to establish a sanctuary. For all of these actors, the struggle has depended to a large degree on the precise use of violence.[64] In many ways, it is a war in which the side that kills the most civilians loses.

The first is variation in the counterterrorism strategy of America and its allies. As in most counterterrorism campaigns, the United States has utilized an assortment of strategies. One has been overwhelming force—the deployment of large numbers of conventional forces overseas to destroy terrorist groups and their support networks. This strategy is best illustrated by the large buildup of U.S. and allied military forces in Iraq and Afghanistan after September 11. Another has been a light-footprint approach characterized by a small military presence and a reliance on clandestine law enforcement, intelligence, and special operations forces to help foreign governments dismantle al Qa'ida and to conduct precision targeting.[65] As we shall see, a light-footprint approach has been more effective in weakening al Qa'ida and has minimized Muslim radicalization. But U.S. and allied counterterrorism efforts alone do not explain wave patterns.

A second factor is variation in al Qa'ida's strategy. Terrorist groups have long used attacks to achieve their political goals. Al Qa'ida has sometimes adopted a punishment strategy that involves attacks on civilian populations—a strategy al Qa'ida in Iraq leaders embraced after the U.S. invasion. At other times al Qa'ida leaders have implemented a more selective strategy focused on killing government officials and their collaborators. Over the past two and a half decades, al Qa'ida has lost considerable support when it has adopted a punishment strategy, especially when it has killed Muslims.

A third factor is the ability of local governments to establish basic law and order in their territory when faced with an al Qa'ida presence. Al Qa'ida has established safe havens in countries with a support base of sympathizers and financially, organizationally, and politically weak central governments. Some governments, such as the Taliban in Afghanistan, have actively supported al Qa'ida. Others have tried to counter the group, but their security forces have been too weak or corrupt, as in Yemen. Still others have been effective, as Pakistan was in the aftermath of September 11, when several al Qa'ida leaders were captured in Pakistani cities with the cooperation of the United States. The Arab Spring, popular uprisings that led to the collapse of several North African and Middle Eastern regimes beginning in 2011, was a welcome sign for those fighting for democracy. But it also undermined stability and eroded the strength of several governments, providing an opportunity for al Qa'ida to establish a foothold.

As the past two and a half decades illustrate, there is no single recipe for defeating al Qa'ida. Its organizational structure, strategies, and tactics have evolved over time and in different countries, indicating that counterterrorism efforts must adapt to changing conditions within al Qa'ida sanctuaries. Yet terrorism waves have frequently ebbed when the U.S. and other foreign powers have utilized a light-footprint strategy focusing on clandestine activity, al Qa'ida has embraced a punishment strategy that kills civilians and undermines its support base, and local governments have developed effective police and other security agencies.

Our story begins on the front lines of Sudan, Afghanistan, and Pakistan, where individuals such as Osama bin Laden and Ayman al-Zawahiri prepared for their apocalyptic showdown with the West. From the beginning, however, they faced withering criticism from within the Islamic community about their support of violence. Khartoum would be their first test.

PART I

———

THE FIRST WAVE

2

THE ORIGINS OF DISSENT

THE HEAT IN Khartoum, Sudan, is oppressive. It creeps across the Libyan and Nubian deserts like a blanket, suffocating trees and shrubs, and settles in Sudan's arid, windswept capital. Sun-baked, mud-brick buildings dot the city's landscape, caked in a layer of dirt and dust. The White Nile, which flows north from Lake Victoria into the city, and the Blue Nile, which flows west from Ethiopia, merge in Khartoum. The waters offer solace from the heat. But not for long. Khartoum is perhaps the hottest major city on the planet; temperatures can exceed 117 degrees Fahrenheit in mid-summer. For seven months of the year, the average monthly high hovers around a scalding 100 degrees. There is no rain for at least half the year.

This furnace witnessed one of the most significant schisms among Islamic fundamentalists, a break that had lasting implications for al Qa'ida well after the September 11 attacks. Tensions had been building among Egyptian Islamic Jihad members for several years.[1] Egyptian Islamic Jihad, or al-Jihad, was established in the late 1970s to overthrow the Egyptian government and replace it with an Islamic state. By 1992, when members had settled in rustic farms and guesthouses near Khartoum, the tensions had reached crisis point.[2] Perhaps the most serious friction occurred between Sayyid Imam Abd al-Aziz al-Sharif, the chief ideologue and leader of the group, and Ayman al-Zawahiri, his deputy. Zawahiri would go on to become one of the world's most wanted terrorists and Osama bin Laden's right-hand man within al Qa'ida.

Some members, including Zawahiri, were pushing to begin terrorist operations in Egypt. But Sharif pushed back. "Fighting in Egypt will not bring any benefit, and there is a great deal of harm in it," he cautioned.

He was met with a ferocious reply. "The time for words is over," one member said, "and it is time for action."[3]

Faced with such dissent, Sharif resigned from the group in disgust, handing the reins to Zawahiri. His parting shot was a warning that wanton violence would be counterproductive and ultimately un-Islamic. "Have the fear of God in your heart for the sake of the other brothers," he counseled Zawahiri. "Do not subject them to dangers that they should not have to face in the line of duty."

Zawahiri retorted that he "committed himself in front of the Sudanese brothers to carry out 10 operations in Egypt" and that he "had received from them $100,000 as an initial payment for those operations."

"You have studied the rules of guerrilla warfare and regular combat," Sharif lectured. "What you are doing now in Egypt falls under neither heading. This is senseless activity that will bring no benefit."

"You wish to turn us into a Salafi group," Zawahiri responded. "We are not that. We are a jihadist group. We will continue fighting in Egypt to the last man and to the last dollar we have."[4]

Salafis believe that the early generations of Muslims set the model that all succeeding generations should follow, especially in their beliefs, understanding of the core Islamic texts, methods of worship, piety, and conduct. Many Salafis are opposed to armed jihad and advocate the *da'wa*, or "call" to Islam, through proselytizing and preaching. Zawahiri was pushing for both Salafism and armed jihad.

The break between him and Sharif was significant in several respects. First, it indicated profound and irreconcilable differences between two venerated Islamic fundamentalists about the role of jihad and the legitimacy of violence. Muhammad Hasan Khalil al-Hakim, who later became a senior member of al Qa'ida, showered Sharif with "love and respect" for his works, which were carefully studied "in the training camps of al Qa'ida."[5] So did Zawahiri, who noted that "I have the greatest respect, appreciation, and amity" for Sharif.[6] Yet Sharif was attacking the foundation of Egypt's budding militancy, several of the leaders of which would play a key role in al Qa'ida.

Second, the break marked the first of numerous battles between Sharif and Zawahiri. Over the next several decades, the two Egyptians waged a savage war of words in books, in newspapers, and on the Internet over the soul of Islam and Muslim youth.

Third, it served as a microcosm for a broader and more significant debate within Islam that reemerged in the years following September 11. The arguments first articulated by Sharif would prove an enduring challenge to al Qa'ida and precipitated counterwaves of anti-jihadist activity. "We are in a media battle," Zawahiri later wrote, "for the hearts and minds" of Muslims.[7]

A Temporary Alliance

Sharif and Zawahiri came from different molds. Sharif was born on August 8, 1950, in Bani Suef, Egypt, a city 72 miles south of Cairo. Situated on the west bank of the Nile, it produces linen, refined sugar, and alabaster, which is quarried in the nearby hills. Islam had a profound childhood impact on Sharif, and he learned from his father to be conscientious about his religious studies.[8] He was a voracious reader and an admirer of the Muslim Brotherhood, the Sunni movement established in Egypt in 1928 that is committed to using the Qur'an and the hadith (the recorded traditions and sayings of the Prophet Muhammad) as guidelines for a modern Islamic state. Sharif graduated with honors from the Faculty of Medicine at Cairo University in 1974 and was appointed to the surgery department at Qasr al-Ayni hospital.

By 1992, when his relationship with Zawahiri soured, Sharif sported a neatly trimmed graying beard. His skin was light, his cheeks were bony, and his ears were long and thin. But it was his thick eyebrows, which arched when he spoke, and his penetrating dark eyes that gave his face its vitality. Sharif was an introvert. Unlike Zawahiri, he was more interested in burying himself in stacks of religious and medical books than in deploying to a war zone.

Zawahiri, on the other hand, came from revolutionary blood. He was the scion of two influential families. On his father's side, one of his relatives, Muhammad al-Ahmadi al-Zawahiri, was the imam of Al-Azhar Mosque in Cairo, a bastion of Sunni Islam, where his grandfather and great-grandfather also studied. His mother's side included a long list of respected individuals. One was Abdul Rahman Azzam, the first secretary-general of the Arab League, who was a passionate advocate of pan-Arabism and an active participant in the Libyan resistance against Italy from 1915 to 1923. Ayman al-Zawahiri was born in 1951 in Maadi.[9] A chic suburb of Cairo, it is situated at the southern end of the Hod al-Bassatine basin, which is bounded to the west by the Nile River and to the east by wadis, or valleys, that come down from the Mokattam Hills. In past centuries the area was populated by farmers and traders. At the end of each annual flood season, the farmers scuttled down from the hills to cultivate the lush, fertile land. The traders ferried goods, many of which came by desert caravan through the Sinai, across the Nile to the west bank and transported them to Upper Egypt.[10]

During Zawahiri's childhood, Maadi boasted many Western allurements. It was home to the annual Egyptian Open Tennis Championship, a nucleus of international schools, and the prestigious Maadi Sporting Club. Despite living in a stronghold of Western culture, Zawahiri's parents, Rabi and Omayma, lived modestly and were more pious and socially conservative than many members of their generation.[11] Zawahiri shunned the Western temptations in Maadi and turned toward religion. As a child, he had a sensitive and pious temperament. Intellectually precocious, he was a poor athlete and, by some accounts, believed that sports like boxing and wrestling were "inhumane."[12]

By the time of his break with Sharif, Zawahiri had filled out considerably and was a slightly heavyset five feet, seven inches tall. His religious devotion was evident in his face. He sported a *zebiba*, which translates literally as "raisin" and refers to the patch of hardened skin on a devout Muslim's forehead where it touches the mat during prayers. It gave Zawahiri an air of religious piety that complemented his dark beard, round spectacles, and olive complexion. He was a gifted speaker. "His ideas are always organized," noted one colleague, "so when he speaks, he expresses himself very well. He is very cool-headed."[13]

In his early teens, Zawahiri formed a secret cell committed to overthrowing the Egyptian government and replacing it with an Islamic regime. As he told Egyptian authorities several years later, the government was guilty of apostasy—of abandoning its fidelity to Islam. Zawahiri was particularly disturbed by the arrest of Muslim Brotherhood members in 1965. Around 1966 or 1967, he began thinking of forming a cell.[14] When the Egyptians later inquired about his objectives, he said simply, "We wanted to establish an Islamic government."

His Egyptian government interrogator then followed up: "What does an Islamic government mean according to this cell?"

"A government that rules according to the shari'a of God Almighty," Zawahiri responded.

"What is the meaning of 'jihad' according to your cell?" he was asked.

Zawahiri answered, "'Jihad' means removing the current government through resisting it and changing the current regime to establish an Islamic government instead."

The Egyptian official pressed him. "How would you replace the current government with an Islamic one?"

"Through a military coup," Zawahiri responded, unmoved. "We were convinced that civilians and the military should cooperate to achieve this end."

"Why did you want to remove the current government?" the official continued.

Zawahiri repeated his mantra: "Because it does not rule according to the shari'a of God, glorified be His name."[15]

It was at this time that Sharif first met Zawahiri. Both attended Cairo University, where they were studying to become doctors. "I got to know Ayman al-Zawahiri in 1968," Sharif recalled. "He was a colleague in the Faculty of Medicine, and we together with other colleagues used to discuss various Islamic issues. I knew from another colleague that Ayman was involved with an Islamic group in which splits had occurred, but he did not broach the subject of joining that group" until the following decade.[16] As Zawahiri explained, Sharif "joined the cell in 1975 or 1976 when he was training with me to be a practicing doctor at the Qasr al-Ayni Hospital, after finishing our last year of medical school. I was the one who recruited him as well."[17] Not only did they forge a close working relationship, but they developed a tight personal bond as well. Their kids played together in the neighborhood streets and they attended many of the same wedding parties.[18]

Sharif soon became involved in Zawahiri's circle of collaborators. The assassination of President Anwar Sadat on October 6, 1981, however, changed everything. Although Sharif and Zawahiri did not appear to be directly involved, Egyptian security services threw a net around a wide range of militants. Perhaps the most damning connection was Zawahiri's relationship with Esam al-Qamari, a decorated tank commander and major in the Egyptian army who smuggled weapons and ammunition from army strongholds for Egyptian Islamic Jihad. "Do you know why I joined the Military College?" Qamari once asked his father, who shook his head. "To carry out a military coup," he answered.[19] His father was speechless.

Both Zawahiri and Sharif were involved in supporting Qamari's efforts against the government, including stockpiling weapons, explosives, and ammunition.[20] Unsurprisingly, both were accused of participating in the assassination of Sadat. Sharif, who was later exonerated, managed to slip out of Egypt in 1982. He moved to the United Arab Emirates, then to Saudi Arabia, and finally landed in Pakistan in 1983. Zawahiri was not so fortunate. He was arrested and spent several years in prison, where he was tortured and humiliated. The experience had a searing impact on his psyche—so much so that he published a book on the subject, *The Black Book: Torturing Muslims Under President Hosni Mubarak.*[21]

Zawahiri's experience in prison produced the first stirrings of his drive for leadership and power. While in prison he spoke openly on behalf of other prisoners. Talking to foreign journalists from his cramped jail cell, which he shared with dozens of other Egyptian militants, he chastised the Egyptian government for torturing prisoners and declared his fidelity to Islam. "Now, we want to speak to the whole world. Who are we?" he asked rhetorically, his raspy voice shaking with rage. "We are Muslims. We are Muslims who believe in their religion, both in ideology and practice, and hence we tried our best to establish an Islamic state and an Islamic society."

The prisoners responded in chorus: "There is no god but God."

Zawahiri continued: "We are not sorry, we are not sorry for what we have done for our religion, and we have sacrificed, and we stand ready to make more sacrifices."[22]

In 1984, Zawahiri was released from prison and left Egypt for Saudi Arabia. He too eventually ended up in Pakistan. Sharif was already there.

The Afghan Jihad

When Sharif arrived in the Pakistani city of Peshawar in 1983, it was a bustling frontier town 30 miles from the Afghanistan border. He had trekked to Pakistan to assist the mujahideen against the Soviet Red Army and work for the Kuwaiti Red Crescent Hospital. An ancient stop on the Silk Road and the much-coveted capital of successive Buddhist and Hindu kingdoms, Peshawar contained bazaars that had attracted visitors for centuries with their rich assortment of carpets, pottery, arms, and artwork. Bearded tribesmen walked the streets in their colorful native robes, crowding between garishly painted buses and taxis. One of the great bazaars, Qissa Khwani, or Market of the Storytellers, featured professional balladeers who recited tales of love and gallantry. "Conspiracy, rebellion, spying, propaganda, arms sales, and smuggling," wrote one traveler, "those were the cottage industries of the storytellers' bazaar."[23]

Following the Soviet invasion of Afghanistan in December 1979, Afghan refugees flooded into Peshawar. So did jihadists, who wanted to assist in the anti-Soviet campaign. Zawahiri arrived in Peshawar in 1986, though it was not his first trip to Pakistan.[24] He had visited in 1980 and worked in the Sayyida Zeinab Hospital, which belonged to the Muslim Brotherhood's Islamic Medical Society. He returned again the following year. The anti-Soviet jihad had an important symbolic meaning for Zawahiri. A Communist superpower that shunned religion had invaded a Muslim country. This was the essence of jihad—and an easy sell to young Muslim recruits from abroad. "In Afghanistan the picture was completely clear," Zawahiri wrote. "A Muslim nation carrying out jihad under the banner of Islam, versus a foreign enemy that was an infidel aggressor backed by a corrupt, apostate regime at home."[25]

Zawahiri joined Sharif at the Kuwaiti Red Crescent Hospital to work as a surgeon. He had not served an internship in surgery at any hospital, so he asked Sharif for help.[26] Zawahiri then floated an invitation to Sharif: Would he be interested in joining Egyptian Islamic Jihad? The organization's goal was to overthrow the Egyptian government and replace it with an Islamic state.

"The matter calls for exhaustive canon law study and is not as simple as you imagine," Sharif mused, noting that it was critical to ground the group in a proper understanding of Islam.

But Zawahiri insisted that Sharif join, pointing out "the importance of exploiting the Afghan jihad and the importance of bringing young men from Egypt to participate in it." For Zawahiri, the Afghan war offered an extraordinary opportunity to train members of Egyptian Islamic Jihad, who could eventually use their skills to overthrow the Egyptian government.

Sharif eventually caved in to Zawahiri and agreed to serve as leader of the group, saying, "That is all right, but I will have nothing to do with them administratively or with their living conditions."[27]

From 1987 to 1993, Sharif was leader of Egyptian Islamic Jihad from his base in Pakistan, and Zawahiri served as his deputy. But Zawahiri still wielded significant power, and some who joined Egyptian Islamic Jihad and pledged allegiance to "the doctor" assumed they were swearing obedience to Zawahiri, not Sharif.[28] Both used noms de guerre. Sharif went by Abd-al-Qadir Bin Abd-al-Aziz Fadl, or simply Dr. Fadl. Zawahiri adopted Dr. Abdel Mu'iz. According to some individuals close to Zawahiri, his decision to hand over the reins of the organization to Sharif was significant. "A closer look at their relationship reveals that [Sharif] deeply influenced the way Zawahiri thinks," one of them said. "The very length of their good relationship—from the 1960s until the second half of the 1990s—suggests its importance. Zawahiri prioritized [Sharif] over himself by choosing him to be the first leader of Islamic Jihad."[29] Sharif was also the chief ideologue and headed the group's sharia committee, which outlined the religious justification for its armed operations.

One of Sharif's most important contributions was the 1988 publication of a 500-page book, *Al-Umdah fi 'Idad al-'Uddah* (The Primer in Preparing for Jihad). Originally written in Arabic, it was translated into nine languages and read by militants from Afghanistan to Indonesia. The book's five chapters outline Egyptian Islamic Jihad's objectives, highlight its ideological underpinnings, and offer strategic and operational tenets. Sharif argued that Muslims who did not join the fight against "apostate" rulers were "impious" and must be defeated.[30] The book was used as justification for militants to commit atrocities against civilians, including women and children, under the façade of defending Islam.[31]

Led by Sharif, Zawahiri, and others—most notably Osama bin Laden and Abdullah Azzam—the Afghan jihad brought Islamic radicals together. Muslim ulema (Islamic scholars) issued fatwas (legal rulings) interpreting the Soviet intervention as a sinful invasion of Islamic territory. This made it possible to proclaim a "defensive" jihad, which, according to Islamic law, not only exonerated those who committed violence but also obliged every Muslim to participate.[32] These first-generation volunteers were mainly Arabs from the Middle East and North Africa. Once in Afghanistan, they were generally divided into small groups in the eastern part of the country, along the Pakistan border.[33]

By the late 1980s, elite foreign fighters began to congregate in a camp near Khowst called Al-Maasada (the lion's den). Osama bin Laden was the leader of this group; he said he had been inspired to call the place Al-Maasada by lines of one of the Prophet's favorite poets, Hassan Ibn Thabit.[34] In August 1988 a group gathered together in bin Laden's house in Peshawar to form a new organization, which they referred to as al Qa'ida al Askariya (the military base). They created an advisory council and membership requirements.[35] According to notes taken during the meeting by one of the participants, "al-Qa'ida is basically an organized Islamic faction, its goal is to live the word of God, to make His religion victorious." Al Qa'ida leaders separated foreign fighters involved in the Afghan war into two components: "limited duration" fighters would assist the Afghan mujahideen for the remainder of the war; "open duration" recruits would be sent to a separate training camp, and "the best brothers of them" would be chosen to join al Qa'ida.[36]

Members were expected to pledge loyalty to the leadership: "The pledge of God and His covenant is upon me, to listen and obey the superiors, who are doing this work, in energy, early-rising, difficulty, and easiness, and for His superiority upon us." Their goal would be "to lift the word of God, to make His religion victorious" across the Arab world through armed jihad. But members were urged to be patient, pious, and obedient, since the struggle would be long and challenging.[37]

Cracks in the Foundation

By 1992, with the departure of Soviet troops, Afghanistan had deteriorated into a frenzied civil war, and Pakistan began to arrest the foreign militants who stayed behind. Many, such as Sharif, were deported.[38] Some dispersed to Bosnia, Algeria, Egypt, and other countries. In each location they attempted to transform domestic conflict into jihad. In some cases, as in Bosnia, they failed to make their radical interpretation of Islam a relevant component of the civil war. In others, such as Algeria, they were more successful. Most Arab states viewed the veterans of Afghanistan as a serious threat: a kind of decentralized army of several thousand radicalized warriors. Egypt, Saudi Arabia, Jordan, and others established border controls to keep them out.[39]

In Sudan, however, a coup d'état in 1989 had brought the military to power. The new leader, Omar al-Bashir, had the support of Islamic fundamentalists, which made the country palatable to Osama bin Laden's strict religious lifestyle. Sudanese authorities were seeking funds to develop the country, and bin Laden agreed to provide some financing. In late 1991 he moved to Khartoum, along with several hundred veterans of the Afghan war, and resumed operations. As one CIA assessment concluded, "In addition to safe haven in Sudan, Bin Laden has provided financial support to militants actively opposed to moderate Islamic governments and the West."[40] The bin Laden family and some of their associates lived in several beige-colored homes in a well-to-do suburb of Khartoum known as al-Riyadh Village. Bin Laden forbade the use of most modern amenities on the compound—including refrigerators, electric stoves, and air conditioning—arguing that Muslims must scorn modern conveniences.[41]

About this time, Zawahiri and Sharif also arrived in Sudan. The country was supposed to provide a refuge from international intelligence pressure, but fissures quickly developed between Zawahiri and Sharif about the legitimacy of violence, especially in Egypt.[42] "Do not become involved in a confrontation in Egypt," Sharif warned, discouraging his comrades from engaging in "excesses of Islamic action" in foreign countries. He prepared to leave the group.

Members worried that Sharif's departure would fracture Egyptian Islamic Jihad. "If you sever your ties with these brothers," one warned him, "they will split into several groups."

But Sharif was insistent, noting that "they had no obligation to conduct jihad inside Egypt" and "that they would not be sinning if they did not carry out armed attacks."[43]

Sharif's opposition to a violent campaign against the Egyptian government provoked radical members, who preferred an activist approach. "We did not join the group just to watch from the sidelines," one member complained.[44] Many revolted against Sharif and pushed for his dismissal.[45]

Quoting from the Qur'an, Sharif berated Zawahiri: "Who is further astray than the one who follows his own whims with no guidance from God? Truly God does not guide those who do wrong."[46]

But Zawahiri was not persuaded and argued that the Egyptian government was illegitimate. "An analysis of the political situation in Egypt would reveal that Egypt is struggling between two powers," he noted. "An official power and a popular power that has its roots deeply established in the ground, which is the Islamic movement in general and the solid jihad nucleus in particular." This meant an all-out, violent war. "It is a battle of ideologies, a struggle for survival, and a war with no truce."[47]

Zawahiri, who had a flair for the apocalyptic, won the argument. Egyptian Islamic Jihad then joined with other violent groups and went on a killing spree. In 1992 they gunned down Farag Fodah, one of Egypt's best-known authors, who was a secularist and supported the Israeli-Egyptian peace process. The following year they attempted to kill the Egyptian interior minister, Hasan al-Alfi. Al-Alfi escaped, but five others died. In November 1993, Egyptian Islamic Jihad attempted to kill the Egyptian prime minister, Aref Sidqi. They failed, but one bystander was killed and eighteen were injured. In June 1995 members of Egyptian Islamic Jihad and al-Gama'a al-Islamiyya, another Egyptian Islamist group dedicated to overthrowing the government and replacing it with an Islamic state, tried to kill Egyptian president Hosni Mubarak while he was in Ethiopia for a conference of the Organization of African Unity but botched the effort. Later that year the group bombed the Egyptian embassy in Islamabad, Pakistan, killing seventeen people and wounding sixty.

For many, including Sharif, the wanton violence was proof that Zawahiri had overstepped the boundaries of human decency. More important, he had grossly misinterpreted Islam. A growing number of leaders from Egyptian Islamic Jihad and religious-political groups such as the Muslim Brotherhood advocated a return to *da'wa* and a move away from violence. War against the Egyptian government had to end, they concluded.[48] Rather than rush to armed confrontation, Sharif believed, Egyptian Islamic Jihad should focus on recruiting competent cadres—including some within the Egyptian military—and waiting until conditions ripened for a swift coup d'état. Of course, Sharif had not suddenly become a pacifist. Rather, he had begun to question the efficacy of violence, especially when civilians were involved, and he wondered whether now was the appropriate time to attack the Egyptian government.

Zawahiri was infuriated with Sharif and others, including the Muslim Brotherhood, for considering a truce with the Egyptian government. He devoted an entire book, *Bitter Harvest*, to accusing the

Muslim Brothers of transgressing Islam's fundamental principles by eschewing violence and supporting democracy.[49]

Sharif had another, more personal reason for his break. Zawahiri had edited Sharif's 1993 manuscript of *Al-Jami' fi Talab al-'Ilm al-Sharif* (The Compendium for the Acquisition of the Noble Knowledge). The book expanded the definition of what constituted a nonbeliever. But Zawahiri altered it, rewriting portions of the document before publication. He also removed Sharif's critiques of the jihadist movement, including specific organizations like al-Gama'a al-Islamiyya, for their overzealous reliance on violence. Sharif was bitter, and his loathing of Zawahiri became effusive and personal. "I do not know anyone in the history of Islam prior to Ayman al-Zawahiri," he lamented, "who engaged in such lying, cheating, forgery, and betrayal of trust by transgressing against someone else's book and distorting it."[50] He was particularly incensed that Zawahiri, who had no religious credentials, had altered a profoundly religious document. Nonetheless, Zawahiri's defenders within Egyptian Islamic Jihad welcomed the edits as a refinement of Sharif's initial draft.[51]

Sharif's and Zawahiri's divorce was anything but amicable. Sharif's departure from the group left Egyptian Islamic Jihad without a serious religious voice on the sharia committee.[52] Zawahiri remained in Sudan until 1994, when the government expelled him. After traveling widely, including to the United States and Europe, he returned to Afghanistan, in the late 1990s.

Hardened Battle Lines

For Zawahiri, the return to Afghanistan symbolized a rededication to the pure form of jihad he had experienced in the 1980s. Even more appealing, however, was the Taliban and its leader, Mullah Muhammad Omar, whom Zawahiri warmly referred to as "Amir al-Mu'minin" (Commander of the Faithful). Operating side by side with Osama bin Laden, Zawahiri underwent a major transformation. Not only did he continue to support violence, but he increasingly broadened his scope to include the United States, in accordance with bin Laden's more global views. Indeed, Zawahiri played the sycophant, often refraining to speak in front of bin Laden unless given permission. "Sheik Osama," he would ask, "may I please speak?"[53]

Zawahiri was particularly enthused by the Egyptian scholar Sayyid Qutb, who had been executed on August 29, 1966, for plotting to overthrow the Egyptian government. In his iconic book *Milestones*, Qutb argued that Western values hindered humanity's progress. Modern-day Islam, he wrote, had also become corrupt, and he compared the modern Muslim states with *jahiliyya*.[54] As used in the Qur'an, *jahiliyya* describes the state of ignorance in which Arabs were supposed to have lived before the revelation of Islam to the Prophet Muhammad at the beginning of the seventh century.[55] In two of Qutb's key works, *In the Shadow of the Qur'an* and *Signposts on the Road*, he pleaded for contemporary Muslims to build a new Islamic community, much as the Prophet had done a thousand years earlier.[56] One problem was that he never clearly specified what the Prophet's experience had been and how it should be replicated in the modern era.[57] But building a new community would mean casting out Muslims who were not pious enough, which meant that most Muslims could not be viewed as true Muslims.

In Islamic doctrine, denying a Muslim his faith is a serious accusation, referred to as *takfir*. The term derives from the word *kufr* (impiety) and means that one is impure and should therefore be excommunicated. For those who interpret Islamic law literally and rigorously, *takfir* is punishable by death. According to Qutb, the only just ruler is one who administers Islamic law "without any question and rejects all other laws in any shape or form."[58] Qutb also sanctioned offensive jihad against governments that stand in the way of Islam. His work found an eager readership among some of the younger generation because of its stunning and drastic break with the status quo. After his execution, Qutb's fiery ideology gradually emerged as the blueprint for Islamic radicals from Morocco to Indonesia. It was later taught at such places as King Abdul Aziz University in Jedda and Cairo's Al-Azhar University.[59]

According to Qutb, most leaders of Islamic governments were not true Muslims. "The Muslim community has been extinct for a few centuries," he wrote. It was "crushed under the weight of those false laws and customs which are not even remotely related to the Islamic teachings."[60] In the mind of Qutb—and subsequently Zawahiri—any regime that did not impose sharia on the country was guilty of apostasy. The Prophet Muhammad argued that the blood of Muslims cannot be shed except in three instances: as punishment for murder, for marital infidelity, or for turning away from Islam. Zawahiri took this third line of argument to its extreme. He accused regimes in Egypt and several other countries of departing from Islam and failing to establish sharia law, which opened them up to attack.[61] Indeed, even Muslims could be punished if they did not obey conservative Islamic law.[62]

Qutb's and Zawahiri's extreme interpretation of the Prophet's words explains why al Qa'ida leaders wanted to overthrow successive regimes in the Middle East (the near enemy, or *al-Adou al-Qareeb*) to establish a pan-Islamic caliphate, as well as to fight the United States and its allies (the far enemy, or *al-Adou al-Baeed*) who supported them.[63] As Zawahiri wrote, the "establishment of a Muslim state in the heart of the Islamic world is not an easy or close target. However, it is the hope of the Muslim nation to restore its fallen caliphate and regain its lost glory."[64] Zawahiri argued that "the issue of unification in Islam is important and that the battle between Islam and its enemies is primarily an ideological one . . . [It] is also a battle over to whom authority and power should belong—to God's course and sharia, to man-made laws and material principles, or to those who claim to be intermediaries between the Creator and mankind."[65]

The United States was the most significant far enemy. "The white man" in America is the primary enemy, Qutb wrote. "The white man crushes us underfoot while we teach our children about his civilization, his universal principles and noble objective . . . We are endowing our children with amazement and respect for the master who tramples our honor and enslaves us." The response to this enslavement, Qutb argued, had to be anger and violence. "Let us instead plant the seeds of hatred, disgust, and revenge in the souls of these children. Let us teach these children from the time their nails are soft that the white man is the enemy of humanity, and that they should destroy him at the first opportunity."[66]

Zawahiri picked up this theme, distancing himself from his earlier works, such as his 1995 essay "The Road to Jerusalem Goes Through Cairo," in which he had advocated attacking Arab regimes.[67] For Zawahiri, the United States only knew "the language of interests backed by brute military force. Therefore, if we wish to have a dialogue with them and make them aware of our rights, we must talk to them in the language they understand."[68] This language was violence and force. Osama bin Laden repeated this message regularly.

The United States specifically, and the West more broadly, was a corrupting influence on Islam, they argued. Zawahiri also accused the United States of propping up apostate Arab countries. In order to reestablish the caliphate, al Qa'ida had to target these countries' primary backers. The conflict with the United States, then, was a "battle of ideologies, a struggle for survival, and a war with no truce."[69] In his book *Loyalty to Islam and Disavowal to Its Enemies*, Zawahiri argued that Muslims must make a choice between their religion and those who opposed it.[70] In *Knights Under the Prophet's Banner*, he similarly wrote that the overthrow of governments in such countries as Egypt would become a rallying point for the rest of the Islamic world. "Then history would make a new turn, God willing," he noted, "in the opposite direction against the empire of the United States and the world's Jewish government."[71] In his mind, and in those of several of his followers, the United States was primarily interested in "removing Islam from power."[72]

In February 1998, bin Laden, Zawahiri, and others published a fatwa to kill Americans: "The ruling to kill the Americans and their allies—civilians and military—is an individual duty for every Muslim who can do it in any country in which it is possible to do it."[73] The fatwa cited three main grievances against the United States. One was the presence of American troops in the Arabian Peninsula, the second was America's intention to destroy the Muslim people of Iraq through sanctions, and the third was the U.S. goal of incapacitating the Arab states and propping up Israel. Bin Laden accused the United States of plundering Arab riches, dictating to Arab rulers, and humiliating Arab people.

Meager Efforts

With the publication of the fatwa, some U.S. government officials began to take notice. One was Henry "Hank" Crumpton. He had wanted to be a spy since childhood and wrote to the CIA. "And they responded—on letterhead," he said. "In a small rural community in Georgia, to get a letter from the CIA, that was pretty cool." After joining the CIA in 1981, Crumpton cut his teeth in Liberia. "That was a good place to start, dealing with chaos and trying to understand the different political and tribal tensions," he said. He learned more from African insurgents than he had learned during his initial training at home. "They were people working with nothing."[74]

Born in Georgia and soft-spoken, Crumpton can be deceiving in his demeanor. "There's a twinkle in his eyes, and he's an aw-shucks guy, but he's one tough intelligence officer," said James Pavitt, former deputy director of operations, the CIA's clandestine wing. "He was not afraid to look people in the eye and say they were wrong. That was his great strength. And that's the kind of thing that started making things happen" after the September 11 attacks.[75] In 1998, Crumpton was reading CIA intelligence assessments and growing alarmed at the al Qa'ida threat.

So was Philip Mudd, then an intelligence analyst at the CIA. Mudd was a young, energetic, and notoriously intense man with short-cropped hair and a smattering of freckles on his face. He had graduated in 1984 from the University of Virginia with a master of arts in English literature, specializing in Victorian-era fiction. "I went into English literature, unfortunately, when the David Letterman show was starting," he said. "And Budweiser was $2.99 a case. That combination was lethal." He could speak French and was passionate about fishing, but he wasn't entirely sure what to do after he got his degree. The CIA intrigued him.

"My father called me one day," Mudd said. His dad had attended a Miami Dolphins football game—in those days Miami actually *won* football games—and had been sitting next to someone who said the CIA was advertising for recruits. "It was in the 'knowing nothing about foreign affairs and having even less interest' category," Mudd said. So he put together a résumé and submitted it. "I had a degree from the University of Virginia, got in my Chevy Chevette—the worst car ever. And when I got there, the security guard looked at me as if I should be committed."[76]

Mudd never looked back. He joined the Central Intelligence Agency in 1985 as an analyst specializing in South Asia and, later, the Middle East. In 1995 he became the deputy national intelligence officer for the Near East and South Asia, and by 1998 he had seen the growing number of intelligence reports on al Qa'ida plotting.

At that time few in the United States government were listening, despite repeated warnings from the intelligence community. It took gruesome terrorist attacks to spur the government to move against bin Laden and Zawahiri: the beginning of al Qa'ida's initial wave, which peaked three years later, on September 11. At 5:35 a.m. on August 7, 1998, national security adviser Sandy Berger woke president Bill Clinton to inform him that simultaneous attacks had been carried out against the U.S. embassies in Nairobi, Kenya, and Dar es Salaam, Tanzania. The destruction was horrific. In Nairobi the blast leveled a three-story building, gutted the rear half of the U.S.

embassy next door, and incinerated dozens of people in their seats in nearby buses. The operatives had packed 400 to 500 cylinders (each about the size of a soda can) with TNT, aluminum nitrate, and aluminum powder and placed them in specially designed wooden crates, which were then sealed and put in the bed of a truck. The area around the U.S. embassy was a maze of narrow streets and alleys, which trapped and intensified the blast. Pedestrians, motorists, and embassy workers were battered from every side by shards of flying concrete, steel, glass, furniture, and other debris.[77]

President Clinton settled on a straightforward, though ultimately ineffective, response: Tomahawk cruise missiles. The day after the embassy bombings, CIA director George Tenet informed policymakers at a White House meeting that the CIA had intelligence indicating an imminent terrorist meeting at al-Farouq training camp in Khowst Province in eastern Afghanistan. Several hundred leaders were expected to attend, including bin Laden. The officials quickly reached a consensus on attacking the gathering.[78] On August 20, U.S. Navy vessels in the Arabian Sea fired cruise missiles. The bombs hit their intended targets. As one of bin Laden's sons explained, "The air was suddenly full of menace, with bright flashes and crashes so loud that their eardrums were bursting . . . Wherever the missiles hit, life was obliterated. Buildings evaporated and large craters opened in the earth."[79]

Though the attack achieved several direct hits, neither bin Laden nor any other senior terrorist leader was killed. Some classified U.S. assessments suggested that the missile barrage actually brought al Qa'ida and the Taliban closer together.[80] One State Department cable reported, "Taliban leader Mullah Omar lashed out at the U.S., asserting that the Taliban will continue to provide a safe haven to bin Laden."[81] After all, bin Laden sometimes stayed at Mullah Omar's residence in Kandahar.[82]

Still, the embassy bombings had a profound impact on U.S. counterterrorism efforts. What is striking is not how little U.S. officials knew but how concerned many were about bin Laden and

Zawahiri. The CIA established a special unit of a dozen officers to assess intelligence on and plan operations against bin Laden. It also established a covert action team in Afghanistan, with presidential support to use lethal force if necessary.[83] State Department cables echoed this theme, often warning that al Qa'ida might strike the homeland. "In our talks," one State Department report noted, "we have stressed that [Osama bin Laden] has murdered Americans and continues to plan attacks against Americans and others and that we cannot ignore this threat."[84] A memo from Assistant Secretary of State Karl Inderfurth to Secretary of State Madeleine Albright warned that "bin Laden and his network continue to threaten U.S. interests. Our people remain in jeopardy. We cannot allow this to continue."[85] A startlingly prescient daily brief to President Clinton on December 4, 1998, warned that intelligence reporting "suggests Bin Ladin and his allies are preparing for attacks in the US, including an aircraft hijacking."[86]

In July 1999, Clinton issued Executive Order 13129, which blocked financial and other support to the Taliban. The order also concluded that "the actions and policies of the Taliban in Afghanistan, in allowing territory under its control in Afghanistan to be used as a safe haven and base of operations for Usama bin Ladin and the Al-Qa'ida organization . . . constitute an unusual and extraordinary threat to the national security and foreign policy of the United States."[87]

If many U.S. government officials recognized the magnitude of the threat, they were still guilty of a paltry response. They would not risk an attack on al Qa'ida, they did not always have enough good actionable intelligence, and there was virtually no strategy to counter al Qa'ida's ideology.[88] Some plans to capture or kill Osama bin Laden were made, but they fell prey to excessive caution. In late 1997 and early 1998, the CIA organized several rehearsals of a plan to capture bin Laden in Afghanistan with the aid of locals. In a May 1998 cable to headquarters, CIA officer Gary Schroen observed that planning was "almost as professional and detailed . . . as would be done by any U.S. special operations element."[89] But senior CIA officials were concerned about the risk of civilian casualties and scrapped the plan.

In September 1998, Richard Clarke, the president's national coordinator for security, infrastructure protection, and counter-terrorism, drew up a plan to capture bin Laden called Political-Military Plan Delenda. The goal was to "immediately eliminate any significant threat to Americans" from the bin Laden network through a campaign of rolling strikes against bin Laden's bases in Afghanistan and other countries.[90] Again, however, U.S. policy-makers deferred action, with Deputy National Security Adviser James Steinberg pushing back against the plan because it offered "little benefit, lots of blowback against bomb-happy U.S."[91] In early 1999, another plot to assassinate bin Laden was scrapped because policymakers were concerned that a strike might kill a United Arab Emirates prince who was suspected of accompanying bin Laden at the time.[92] Schroen, who was the CIA station chief in Pakistan, had vehemently pressed for a strike.[93] But again he was overruled.

The best chance to get bin Laden came in May 1999. Multiple CIA reports indicated that he was staying around Kandahar for several days.[94] But senior military officials were concerned about the quality of the intelligence and worried about collateral damage. In a frustrated e-mail, the head of the CIA's bin Laden unit noted: "Having a chance to get [bin Laden] three times in 36 hours and foregoing the chance each time has made me a bit angry . . . [The director of Central Intelligence] finds himself alone at the table, with the other princip[als] basically saying 'we'll go along with your decision Mr. Director,' and implicitly saying that the Agency will hang alone if the attack doesn't get Bin Ladin."[95]

U.S. diplomatic attempts were equally feeble. The State Department pressed the Taliban to expel Osama bin Laden more than thirty times between 1996, when the Taliban took Kabul, and the summer of 2001.[96] Hundreds of State Department memos and cables outlined U.S. government discussions with Taliban officials to take this action.[97] But the Taliban refused to budge. One National Security Council memo admitted that "frequent direct diplomatic contact with the Taliban by the US has failed to gain any cooperation on ending the al Qida presence in Afghanistan."[98] This should not have been a surprise. Despite occasional differences, Osama bin Laden and Mullah Omar had developed a close relationship. Bin Laden provided money and other benefits. In return, al Qa'ida enjoyed a sanctuary. Its operatives could travel freely within Afghanistan, enter and leave without visas or immigration procedures, purchase and import vehicles and weapons, use official Afghan Ministry of Defense license plates, and establish training camps.[99]

When the Bush administration took office, concerns about al Qa'ida reached a crescendo. In a desperate memorandum to the new national security adviser, Condoleezza Rice, Richard Clarke said that "we *urgently* need such a Principals level review on the al Qida network" and bluntly warned that "we would make a major error if we underestimated the challenge al Qida poses, or overestimated the stability of the moderate, friendly regimes al Qida threatens."[100]

Deviating Paths

Al Qa'ida's first wave, which crested with the September 11 attacks, was caused by several factors. One was the group's initial decision to adopt a strategy that focused on targeting government installations. In November 1995, al Qa'ida operatives packed a van with plastic explosives and attacked the office of the program manager of the Saudi Arabian National Guard, killing seven and wounding sixty. On August 7, 1998, al Qa'ida conducted attacks against the U.S. embassies in Nairobi and Dar es Salaam. In October 2000, al Qa'ida attacked the U.S. Navy destroyer USS *Cole*, which was docked in the Yemen port of Aden, killing seventeen U.S. Navy personnel and wounding thirty-nine others. And then came September 11. As noted, al Qa'ida leaders benefited from a supportive Taliban government, and the United States failed to implement any systematic counterterrorism strategy, especially against al Qa'ida in Afghanistan.

The United States also missed a chance to exploit divisions among radicals. As U.S. government officials debated a response to al Qa'ida after September 11, Sharif and Zawahiri were pursuing divergent pathways. A dedicated ideological campaign against Zawahiri's radical interpretation of Islam might have disrupted the support networks protecting al Qa'ida. Instead, U.S. officials allowed the more moderate leaders to be pushed to the side. Sharif had moved his family to Yemen in 1994 and begun working as a doctor in the General Al-Thawrah Hospital. In 1999 he divorced his wife, Nabihah al-Tamimi, and married a Yemeni woman, Samah Muhammad Ghalib.[101] Zawahiri had moved back to Afghanistan and continued to plot against the United States and write about al Qa'ida's religious doctrine. In the wake of the U.S. embassy bombings and the attack against the USS *Cole*, Zawahiri and other al Qa'ida leaders anticipated U.S. military retaliation and developed countersurveillance techniques. Among a variety of tactics, they rotated between several residences in Nangarhar, Khowst, Kandahar, and other provinces. And they frequently stayed in different locations so they couldn't be killed in the same strike.

Afghanistan was now the hub of al Qa'ida's global terrorist enterprise. The CIA and U.S. special operations forces had been among the American organizations most actively monitoring Osama bin Laden's activities and weighing a strike. They would now be called on to respond to the most significant attack on American soil.

3

HUNTING IN THE HINDU KUSH

THE CH-47 CHINOOK'S helicopter blades sliced through the frigid mountain air. The chopper was carrying nearly four dozen soldiers, with 80-pound rucksacks and weapons on board. They were headed to the Shah-i-Kot Valley of eastern Afghanistan. U.S. intelligence intercepts in early 2002 had detected a large contingent of al Qa'ida and Taliban fighters taking shelter there after U.S. ground and aerial bombardment. In the Chinook, the dim cabin lights cast dancing shadows across the floor. Sergeant Major Frank Grippe and his crew felt a nervous tension.

When they hit the ground, all hell broke loose. "We started taking fire," Grippe explained. Rocket-propelled grenades, small arms fire, heavy machine gun fire, and 82-millimeter mortar rounds rained down on the Americans. "We returned fire and we moved under some cover."[1]

Grippe was the command sergeant major for the 1st Battalion, 87th Infantry Regiment of the 10th Mountain Division. He had grown up in the Mohawk Valley of upstate New York, sandwiched between the Adirondack and Catskill Mountains. But rural New York was a distant memory. Grippe maneuvered his force to a small ridge that separated the landing zone from the al Qa'ida location.

Lieutenant Brad Maroyka, commander of Charlie Company's First Platoon, was watching his two squads hit al Qa'ida targets from his position about 150 yards away. "We've got enemy moving up on the west side," he radioed to company commander Captain Nelson Kraft, who was back near the command post. "We are destroying them, but they are returning fire."[2] U.S. soldiers in the northern blocking position fired back with 7.62-millimeter sniper rifles, M4s, and squad automatic weapons.

"Incoming fire!" screamed Sergeant First Class Robert Healy, the battalion operations sergeant. A mortar round landed nearby, spraying several of his soldiers with shrapnel. Ten seconds later another mortar round landed, wounding six more soldiers.

"I'm hit," yelled Grippe. A piece of shrapnel the size of a quarter had lodged in the back of his thigh. Grippe continued fighting, but the shrapnel remained in his leg. "I guess you could say I'll be setting off airport detectors, metal detectors, for the rest of my life," he said.[3]

The fighting was intense. As the day progressed, the Americans called in air support. A Predator controller observed a group of enemy fighters in the valley and reported, "They are coming down off the hills and it looks like they are saddling up."[4]

The MQ-1 Predator, a pilotless drone equipped with video cameras and forward-looking infrared sensors, had made its combat debut in 1995 in the Balkans. But U.S. officials such as Richard Clarke, the president's counterterrorism czar, had foreseen its usefulness in targeting terrorists. In December 2000, Clarke wrote a White House memo announcing that "the CIA began covert flights into Afghanistan using the Predator [unmanned aerial vehicle] operating out of Uzbekistan." More important, he wrote of the new advantage the drones gave U.S. forces. "The Spring flights may be able to incorporate a new capability: Hellfire anti-tank missiles mounted aboard the Predators. This new capability would permit a 'see it/shoot it' option."[5]

For the next several days after Grippe and his crew landed in the valley, U.S. planes and ground units unleashed withering firepower in the Shah-i-Kot. A-10 Thunderbolts strafed al Qa'ida and Taliban positions. "I put down about 250 rounds of 30mm," boasted an A-10 pilot from the 74th Expeditionary Fighter Squadron, "and then another A-10 pilot put down another 200–250 rounds of 30mm, right into the area, just to let them know that we were there, in case anybody was still alive at that point."[6]

A U.S. special operations team in the valley described a scene of "unbelievable carnage" with "pink mist still in the air." "I mean, to put it bluntly, when you air-burst MK-82 against human flesh, it's got an amazing effectiveness," an A-10 pilot remarked. "The next morning," one Predator controller noted, they "were following a trail of dead up that valley."[7]

The battle of Shah-i-Kot was one of the largest battles against al Qa'ida fighters at any point after September 11 and spurred on the first reverse wave against al Qa'ida. Americans were still reeling from the attacks on the Twin Towers in New York City and the Pentagon in Washington and the downed United Airlines flight in Shanksville, Pennsylvania. Known as Operation Anaconda, the Shah-i-Kot attack was largely successful. U.S. intelligence reports indicated that several hundred al Qa'ida and Taliban fighters were killed, and several hundred more fled to Pakistan. In general, U.S. operations against al Qa'ida in the immediate aftermath of September 11 were remarkably efficient in capturing or killing most fighters in Afghanistan—or forcing them to flee to Pakistan, Iran, and other countries. U.S. forces achieved this by effectively leveraging Afghan forces and orchestrating good cooperation between intelligence and military personnel, particularly special operations forces. Such elements would not always be present in future fights.

Place of the King

The landscape of eastern Afghanistan rises up to challenge foreign invaders. Its soft limestone caverns, majestic granite mountains, and subterranean streams offer an ideal refuge for militants. The desiccated earth boasts horizontal layers of rock—green shale, schist, sandstone, limestone, dark chert, and altered volcanic rocks—deposited over millions of years as an ocean evaporated. Soviet forces in the 1980s encountered a stunning network of cave complexes dug into the soft rock. Afghan rebels had built an underground mosque with an ornate brick façade, a hospital with an ultrasound machine, a library stuffed with bound books, and living quarters furnished with plush chairs and carpets. Some cave complexes contained surprisingly modern ventilation and heating systems, electricity generators, weapons and fuel depots, and a water supply. In the late 1990s, Osama bin Laden used hard-rock mining techniques to expand many of the caves and tunnels, reinforce rooms and corridors, and obfuscate cave entrances.

The Shah-i-Kot Valley, or "place of the king," lies 30 miles from the Pakistan border in Paktia Province, in the foothills of the Hindu Kush. It is 5 miles long and nearly 3 miles wide, with an arrowhead-shaped ridgeline to the south, snowcapped mountains to the east, and a humpbacked set of peaks marching as high as 9,000 feet to the west. The tallest mountain in the vicinity is Takur Ghar, which towers over 10,000 feet and casts a shadow over the valley. The terrain is rugged, with little vegetation except occasional clumps of juniper trees. In late winter the Shah-i-Kot is sprinkled with patches of snow and ice extending down from the solid snow line, which begins several hundred feet above the valley floor. In early March temperatures undergo huge swings, from 60 degrees during the day to minus 20 with wind chill at night—an 80-degree drop. There are a handful of villages in the valley, though most of the residents fled when the fighting began.

Al Qa'ida and Taliban fighters took advantage of the valley's natural and manmade crevices for protection. "We mostly found holes or natural ravines that had been built over into large bunkers," explained Frank Grippe. "The bunkers were not just set up randomly. They were interlocked. Whoever designed the scheme for their defensive position, they knew what they were doing. They were well emplaced."[8]

An al Qa'ida manual recovered from the Shah-i-Kot, titled *The Black Book of Mountainous Operations and Training*, explained how such terrain limits the effectiveness of conventional forces. It encouraged al Qa'ida and other fighters to break "into small units (platoon-size) that fight independently from each other" and to ensure "control of high elevations."[9] More than one hundred caves were detected on the eastern ridge alone, and more than thirty caves on the western ridge. The largest cave was about 100 feet deep and was filled with weapons and ammunition.

After the fall of Kabul in November 2001, U.S. military intelligence reports indicated that "thousands of vehicles leaving Kabul" were on the road to Khowst and Paktia Provinces.[10] U.S. air strikes had to be curtailed because of concerns about civilian casualties. On January 1, 2002, a U.S. military assessment concluded that militants in the region were attempting to reconstitute a viable force.[11] Over the next several weeks, U.S. military and CIA reports indicated that a sizable contingent of Arab, Chechen, Uzbek, and Afghan fighters—perhaps several hundred—was gathering in the Shah-i-Kot Valley.

The force was nominally led by Saifullah Rahman Mansour, a Taliban commander, with support from his brother, Abdul Latif Mansour, a future Taliban leader. Saifullah was an experienced, hardened warrior who considered American soldiers to be infidels. He also had close ties with the legendary mujahideen fighter Jalaluddin Haqqani, who provided him with a security belt around the valley. Haqqani had been described by the Soviet government, which had a high threshold for violence itself, as "a cruel and uncompromising person" who "displays exceptional brutality toward people suspected of loyalty to the ruling regime."[12] This mixture of fighters was a good illustration of the close links the Taliban and other Afghan militant groups had with al Qa'ida. In the Shah-i-Kot, they communicated through couriers as well as on VHF and HF radios.

They also used more arcane ways to send messages, such as blankets and smoke and flares.

The enemy, led by Mansour and supported by al Qa'ida fighters, planned to employ a "defense in depth" strategy if they were attacked, inflicting as many casualties as possible on American and allied soldiers instead of denying access. They would permit U.S. and allied forces to enter the lower Shah-i-Kot Valley, draw them in, and engage targets of opportunity. Enemy observation posts provided early warning of approaching U.S. forces. Mansour's Taliban forces were arrayed in two outer security belts, where they manned checkpoints and lookout positions. Al Qa'ida fighters were dug in at higher elevations.

"We found mortar base plates that were cemented in, allowing the al Qaeda to move tubes easily in and out of the caves," explained Major General Franklin L. "Buster" Hagenbeck, the ground tactical commander of the operation.[13] Hagenbeck was a tough soldier and a skilled athlete who had played defensive back on the West Point football team, was a Golden Gloves boxer, and had briefly served as an assistant football coach under the legendary Bobby Bowden at Florida State University.[14] He organized Operation Anaconda as a brigade-sized operation. The initial concept of operations, which was completed in early January 2002, emphasized the need to "destroy al Qa'ida" in the area and block escape routes to Pakistan.[15] The plan came together in a two-week period in February. Special operations forces and CIA operatives met in a safe house in Kabul on February 6, and a small group of planners from Combined Force Land Component Commander (CFLCC), which was based in Kuwait and had tactical control of all ground forces operating in the theater except for a handful of units conducting clandestine operations, joined them on February 9.

On February 17 the team briefed their plan to Hagenbeck. Special operations teams and two Afghan blocking forces would surround the valley while U.S.-trained Afghan forces under General Zia Lodin moved in. At the same time air assault teams would occupy blocking positions along the eastern ridge. Their ultimate objective was "the destruction of identified al Qaeda leadership, organization, and infrastructure and [the prevention of] their escape to Pakistan."[16] It was hoped that effective blocking positions would solve the problem U.S. military and CIA operatives had encountered back in December, when al Qa'ida operatives had escaped across the border at Tora Bora. Combat operations were expected to take about seventy-two hours.[17]

The concept of operations, a 126-slide PowerPoint briefing, indicated that "several hundred Taliban fighters" were in the area, along with al Qa'ida members "dedicated to [the] cause of Jihad; eager to fight to the death if confronted."[18] New intelligence continued to arrive as the start date drew nearer. On February 25, U.S. Central Command reported, "The Taliban and al-Qaeda groups know we're looking for them, and aren't moving. We did first good surveillance last night. Will refine shots now until the 28th. As usual, terrain in the area made taking good shots difficult (deep, narrow valleys)."[19] The final plan for Operation Anaconda was briefed to the head of U.S. Central Command, General Tommy Franks, on February 26.

Executing the Plan

On March 1, Afghan forces and U.S. special operations forces from Task Force Anvil moved into blocking positions along enemy routes of retreat south and east of the valley. On March 2 the combat phase of Operation Anaconda began at 5:30 a.m., when several reconnaissance teams—Task Force Rakassan, Task Force 64, and Task Force K-Bar—moved into blocking positions. At the same time Afghan and special operations forces from Task Force Hammer drove south into the valley from the city of Gardez. Their mission was to attack along the western ridge and force the enemy into "kill zones" where 10th Mountain troops and more special operations forces were waiting.[20]

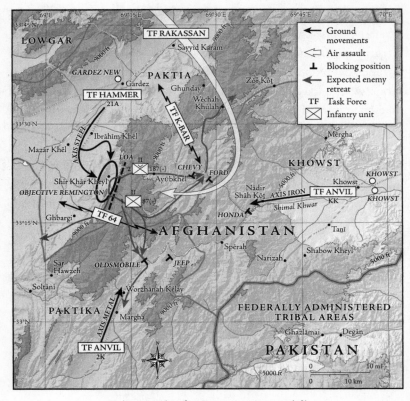

Figure 3: Plan for Operation Anaconda[21]

Things did not start well. Unexpected fire, initially believed to be from al Qa'ida mortars but later determined to be accidental fire from a U.S. AC-130 gunship, turned back the Afghan force. AH-64 Apache helicopters did preliminary sweeps of the landing zones, but air assault forces came under immediate attack and were pinned down as they entered the valley by fire from al Qa'ida fighters on the mountain slopes above them. "Each group," chronicled an initial intelligence report, "poses a significant threat to our ground forces and helos."[22] AH-64s made a pass through the valley floor to clear the way for additional air assault troops. In the Shah-i-Kot, they carried lethal weaponry, including a 30-millimeter M230 chain gun and a mixture of AGM-114 Hellfire and Hydra 70 rocket pods. Enemy fire was intense nevertheless. "Flew in to [landing zone] . . . Under fire when we stepped off the helicopter," one soldier wrote.[23] Several of the Apaches returned to base full of holes, and one took a rocket-propelled grenade in the nose.

Another air assault wave, bringing in the 10th Mountain Division's 1-87 Infantry Battalion, headed for the three southern blocking positions. They took two blocking positions, but "a heavy concentration of fire" prevented them from taking the third. The soldiers landed "at the base of an al-Qaeda stronghold and literally within a minute of being dropped off began taking sporadic fires as they moved to cover."[24] Mortar fire, rocket-propelled grenades, heavy machine-gun fire, and small arms fire emanated from the hills above the troops' positions. The soldiers took fire all morning. "I didn't really expect them to try and duke it out with us," said the 1-87 Infantry Battalion commander. "I was just surprised at the intensity of what I saw on the valley floor."[25]

The first major air strike came when a B-52 bombed a series of al Qa'ida and Taliban targets in the early morning. Within an hour a B-52 hit a building in the deserted town of Marzak, situated in the heart of the Shah-i-Kot. A few minutes later a B-52 dropped a string of 500-pound bombs on al Qa'ida fighters in the open.[26]

Air force documents tell the story in gripping fashion. "Enemy continues to control the high ground in [vicinity of] whaleback and small fortified pockets through the area of operations," one report declared. "Numerous bombing strikes were made against dug-in enemy forces [around] Babulkeyl," another deserted Shah-i-Kot town, "resulting in moderate to heavy enemy casualties."[27]

CIA human intelligence reports, or HUMINT from individual sources, helped determine where the Taliban and al Qa'ida fighters were concentrated, though not necessarily their tactical positions. The mountain terrain discouraged reconnaissance and surveillance from military aircraft and satellites, as did the dispersal of enemy fighters in caves and crevices, and poor weather. Even signals intelligence, or SIGINT, which involved radio and other communications intercepts, was challenging, since Taliban and al Qa'ida fighters had improved their communication discipline. They used cell phones and satellite phones infrequently and adopted code words. "The CIA nevertheless collected unique intelligence," Hank Crumpton explained, such as by deploying "unilateral Afghan assets with modified GPS devices into the [Shah-i-Kot] area to mark key sites and routes." They illuminated enemy positions for U.S. strike aircraft.[28] Yet intelligence remained a problem during Operation Anaconda. Preliminary reports estimated that there were between 168 and well over 1,000 enemy fighters in the valley, but the smaller number had driven the operational plans. In addition, the intelligence analysis failed to identify where most of the fighters, especially al Qa'ida fighters placed in higher elevations, were located.[29]

Nowhere were these challenges more acute than on Takur Ghar mountain on March 4. Rocket-propelled grenades hit an MH-47 Chinook helicopter attempting to deposit a special reconnaissance team on what turned out to be a position held by al Qa'ida. Machine-gun fire struck the Chinook, severing the hydraulic and oil lines.[30] It lifted off rapidly, causing Petty Officer First Class Neil C. Roberts, a U.S. Navy SEAL, to fall from the aircraft. Roberts activated his infrared strobe light and returned fire on the enemy with his squad automatic weapon, but he was soon captured and killed by al Qa'ida forces. The lead Chinook from the rescue force, call sign Razor 01, was also hit by a rocket-propelled grenade.[31] Close air support and ground combat continued throughout the battle on Takur Ghar.

Al Qa'ida and Taliban forces were clearly taking casualties. Reports on the number of enemy killed climbed to 353 after the first four days of Operation Anaconda.[32] According to one report, enemy fighters were "staggering from three nights of airstrikes and facing new daylight strikes."[33] A series of air strikes on al Qa'ida reinforcements helped turn the tide on March 5. Late in the afternoon, an MQ-1 Predator spotted vehicles and al Qa'ida fighters in a ravine on the southern cusp of the valley. Over the next several hours, A-10s, F/A-18s, and AC-130 gunships attacked al Qa'ida forces.³⁴ The air support had a direct impact on the battle. "Due to increased bombing and [close air support] the enemy was unable to sustain any effective fires upon our forces," concluded a report on March 7.³⁵

Activity in Operation Anaconda tapered off after March 14. Two days later U.S. intelligence estimates indicated that there were fewer than fifteen enemy personnel in the valley.³⁶ U.S. military and CIA estimates calculated that between two hundred and three hundred Taliban and al Qa'ida fighters had been killed, and several hundred more, including Saifullah Rahman Mansour, had fled to Pakistan. Specific numbers were impossible to confirm because the heavy bombardment, including 2,000-pound bombs, had obliterated bodies. Some fighters were trapped inside collapsed caves, and others had been buried by their comrades before nightfall, as Muslim custom dictates. There were some U.S. casualties as well. Five U.S. Army soldiers, two U.S. Air Force personnel, and one Navy SEAL died, and as many as eighty soldiers were wounded.

Though it had inflicted casualties and fought viciously, al Qa'ida never made an attempt to face the U.S. military directly during Operation Anaconda. The Shah-i-Kot was largely cleared of al Qa'ida fighters, at least for the moment.

Jawbreaker

On September 11, Art Cummings, who was running the FBI's counterterrorism squad in the Richmond field office, received a phone call from Dale Watson, the assistant director for the Counterterrorism Divison at FBI Headquarters in Washington. *We need you in Washington,* Watson said. He gave Cummings until midnight to get there.

Cummings arrived shortly before midnight and dropped his bags at the Marriott Hotel at 9th and F Streets in Northwest

Washington. He would live there for three months. By this time Cummings had been in the FBI for nearly a decade and a half. After serving as a Navy SEAL, he spurned an offer from the Drug Enforcement Agency and chose the FBI, in part because the Bureau offered more money. He started as an agent in 1987 and worked virtually every type of FBI case, from counterintelligence to drugs, which gave him a wide-ranging appreciation of the threats faced by the United States as well as of the tactics and techniques necessary to collect information and arrest suspects.

Cummings became increasingly valuable to the FBI after the September 11 attacks, when he was assigned to the Counterterrorism Division at FBI Headquarters and charged with the development and oversight of the Bureau's operations in foreign theaters such as Afghanistan. He was later given responsibility for the development and management of FBI operations against al Qa'ida and other terrorist groups.[37] Cummings stayed in Washington and returned to his wife and family in Richmond on the weekends. The war against al Qa'ida took over his life.

As Cummings and the FBI tried to piece together the September 11 plot, the CIA and U.S. special operations forces were engaged in one of the most successful efforts to overthrow a government in modern U.S. history. "We're getting ready to do something that hasn't been done since World War II and the days of the OSS," Hank Crumpton explained. Crumpton, who had just been appointed to run the Afghan war within the CIA's Counterterrorism Center (CTC), was referring to the Office of Strategic Services, which was involved in a number of espionage and subversive activities behind enemy lines during World War II. "We here at CTC are assembling teams of case officers and paramilitary officers to drive the fight into Afghanistan. The rules have finally changed," Crumpton continued, "which means we get a full shot at bin Laden and al Qa'ida."

Crumpton outlined how the CTC teams would work. Separate teams would deploy to different parts of Afghanistan and embed with Afghan field commanders. A Farsi- or Dari-speaking case officer would lead each team, while a paramilitary officer from the Special Activities Division, the CIA's covert paramilitary operations unit, would serve as his deputy. The CIA teams would produce intelligence on enemy positions and capabilities, which CTC headquarters would use to help coordinate the war. Each CTC team on the ground would have a special operations team attached to it, with a combat air controller to coordinate close air support.

Crumpton was an extraordinarily competent CIA officer. But he also had a sense of humor. When he took over the Afghan operation, he posted a sign on his office door that borrowed the words of Antarctic explorer Ernest Shackleton: "Officers wanted for hazardous journey. Small wages. Bitter cold. Long months of complete darkness. Safe return doubtful."[38] Crumpton's vision of the war was straightforward. Since power and politics in Afghanistan were very localized, success hinged on effectively cooperating with Afghanistan's tribes, subtribes, clans, and communities. Many were currently allied with the Taliban, so the CIA's and the U.S. military's task was to orchestrate widespread defection. The strategy, he said, depended on recognizing that "the center of gravity rested in the minds of those widespread tribal militia leaders, who were allied with the Taliban and al-Qaeda out of political convenience or necessity," and "convincing potential allies that their future rested with the small CIA and U.S. military teams."[39]

On September 13, 2001, George Tenet had briefed President Bush on the CIA's plan for conducting operations in Afghanistan. He took with him his counterterrorism chief, Cofer Black, and together they outlined a strategy that merged CIA paramilitary teams, U.S. special operations forces, and air power to bring down the Taliban regime. "Mr. President," Black noted at the briefing, staring intently at Bush, "we can do this. No doubt in my mind. We do this the way that we've outlined it, we'll set this thing up so it's an unfair fight for the U.S. military. But you've got to understand," he continued, choosing his words carefully, "people are going to die."[40]

Two days later, at Camp David, Tenet explained that the plan "stressed one thing: we would be the insurgents. Working closely with military special forces, CIA teams would be the ones using speed and agility to dislodge an emplaced foe."[41]

General Tommy Franks also began working on war plans. On September 20, Franks arrived at the Pentagon from Tampa, Florida, to brief Secretary of Defense Donald Rumsfeld, Deputy Secretary of Defense Paul Wolfowitz, and the Joint Chiefs of Staff on his plan for invading Afghanistan. Wolfowitz outlined his views in a classified September 23 paper for Rumsfeld entitled "Using Special Forces on 'Our Side' of the Line." He argued that U.S. Army special forces should be deployed on the ground with Northern Alliance forces to help direct U.S. air attacks, gather intelligence, and deliver humanitarian aid where needed. Wolfowitz was aware of the Soviet experience in Afghanistan in the 1980s and was concerned that the United States would suffer a similar fate.[42] The thinking was that blending U.S. and Afghan forces would limit American exposure.

A CIA team led by Gary Schroen, appropriately code-named Jawbreaker, landed in the Panjshir Valley in northeastern Afghanistan on September 26, 2001, only two weeks after the September 11 attacks. The team was part of the Special Activities Division, which had no more than a few hundred officers with classic intelligence and special operations backgrounds. Schroen and his team were soon joined on the ground by several special operations force A-teams, including Operational Detachment Alpha (ODA) 555, known as "Triple Nickel." These forces worked with local Afghan commanders and coordinated U.S. air strikes while providing arms, equipment, and military advice. They furnished money to buy— or at least rent—the loyalty of local commanders and their militia forces. As Schroen once noted, "Money is the lubricant that makes things happen in Afghanistan."[43]

The U.S. bombing campaign began on the night of October 7. The objective was to destroy the Taliban's limited air defense and communications. American and British special operations teams had been conducting scouting missions in Afghanistan. Al Qa'ida played a limited, though still important, role in the Taliban's defense. Of particular note was al Qa'ida's 055 Arab Brigade, which included an influential group of foreign fighters. The group was commanded by Juma Namangani, a flamboyant Uzbek militant and founder of the Islamic Movement of Uzbekistan, who was killed the next month during a U.S. air strike in northern Afghanistan. Namangani was aided by Abd al-Hadi al-Iraqi, who was born in Mosul, Iraq, in 1961 and had served in the Iraqi military. The U.S. Defense Department considered Abd al-Hadi al-Iraqi one of al Qa'ida's "key paramilitary commanders in Afghanistan" and said he "was known and trusted by Bin Ladin and Ayman al-Zawahiri."[44] Prior to September 11 he had served on bin Laden's ten-person advisory board and al Qa'ida's military committee, which oversaw military operations and training. The 055 Brigade, which was believed to have between five hundred and a thousand fighters at its disposal—though some estimates projected as many as twenty-five hundred—provided the Taliban with a cadre of elite, well-trained soldiers. They were integrated into the Taliban army and were used to conduct commando-style operations. Abd al-Hadi al-Iraqi had also been involved in al Qa'ida's advanced training in chemical and explosives.

Some of the first major combat actions of the war occurred in the mountains near Mazar-e-Sharif in northern Afghanistan. Special operations teams working with Northern Alliance generals Abdul Rashid Dostum and Atta Mohammed fought their way north up the Dar-ye Suf and Balkh River Valleys toward the northern capital.[45] The terrain and conditions were unlike anything the Americans had ever seen. They found themselves traversing steep mountain paths next to thousand-foot precipices. Since even four-wheel-drive vehicles couldn't effectively maneuver on the winding mountain trails, military and intelligence forces used Afghan horses to haul their equipment. Many of the Americans had never been on a horse before. Because of the sheer dropoffs, they were told to keep one foot out of the stirrup, so that if the horse stumbled, they could fall onto the trail as the horse slid off the cliff. In especially steep areas, U.S. forces were prepared to shoot any horse that stumbled before it could drag its rider to his death.[46]

The first forays against the Taliban were in northern Afghanistan because Tajik and Uzbek opposition to the Pashtun Taliban was strongest there. In late October and early November, Dostum's forces took several villages near Mazar-e-Sharif, which they overran on November 10.[47] Al Qa'ida's 055 Brigade sustained a major blow in the north. When the Taliban commander Mullah Mohammad Fazl surrendered to Dostum in late November, al Qa'ida fighters with him were detained and transported by truck to the Qala-e-Jangi fortress. The al Qa'ida fighters at Qala-e-Jangi rose up not long after, triggering a battle in which CIA operative Johnny "Mike" Spann, who was serving in the clandestine service's Special Activities Division, was killed. The uprising brought intense fighting. Some al Qa'ida fighters died during the U.S. aerial bombardment of Qala-e-Jangi. Others died when Northern Alliance forces poured oil into the basement of the prison and ignited it, and still others drowned when the basement was flooded with frigid water.

Those who escaped U.S. bombardment, led by Abd al-Hadi al-Iraqi, headed to Pakistan, where they fled across the border or regrouped in areas like the Shah-i-Kot Valley. The fall of Mazar-e-Sharif and the dispersal of the 055 Brigade unhinged the Taliban position in northern Afghanistan. Taliban defenders near Bamiyan in the central part of the country briefly resisted before surrendering on November 11, and Kabul fell without a fight on November 13. The Taliban collapse was remarkable. Only two months after the September 11 attacks, the most strategically important city in Afghanistan—Kabul—had been conquered. American and Afghan forces then encircled a force of some five thousand Taliban and al Qa'ida survivors in the city of Kunduz; they surrendered following a twelve-day siege on November 26.[48]

One of al Qa'ida's most significant losses at the time was Muhammed Atef, better known to his friends as Abu Hafs al-

Masri. He was killed outside Kabul when U.S. F-15s dropped bombs on his position, as identified by MQ-1 Predator drones.[49] Atef could almost have been Osama bin Laden's body double. He had a large nose, a slightly heavier build than bin Laden, and stood over six feet, four inches tall. His olive complexion and dark brown hair gave away his Mediterranean heritage. The hair in his beard had a neat line of gray from the base of his neck to the lower portion of his cheeks and then sharply switched to dark brown on the upper part of his cheeks, his chin, and above his mouth. It made him look a bit like a skunk.

Atef was born in Menoufya, Egypt, on June 17, 1944, and studied at Asyut University. He had served in the Egyptian Air Force and then, beginning in the early 1980s, as a deputy and close confidante of bin Laden. In 1992, Atef personally selected a cadre of talented individuals from al Qa'ida training camps to attend advanced classes at bin Laden's home in the Hyatabad neighborhood of Peshawar.[50] Several years later, the bin Ladens became indebted to Atef when he seized a grenade that one of Osama bin Laden's sons had accidentally armed and tossed it out of an airplane flying the family from Kabul to Kandahar. The grenade would have brought down the plane, killing bin Laden's wives, sons, and daughters.[51]

Atef's relationship with bin Laden grew deeper in early 2001, when his daughter Khadija married bin Laden's son Muhammad. They celebrated at bin Laden's Tarnak Farms compound outside Kandahar City. Atef was a possible successor to bin Laden and argued that al Qa'ida should procure weapons of mass destruction. In an e-mail to Atef in April 1999, Ayman al-Zawahiri encouraged him to continue looking into using chemical and biological weapons against the United States. "The destructive power of these weapons is no less than that of nuclear weapons," he explained. "I would like to emphasize what we previously discussed—that looking for a specialist is the fastest, safest, and cheapest way" to embark on a biological and chemical weapons program.[52]

Atef's death was a significant blow to bin Laden. As bin Laden's son Omar confided in his memoir, "I believe that my father loved Mohammed Atef as much as one man can love another. Due to their indestructible friendship, Mohammed became like a favored uncle to my father's children."[53]

With the fall of Kabul and Kunduz and the killing of such senior al Qa'ida leaders as Muhammed Atef, attention shifted to the Taliban's southern stronghold, Kandahar. Special operations forces in support of Hamid Karzai, a Popalzai tribal leader and the future president of Afghanistan, advanced on Kandahar from the north.[54] In addition, special operations forces in support of Gul Agha Shirzai, who was nicknamed "Bulldozer" for his coercive tactics, advanced from the south. The first clashes occurred in late November at Tarin Kowt and Sayed Slim Kalay, which lay just north of the city. There were also several fights along Highway 4 south of Kandahar from December 2 to December 6. On the night of December 6, Mullah Omar and the senior Taliban leadership fled the city and went into hiding, effectively ending Taliban rule in Afghanistan.[55]

Allied forces subsequently tracked a group of al Qa'ida survivors thought to include Osama bin Laden to a series of caves in the White Mountains near Tora Bora. The caves were taken in a sixteen-day battle ending on December 17, but many al Qa'ida defenders, including bin Laden, escaped and fled across the border into Pakistan.[56]

Picking Up the Pieces

After the Taliban was overthrown, a small group of Americans, including Philip Mudd at the CIA, helped put together a government in Afghanistan. Early in November, Ambassador James Dobbins, the Bush administration's envoy to Afghanistan, took a secure call from Hank Crumpton, who was still overseeing the CIA's operations in Afghanistan. Crumpton offered to send over Mudd, who had just served on the White House staff. Dobbins gladly accepted.

Mudd's job, as Dobbins envisioned, would be to connect the U.S. negotiating team to Afghan field commanders, Northern Alliance officials, and CIA teams on the ground. "Phil was easy to get along with," said Dobbins, "very understated, and extremely competent." Mudd also earned a reputation for securing the best accommodations in Afghanistan, working his CIA contacts to find an aboveground bedroom, heat, light, plumbing, and hot meals. "After the first night," said Dobbins on one of their visits to Afghanistan, "I considered moving in with him, but my security team scotched the idea. I was living in a bunker in the old U.S. embassy in Kabul surrounded by something like five hundred U.S. Marines, all guarding me. And Phil had prime real estate in a building that had once been a hotel. My security took one look at it and said, 'Forget it. It's too vulnerable to an attack.'"[57]

As the Taliban's power base collapsed, international and local attention turned to reconstruction. Dobbins, Mudd, and their team helped organize a meeting of Afghan and international political leaders in Bonn, Germany, late in November. On December 5, with coalition troops about to take Kandahar, Afghan leaders signed an agreement that established a timetable for the creation of a representative and freely elected government.[58] Under the Bonn Agreement, the parties agreed to establish an interim authority comprising three main bodies: a thirty-member acting administration headed by Hamid Karzai, a Pashtun, which took power on December 22; a Supreme Court; and a Special Independent Commission for the Convening of the Emergency Loya Jirga, the name for a traditional meeting of Afghan tribal, political, and religious leaders.

As Afghanistan began to recover from the shock of invasion, there was extraordinary upheaval across the Muslim world. American Muslim groups and most governments worldwide, including several surprising leaders, had denounced the September 11 attacks. Mohammad Khatami, the Iranian president, said that he felt "deep regret and sympathy with the victims," and Libyan leader Moammar Gadhafi denounced the attacks as "horrifying."[59] Yet there were jubilant crowds in some Palestinian areas, and Saddam Hussein's government in Iraq issued an immediate statement gloating that "the American cowboys are reaping the fruit of their crimes against humanity." Under the headline "America Burns," the official newspaper *Al-Iraq* said that "what happened in the United States yesterday is a lesson for all tyrants, oppressors and criminals."[60] Still others across the Muslim world expressed skepticism that al Qa'ida, a fringe organization in Afghanistan, could have perpetrated sophisticated multipronged attacks against the world's only superpower. Across the Middle East, conspiracy theories gained currency, including one that the CIA or the Israeli intelligence service, the Mossad, had orchestrated the attacks to justify a war in the region.[61]

Yet beneath the surface there was a roiling debate among Muslims. Credible conservative voices denounced the attacks. Some had worked alongside Zawahiri and bin Laden over the years. For Sayyid Imam Abd al-Aziz al-Sharif, the former leader of Egyptian Islamic Jihad and friend of Zawahiri, the September 11 attacks were barbaric and un-Islamic. He wrote that bin Laden had betrayed Mullah Omar and the Afghan people by orchestrating an international terrorist attack while living on Afghan soil under Omar's protection. This left the Taliban vulnerable to America's military response. "Afghanistan and its people were the ones who paid the price," he wrote.[62]

Sharif had an esoteric and historically grounded claim: the al Qa'ida hijackers had attacked a country that had allowed them on its soil. "They entered the United States with a visa," Sharif explained. "This is a contract of safety on which there is not dispute among the ulema." Sharif cited Muhammad ibn al-Hasan al-Shaybani, a venerable Muslim scholar from what is now Iraq, who died in A.D. 805. In his book *Kitab al-Siyar al-Kabir*, Shaybani argued that it is un-Islamic to betray a country—in blood, honor, or money—which allows individuals to enter its territory.[63] Bin Laden's and Zawahiri's punishment, Sharif said, would not be pleasant. "On the Day of Judgment," he noted, "every double-crosser will have a banner at his anus proportionate to his treachery."[64]

Sharif also feared that the September 11 attacks would initiate violence against Muslims. "They were a disaster for Muslims," he acknowledged. "They have sown sedition within every house."[65] War and violence would proliferate across the Muslim world, he argued, affecting innocent women, children, men, and families.

Though he had left al Qa'ida, Sharif was targeted by the government in Yemen because of his past association with extremist groups. In late September 2001 he began to suspect that Yemeni intelligence agents were monitoring his movements, and he grew increasingly concerned about his security. On October 28, Yemeni authorities seized him while he was working at the Al-Shiffa Hospital in Ibb governorate, south of Sana'a. His family was not informed of his arrest, and it took them three weeks to locate him. Sharif was initially held incommunicado, but eventually family members had irregular access to him. During his three years in detention in Yemen, he was held without charge, without trial, and without access to an attorney. According to a Human Rights Watch investigation, his cell was dirty and his food substandard, though he was not physically abused.[66] Despite the urgings of prominent Yemeni politicians, including parliamentary speaker Abdullah al-Ahmar, and tribal leaders, the Yemeni government refused to release Sharif.

For many others, including conservative Muslims, the September 11 attacks were barbaric. One was Salman al-Awdah, a Salafi cleric born in 1955 in the Saudi village of al-Basr. He had served five years in jail for taking part in the Sahway, or Awakening, a clerical movement that opposed the Saudi government's 1991 decision to allow U.S. military forces on its soil after Iraq invaded Kuwait. In 1994, Osama bin Laden had praised Awdah in his "Open Letter to Shaykh Bin Baz on the Invalidity of His Fatwa on Peace with the Jews."[67] Yet Awdah denounced the September 11 attacks. In an open letter to bin Laden, he noted, "My brother Osama: How much blood has been spilt? How many innocent people, children, elderly, and women have been killed, dispersed, or evicted in the name of al Qa'ida?" Referring to Judgment Day, he asked bin Laden, "Will you be happy to meet God Almighty carrying the burden of these hundreds of thousands or millions on your back?"[68]

Surprisingly, even some of al Qa'ida's leaders condemned the attacks. Perhaps the most intriguing was Saif al-Adel, who was Osama bin Laden's security chief in Sudan and continued to be a close confidant. Adel had served in the Egyptian military and had a long pedigree of violent jihad. He had worked as an instructor in the Sa'adah training camp in Lebanon in 1988 and 1989 before joining al Qa'ida. He also helped plan the 1998 U.S. embassy bombings in Tanzania and Kenya.[69]

Adel stood five feet, five inches tall, weighed roughly 160 pounds, and had a receding hairline. He wore glasses with heavy black frames and large square lenses and had a baby face that gave him a youthful appearance. His militant career, including actions with Egyptian Islamic Jihad, had left him with a noticeable scar on one of his arms and hands, and two of his fingers had been permanently injured. But al Qa'ida leaders found him abrasive. "Other members of the organization did not want to work with or for Saif al-Adel," said one, "because he did not get along with people, nor did he trust people."[70] Others accused him of being chauvinistic about his heritage and showing favoritism to Egyptians. "His narrow Asian eyes," another colleague claimed, "reflected malicious cleverness, and his lean and strong body was full of energy."[71]

Adel objected to the September 11 attacks. According to Khalid Sheikh Mohammed, one of the masterminds of the attacks, Adel had not even been informed of the details during the planning stage.[72] In one particularly blunt letter, dated June 13, 2002, Adel wrote to Khalid Sheikh Mohammed that bin Laden's actions would take al Qa'ida "from misfortune to disaster." He complained of bin

Laden's autocratic leadership, writing that "if someone opposes him, he immediately puts forward another person to render an opinion in his support, clinging to his opinion."[73]

Others followed suit. One was Abu Mus'ab al-Suri, a Syrian whose writings on military strategy were widely read among al Qa'ida operatives and sympathizers.[74] He criticized the decision to engage in "the battle of Shah-i-Kot, which has the American name 'Operation Anaconda,' where hundreds were killed." Al Qa'ida paid a "high strategic price," Suri concluded, which confirmed that "confronting the campaigns of American and allied forces in an overt way . . . is still in its wrong time."[75] Another was the Egyptian Islamic extremist and journalist Shaykh Abu al Walid al-Masri, whose daughter was married to Saif al-Adel and who was a senior member of the al Qa'ida shura council, its leadership body. He had been involved in jihadist movements around the globe for over four decades, including against the Soviets in Afghanistan.[76] Shaykh Abu al Walid al-Masri published a rare critical document about bin Laden titled "The Story of the Afghan Arabs: From the Entry to Afghanistan to the Final Exodus with the Taliban." Bin Laden's leadership, he argued, "encourages recklessness and causes disorganization, characteristics which are unsuitable for this existential battle in which we confront the greatest force in the world, the USA."[77] He also discussed in colorful detail many of the debates and divisions within al Qa'ida and concluded that al Qa'ida "was a tragic example of an Islamic movement managed in an alarmingly meaningless way."[78]

It is not entirely clear what Osama bin Laden's objectives were in conducting the September 11 attacks, in part since there is little primary-source evidence from bin Laden himself. It is unlikely that he expected to chase the United States out of the Middle East with a single terrorist blow. Instead, he may have hoped that the United States would end its support of Arab regimes and pull its forces out of the Middle East, including Saudi Arabia, following a broader campaign of violence. What is more apparent, however, is that bin Laden was not well prepared for the American response or the harsh reaction from some al Qa'ida leaders.

A Painful Lesson

Al Qa'ida had pulled off the most successful terrorist attack on U.S. soil up to that point, killing nearly three thousand people and wounding thousands more. Yet the American response was swift and decisive. Kabul had fallen; the Taliban and al Qa'ida were on the run. Now U.S. forces turned their attention to individual al Qa'ida leaders.

Senior al Qa'ida member Saif al-Adel described his trepidation: "On Sunday night, the third night of the blessed month and after 0100 in the morning, I woke up feeling anxious and sensed there was a danger close to me," he recalled. "I woke up the brothers with me, Abu-Muhammad al-Abyad, Abd al-Rahman al-Masri, and Abu-Usamah al-Filastini, and told them of my anxiety."

Suddenly they heard explosions in the distance from U.S. air strikes. The explosions came closer.

"We heard a missile passing over our heads immediately before we had finished eating and it exploded 100 meters from the house," Adel noted. "We looked at the aircraft and saw it fire the second missile and we took cover. It fell in the middle of the road. When we finished removing the young men and Abd-al-Wahid [from under the debris], the brothers consulted each other and feared that their house was also being watched," he said.

The U.S. attack took place on the morning of November 19, 2001, at Adel's residence in Kandahar Province. Several al Qa'ida fighters were killed that day by U.S. strike aircraft and AH-64 Apache helicopters. Asim al-Yamani, a trainer at al Qa'ida's al-Farouq camp, and Abu-Ali al-Yafi'i, one of Adel's guards, were among the dead.

"We saw the tragedy on the road," Adel summed up, "and it was a story and lesson."[79]

It had been a difficult few months for Adel and other senior al Qa'ida leaders. Around September 18, bin Laden had arrived at one of al Qa'ida's safe houses in Kabul with Ayman al-Zawahiri, Abu Hafs al-Masri, and several others to prepare for the imminent U.S. retaliation for September 11. He gave orders. Al Qa'ida would have an initial front line of fighters to defend Kabul, led by Abd al-Hadi al-Iraqi and Abdul Wakil al-Masri. Abu Zubaydah and Ibn al-Shaykh al-Libi would organize the defense of Khowst Province, and others would defend key Afghan fronts.

By December, however, the organization was in disarray. One quarter of Osama bin Laden's top commanders had been killed or captured.[80] The situation was particularly troubling in southern Afghanistan, where al Qa'ida had been headquartered. Saif al-Adel told the remaining foreign fighters that he had no more instructions from bin Laden, who had not communicated with him, and there were no serious contingency plans for the loss of Afghanistan. To make matters worse, Taliban leaders were demanding that al Qa'ida and the rest of the Arabs leave the country. Adel said there was no choice but to try to save themselves by escaping and reorganizing at some later point. It was one of al Qa'ida's darkest hours.

Al Qa'ida's first wave began to ebb, in part because the organization had shifted to a punishment strategy, killing more than three thousand civilians and causing worldwide outrage on September 11. In addition, the United States adopted a light-footprint strategy, utilizing a small number of CIA and U.S. special operations forces to overthrow the Taliban government, undermining al Qa'ida's sanctuary. By 2002 al Qa'ida fighters had largely been eliminated from Afghanistan thanks to Operation Anaconda and other efforts, though bin Laden briefly trekked to Konar Province, undetected, before returning across the border to Pakistan. As the CIA's Hank Crumpton proudly announced, "Several teams of

CIA and U.S. Army Special Forces personnel, scores of clandestine U.S. military raiders, and U.S. airpower had destroyed the Taliban regime and disrupted al Qaeda, killing or capturing approximately 25 percent of the enemy's leaders."[81] The United States had seized over twenty terrorist training camps, killed thousands of enemy fighters, and forced hundreds of al Qa'ida members and thousands of Taliban to flee across the border.

The fight then moved to neighboring Pakistan.

AL QA'IDA IN PAKISTAN

THE MANHUNT FOR Khalid Sheikh Mohammed, one of the masterminds of the September 11 attacks, grew hot in Pakistan in 2003. U.S. intelligence agencies had been desperate to find the al Qa'ida leader, whom colleagues referred to by his code name, Mukhtar. Agents had been contacting every imaginable human source and culling through huge caches of signals intelligence. Just after the September 11 attacks, George Tenet had urged his staff to move outside their comfort zones. "All the rules have changed," he warned in a memo titled "We're at War." "Each person must assume an unprecedented degree of personal responsibility."[1] U.S. and Pakistani intelligence agents had mapped out a network of contacts close to Khalid Sheikh Mohammad, yet they still lacked enough information to capture him.

The situation changed early in 2003. The hunt centered on Rawalpindi, a bustling Pakistani city of nearly 1.7 million located on the Potwar Plateau, 9 miles southwest of Islamabad, the nation's capital. Rawalpindi lies along the ancient trade routes that connected Persia and the Central Asian steppes to India. Sikhs settled the area in 1765 and invited nearby traders to take up residence as well. It became a strategic military outpost after the British occupied the Punjab in 1849. The old parts of Rawalpindi boast densely packed houses decorated with intricate woodwork and cut brick corbels, with narrow streets that open up into a series of bazaars. The city also has a tradition of sheltering fugitives. Early in the nineteenth century, Shah Shuja, the exiled king of Afghanistan, fled to Rawalpindi after he was deposed by Mahmud Shah. Rawalpindi was an ideal place for al Qa'ida terrorists to hide.

On February 28, 2003, Pakistani intelligence received a tip that an associate of Khalid Sheikh Mohammed who was willing to assist in his capture was arriving at Islamabad International Airport. The informant was scheduled to meet Khalid Sheikh Mohammed, or KSM, as U.S. operatives referred to him, that night in a house on Peshawar Road. Khalid Sheikh Mohammed was the opposite of the pious al Qa'ida militant exemplified by Ayman al-Zawahiri and Osama bin Laden. He had thick black hair, brown eyes, and a plump physique, and he led a lavish lifestyle. While in the Philippines in late 1994 and early 1995, he apparently attended a number of parties where alcohol was consumed and he spent generously on women, frequenting go-go bars and karaoke clubs in Manila. He reportedly gave large tips. He also purportedly buzzed a tower with a rented helicopter to impress a female dentist he was dating.

Yet Khalid Sheikh Mohammed was involved in some of al Qa'ida's most notorious terrorist attacks and plots, from the September 11 attacks to the 2002 Bali bombings and the assassination of the *Wall Street Journal*'s Daniel Pearl. "I decapitated with my blessed right hand," he bragged, "the head of the American Jew, Daniel Pearl, in the city of Karachi, Pakistan."[2] Some intelligence analysts dubbed him the Forrest Gump of terrorists. CIA reporting had indicated that he was "the driving force behind the 11 September attacks as well as several subsequent plots against U.S. and Western targets worldwide."[3]

Sensing that the capture of Khalid Sheikh Mohammed was imminent, Marty Martin, who was at the CIA's Counterterrorist Center, pulled aside George Tenet late on the afternoon of February 28. "Boss, where are you going to be this weekend?" he asked. "Stay in touch. I just might get some good news."[4]

Then came the information they needed.

"I am with KSM," the informant said in a text message, after slipping into a bathroom in the squat two-story white house in Rawalpindi.[5]

The Pakistanis and Americans shifted into overdrive. At 4:45 a.m. on March 1, they surrounded the home of Ahmed Abdul Qudoos, a pale, white-bearded man who was a member of the Pakistani Islamic political party Jamaat-e-Islami. Pakistani forces broke down the front door and rushed in, brandishing weapons and shouting. In one of the rooms, a man on the ground floor pointed upward. "They are up there," he yelled.[6]

Pakistani forces dashed upstairs and found Khalid Sheikh Mohammed and several accomplices, including Mustafa al-Hawsawi, a Saudi member of al Qa'ida who had helped organize and finance the September 11 attacks. KSM quickly grabbed his Kalashnikov; a Pakistani agent tried to wrestle it from him, but the gun went off, shooting the agent in the foot. Before Khalid Sheikh Mohammed and Mustafa al-Hawsawi could do further damage, they were overpowered, hooded, bound, hustled from the house, placed in a vehicle, and quickly driven away, as was Ahmed Abdul Qudoos.

Tenet's phone soon rang, waking him up. It was Marty Martin. "Boss," he said, "we got KSM."[7]

The capture of Khalid Sheikh Mohammed was a major intelligence victory. Despite the billions of dollars the United States had spent on technical intelligence, it was old-fashioned human intelligence that secured the target. This is what Hank Crumpton had been preaching. "Distance and remote technology may reduce physical risk and protect our consciences, but we lose the tactile sense of the human battlefield," he had warned.[8] The informant, who was "a little guy who looked like a farmer," according to one American official who met him, was attracted by the $25 million bounty on Khalid Sheikh Mohammed's head.[9] He was duly rewarded.

Sometime later Tenet congratulated him in person. The informant wore one of his best suits, which was neatly pressed, to the meeting. "Do you think President Bush knows of my role in this capture?" he asked Tenet, somewhat innocently.

"Yes, he does," Tenet replied, "because I told him."

"Does he know my name?" the informant asked.

"No," Tenet answered. "Because that is a secret that he doesn't need to know."[10]

Movement into Pakistan

After the Taliban was overthrown, al Qa'ida operatives fled en masse to Pakistan. "The movement of al Qa'ida fighters into Pakistan came in waves," noted Robert Grenier, the CIA's station chief in Islamabad.[11]

A polished operator, always impeccably dressed, Grenier was a passionate Boston Red Sox fan who had a bachelor's degree in philosophy from Dartmouth College. His aura in the CIA community grew after the September 11 attacks, when he engaged in face-to-face discussions with Mullah Osmani, the deputy of Taliban leader Mullah Omar, in the mountains of Baluchistan Province in Pakistan. After Osmani declined to help the CIA by handing over bin Laden, Grenier had another idea. Would he help overthrow Mullah Omar? As Grenier explained, Osmani "could secure Kandahar with his corps, seize the radio station there, and put out a message that the al Qa'ida Arabs were no friends of the Afghans and had brought nothing but harm to the country and that Bin Laden must be seized and turned over immediately."[12] It would have been a bold move, but Osmani declined.

Fortunately, the Pakistani government was more supportive. On the morning after the September 11 attacks, the U.S. ambassador to Pakistan, Wendy Chamberlin, went to see Pakistan's president, Pervez Musharraf. She had been sent to pose a question asked by President Bush: "Are you with us or against us?" The meeting, which took place in one of Musharraf's Islamabad offices, was tense. America was reeling from the events of the preceding day, and President Bush wanted a quick answer from Musharraf. After an hour, Musharraf appeared to be waffling on his commitment to the United States, so Chamberlin resorted to a bit of Hollywood drama. Sitting close to him, she half turned away and looked down at the floor in a display of exasperation.

"What's wrong, Wendy?" he asked.

"Frankly, General Musharraf," she responded, "you are not giving me the answer I need to give my president."

Musharraf quickly replied, "We'll support you unstintingly."[13]

They agreed to discuss more details on September 15. On that day, Chamberlin presented a series of discussion points. One of the most important was capturing al Qa'ida operatives streaming into Pakistan from Afghanistan.

Musharraf had his own negotiating points. "We want you to pressure the Indians to resolve the Kashmir dispute in our favor," he said.

"We can't do that," Chamberlin responded. "This is about the terrorists who attacked America on our soil and not about Kashmir."

Musharraf was not finished. "We'd also like you to ensure that U.S. aircraft do not use bases in India for operations in Afghanistan," he insisted.[14]

His request was not altogether surprising. Pakistan and India had been involved in at least three major wars over the status of Kashmir—in 1947–1948, 1965, and 1971—as well as multiple skirmishes. The most recent border skirmish had, ironically, been initiated by Musharraf in 1999. Pakistani troops and Kashmiri insurgents crossed the Line of Control, which separates Indian- and Pakistani-controlled parts of Jammu and Kashmir, and occupied Indian territory in Kargil. The incident sparked furious artillery clashes, air battles, and costly infantry assaults by Indian troops against dug-in Pakistani forces.[15]

"We can do that," Chamberlin told Musharraf. The United States considered Indian bases militarily unnecessary and recognized how provocative their use might be for Pakistan.[16]

In the end, Musharraf agreed to many of America's requests.

He permitted overflight and landing rights for U.S. military and intelligence units, allowed access to some bases in Pakistan, provided intelligence and immigration information, cut off most logistical support to the Taliban, and broke diplomatic relations with the Taliban.[17] The United States used several bases (such as those near Jacobabad, Dalbandin, and Shamsi), set up a joint Pakistani-American facility in the U.S. embassy in Islamabad for coordinating U.S. aircraft flying through Pakistan, and shared intelligence on key Taliban and al Qa'ida leaders.[18] The U.S. military also installed radar facilities in Pakistan, which provided extensive coverage of Pakistani airspace.[19]

Similarly, the United States agreed to many of Musharraf's requests. U.S. aircraft could not fly over Pakistani nuclear facilities, the U.S. military could not launch attacks into Afghanistan from Pakistan, and the United States would provide economic assistance to the country. These concessions provided a solid foundation for U.S. actions in the fall of 2001 against the Taliban and al Qa'ida. U.S. successes in Afghanistan in 2001, however, had an unpleasant consequence: al Qa'ida forces began to scatter. U.S. intelligence assessments indicated that the bulk of al Qa'ida fighters were flowing into Pakistan's tribal areas. But many went to such cities as Peshawar and Karachi, while others migrated to Iran.

In December 2001 a U.S. government assessment examined possible al Qa'ida routes from Afghanistan to Pakistan and Iran through several Afghan locations: Konar, Jalalabad, Gardez, Kandahar, and Zaranj.[20]

Al Qa'ida operatives ended up using all of them. In a meeting in Kandahar that month, al Qa'ida leaders who had remained in southern Afghanistan, led by Saif al-Adel, instructed a group of roughly five hundred fighters to go to Pakistan through Afghanistan's eastern Paktia Province, near Gardez. They were mainly Arabs, although a smaller number were Uzbeks and Tajiks. Some were temporarily housed in the city of Zormat, while others fled to the Zormat Mountains and then continued into Pakistan.

Figure 4: U.S. Assessment of Potential al Qa'ida Routes

The Management Council

Others fled to Iran and formed al Qa'ida's "Management Council," a group of senior officials who supported Osama bin Laden and other leaders in Pakistan. They included Abu al-Khayr al-Masri, Abu Muhammad al-Masri, Saif al-Adel, Sulayman Abu Ghayth, and Abu Hafs al-Mauritani. The exodus of some al Qa'ida members to Iran posed a particular problem for the United States. There was no U.S. military and intelligence presence in Iran, at least not overtly, and the United States had an openly adversarial relationship with the Iranian government. Grenier told CIA headquarters, "Many al Qa'ida fighters were trying to get to Iran. They were interested in temporarily settling in Iran, or else moving on to Gulf states or other sanctuaries. They didn't want to stay in Pakistan because the government was cooperating with the United States."[21] While the Shi'ite Iranian leadership was generally opposed to Sunni al Qa'ida militants, Iranian officials, motivated by the old adage "my enemy's enemy is my friend," provided some aid to anti-American groups.

The Iranian government considered the U.S. presence in neighboring Afghanistan a threat to its security. Iranian intelligence officials soon initiated a meeting with al Qa'ida leaders. Ramzi bin al-Shibh, who was at a December 2001 meeting, reported that Iranian officials expressed their willingness to allow transit and give shelter to some members of al Qa'ida, though under tight scrutiny.[22] Beginning in late 2001, Iran's Islamic Revolutionary Guard Corps Qods Force, whose mission is to organize, train, equip, and finance foreign Islamic revolutionary movements, sheltered over two dozen al Qa'ida members in hotels and private residences.

But in 2002, Iran's intelligence agency, the Ministry of Intelligence and Security, took charge of relations with al Qa'ida and began rounding up operatives and their families in such cities as Zahedan. Early in 2003, Iran seized members of the Management Council and as many as sixty leaders and associates who had sought refuge there after September 11. Most al Qa'ida leaders and their families were placed under house arrest in crowded conditions. In several instances al Qa'ida prisoners, including women and children, complained to Iranian officials about their conditions and staged protests. In 2003, Osama bin Laden apparently sent a letter to Tehran threatening attacks if al Qa'ida leaders and his own family members were not released. But Iran did not comply and bin Laden did not follow through with the attacks.

Saif al-Adel, who was a member of al Qa'ida's inner shura, had escaped to Iran through Afghanistan's western border.[23] Like most other al Qa'ida leaders in Iran, Adel was placed under house arrest, though he retained access to the Internet and telephones. Using money provided by wealthy donors from the United Arab Emirates, Saudi Arabia, and Kuwait, Adel rented apartments in Iran for some al Qa'ida members and their families. He also reestablished contact with the al Qa'ida leadership and began to organize groups of fighters to return to Afghanistan and support the overthrow of the Karzai regime. In 2003, according to Saudi and U.S. officials, Adel was in communication with the al Qa'ida cell in Saudi Arabia that carried out bombings in Riyadh on May 12.[24] He was also in touch with the Arabic-language newspaper *Al-Sharq al-Awsat* and told it that he believed around 350 "Afghan Arabs" had been killed in Afghanistan since the U.S. invasion and around 180 had been captured. He contributed articles to *Mu'askar al-Battar*, a jihadist magazine published under the auspices of al Qa'ida's affiliate in the Arabian Peninsula.[25]

Sa'ad bin Laden, the third of bin Laden's sons, and Abu Mus'ab al-Zarqawi, the future leader of al Qa'ida in Iraq, also fled to Iran, as did a handful of other al Qa'ida fighters. Sa'ad bin Laden had developed a close relationship with his father. From Iran he continued to assist al Qa'ida, apparently helping with the truck bombing of a synagogue in Djerba, Tunisia.[26]

Back at the CIA's Counterterrorism Center, Philip Mudd and other senior officials were concerned that al Qa'ida leaders were in Iran. Al Qa'ida and Iran did not like each other, Mudd believed, and they certainly didn't share a common ideological view. But their mutual support did not help the United States. Al Qa'ida leaders didn't like the situation either, but they didn't have a better option. If they staged an attack against Iran, some of their leaders might be executed. For Iranian officials such as Ahmad Vahidi, a commander in the Islamic Revolutionary Guard Corps and later minister of defense, holding and monitoring several al Qa'ida leaders was a wild card.[27] Iran could provide them with a safe haven from their bitter enemy, the United States. British Prime Minister Winston Churchill had used similar logic when he declared to his personal secretary, John Colville, that "if Hitler invaded Hell, I would make at least a favorable reference to the devil in the House of Commons."[28]

Pakistan's Struggles

Most al Qa'ida leaders, however, went to Pakistan. In cooperation with the United States, the Pakistani government deployed units from the regular army, Special Services Group, Frontier Corps, and Directorate for Inter-Services Intelligence to conduct operations along routes from Afghanistan to Pakistan. Two brigades of infantry forces from the Ninth Division of the XI Corps were deployed for border and internal security operations for much of 2001 and 2002. Pakistan also established two quick reaction forces from the Special Services Group to provide local commanders with the ability to deploy troops quickly. In addition, approximately four thousand Frontier Corps forces were used to conduct operations in Pakistan's Federally Administered Tribal Areas.[29]

In October 2001, Frontier Corps forces clashed with militants crossing the border around Nawa Pass in Bajaur Agency, one of the tribal districts. In December 2001, Pakistan deployed a mixture of forces to Khyber and Kurram Agencies during U.S. operations at Tora Bora and helped capture a small number of al Qa'ida and other foreign fighters.[30] Early in 2002, Pakistan increased force levels in North and South Waziristan to target militants during Operation Anaconda. In May, Pakistani forces raided a suspected weapons cache in North Waziristan, netting mortar rounds, antipersonnel mines, and ammunition. The next month soldiers from the Special Services Group, Frontier Corps, and Pakistan's regular army conducted an assault against al Qa'ida operatives during Operation Kazha Punga in South Waziristan. Pakistani troops entered Khyber and Kurram Agencies to capture al Qa'ida fighters coming from Afghanistan.[31]

The United States viewed these initial Pakistani military operations as a limited success, even though Pakistan allowed Taliban leaders to establish a sanctuary in Baluchistan Province. Over the course of 2002, Pakistan's security agencies picked up thousands of militants, though many were eventually released.[32] In some cases the militants were released at the cutoff period for detention under the Maintenance of Public Order law or by the relevant courts on bail. Despite these drawbacks, Pakistan played a role in achieving one of the most significant objectives: the overthrow of the Taliban regime. "Musharraf became an international hero," remarked Ambassador Chamberlin. "Money was flowing into Pakistan. And Pakistan was no longer a pariah state. The situation was euphoric. Musharraf was on the cover of every magazine and newspaper."[33]

Yet these large conventional operations netted few major al Qa'ida figures. As President Musharraf later acknowledged, Pakistan's military forces could not "control a border belt which is so mountainous, treacherous," and facilitated al Qa'ida's movement into Pakistan. "They went in unnoticed," he remarked, "and they went into the cities."[34] The challenge was clear. Large numbers of conventional military forces like those deployed by Pakistan could not win this shadow war. Instead the hunt required lethal clandestine operations from agencies that could operate with speed and stealth in rural and urban areas. It was a mission better suited for police, intelligence units, and special operations forces.

The Manhunt Begins

While al Qa'ida fighters slipped into Pakistan, a clandestine manhunt began across the country's settled areas. One of the first major captures was Abu Zubaydah, who was born on March 12, 1971, to Palestinian parents in Riyadh, Saudi Arabia.[35] His six-volume diary, which was seized when he was captured in 2002, revealed a troubled childhood. Zubaydah was rejected by colleges in Saudi Arabia,

Egypt, the Philippines, and the United States before he entered a program in New Delhi. Homesick and dejected, he struggled to find direction, writing that "a Palestinian is born in a country not his [and] has to coexist in a country whose citizens first look toward him as one of a displaced people. Their looks sometimes speak out and hurt you."[36] Zubaydah recounted painful experiences of prejudice and rejection associated with his Palestinian heritage. He also suffered from bouts of loneliness.

His biggest struggle was with his father, a schoolteacher and administrator. Zubaydah wanted to please his father but also wanted to establish his own identity. "I simply believe in my independence from everything, even from my father," he wrote. "Aren't you going to finish your medical school to please your Dad?" he queried, somewhat rhetorically, in another entry. "Well, I decided to get my martyrdom certificate instead. I do not think my father will be happy about it."[37]

Zubaydah turned to jihad. With a neatly trimmed black beard and spectacles, he looked more like a graduate student than a terrorist. He first traveled to Afghanistan to participate in the anti-Soviet war in 1990, feeling that this would bring him closer to God. After mingling with the radicalized contingent of foreign fighters, he became obsessed with destroying Israel and the United States. His initial request to join al Qa'ida in 1993 was rejected, apparently because he was a "generalist" and al Qa'ida leaders were looking for someone with "niche skills."[38] But he was obstinate. He received a shrapnel wound to the head in the early 1990s while fighting on the front lines in Afghanistan, a testament to his commitment to jihad.

Over the next decade Zubaydah became one of the most ruthless international terrorists, with a close connection to senior al Qa'ida officials. Though not a formal member of al Qa'ida, he developed a personal relationship with Khalid Sheikh Mohammed, Ayman al-Zawahiri, Abu Mus'ab al-Zarqawi, and even Osama bin Laden. In the late 1990s he played a role in the millennium plots, including the plans to bomb Radisson hotels in Amman, Jordan, and three other sites. On November 30, 1999, Jordanian intelligence intercepted a call between Abu Zubaydah and Khadr Abu Hoshar, a Palestinian militant, and determined that an attack was imminent; Jordanian police arrested twenty-two conspirators and foiled the attack. Abu Zubaydah was sentenced to death in absentia by a Jordanian court for his role in the plots. He also developed a relationship with Ahmed Ressam, who was captured in December 1999 at the U.S.-Canadian border in Port Angeles, Washington, and later convicted of planning to bomb the Los Angeles International Airport on New Year's Eve. Ressam had stayed at Zubaydah's guesthouse in Islamabad in January of that year.[39]

By 2001, Zubaydah was running several training camps and guesthouses for foreign fighters in Afghanistan, including the Khaldan training camp near Khowst Province, as well as a series of guesthouses in Pakistan, primarily in Islamabad.[40] The guesthouses were used as temporary residences by foreign fighters on their way to—or back from—the Khaldan camp. Khaldan was not under the control of al Qa'ida, though Zubaydah knew many of the members. He pulled the plug around April 2000, not long after bin Laden told him that "it would be better if Khaldan camp remains closed."[41] Bin Laden wanted to unify the unwieldy network of foreign fighters operating in Afghanistan under his umbrella.

But Zubaydah kept popping up in U.S. and British intelligence reports. On May 30, 2001, senior CIA officials, led by George Tenet, briefed Condoleezza Rice that Zubaydah was working on a number of attack plans, some of which appeared to be close to execution. In June, British intelligence briefed the CIA that Zubaydah was planning suicide car bomb attacks against U.S. military targets in Saudi Arabia.[42] In August a Presidential Daily Brief entitled "Bin Laden Determined to Strike in U.S." stated that Zubaydah was in touch with the millennium bomber Ahmed Ressam. "Convicted plotter Ahmed Ressam has told the FBI," the brief noted, "that he conceived the idea to attack Los Angeles International Airport himself, but that in [REDACTED], Laden lieutenant Abu Zubaydah encouraged him and helped facilitate the operation. Ressam also said that in 1998 Abu Zubaydah was planning his own U.S. attack."[43]

On September 11, 2001, Zubaydah was in a safe house in Kabul with a group of foreign fighters watching video footage of the twin towers burning. The group slaughtered several sheep to celebrate the attacks. He went into hiding soon after, as the manhunt for al Qa'ida fighters began. In December he escaped to Karachi, Pakistan, through Afghanistan's eastern Paktika Province, moving among safe houses and using more than thirty-five aliases. Pakistani and U.S. intelligence agencies began to piece together his movements based on human sources, signals intelligence, interrogations of lower-level operatives, and the clandestine monitoring of e-mails. U.S. intelligence agencies, including the National Security Agency and the Central Intelligence Agency, provided much of the signals intelligence and other technical intelligence by tracking cell and satellite conversations.[44]

In February 2002, CIA station chief Robert Grenier learned that Zubaydah had frequented thirteen safe houses in three cities: nine in Faisalabad, one in Karachi, and three in Lahore. Armed with one of Zubaydah's cell phone numbers, the CIA and FBI began tracking his movements. But Zubaydah was careful about security. He turned on his phone only briefly, to collect messages. On a wall at the U.S. embassy in Islamabad, U.S. intelligence officials posted a large blank piece of paper with Abu Zubaydah's phone number at the center. Over the next several weeks they linked phone numbers and data points from U.S. and Pakistani intelligence files, creating a map of Zubaydah's social network.[45]

In the early morning hours of March 28, 2002, Pakistani and American security officials raided all thirteen sites simultaneously. The site in Faisalabad, an industrial city in Punjab Province, was a sizable coffee-colored, two-story building with large pillars at the front door, white trim around the outside windows, and razor wire atop the outer wall—not exactly a rustic cave. The Pakistanis took the lead, breaching the perimeter fence and breaking the reinforced front door with a ramrod. A soldier confronted Zubaydah with an AK-47.[46]

"The first thing the guy does is, he grabs the barrel of it and tries to wrestle the gun away," said an FBI official. "This turns out to be Abu Zubaydah. So he is at the other end of the gun. The Pakistani soldier, judging the path of least resistance, he pulls the trigger. So Abu Zubaydah's pulling the gun, which shoots him in the stomach and groin and puts numerous rounds through him, and he goes down."[47]

The CIA suddenly had a bizarre situation. Deciding that Zubaydah could provide useful information on past and future terrorist attacks, the CIA leadership moved to keep him alive. Alvin Bernard "Buzzy" Krongard, the CIA's executive director, was on the board of directors at Johns Hopkins Medical Center. He arranged for a doctor to fly a CIA-chartered aircraft to Pakistan and save Zubaydah's life.[48]

The raid on Zubaydah's house and the attempt to save his life were both successful. Pakistani authorities captured roughly two dozen al Qa'ida members. The raid—and eventually Zubaydah—provided a wealth of information. First, Zubaydah was captured at a safe house operated by Lashkar-e-Taiba, or Army of the Righteous, a terrorist group established in the 1980s to liberate Indian-controlled Kashmir through violence. Zubaydah's presence at the safe house indicated that Lashkar members were facilitating the movement of some al Qa'ida members in Pakistan. This discovery was disturbing to some U.S. officials, since Lashkar-e-Taiba had close links with Pakistan's spy agency, the ISI. Zubaydah frequently used a computer that belonged to Lashkar-e-Taiba in Faisalabad from late 2001 until early 2002.[49]

Second, several key pieces of intelligence captured at the Faisalabad safe house led to other al Qa'ida operatives. These included two bank cards, one from a bank in Kuwait and another from a bank in Saudi Arabia, as well as Zubaydah's diary, computer disks, notebooks, and phone numbers. The diary was particularly illuminating and became a rich source of information. In one entry, for example, Zubaydah noted that he was preparing for follow-on attacks within days after September 11. A diary entry in 2002 described plans to wage war in the United States by instigating racial wars, initiating timed explosive devices, attacking gas stations and fuel trucks, and starting timed fires.[50] A Saudi captured with Zubaydah, Ghassan al-Sharbi (also known as Abdullah al-Muslim), who was in his early twenties, was planning to hack the New York Stock Exchange.[51]

Third, Zubaydah provided considerable detail to his FBI and CIA interrogators about al Qa'ida.[52] As one CIA report concluded, "Within months of his arrest, Abu Zubaydah provided details about al Qa'ida's organizational structure, key operatives, and modus operandi. It was also Abu Zubaydah, early in his detention, who identified KSM as the mastermind of the 11 September attacks."[53] Zubaydah provided more intelligence than almost any other operative, telling his interrogators that "brothers who are captured and interrogated are permitted by Allah to provide information when they believe they have 'reached the limit of their ability to withhold it' in the face of psychological and physical hardships."[54]

"Take Me on Your Journey"

In early 2002, Art Cummings traveled to Guantánamo Bay, Cuba. Located at the southeastern end of the island, Guantánamo Bay boasts a spacious harbor surrounded by verdant hills. In 2002 the U.S. military constructed a detainment camp there for captured al Qa'ida and other terrorists. Cummings had been sent by the FBI to interview U.S. citizens and others involved in plots against the U.S. homeland. He wanted to know why these individuals were radicalizing and fighting the United States.

"Take me on your journey," he said to one young detainee, "on how you went from college in the United States to the battlefield of Afghanistan."

The reply stopped Cummings short.

"Well," the detainee explained, "I had a choice of doing what my parents told me to do: go to college and get a job. Or I could go to Mindanao, shoot rocket-propelled grenades, and blow things up."

Joining a militant group was exhilarating for a young man. The detainee suddenly had the opportunity to travel to exotic places and take courses in weapons training, learn intelligence skills, and bond with other youths committed to a common cause. Cummings could relate; he had joined the Navy SEALs for similar reasons. Still, he was perplexed.

"What about Islam?" he asked.

"Couching this whole thing in terms of Islam," the detainee answered, "was what made my parents happy."

Religion was a secondary motivation for joining the fight.

"But once I joined," the detainee explained, "I couldn't get out. If I returned to my native country, they would have arrested me and thrown me into prison."[55]

Cummings wanted to understand the detainees' motivations, but he also needed to collect information on terrorist plots and the al Qa'ida network. His interviews with captured al Qa'ida fighters reinforced his conviction that coercive techniques were generally unnecessary and often counterproductive. He argued that what drove some terrorists to talk was forcing them to ponder their future.

"You understand, you're going to die in this steel box," Cummings told several of them. "And when you're dead, your life is nothing. You will die, and you will be nothing to anyone. When you die, you will be in an unmarked grave, and no one will know how you died, when you died, or where you're buried."

For others, it was manipulating basic human needs. "Eventually these guys just get tired of living in austere conditions, and the government offers them different accommodations based on different levels of cooperation," said Cummings.

One detainee was blunt. "He saw a little snuff on my lip," explained Cummings. "He asked for some, so I said, 'Sure.' I gave him some."

The doctors at Guantánamo Bay were outraged.

"Okay," Cummings replied, "enlighten me here. What's the problem?"

"Well, it's not healthy," one doctor lectured him.

"The only reason he's talking to me is because I'm supplying him with snuff," Cummings retorted. "So I'm going to be bringing a tin of Copenhagen every time I interrogate this guy. And I guarantee you that every time before he starts talking, he's going to put a big ol' mighty healthy dip in his lip."[56]

Cummings's concern about coercive techniques spoke to a much broader debate within the U.S. government and across the American public. In a letter to President Bush in December 2002, for example, Human Rights Watch executive director Kenneth Roth said that he was "deeply concerned by allegations of torture and other mistreatment of suspected al-Qaeda detainees."[57] Human Rights Watch reported that eleven suspects, including Khalid Sheikh Mohammed, had "disappeared" in secret prisons and might have been tortured under the direction of the CIA.[58] A 2005 U.S. Justice Department memo stated that Khalid Sheikh Mohammed had been waterboarded 183 times and Abu Zubaydah 83 times. The memo concluded that the "CIA used the waterboard extensively in the interrogation of KSM and Zubaydah, but did so only after it became clear that standard interrogation techniques were not working."[59]

The reality was complicated. In a few instances, as with Khalid Sheikh Mohammed, coercive measures appeared to provide some information on homeland plots. But whether these techniques were *necessary* is unclear, and determining that would require proving the counterfactual argument that more traditional techniques could have been as effective. The divide was particularly acute between some CIA officials, who insisted that coercive measures were necessary and effective, and many FBI officials, who asserted that they were counterproductive.[60] In the vast majority of cases, coercive techniques appeared to be unnecessary and al Qa'ida operatives provided information in response to more traditional interrogation techniques.

Despite the controversy, the interrogation of al Qa'ida detainees and, more important, the capture of millions of documents and other information from raids led to additional arrests. "High and medium value detainees have given us a wealth of useful . . . information on al-Qa'ida members and associates," concluded one CIA assessment, "including new details on the personalities and activities of known terrorists."[61] The CIA took pride in the fact that "the intelligence acquired from these interrogations has been a key reason why al Qa'ida has failed to launch a spectacular attack in the West since 11 September 2001."[62] Detainee interrogations were a critical source of human intelligence. In 2004, for instance, the CIA counted a total of 6,600 human intelligence reports on al Qa'ida, half of which were from detainee reporting.[63]

As the debate raged on, however, al Qa'ida members continued to fall.

Falling Dominoes

Born on May 1, 1972, in Yemen, Ramzi bin al-Shibh grew up in a working-class neighborhood in Sana'a, the capital city. Sana'a is situated at the foot of Mount Nuqum, at an elevation of more than 7,200 feet above sea level, in the western part of the country. For centuries it has been the chief economic, political, and religious center of the Yemen Highlands. In 1987, bin al-Shibh's father died and his mother and older brother, Ahmed, looked after him. In 1987, while still in high school, he worked as a part-time clerk for the International Bank of Yemen. While he first became a devoted Muslim, at the age of twelve, he did not appear to be radical.[64] A childhood friend described him as "religious, but not too religious."[65]

Bin al-Shibh first attempted to leave Yemen in 1995, when he submitted an application for a U.S. visa but was rejected. He then went to Germany, applying for asylum under the name Ramzi Omar. In Hamburg he met Mohammed Atta, who became the lead al Qa'ida operative in the United States, coordinating the attacks with bin al-Shibh.[66] The two became close friends, and bin al-Shibh began to show signs of radicalization. He increasingly complained about a "Jewish world conspiracy" and argued that the most important duty of every Muslim was to pursue jihad.[67] By 1998, bin al-Shibh and Atta shared an apartment in the Harburg section of Hamburg and had begun to associate with two other September 11 hijackers, Marwan al-Shehhi and Ziad Jarrah. By that time bin al-Shibh was wiry, with recessed eye sockets, black hair, and a scraggly beard. He often wore a white and red kaffiyeh, or headscarf, typical of Yemeni men. Friends and acquaintances described him as charismatic and self-confident.

"His philosophy, even his vocabulary, is very much like bin Laden's," remarked Yosri Fouda, an Al Jazeera reporter who interviewed him. "He also has the sheikh's serene charm, zest, and religious knowledge."[68]

In late 1999, bin al-Shibh traveled with Atta, al-Shehhi, and Jarrah to Kandahar, where they were trained at al Qa'ida camps. The four met Osama bin Laden and pledged *bayat*, or loyalty, to him. They also accepted his proposal to martyr themselves in an operation against the United States.[69] "I swear allegiance to you," they repeated, "to listen and obey, in good times and bad, and to accept the consequences myself. I swear allegiance to you, for jihad and hijrah, and to listen and obey. I swear allegiance to you, to listen and obey, and to die in the cause of God."[70]

As bin al-Shibh later acknowledged, bin Laden was an alluring figure, revered by al Qa'ida members. He generally had a calm demeanor, even during stressful situations, and was viewed as a pious Muslim. Bin Laden was humble and talked to those around him with a sincere and respectful demeanor. He rarely talked down to people, and he interacted with fighters from all levels of al Qa'ida, sharing meals with the lowest-level foot soldiers. He listened carefully. When discussing the tactics of an operation, for example, bin Laden would consider the opinions of everyone involved, giving each person his attention.[71] But when he made up his mind, he could be myopic and bullheaded. As his son Omar recalled, "His stubbornness had brought him many problems. Once he wished for something, he never gave up."[72]

Bin al-Shibh was apparently chosen to be one of the September 11 hijackers and traveled with Atta to Karachi at the end of 1999 to meet with Khalid Sheikh Mohammed and discuss the plot in more detail.[73] He returned to Germany early in 2000. Bin al-Shibh attempted to obtain a U.S. visa to attend flight school on four occasions from May to November of that year. But the U.S. Department of State rejected each application.[74] He was apparently so desperate to get into the United States that he e-mailed a U.S. citizen in San Diego and asked her to marry him, but that failed as well.[75]

In the eight months before the attacks, bin al-Shibh was the primary intermediary between the hijackers in the United States and al Qa'ida leaders in Afghanistan. He relayed orders from al Qa'ida operatives to Atta via e-mail or phone and met with Atta in Germany in January 2001 and in Spain in July 2001 to discuss the operation's progress.[76] The CIA made it clear that "Ramzi Bin al-Shibh, not KSM, was in direct contact with the 11 September hijackers once they were in the United States."[77]

In August 2001, Mohammed Atta and bin al-Shibh discussed the impending attacks via e-mail. Atta pretended that he was a young man in the United States talking to Jenny, his girlfriend in Germany.

"The first semester starts in three weeks," he wrote to bin al-Shibh. "Nothing has changed. Everything is fine. There are good signs and encouraging ideas. Two high schools and two universities. Everything is going according to plan. This summer will surely be hot. I would like to talk to you about a few details. Nineteen certificates for private study and four exams. Regards to the professor. Goodbye."[78]

As U.S. intelligence officials later realized, the four schools meant the intended targets in the United States and the "nineteen certificates" indicated the nineteen hijackers. A week before the attacks, bin al-Shibh left Germany and arrived in Afghanistan, where he soon celebrated what he called the "Holy Tuesday Operation." After the U.S. bombing campaign began in the wake of the attack, he fled Afghanistan and spent about six weeks in Iran. In early 2002, bin al-Shibh traveled to Karachi and began working with Khalid Sheikh Mohammed on follow-on plots against the West, including an attack against London's Heathrow Airport.[79] The plot involved hijacking two aircraft from Heathrow and crashing them into the terminal buildings. He also worked on a manuscript justifying the September 11 attacks, titled "The Truth About the New Crusade: A Ruling on the Killing of Women and Children of the Non-Believers." It was a rambling document that tried to justify civilian casualties.

"Someone might say that it is the innocent, the elderly, the women, and the children who are victims, so how can these operations be legitimate according to sharia?" bin al-Shibh asked rhetorically. "They are legally legitimate," he answered, "because they are committed against a country at war with us, and the people in that country are combatants."[80]

As the manhunt for al Qa'ida leaders in Pakistan intensified in 2002, bin al-Shibh grew increasingly wary about personal security. During an interview with journalist Yosri Fouda, he became incensed when he discovered that Fouda had brought along his mobile phone. Bin al-Shibh grabbed the phone from him, removed the SIM card and battery, and placed it in another room to ensure that U.S. and Pakistani officials couldn't track it.[81]

He was right to be worried. Much as with Khalid Sheikh Mohammed and Abu Zubaydah, patient intelligence analysis by Pakistani and American operatives—using human sources, intercepts, and information collected from other raids—paid off. The U.S. interrogation of Abu Zubaydah provided critical information on bin al-Shibh's travel patterns and associates.[82] But the biggest break came on September 10, 2002, when ISI officers detained Mohammad Ahmad Ghulum Rabanni, an al Qa'ida operative and Pakistani citizen, along with his driver. During interrogations that day, they provided information about al Qa'ida safe houses in Karachi, including the one where bin al-Shibh was hiding.

Pakistani forces moved quickly. In the early morning hours of September 11, 2002—one year after the attacks in New York City and Washington—Pakistani ISI officers, Army Rangers, and police conducted raids of three suspected al Qa'ida residences in two sections of Karachi. The first safe house was located on Tariq Road in the Pakistan Employees Cooperative Housing Society area, an affluent section of the city, home to nearly one million people. When Pakistani forces began the raid, three individuals present, including Ramzi bin al-Shibh, held knives to their throats and threatened to kill themselves rather than be taken into custody. The standoff lasted four hours before Pakistani officers overpowered and seized them.[83] Pakistani and U.S. officials discovered a wealth of information when they combed through the safe house, including high explosives, nearly two dozen remote radio detonators, individually wrapped documents belonging to various members of Osama bin Laden's family, a handwritten note to a senior al Qa'ida operative, identification cards for Ahmad Ibrahim al-Haznawi (a September 11 hijacker), and contact information for several known al Qa'ida operatives.[84]

The two other safe houses were located in the defense II commercial area of Karachi. ISI officers had information that six to eight al Qa'ida operatives who were part of a special terrorist team deployed to attack targets in the city were staying there. Preparing for the worst, the ISI called in backup. The raid began around 10 a.m. on

September 11, and a two-and-a-half-hour firefight ensued between al Qa'ida fighters and Pakistani security forces. The terrorists, who were mostly Arabs, threw four hand grenades and fired hundreds of rounds at Pakistani forces, who returned fire. Two Arabs were killed, five were captured, and several ISI operatives, police, and Rangers were injured. During a search of the safe houses in this area, Pakistani authorities seized a laptop computer that contained a variety of manuals and files describing al Qa'ida ideology and tactics.[85]

As with other captures, intelligence collected at the three safe houses was critical in tracking down al Qa'ida operatives. Bin al-Shibh led to Khalid Sheikh Mohammed, who was seized on March 1, 2003. Not all Pakistanis supported their government's decision to deliver him, or any al Qa'ida fighters, to the United States, however. One Pakistani newspaper published an article called "FBIistan," complaining about the raid and saying that if "any foreign person has committed a crime in Pakistan, he should be tried under the law of the land. But we have been playing the role of a mercenary for the United States."[86] Musharraf's government ignored these objections, however, and continued to cooperate with the United States, receiving millions of dollars in reward money. The press continued to prove nettlesome to counterterrorism operatives: on March 2, 2003, some media outlets showed photos of Khalid Sheikh Mohammed as a suave and dashing fighter, painting him as al Qa'ida's James Bond. Marty Martin from the Counterterrorism Center phoned George Tenet. "Boss," Martin noted in palpable disgust, "this ain't right. The media are making the bum look like a hero. That ain't right. You should see the way this bird looked when we took him down. I want to show the world what terrorists look like."[87]

CIA officers on the scene of Khalid Sheikh Mohammed's arrest had taken digital pictures of him and sent them back to CIA headquarters. Tenet suggested that Martin and Bill Harlow, the CIA's spokesman, look through the photos. They found the most evocative one, and Bill called an Associated Press reporter and told him, "I'm about to make your day."[88] The photo showed a disheveled Khalid Sheikh Mohammed, moments after the capture, still groggy from being awakened in the middle of the night and dragged out of his house. It was not a good hair day. He had bloodshot eyes, day-old stubble, and a sizable mat of chest hair showing under his grimy white T-shirt.

His capture produced a trove of new intelligence. U.S. and Pakistani officials seized a hard drive that had information about the four airplanes hijacked on September 11, including code names, airline companies, flight numbers, and names of the hijackers. It also had transcripts of chat sessions belonging to at least one of the September 11 hijackers, three letters from Osama bin Laden, spreadsheets that described financial assistance to families of known al Qa'ida operatives, a letter to the United Arab Emirates threatening attack if that country's government continued to help the United States, and a document summarizing operational procedures and training requirements of an al Qa'ida cell.[89] The CIA's interrogation of Khalid Sheikh Mohammed was also useful, shedding light on al Qa'ida's strategic doctrine, plots, key operatives, and probable methods of attacks on the U.S. homeland.[90]

Other dominoes began to fall. Khalid Sheikh Mohammed provided critical information that aided in the 2003 capture of Majid Khan, an al Qa'ida official who was involved in planning multiple attacks in the United States.[91] In an example of how information from one detainee can be used in debriefing another, Khalid Sheikh Mohammed detailed Majid Khan's role in delivering $50,000 in December 2002 to operatives associated with Hambali, the military leader of the Indonesian terrorist organization Jemaah Islamiyah. U.S. officials then confronted Majid Khan with this information, and he acknowledged that he had delivered the money to an al Qa'ida and Jemaah Islamiya operative named Mohd Farik bin Amin, better known as Zubair.[92] Khan provided Zubair's physical description and contact number.[93] Because of that information, Zubair was captured in June 2003.[94] In addition, Khalid

Sheikh Mohammed led the CIA and FBI in August 2003 to Hambali, who was hiding in Thailand. Hambali had developed a close relationship with al Qa'ida operatives and was intimately involved in the 2002 terrorist attack in Bali, which killed more than two hundred tourists.[95]

A Laughingstock

Al Qa'ida leaders were now under intense pressure in Pakistan. U.S. intelligence agencies, including the CIA and the FBI, were sharing information and coordinating efforts better than they had before September 11. The relationship wasn't perfect, but it had improved. The director of the Counterterrorist Center chaired a meeting each evening that included CIA officers and representatives from other agencies across the U.S. government.[96]

In this season of success for U.S. and Pakistani forces, al Qa'ida suffered a staggering number of losses. In addition to Abu Zubaydah, Ramzi bin al-Shibh, and Khalid Sheikh Mohammed, dozens of leaders were captured: Abdu Ali al Haji Sharqawi in Karachi in February 2002; Yassir al-Jazeeri in Lahore in March 2003; Mustafa al-Hawsawi in Rawalpindi in March 2003; Walid bin Attash and Ammar al-Baluchi in Karachi in April 2003. Key al Qa'ida leaders were also captured or killed in other countries, including in Thailand, Yemen, Saudi Arabia, and Morocco. Most of these operations, such as the capture of Abd al-Rahim al-Nashiri in 2002, were the result of careful intelligence work, not the use of large-scale military force.

The United States now possessed a more nuanced understanding of its enemies. Al Qa'ida was composed of a shura council and several core committees: military, media, finance, religious, families, documents, radio communications, and external support. It was hierarchically structured, much like a multinational corporation. The shura council was the most powerful committee and served as an advisory body to Osama bin Laden, who acted as its chairman, asking questions and listening to the discussions at hand. The council met regularly, sometimes once a week, to discuss important issues. Key members included Ayman al-Zawahiri, Abu al-Khayr al-Masri, Abu Ghayth al-Kuwaiti, Saif al-Adel, Abu Muhammad al-Masri, Abd al-Hadi al-Iraqi, and Shaykh Sa'id al-Masri.

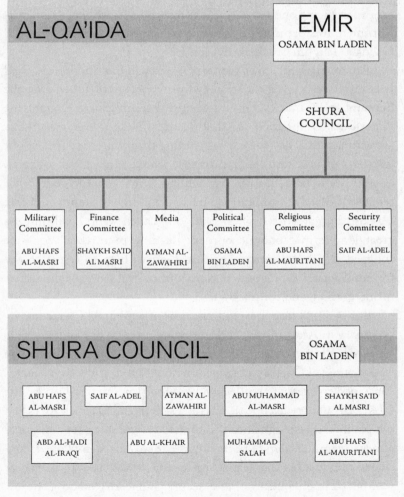

Figure 5: Al Qa'ida Organizational Structure, 2001

As leader, bin Laden was primarily concerned with the shura council and the military committee, especially its external operations subcommittee. By 2003 some of the shura members, such as Muhammed Atef, had been killed. The rest had fled to Pakistan, Iran, and other locations.

Al Qa'ida's difficulties were captured in a letter from Saif al-Adel to Khalid Sheikh Mohammed on June 13, 2002. "Today, we are experiencing one setback after another and have gone from misfortune to misfortune," he wrote. It was embarrassing and made al Qa'ida a "laughingstock of the world."[97]

Part of the problem, Adel explained, was bin Laden, who had failed to develop a cogent strategy for what would happen *after* the September 11 attacks, beyond a general commitment to fight the Americans. On October 2001, bin Laden made at least two public appearances in Khowst Province, noting that while al Qa'ida might lose part of northern Afghanistan, it would surely hold southern Afghanistan. In a message to Mullah Omar on October 3, he remarked that U.S. military operations in Afghanistan would fail. "A campaign against Afghanistan," bin Laden wrote, "will impose great long-term economic burdens, leading to further economic collapse, which will force America, God willing, to resort to the former Soviet Union's only option: withdrawal from Afghanistan, disintegration, and contraction."[98]

But by 2003 he appeared to have been wrong. Al Qa'ida lost its sanctuary in Afghanistan, and a growing number of members were captured or killed because of clandestine U.S. operators. The reverse wave against al Qa'ida had gained momentum as the United States continued to execute an effective light-footprint strategy led by the CIA, FBI, and special operations forces. Senior al Qa'ida leaders had not planned far enough ahead. They had no real plans for additional attacks against the United States. Bin Laden, Adel complained, continued to pressure other leaders to "attack, attack, attack." But there was no clear organization, and security concerns made it almost impossible for al Qa'ida leaders to communicate with each other. It was time, he argued, to pull back and reconsider the group's goals and missions. "I say today we must completely halt all external actions until we sit down and consider the disaster we caused," he concluded. "My beloved brother, stop all foreign actions, stop sending people to captivity, stop devising new operations, regardless of whether orders come or do not come from [bin Laden]."[99]

Al Qa'ida leaders had hoped to attack the United States again. But the FBI and other U.S. government agencies, working desperately to prevent another attack on the homeland, now faced their most significant test in the United States.

5

COMING TO AMERICA

MAY 8, 2002, was a typical spring day in Chicago. A blustery east wind swept across Lake Michigan and into the city, snatching empty soda cans and candy wrappers on Michigan Avenue and swaying the burr oak and sugar maple trees along Lake Shore Drive. The Chicago Cubs had lost—again—in a lazy afternoon game to the St. Louis Cardinals, 3–2. The Cubs hadn't won a World Series since 1945, the last year of Franklin D. Roosevelt's presidency, and they were off to another discouraging start. An intermittent haze and drizzle began in the afternoon. The temperature crept above 60 degrees, though it felt much colder to FBI agents at O'Hare International Airport. They were tracking an inbound flight from Zurich, Switzerland. On board, they believed, was an operative named José Padilla.

Padilla was born in Brooklyn on October 18, 1970, to Puerto Rican immigrants. As a child he had been known as "Pucho" because of his plump cheeks. He now stood five feet, ten inches tall and weighed 170 pounds, and he had *José* tattooed on his right arm.[1] With olive skin, a fleshy face, and a patchy mustache, he had a tendency to tighten his lips and slightly push up the corners of his mouth in a look of defiance. His body language betrayed contempt for others. As a child in Chicago, he had joined the Latin Disciples street gang and been arrested several times for criminal trespassing, battery, attempted theft, and resisting arrest. What brought him to the attention of U.S. government officials, however, was his connection to senior al Qa'ida officials.

Nearly eight months after September 11, CIA and FBI intelligence reports were still blinking red about another terrorist attack in the United States. In a December 2001 statement, Osama bin Laden had warned of future operations in the United States:

> When the darkness comes upon us and we are bit by a
> Sharp tooth, I say,
> "Our homes are flooded with blood and the tyrant
> Is freely wandering in our homes."
> And from the battlefield vanished
> The brightness of swords and the horses
> And over weeping sounds now
> We hear the beats of drums and rhythm
> They are storming his forts
> And shouting: "We will not stop our raids
> Until you free our lands."[2]

U.S. officials such as Art Cummings believed that bin Laden was planning an attack on public transportation targets. The CIA concluded that al Qa'ida was targeting "railways and subways as a means to hurt the U.S. economy and incite mass hysteria." Al Qa'ida had chosen these targets "after observing the economic impact of the 11 September attacks on the U.S. airline industry."[3] But a second attack in the United States would require substantial planning.

Partly in response to widespread criticism of intelligence failures leading up to September 11, the Bush administration had created the Department of Homeland Security, merging unconnected agencies such as the Coast Guard and Immigration and Naturalization Service and placing them under a common umbrella. Screening at airports had increased, and government agencies now reviewed the names of travelers coming into the United States, looking for potential terrorists. Senior al Qa'ida officials, including Khalid Sheikh Mohammed, knew that American intelligence agencies would be on the lookout for Arabs.[4] So a second wave of operatives, they figured, should be people holding passports from non-Arab countries, and their eventual targets would be in the central or western United States.[5] The CIA and FBI had anticipated this step. A CIA report warned that al Qa'ida might be recruiting people "who possess visa-waiver status in the United States and Canada and have a non-Arab appearance."[6]

Over the next several years, al Qa'ida pursued a robust offensive campaign in the United States, attempting to blow up apartment buildings and bridges, detonate bombs on public transportation, and recruit American citizens in New York, Ohio, Oregon, and other states. In 2004, al Qa'ida thought it had access to a nuclear device—which later turned out to be a hoax—and approached an associate who claimed he could move illicit substances via Iran, Turkey, and Europe to the United States.[7] Art Cummings saw an FBI assessment that counted at least fifty-two al Qa'ida or al Qa'ida–affiliated operatives in the United States between 1998 and 2007. Approximately twenty-two were detected by the FBI in the early stages of their plots. Another thirty, including the nineteen September 11 hijackers, went undetected until they carried out an attack or intelligence gathered after their departure revealed that they had been in the United States.[8]

As early as 1997, José Padilla had been ruminating about an attack. He had discussed training at an al Qa'ida camp in Afghanistan with Adham Hassoun, a computer programmer in Broward County, Florida. Hassoun volunteered to pay for the excursion. It would be a good way to meet "some nice, uh, brothers," he said. "We take the whole family and have a blast. We go to, uh, our Busch Gardens, you know. You won't regret it. Money-back guarantee."

Padilla chuckled but suggested they stop discussing the issue on an open phone line.

"Why?" Hassoun said. "We're going to Busch Gardens. What's the big deal?"[9]

Padilla was right to be worried. Even in 1997 the FBI was listening to his phone calls, suspicious about his activities and his connections to extremist groups overseas.

After several years of networking and training at an al Qa'ida camp in Afghanistan, Padilla eventually met with Abu Zubaydah, Muhammed Atef, and ultimately Khalid Sheikh Mohammed while they were planning follow-on attacks. Khalid Sheikh Mohammed offered to support Padilla and provide guidance for an attack. The CIA, FBI, and other U.S. intelligence agencies had confirmed that there was a plot. Now it was up to a small group of intelligence operatives to find out what the plot entailed, understand what Padilla's role was, and hunt him down before the attack occurred. American lives were at stake. Much like the raids on al Qa'ida targets in Pakistan, success would hinge on patient, clandestine, and coordinated operations from U.S. intelligence and law enforcement agencies. But it would also require help from increasingly alert American citizens who were willing to risk their lives to stop an attack.

A Sordid Past

For al Qa'ida, José Padilla was an adequate candidate for an attack, though perhaps not ideal. He had grown up in the United States, so he understood American culture and could blend in better than a foreigner. He was also a U.S. citizen, making it easy for him to enter the country and move around undetected. But as an operative, Padilla was raw. As a recent convert from Catholicism to Islam, he had to prove his dedication to violent jihad. He had spent part of his troubled youth in prison. Moreover, he lacked the community and kinship networks in the Arab world to verify his credentials and commitment. Still, he was eager to conduct an attack and had valuable attributes.

Padilla had been raised in a small gray stone building in Chicago's Logan Square neighborhood. He played baseball in the schoolyard across the street and attended nearby St. Sylvester Church with his mother, brother, and two sisters.

"You always got the feeling that he wasn't looking for trouble," said Art Ryder, a school counselor at Darwin Elementary School, which Padilla attended. "But if you started it, he'd finish it. He had eyes that could stare right through you."[10]

Padilla joined a local street gang when he was thirteen years old. During his gang years he maintained several aliases, including José Rivera, José Alicea, José Hernandez, and José Ortiz. In 1985, in his midteens, he began to show signs of savage violence, not just everyday criminality. On August 15, 1985, Padilla and a colleague, Andre Boulrece, were arrested by Chicago police after attacking and robbing three youths. One of the victims, Elio Evangelista, chased them down, but Boulrece turned and stabbed him in the abdomen during the ensuing struggle. Boulrece and Padilla then knocked Evangelista to the ground, took $107 from his wallet, and repeatedly kicked him in the head, eventually killing him. Boulrece was convicted of murder. Padilla was convicted as a juvenile of aggravated battery and armed robbery and spent the next several years in a juvenile detention center. In 1989, after he was released, he was arrested for punching a clerk who tried to stop him from stealing a doughnut.[11]

Padilla moved to southern Florida in 1991. In October he brandished a .38 revolver at another driver during a traffic encounter. When the other driver followed him to a gas station, Padilla fired a shot. No one was hurt. Police traced Padilla's license plate and staked out his home at 2315 NW 55th Way in Lauderhill, Florida. When the officers moved in to arrest him, Padilla reached into his waistband for his revolver, but he was disarmed by the officers.[12]

"That was the first time I thought I was going to have to shoot someone," remarked police officer Charles Vitale, who wrestled Padilla to the ground. "He was just turning 21 when I arrested him, and he had no fear of pulling a gun on a police officer. You just knew he was going to turn out really bad."[13]

Padilla was convicted and sent to a Broward County prison, where he converted to Islam.[14] Broward County court records show that on July 1, 1994, he changed his name to Ibrahim. After his release he attended several mosques in the Broward County area, the Darul Uloom Islamic Institute in Pembroke Pines, and the Al-Iman Mosque in Fort Lauderdale, which he joined in 1994. The imam at the Al-Iman Mosque, Raed Awad, was a fundraiser for the Holy Land Foundation, which had links to the Palestinian militant group Hamas. Padilla and his girlfriend, Cherie Maria Stultz, found jobs at a Taco Bell in Davie, Florida. They also found a mentor in the restaurant's manager, Mohammad Javed. "They were poor but trying to make something of their lives," recalled Javed. "Buy a car, establish a good credit rating, things like that."[15]

After Padilla's conversion to Islam, he began to wear a red-and-white-checked kaffiyeh and met several individuals who had a profound impact on his life. Two of them, Adham Hassoun and Kifah Wael Jayyousi, were associates of Umar Abd al-Rahman, the "blind sheikh," who had been involved in several terrorist plots, including the 1993 World Trade Center bombing.[16] Along with other members, including Mohammed Hesham Youseff and Kassem Daher, this loose network sent money, equipment, and individuals to overseas conflicts to wage violent jihad and support terrorist groups. Jayyousi also edited a magazine, *Islam Report*, which urged readers to resist Arab regimes and send donations to those involved in jihad. In one article he preached, "May Allah help the mujahideen topple these un-Islamic and illegal puppet regimes in our Muslim lands."[17]

For Padilla, associating with this social network was critical to radicalization. The formation of a cell among friends has often been pivotal in the incubation of al Qa'ida terrorists.[18] Indeed, Padilla was never subjected to a top-down al Qa'ida recruitment and brainwashing campaign. Instead, he gradually became radical through his association with Hassoun, Jayyousi, Youseff, Daher, and their broader network. When he left prison in 1994, he had just become interested in Islam and was particularly vulnerable to new ideas. Because of the social bonds he developed, Padilla eventually accepted the global Salafi ideology preached by Sayyid Qutb and supported by Osama bin Laden and Ayman al-Zawahiri.

Padilla's new friends also put him on the FBI's radar. The Bureau had begun monitoring the group in 1993. They were part of a wave of new cells forming across North America to fundraise for—and recruit—individuals to train and fight in Bosnia, Chechnya, Somalia, and other locations.[19] Padilla's network supported the Benevolence International Foundation (BIF), a nongovernmental organization that provided financial aid to al Qa'ida and other Islamic extremist groups. On February 4, 1995, FBI officials listened to Jayyousi and Daher discussing their plans.

"This business, the profit generated from this business, will be for the brothers," said Daher. "I mean we have to support the mujahideen brothers."

Daher then described his organization, the Canadian Islamic Association, as a "cover—I mean it's very good."[20]

Aware of current counterterrorism techniques, the group used coded language when talking on the phone to disguise their planning, such as "getting some fresh air," "participating in tourism," "opening up a market," and "playing football." Their clandestine efforts led to humorous and sometimes bizarre conversations in which they discussed going on "picnics" in Afghanistan or Chechnya "to smell fresh air and to eat cheese," or using $3,500 to buy "zucchini." Still, FBI officials monitored their phone calls, collecting information and trying to understand their intentions. As Hassoun explained, coordination was critical among those in the network: "The important thing is that each one of us completes the other . . . so if you can't finish something your brother will complete it for you, and the other brother will complete it for him, and so on . . . so we are all a connected link . . . if someone splits from this link, the link is no longer connected, and each one is on their own. We don't want to get to that point . . . especially that tourism work is a good work, because there are a lot of tourists and a lot of people who would like to go do tourism . . . so we work toward, of course, to always inform them of the nice places for tourism and so on . . . and 'resort places' and so on."[21]

Over the next several years the group provided assistance to fighters conducting violent jihad overseas. They envisioned themselves as modern-day versions of Abdullah Azzam and Osama bin Laden, who had helped mujahideen trek to Afghanistan in the 1980s to fight the Soviets. By 1998, however, Padilla had grown restless in the United States and was pressing the group to let him travel abroad. In a June 25 phone conversation overheard by the FBI, Hassoun and Youssef discussed sending another individual overseas to commence training.

Youseff suggested sending "Doctor Ibrahim. Ibrahim Padilla."

"I understand what you mean," Hassoun responded. "He is a good surgeon."[22]

A few days later, on July 18, Youssef and Hassoun spoke again. Youssef was on a satellite phone in Kosovo, where he was "under bombing from the Serbs, and we have casualties."[23] Hassoun stated that he would send Padilla to Egypt but first had to find a donor willing to fund the trip.

On September 5, 1998, after securing the funds, Padilla flew from Florida to Cairo, where he studied Arabic, earned a subsistence income as a handyman, and agreed to an arranged marriage with an Egyptian woman named Shamia'a. In February 2000 he traveled to Saudi Arabia to perform the hajj, the traditional pilgrimage to Mecca—a sign of his growing dedication to Islam and a demonstration of his solidarity with other Muslims. The trip, however, had a double purpose. During his travels, Padilla met a Yemeni al Qa'ida recruiter to discuss training opportunities in Afghanistan.[24] On April 10, Hassoun spoke to Padilla by phone as the FBI continued to monitor. Padilla said he wanted to travel to Yemen. "But I need a recommendation to connect with the good brothers, with the right faith," he explained.[25]

After establishing a contact, Padilla traveled to Yemen in May and stayed with the al Qa'ida recruiter he had met in Saudi Arabia.[26] In Sana'a the recruiter turned him over to an associate, who helped organize Padilla's trip to Afghanistan. Padilla entered Pakistan on June 26, 2000, traveled from Karachi to Quetta, and then drove to Kandahar, Afghanistan, on Highway 4. To prepare for his training, he filled out a "Mujahideen Data Form." He wrote that he had traveled to Egypt to study Islam, Saudi Arabia for the hajj, and Yemen "as a way to go through for Jihad."[27] The application was later recovered by the FBI in Pakistan in a box containing more than a hundred similar applications.[28]

On September 3, Hassoun spoke to Youssef, who was in Egypt, and indicated that Padilla had traveled to Kandahar and "entered into the area of Osama."[29]

FBI officials listening to the conversation felt chills. Padilla was an American citizen headed to training camps run by the world's preeminent terrorist. On October 15, FBI officials heard Hassoun tell a colleague in the Republic of Georgia that Padilla was still "in Afghanistan."[30]

In fact, Padilla had entered the al Qa'ida–affiliated al-Farouq training camp in Kandahar Province under the name Abdulla al-Espani. He went to al-Farouq with the understanding that he "would go to Chechnya afterwards" to fight against the Russians.[31] Padilla received training on Kalashnikovs, AK-47s, G-3 rifles, M16s, Uzis, and submachine guns. He also learned key skills of an al Qa'ida operative, such as clandestine communications, camouflage, surveillance, countersurveillance, and explosives using C-4, dynamite, and improvised devices. In his spare time, he and his fellow recruits engaged in rigorous physical fitness training and religious indoctrination.[32]

From Training to Operations

Padilla's American citizenship made him particularly useful for al Qa'ida leaders, who were looking for Americans to recruit other radicals and conduct attacks in the United States. Senior al Qa'ida operative Muhammed Atef approached him at the al-Farouq camp and asked about his faith. Padilla believed that Atef was "evaluating his commitment and suitability for al Qa'ida operations," and he was excited about the prospects.[33] He had several meetings with Atef, who gave him $1,400 in late 2000 to travel to Egypt, with the understanding that Padilla would later return to Afghanistan.

Under Atef's tutelage, Padilla began the final stage of his transition from juvenile miscreant to violent terrorist and changed his name to Abdullah al-Mujahir. He had started to radicalize through his network, but his association with senior al Qa'ida leaders cemented his transformation.[34] In preparation for his role as an al Qa'ida operative, Padilla was ordered to get a new passport. The purpose, he was told, was to erase the trail of visas and stamps that showed he had traveled to Afghanistan, Pakistan, Yemen, and Egypt, all destinations that would elicit suspicion from foreign intelligence agencies. On February 16, 2001, Padilla sought a replacement passport from the U.S. consulate in Karachi, stating that his passport had been lost in a market. He obtained the replacement on March 21.[35]

Padilla returned to Afghanistan two months later and tracked down Atef, who met him at a safe house in Kandahar. Over the next several months they discussed the possibility of a terrorist attack in the United States. In the summer of 2001, Atef asked him to blow up apartment buildings in the United States. Padilla accepted the mission. Atef then sent him to a site near the Kandahar airport where he trained with an al Qa'ida explosives expert and another operative, Adnan el-Shukrijumah. Also known as Jafar al-Tayyar, Shukrijumah had lived in Florida and would eventually resurface in several plots against the U.S. homeland. Padilla and Shukrijumah trained at the Kandahar airport site on switches, circuits, and timers and learned how to prepare and seal an apartment to obtain the highest explosive yield. Their mission was eventually abandoned, however, because they did not get along.[36]

I cannot do the operation on my own, Padilla told Atef.[37] Then came the upheaval of September 11.

After the attacks Padilla stayed at a number of safe houses in Afghanistan with Atef, including the site where Atef was killed by U.S. aircraft in November 2001. Padilla was there that day. After running for cover, he returned to help dig Atef's body out of the rubble. Armed with an assault rifle, he then fled to Khowst Province with other al Qa'ida operatives seeking to avoid capture by U.S. forces. At the Afghanistan-Pakistan border in January 2002, Padilla met Abu Zubaydah for the first time.[38] He also linked up with Binyam Ahmed Muhammad, whose nom de guerre was Talha al-Kini. He was a tall, lanky Ethiopian national and a trained electrical engineer who had attended the al-Farouq camp with Padilla.[39] Padilla and Binyam Muhammad approached Abu Zubaydah and proposed an operation that involved traveling to the United States and detonating a nuclear bomb. Zubaydah was skeptical of the idea. It is not feasible, he said, noting that Padilla didn't have the physics background to pull it off.

Their other idea, an explosive wrapped in uranium—a "dirty bomb"—was intriguing, Zubaydah remarked. But ultimately "the dirty bomb plan would not work either, could cause too much of a problem for al Qa'ida," and "Khalid Sheikh Mohammed would not think it viable."[40] Plus, Zubaydah noted, the U.S. government would probably discover that radioactive material was missing from American laboratories before Padilla and Binyam Muhammad could execute the operation.

Zubaydah inquired how they planned to enter the United States. It was simple, Padilla explained. They would go through Mexico.

Zubaydah was puzzled. Why wouldn't Padilla go directly into

the United States, since he had a valid U.S. passport? Putting that aside, he then turned to specifics about the plot. How would they obtain the necessary materials?

We will steal the ingredients, Padilla responded, to make conventional explosives from stores in the United States. And we can acquire the radioactive materials, he continued, from "factories that use uranium" or from laboratories at U.S. universities.

Zubaydah was again incredulous and said that it would not be as easy as they believed.[41]

They continued to discuss the idea of an attack inside America. Maybe blowing up gas tankers? Or spraying people with cyanide in nightclubs? In mid-February 2002, Zubaydah telephoned a colleague and asked for $20,000 to support their operations. On February 16, an associate of Khalid Sheikh Mohammed arrived in Lahore and delivered $30,000 to Zubaydah.[42] At the time, al Qa'ida operatives in Pakistan had noted the extensive discussion in the American press about the danger of a dirty bomb and were researching the possibility. Though al Qa'ida leaders were under enormous pressure in Pakistan, they remained resilient and adaptable.

"The dirty bomb concept was receiving speculative coverage in the international media," noted Zubaydah. "As a result, many other al Qa'ida brothers said openly that this was a very good idea and that such an attack would be very effective if conducted in a subway."[43]

Still, Zubaydah continued to have reservations and wanted al Qa'ida's most competent operative, Khalid Sheikh Mohammed, to evaluate both Padilla and the plot. He wrote a reference letter for Padilla, explaining the dirty bomb project and arguing that it was impractical. But he asked Khalid Sheikh Mohammed to assess it anyway. Padilla traveled to Karachi in mid-March 2002 with Binyam Muhammad.[44] They were taken to a safe house by Ammar al-Baluchi, Khalid Sheik Mohammed's nephew, and presented their plans.[45] Khalid Sheikh Mohammed was skeptical of the dirty bomb plot and suggested that Padilla and Binyam Muhammad undertake the apartment operation originally conceived by Muhammed Atef.

"Once in the U.S.," he explained, Padilla and Binyam Muhammad were "to locate as many as three high-rise apartment buildings which had natural gas supplied to the floors. They would rent two apartments in each building," he continued, "seal all the openings, turn on the gas, and set timers to detonate the buildings simultaneously at a later time."[46]

The selection of the target city in the United States would be left to Padilla, who accepted the mission. Ramzi bin al-Shibh provided some last-minute tips on telephone and e-mail security.[47] In April 2002, Khalid Sheikh Mohammed gave Padilla over $10,000, travel documentation, a cell phone, and an e-mail address so he could be notified when Padilla arrived in the United States. Binyam Muhammad was given approximately $6,000.[48]

The night before their departure, Padilla and Binyam Muhammad attended a dinner with Khalid Sheikh Mohammed, Ammar al-Baluchi, and Ramzi bin al-Shibh. They went over the plot again and reinforced careful communications practices and countersurveillance techniques. Once in Chicago, Padilla was to conduct an Internet search on buildings that had natural gas heating, open a bank account, and rent an apartment. Binyam Muhammad was to return to the United Kingdom, obtain valid travel documents, and then fly to the United States to link up with Padilla.[49]

FBI and CIA officials had been aware of Padilla and his network for several years, though they had periodically lost track of him during his travels in Afghanistan and Pakistan. But the capture of Abu Zubaydah on March 28, 2002, revealed to investigators exactly how far along the plot had gotten. U.S. interrogators showed Zubaydah two photographs, one of which was from José Padilla's passport. The other photograph was from a fake passport of Binyam Muhammad, whom Abu Zubaydah identified as Padilla's accomplice. According to CIA and FBI reports, Zubaydah was pivotal in identifying Padilla.[50] CIA officials like Philip Mudd had now realized that a "plot" was bigger than one operation. Their job was to understand—and ultimately destroy—the "spiderweb."

There were operatives involved in executing the plot, like Padilla and Binyam Muhammad, as well as networks involved in training, money, weapons and explosives, radicalization, targeting, and communications.

"The big question," said Mudd, "is can we find anything else? Do they have co-conspirators?"[51]

The FBI then caught a break. On April 4, Binyam Muhammad and José Padilla were both stopped at passport control in Karachi. Binyam Muhammad was detained for a forged passport and José Padilla for multiple visa violations. They were released the next morning, but Pakistani intelligence officials alerted the United States.[52] Padilla left Pakistan on April 5. After spending a month in Egypt, he went to Zurich, Switzerland, and boarded a flight bound for Chicago's O'Hare International Airport. Binyam Muhammad, who had remained in Pakistan to acquire a new passport, was arrested at the Karachi airport on April 10 on his way to London.[53]

On May 8, Padilla landed in Chicago. He was carrying $10,526 in U.S. currency that he had received from al Qa'ida, but he declared only $8,000.[54] He had the cell phone provided by Ammar al-Baluchi, the names and telephone numbers of his training camp recruiter and sponsor, and e-mail addresses for Ammar al-Baluchi and Binyam Muhammad.[55] Several minutes before his flight landed, U.S. District Court judge Michael Mukasey signed a material witness warrant authorizing Padilla's arrest. In August 2007 a federal jury in the Southern District of Florida convicted José Padilla of conspiracy to murder, kidnap, and maim individuals in a foreign country, conspiracy to provide material support to terrorists, and providing material support to terrorists.[56]

The capture of José Padilla was significant. His personal relationship with senior al Qa'ida leaders such as Muhammed Atef, Abu Zubaydah, and Khalid Sheikh Mohammed indicated that he was not a lone wolf. What made him particularly dangerous was his access to a radicalized social network in the United States *and* his success in coordinating with al Qa'ida leaders. U.S. government agencies, including the FBI, had been aware of him through his involvement in his North American jihadist network. He did not appear to be an imminent threat, however, especially in the context of numerous other extremists operating in the United States. It took actionable intelligence from captured al Qa'ida leaders, including Abu Zubaydah, to comprehend the significance of the threat that Padilla posed.

A Narrow Miss

In the first year after September 11, the FBI struggled to adapt to a changing environment. For decades a "successful" case for an FBI agent meant prosecuting and ultimately convicting the criminals or terrorists he or she was tracking. But for FBI agents like Art Cummings, this strategy was no longer sufficient. The FBI had been working on terrorism for decades and had successfully dismantled a range of terrorist organizations, from right-wing groups like the Aryan Nations to left-wing groups like the Black Panthers. However, several senior FBI officials believed that the September 11 attacks provided indisputable evidence that the Bureau needed to focus more aggressively on uncovering cells and plots, collecting additional intelligence, and letting go of the obsession with convictions.

"We began to shift from a disruption to a prevention strategy by early 2003," Cummings explained. Being familiar with so many FBI activities—he had worked counterintelligence, violent crime, drug, child molestation, and finally terrorism cases—Cummings knew what would have to change. But nothing came easily. "It took so long because we focused so heavily after September 11 on capturing additional terrorists, including disrupting the early Khalid Sheikh Mohammed plots," he said.

Part of the new paradigm meant rethinking intelligence collection and analysis. It wasn't good enough anymore to disregard a suspect simply because there was little or no reporting from the CIA, National Security Agency, or other intelligence agencies. "We had to dig deeper," Cummings explained. "Who were their contacts? Where were they traveling? What were they doing? Did it make sense that they were an operative? After walking down this road and still finding nothing, we could at least say, 'Either this individual is damn good, or he's not a terrorist.'"[57]

In addition, Cummings observed that the United States generally denied entry to suspected terrorists trying to enter the country at the borders. But this was unhelpful in some cases, since it would actually be useful, if not critical occasionally, to track and collect intelligence on the subjects. Who were they? What were they doing? To whom were they talking? Where were they going? Several FBI officials, including Cummings, proposed approaches that were virtually unthinkable for some Department of Justice officials and members of Congress.

"We need to let some of them into the country," Cummings argued, "and watch where they go, who they talk to, and what they talk about."[58] Such a strategy would require around-the-clock coverage of the suspects and faith that the FBI would not lose them while they traveled in the United States. Members of Congress told Cummings that such activity was reckless. It was certainly risky. But if the FBI was careful and meticulous in conducting surveillance, it would have the opportunity to collect priceless intelligence leads.

Cummings eventually got his way, but not before a narrow miss. Padilla was not the first serious threat to the U.S. homeland after the September 11 attacks. That distinction belongs to Richard Colvin Reid, who nearly pulled off a successful airplane bombing. Born on August 12, 1973, in South London, Reid was a peculiar figure. He stood six feet, four inches tall and weighed over 200 pounds but was hardly imposing. What stuck with people who met him was his disheveled physical appearance and disregard for personal hygiene. He had thick, scraggly brown hair that he wore in a ponytail and irregular patches of facial hair. French airport security officials, who had temporarily detained him in late 2001, described him as "filthy, very unkempt, emotionless."[59]

Reid had trouble with authority. Even while attending al Qa'ida training camps in the late 1990s, he revolted against leadership. As he acknowledged, his "inability to get along with people in positions of authority was problematic" during his "entire time in Afghanistan," especially with those younger or with less experience in jihad. Reid was also an introvert, preferring to spend time alone reading when he wasn't taking classes in Afghanistan. He was frustrated in love and never married. He considered it heartless that his Arab and Afghan contacts with female relatives were reluctant to offer them as prospective wives to him. He believed that this was because he was not an Arab and did not come from an established family.[60]

Reid was the product of a marriage between a lower-class, black, Protestant father and a middle-class, white, Catholic mother. He didn't fit in from birth. Protestants hated Catholics. Whites hated blacks. The middle class hated the working class. And Reid was caught in the middle. Much like José Padilla, he had a troubled youth. His father was serving jail time for stealing a car when Reid was born. Reid followed in his father's footsteps, serving sentences at Feltham Young Offenders Institution and the Blundeston Prison for a series of crimes. At Feltham, at age nineteen, Reid converted to Islam under the tutelage of the radical imam Abdul Ghani Qureshi. Upon his release in 1996, he joined the Brixton Mosque in London, where an acquaintance provided him with a letter of introduction to attend a training camp in Afghanistan.[61]

In 1999, Reid went to the Khaldan training camp, which Abu Zubaydah eventually ran. He obtained a few donations but funded the trip by selling incense and saving his welfare payments. At Khaldan he worked with one of al Qa'ida's preeminent bomb makers, Midhat Mursi, also known as Abu Khabab al-Masri. Reid also met several individuals involved in plotting terrorist attacks in the

United States, such as the millennium bomber, Ahmed Ressam, who was arrested in December 1999, and Zacarias Moussaoui, an al Qa'ida operative who had attended several flight schools in the United States and who was arrested in August 2001.[62] After Khaldan, Reid joined Taliban field units in Afghanistan as they fought the Northern Alliance between April 1999 and March 2001, alternating between the front lines and al Qa'ida training camps.[63] He believed that fighting with the Taliban was a way to demonstrate his devotion to al Qa'ida, since he understood that individuals who fought for the Taliban "earned Osama bin Laden's respect."[64]

Al Qa'ida's chief of operations, Muhammed Atef, helped conceptualize the shoe bomb plot and provided initial training to Reid. Late in 2001, Reid was given a shoe bomb in Afghanistan to smuggle onto an aircraft and detonate in midair.[65] Reid believed that a shoe bomb was perfect. Before the attack he took numerous flights and observed security procedures, noting that even on Israel's El Al Airlines security officers did not check inside his shoes.[66] He also continued to receive guidance from Ammar al-Baluchi, Khalid Sheik Mohammed's nephew, on the airline bombing.[67]

On December 5, 2001, Reid applied for a new passport, al Qa'ida's standard method for erasing travel history—a strong indication that he was getting ready to execute the operation. "I was drunk and washed my passport," Reid told a British consulate official.[68]

During the final weeks before his suicide attack, Reid wrote an e-mail to his mother justifying the operation. "What I am doing is part of the ongoing war between Islam and disbelief," he told her. "I didn't do this act out of ignorance nor did I do [it] just because I want to die, but rather I see it as a duty upon me to help remove the oppressive American forces from the Muslim lands. We do not have other means to fight them. We are ready to die defending the true Islam rather than just sit back and allow the American government to dictate to us what we should believe and how we should behave. This is a war," he concluded, "between Islam and democracy."[69]

It was a passionate e-mail. But it was also deeply troubling. Reid's rhetoric reflected a common charge that the U.S. government was "oppressing" Muslims and "dictating" what they should believe. The U.S. military had, of course, come to the aid of beleaguered Muslims in Afghanistan in the 1980s, Somalia in the early 1990s, Bosnia in the 1990s, and Kosovo in 1999. But this reality did not fit with the al Qa'ida worldview, especially as it was manifested in Reid.

On December 21, 2001, Reid attempted to board an American Airlines flight bound for Miami at Charles de Gaulle Airport. But French security personnel were suspicious of him, and extra searches and questioning caused him to miss his flight.[70] Security officials searched his luggage and found a Walkman, a cassette tape with recordings of the Qur'an, anti-Israel propaganda, a copy of a *Time* magazine titled "Islam in Europe," and an issue of *Newsweek* with a picture of Osama bin Laden.[71] But they failed to detect his shoe bomb. After a final pat-down the next day, Reid was allowed to board an American Airlines flight to Miami.

Three days before Christmas, on December 22, Richard Reid left Charles de Gaulle Airport on American Airlines Flight 63, a Boeing 767-300, with 183 passengers and a crew of 14.[72] He was seated in 29J, a window seat. Several hours after the flight left Paris, the passenger in seat 29H got up to use the bathroom.[73] Reid quickly removed his ankle-high Aspen hiking shoes, each of which was rigged to explode. A chemical analysis later indicated that he used a pentaerythritol tetranitrate–based plastic bonded explosive as the main charge.[74] Both the right and left shoes contained a black safety fuse. One end of the fuse was taped to an improvised detonator, which consisted of a piece of paper rolled into a tube measuring approximately 2 inches in length. The tubes contained one and a half grams of the explosive triacetone triperoxide (TATP), a white crystalline material commonly produced from hydrogen peroxide, acetone, and sulfuric acid.[75]

Reid took off his right shoe, pulled the free end of the safety fuse out of the shoe, and attempted to ignite the fuse using matches he had brought onto the aircraft.[76] Flight attendant Hermis Moutardier, who was picking up trays after the meal service, cruised the aisles searching for the burning smell. A passenger pointed to Reid.

Smoking is not allowed on the airplane, she said to Reid.

I promise to stop, responded Reid.

A few minutes later, Moutardier saw Reid bend over in his seat. "Excuse me," she said, furious that he was apparently trying to smoke again. "What are you doing?"

What she saw made her stomach churn. Reid was frantically trying to light one of his shoes, and she could see the wires protruding from it. Moutardier grabbed at the shoe, but Reid shoved her into the bulkhead. She made a second attempt, and he pushed her to the floor. "Get him! Go!" she screamed, alerting another flight attendant, Cristina Jones, who came running over.

"Stop it!" Jones yelled and grabbed Reid's upper body.[77] But he bit her finger. When she screamed, several passengers came to her aid and tackled Reid. They restrained him for the rest of the flight with a makeshift combination of plastic cuffs for his hands, a seatbelt extension for his feet, and an odd assortment of belts, headphone cords, and other makeshift items to tie up his body. A doctor on board gave him Valium, which was kept in the flight kit.[78]

The FBI was alerted to the disturbance and the flight was diverted to Boston, landing at 12:53 p.m. FBI special agent Margaret Cronin, FBI special agent Charles Gianturco, and Massachusetts State Police troopers boarded the aircraft. The captain outlined the struggle on board and provided the FBI with Reid's British passport, which he had confiscated after the altercation. Cronin and Gianturco then took Reid into custody.

A small group of vigilant flight attendants and passengers had preempted certain catastrophe. The FBI conducted a series of tests to assess the viability of Reid's shoe bombs and determined that they "were functioning explosive devices capable of exploding if the safety fuse had been properly ignited." The FBI also reported that "if either device had been placed near or against the interior wall of the aircraft at seat 29J . . . the resulting explosion would have breached the outside skin of the aircraft."[79] Boeing conducted a series of tests and concluded that Reid's bomb would have been lethal in a pressurized cabin at 32,000 feet, and would probably have destroyed the plane in midair.

Reid expressed no remorse for his failed attack and unleashed a chilling diatribe during his sentencing: "I admit my allegiance to Osama bin Laden, to Islam, and to the religion of Allah. With regards to what you said about killing innocent people, I will say one thing. Your government has killed two million children in Iraq. If you want to think about something, against two million, I don't see no comparison. So, for this reason, I think I ought not apologize for my actions. I am at war with your country. I'm at war with them not for personal reasons but because they have murdered so many children and they have oppressed my religion and they have oppressed people for no reason except that they say we believe in Allah."[80]

The presiding judge, William Young, shot back: "We are not afraid of any of your terrorist co-conspirators, Mr. Reid. We are Americans. We have been through the fire before. You are not an enemy combatant. You are a terrorist. You are not a soldier in any war."

In a firm tone, Judge Young then delivered his summation: "You're a big fellow. But you're not that big. You're no warrior. I know warriors. You are a terrorist. A species of criminal guilty of multiple attempted murders. It seems to me you hate the one thing that to us is most precious. You hate our freedom. Our individual freedom. Our individual freedom to live as we choose, to come and go as we choose, to believe or not believe as we individually choose. Here, in this society, the very winds carry freedom. They carry it everywhere from sea to shining sea. It is because we prize individual freedom so much that you are here in this beautiful courtroom. So that everyone can see, truly see that justice is administered fairly, individually, and discreetly."

Young wasn't finished. "See that flag, Mr. Reid? That's the flag of the United States of America. That flag will fly there long after this is all forgotten. That flag still stands for freedom. You know it always will. Custody, Mr. Officer," he said, ending his speech. "Stand him down."

But Reid had more to say. "That flag will be brought down on the day of judgment," he said, "and you will see in front of your Lord and my Lord and then we will know."[81]

Reid was then removed from the courtroom. Though the victory did not belong to the government agencies, the result was a triumph. French, American, and even British officials had failed to identify Reid and stop him from blowing up an airplane. Instead, brave citizens steeled by the September 11 attacks had done so.

"I don't believe I would have grabbed him the way I did had I not known about September 11," said Hermis Moutardier. "I don't know that the passengers would have come to my aid so quickly had they not known about September 11."[82]

The Lackawanna Threat

Reid had been arrested in Boston. The drowsy, blue-collar city of Lackawanna could not be more different. Lackawanna rests on the eastern shore of Lake Erie in upstate New York, just south of Buffalo, with a mostly white population of 20,000. Vacant grain elevators and dormant railroad tracks line the shore, interspersed with fields overgrown with gnarled shrubbery. Test wells that monitor decades of buried industrial waste dot the landscape. The area was a steel manufacturing hub for much of the twentieth century, beginning in 1899, when the Lackawanna Steel Company purchased land along the West Seneca shore of the lake. In 1909 residents split off from West Seneca and formed their own city. By 2002, Lackawanna was home to an amalgam of Protestant and Roman Catholic churches, along with the Masjid Alhuda Guidance Mosque, the largest mosque in the Buffalo area. It was situated among rows of dilapidated apartments on Wilkes Barre Avenue, a narrow thoroughfare running between razed steel mills to the west and railroad tracks to the east.

Like the case of José Padilla, the threat in Lackawanna emerged from a close network of friends. In this instance they were Yemeni-Americans, all of them U.S. citizens. Unlike with Padilla, however, top-down al Qa'ida recruitment contributed to their radicalization. The focal point was Lackawanna native Kamal Derwish, a charismatic preacher and al Qa'ida recruiter. Sahim Alwan, who came under Derwish's mentorship, described him as "very articulate, very impressive, very knowledgeable of the religion . . . he was very likable."[83] Other friends described him as friendly and alluring.

Derwish was born at Mercy Hospital in southern Buffalo, raised in Saudi Arabia, and conducted training in Afghanistan and Bosnia in the 1990s. He served as both a catalyst and a spiritual adviser for a small cell of impressionable individuals: Faysal Galab, Sahim Alwan, Yahya Goba, Shafal Mosed, Yasein Taher, and Jaber Elbaneh.[84] Several members of the network were second-generation children of immigrants who had come to work at Lackawanna's steel plants in the 1970s. None were particularly religious. Six were graduates of Lackawanna High School, known by their peers and family as being more interested in playing soccer and ice hockey than conducting jihad.

When Derwish returned to Lackawanna from overseas around 1998, he had developed a close relationship with several al Qa'ida operatives and was on a dedicated mission to motivate young Muslims to participate in violent jihad. He held private meetings in several venues. "Sometimes at his apartment, or sometimes in the mosque, like after the prayers and stuff, we'll just hang out there, just come," said Sahim Alwan. "He also taught the Qur'an to the kids in the mosque."[85]

The location was important. For Derwish, recruitment and incitement were better in private, informal settings where operational security could be maintained, rather than at public mosque services which law enforcement agencies could be monitoring. These clandestine meetings drew as many as twenty regular attendees, most of whom were in their late teens and early twenties. Lackawanna's young Muslims were captivated by Derwish. Since few Yemenis in the Lackawanna community practiced Salafi Islam, they were awestruck by Derwish, whom one follower called a "music man of religion."[86]

According to a member of the network, "I really was, you know, starting to learn my religion, and I didn't see, I never really saw the mujahideen part of it."[87]

To aid in recruitment, Derwish introduced his network to Juma al-Dosari, an imam from Indiana who had connections with al Qa'ida and had fought in Bosnia. According to one participant at the meetings, Dosari was brought in to "close the deal" on their recruitment.[88] In April 2001, Dosari delivered a heavily politicized sermon at the Lackawanna mosque, stressing the need to help Muslims suffering in Kosovo, Chechnya, and Kashmir. According to an FBI profile of their recruitment strategy, Derwish and Dosari would develop a friendship with each individual and identify his interests, emotional state, strengths, and weaknesses. They then repeated a common theme: Muslims are being persecuted across the globe, and "true" Muslims fight for their faith. It was a mesmerizing message. Both Derwish and Dosari also argued that Lackawanna's young Muslims were not leading a proper Islamic lifestyle and suggested that they attend a four-month training program in Afghanistan.[89]

"I was hungry for knowledge of the religion itself," noted Sahim Alwan. "It was a religious quest."[90]

Derwish's and Dosari's recruits began to withdraw from Lacka-wanna and its secular community. The travel was the first major step. They left in two groups. The first departed in April 2001 and con-sisted of Shafal Mosed, Yasein Taher, and Faysal Galab; the second left in May 2001 and included Sahim Alwan, Yahya Goba, Mukhtar al-Bakri, and Jaber Elbaneh. Alwan's group traveled through Toronto to the United Arab Emirates and finally landed in Karachi. They were met by Derwish, who arranged their transportation to Afghan-istan. After about six days they traveled to Quetta, where they stayed at a guesthouse and listened to lectures on jihad and sermons on suicide operations. After several days they departed for al-Farouq training camp in a bus crammed with ten other individuals.[91]

Taher, Galab, and Mosed arrived in Pakistan on April 29 and also traveled to Quetta, where they stayed at a guesthouse. They then drove to al-Farouq camp, where they received training and instruction in the use of Kalashnikovs, 9-millimeter handguns, M16 automatic rifles, and rocket-propelled grenade launchers.[92] The group took classes on combat tactics and explosives, including plastic explosives, TNT, detonators, landmines, and Molotov cock-tails.[93] There were approximately two hundred others at the camp, divided into groups of twenty. All of the individuals had—or were assigned—code names.[94] Osama bin Laden visited the camp during their stay and spoke about the importance of targeting the United States and Israel, as well as the need for patience.[95]

But al Qa'ida training did not convince the entire Lackawanna contingent to become involved in terrorism. Yasein Taher did not complete the training and left shortly after bin Laden's speech. According to one member of the network, they discussed the importance of keeping their experience quiet when they reunited in Lackawanna later that summer. After September 11 they low-ered their profile in the community out of concern that U.S. law enforcement and intelligence agencies would discover their Afghan travels. Still, some members of the group remained committed to violent jihad. As one individual noted, "[Elbaneh] was planning on going to the fighting against the Northern Alliance, and stuff like that. Basically his mindset was 'I want to be a martyr. I want to die.'"[96] Elbaneh just needed to be patient.

One of the FBI's first indications of a potential terrorist threat came in June 2001, when a "concerned Yemenite" sent an anonymous letter to the FBI's Buffalo field office noting that Derwish and several others were connected to al Qa'ida and had traveled to Afghanistan.[97] On September 10, 2002, Mukhtar al-Bakri was arrested in Bahrain after sending two e-mails to an associate in New York State suggesting that a suicide operation was imminent. The FBI and CIA scrambled to piece together information on the Lackawanna network. On July 8, 2002, the FBI had interviewed Shafal Mosed, and on July 26 FBI agents had interviewed Yasein Taher. Both acknowledged that they had been in Pakistan for three months between April and July 2001.[98] But the FBI had not appreciated the extent of their travels in Afghanistan, including al-Farouq.[99] September 2002 searches of the Lackawanna residences of Goba, Alwan, Mosed, and Bakri turned up U.S. passports used for travel to Afghanistan in 2001.

On September 13, 2002, the FBI arrested five of the suspects. In 2003 six members of the network were sentenced to prison terms ranging from seven to ten years for providing material resources to a foreign terrorist organization. While they had trained at an al Qa'ida camp, their experiences had not transferred into an operation—at least not yet. Unlike the Padilla and Reid cases, there was no evidence of an imminent attack.

Following his time at al-Farouq, Elbaneh never returned to the United States, traveling instead to Yemen and participating in extremist operations overseas. Kamal Derwish was killed in Yemen by a Hellfire missile from a CIA drone in November 2002, along with five other al Qa'ida operatives traveling in a vehicle. Dosari was captured by Pakistani authorities in January 2002, fleeing from Afghanistan, and was turned over to U.S. custody and sent to Guantánamo Bay.

Gas Stations and Bridges

Back at FBI Headquarters in Washington in 2002, Robert Mueller and his senior staff, including Art Cummings, were bracing for another attack. So was the CIA. "Recent information," read one CIA assessment, "demonstrates al-Qaida's ongoing interest to enter the United States over land borders with Mexico and Canada."[100] In October 2002 a cell of American Muslims from the Portland, Oregon, area were arrested for attempting to join al Qa'ida. In June 2003, eleven individuals were indicted in northern Virginia for inciting terrorism.

Perhaps the most serious U.S. homeland plot, however, was led by Majid Khan. In 1996, Khan had moved with his family to the United States from Pakistan and settled in Baltimore, but he had never obtained U.S. citizenship. After graduating from high school in 1999, he became involved in a local Islamic organization, and in early 2002 he traveled to Pakistan. Khan's uncle and cousin introduced him to Khalid Sheikh Mohammed, who selected Khan as an operative for a possible attack inside the United States.

Khan spoke excellent English, had extensive knowledge of the United States, and had worked at his family's gas station. The latter detail was particularly useful for Khalid Sheikh Mohammed, who asked Khan to return to the United States and collect information on gas station operations, including fuel delivery schedules, tanker routes, and procedures for filling underground tanks. Khan was to assume the role of a businessman interested in buying a gas station. The ultimate goal was to blow one up.[101] In support of the plot, Khan attended a training course where he learned how to construct explosive timing devices. Khalid Sheikh Mohammed also asked Khan to conduct research on poisoning U.S. water reservoirs and considered Khan for an operation to assassinate Pakistan's president, Pervez Musharraf.[102]

Early in 2003, Khan tapped Uzair Paracha, a U.S. permanent resident alien he met in Pakistan, to impersonate him in the

United States. His goal was to make it appear that he had never left the country and enable him to gain immigration documents that would facilitate reentry.[103] Khan also recommended to Khalid Sheikh Mohammed that Iyman Faris, an Ohio-based truck driver and naturalized U.S. citizen, be tasked with conducting an al Qa'ida operation. At Khalid Sheikh Mohammed's request, Faris researched suspension bridges in New York and looked into obtaining the tools that would be necessary to cut the suspension cables.[104]

But again patient intelligence work paid off. A significant break came from the March 2003 capture of Khalid Sheikh Mohammed. As the CIA reported, KSM "provided information about an al-Qa'ida operative, Majid Khan," and admitted to having "tasked Majid with delivering a large sum of money to individuals working for another senior al-Qa'ida associate."[105] In addition, the FBI pulled off a coup with Iyman Faris, which highlighted the paradigm shift that officials like Art Cummings had led at the Bureau. Cummings went to Attorney General John Ashcroft with a pitch.

"Faris is a militant with the capability and intent to kill Americans. But he would be perfect to recruit," Cummings said. "In fact, I can't do my job if we take Faris off the streets now." Cummings needed more time. He wanted Faris to lead him to the "spider-web"—the broader network.

"What's the chance he'll get away from us if we don't capture him right now?" Ashcroft asked.

"Probably fifteen percent," responded Cummings. But he was willing to take the chance and attempt to flip Faris in return for a reduced sentence.

Cummings and other FBI agents felt that one of Faris's biggest weaknesses was his ego—his desire to be important. They worked to exploit this vulnerability. "We told him that because of his unparalleled relations with senior al Qa'ida leaders," said Cummings, "he would be an extraordinary asset to the U.S. government. He'd be a star. I think he even believed he'd be an FBI agent one day."

In March the FBI approached Faris with information newly

gleaned from Khalid Sheikh Mohammed, implicating him in terrorist activity. They dangled an offer to move his extended family from Pakistan to reduce the risk of al Qa'ida retaliation. Faris agreed. Soon afterward the FBI took him to a safe house in Virginia. With agents directing and monitoring his communications, Faris served as a double agent and sent messages to his bosses via cell phone and e-mail. "Our focus was not to prosecute Faris," explained Cummings, "it was to stop individuals from killing Americans. With Faris, this meant trying to convince him to work with us."[106]

With the help of Faris, the FBI arrested Majid Khan and Uzair Paracha in March 2003, as well as several others, including Uzair's father, Saifullah. The arrests were a severe blow to al Qa'ida leaders, including Khalid Sheikh Mohammed, who had desperately tried to conduct follow-on attacks in the United States. Khalid Sheikh Mohammed's arrest had also disrupted plots to hijack aircraft to attack the Library Tower in Los Angeles and other targets on the West Coast. U.S. intelligence and law enforcement agencies had information on virtually every major terrorist targeting the U.S. homeland. The problem, it turned out, was deciding which ones were most significant. They received a cluttered mass of raw intelligence every day. Agents had to connect the dots but also weigh which dots were most important and focus on them. The triggering event that led to arrests was different in each case. Abu Zubaydah's capture led to José Padilla, vigilant passengers neutralized Richard Reid, a concerned community member upended the Lackawanna cell, and Khalid Sheikh Mohammed's capture undermined Majid Khan and his network.

"Since the security situation in the United States was strong and al Qa'ida's capabilities had weakened," remarked senior al Qa'ida leader Abu Faraj al-Libi, "al Qa'ida had to return to easier ideas and methods in order to execute an attack in the United States."[107]

The first al Qa'ida wave was now over. U.S. intelligence agencies and special operations forces had delivered major setbacks to al Qa'ida in Afghanistan, Pakistan, and now the United States.

After September 11, al Qa'ida had failed to launch a successful attack against the United States despite several attempts by Khalid Sheikh Mohammed, and it had lost its sanctuary in Afghanistan. The organization's punishment strategy, which involved targeting civilians, had also backfired and created major fissures within even conservative Islamic circles. Al Qa'ida had crippled itself. Nothing seemed to be going well. But it would now get a break from Iraq, where the U.S. invasion provided an opportunity for redemption.

PART II

THE SECOND WAVE

6

AL QA'IDA IN IRAQ

I N JULY 2003, militants loyal to Abu Mus'ab al-Zarqawi congregated at a house in the Al Qahira district of Baghdad to discuss clandestine operations against U.S. and other international targets. Al Qahira is a busy neighborhood east of the Tigris River, home to both Sunnis and Shi'ites. The cell met again several days later.

"We should perform jihad and attack the occupier," one of the members, Abu Azzam al-Filistani, suggested.[1]

The cell then turned to a key question: Which target?

Discussions continued over the next several days and zeroed in on the United Nations headquarters at the Canal Hotel in Baghdad. Most senior UN officials had opposed the March 2003 U.S. invasion of Iraq, though the UN had reluctantly established a presence in Iraq to assist in reconstruction efforts after the overthrow of Saddam Hussein. This was enough to draw Iraqi ire. Iraqis also resented the UN for imposing an economic embargo in the 1990s in response to Saddam's program of weapons of mass destruction. To repay these grievances, cell members prepared an attack. Operational planning for the UN plot was led by Ali Hussein al-Azzawi, a former pilot for Iraqi Airways, and Thamir Mubarak Atrouz al-Rishawi, whose family eventually became a major supporter of al Qa'ida in Iraq.[2] Most important, the operation had the backing of Abu Mus'ab al-Zarqawi.

Zarqawi was a rock star. When he walked into a room, he didn't just meet people, he engulfed them. Forget his security detail and his high-profile status as a senior commander. He shouldered past his aura, built on fame and reputation, and connected with the lowest-ranking fighters, the grunts who had trekked from Libya, Saudi Arabia, and Yemen to fight the Americans. He was "kind in dealing with his driver and those around him, treating them like his brothers," explained one of his colleagues. Take his obsession with Kraft cheese: he carefully unwrapped each piece from its plastic packaging and placed it in his mouth, savoring every bite. As one of his admirers pointed out, however, he "refused to take any until his fighters could have some."[3] To preserve this "man of the people" image, Zarqawi participated in grisly actions, bragging that he had beheaded Nicholas Berg, a kidnapped American businessman, with his own blade in 2004. Through such exploits Zarqawi became legendary among al Qa'ida operatives.

"Had I known of all of Zarqawi's activities and capabilities when he first came to al Qa'ida with a desire to pledge *bayat* to Osama bin Laden," joked senior al Qa'ida leader Abu Faraj al-Libi, "I would have written a letter to bin Laden advising that the sheikh pledge *bayat* to Abu Mus'ab instead."[4]

By mid-August 2003, Zarqawi's terrorist cell was ready to execute the operation against UN headquarters. Members of the cell planned the attack in a Pepsi factory in the Al Mashtal area of Baghdad. They recruited several informants who provided a blueprint of the UN compound and accessed the daily calendars of some UN officials. "We brought in a suicide bomber from the Arab Maghreb," one cell member explained, "and my role was to help them in giving them the mortars and the rockets."[5]

They carefully packed a large cement truck with plastic explosives, artillery shells, and other ammunition. Cell members, several of whom were North African, conducted rehearsals and finalized preparations. "Hajj Ali drove the vehicle," another cell member noted. "They went to the UN headquarters and carried out the operation."[6]

The truck drove through the barrier at the main entrance of the UN headquarters at 4:30 p.m. on August 19, 2003, pulled up to the security wall under the corner office of Sergio Vieira de Mello, the UN secretary-general's special representative to Iraq, and detonated.

"There was a huge, shattering explosion," remarked Salim Lone, the UN's spokesman, who was in his office. "I was working on the computer. The glass in the window blew—the woodwork, everything came out of the roof. I ran into the corridor," he continued. "Everybody was very severely wounded, very badly hurt, bleeding, people with blood on their face."[7]

The bomb shredded the façade of the UN headquarters. Little was left of the truck except for a rear axle at the bottom of a deep crater. The blast killed twenty-two people and injured hundreds.[8] American forces had blocked off the road with a five-ton truck, but UN officials had asked that it be removed, along with an observation post on the roof and armored vehicles in front of the compound, because they were uncomfortable with a heavy U.S. military presence.

Vieira de Mello was sitting at a table with several staff members when the bomb exploded, leaving a six-foot-deep crater in the ground. His office collapsed into a smoking pile of concrete slabs, shredded steel, and shattered glass.

"Sergio, *courage*," screamed Ghassam Salamé, his political adviser. "We're coming to help you." A ray of sunlight illuminated Vieira de Mello, and Salamé could see him waving his right hand. He was trapped upside-down, wedged under several enormous slabs of concrete.

"Sergio, answer me," Salamé said. "Are you alive?"

"*Oui*, Ghassan," he replied.[9]

But rescue workers couldn't get to Vieira de Mello in time. That evening, when U.S. and Iraqi soldiers finally cleared away the debris, Salamé identified his body. His last words, according to a U.S. soldier who was furiously trying to dig him out, were "Don't let them pull the UN out."[10]

Vieira de Mello's death was a devastating blow for the UN and those who knew him. In a poignant letter to his widow, U.S. ambassador Paul Bremer wrote that "like you, I will miss his buoyancy, his optimism, his refined intellect and his sense of humor."[11]

The attack had wide-ranging repercussions. The UN withdrew most of its staff because of security concerns, relocating many of them to the nearby country of Oman. Several international monetary agencies, including the World Bank and the International Monetary Fund, refused to set up shop in Iraq until the situation improved. And the ability of development agencies, such as the United Kingdom's Department for International Development and the U.S. Agency for International Development, to go "outside the wire"—to leave their compounds—was so severely restricted that work virtually halted.[12]

The attack symbolized the beginning of a second wave of terrorism. Al Qa'ida was headquartered in Afghanistan when it targeted the United States on September 11, but it had no serious presence in Iraq. America's invasion galvanized numerous Muslims and became a superb recruitment tool for al Qa'ida. Opinion of the United States plummeted in polls across the Muslim world. U.S. intelligence and law enforcement agencies, including the CIA and the FBI, saw that Iraq was becoming an incubator of international terrorism. Instead of decreasing the terrorism problem, as many U.S. policymakers had hoped, the Iraq war exacerbated it. The steady gains made by small numbers of covert U.S. intelligence operatives, special operations forces, and law enforcement officials in Afghanistan, Pakistan, and even the U.S. homeland were now in jeopardy. Many al Qa'ida leaders had hoped for a large conventional U.S. army in Iraq; the U.S. invasion delivered it. Before the 2003 invasion, al Qa'ida had failed to secure a foothold in Iraq. Now the gates had swung open. Zarqawi would be the Trojan horse.

A Growing Vacuum

Zarqawi was born on October 20, 1966, in Zarqa, Jordan. His house was located in a squalid area near the town cemetery and an abandoned quarry. After his father died, in 1984, Zarqawi dropped out of school, and his life degenerated into drug abuse and violent crime. He then drifted into Palestinian refugee camps, where he became interested in Salafism, eventually trekking to Afghanistan in 1989 to fight against the Soviet army. In 1992 he returned to Jordan, and in March 1994 he was arrested for plotting to overthrow the government. During the trial, Zarqawi heaped scorn on the judge and King Hussein, illustrating his voluble and frequent defiance of Middle Eastern rulers. He was given fifteen years of hard labor. But in 1999 Jordan's new king, Abdullah II, granted a general amnesty and released Zarqawi. He returned to Afghanistan to establish a terrorist organization called Tawhid wa'l Jihad (Monotheism and Struggle) in the western province of Herat.[13]

In November 2001, two months after the September 11 attacks, Abu Zubaydah helped smuggle Zarqawi and roughly seventy other Arabs out of Kandahar into Iran.[14] But Zarqawi didn't stay there long. In the summer of 2002 he settled in northern Iraq, with help from the terrorist group Ansar al-Islam.[15] He was proudly not a member of al Qa'ida, preferring to run his own group, though he had contacts with several senior al Qa'ida members.[16] When the United States invaded Iraq, Zarqawi was well positioned to run operations targeting American and UN infrastructure, and he had established relationships with sheikhs such as Thamir Mubarak Atrouz al-Rishawi and Abdullah al-Janabi.

Zarqawi explained to al Qa'ida leaders that setting up an organization in Iraq would provide an opportunity to expand his power and influence. "Then the mujahidin will have assured themselves land from which to set forth," he wrote, and achieve "strategic depth and reach among the brothers outside [Iraq] and the mujahidin within."[17]

Zarqawi even made an impression on senior American officials, including John Negroponte, who became U.S. ambassador to Iraq and later the first director of national intelligence. "He was a phenomenon," said Negroponte. "I felt like Inspector Clouseau trying to understand him. He was a fascinating guy, and built an entire enterprise almost entirely around himself."[18]

For Zarqawi, the March 20, 2003, U.S. invasion of Iraq and the resulting insurgency created an opportunity. By the summer of 2003, CIA officials in Iraq had become concerned about growing violence. According to U.S. government estimates, insurgent activity was "centered on U.S./Coalition targets, ranging from checkpoints, and increasingly, to higher profile targets such as helicopters and tactical level military headquarters. These are still locally organized, indigenous attacks. However, all current indicators point to ingress of experienced external forces . . . that may be planning for more intensified attacks or for organization of disparate groups."[19]

While U.S. government officials publicly assured Americans that the security situation was not as bad as press reports indicated, internal U.S. documents showed alarm. In a memo to Secretary Rumsfeld, Ambassador Bremer, head of the Coalition Provisional Authority (CPA), identified several threats to U.S. forces. The first included elements of the former regime, such as Ba'athists, Fedayeen Saddam, and intelligence agencies. They attacked coalition forces, infrastructure targets, and Iraqi employees of the coalition. "To date," Bremer wrote, "these elements do not appear to be subject to central command and control. But there are signs of coordination among them."[20] Former officers from the Mukhabarat, Iraq's intelligence service, specialized in making radio-detonated Kaneen bombs. They used money channeled through radical Islamic clerics, who had been funded by wealthy donors in the United Arab Emirates and other Gulf countries.[21]

The second threat included groups like Zarqawi's Tawhid wa'l Jihad, which incorporated foreign fighters from Saudi Arabia, Syria, Yemen, and other countries. The third threat was foreign subversion. Iran was a particular worry: "Elements of the Tehran government are actively arming, training and directing militia in Iraq. To date, these armed forces have not been directly involved in attacks on the Coalition. But they pose a longer term threat to law and order in Iraq."[22] In a May 29 briefing to President Bush, Bremer noted that he faced emerging threats that included "Iranian-sponsored Islamic extremism."[23] The United States tracked the movement of Iranian intelligence officials into and out of Iraq.[24]

Syria also provided support to insurgent groups and helped funnel al Qa'ida and other foreign fighters into Iraq. "I was actually more concerned about the Syrians than the Iranians," Bremer recalled, "because of the transit of foreign fighters coming into Iraq from Yemen, Saudi Arabia, Sudan, and other countries, who came through Damascus."[25] An assessment produced for Iraq's Ministerial Committee for National Security, which was chaired by Bremer, pointed to "a substantial body of evidence that Syrian nationals, and possibly agents of the Syrian government, are providing aid to insurgents in Iraq. This assistance is coming in a number of forms including weapons, cash, aid and refuge, and training."[26] Syrian intelligence agents also operated front companies in Iraq.[27]

Iraqi intelligence estimates "reported that enemy cells, associated with the Zarqawi Group, were moving out of Syria that possibly had the Green Zone on their target list."[28] In briefings for the new Iraqi leadership, CPA officials warned that Syria "has been the most politically antagonistic of Iraq's neighbors since liberation" by providing refuge for former regime members and smuggling weapons, money, and fighters into Iraq.[29] The CPA responded with several strategies: monitoring the activities of companies associated with the Syrian government, especially those that had "connections with the Syrian intelligence services"; intensifying border patrols along the Iraqi-Syrian border; periodically shutting down Syrian border crossings; and filing lawsuits in international courts against Syria's seizures of Iraqi assets.[30] None of this proved very effective, and Syria remained the principal pipeline for foreign terrorists for several years.

As the insurgency worsened, public opinion polls highlighted growing dissatisfaction among Iraqis. According to one poll from the State Department's Bureau of Intelligence and Research, "Iraqis are unhappy with the conditions in their country after the end of Saddam's regime."[31] In one Gallup poll shared among U.S. government officials, 94 percent of Iraqis in Baghdad believed that the city was a more dangerous place to live in after the U.S.-led invasion. Majorities also said that they were afraid to go out of their homes during the day (70 percent) and at night (80 percent) because of safety concerns. And anti-American sentiments in much of Iraq were extremely high.[32]

Through the fall, the security situation continued to deteriorate. The Coalition Provisional Authority's Office of Policy Planning, for example, argued that street crime had increased from prewar levels and insurgents were getting smarter about conducting attacks.[33] Meghan O'Sullivan, a senior adviser to Bremer, wrote in a memo to him that "recent intelligence suggests that terrorists are seeking to use 'official' vehicles to target their victims."[34] Insurgents also targeted key infrastructure such as pipelines—which disrupted oil exports, electricity production, and fuel distribution—and railroads. One U.S. report concluded that "the extent to which normal operations are disrupted remains unacceptable if the railway is to function as a vital transport element in the movement of cargoes."[35] In mid-2003, U.S. Central Command reported to Secretary Rumsfeld that "the emerging threats and attacks against the Iraqi infrastructure are reaching a level that requires immediate and unprecedented action. We are losing the consent of the Iraqi people by failing to meet their expectations in some of the most basic areas of life support. As such we risk losing the peace."[36]

The CIA, which had been so instrumental in disrupting al Qa'ida in Pakistan and the United States, suffered from a significant lack of intelligence on the insurgency. Its agents were focused on finding Iraq's elusive weapons of mass destruction. The CIA station chief oversaw the Iraq Survey Group, an intelligence organization under CIA official David Kay and Army Major General Keith Dayton, which had roughly 1,400 coalition civilians and military personnel searching for weapons of mass destruction. In a briefing to President Bush, Bremer argued that the United States needed to "increase and sharpen Intel collection—esp. local HUMINT."[37] Few people had any understanding of the insurgency and its causes, and Bremer was "deeply frustrated."[38]

"We never had a good handle on the insurgent command and control network," he said. "We had lots of good information at the tactical level, such as where a specific insurgent lived. But we didn't have a good picture at the strategic level. We were flying blind."[39]

Al Qa'ida in Iraq

Back at the FBI, senior officials were uneasy about the Iraq war's impact on counterterrorism efforts. FBI agents began hearing complaints from Muslim communities across the United States who objected to the invasion. Even worse, al Qa'ida and allied groups made the Iraq war a centerpiece of their aggressive propaganda and recruitment campaign. "Before Iraq," observed Art Cummings, "we weren't seeing many homegrown terrorist groups. But after the Iraq invasion, they exploded."

In 2003, Cummings was promoted to chief of the FBI's International Terrorism Operations Section 1, or ITOS 1, which was responsible for the Bureau's investigation of all terrorist organizations in the United States—especially al Qa'ida and its affiliated networks. After reviewing intelligence reports coming into FBI Headquarters, Cummings could state that "Iraq was a contributing factor to radicalization in the United States."[40]

British intelligence had come to a similar conclusion about the UK's Muslim population. Al Qa'ida waged an intense campaign on the Internet to influence troubled young Muslims. The head of MI5, Dame Eliza Manningham-Buller, warned that the "propaganda machine is sophisticated and al Qa'ida itself says that 50 percent of its war is conducted through the media. In Iraq," she continued, "attacks are regularly videoed and the footage downloaded onto the Internet within thirty minutes. Virtual media teams then edit the result, translate it into English and many other languages, and package it for a worldwide audience. And, chillingly, we see the results here, young teenagers being groomed to be suicide bombers."[41]

Al Qa'ida's use of the Internet disturbed Cummings. But what should the FBI do? FBI leaders struggled to answer the question. "We went back and forth on what do or what our options were," said Cummings. "We clearly needed to shut some of the sites down. But they'd pop up again in a week or two somewhere else. Maybe we'd find the next site, maybe we wouldn't."[42]

There were also legal questions about shutting down sites, since Internet laws were vague. To make matters worse, there was no U.S. government cyber strategy or single organization that pulled together military, intelligence, and law enforcement programs. So cyber efforts were haphazard and ad hoc.

As the United States struggled to respond, al Qa'ida took advantage of a vacuum in Iraq that its leaders had prepared to fill. "Our analysis," wrote Saif al-Adel from Iran, "was that the Americans were going to make the mistake sooner or later to invade Iraq." The goal, he continued, should be to use Iraq to help establish an Islamic caliphate. Even though Al Qa'ida's sanctuary in Afghanistan had disappeared and its leaders were being rounded up in Pakistan, the United States, and other countries, gaining a grip in Iraq was now a legitimate possibility. "We should play an important role in the confrontation and resistance," Adel argued, since "this is our historical chance to establish the Islamic State who will have the biggest role in removing injustice and establish justice in this world allah willing."[43]

But there was one problem. For some al Qa'ida leaders, including Osama bin Laden, Abu Mus'ab al-Zarqawi was not the ideal person to run operations in Iraq. He was not an al Qa'ida member and had never sworn *bayat* to bin Laden. Even worse, he had a reputation as a gangster who pursued his own agenda. Indeed, Zarqawi's vision in Iraq was somewhat different from al Qa'ida's goals. In a letter to al Qa'ida leaders, Zarqawi explained that he wanted to expel U.S. forces from Iraq, establish an Islamic emirate, and—here was the rub for some al Qa'ida leaders—foment sectarian war by attacking Shi'ites. He saved his harshest words for the Shi'ites, not the Americans: "[They are] the insurmountable obstacle, the lurking snake, the crafty and malicious scorpion, the spying enemy, and the penetrating venom. We here are entering a battle on two levels. One, evident and open, is with an attacking enemy and patent infidelity. [Another is] a difficult, fierce battle with a crafty enemy who wears the garb of a friend, manifests agreement, and calls for comradeship, but harbors ill will and twists up peaks and crests. Theirs is the legacy of the Batini bands that traversed the history of Islam and left scars on its face that time cannot erase. The unhurried observer and inquiring onlooker will realize that Shi'ism is the looming danger and the true challenge. They are the enemy. Beware of them. Fight them. By God, they lie."[44]

The goals of Zarqawi's terrorist group, Tawhid wa'l Jihad, had broadened considerably over the years. In the 1990s, Zarqawi's primary obsession was overthrowing the Jordanian government. But after interacting with other foreign fighters in Afghanistan, he expanded his goals to include the United States. As one al Qa'ida sympathizer contended, the objective was to "force America to abandon its war against Islam by proxy and force it to attack directly."[45]

Zarqawi had arrived in northern Iraq in 2002. By the summer of 2003, after the U.S. invasion, he had already begun spreading mayhem among the United States, its allies, and Shi'ites through a lethal campaign of car bombs and gruesome beheadings. On August 8 a cell allied with Zarqawi helped plan and carry out a car bombing at the Jordanian embassy in Al Andalus district of Baghdad, which killed nineteen people and injured over fifty more.

The roof of the vehicle landed on a neighboring house, and one of the outer walls of the compound collapsed. On August 19, Zarqawi was involved in the UN bombing that killed Sergio Vieira de Mello. And on August 29, Zarqawi's network exploded a car bomb outside the Imam Ali Mosque in Najaf, killing the Shi'ite chairman of the Council for the Islamic Revolution in Iraq, Ayatollah Muhammad Baqr Al-Hakim.

Ambassador Bremer and senior CIA and FBI officials in Iraq became increasingly concerned. Bremer called George Tenet, who was on a beach in New Jersey. "George, we need help," Bremer pleaded. "The FBI is telling me we are facing something new with a growing number of more sophisticated car bombs. But I don't have particularly good intelligence about who the insurgents are and what is motivating them."

"We will do what we can to help," Tenet replied. "But we are already overworked because of the search for weapons of mass destruction. This is our primary focus, not the insurgency."[46]

As U.S. officials wandered in the dark, Zarqawi cautiously began to reach out to al Qa'ida. A formal alliance had risks, especially if it meant losing his independence. But it also had potential benefits. Bin Laden and Zawahiri were household names. A poll conducted by the Pew Charitable Trust in 2003 indicated that a shocking 55 percent of Jordanians, 50 percent of Indonesians, and 45 percent of Pakistanis had "a lot" or "some" confidence in Osama bin Laden to do the right thing regarding world affairs.[47] Even in Iraq, bin Laden had a prominent following. Zarqawi began to think in business terms. A merger with al Qa'ida, he thought, would give him the option of tapping into more fighters, more money, and greater brand recognition.

In January he wrote a note to Osama bin Laden and other senior leaders. "We do not see ourselves as fit to challenge you," Zarqawi said, "and we have never striven to achieve glory ourselves. All that we hope is that we will be the spearhead, the enabling vanguard to the victory that is promised and the tomorrow to which we aspire." He then extended an olive branch. "If you agree with us on [our vision], we will be your readied soldiers, working under your banner, complying with your orders, and indeed swearing fealty to you publicly and in the news media, vexing the infidels and gladdening those who preach the oneness of God."[48]

Zarqawi would agree to swear *bayat* to bin Laden, but only on his terms. It was a deal that would later haunt al Qa'ida. For now, al Qa'ida leaders desperately wanted a place in the Iraq insurgency, recognizing it as a magnet for jihadists. Despite concerns about Zarqawi, bin Laden sent Abd al-Hadi al-Iraqi to oversee negotiations. Iraqi served as the principal communications liaison between al Qa'ida senior leadership in Pakistan and Zarqawi in Iraq.

One of Zarqawi's colleagues, Shaykh Maysarat al-Gharib, described Zarqawi as excited at the prospect of joining al Qa'ida. "I had never before witnessed him to be that focused or engaged," said Gharib. "I do remember when he entered wearing his beautiful white robe, asking me about the drafting of the official announcement, the highlights of which he had previously laid out for me."[49]

By October 2004 they had reached a deal. Zarqawi agreed to come under the command and control of al Qa'ida and to rename his group Tanzim Qa'idat al-Jihad fi Bilad al-Rafidayn (Al Qa'ida in the Land of the Two Rivers). On October 17, Zarqawi released a statement using the online Arabic magazine *Mu'askar al-Battar*, swearing allegiance to bin Laden. As promised, he advocated the subjugation of Shi'ites and the creation of a worldwide caliphate governed by sharia law. "By God, O sheikh of the mujahideen," Zarqawi wrote, "if you bid us plunge into the ocean, we would follow you. If you ordered it so, we would obey!"[50]

Bin Laden publicly responded on December 27, welcoming Zarqawi into al Qa'ida and identifying Iraq as the central battleground against the United States.[51] Zarqawi's new organization, which became colloquially known to Americans as al Qaʾida in Iraq, brought in foreign fighters at unprecedented levels. According to documents captured in a raid near Sinjar, along Iraq's border with Syria, al Qaʾida in Iraq's foreign contingent came primarily from Saudi Arabia, Libya, Yemen, Algeria, and Syria. Most were young, averaging twenty-four to twenty-five years old. Some had been students, while others held full-time jobs. One al Qaʾida recruit had been a massage therapist before deciding to travel to Iraq and blow himself up as a suicide bomber.[52] Virtually all of the foreign fighters entered Iraq through Syria, with the aid of smuggling and criminal networks rather than al Qaʾida's own personnel. Al Qaʾida in Iraq relied heavily on voluntary donations and kept meticulous records of financial expenses. Captured documents suggested that the group relied almost entirely on transfers from foreign supporters, money that foreign suicide bombers brought with them, and fundraising from local Iraqis.[53]

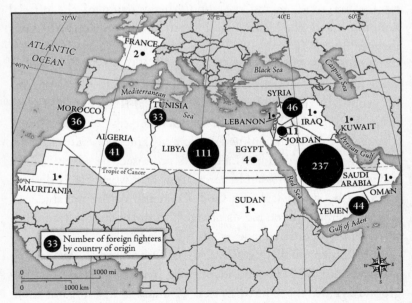

Figure 6: Foreign Fighters in Iraq by Country of Origin[54]

By 2004, al Qa'ida in Iraq had roughly fifteen brigades operating under its banner, including two "martyrs" brigades dedicated to suicide operations. The group released daily communiqués, ran two official websites (both of which were periodically shut down by U.S. cyber operations), and published two magazines. One was a short monthly magazine, *Siyar A'lam Al-Shuhada'* (Biographies of Great Martyrs), and the other, *Sawt al-Jihad* (Voice of Jihad), appeared more erratically.[55] For Zarqawi, the merger with al Qa'ida paid huge dividends. He could leverage the star power of bin Laden and his access to resources, but he was his own man.

"Al Qa'ida was not the Communist Party with rigid discipline," observed U.S. Ambassador to Iraq John Negroponte. It was "sui generis. It adopted the mantra of *Zarqawi*, not bin Laden or Zawahiri."[56]

Blowback

For Sayyid Imam Abd al-Aziz al-Sharif, the former leader of Egyptian Islamic Jihad and childhood friend of Ayman al-Zawahiri, the Iraq invasion was a bridge too far. Before the invasion he had opposed al Qa'ida. Sharif believed that al Qa'ida had been wrong to kill civilians, but jihad was still legitimate in cases where Muslim populations were oppressed by non-Muslims. One was Israel's occupation of Palestinian territories. "If it were not for jihad in Palestine," he wrote, "the Jews would have crept toward the neighboring countries a long time ago and they would have enslaved the people of the region." The same was now true in Iraq, he concluded, where "if it were not for jihad in Iraq, America would have . . . enslaved the people of the region."[57]

Sharif was critical of the U.S. invasion, which he viewed as unprovoked, aggressive, and destined to undermine U.S. interests. Others felt the same way. Salman al-Awdah, the Saudi cleric who had once accused bin Laden of massacring women and children, signed a statement with twenty-five others supporting jihad in Iraq. "All forms of resistance—be they political, social, intellectual, or military—that lead to expelling the occupation authorities and lifting their injustice have been sanctioned by all religions," it read.[58]

Awdah was troubled because the United States had not been attacked by terrorist groups operating in Iraq. It was a preventive war, and therefore illegitimate. Perhaps more important, he was concerned that the occupation would radicalize Muslim youths throughout the region, including Saudi Arabia. "The terrorist attacks in the kingdom," he concluded, "are linked to Iraq, and they were born from the U.S. war drums calling to invade that country, because the youths thought that the United States was in Iraq today, and would be in Riyadh tomorrow."[59]

Things got worse in April 2004. The U.S. military siege of Fallujah and its onslaught against Muqtada al-Sadr's Shi'ite militia, Jaysh al-Mahdi, boosted popular sympathy for the insurgents. At that time, disillusionment with the political process was intensifying. But it was the published photographs of U.S. actions at Abu Ghraib prison that aided al Qa'ida in Iraq. Abu Ghraib burst into the headlines when the U.S. television show *60 Minutes II* broke a story involving abuse and humiliation of Iraqi inmates by a group of U.S. soldiers.

Ambassador Bremer was in Washington at the time, and Dan Senor, his spokesman, greeted him with the news. "Apparently some MPs guarding detainees forced them to engage in homosexual acts," he reported, horrified. "They made one of them crawl around on the ground with a dog's leash around his neck," Senor wrote. "There may have also been women involved, whether our women MPs or women detainees isn't clear."[60]

Bremer's immediate response was to get out in front of the story. He announced a full investigation and ordered the immediate reform of detainee policy "to promote fair, speedy, and transparent procedures for dealing with detainees and reviewing their status without compromising the overall security of the Iraqi population."[61] This included the release of several high-profile Sunnis who had been in custody for an extended period without clear charges.[62]

Despite efforts to control the crisis, internal U.S. documents show that the scandal was a bombshell—it even affected members of Iraq's Governing Council. In meetings with U.S. officials, they denounced the abuses, requested information about what the U.S. military was doing to correct them, and decided to "form a committee by Iraq Judges and public prosecutors to investigate the anti-humanitarian violations committed by those in charge of Abu Ghraib prison."[63] In addition, the Governing Council proposed that Abu Ghraib "be razed to the ground and a housing complex be built on the property to house those who were imprisoned or tortured by the past regime."[64]

Most senior U.S. policymakers understood the strategic implications for the United States and its image abroad. In preparing President Bush for a phone call with Governing Counsel president Shaykh al-Yawr, National Security Adviser Condoleezza Rice cautioned that the Abu Ghraib scandal had "heightened feelings of anxiety among Iraqis."[65]

Edward Schmults, Ambassador Bremer's senior adviser to the Ministry of Justice, said the United States was "overwhelmed" by negative publicity.[66] These concerns triggered an effort to close down Abu Ghraib immediately.[67] The uncensored Abu Ghraib photographs began to appear on jihadist websites and be used for recruitment purposes.

Abu Ghraib also highlighted another challenge: a number of detainees were becoming significantly *more* radicalized after spending time at Abu Ghraib. A memo to Bremer described the plight of a man who eventually was involved in a suicide attack in Arbil. Coalition forces had arrested him for support to insurgent groups and sent him to Abu Ghraib, "where a group of devout Muslims adopted, clothed, fed, and protected him from other prisoners. Because this group lived separately from the rest of the prison population," the cable continued, "they provided a nurturing environment that allowed them to brainwash potential recruits. When the young man transferred to the facility in al Qassim, another group of extremists were waiting for him. After two months, they had successfully converted the young man and given him a list of contacts on the outside to pursue when he was released. A few days later the young man had found himself in a car bombing plot that nearly succeeded."[68]

By 2004, Iraq was the most violent country on earth, and al Qa'ida had seized control in key areas.

A New Wave

Officials like Art Cummings were starting to realize that al Qa'ida was evolving new ways of fighting back. Al Qa'ida's suicide campaign was intense, widespread, and effective, and the organization developed a lethal capacity to kill or maim people using vehicle and roadside bombs.[69] The daily average number of terrorist attacks rose from fifteen in June 2003 to a shocking seventy by June 2004, an increase of nearly 500 percent.[70] Al Qa'ida in Iraq's tactics were innovative. The group mastered the art of using several simultaneous suicide attackers and experimented with bombers of different demographics. They also manufactured a wide range of bombs, from remote-controlled devices to pressure plates and infrared triggering mechanisms.

To keep up with al Qa'ida's developments, the FBI deployed to Iraq a growing number of agents to conduct forensics after major attacks, analyze material confiscated from al Qa'ida operatives (such as cell phones, computers, and items left in their pockets when they were seized), and interrogate detainees. By 2003 the FBI's overseas presence had risen by 12 percent; there were now forty-six FBI legal attaché offices around the world, up from forty-one in 2000.[71] And the number of FBI offices and agents overseas would continue to increase over the next several years. Despite the global surge, however, the FBI remained hamstrung in recruiting Muslims into the Bureau. They had fewer than a dozen Muslim agents out of a total of twelve thousand. "Well, it's not for lack of trying," Cummings said, shrugging. "It's not for lack of recruiting."[72] The FBI also struggled to recruit agents who could speak Arabic, Pashto, Urdu, and other languages in countries where al Qa'ida was operating, including Iraq.

The bitter irony was that al Qa'ida established a foothold in Iraq after—and indeed *because of*—the U.S. invasion, beginning a dramatic wave of violence. The large number of conventional U.S. military forces drew al Qa'ida and other foreign fighters. One U.S. intelligence report warned that this made the U.S. homeland increasingly vulnerable to a terrorist attack, saying, "We assess that al Qa'ida will probably seek to leverage the contacts and capabilities of al Qa'ida in Iraq (AQI), its most visible and capable affiliate and the only one known to have expressed a desire to attack the Homeland."[73]

One of the most powerful examples of Iraq's recruitment potential was Muriel Degauque, a thirty-eight-year-old Belgian woman who detonated a bomb as she drove past an American patrol on November 9, 2005, near the town of Baquba in central Iraq. In the bomb crater, investigators found travel documents showing that she had arrived in Iraq from Belgium just a few weeks earlier with her husband, Hissam Goris. The couple had been recruited by al Qa'ida in Iraq. Goris died the following day, shot by U.S. forces as he prepared to launch a suicide attack near Fallujah.[74]

Iraq was a propaganda coup for al Qa'ida. A contributor to the first issue of the magazine *Al Battar* argued that the Iraq war had made jihad "a commandment" for Saudi Arabians because "the Islamic nation is today in acute conflict with the Crusaders."[75] Television images aired daily by Al Jazeera and other channels, which showed suffering Iraqis and Abu Ghraib photos, enraged the Arab population. Public opinion polls reflected deepening anti-Americanism across the Arab world. The percentage of Jordanians who had an unfavorable view of the United States went from 75 percent in the summer of 2002 to 99 percent in May 2003. Unfavorable ratings of the United States jumped from 69 percent to 81 percent in Pakistan, 55 percent to 83 percent in Turkey, and 59 percent to 71 percent in Lebanon over the same time.[76]

Perhaps the most far-reaching repercussion of al Qa'ida's success in Iraq, however, was that it helped inspire a second wave of terrorism. America's decision to adopt a strategy of overwhelming force and deploy large numbers of conventional U.S. soldiers radicalized scores of Muslims. With the collapse of the Iraq government, al Qa'ida established a sanctuary in places like Anbar. Iraqi police and army forces failed to establish order, and the country degenerated into something close to anarchy. Al Qa'ida took advantage of the situation. The rise of al Qa'ida in Iraq triggered a new wave of attacks in the West. The next one, it turned out, would be in Spain.

THE MADRID ATTACKS

MARCH 11, 2005, was a somber day in Spain. Silence spread across train stations and bustling streets at 7:39 a.m. as Spaniards bowed their heads in mourning. In Madrid the weather was crisp and clear, barely above freezing, with a slight wind out of the southwest. A crowd gathered at the Bosque de los Ausentes, the Forest of the Departed, a layered mound of 191 gnarled olive and cypress trees planted to remember each victim of the terrorist attacks one year earlier. The memorial was constructed in Madrid's main park, a sprawling enclave adorned with sculptures and monuments, which now served as a solemn venue. A stream of crystal water, symbolizing life, meandered through the memorial. A narrow path spiraled to the summit, which looked out across the formal gardens. Engraved in stone beside the stream's edge were the words "In homage and gratitude to all the victims of terrorism whose memory permanently lives within us and enriches us constantly. The citizens of Madrid."[1]

Spain's monarchs, King Juan Carlos and Queen Sofia, flanked by rows of foreign leaders, gently placed a wreath of white and purple chrysanthemums at the edge of the grove. Their flowers bore the message "In memory of all the victims of terrorism." A lone cellist, dressed in black, played "Song of the Birds," a piece from the late Spanish composer Pablo Casals. Across Spain, hundreds of church bells chimed. Office workers poured into the streets. Dignitaries stood in grim silence. The majestic Spanish flag, with its brilliant red and yellow colors fluttering in a soft breeze, flew at half staff. Schoolchildren paused to remember the dead.

"Who will give me back my will to live, which died here a year ago?" read a letter stuck to a wall at El Pozo, hardest hit of the four rail stations targeted by backpack bombers.

At the Atocha train station in the center of Madrid, which has a cavernous interior plaza and lush tropical gardens, an anonymous person left a single red rose on the platform and scribbled a note that betrayed anguish and loss. "For you, my love, who are no longer with me," it read.

In the nearby Puerta del Sol, one of Madrid's busiest hubs, dotted with hip boutiques and restaurants, pedestrians paid homage to the dead at a monument dedicated to those who responded to the attacks, which bore an inscription reading "May the memory of the victims and the exemplary behavior of the city of Madrid stay with us always."[2]

The memorials to Madrid's terrorist attacks are ubiquitous. The attack left 191 dead and 1,755 injured, up to that point the largest number of casualties from an attack in continental Europe since World War II.[3] With the situation in Iraq deteriorating, the Madrid attacks were a tremendous blow to the Spanish psyche and to anyone involved in the struggle against al Qa'ida. The second wave was building. Al Qa'ida and its affiliated networks were no longer on the defensive but were lashing out. Spain's deployment of conventional military forces to Iraq had attracted al Qa'ida's attention. European police and intelligence agencies, unprepared to deal with the growing radical Islamic threat within their own borders, struggled to keep pace.

A Gathering Storm

Shortly after 6 a.m. on March 11, 2004, a dozen dark silhouettes exited from two vehicles. The figures that emerged from the white

Renault Kangoo van with the license plate 0576 BRX left behind a pile of cigarette butts and a tape of Qu'ranic recitations and entered the Alcalá de Henares train station.[4] They wore dark scarves, hats, and gloves and walked with self-assurance. The temperature had just passed 40 degrees, and clouds covered the still-darkened city. Central Alcalá, which lies 22 miles northeast of Madrid, has retained a medieval flavor, with winding cobblestone streets and historic buildings. Miguel de Cervantes, the author of *Don Quixote*, was born in Alcalá and baptized in the Church of Santa María. Alcalá's transportation links make it a vital commuter hub, and many of its inhabitants travel to Madrid each day. The morning of March 11 was no different, as commuters filed into the congested train station.

The terrorists—predominantly Moroccans, along with Algerians, Egyptians, Tunisians, and those of other nationalities—carried thirteen improvised explosive devices concealed in blue sports bags into the Alcalá station. They placed the bombs in the luggage and seating areas in four trains. The first, train number 21431, left Alcalá de Henares station on the C-1 track at 7:01, headed for downtown Madrid. The other three followed shortly thereafter: train 17305 left on track C-2 at 7:04, train 21435 departed on track C-1 at 7:10, and train 21713 left on track C-7 at 7:14. After placing the bombs and setting the timers, the terrorists left the trains, which continued toward Madrid.[5]

The bombs required minimal knowledge of explosives. Each included a detonator attached to the vibrator of a cell phone, approximately 10 kilograms of GOMA 2 ECO nitroglycerin-based dynamite, a copper detonator, blue and red wires, and nails and screws for added fragmentation.[6] GOMA 2 ECO is a gelatinous explosive used by Spanish mining companies to blast holes in packed layers of sedimentary rock. The March 11 bombers preferred it because it could be manipulated with a low risk of accidental detonation and it was relatively easy to procure on the black market. Each bomb was set to detonate when the phone's internal alarm triggered the vibrator at approximately 7:40 a.m. The small amount of explosives and the use of nails and screws for fragmentation suggested that the terrorists were more interested in killing commuters than in causing extensive infrastructure damage. Ten kilograms of GOMA 2 ECO can destroy panes of glass and the metal frame of a train but will not significantly damage the structure of train stations.

Several networks collaborated between September 2002 and early 2004 to carry out the attacks.[7] Most of the individuals were first-generation North African Muslim males, approximately thirty years old and younger. Some were financially successful and well educated, while others came from impoverished backgrounds and had long criminal records.

One group was led by a Moroccan national named Jamal Ahmidan, who lived in Madrid's Villaverde district. He was short and stocky, just five feet, four inches, with crooked teeth and somewhat slanted eyes that earned him the nickname El Chino, "the Chinaman." He was born on October 28, 1970, in Morocco, the fourth of fourteen children, in a sparse cinder-block house near the center of Jamaa Mezuak in the Moroccan city of Tetouan.[8] Ahmidan began working for his father, Ahmed, at age fifteen, selling clothes from a stall in one of Tetouan's crowded markets. He was ambitious and pugnacious, his friends recalled. "To his face you had to show respect," remarked one of his childhood friends, Anwar Belaman.[9]

When his older brother Mustafa moved to Europe, Ahmidan followed, entering Spain illegally early in 1990 and settling in Madrid.[10] He built a lucrative business selling hashish and ecstasy. The operation stretched from the Netherlands to Spain, and Ahmidan enjoyed luxury cars, motorcycles, drugs, and women, tearing around Madrid and frequenting late-night clubs. He informed his mother, Rahma, who was living in Morocco, that he was working as a mason. But his drug dealing eventually caught up with him. Ahmidan served jail time in the Netherlands, France, Switzerland, Morocco, and Spain. Much like José Padilla, he was radicalized in prison and eventually became a prison imam, leading prayers five times a day. His rhetoric became more extreme, harping on the idea that "Jews mistreat Muslims" and threatening to "do jihad" against the judges who kept him in prison. In 2003 he was released from prison in Morocco. He followed a more austere version of Islam and professed a newfound respect for Osama bin Laden and al Qa'ida. He told his brothers he had watched videos of mujahideen fighting the Russians in Chechnya and began talking passionately and impulsively about the plight of Palestinians. "Before then, he wanted to be rich," recalled one of Ahmidan's brothers. "After, he wanted a life in another world. He wanted to fight."[11]

Ahmidan was torn between his lust for jihad and his drug-trafficking trade. To live with this paradox, he adopted the *takfir wal hijra* doctrine, which justifies the use of illegal proceeds to fund jihadist operations and accepts non-Muslim practices such as drinking alcohol and drug trafficking as a cover for terrorist activities. For Ahmidan, however, drugs were a way to make money. He traded 25 to 30 kilograms of hashish to a former Spanish miner for 210 kilograms of GOMA 2 ECO dynamite and 260 detonators.

In the late summer of 2003, Ahmidan met Sarhane ben Abdelmajid Fakhet, who led a second cell of terrorists. Known to his colleagues as "the Tunisian" because he had immigrated from Tunisia, just across the Mediterranean Sea from Spain, Fakhet had a plump face and a patchy beard. According to Spanish law enforcement officials, he was "the ideological chief" of the March 11 attacks, viewed by many of the participants as "the emir" and a "charismatic leader."[12] He moved to Madrid in 1994 to pursue a doctorate in economics at one of the city's main universities, Universidad Autónoma de Madrid. The Spanish government awarded him a grant that covered his accommodations and tuition, and he set to work on his doctoral thesis, a comparative analysis of European and Tunisian accounting methods. Eventually he left the university and started selling real estate. "He was very soft and well-educated," remarked

Moneir Mahmoud Aly el-Messery, the imam at the Central Cultural Islámico, popularly known as the M-30 mosque because of its proximity to Madrid's M-30 motorway.[13]

When Fakhet was a student, he worked in the restaurant attached to the M-30 mosque, and he sometimes went to Messery's weekly religion class. He also moved into an apartment building in a working-class neighborhood on Francisco Ramiro Street. Neighbors characterized him as a devout Muslim and said they occasionally heard him praying, sometimes with late-night guests. At the time M-30 was frequented by a handful of radicals, who sometimes held long meetings on the mosque's terrace.[14] But Fakhet and several others eventually left the mosque because it was not sufficiently extreme, and they feared it had been infiltrated by Spanish law enforcement and intelligence services.[15] Fakhet had become acutely sensitive about security measures, taking steps to avoid—or elude—police surveillance. He also changed SIM cards regularly, in one instance using seven different cards in one day.[16]

For Fakhet, an attack was necessary because Spain was "against Muslims and involved in the Iraq war," as he told one colleague.[17] Spain's participation in the war triggered a profound rage among immigrants like Fakhet, a development not entirely surprising to some European police agencies. "The Spanish Government's support of the military intervention in Iraq by the United States and its Allies constitutes without doubt a further risk factor for Spain," concluded the European police agency Europol only months before the Madrid attacks.[18]

During 2003, Fakhet spent time cruising jihadist websites for ideas on terrorist attacks. His particular fetish was information on the types of explosives used during the 2002 Bali and 2003 Casablanca terrorist attacks.[19] He was also influenced by a document titled *Iraq the Jihad: Hopes and Dangers*, which was posted on the Global Islamic Media website in 2003. The document called for U.S. withdrawal from Iraq and attacks against America's European allies and sent a specific warning to Spain: "Therefore we say that in order to force the Spanish government to withdraw from Iraq the resistance should deal painful blows to its forces . . . It is necessary to make utmost use of the upcoming general election in Spain in March next year. We think that the Spanish government could not tolerate more than two, maximum three blows, after which it will have to withdraw as a result of popular pressure. If its troops still remain in Iraq after these blows, then the victory of the Socialist Party is almost secured, and the withdrawal of the Spanish forces will be on its electoral program."[20]

A third group, based in the central Madrid district of Lavapies, was led by Jamal Zougam, an olive-skinned Moroccan born in 1974 in Tangier, located at the northern tip of Morocco, across the Strait of Gibraltar. Zougam had thick black hair and a thin face with full lips and a trimmed goatee. He had a short temper that some-times got him into trouble. In Madrid he became involved in a knife fight when a man brought a dog—considered an unclean animal by Muslims—into a restaurant called Alhambra. Zougam stabbed the man's friend, punched him, and hit him with an iron bar.

Zougam grew up in a poor area of Tangier with narrow, wind-ing streets and dusty buildings with peeling yellow paint. He left for Spain in 1983 with his mother, two sisters, and a half-brother. Around 1996 he and his half-brother, Mohamed Chaoui, opened a fruit shop in Lavapies. On Fridays at noon the brothers would walk to a small, makeshift Moroccan mosque to pray and listen to readings of the Qur'an.[21] In 1999 they closed their fruit shop and opened a cell phone shop called Nuevo Siglo, or the New Century. It sold cell phones and cell phone cards, repaired phones, and rented out booths for long-distance calls.[22]

Spanish police had tapped Zougam's telephones at various periods before the March 11 attacks but did not translate most of the conversations. Spanish authorities did not believe Zougam posed a major terrorist threat, and there weren't enough translators who understood the Arab dialect he spoke.[23] In 2001, Spain's national police stormed his apartment and seized a video of Islamic warriors fighting Russian troops near Chechnya, several Arabic books on jihad, and documents with phone numbers for suspected terrorists. The raid followed a request by a French magistrate who suspected that Zougam was involved in terrorism, but Spanish police believed the evidence they collected wasn't strong enough to arrest him.[24]

Among the pieces of extremist propaganda found at Zougam's house, authorities discovered a video titled *Islamic Jihad in Dagestan* and another titled *The Islamic Movement in the West*, which contained an interview with bin Laden. Zougam also kept books on the alleged campaign by the United States to finish off Islam.[25] Like other members of the three groups, he was paranoid about security, especially about electronic surveillance by Spanish police and intelligence agencies. He obtained material to disable the SIM lock on a cell phone, which enabled him to use a SIM card from a different service provider from the one originally assigned to the phone. He also obtained information to alter his computer's settings and to encrypt and decrypt cell phones.[26]

These three networks—led by Ahmidan, Fakhet, and Zougam—came together through common associations with Islamic extremist organizers, intermarriage among their families, worship at centers such as Madrid's M-30 mosque, and, most important, a desire to conduct violent jihad. Their goal was clear: to kill as many Spaniards as possible. Characteristic of the second wave of terrorism, they were inspired by the U.S. invasion of Iraq and emboldened by the resurgence of al Qa'ida.

The Madrid Attacks

By early March 2004, the network had assembled the bombs. Their base was a rural house nestled among olive groves in Chinchón, roughly 25 miles southeast of Madrid. They packed the GOMA 2 ECO and detonators, used wires to connect them to cell phones, packed nails and screws, and gingerly placed the bombs in blue sports bags. They loaded the bags into the vans, drove to the Alcalá de Henares train station, and placed them on the trains.

At 7:37 a.m. the first of three bombs exploded on train 21431, which was pulling into the Atocha station in central Madrid. Cars three, four, and six of the six-car train were torn apart. At 7:38 there were two explosions on train 21435 near El Pozo train station, destroying car four of the six-car train. Another bomb at 7:38 ripped through train 21713. At 7:39 four explosions rocked train 17305, which was 600 yards from the Atocha station, destroying cars one, five, and six. Train 17305 continued forward another 15 yards before it ground to a halt and the conductor began to hear shouts and groans from the wounded and dying.[27] The bombs split open the train cars, ripping metal and sending body parts through the windows of nearby apartments. Commuters panicked, trampling one another and abandoning their shoes and bags. Cell phones rang unanswered on dead bodies as frantic relatives tried to contact them. Buses were pressed into service as ambulances. Bloody victims crawled from mangled train cars and staggered into the streets.

"There was one carriage totally blown apart. People were scattered all over the platforms. I saw legs and arms. I won't forget this ever. I've seen horror," remarked Enrique Sanchez, a traumatized ambulance worker.[28]

Spaniards mourned in unison. Some lit candles, others placed flowers at the train stations, and still others wrote poetry to the victims. Over the next several days grieving family members buried their dead. In Alcalá de Henares more than eight hundred people attended a funeral for two of the town's forty victims, Air Force Lieutenant Felix Gonzalez and Pilar Cabrejas. Gonzalez's son Marcus, eleven, sobbed uncontrollably as he laid flowers on his father's coffin. Gonzalez's father clung to his wife and wept. "We have buried a son . . . a son full of future," he said. "We are all overwhelmed."[29]

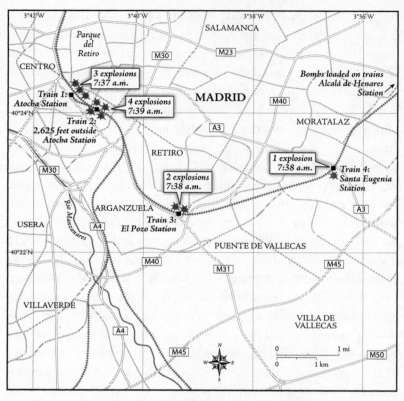

Figure 7: Map of Madrid Bombings, March 2004

After desperately searching for his wife in hospitals across Madrid, Jesus Antonio Muñoz eventually located her body. She had been killed in the attacks. "It's absurd," he said. "I don't feel any repulsion. I don't know—indifference. The only thing I know is that they've torn out my heart. And now I'm like a child of five years old. Now I've got to start everything again—becoming an adult all over again. When you bury a person, the pain is that it is the last moment when you have that person next to you, and when the ceremony ends you hand that person over to God."[30]

The blast occurred three days before the Spanish general elections, which the Popular Party government appeared likely to win, despite having led the country into the highly unpopular war in Iraq. But media reports blamed the attacks on Spanish involvement in Iraq. On March 14 voters elected the Socialist Party. In response to a poll asking if the attacks caused Spaniards to change their vote, 9 percent said yes. Most of those in the 9 percent said they had switched to the Socialist Party, whose narrow margin of victory (43 percent to 38 percent) suggested that the bombing may have tipped the elections.[31] It didn't help the Popular Party that Spain's incumbent president, José María Aznar, initially claimed that the Basque terrorist group ETA was responsible for the bombings, even though there was no evidence.

Terrorism was not new to Spain. The country had suffered through several decades of terrorist attacks at the hands of ETA, whose goal was to establish an independent Basque homeland in the northeastern part of the country. The group had killed more than eight hundred Spaniards between 1968 and 2004, including Prime Minister Luis Carrero Blanco in 1973, whose vehicle was blown from the road and lodged in the second-floor terrace of a Madrid building following a bomb attack.[32] But the 1980s and 1990s saw an influx of North Africans, especially Moroccans, who were targeted for recruitment by Islamic terrorist organizations such as al Qa'ida, the Moroccan Islamic Combatant Group, the Salafist Group for Preaching and Combat, and the Armed Islamic Group.[33] Spanish police and intelligence agencies had failed to penetrate many of these groups, believing that the main terrorist threat to Spain came from ETA. Consequently, Spanish police had devoted few resources to countering al Qa'ida and other radical Islamic groups.[34] "The very successes achieved in the struggle against ETA in recent years," President Aznar later reflected apologetically, "may have led us to lower our guard against the fundamentalist threat."[35]

After the March 11 attacks, Spanish National Police took the lead in the investigations. One of their first major breaks came when a young officer discovered 22 pounds of GOMA 2 ECO in a sports bag, packed with nails, screws, and two wires that ran from a blue mobile phone to a detonator. It contained all of the bomb's components—a priceless find. Spanish police traced calls to and from the phone and quickly began to map out the network. Data stored on the chip revealed that a calling plan had been set up at the telephone and copy shop in Lavapies owned by Jamal Zougam. Law enforcement officials arrested him on March 13.[36]

Spanish police and intelligence agencies then traced the purchase of the phones back to a business named Bazar Top SL in Pinto, a small town 12 miles south of downtown Madrid. Investigators estimated that the cost of the phones—procured by a member of the Madrid network—was $730. SIM cards were acquired through Jawal Mundo Telecom, a Madrid-based company managed by several individuals tied to the Madrid bombings, and cost the terrorists approximately $790. The network used three safe houses, costing roughly $9,800. In late January 2004, Jamal Ahmidan had rented the Chinchón Farm, where the network met and built their bombs. In early March, Abdennabi Kounjaa paid one month's rent, $975, for a cottage in Granada, and Mohamed Belhadj paid $2,200 deposit for rent on an apartment in the Madrid suburb of Leganés. The attacks had been relatively cheap to execute; Spanish police estimated that they cost between $43,000 and $68,000.[37]

At three o'clock on the afternoon of April 3, nearly a month after the attacks, police approached an apartment building on Calle Carmen Martín Gaite in Leganés. They saw a young Moroccan man with a backward baseball cap taking out trash. He yelled something in Arabic, then ran away at an impressive pace. He turned out to be a track champion, and the police did not catch him. A moment later voices cried out, "Allahu Akhbar!" and machine-gun fire from the second floor of the apartment house raked the street, scattering the police. Over the next few hours the police tactical unit, Grupo Especial de Operaciones, evacuated the residents of nearby apartments. Tanks and helicopters moved in, and the siege of Leganés began. Inside were seven terrorists, including Sarhane ben Abdelmajid Fakhet.[38]

"Allah is great, we are messengers of Allah," someone yelled from inside the house.[39]

At 6:05 p.m., Fakhet faxed a handwritten note to *ABC*, a conservative daily newspaper in Madrid. He warned that "we have the power and capacity, with the permission of Allah, to attack you when and how we want." The letter demanded that Spain withdraw its troops from both Iraq and Afghanistan by the following Sunday. Otherwise, "we will turn Spain into an inferno and make your blood flow like rivers."[40]

Jamal Ahmidan then phoned his mother in Morocco. "This is my last day," he said. "At the end of the day, we all have to die."

Ahmidan's mother asked why he was going to kill himself.

"I don't know, Mother," he replied. "It's God's will."

He hung up and she phoned back immediately. Another terrorist picked up the phone and passed it to Ahmidan.

"It's enough, Mother," he yelled. "Do not worry about me and give me your blessing. Do not phone me back."[41]

That was it. Outside the Leganés apartment, the police attempted to negotiate, but the terrorists cried out, "We will die killing!"

The police then ordered the terrorists to come out "naked and with your hands up."

"Come in and we'll talk," one of the occupants responded.[42]

At 9:05 p.m., the police blew the lock on the door and fired tear gas into the room. But it was too late. Fakhet, Ahmidan, and the rest of the group had decided to commit collective suicide. They detonated a bomb, killing themselves and a police officer. The body of Jamal Ahmidan was hurled through the wall and into a swimming pool. In the ruins police found another 22 pounds of GOMA 2 ECO and 200 copper detonators similar to those used in the train bombings.[43] They also found the shredded remains of a videotape. The police painstakingly reassembled the fragments, which enabled them to view the final statement of Fakhet and two other members of the cell, which called itself "the brigade situated in Al Andalus." Unless Spanish troops left Iraq within a week, the men had declared, "we will continue our jihad until martyrdom in the land of Tariq ibn Ziyad."[44]

The U.S.-led war in Iraq continued to motivate al Qa'ida–affiliated and –inspired terrorists. It hit a raw nerve for many impressionable young Muslims and was used to illustrate the American "oppression" of Muslims. Radical recruiters may have exaggerated or fabricated information, but the war indisputably fomented rage against America and its allies.

Ties to Al Qa'ida

For senior CIA officials, the Madrid bombings proved that al Qa'ida and its affiliated groups were still capable of conducting spectacular attacks.

"Where is this going?" asked Philip Mudd, who was now deputy director of the CIA's Counterterrorism Center. "We sat around the table and looked back at the past thirty-six months," he remarked. "Al Qa'ida had certainly made it a fight."[45]

Seen from that perspective, the situation troubled them. In October 2002, al Qa'ida–affiliated operatives from Jemaah Islamiyah killed 202 people, 88 of them Australians, on the Indonesian island of Bali. In May 2003 a group with ties to al Qa'ida killed 45 people in Casablanca during a series of suicide bombings. The same week, al Qa'ida operatives were involved in multiple attacks in Riyadh, Saudi Arabia, killing 34 people and wounding 60 others. In August a suicide car bomb detonated in front of a Marriott hotel in Jakarta, Indonesia, killing 13 and wounding 149 others. In November there were multiple attacks in Istanbul, which killed over 40 people and wounded more than 750. Then came the Madrid attacks.

During the CIA's nightly al Qa'ida threat briefings, several questions hung over senior officials like Mudd. Was a second catastrophe in progress? Were its perpetrators deployed? Might they use chemical, biological, or nuclear material? "The sense of the unknown," Mudd said, "was pervasive." The CIA's understanding of al Qa'ida had dramatically improved. "But we knew that our window into the group was nowhere near good enough to assure policymakers, legislators, and the American people that we in the agency . . . could prevent another attack."[46]

Spanish police and intelligence agencies were struggling with the same questions. At the time of the Madrid attacks, there was no al Qa'ida command structure in Spain, at least as far as the Spanish intelligence community was aware. But the Madrid attacks, it turned out, did not emerge solely from local networks. They were connected to al Qa'ida in several ways. The first was inspirational. After the U.S. invasion of Iraq, Osama bin Laden began to include Spain in his list of targets because Spain deployed troops to Iraq. "We reserve the right to retaliate at the appropriate time and place," he thundered, "against all countries involved, especially the UK, Spain, Australia, Poland, Japan, and Italy."[47]

In April 2004, bin Laden issued a stern warning. "There is a lesson," he said, "regarding what is happening in occupied Palestine and what happened on September 11 and March 11: These are your goods returned to you."[48]

Spain was particularly symbolic for Osama bin Laden and Ayman al-Zawahiri, because it represented the northwestern cusp of the caliphate they were trying to resurrect. Early in the eighth century A.D., an army led by Ibn Abd-el-Hakem had crossed from North Africa and conquered most of Spain, giving Muslim leaders a foothold in continental Europe. For seven hundred years Spain belonged to one of the great Muslim civilizations, reaching its apex with the Umayyad Caliphate in the tenth century.[49] On March 11, 2004, shortly after the Madrid attacks, a group calling itself the Abu Hafs al Masri Brigades sent a communiqué by e-mail to the editor of *Al-Quds Al-Arabi*, the pan-Arab newspaper published in London, which Spanish National Police traced back to Iran, though it could have originated in Yemen, Egypt, or Libya. "The death squad has managed to penetrate the bowels of Crusading Europe, striking one of the pillars of the Crusader alliance, Spain, with a painful blow," it stated. "This is part of the settling of old scores with the Crusading Spain, the ally of America in its war against Islam."[50]

Al Qa'ida's role was not purely inspirational, however. The Madrid attackers' most significant connection to al Qa'ida was through Amer Azizi, a deputy to Hamza Rabi'a, al Qa'ida's head of operations in Europe and North America.[51] Amer Azizi, whose nom de guerre was Jafar al-Maghrebi, was born on February 2, 1968, in Hedami, Morocco. He was an active member of an al Qa'ida cell in Spain established during the 1990s and led by Abu Dahdah, better known as Imad Eddin Barakat Yarkas, who was arrested in 2001. Azizi had spent time at terrorist training camps in Afghanistan and fought with Islamic militants in Bosnia. By 2002 he was serving as a conduit between senior al Qa'ida leaders and the Madrid operatives. He had also developed a relationship with several of the Madrid bombers, including Sarhane ben Abdelmajid Fakhet.

In late 2002 or early 2003, as Spanish intelligence officials later discovered, Fakhet had traveled to Turkey and met with Amer Azizi. At the meeting Fakhet outlined plans for an attack in Spain and told Azizi he needed manpower and other support to carry it out. Azizi responded that al Qa'ida would not offer direct assistance, perhaps because it was unnecessary; Fakhet seemed to have the plotting under control. But Azizi nonetheless supported the plan and told Fakhet he could assert responsibility for the attack in the name of al Qa'ida. The two kept in touch via e-mail.[52] Azizi also offered the name of a Moroccan immigrant living in Madrid, Jamal Zougam.[53] Azizi had developed close links with Zougam and several other future perpetrators of the Madrid attacks, such as Moroccan-born Said Berraj.[54] In fact, many of the Madrid attackers belonged to a broader network of violent jihadist activity that involved al Qa'ida, the Libyan Islamic Fighting Group, Moroccan Islamic Combatant Group, and other groups.[55]

The Madrid attacks also had an important impact on al Qa'ida and inspired its senior leaders to perpetrate similar attacks, especially after their setbacks in Afghanistan, Pakistan, and even the United States after September 11. According to the CIA, al Qa'ida believed that the attacks had brought down the Aznar government.[56] In an April 2004 meeting in Abbottabad, Pakistan, Hamza Rabi'a raised the idea of duplicating the Madrid attacks in the United States or the United Kingdom. "We should strike an aboveground passenger train traveling between two major cities," Rabi'a remarked to Abu Faraj al-Libi.[57]

Following the capture of Khalid Sheikh Mohammed, Libi had taken over as al Qa'ida's most senior operative.[58] He had dark, thinning hair, exposing much of his forehead, and a neatly trimmed beard tinged with gray. His most notable feature, however, was the blotchy patches of skin under his eyes, which resembled the eye black used by professional baseball players. Libi's skin discoloration made him easier to track than others. He became a jack-of-all-trades, caring for al Qa'ida families residing in Pakistan, vetting and transporting al Qa'ida fighters to Afghan training camps, and assisting in external operations.

At some point after the September 11 attacks, Libi had received a letter from Osama bin Laden, which he passed to Rabi'a, requesting that "Rabi'a follow through with the details about operational planning against the United States and . . . share these ideas with Abu Mus'ab al Zarqawi" in Iraq. Rabi'a was also to provide Zarqawi with information about the types of people who could work in the United States.[59] Rabi'a and Libi discussed the possibility of targeting the corridor between New York City and Washington, D.C., but decided that the ultimate target would depend on detailed surveillance by operatives on the ground.

"A train," Libi remarked, "would be the easiest to plan, prepare, and conduct." Rabi'a's preference was a powerful explosion in a single passenger car, while Libi preferred explosions in several trains, much like the Madrid attacks, triggering a wave of fear through

America and harming the U.S. economy. "But our main problem," Libi later noted, "was identifying operatives who could actually travel to Western countries to perpetrate the attacks."[60]

Back to Pakistan

As European police and intelligence agencies struggled to cope with the growing radical Islamic threat, there were some bright spots. One of the most significant was the capture of Abu Faraj al-Libi on May 2, 2005. Libi, whose real name was Mustafa al-'Uzaybi, was born in Tripoli in 1970. He first developed ties with bin Laden in the early 1990s in Sudan and gradually worked his way up the al Qa'ida echelons. U.S. intelligence agencies had been watching his rise, thanks in part to a well-placed FBI informant who met Libi in the late summer of 2001 at an al Qa'ida guesthouse in Kabul which doubled as a communications hub.[61]

"Al-Libi was a senior al Qa'ida leader," one FBI paper observed, "reporting directly to the group's leader, Usama bin Laden, and his deputy, Ayman al-Zawahiri."[62] His position gave him virtually unprecedented access to al Qa'ida's leadership. He received courier messages and public statements from bin Laden for internal and external distribution.[63] In November 2003, Libi met with Zawahiri in Shakai, South Waziristan, to discuss operations. Later that year, however, he was involved in an attempt to assassinate Pervez Musharraf, which pushed him to the top of the Pakistan government's list of targets. He was already there for the United States. In December 2003, U.S. intelligence agencies became aware of his efforts to plan operations against U.S. forces in Afghanistan, and in 2004, he became involved in al Qa'ida meetings in Syria to discuss terrorist attacks in the United States, Europe, and Australia.[64]

After his failed attempt on Musharraf, Libi fled to the southern part of Pakistan's tribal areas. When Pakistan sent army and Frontier Corps forces into South Waziristan in March 2004, he took shelter in various mosques and safe houses, moving from Karachi to Punjab and then back to the Federally Administered Tribal Areas.[65] Pakistani police and intelligence operatives, with help from the United States, hunted him down. Relying on human and signals intelligence, they tracked Libi across the country and finally caught him after a wild chase that ended in a graveyard. Amjad Faruqi, an al Qa'ida operative who had been the chief planner of one of the assassination attempts on Musharraf, led the investigators to him. "We started by tracking Faruqi's phone," explained President Musharraf. "He kept changing numbers and would often go quiet for some time. But we kept at it."[66]

They finally hunted down Faruqi in Pakistan's North West Frontier Province and killed him in a gunfight in September 2004, but along the way they collected a significant amount of intelligence on Libi's movements, associates, and general pattern of life. An additional source of information was Central Asian militants in the Waziristan tribal areas. Libi's disdain for Central Asians created an exploitable opportunity: captured Uzbek, Tajik, and Chechen fighters willingly provided information on his habits, associates, and lifestyles. One of those leads took the Pakistanis to Libi's courier. "Under interrogation," Musharraf said, "he revealed that he had rented a house in Abbottabad, and that was where Libi was living right then."[67]

Abbottabad is a major hub of tourism in Pakistan's Khyber Pakhtunkhwa province and the town where U.S. Navy SEALs eventually killed Osama bin Laden. What the courier failed to clarify, however, was that Libi actually used three houses in Abbottabad. Pakistani agents raided the first one, but Libi, who was in the third house, escaped. Pakistan missed again not long after, when police and intelligence services received information that Libi was probably meeting with a senior al Qa'ida official at a house in Abbottabad. When the visitor—presumably Libi—arrived, the person in the house came out to meet him. But the visitor became suspicious that the meeting was a setup, tried to run away, and was killed in a shootout. It was not Libi; he had sent a decoy and stayed behind to observe.

The United States and Pakistan soon had another opportunity. Pakistan recruited one of Libi's colleagues, Abd al-Khaliq, and asked him to link up with Libi. They set up a meeting at 4:30 p.m. on May 1, 2005—a little over a year after the Madrid attacks— in Mardan, an agrarian town 40 miles north of Peshawar whose tribesmen grew wheat, sugarcane, rice, and vegetables. U.S. intelligence agencies, including the National Security Agency, helped locate Libi in the Mardan area by monitoring his cell phones and passed the information over to Pakistan authorities. In addition, Pakistani intelligence officers knew from informants that Libi traveled on the back of a motorbike while somebody else drove. "Our people were camouflaged, hiding and ready, with three men on motorbikes," explained Musharraf.[68]

As 4:30 approached, Libi repeatedly called Khaliq, asking in coded language whether everything was satisfactory, worried that the meeting might be compromised. "Our men took their informant to a bazaar so that Libi would hear the background noise and be assured that he wasn't in custody," said Musharraf. "We played other such games with him. But still, he did not appear at four thirty. Then the line went dead."[69]

The chase continued. On the morning of May 2, Libi had someone phone Khaliq to meet at 9:30, giving Pakistani police and intelligence agencies virtually no time to respond. The setting was a graveyard at the shrine of Shah Dhand Baba in Mardan.[70] In a bizarre twist, ISI agents donned flip-flops and burqas, the dark robe worn by some conservative Islamic women to cover their bodies.

Libi arrived at 9:30 and slid off the back of the motorcycle. For some reason he broke with his standard procedure of sending a decoy first and started walking toward Khaliq.[71] Though disguised in oversized sunglasses, a Sindhi cap, and a shalwar kameez, he was given away by the blotchy patches of skin under his eyes.[72] His driver stayed on the bike while a gunman named Ibrahim followed at a distance. As Libi approached, one of the burqa-clad Pakistani agents jumped on him. It was quite a scene. In a place as conservative as the North West Frontier Province, a woman in a burqa tackling a man in public is unthinkable.

Libi's capture was primarily "an ISI show" with some help from the police, according to Amanullah Khan, deputy superintendent of police in Mardan. "We got to the place after hearing a few gunshots."[73]

ISI agents bundled Libi into a vehicle and whisked him away. Like the CIA's public relations efforts after Khalid Sheikh Mohammed's capture, Pakistan released photos of Libi showing him disheveled and with an ill-kempt beard, a stark contrast to the well-groomed, smartly suited man whose portrait appeared on Pakistan's most-wanted list. President Musharraf then informed General John Abizaid of U.S. Central Command, who was visiting Pakistan.

"I have good news for you," Musharraf said. "We have Libi."

"Really? When?" asked Abizaid, visibly surprised.

"A few days ago," Musharraf replied.

"Where is he now?" asked Abizaid.

"Oh, he's here in Islamabad," Musharraf responded nonchalantly. "Please tell President Bush—or should I?"

"It would be better if you informed him," remarked Abizaid, his excitement growing.

"I don't know," said Musharraf. "You tell President Bush."

"No, I can't," Abizaid retorted. "You please tell him."[74]

Musharraf phoned Bush that night. A month later, on June 6, 2005, Libi was transferred to U.S. custody. He eventually landed in Guantánamo Bay. As with previous al Qa'ida captures, the United States gained a gold mine of information from him. A computer seized during his capture contained manuals related to explosives, detonator circuits, chemicals, military tactics, missiles, and tanks.[75] The United States and Pakistan also found names, phone numbers, and other contact information, which they could use to target other al Qa'ida leaders.

Ripples in Europe

Another encouraging sign after the Madrid attacks was the stirring response among Spanish Muslims. Spain's leading Muslim clerics issued a religious order condemning Osama bin Laden. "We declare," they stated, "that Osama bin Laden and his al Qa'ida organization, responsible for the horrendous crimes against innocent people who were despicably murdered in the 11 March terrorist attack in Madrid, are outside the parameters of Islam." They wrote that the attacks were "totally banned and must be roundly condemned as against Islam."[76]

Their reasoning was remarkably similar to that used by Sayyid Imam Abd al-Aziz al-Sharif, or Dr. Fadl, in his increasingly frequent denunciations of al Qa'ida. Other prominent Muslims in Spain had a similar reaction. At Madrid's Cultural Islamic Center, where some of the attackers had worshipped, director Mohamed Saleh denounced the attackers as apostates. Some of the attackers had worshipped at the mosque.

"These people are terrorists, and terrorists are criminals wherever they are from," he remarked. He then went further. "They cannot have real faith or know Allah. For a Muslim to kill a person unjustly is to kill everyone. There is no justification to kill."[77]

Spanish police and intelligence officials also responded with renewed vigor and a deeper appreciation of the fundamentalist Islamic threat to Spain—and to Europe more generally. In the four years after the Madrid attacks, Spain added 1,000 police and Guardia Civil personnel to conduct counterterrorist operations, boosting their staffs by nearly 35 percent.[78] These efforts had an immediate impact. Within two days of the attacks, the central external information unit of the National Police had identified most of the perpetrators. More than sixteen members of the Madrid network were tried and convicted: thirteen in Spain, two in Morocco, and one in Italy. Seven others committed suicide in the Leganés siege. Several others were eventually killed or captured. Amer Azizi and Hamza Rabi'a were killed in December 2005 by a Hellfire missile from a CIA Predator after U.S. intelligence operatives had tracked them to the area around Miram Shah in North Waziristan.

The Madrid attacks, it turned out, were only the tip of the iceberg. On April 2, 2004, just weeks after the Spanish tragedy, individuals belonging to the same terrorist network tried—and failed—to attack a high-speed train bound for Seville using similar bombs. In October and November 2004, Spanish police executed Operation Nova, detaining nearly forty members of an Islamic terrorist network plotting to attack the Spanish National High Court, where many of the terrorist cases were tried. The dismantling of this group highlighted the problem of radicalization of inmates in the Spanish prison system, particularly among Islamic inmates. Many were serving sentences for common criminal offenses and had no terrorist associations prior to their incarceration. Several of the terrorists had corresponded by mail for years with three U.S. prisoners at the maximum-security prison in Florence, Colorado. The three prisoners—Mohammad Abou Halima, Mohammad Amin Salameh, and Nidal Ayyad—had been incarcerated for their involvement in the 1993 World Trade Center bombings.[79]

In October 2004, Spanish police arrested a group of Pakistani nationals and charged them with drug trafficking and terrorism. They had links to al Qa'ida and the Pakistan-based group Lashkar-e-Taiba, which later perpetrated the spectacular November 2008 attacks in Mumbai. During Operation Tigris in June 2005, Spanish police dismantled a jihadist facilitator network that funneled suicide bombers from Spain to Iraq. Eight of the thirty-nine suspects were sent to prison on terrorism charges, while seven others were deported to their countries of origin. Still, these successes had come at a steep price: the extent of the country's radicalization problem had become clear only after 191 tragic deaths.

The events in Madrid were the first major attack on European soil by a network affiliated with or inspired by al Qa'ida. But it would not be the last. Across the English Channel, British intelligence agencies had picked up indications that British-based extremists were impressed by the scope and perceived success of the Madrid attacks. British officials accurately feared a similar plan was unfolding in the United Kingdom, as extremists like Omar Khyam became inspired by the Madrid attacks.

"That's amazing, isn't it," remarked Khyam on March 23, 2004, referring to the Madrid bombings. He was a British citizen whose family had emigrated from Pakistan and who was now being monitored for terrorist plotting. "Everything turns around." The UK's domestic intelligence agency, MI5, had placed an eavesdropping device in Khyam's car.

"Look on the success of the Madrid bombing, change of power," responded Shehzad Tanweer, one of his colleagues in the car.[80] It was now a common belief among terrorists that attacks could affect domestic politics.

Like Spain, the UK had deployed conventional military forces to Iraq. In May 2005 the Joint Terrorism Analysis Centre (JTAC), which had been established two years earlier to analyze and assess all intelligence relating to international terrorism, issued a report on the threat to the British rail and subway networks. It concluded that "rail and underground networks have been attractive targets to terrorists worldwide; Madrid attacks offer inspiration for further attacks against rail networks; attacks on UK rail networks feature highly in terrorists' menu of options; but no suggestion of a current tangible threat to UK rail or underground."[81]

The second wave continued to build. The next attack, it turned out, would be just as deadly as the one in Madrid. Al Qa'ida leaders turned their focus to London.

THE LONDON ATTACKS

HASINA PATEL LEFT her house in Leeds, England, promptly at 9 a.m. on Thursday, July 7, 2005. Leeds is situated beside the River Aire about 170 miles northwest of London, in Yorkshire. That morning the weather was overcast and soggy, with heavy showers scattered across the area, but locals were in an unusually cheery mood. The day before, the International Olympic Committee had announced that London would host the 2012 Summer Olympics, beating out Paris in the final round of voting. Yet Patel was distraught. She was having problems with her pregnancy and had made an emergency appointment at a local hospital. It was her second pregnancy in two years. In May 2004 she and her husband, Mohammad Sidique Khan, had a beautiful baby girl. But she was having trouble reaching Khan. She hadn't seen him for several days and had left repeated messages on his cell phone. "Are you going to come for the scan?" she asked in one message, growing frantic because he wasn't returning her calls.

Patel grabbed her mother instead. When she arrived at the hospital, the news was heartbreaking. "It seems that the baby stopped growing at six or seven weeks," she was told. Patel walked back into the waiting room and gave her mother the news. "Mum," she said, "I think the pregnancy is not going to go ahead—the baby had stopped growing."[1]

Devastated, Patel returned home and clicked on the television. There was more bad news: beginning at 8:50 a.m., four suicide bombers had conducted separate attacks in central London. Three were on London's subway system, the Underground, and one was on a Number 30 double-decker bus traveling east from Marble Arch. London was in chaos. Fifty-six people had been killed, including the four suicide bombers, and more than seven hundred were injured, many of them losing limbs.

One of the bombers, it turned out, was Patel's husband. The news was unbearable—two life-changing events within hours.

"He had committed a terrorist attack in London, I couldn't believe it, and I had lost my child," she said. "I felt quite ashamed really that, you know, I was always going to be associated with this now and how could he do such a thing? It is difficult, he has left me to pick up the pieces really."[2]

Patel came from a prominent Indian family, while Khan was Pakistani. Their families had opposed the marriage, in part because they had not arranged it, but Patel and Khan had defied them. Now Patel was caught at the center of what was then Europe's largest-ever suicide attack.

UK police and intelligence agencies had grown increasingly concerned about the radical Islamic threat to the country. One report from MI5 noted in early 2005, "We know that both British and foreign nationals belonging to Al Qaida cells and associated networks are currently present throughout the UK, that they are supporting the activities of terrorist groups, and that in some cases they are engaged in planning, or attempting to carry out, terrorist attacks."[3] What they had underestimated, however, was the scope of the threat and the degree of animosity felt by young British Muslims toward the state.

The Madrid attacks had been symptomatic of the second wave of terrorism by al Qa'ida and its broader network, which was now reaching British shores. Since several al Qa'ida leaders, including external operations chief Abu Ubaydah al-Masri, were involved in the attacks, they couldn't be considered isolated, homegrown incidents. Eliza Manningham-Buller, the director-general of MI5, acknowledged that British intelligence had identified some of the potential terrorists but had enough resources only to "hit the crocodiles nearest the boat."[4] Mohammad Sidique Khan and his colleagues, it turned out, were lurking an oar's length outside the perimeter.

The Extremist Underground

Khan was the oldest of the group. He stood five feet, eight inches tall and had soft hazel eyes, thick black hair, dark bushy eyebrows, and a neatly trimmed beard. He spoke calmly and eloquently, with a slight Yorkshire accent, and emphasized important words by lightly raising his tone and gesturing with his hands.[5] A talented public speaker, Khan could be persuasive, a trait that helped him recruit potential suicide bombers. His friends called him Sid. He was rarely in trouble and kept fit by playing cricket and practicing jujitsu.

Born at St. James Hospital in Leeds on October 20, 1974, Khan was the youngest of four children. His father, Tika Khan, was a foundry worker and one of the first Pakistanis to settle in Yorkshire. The Khan family grew up in Beeston, an impoverished, ethnically mixed area of the city. Headingley is famous for its cricket ground; Kirkstall is known for its medieval abbey; Beeston is one of the most isolated suburbs and is situated on a hill overlooking the city, separated from Leeds by the M621 motorway. The area is largely residential, close-knit, and densely populated, with back-to-back terraced housing, some of which is drab and grungy. By the late 1990s there were several mosques, a large, modern community center, an Islamic bookshop, and a large park where kids played soccer and cricket. Average income was low, but there was little to distinguish Beeston from many other poor areas in the UK.[6]

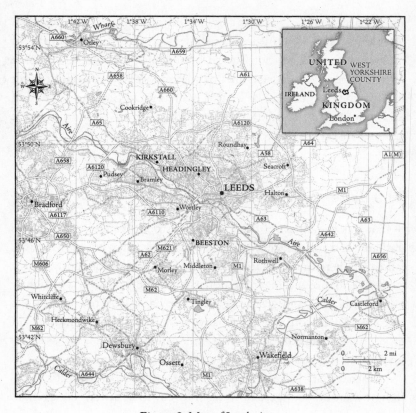

Figure 8: Map of Leeds Area

In 1996, Mohammad Sidique Khan enrolled in Leeds Metropolitan University, where he was an average student. He received a
degree in business studies, but his most notable success at the university, it turned out, was meeting his future wife. "He stood out
because he was more mature, I thought, than the other lads, more
into fitness and health, and he used to pray five times a day," said
Hasina Patel. "I saw potential for marriage really—he just seemed
sensible and polite, that sort of thing, a good family man and he
came from a good family."[7]

They were married on October 22, 2001. Khan's parents moved
to Nottingham, about 60 miles southeast of Leeds, but he and sev-

eral siblings remained in the Leeds area. That year Khan joined the staff of Hillside Primary School, where he worked with special-needs children and those with language and behavioral difficulties. The school had students from a variety of ethnic backgrounds and a high pupil turnover. Khan gave an interview to the *Times Educational Supplement* in 2002 in which he spoke passionately about the kids he worked with, noting that "a lot of them have said this is the best school they have been to."[8] He and his wife shared a zeal for education. "We both liked working with children, which we did later on," Patel confided. "We both took different types of careers working with children and we were thinking of doing our [postgraduate certificate in education] at one point as well."[9]

On the surface Khan struck most people as mature and genteel. But he was a chameleon. There was a noxious, sinister side that he hid from most people, including his wife. Beginning in the late 1990s, he began spending time in Beeston's extremist underground, especially its youth clubs, gyms, and Islamic bookshop. In 2001 he attended the Hamara Youth Access Point, where he played pool, boxed, and socialized. He had attended several mosques in Beeston: the Hardy Street mosque, run by Kashmiri Muslims; the Stratford Street mosque, run by Pakistani Tablighi Jamaat members; and the Bengali mosque on Tunstall Road, run by Bangladeshis. Khan eventually migrated to the Stratford Street mosque, which followed the more rigid, orthodox, Deobandi school of Islam.[10] But his stay at the mosque didn't last long, and he gradually became interested in Wahhabi fundamentalism. Some members of his family, such as his brother Gultasab, became concerned about his new passion. But in an area rife with drug dealers and other dangers, his family had other things to worry about. "Better being Wahhabi than on drugs," said Gultasab.[11]

Khan's transition to Wahhabism paralleled a growing militancy. In January 2001 he attended an outdoor training session organized by extremists in West Yorkshire. Police covertly monitored the forty attendees, took photographs, and showed them to a number of sources, who could identify only nine of them. Khan was not among those identified.[12] By 2002 he was leading paintball outings with youth groups from the Leeds area, events that served as bonding and vetting opportunities and were often preceded by Islamic lectures.[13] But he kept his wife at a distance.

"We were trying to be good Muslims, and in our religion we are told that men and women have to be segregated," said Patel. "I never sat in the same room with his friends; he never sat in the same room as my friends. So it is a completely different life, his social life and my social life was completely separated, we would never speak."

The distance between them put a growing strain on their marriage. "We did used to argue a lot because he was spending more and more time away from me, sometimes for days at a time, and we did have a lot of arguments and we were growing apart," remarked Patel. "I thought maybe it is a phase, maybe he is depressed, he is always out with his friends, but I couldn't put my finger on it, why he was always out and not spending a lot of time with me and my daughter."[14]

Instead of devoting time to his family, Khan associated with a small network of individuals, including Shehzad Tanweer, who went by the nickname Kaka. Tanweer was tall and wiry, with dark curly hair, glasses, and a prominent nose. He was born on December, 15, 1982, in Bradford but spent most of his life in Beeston. Like Khan, he was a second-generation British citizen whose parents were from Pakistan. "He was proud to be British," said one of his uncles, Bashir Ahmed. "His parents were loving and supportive. He was a very kind and calm person. He was respected by everyone."[15]

Tanweer was the second of four children and the oldest son. He did well academically and was a gifted sportsman, excelling at cricket. Also like Khan, he studied at Leeds Metropolitan University. He left the university in 2003 before completing his Bachelor of Science course and worked part-time in his father's fish and chip shop. Neighbors described him as a "nice lad" who could "get on with anyone," though he had his rougher moments.[16] Hours before he blew himself up on London's Underground, his polite conversation with a cashier at a Woodall gas station degenerated into an argument when he complained that he was being short-changed.

West Yorkshire Police first came across Tanweer in 1995, when he was arrested for a reported burglary. The police took his personal details but did not take fingerprints, photographs, or a DNA sample, and he was released without charge. They next encountered him in April 2004, when he was cautioned for public disorder. This time the police took a photograph, fingerprints, and DNA and entered his name on the Police National Computer system.[17]

Tanweer lived about half a mile from Hasib Hussain, the third bomber. Hussain had a crooked nose that looked like it had been broken in a bar fight, and he had been one of the tallest boys in his class. Like Tanweer and Khan, Hussain grew up in Leeds and was still living there with his parents before the attack. He grew up on the outskirts of the city, in a neighborhood of dilapidated brick houses. As a teenager he was a quiet, not particularly gifted student with few friends. He went on to Thomas Danby College for an advanced business program, and although his attendance record was patchy, he stayed to the end.[18]

Some of his fellow students began to notice a change in Hussain in 2002, after he returned from the hajj to Mecca. He scribbled "Al Qaeda—No Limits" on his religious-school book and spoke openly of his support for its senior leaders. In October 2004, Hussain received a police caution for shoplifting, but otherwise he was not on the radar screen of police and intelligence officials.

Germaine Lindsay was the only one of the July 7 bombers born outside the United Kingdom, which made him something of an outsider in the group. He spent the first year of his life in Jamaica and moved to the United Kingdom with his mother in 1986. The family settled in Huddersfield, a mixed community in West Yorkshire, halfway between Leeds and Manchester. Lindsay was a bright child and a good athlete who enjoyed martial arts and kickboxing, but his home life was unstable. His father, who remained in Jamaica, did little parenting, and his mother moved in with another man in West Yorkshire and then with another boyfriend in 1990. The following year Lindsay and his mother converted to Islam and he took the name Jamal. In Islamic groups around Huddersfield and Dewsbury, he was admired for the speed with which he achieved fluency in Arabic and memorized long passages of the Qur'an, showing unusual ardor and maturity.[19]

In 2002, Lindsay's mother moved to the United States to live with yet another man, leaving him alone at the family home in Huddersfield. He left school and did odd jobs, selling mobile phones and Islamic books. On an Internet chat room he met Samantha Lewthwaite, a white British convert to Islam who changed her name to Asmantara. Their relationship progressed from Internet discussions to speaking on the phone, exchanging photographs, meeting in person in October 2002, and then marrying. They moved from Huddersfield to Aylesbury in Buckinghamshire, near her parents, and had their first child six months later.

Lindsay had some run-ins with the police. A Fiat Brava registered to him drove off from the scene of a robbery in Luton in May 2005, and he was subsequently named as a suspect. The vehicle was not located, and it appears that Lindsay was never interviewed regarding the matter.[20] Like several of the other bombers, he had not previously come to the attention of police and intelligence agencies for involvement in terrorism.

Lindsay became increasingly interested in extreme interpretations of Islam and was influenced by Abdallah al-Faisal, a Jamaican who later served a prison sentence for inciting murder and race hate. Not long after Lindsay's marriage to Samantha, he refused to pray with her any longer. "He was snappy and verbally aggressive," she noticed. "It was a turning point—a different Jamal I saw from now on. It was nothing instant, but gradual over the months as his attitude to me changed. It was as if he was driving me away." He also changed his clothes. "He was dressed in trendy designer clothes and had ditched all his Arab-style gowns," she continued.

"He shaved off the beard he had grown since he was fourteen and had never even trimmed."[21]

In many ways, Khan, Tanweer, Hussain, and especially Lindsay had been normal—even anodyne—English boys in their younger years. What brought them together, however, was collective participation in Leeds' radical underground and Khan's charismatic leadership. In 2001, Khan left the Stratford Street mosque, complaining that its approach to outreach was too narrow and its focus apolitical. The mosque's imams, Khan concluded, knew little of the challenges British Muslims faced, partly because they were from South Asia and barely spoke English. He wanted to discuss current politics, but many officials discouraged such delicate subjects. Khan gravitated to the Iqra Learning Center in Beeston, where he and his colleagues were free from their parents' version of Islam. Khan and his small network had political discussions about Iraq, Afghanistan, Kashmir, and Chechnya, and they produced jihad videos depicting crimes committed by the West against Muslims. The bookshop at the Iqra Learning Center was a central node for radical Islam. Not only did it sell Islamic books, tapes and DVDs, but it also hosted lectures and discussion groups on Islam.[22]

Much like the young Muslims in Lackawanna, Khan and his network became radicalized *outside* of the mosques, which they considered too moderate, detached, and infiltrated by government agencies. Khan's radicalization should have been a sign to family members—and intelligence agencies—that something was wrong. During a 2004 conversation in a friend's apartment, which was bugged by UK police and intelligence agencies, Khan outlined his disdain for the current crop of scholars and Muslim leaders in the Leeds area. "I've placed a lot of emphasis on the scholars that we have today," he said. "They're not doing their jobs. If they were, we would not be in the situation. We sit on our backsides moaning and munching for the rest of our lives."[23]

The UK's Growing Threat

While Khan, Tanweer, Hussain, and Lindsay were slipping into the Leeds extremist underground, British police and intelligence units had their hands full with other, more pressing matters. Early in 2003, MI5 obtained intelligence that an individual named Mohammed Qayum Khan, from Luton, was the leader of an al Qa'ida facilitation network in the UK. MI5 and police agencies began investigating Mohammed Qayum Khan, who was later arrested and sentenced to life in prison, in an operation code-named Crevice. They quickly identified another key member of the group, Omar Khyam, who appeared to be acting as a courier. MI5 put him under limited surveillance.[24]

On February 20, 2004, an electronics expert arrived from Canada to meet Khyam. Surveillance showed that he was advising Khyam and his associates on how to build remote detonation devices, which suggested that Khyam was actively planning an attack. At this point Khyam became one of MI5's top targets and Crevice became their main operation. In fact, it was the largest operation MI5 and the police had ever undertaken up to that point. MI5 searched 30 addresses, devoted 45,000 man-hours to monitoring and transcribing bugged conversations, conducted 34,000 man-hours of surveillance, performed countless covert searches of targets' property and baggage, and deployed an enormous number of eavesdropping devices.[25]

Mohammad Sidique Khan occasionally surfaced during the investigation but did not participate in discussions about terrorist operations—at least, not in discussions picked up by MI5 or the police. For example, at 8:50 p.m. on February 21, 2004, MI5 covertly recorded a conversation in Omar Khyam's Suzuki Vitara between Khyam and Mohammad Sidique Khan.

"Are you really a terrorist?" Mohammad Sidique Khan inquired.

"They are working with us," Omar Khyam responded. "I am not a terrorist, they are working through us."

"There is no one higher than you," said Khan.

Khyam then changed subjects, referring to pressure from British police and intelligence services. "I do not live in Crawley any more. I moved out because in the next month they are going to be raiding bigtime all over the UK."[26]

Mohammad Sidique Khan had begun to associate himself with one of the UK's most dangerous terrorists. But MI5 needed to prioritize. In the case of Crevice, all their time and money went to monitoring Omar Khyam. Any spare resources were focused on the rest of the core Crevice group who were directly involved in the attack plan. There were limited funds and manpower to follow up on other individuals.[27]

To provide a better understanding of Omar Khyam's planning, MI5 bugged his house, Flat 4 at 56 Hencroft Street in Slough, just west of London. On the evening of March 23, 2004, police and intelligence officials listened to a conversation between Khyam, Mohammad Sidique Khan, and several others. The meeting appeared to center on raising money for a trip to Pakistan. Khan and others discussed a variety of fraud scams. One involved purchasing equipment on credit, defaulting on payment, and then selling the goods for cash. But there is no record of Khan discussing terrorist activity.

"I can't find my passport," Khan explained. "Do you think they will let me in?"

"You can get one in a day," said Omar Khyam.

"Have you got cheap tickets?" inquired Khan. "These two—it's costing like £1100."

"Yeah," replied Khyam.

"Two of them, yeah," Khan affirmed.

"We got £580 for two people, that's including one night in Dubai as well as the hotel," said Khyam.

They then began to discuss ways of raising money to travel, including borrowing from banks, stealing and selling cars, and running credit card scams.

"They're asking for wage slips and bank statements. I blagged the amount, didn't I? Over the phone I said my father's had a stroke, kill my father off again," Khan remarked, as everyone broke into laughter. "My father had a stroke and I can't think about it, so I'll leave it for a little while and get back to you, when things have settled down again. They were very apologetic and sympathetic."

"To be fair to you, he did give you some advice," said an unidentified male in the room. "He says if you, like, went straight into, like, a bank and applied for an unsecured loan. He said there's no reason why, because he says their lending criteria is stricter than some banks."

"I'm gonna tap HSBC," Khan announced, referring to the London-headquartered bank. "I've got myself onto their register and I'm gonna tap one of my leads and take it from there. It's not a problem. Whatever comes, comes apart from that, I'll just go with a balaclava and a shotgun. I'll just need a driver, any offers?"

The room erupted in cackles and hoots.[28]

At the time, Mohammad Sidique Khan appeared to be on the fringes of the Crevice plotters, more interested in criminal activity than in terrorism. Surveillance teams are often tasked by investigators with establishing patterns of activity involving the main targets. When a primary target such as Omar Khyam came into contact with other individuals, the surveillance team had to decide whether to follow the new contact or ignore him and stay with the main target. A whole series of factors are taken into consideration to make what is often a split-second decision, though it will later be reviewed as part of the wider investigation. This dilemma became acute in March 2004. In eavesdropped conversations, Khyam appeared to be growing jumpy. He and the other Crevice plotters were heard talking about leaving the country. MI5 thought this might be an escape plan and that the attack might be imminent. Between March 29 and April 1 they arrested the core Crevice suspects, including Omar Khyam.[29]

Once the Crevice plotters had been arrested, MI5 returned to the group's contacts in an operation code-named Rhyme. In early 2003, UK intelligence came across a plot led by Abu Issa al-Hindi, who also went by Dhiren Barot. The Rhyme plotters were planning to pack three limousines with gas cylinders and explosives, and then set them off in underground car parks. The group also investigated the use of radiological material in bombs. MI5 and the police provided six weeks of twenty-four-hour coverage, deployed up to 15 surveillance teams, installed and monitored 20 closed-circuit television cameras, devoted 25,000 man-hours to monitoring and transcribing bugged conversations, conducted 60 property searches, and seized and analyzed hard drives containing 2.5 terabytes of data (roughly twelve times the height of Mount Everest if printed out and stacked). On August 3, 2004, thirteen individuals, including Barot, were arrested; eight of those faced trial. Barot pleaded guilty and was sentenced to life imprisonment in November 2006. The seven other members of the group were convicted of terrorist offenses in June 2007.[30]

The UK clearly had a domestic terrorist problem. Young Muslims from Luton, Leeds, Walthamstow, and other locations were radicalizing and preparing to conduct terrorist attacks. In April 2003 the Joint Intelligence Committee specifically identified the London Underground as a potential target.[31] UK and U.S. intelligence assessments indicated that al Qa'ida had learned from past successes and failures and believed there were exploitable vulnerabilities in the UK and other Western public transportation systems.[32]

As in Spain, the war in Iraq was a primary motivation of the impressionable young Muslims. An alarming report in May 2005 from the government's Joint Terrorism Analysis Centre, which was based at MI5's headquarters and responsible for assessing terrorist threats to Great Britain, concluded that the "threat from Al Qaida (AQ) leadership directed plots has not gone away and events in Iraq are continuing to act as motivation and a focus of a range of terrorist related activity in the UK."[33] In early 2005 the Joint Intelligence Council argued that suicide bombs could become the preferred technique for extremist attacks in some parts of the world, following their effective use in Iraq. But suicide attacks would probably not become the norm in Europe, it surmised. Still, MI5 warned that "the most significant threat to the UK and to UK interests overseas comes from Al Qaida and associated networks. The threat to the UK remains real and serious."[34]

Ongoing UK counterterrorist operations placed an extraordinary burden on MI5, which could cover less than one percent of its targets well. According to MI5's estimates, it could cover another 6 percent of its targets fairly well (but with gaps), 33 percent adequately (with even bigger gaps), and 42 percent inadequately; 19 percent had no coverage at all.[35] Khan, Tanweer, and their network fell in the no-coverage category. To make matters worse, the terrorist threat appeared to be getting more serious. In 2001, MI5 knew of approximately 250 primary investigative targets within the UK. There were over 500 targets by July 2004 and 800 by July 2005. To deal with the threat, government agencies ramped up their coverage of Islamic extremists. Roughly 56 percent of MI5's resources went to Islamic groups in July 2005, up from 23 percent in 2002. At MI6, the UK's external spy agency, and the Government Communications Headquarters (GCHQ), the UK's primary signals intelligence collection agency, operational effort against the range of threats rose from single digits before September 2001 to double digits by 2005.[36]

With British services busy with operations and proliferating targets, Khan and his colleagues slipped into Pakistan.

Training in Malakand

Back in the United States, Art Cummings and other FBI officials had watched the radicalization of British Muslims with alarm. The problem was twofold. First, al Qa'ida leaders based in Pakistan could potentially leverage the large number of British Pakistanis traveling to Islamabad and other cities; about 400,000 British residents traveled to Pakistan every year.[37] The vast majority visited family, attended weddings, or went on vacation. Only a tiny percentage were involved in terrorist activity. For the few terrorists, however, trips to Asia gave them the chance to visit a training camp and mingle with some of al Qa'ida's most accomplished operatives.

"Our Muslim community is at least assimilated," said Cummings, who had been appointed deputy director of the National Counterterrorism Center. "The Pakistan community in the UK is a *Pakistan* community. They all know each other, they're all related, they know all the tribal relationships. And they claim their opportunity is minimal." This perceived economic disparity created a situation in which they "live in England," Cummings calculated, "but they hate the English."[38]

Second, British citizens did not need a visa to get into the United States for stays of ninety days or less. Consequently, a British Pakistani could fly to Pakistan, attend an al Qa'ida training camp, and enter the United States on a British passport fairly easily, unless U.S. or other intelligence agencies gained information about his or her involvement in terrorism.

Cummings was right to be concerned. In July 2003, Mohammad Sidique Khan traveled to Pakistan under the radar of British intelligence. He was picked up at Islamabad International Airport by Omar Khyam and Mohammad Junaid Babar, a Pakistani-American who ran training camps in Pakistan for al Qa'ida and other Islamic militants. Both had ties to an al Qa'ida facilitator named Abu Munthir al-Mughrebi. A few days later they met at the Capitol Hill Lodge in Rawalpindi to trek to the Malakand training camp, near the Afghanistan-Pakistan border. The camp was situated in an area immortalized by Winston Churchill in *The Story of the Malakand Field Force*. "Except at the times of sowing and of harvest, a continual state of feud and strife prevails throughout the land," he wrote. "Every tribesmen has a blood feud with his neighbour. Every man's hand is against the other, and all against the stranger."[39]

In the town of Timergara, about 40 miles from the Afghanistan city of Asadabad, Khyam and Babar purchased ammonium nitrate and other items. They then traveled in a rickety pickup truck, with Khyam, Babar, and Khan jammed in the back. They discussed jihad while the truck kicked up thick clouds of dust as it rattled along Pakistan's winding roads. The group traveled the last leg on foot through the mountains. After settling in, Khan fired AK-47s and Pika long-range light machine guns. He also went through courses on physical conditioning, weapons training, and explosives use, including how to manufacture and detonate homemade explosives using ammonium nitrate and aluminum powder. Senior al Qa'ida leader Abd al-Hadi al-Iraqi oversaw the training of this network and others in the camp, and al Qa'ida's external operations chief, Abu Ubaydah al-Masri, helped plan their operation.

When they had completed training, the group traveled to Peshawar together. Khan and several others took a Daewoo bus to Lahore because it wouldn't get checked by Pakistani authorities.[40] They rented 13 Ilyas Street, known as the Sufi House, in one of Lahore's densely populated areas. The group left early every morning, and when they returned after dark, they gathered outside in the courtyard, talked noisily, played music, and kept the neighbors awake. "We knew what they were doing," remarked a neighbor, "and we were afraid at those boys being here, but we couldn't do anything about it."[41]

It was not Mohammad Sidique Khan's first trip to Pakistan. He had trained with militants in Kashmir back in 2001 and had also made a short trek to the Taliban's front line with the Northern Alliance near Kabul.[42] After he returned to Leeds in 2003, he made preparations to travel back to Pakistan, this time with Shehzad Tanweer. On February 21, 2004, he spoke to Omar Khyam in a car that was bugged by MI5.

"Are these lot ready, bruv?" Khyam inquired, referring to Shehzad Tanweer and others.

"Yeah," said Khan.

"What I'll do is, I will talk to you tonight, inshallah," responded Khyam. "How quickly can these guys go?"

"It's down to you," said Khan. "We have a lot of questions to ask. I know that this is like really out of order. I was hoping for a slight extension. You know my wife is having a kid, yeah? I was hoping so that I can get to the hospital. But these guys are good to go as soon as you say."[43]

They parked the car and walked into Khyam's apartment, which had also been bugged by MI5.

"There was a time you could land and Afghanistan was like a terrorist training camp," said Khyam. "You can come out and come back but obviously we know that time is finished. That's it cause every time you come back, you are going to make yourself hotter because you're a youth travelling into Pakistan and out of Pakistan and they watch that. So when you come back," he continued, "and when you link up with some brothers here, they become hot as well. And when you meet brothers involved in financing it makes them hot. So overall, it's worse, right now.

"Second thing," said Khyam. "Because you are going to leave now you may as well rip the country apart, economically as well. All the brothers are running scams and I advise you to do the same. Run them, you will probably walk away with 20 grand and that's really easy money bruv. I can set it all up for you. And I will get a brother to run it. All the brothers leaving are doing it because the government—we might as well take their wealth . . . They are taking it from us and we are just taking it back. Any questions you want to ask—fire away."

"Any extra risks getting into Pakistan?" asked Shehzad Tanweer, who had not been to Pakistan.

"We had five Bengalis last year," Khyam noted, obviously impressed with himself. "Guess how we got them in? From Bangladesh all the way across India into Pakistan. We bribed the guy. You know when you go to the check-in, it would all be set up."

"Going through the airport," Mohammad Sidique Khan reaffirmed. "Normal tickets."

"Yeah, just walk straight through, bruv, normal," said Khyam. "Just act as if you are a Pakistani. And if they say something to you in Urdu just say 'I don't speak Urdu.'"

Tanweer then inquired about items to take to the al Qa'ida camp. "What do we need to buy?"

"I think you need to buy the sleeping bag," said Khyam. "You need a rucksack. A 45 liter one, you need a sleeping bag, one that has strips on the side and becomes really compact. Some Merrells—or boots."

"What about thermal, waterproof?" asked Tanweer.

"Nah," noted Khyam. "All you need is a jacket which is waterproof and breathable. Forget the Gore-Tex."

Tanweer continued to pepper him with questions, "How much money is needed?"

"Well," Khyam responded, thinking for a moment, "if you are going to put this stuff through, you will leave with about £20k."

Tanweer then asked about passports.

"Take your own passports through the airport," Khyam told him. Then he outlined the role of an al Qa'ida handler, or emir, in Pakistan. "Whoever is your emir he will take all the wealth. If you or your brother need a doctor he will arrange for you to see a doctor. He will pay for it. If you need to make a phone call home he will arrange for the telephone call. Anything you think needs to be done he will do it. But Islam works through the emir. Everything goes through him. Don't tell your real name to no one, even to your emir," he continued. "Just say you are from Manchester. The only thing I will advise you, yeah, is total obedience to whoever your emir is. Whether he is Sunni, Arab, Chechen, Saudi, British—total obedience. I'll tell you up there you can get your head cut off."[44]

On November 10, 2004, Shehzad Tanweer received his visa from the Pakistani consulate in Bradford, England, using his UK passport, number 453897014. The purpose of the trip, he wrote, was to "visit family." That day the Pakistani consulate also issued a visa to Mohammad Sidique Khan for his UK passport, number 040169095, for the purpose of a "holiday" and "a friend's wedding."[45] Hasib Hussain had been to Pakistan earlier that year, arriving in Karachi from Saudi Arabia on Saudi Airlines Flight SV714 on July 15.[46] Khan and Tanweer traveled to Pakistan around November 19. After arriving they split up, and Tanweer stayed with his uncle's family in Faisalabad. After a week or so, Khan picked up Tanweer, who told his family that they were checking out a school near Lahore.[47] They then traveled to camps run by Abd al-Hadi al-Iraqi, where they were groomed to be bombers, encouraged to recruit other martyrs, and taught how to make explosives.[48] Both Tanweer and Khan left Karachi on Turkish Airlines Flight TK-1057 on February 8, 2005, at 3 a.m. and returned to the UK.[49]

The ability of Khan, Tanweer, and others to undergo training in al Qa'ida–affiliated camps in Pakistan was critical, and separated them from purely homegrown terrorists. The value of training may have been more in the indoctrination and bonding that occurred than in the rudimentary combat skills learned. Spending time in a militant training environment conditioned recruits like Khan, many of whom already had extremist leanings, to use violence. Recruits committed to the extremist cause cemented personal ties with other extremists. These conditions are more difficult to create over the Internet or during camping or rafting excursions in the West. Participating in Pakistani training camps also improved the operational tradecraft of recruits like Khan and Tanweer. They learned how to case targets, communicate clandestinely, and develop and live with cover stories. Extremists could also share security and tradecraft procedures and lessons. While the technical skills needed to conduct attacks are often learned from years of practice rather than from a few days or weeks in a camp, the experience in the camps concluded the radicalization process for the July 7 bombers.

For Mohammad Sidique Khan, the value of attending al Qa'ida–affiliated camps was perhaps most evident in the martyrdom video he taped, in which he ranted against UK and other Western "oppression" of Muslims.

"Our words have no impact upon you, therefore I'm going to talk to you in a language that you understand," he seethed. "Our words are dead until we give them life with our blood."

He viewed himself as a martyr and compared his devotion to that of the Prophet Muhammad: "I and thousands like me are forsaking everything for what we believe. Our driving motivation doesn't come from tangible commodities that this world has to offer. Our religion is Islam, obedience to the one true God, Allah, and following the footsteps of the final prophet and messenger Muhammad. This is how our ethical stances are dictated," he continued, speaking calmly and deliberately and wagging his index finger at the camera for emphasis.

"Your democratically elected governments continuously perpetuate atrocities against my people and your support of them makes you directly responsible, just as I am directly responsible for protecting and avenging my Muslim brothers and sisters." Khan concluded with a menacing threat to the West: "Until we feel security, you will be our target. Until you stop the bombing, gassing, imprisonment, and torture of my people, we will not stop this fight. We are at war and I am a soldier. Now you too will taste the reality of this situation."[50] Shehzad Tanweer made a similar statement, threatening that attacks would continue "until you pull your forces out of Afghanistan and Iraq."[51]

After the attacks on the Underground, many Muslims would denounce Khan and his colleagues as un-Islamic. Khan's use of the words *my people* in reference to the *ummah*, or Muslim community, angered those who did not share his beliefs.

With their martyrdom videos completed, the group made final plans for the attack shortly after their return from Pakistan. In the final months they kept in regular contact with their al Qa'ida handlers in Pakistan.[52]

Executing the Attacks

By May 2005 both Tanweer and Khan had left their jobs and could devote all of their time to making the bombs and selecting the target. They rented an apartment from an Egyptian chemistry Ph.D. student at Leeds University. Lindsay met the student at Leeds Grand Mosque in November 2004. Next door to the mosque was a ground-floor apartment in a two-story block at 18 Alexandra Grove.[53] They did not stand out amid the transitory student population.[54] As the 2006 transatlantic plotters would later do, and as their al Qa'ida handlers had advised, Khan and his network built the bombs in a different location from where they lived to minimize detection.

Tanweer and Lindsay bought face masks to make the bombs, as instructed by their al Qa'ida trainers, and began boiling the homemade explosive—a thick yellow hydrogen peroxide mixture—and storing it in a cast-iron bathtub.[55] They connected fans to the hot plates, kept the windows open, and taped the curtains to the walls to avoid being spotted. The fumes singed the tops of plants just outside the windows and partially bleached the plotters' hair, a development they explained to inquisitive family members and friends as the result of exposure to chlorine in a swimming pool.[56] Tanweer and Lindsay constructed the four bombs with 2 to 5 kilograms of concentrated hydrogen peroxide mixed with black pepper and hexamethylene triperoxide diamine, a high-explosive organic compound used as the initiator.[57] Unlike the Madrid bombers, they did not add nails or ball bearings to maximize fragmentation.

On June 28, Khan, Tanweer, and Lindsay conducted a reconnaissance trip to London and discussed how they would perpetrate the attacks.[58] They also scrambled to tie up loose ends. Germaine Lindsay had spent increasingly less time at home, and when he was there, he locked himself away in the computer room. His wife, who suspected that he was having an affair, confronted him about text messages on his cell phone and kicked him out of their three-bedroom house. "He left with a holdall and a bunch of door keys," she said. "I went to bed. Later that night I'm sure I heard him on the stairs and going into Abdullah's room," she continued. "He must have been there in the dead of night to kiss his little boy goodbye."[59]

Hasib Hussain's last few days were routine. On Monday, July 4, he told his mother that he was traveling to London in the next day or two. His mother saw him asleep in his room early on July 5, and again in the evening when she offered to make him sandwiches for the London trip. She again saw him asleep during the morning on July 6. At around 3:30 p.m., his sister-in-law caught a glimpse of him getting ready to go out after eating a bowl of cereal.

Shehzad Tanweer went to see some old school friends on the evening of July 4. On July 6 he played cricket in a local park until late in the evening and then returned home, saying he had lost his mobile phone. He was last seen at home just before midnight on July 6.[60]

Mohammad Sidique Khan had been away from his wife, Hasina Patel, for most of that week. On Tuesday, July 5, he took Patel to the hospital. "I'll see you later," he said. "I'll be back in a few hours." "He dropped me off at home," remarked Patel, "and that was the last time I saw him."[61]

At 3:58 a.m. on July 7, Khan, Tanweer, and Hussain departed from Leeds in a light blue Nissan Micra. An hour later they stopped at Woodall services on the M1 highway to fill up with gas. Closed-circuit television footage showed Tanweer nonchalantly walking into the gas station wearing a white T-shirt, dark jacket, white tracksuit bottoms, and a baseball cap. At 5:07, Germaine Lindsay pulled up to Luton station in a red Fiat Brava. During the ninety minutes or so before the others arrived, he got out of his car, entered the station, peered up at the departure board, and returned to his car. Again, closed-circuit television at the train station captured the events on camera.

At 6:49 a.m., Khan, Tanweer, and Hussain arrived at Luton and parked next to Lindsay's Fiat. They stepped out of their car and dug through their backpacks, double-checking the bombs. They hoisted the full backpacks as if they were going on a camping trip. At 7:15 the four men entered Luton station and walked through the turnstiles together. They were casually dressed and appeared relaxed. At 7:40 they boarded a train for London King's Cross Station. They stood out a bit from commuters because of their luggage and casual clothes, but not enough to cause suspicion. The train arrived at King's Cross at 8:23, slightly late because of a delay further up the line. The four men hugged and appeared happy, even exhilarated, according to eyewitnesses. They then split up.[62]

Khan boarded a westbound Circle Line train, Tanweer an eastbound Circle Line train, and Lindsay a southbound Piccadilly Line train on the Underground. At 8:50 a.m. the train carrying Shehzad Tanweer exploded. Forensic evidence suggested that Tanweer was sitting toward the back of the second carriage, with the backpack next to him on the floor. The blast killed 8 people, including Tanweer, and injured 171 others. At Edgware Road, Mohammad Sidique Khan was also in the second carriage from the front, most likely near the standing area by the first set of double doors. Shortly before the explosion he was seen fiddling with the top of the backpack. The explosion killed 7, including Khan, and injured 163 people. On the Piccadilly Line, Germaine Lindsay was in the first carriage as it traveled between King's Cross and Russell Square. The train was crowded, and forensic evidence suggested that the explosion occurred on or close to the floor of the standing area between the second and third set of seats. The explosion killed 27 people, including Lindsay, and injured more than 340.[63]

At 8:55 a.m., Hasib Hussain walked out of King's Cross Underground onto Euston Road. Telephone records show that he tried unsuccessfully to contact the three other bombers on his cell phone over the next few minutes. "I can't get on the Tube, what should I do?" he inquired.[64]

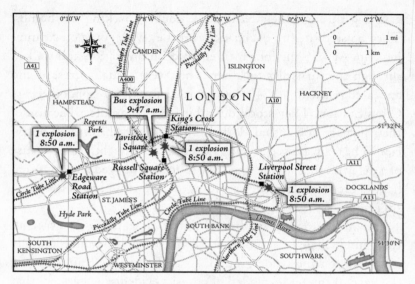

Figure 9: Map of London Bombings

Hussain's bomb had apparently malfunctioned, and now the trains had stopped because of the attacks. His demeanor over this period appears to have been relaxed and unhurried. Five minutes later he walked back into King's Cross Station, went into W. H. Smith on the concourse, and bought a nine-volt battery for the bomb. At 9:06 he walked into a McDonald's on Euston Road; he left about ten minutes later. He boarded a Number 91 bus traveling from King's Cross to Euston Station, looking nervous and pushing past people, and then switched to a Number 30 bus traveling eastward from Marble Arch. The bus was crowded following the closures on the Underground. Hussain sat on the upper deck, toward the back. Forensic evidence suggests that the bomb was next to him in the aisle or between his feet on the floor. He detonated the bomb at 9:47 a.m., killing 14 people and injuring more than 110.[65]

Liza Pulman had just left King's Cross on the Underground when her train was rocked by a huge explosion. The girl next to

Pulman grabbed her hand. Someone began to cry, saying, "Help us, Mary, mother of Jesus. Save us, Lord Jesus. Please save us."

Pulman tried to sit up, but the girl next to her squeezed her hand even tighter. "Oh God!" she screamed, beginning to sob. "What's happened? I'm so frightened, I'm so frightened."

"What's your name?" inquired Pulman.

"Michele," the girl said.

"It's okay, Michelle," Pulman responded, trying to console her. "We'll be okay."

"You're very calm," Michelle remarked.

"No I'm not," said Pulman. God, my heart's racing, Pulman thought to herself. What are we going to do? There are so many of us.[66]

Emergency responders reacted quickly, assisting the wounded and finding the dead in the intense heat and darkness, with hoards of rats, mangled wreckage, and body parts in the tunnels. The British set up a mortuary on the grounds of the Honourable Artillery Company, where they came across some of the first clues identifying Mohammad Sidique Khan as a suicide bomber, after combing through pocket litter.

Al Qa'ida leaders were jubilant about the attack. Al Jazeera aired a video statement from Ayman al-Zawahiri containing footage of Mohammad Sidique Khan. During the video, Khan praised Osama bin Laden, Abu Mus'ab al-Zarqawi, and Zawahiri.[67] In a second video, broadcast on September 19, Zawahiri went further, stating that al Qa'ida had helped launch the attacks: "London's blessed raid is one of the raids which Jama'at Qa'idat al-Jihad (Al Qaidah of Jihad Group) was honored to launch . . . In the Wills of the hero brothers, the knights of monotheism—may God have mercy on them, make paradise their final abode and accept their good deeds."[68]

In an extraordinary, and perhaps unprecedented, copycat attack, four bombers attempted attacks two weeks later, on July 21, at the Shepherd's Bush, Oval, and Warren Street Underground stations in London and on the top deck of a Number 26 bus traveling from Waterloo to Hackney. But the bombs malfunctioned. Although the trigger detonators created minor explosions, the main charges failed to detonate. No one was killed. A fifth device was recovered two days later, abandoned near Wormwood Scrubs in west London. Subsequent investigations by British authorities led to the arrest of five perpetrators. Material recovered from the July 21 attacks indicated that the detonators were made of triacetone triperoxide. The devices, unlike those of July 7, contained screws, bolts, and washers intended to produce fragmentation and maximize casualties.

The four bombers—Yasin Hassan Omar, Muktar Said Ibrahim, Ramzi Mohammed, and Osman Hussain—were quickly captured. They were an entirely separate cell of immigrants and British citizens originating from Somalia, Ethiopia, and Eritrea, with no known links to al Qa'ida. There were no forensic links between the July 7 and July 21 attacks. The difference in device construction and the explosive material recovered suggested that different bomb makers were involved in each of the attacks.

Cold Comfort

Al Qa'ida's second wave had now reached the UK. At 4 a.m. back in Washington, Director of National Intelligence John Negroponte's home phone rang, waking him up. It was Andy Card, President Bush's chief of staff.

"What the hell is going on in London?" Card asked.

What struck Negroponte, as it had the FBI's Art Cummings, was that these attacks were not conducted by Arabs. The perpetrators were British Pakistanis with British passports and easy access to the United States. "The game was changing," he later said. "And it was changing fast."[69]

For Cummings, the London attacks showed how extremists might plot a terrorist attack in the United States. Unlike the British population, which had become accustomed to several decades of Irish Republican Army attacks, the United States had seen far less terrorism. "Stopping [every] attack is not realistic," Cummings believed. "We will do everything we can, and we will succeed a large number of times. We won't win every one."[70]

The London attacks produced a strong reaction, but they did not bring down the government, as the attacks in Spain the previous year had done. Still, the British government was reminded that it faced a wave of terrorism from a small number of radicals affiliated with al Qa'ida. With conventional British forces in Iraq, there was also an increase of disaffected British Muslims. However, the bulk of the UK's Muslim population strongly condemned the attacks—and the attackers—as un-Islamic. Sir Iqbal Sacranie, secretary-general of the Muslim Council of Britain, sent a clear message: "There can never, ever be justification for killing civilians, full stop."[71]

Perhaps the most surprising condemnations came from the families of the bombers. Germaine Lindsay's wife, Samantha Lewthwaite, was eight months pregnant and had a seventeen-month-old child, Abdullah. Her husband's violent actions had destroyed her life. Ironically, the couple had first met face-to-face at a peace march in London. "He wanted to qualify as a human rights lawyer and I was a member of an Amnesty International group at school," she said. "We wanted to make a difference to the world by peaceful means.[72]

"When Jamal and I got married we were two peas in a pod and I thought I had found the world's best husband," she said. "Jamal is accountable for his actions 100 percent and I condemn with all my heart what he has done." But she and her children had to pay a heavy price for his atrocities. "The day will come," she glumly realized, "when I'll have to tell them what their father did."[73]

Hasib Hussain's family issued a collective statement denouncing the attacks. "Our thoughts," they wrote, "are with all the bereaved families and we have to live ourselves with the loss of our son in these difficult circumstances." They continued, "We had no knowledge of his activities and if we had, we would have done everything in our power to stop him."[74]

Shehzad Tanweer's uncle, Bashir Ahmed, said his family was "left shattered" by the young man's involvement in the attacks.[75]

Mohammad Sidique Khan's family was equally devastated. Police found a home video of Khan bidding farewell to his infant daughter several days before the attacks. He wore a bland white T-shirt and gently cradled his daughter in his arm as he repeatedly kissed her forehead. He spoke softly but with an air of self-confidence. "Sweetheart, not long to go now and I'm going to really, really miss you a lot," he said. "I'm thinking about it already. Look, I absolutely love you to bits and you have been the happiest thing in my life. You and your mum, absolutely brilliant. I don't know what else to say. I just wish I could have been part of your life, especially these growing up, these next months, they're really special with you learning to walk and things. I just so much wanted to be with you but I have to do this for our future and it will be for the best, inshallah, in the long run."[76]

Khan's wife, Hasina Patel, found little solace in his words. Khan had abandoned his responsibility as a father and a husband to kill civilians—including twenty-eight women—in an attack roundly condemned by Muslims, especially his own family members. She was left confused and vexed. "It has been really, really difficult," she acknowledged. "I can't believe people can do that kind of thing," she said. "How can you be so calculated and cold and not have any emotions, how can people do that?"[77]

Not long after the attacks, UK officials showed Patel a will that Khan had written. There were sections for his wife, daughter, family, and the general public, including funeral arrangements. Perhaps the most disconcerting part was the section for his wife. "I am really sorry for all the lies and deceit," Khan wrote. "I hope you can forgive me and I hope you can try to understand why I did what I did. You have tried to be a good wife but I have deceived you."[78]

He also left money for "the children," unaware that their unborn child had not survived.

Khan and Patel had once dreamed of helping British society by working with disadvantaged children. "We had the same sort of hopes and dreams," she recalled, fighting back tears and struggling to understand how it had all gone wrong.[79]

U.S. and British counterterrorism agencies now redoubled their efforts; all roads led back to Pakistan.

9

RESURGENCE IN PAKISTAN

Ayman al-Zawahiri fixed his eyes on the camera, paused slightly, and began to speak in a measured voice, almost a monotone. "Among those who have responded to this noble, divine call," he said, "is our brother Azzam the American, whom we ask Allah to count among those in whom is realized the statement of the truth, exalted is he."

Zawahiri, al Qa'ida's second-in-command, was dressed in a neatly pressed white shalwar kameez and turban and sat somewhat stiffly before the camera. His graying beard was tinged with white, and he peered through round spectacles, which gave him a cerebral, professorial aura. He spoke softly, angling his head to the right and occasionally rocking forward in his chair, appearing stilted in front of the camera. The video, which was released in September 2006 by As-Sahab Media, al Qa'ida's media wing, was unpretentious but professional. The producers juxtaposed Zawahiri's white garb, perhaps a symbol of religious purity, with a jet-black background and included lucid subtitles in English and Arabic. On the surface the video appeared no different from any of al Qa'ida's ubiquitous diatribes. But this was a paradigm shift. Zawahiri was directing the viewer's attention to an American, who was making an unusual plea for support.

"As our brother Azzam the American talks to you," Zawahiri continued, "he talks to you as one who is concerned about the fate which awaits his people and as a perceptive person who wishes to lead his people out of the darkness into the light." As Adam Gadahn, the American, later explained, "his people" referred to Americans, though he also directed the message at other Westerners and "unbelievers" as well.

"So listen," Zawahiri urged viewers, "because what he is talking to you about is serious and significant. He is talking to you about the fate which awaits every human, an extremely grave issue in which there is no joking, procrastination, or backtracking."

It was a remarkable moment. Al Qa'ida's deputy was lauding an American, inviting him to deliver a message for the organization. Gadahn, who was similarly outfitted in a starched white shalwar kameez and turban, sat in a room sparsely furnished with a Compaq computer monitor and leather-bound religious texts embroidered in gold. He spoke deliberately, though with more passion than Zawahiri, occasionally lifting his right hand for emphasis. He began with a standard al Qa'ida charge that the West, and the United States in particular, was guilty of barbarities against Muslims and others. Yet the purpose of his talk, he quickly clarified, was to invite Americans and other Westerners to join al Qa'ida.

Gadahn asked Americans to examine themselves. "I know that even the hearts of the most hardened of enemies can be softened if God so wills," he said, slowly tilting his head from side to side and occasionally stroking his beard. "I would like to devote this talk to making a heartfelt invitation to my religion, Islam. Islam, the religion of justice and charity, is for everyone, regardless of race, gender, or nationality."[1]

Gadahn was one of the few non-Arabs ever to appear on an al Qa'ida video. He was five feet, eleven inches tall and was slightly overweight at 200 pounds. He had a light complexion, hazel eyes, bushy eyebrows, and a reddish brown beard that was neatly trimmed.[2] Gadahn's lecture, simply titled "An Invitation to Islam," was full of the ordinary non sequiturs and historical embellishments that blight the reasoning of ideological zealots. He also spoke with the air of an Islamic religious scholar, or ulema, though he had no formal training and had only recently converted to Islam. Ironically, Gadahn's grandfather was a Jewish physician and his parents were both Christian, though not particularly religious. Nevertheless, he urged Americans and other Westerners to make a choice between good and evil, right and wrong.

"Why not surrender to the truth? Escape from the unbelieving army and join the winning side," he argued, sounding like a seasoned politician. "Time is running out, so make the right choice."[3]

The arrogance and self-confidence exuded by Zawahiri and Gadahn were striking. Al Qa'ida had rebounded from being an organization that was nearly eliminated after the September 11 attacks to being one buoyed by resistance to the war in Iraq and a second wave of attacks. More important, it had experienced an amazing resurgence in Pakistan.[4] The 2004 Madrid attacks, 2005 London bombings, and 2006 transatlantic airlines plot were either planned or facilitated by al Qa'ida operatives in Pakistan.

But who was this relatively obscure American? And how did he make his way from rural California to the savage mountains of Pakistan's Federally Administered Tribal Areas, the center of the revived al Qa'ida?

From Death Metal to Islam

Adam Gadahn was born on September 1, 1978, and grew up on a goat farm near Winchester, California, where his family raised between 150 and 200 goats for milk, cheese, and meat.[5] Winchester is a quaint agricultural community 70 miles southeast of Los Angeles. The San Gabriel, San Jacinto, and San Bernardino Mountains rise in the distance, home to creosote bushes, desert willow, scrub oak, and ironwood trees. To the east is the San Jacinto Fault, one of the most active earthquake epicenters in California. Gadahn's mother, Jennifer, and father, Phil, built a primitive cabin with no running water where they home-schooled Gadahn and his brother, Omar. Phil drove a rusty white pickup truck but stripped out most of the comfort items. "It was a stick-shift, headlight-switch-only affair, with gaping holes where radio, air conditioner, or glovebox might reside," recalled a family friend. "Even the window behind the driver between the bed and the cab was missing."[6]

Gadahn's childhood was iconoclastic and, as it turned out, prepared him for settling in the arid mountains along the Afghanistan-Pakistan border. His parents had few modern amenities, preferring a simple life for their children.

"He was very much a loner," said Carol Koltuniak, whose son was on the same Little League baseball team as Adam. Gadahn's family, which enjoyed playing board games together, came to every game and practice. "They seemed very happy in their lifestyle," she said.[7]

At age fifteen, Gadahn became interested in death metal, a musical genre that emerged in the 1980s, with ghastly named bands like Obituary, Morbid Angel, Necrophagia, and Cannibal Corpse. Death metal employed heavily distorted guitars, aggressive picking, growling vocals, and pounding drums. "Death metal was music that went farther than any before it in rejecting society in its whole and claiming that only death is real," explained Chris Blanc, who was in contact with Gadahn at the time and had a weekly radio show on KSPC 88.7, a Pomona College radio station. "No matter how much plastic you buy or paper that says you're important, death triumphs in the end; so maybe there should be a value to life outside the tangible?"[8] Gadahn's interest in death metal opened him up to songs filled with torture, necrophilia, mutilation, and other dark images, though he remained polite, even urbane, in his daily interactions.

"I remember him as a passionate, courteous, intelligent kid excited about life, but somewhat cowed by its unnecessary human-induced dark side, thus prone to listen to lots of quality death metal," said Chris Blanc. "Call it compassion, or call it empathy, but a lot of kids like Y. A. Gadahn resonated with me in spirit."[9]

In 1993, Gadahn contacted Jon Konrath, publisher of the

now-defunct death metal magazine *Xenocide*, to contribute album reviews and drawings. Gadahn's reviews were unsophisticated, though his writing exuded vibrancy. "Autopsy's newest and sickest!" Gadahn wrote in reference to an album by the group Autopsy; "18 tracks to mangle your mind. Although they have mostly been known for slow to mid-paced Doom/Death on their 4 previous releases, the bay area quartet crank it up to a good fast grind on many of these tunes, notably 'Tortured Moans of Agony,' 'Battery Acid Enema,' 'Blackness Within' and 'Skullptures.'"[10] After listening to a seven-song demo tape released by a group named Enraptured, he offered some guidance to record companies. "Pick up this demo for the 5 excellent bonus tracks," he wrote, "and ignore the 2 cheesy fag songs."[11]

At the time, Jon Konrath was at the University of Indiana and interacted with Gadahn through letters. "We never talked on the phone," he said later. "He wrote some stuff. He seemed pretty decent and a creative guy. I didn't do anything to change his copy. He did some drawings, too, just scribbled stuff."[12]

Gadahn became consumed with death metal and plastered posters and fliers of death metal bands on his bedroom walls. He also received letters from death metal fans around the world. Much of his correspondence involved sending and receiving music cassettes of new or up-and-coming bands that had not yet been signed to a music label. At one point he received so much mail that his parents rented a new post office box dedicated to his pen pals. Death metal was a fad for Gadahn, however, and his interest quickly waned.

"My entire life was focused on expanding my music collection," Gadahn later noted with some remorse. "I eschewed personal cleanliness and let my room reach an unbelievable state of disarray. My relationship with my parents became strained, although only intermittently so. I am sorry even as I write this."[13]

Gadahn was also exposed to media equipment during his teenage years, a bonus when he later became involved in al Qa'ida's propaganda operations. His aunt broadcast a public radio talk show focused on environmental issues, and he regularly visited the studio and assisted with pledge drives. In 1995 he finished home schooling and moved in with his grandparents, Carl and Agnes Pearlman, in a cozy house on North Westwood Avenue in Santa Ana. It was time to explore the world, he had decided. He used his grandmother's computer to surf the Internet, spending hours in America Online chat rooms. Gadahn also searched for religious information and frequented websites dedicated to Islam. Later that year he trekked to the Islamic Society of Orange County in Garden Grove, California, to learn more.

"I began to listen to the apocalyptic ramblings of Christian radio's 'prophecy experts,'" he wrote, but he was turned off by their conspiracy theories, support for Israel, and fiery preaching. He continued to ask questions and search for answers. "I suppose it was simply the need I was feeling to fill that void I had created for myself," he said.

It is not entirely clear what "void" Gadahn felt, but he was searching for a purpose in life and had experimented with death metal, Christianity, and Islam. In November 1995 he converted to Islam. "You see," he explained, "I discovered that the beliefs and practices of this religion fit my personal theology and intellect as well as basic human logic. As I began reading English translations of the Qur'an, I became more and more convinced of the truth and authenticity of Allah's teachings contained in those 114 chapters. I can't say when I actually decided that Islam was for me. It was really a natural progression."[14]

Radicalization

In the fall of 1996, Gadahn moved into a small apartment with a half-dozen other Muslims a block from the Islamic Society. He needed money and asked Haitham Bundakji, the mosque's chairman, for a job, and he soon began working as a security guard. That job did not last long. One night Bundakji stopped by at 2 a.m. to check on his staff and found Gadahn fast asleep. "So I let him go," Bundakji said.[15]

In 1997, Gadahn worked at a nongovernmental organization, Charity Without Borders, and came into contact with Khalil al-Deek, a Palestinian-born American citizen, and Hisham Diab, an Egyptian national. Deek, also known as Joseph Jacob Adams, had migrated to the United States in 1981 to complete his university studies in computer science. He would go on to work as an al Qa'ida facilitator and put together an electronic version of the *Encyclopedia of Jihad*, a manual created by Islamic radicals in Afghanistan in the 1980s that provided such information as how to build bombs.[16] Deek was arrested in connection with the 1999 millennium bomb plot, released from a Jordanian prison in 2001, and eventually killed in Pakistan in April 2005. He welcomed Gadahn into his circle and gave him a new identity, though mosque officials viewed this network with growing suspicion. "They were very rigid, cruel in talking to people," Bundakji said. "They were radicals, super-orthodox."[17] And it rubbed off on Gadahn. "He was becoming very extreme in his ideas and views," said Musammil Siddiqi, the society's religious director.[18]

In May 1997, Gadahn was arrested by Orange County police for assault and battery after attacking Bundakji; he later pleaded guilty.[19] He spent hours drinking tea and talking about religion in Diab's apartment, and he joined a discussion group led by Deek and Diab that met in offices and apartments. They avoided the Islamic Society in Garden Grove because of security concerns.[20] Gadahn quickly began to show signs of radicalization, following a pattern observed in other cases. "This stage, which is largely influenced by both internal and external factors," concluded a New York Police Department intelligence report on radicalization, "marks the point where the individual begins to explore Salafi Islam, while slowly migrating away from their former identity—an identity that now is re-defined by Salafi philosophy, ideology, and values."[21]

In 1998, Gadahn took a camping trip with Deek and several others to the Mojave Desert, an expansive area that covers more than 25,000 square miles in southeastern California and portions of Nevada, Utah, and Arizona. Camping was a common practice among Western militant networks, including the one led by Mohammad Sidique Khan in England. It is unclear what they did during the trip, but the conditions approximated the isolation and harsh environment of an extremist training camp, which promote team building, physical fitness, and indoctrination.

When Gadahn returned, he visited his parents in Winchester. He insisted on staying in a tent on their property, even though there was snow on the ground, and hunted and killed a rabbit on the farm using a stone. His parents began to notice an alarming transformation in his disposition and outlook. He had become concerned about the plight of Muslims in the world and the need to fight back. This marked another step in his acceptance of the al Qa'ida worldview. "The factors of radicalization," noted a report by the Canadian Security Intelligence Service, "include a belief in the need to defend Islam from perceived aggression by the West, influence from a spiritual leader, influence from a radicalized family member, and attending overseas training."[22]

Gadahn increasingly fit this profile. But he bristled at the assertion that he was duped into radicalization. In response to a later article titled "Azzam the American" written by Raffi Khatchadourian for *The New Yorker*, Gadahn wrote an animated letter and an e-mail to the magazine protesting several assertions. *The New Yorker* passed the letter to the FBI and declined to publish it. Gadahn was incensed by quotes saying that Khalil al-Deek and Hisham Diab treated him like "their new pet" and chided him for wearing jeans. "No one—and I mean no one—told me to stop wearing jeans," Gadahn wrote, "chiefly because I never wore them in the first place, whether before or after my conversion to Islam.

On the contrary, Hisham and Khalil would often wear rather tight Levis, much to my dislike."

He also objected to the implication that he was acting as "their little rabbit," endlessly doing chores at their behest. "As for my supposed running of errands for them, that too is patently false," he argued. "I purchased the $800 Audi with my own money for my own personal use, paid my share of the rent for whatever apartment I was sharing when I wasn't staying with my grandparents, and paid back the money which I had borrowed for my first trip to Afghanistan by working—I repeat, working—for Charity Without Borders."[23]

The FBI believed that Gadahn sent the letter, which was signed "Adam Gadahn, Member, Qaida Al Jihad Organization," from a computer in Lahore, Pakistan. In 1997, Gadahn had traveled to Pakistan and Afghanistan "to live in an Islamic country and to witness Islam in its heartland."[24] While there, he did not maintain regular contact with his family. Using the nom de guerre Abu Suhayb al-Amriki, Gadahn was introduced to al Qa'ida operative Abu Zubaydah at the Azzam Media Center in Peshawar by Khalil al-Deek. Zubaydah sent Gadahn to the Khaldan training camp in Afghanistan, where he underwent weapons training. Gadahn interacted with militant networks, including al Qa'ida, and became increasingly devoted to violent jihad. In e-mail communications with family members, he discussed political matters and revealed a strong distaste for the U.S. government. He also requested $500 for normal living expenses.[25]

Gadahn returned to California after becoming ill with a parasitic disease. His family and friends barely recognized him. He had grown a long black beard, dressed in a shalwar kameez, ate only halal meals (food that is permissible according to Islamic law), and was uncharacteristically concerned about his personal security. He was vague about his trip to Pakistan and Afghanistan when talking to his parents, and never mentioned the names of individuals he had met or the places where he had stayed. At his grandfather's birthday party, he strongly objected when a family member attempted to take his photograph.

Unlike other radicalized individuals, such as Abdulla Ahmed Ali, José Padilla, and Mohammad Sidique Khan, Gadahn did not appear to be developing into a fighter. He never completed military training and was more of a scholar than an operative. Abu Zubaydah and other al Qa'ida leaders had recommended that he assist in translations and narrate films and videos, since he had an "authoritative voice" and spoke excellent English and Arabic.[26] "Abu Suhayb was not an operative," said Khalid Sheikh Mohammed, using Gadahn's nom de guerre, "was not ready for martyrdom, was merely a translator and a scholar, and was a Salafi, not a mujahid."[27]

Red with Blood

In 2000, Gadahn told his parents he was returning to Pakistan and would probably not be coming back. After he left, his family did not hear from him again for a year, but then he phoned from Pakistan. His parents told him that the FBI was asking about him and had seized a computer owned by Khalil al-Deek that Gadahn had left at the house. He called his family again in 2002 and told them it was the first time he had spoken English in a long time, that he had married an Afghan woman and they were expecting a child. By this time U.S. intelligence agencies were concerned that Gadahn posed a serious threat to U.S. security. While he was not a senior al Qa'ida operative—at least not yet—he had associated with al Qa'ida leaders, including Abu Zubaydah and Khalid Sheikh Mohammed. He appeared particularly close to Abu Zubaydah.

In May 2004 the FBI sent out a "Be on the lookout" (BOLO) warning for Gadahn because of his association with al Qa'ida and his increasingly anti-American rhetoric.[28] Several months later, al Qa'ida's media wing released a video in which Gadahn warned of impending violence. Wearing glasses, with his head wrapped in a kaffiyeh, he spouted phrases and themes similar to those from his death metal days. "People of America," he said, wagging his finger at the camera and cradling an AK-47 in his left arm, "I remind you of the weighty words of our leaders Sheik Osama bin Laden and Doctor Ayman al-Zawahiri that what took place on September eleventh was but the opening salvo of the global war on America. The streets of America shall run red with blood. Casualties will be too many to count and the next wave of attacks may come at any moment."[29]

In September 2005, Gadahn offered a similar warning on another As-Sahab video. "Yesterday, London and Madrid," he thundered. "Tomorrow, Los Angeles and Melbourne, Allah willing."[30] In the video, Gadahn's face was largely covered with a black turban and scarf, though his eyes, his forehead, and the bridge of his nose were still visible. The FBI Laboratory reviewed the videotape and, using several forensic techniques, identified him as Gadahn. The FBI also presented the videotape to some of Gadahn's relatives and captured al Qa'ida leaders, including Khalid Sheikh Mohammed, Ramzi bin al-Shibh, and Majid Khan, for help in identification.

In 2006, Gadahn was indicted in the Central District of California for treason and material support to al Qa'ida and the U.S. government offered a $1 million reward for his capture.[31] He was the first person to be charged with treason in the United States since the 1950s, when Tomoya Kawakita was convicted of treason and deported to Japan.[32] Gadahn would eventually become a deputy for Abu Yahya al-Libi, the head of al Qa'ida's media shura, and he continued to release propaganda videos promising bloodshed in the United States.

Gadahn had settled in Pakistan's Federally Administered Tribal Areas, where al Qa'ida leaders were experiencing a breathtaking run of success. The area was key to this new wave of activity. Its jagged limestone mountain ranges, cavernous gorges, sparse population, and parched landscape make it inhospitable terrain and, rather unsurprisingly, an ideal place for sanctuary. The area has a haunting, isolated feel. "The quietness of the place is uncanny," wrote T. E. Lawrence, better known as Lawrence of Arabia, during a short visit in the 1920s; "no birds or beasts except a jackal concert for five minutes about ten p.m."[33]

For Philip Mudd, who had moved from the CIA to the FBI, the ability of terrorists to establish overseas connections had a multiplier effect. "Their operational security capabilities are often better than those of purely homegrown terrorists," he concluded. Part of the reason was that the individuals they interacted with had developed sophisticated countersurveillance and counterintelligence capabilities just to survive. "In short," he noted to colleagues, "counterintelligence improves when they go overseas."[34]

From 2003 to 2005, when the United States was engrossed by Iraq, the tribal areas were largely ignored. With al Qa'ida's resurgence, however, the U.S. government began to take increasing notice.

Al Qa'ida's Resurgence

On January 13, 2006, an MQ-1 Predator drone flown by the CIA honed in on a target in Damadola, Pakistan. Powered by a Rotax engine, the Predator can fly up to 400 nautical miles to a target and loiter overhead for fourteen hours, performing surveillance or launching an attack before returning to its base. Damadola consists of a cluster of villages amid the narrow valleys and swelling rivers of the Hindu Kush, along Pakistan's border with Afghanistan.

"Osama bin Laden was like a ghost," said one CIA operative working in the region.[35] But U.S. intelligence agencies had somewhat better luck with Ayman al-Zawahiri. In search of Zawahiri, they had contacted human sources and conducted communications intercepts. But Zawahiri was wily. He moved regularly among a trusted network of safe houses and shunned satellite and cell phones, making it difficult to get precise information on his location—what intelligence analysts called "actionable information." In this case, however, U.S. agencies received intelligence that several senior al Qa'ida officials, possibly even Zawahiri, were attending a meeting. Mixed into the group were militants from the radical Sunni group Tehreek-e-Nafaz-e-Shariat-e-Mohammadi (TNSM), whose leader, Faqir Mohammed, had publicly declared his affinity for al Qa'ida. CIA operatives in Pakistan requested that Predators be moved to the area immediately. TNSM officials with known ties to al Qa'ida, communications intercepts, and reliable human intelligence all pointed to the attendance of key figures. So the CIA took action. Hellfire missiles pounded the meeting houses and their *hujras* (guesthouses), badly damaging them.

"I ran out and saw planes," said Shah Zaman, a resident of Damadola. "I ran toward a nearby mountain with my wife. When we were running we heard three more explosions and I saw my home being hit. The houses have been razed," Shah Zaman explained. "There is nothing left. Pieces of the missiles are scattered all around. Everything has been blackened in a 100-yard radius."[36]

Zawahiri was not there. But the strike still killed several fighters, including Zawahiri's son-in-law, Abdul Rahman al-Maghribi. Several weeks later, Zawahiri responded in a video. "The U.S. aircraft, with the collusion of traitor Musharraf and his security services, the slaves of the Crusaders and Jews, have launched an attack on the village of Damadola in the Bajaur district," he taunted, "on the pretext of seeking to kill my weak person and four of my brothers."[37]

Despite missing Zawahiri, U.S. intelligence agencies increasingly focused their collection efforts on Pakistan's tribal areas. In 2001 and 2002 the CIA and special operations forces had pursued al Qa'ida out of Afghanistan. By 2003 many high-ranking al Qa'ida leaders were situated in Pakistan's settled areas. By 2004 those who remained moved to the Federally Administered Tribal Areas. A few, such as Zawahiri, traveled north to Bajaur Agency and other parts of the North West Frontier Province. But the vast majority of the CIA's intelligence efforts focused on North Waziristan.

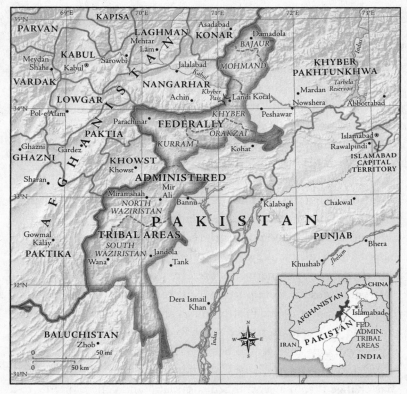

Figure 10: Map of the Federally Administered Tribal Areas

The CIA had identified dozens of compounds in North Waziristan with ties to al Qa'ida operatives. The large Taliban training camps housed a substantial number of fighters and looked almost like military bases, but al Qa'ida structures were very different. Operatives tended to stay inside small compounds, except perhaps at night, rarely wandering outside in daylight for fear they were being monitored—which they were. These camps focused on bomb making, assassination, and small-scale ambushes rather than fighting an insurgency. In addition to occupying North Waziristan, al Qa'ida and other militant groups scattered their training camps across the border region in places like Malakand, which the 2005 London bombers visited.

Still, the CIA was handicapped in Pakistan. It had a small number of Predator orbits and a small number of case officers. Most of its resources, including personnel, had been pushed to Iraq. Al Qa'ida had taken full advantage. A National Intelligence Estimate reported that "the group has protected or regenerated key elements of its Homeland attack capability, including: a safe haven in the Pakistan Federally Administered Tribal Areas (FATA), operational lieutenants, and its top leadership."[38]

Yet al Qa'ida was a notably different organization from the one that had existed on September 11, 2001. By 2006 it had decentralized. Some CIA analysts had begun calling it a "complex adaptive system."[39] The term refers to systems that are diverse, comprise multiple networks, and possess the capacity to evolve and learn from experience. Multiple networks represent perhaps the most important element. These networks are often dispersed and small, but different nodes can communicate and coordinate their campaigns. Terrorism expert Bruce Hoffman has argued that al Qa'ida at this time was "in the main flatter, more linear, and more organizationally networked" than it had been.[40] "The organizational structure of AQ and its affiliates," one Canadian intelligence report asserted, "has changed from a centralized command and control model to a decentralized and loosely tied system. It has been transformed into more of a global movement, which incorporates hundreds of groups or networks and thousands of individuals."[41]

For Philip Mudd, who had become deputy director of the FBI's National Security Branch in 2005, the intelligence picture suggested that al Qa'ida consisted of three tiers. The first included core, or central, al Qa'ida.[42] Despite the capture of key al Qa'ida figures such as Khalid Sheikh Mohammed and Abu Zubaydah, the core leadership included many old faces, including Osama bin Laden and Ayman al-Zawahiri.[43]

"Al Qa'ida's goal is to return the war to a direct conflict between the entire Muslim *ummah* and the United States," remarked al Qa'ida operative Abu Faraj al-Libi around this time. The group's strategy would also be characterized by the "use of affiliated mujahideen groups as proxies to pin the United States down in Iraq, Afghanistan, and elsewhere."[44]

Much of al Qa'ida's founding core was scattered across Pakistan, with a smaller contingent, such as Saif al-Adel, in Iran. Other senior al Qa'ida leaders in Pakistan, who had replaced those captured or killed by U.S. and Pakistani forces, included Abu Faraj al-Libi, director of operations; Hamza Rabi'a, chief of external operations; Abd al-Rahman al-Muhajir, a senior operational coordinator; Shaykh Sa'id al-Masri, al Qa'ida's general manager; Atiyah Abd al-Rahman al-Libi, Shaykh Sa'id's deputy; Abu Layth al-Libi, a senior military commander; and Abd al-Hadi al-Iraqi, a senior military commander. While still a midlevel official, Adam Gadahn had worked his way up in al Qa'ida's hierarchy, translating propaganda material and occasionally surfacing on videos.

CIA operatives in Pakistan concluded that most of the organization could not directly contact their senior leaders, especially Osama bin Laden, because of security concerns. Still, CIA officials watched with alarm as al Qa'ida gradually became better integrated into local networks in towns like Mir Ali, where many had intermarried with the population and developed close personal relationships with the natives. A key piece in taking down al Qa'ida, then, was to understand those personal relationships.

Mudd's second tier comprised the affiliated groups. These groups benefited from bin Laden's financial assistance and inspiration and received at least some direct training, arms, money, or other support from central al Qa'ida. In some cases, like Abu Mus'ab al-Zarqawi's al Qa'ida in Iraq, these groups also sent money that they had raised from donations, kidnappings, and other activities back to al Qa'ida central. In addition to al Qa'ida in Iraq, there were several affiliated groups by 2006, including the Libyan Islamic Fighting Group, Jaish-e-Mohammad, Islamic Movement of Uzbekistan, and others in Asia, Africa, and the Middle East. These relationships allowed al Qa'ida to bloom into a wide global network. As one U.S.

intelligence assessment warned, "Other affiliated Sunni extremist organizations, such as Jemaah Islamiya, Ansar al-Sunnah, and several North African groups, unless countered, are likely to expand their reach and become more capable of multiple and/or mass-casualty attacks outside their traditional areas of operation."[45]

Mudd's third tier consisted of like-minded individuals. They had no direct contact with al Qa'ida central but were inspired by the al Qa'ida cause and outraged by perceived oppression in Iraq, Afghanistan, Chechnya, and Palestinian territory. Examples included cells arrested in Oregon and Virginia in October 2002 and June 2003, respectively. Without direct support, these groups tended to be amateurish, though they could occasionally be lethal. In November 2004, for example, a member of the Hofstad Group in the Netherlands, Mohammed Bouyeri, murdered the Dutch filmmaker Theo Van Gogh in Amsterdam.[46]

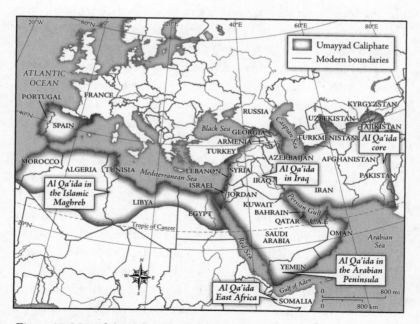

Figure 11: Map of al Qa'ida in 2006 and the Umayyad Caliphate (A.D. 661–750)

Altogether, al Qa'ida had transformed itself by 2006 into a global terror network. While the Afghanistan-Pakistan border region was its home base, it had a growing array of allied groups and networks on several continents. Al Qa'ida's strategy was to expand into areas once part of the caliphate: Iraq, North Africa, East Africa, the Arabian Peninsula, and even Spain. As al Qa'ida expanded into other regions, however, the Pakistani government's response began to waver.

Pakistan's Efforts

Al Qa'ida's second wave was aided by Pakistan's inability to clear al Qa'ida's sanctuary. Between 2004 and 2006, Pakistani security forces, with U.S. support, conducted nearly two dozen major operations against militants but with minimal effects. In March 2004, Pakistani forces launched Operation Kalosha II, a thirteen-day cordon-and-search effort across a 22-square-mile area west of Wana, South Waziristan. The area had come under the command of several local militants who were suspected of harboring al Qa'ida and other foreign fighters.[47] Pakistan employed Frontier Corps and the XI Corps, based in Peshawar, and sent them into the raids under the command of Lieutenant General Muhammad Safdar Hussain.

On March 16, Frontier Corps forces surrounded three fortress-like houses in Kalosha village, 10 miles west of Wana. One was owned by Nek Muhammad, a charismatic young Waziri tribal leader who served as a commander for al Qa'ida and the Islamic Movement of Uzbekistan. Nek Muhammad was an upstart jihadist born in 1975. Just three years older than Adam Gadahn, he had a youthful handsomeness, a thick black beard, and long, wavy hair. But it was his extraordinary confidence and tribal mien that catapulted him to power in South Waziristan. "Nek never had an intellectual mind but some other traits of his personality became evident during his stay at the Darul Uloom," a madrassa in Waziristan, recalled one of his teachers. "He showed himself to be a hard-headed boy, endowed with an impenetrable soul and an obstinate determination to carry out his will no matter how mindless it might be."[48]

At 6:30 a.m., Pakistani forces burst in to the house of Nek Muhammad and the others. Militants from the Ahmadzai Wazir tribe threw a siege around the Frontier Corps' outer cordon, and fighting ensued. By the end of the day, fifteen Frontier Corps and one Pakistan Army soldier had been killed and fourteen others had been taken hostage. The militants also damaged or destroyed roughly a dozen army trucks, as well as pickups, armored personnel carriers, and light artillery. The cordon drawn around Kalosha and the surrounding villages failed to contain the militants, some of whom dispersed through a network of tunnels, which later proved to be full of high-tech gear. Pakistan had initially deployed seven hundred soldiers, but by March 19 roughly seven thousand army and Frontier Corps troops were battling militants at several locations in a 30-square-mile stretch south and west of Wana. The operation also involved more than a dozen Cobra helicopters and Pakistan Air Force fighter jets.

On March 26, Lieutenant General Safdar Hussain declared victory: "We have accomplished the mission that was given to us."[49] This was an overstatement. During Operation Kalosha II, Pakistani forces killed a number of local and foreign fighters and disrupted a major al Qa'ida command center. But they also triggered numerous attacks against Pakistan Army and Frontier Corps bases and failed to capture or kill al Qa'ida fighters in the area.[50] The Pakistan Army also demolished a number of houses and used private residences as fortifications and barracks. Some locals were enraged at such scorched-earth tactics.[51] As one local lamented, "The army took away everything from my house: jewelry, clothes, toiletries, even pillow covers and shoe polish."[52]

Over the next several years, with Frontier Corps and army casualties mounting, Pakistan pursued several peace deals. In March

2004 it signed the Shakai Agreement, under which Pakistan Army troops agreed not to interfere with locals and to stay in their cantonment areas, insurgents would not attack Pakistani government personnel or infrastructure, and all foreigners would have to register themselves with the government.[53] The deal compensated the militants for their losses and did not require them to compensate their victims. Weapons were not "surrendered," but some were "offered" to the military as a token, ceremonial gesture.[54]

The most troubling aspect, however, was the way the army reached the deal. The Pakistani officials met Nek Muhammad at a Deobandi madrassa, the Jamia Arabia Ahsanul Madaris. This was viewed by locals as a tacit surrender by the army. Indeed, Lieutenant General Safdar Hussain, decked out in his uniform, bestowed a garland on Nek Muhammad, exchanged gifts with him, and called him "brother."[55] Donning a tribal headdress, he addressed the assembled tribesmen and condemned U.S. operations in Afghanistan, noting that no Afghan pilots had been involved in the September 11 attacks.[56]

Nek Muhammad characterized the transaction as an army surrender. "I did not go to them, they came to my place," he boasted. "That should make it clear who surrendered to whom."[57] Confident in his victory, he soon violated the agreement, and he was killed in June 2004 by a U.S. missile strike near Wana.[58]

Over the next few years, Pakistan scrambled to broker peace deals in the tribal areas. In September 2006 the governor of the North West Frontier Province, Lieutenant General (ret.) Ali Mohammad Jan Orakzai, reached an agreement in Miramshah, North Waziristan, with a group of tribal elders. As part of the agreement, militants promised that they would stop conducting attacks against the Afghan and Pakistani governments, halt targeted killings of progovernment *maliks* (tribal chiefs), and refrain from imposing their Taliban lifestyle on others by force. Like many previous efforts, however, the deal had the opposite effect from the intended one. Militant groups invoked the power of the treaty to increase their control. Less concerned than the Pakistanis about pleasing the Americans, they allowed al Qa'ida officials to settle in the tribal areas, including Adam Gadahn, who had moved to North Waziristan.

For many locals, this development was distressing. "There have been more kidnappings, robberies and murders since then as the Khasadar force—a ragtag, untrained tribal force left to man the posts—has neither the teeth nor the wherewithal to rein in the militants or control crime," reported one local assessment. "There is growing evidence that militants are now more assertive than they were before the September 5 agreement."[59]

The same challenges existed in South Waziristan, where the Pakistan Army launched Operation Zalzala. The operation's goal was to clear areas in South Waziristan held by militants loyal to Baitullah Mehsud.[60] As his name suggested, Baitullah Mehsud belonged to the Mehsud tribe. He was short, at around five feet, four inches, with shoulder-length black hair and a dark beard the length of a fist. His beard was patchy and unkempt, and he was a regular user of snuff. Baitullah Mehsud was also a cagey and charismatic leader, whose activities landed him on *Time* magazine's list of the one hundred most influential individuals in 2008. "He nearly routed the Pakistani Army from the country's embattled northwest frontier province," wrote *Time*, "establishing himself as an icon of global jihad—not unlike his idol, fellow Pashtun Mullah Omar."[61] Unlike other tribal leaders, Mehsud was young, uneducated, and hailed from a weak clan; his family reportedly made their living driving trucks.

In May 2007, Frontier Corps and units from the Special Services Group raided a foreign fighter training camp in Zarga Khel, North Waziristan. In August 2007 more than two hundred Pakistani security forces were abducted in South Waziristan. Baitullah Mehsud conducted a relentless suicide bombing campaign, in cooperation with allied Pashtun and Punjabi militants. Some U.S. and Pakistani intelligence assessments concluded that Baitullah

Mehsud's network assassinated Benazir Bhutto in December 2007, with help from al Qa'ida.[62]

Operation Kalosha II, Zalzala, and other Pakistani campaigns ultimately failed to clear South Waziristan and other parts of the tribal areas of al Qa'ida and foreign militants, much to the consternation of U.S. officials. Pakistan conducted sweeps and searches and occasionally engaged in bloody battles, but none of the operations employed enough forces to hold territory. The government's initiatives were hindered by conservative religious parties operating in the tribal areas, who considered Pakistani operations an extension of the American war. The peace deals also failed to achieve their objective. As President Pervez Musharraf eventually acknowledged, "We thought if we reached an agreement, that would be the end of it; they will suppress it to peaceful means. Well, it proved wrong, because the people who got involved on the other side, they double-crossed. While they carried on with their own activities, the army, in fact, became a little complacent that we have reached an agreement. Then we reactivated the same process again. With hindsight one can see, well, that didn't prove to be correct."[63]

U.S. intelligence agencies agreed. "Pakistan's border with Afghanistan remains a haven for al-Qaida's leadership and other extremists," warned a Defense Intelligence Agency assessment. "In a September accord with the Pakistan government, North Waziristan tribes agreed to curtail attacks into Afghanistan, cease attacks on Pakistani forces and expel foreign fighters. However, the tribes have not abided by most terms of the agreement."[64] A Pakistan Ministry of Interior document briefed to President Musharraf and discussed at a Pakistan National Security Council meeting was even more alarming: "Talibanisation has not only unfolded potential threats to our security, but is also casting its dark shadows over FATA and now in the settled areas adjoining the tribal belt. The reality is that it is spreading . . . There is a general policy of appeasement towards the Taliban, which has further emboldened them," it concluded. "Time is of the essence. We must act before it is too late."[65]

Swords into Plowshares

CIA maps of Pakistan showed several sanctuaries, including in Bajaur, South Waziristan, and North Waziristan. It was a boon for al Qa'ida operatives, including Adam Gadahn. While the American-born Gadahn was not a senior al Qa'ida leader, his expanded freedom of movement in Pakistan showcased al Qa'ida's resurgence. Yet Gadahn was controversial. On one jihadist website, Al-Qawl al-Fasl Net, several users posted brooding messages about him.

"Who is Adam Yahya Gadahn?" wrote one participant, calling himself Kuluna Junud. "His real name is Adam Pearlman. As his name indicates, he is a Jew and the grandson of Karl Pearlman, a fanatical Jewish supporter of Zionism."

"Of course, Adam Gadahn is a part of the Zionist media element that hates Islam," responded Muhammad Daghidi. "He is a Mossad player."[66]

Even senior FBI and CIA officials had trouble taking Gadahn too seriously. "He came across as an amateur," remarked Philip Mudd. "He had no theological credibility."[67]

For Adam Gadahn's family, his gradual rise in al Qa'ida was heartbreaking. Gadahn's aunt, Nancy Pearlman, described her nephew as inquisitive and quick to learn languages. "He was raised to be religious, to believe in a God," Pearlman said outside her Los Angeles home. "He made his own choice. We all make our own choices in life."[68]

"Our family are strong believers in nonviolence," she went on. "We are strong believers in peace."[69] Gadahn's father, Phil Pearlman, was a musician whose music had an easygoing California folk-rock psychedelic feel, with traces of Neil Young and the Grateful Dead.

For his album *Relatively Clean Rivers*, Phil inscribed the following lines on the jacket, an appeal to turn swords into plowshares:

Hoping we can all get together, the Arabs and the Jews,
And melt down weapons into water sprinklers,
Tractors, shovels and hoes,
Irrigation pipes

Despite Phil's pleas for peace, his son had moved in the opposite direction.

Back in Washington, some U.S. agencies, including the FBI, were still struggling to adapt to a new era. After joining the Bureau, Philip Mudd had pitched a program called Domain Management, designed to encourage agents to move beyond chasing criminal cases and to think more strategically about intelligence. Drawing on commercial marketing software and other technologies, Domain Management was designed to help the FBI remain ahead of the threats it faced. In February 2006, Mudd pitched the concept to top FBI officials from across the nation. He displayed a map of the San Francisco area with data showing where Iranian immigrants were clustered and where an FBI unit was "hunting."[70] Some officials found Mudd's concept vague and indicative of ethnic and religious profiling, and mocked him as a highbrow, white-collar CIA operative. Arresting bad guys, Mudd had warned, was sometimes less important than collecting intelligence to uncover the next terrorism plot. Such strategic efforts were badly needed now.

Mudd had other concerns with the FBI. "The big problems I see," he said "are not ones that the media talks about," such as improving the FBI's intelligence capabilities and changing its culture. The FBI had decades of experience, he believed, collecting and analyzing intelligence to take down criminal organizations and domestic terrorist groups. But "I see problems in training," he said. "I see problems of resources, how we pay for technology."

There were also challenges in coordinating efforts across the

FBI's vast bureaucracy. "When you're talking about fifty-six field offices, four-hundred-plus regional agencies, a dispersed organization in fifty states and forty-plus elements overseas, that's a daunting prospect."[71] Officials like Art Cummings and Philip Mudd knew they would need a new strategy to counter al Qa'ida's rise. The overthrow of the Taliban regime had shown the effectiveness of shifting to a clandestine strategy from a conventional approach, especially in Iraq. The United States had to alter its strategy again, and Iraq was a good place to start.

10

THE TIDE TURNS IN IRAQ

THE PHONE RANG. It was Sheikh Abdul Sattar Abu Risha, and he was calling from the Iraqi city of Ramadi.

Located 65 miles west of Baghdad on an alluvial plain in Anbar Province, Ramadi is bordered by the Euphrates River as it flows south to the Persian Gulf. Date orchards and farms dot the riverbanks, where local tribes have controlled the smuggling routes for centuries. It was September 2006, and the suffocating summer heat, which had reached a sweltering 118 degrees the month before, was finally beginning to break. But fighting was tearing the city apart. Ramadi had lost entire city blocks, with some structures reduced to rubble and rows of half-charred, pockmarked buildings lining the streets. Denizens boarded up squat storefronts, stifling economic activity, and fled. U.S. soldiers had anointed Ramadi the "heart of darkness" after swaths of the city had fallen under the effective control of al Qa'ida.

The phone call was for Sheikh Wissam Abd al-Ibrahim al-Hardan al-Aethawi. He came from one of the most respected families in Anbar and Salah ad-Din Provinces and was the head of Iraqi tribal affairs in Anbar for Saddam Hussein. Sheikh Wissam lived in a small village about 45 miles from Ramadi.

"Hello?" he said.

"Please," Abdul Sattar started, "I want you to come to Anbar."

Wissam paused. "What do you have in mind?" he inquired skeptically.

Abdul Sattar wanted him to participate in a meeting.

"I do not wish to attend any conferences, because they are to no avail," replied Wissam.[1]

No, Abdul Sattar retorted, it was not a conference. It was more important than that, he said. It was time to fight back.

Al Qa'ida, which officially referred to itself in Iraq as Tanzim Qa'idat al-Jihad fi Bilad al-Rafidayn (al Qa'ida in the Land between the Two Rivers), had become a growing threat to sheikhs such as Abdul Sattar, Wissam, and their tribes, killing off a disturbing number of their peers and forcing others to flee to Jordan, Syria, the United Arab Emirates, and other neighboring countries. Abdul Sattar could be persuasive, though he was the leader of only a small tribe, the Albu Risha. Born in 1971, he had a wiry build, a well-groomed goatee, a scarred nose, and several noticeable moles on the left side of his face. He was a maverick, carrying around a Colt .44 revolver in a leather holster tucked away under his gold-braided robes. Along with the renegade image, Abdul Sattar had indefatigable, contagious charm. He hosted people at his fortresslike compound on the outskirts of Ramadi; Iraqis frequently stayed at his guesthouse. He had an innate ability to connect with people, bringing them into his circle of trust.[2]

Wissam eventually relented and trekked to Ramadi with a host of other sheikhs. When he arrived, Abdul Sattar greeted him. "We are victorious by the God of al-Kaaba," he said, referring to the Kaaba, the small shrine near the center of the Great Mosque in Mecca, Saudi Arabia, the most sacred site in Islam.

Wissam asked him to get to the point.

"We have a huge undertaking," Abdul Sattar replied. He then paused. "I want to fight al Qa'ida," he said. The words hung in the air.

"How many do you have?" Wissam inquired.

"I have seven thousand," responded Abdul Sattar.

Wissam chuckled. He calculated that Abdul Sattar had per-haps seventy, but certainly not seven thousand. Still, he remained respectful: "Your seventy *would* be considered as seven thousand."[3]

A few days later, on September 9, 2006, Abdul Sattar orga-nized a tribal council, attended by more than fifty sheikhs, at which he declared the start of the Sahawa al-Anbar—the Anbar Awak-ening—a movement in which a cadre of determined sheikhs and their supporters came together to fight al Qa'ida. They risked their reputations, their kinsmen, and ultimately their own blood to fight a group that was beheading opponents and slaughtering innocents. The council was a culmination of months of work by U.S. soldiers such as Lieutenant Colonel Tony Deane and Lieutenant Colonel Jim Lechner, CIA operatives, and U.S. Marine forces.

The decline of al Qa'ida in Iraq and the end of the second wave cannot be reduced to a discrete moment or a single individ-ual, including Sattar. Instead, the Anbar Awakening was a result of tribal uprisings throughout the province that had started as early as 2003, had initially been suppressed, but had gathered new momentum by 2006.[4] Al Qa'ida in Iraq had increasingly turned to a punishment strategy, which severely undermined its support base and triggered a revolt among Anbar's tribal sheikhs. But the sheikhs were not alone. A group of Americans came to their aid. Members of the U.S. Army's 1st Brigade of the 1st Armored Divi-sion, Marines from the I and II Marine Expeditionary Force, CIA operatives, U.S. special operations forces, and a host of agencies provided intelligence, firepower, and ultimately trust in the Iraqis to stand up for themselves. In contrast to some accounts of the Iraq war, which credit the U.S. military "surge" in January 2007 as the turning point, a closer look at the decline of al Qa'ida in Iraq indi-cates that America's most significant contribution was clandestine and preceded the surge.

A Cause Célèbre

For senior U.S. policymakers, Iraq was a mess. U.S. intelligence reported that the "Iraq conflict has become the 'cause célèbre' for jihadists, breeding a deep resentment of U.S. involvement in the Muslim world and cultivating supporters for the global jihadist movement."[5] At the FBI, senior officials like Art Cummings were monitoring al Qa'ida's strategy of using the Iraq war for raising funds, recruiting operatives, and distributing propaganda. Virtually every major terrorist plot in the United States and Europe involved someone who had been radicalized because of the Iraq war.

Dissident fighters from all over the world populated the Iraq insurgency, which was a complex, heterogeneous amalgamation of groups. Within a few months of the fall of Saddam Hussein, a tacit alliance of Ba'athists, Sunni nationalists, and Salafists had formed. But it had no central leadership. Dozens of groups grappled for control of their neighborhood blocks. By 2004, Salafists, including those associated with Abu Mus'ab al-Zarqawi, took an increasingly prominent role in the fighting, especially after the abortive U.S. operation to recapture Fallujah in April 2004.[6] In the summer of 2004, the CIA chief of station in Iraq had gone to the U.S. ambassador, John Negroponte, with alarming news. Al Qa'ida was pushing into Fallujah, he said. They were creating shadow courts, executing people, and turning the whole place into a car-bomb manufacturing center. He told Negroponte that "there were garages full of cars used for bombings, almost like an assembly line."[7]

Marine intelligence analysts traced al Qa'ida's growing power to events in Fallujah. As momentum increased, four major groups began to emerge: al Qa'ida in Iraq, Ansar al-Sunnah, the Islamic Army in Iraq, and the Islamic Front of the Iraqi Resistance. They were followed by a smattering of smaller groups, such as the Victorious Sect and the 1920 Revolution Brigade, which filled a governance and security vacuum in various Iraqi cities.

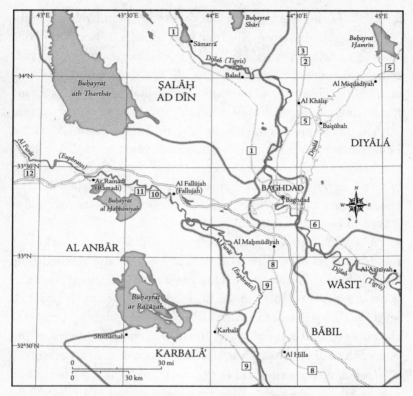

Figure 12: Map of Ramadi and Vicinity

For U.S. Marine intelligence analysts in Anbar Province, however, the most startling development was the emergence of al Qa'ida in Iraq. Major Ben Connable, who was monitoring the insurgency as the senior intelligence analyst and fusion officer for the I and II Marine Expeditionary Force in the province, expressed growing alarm. "Al Qa'ida in Iraq," he warned his colleagues, "is beginning to dominate the insurgency. And other insurgent groups are starting to defect en masse to al Qa'ida."[8]

Marine intelligence reports grew more frantic as al Qa'ida in Iraq became the preponderant organization in the province, surpassing nationalist insurgents, the Iraqi government, and U.S.

forces in its ability to control the day-to-day life of most Sunnis. "Transitioning to a primarily Iraqi organization in late 2004," one Marine assessment concluded, "AQI has become an integral part of the social fabric of western Iraq." Al Qa'ida amassed power by strategically eliminating, subsuming, marginalizing, and co-opting nationalist insurgent groups across Anbar. Zarqawi had accomplished this impressive task by leveraging his association with bin Laden to bring in fighters and raise outside income. "AQI cunningly employed their greater financial resources," the U.S. Marine Corps report continued, "superior organization, proven leadership, and brutal tactics to consolidate their hold on most other nationalist insurgent cells in al-Anbar."[9]

Al Qa'ida's strategy was to paint the United States as a foreign invader and its Iraqi allies as infidel puppets. It also accused Iraqi security forces of being glorified Shi'ite militia and Iranian proxies. "It is not a secret the legality of our Jihad against our occupier," boasted an al Qa'ida letter sent to Iraqi tribal leaders.[10] Its goals were to "unite the ranks of Muslims under one Imam who shall be listened to and obeyed" and to establish "an Islamic State according to Shari'ah."[11]

Couching the struggle as one that opposed American forces and supported Islam—even a fringe interpretation of Islam—brought new recruits and a burgeoning army of suicide bombers. Before the U.S. invasion, Iraq had no recent history of suicide attacks. In 2002, the year before the U.S. invasion, there were no suicide attacks. In 2003 there were 2, but the numbers quickly shot up to 95 in 2004 and 163 in 2005.[12] Many of those committing these attacks were foreigners who refused to become infantry soldiers, preferring to become martyrs. As one would-be suicide bomber, Muhammad Bin-Sabbar Muhammad al-Khuwi Abu Yasir, explained, "My entry in Iraq and my request to perform martyrdom expresses my personal interest and desire, and I do not intend to change this status to fighter after entry, and I swear by God to that."[13] Others wrote similar letters.[14] Many wrote final wills and testaments for their family members, promising to "meet in heaven" and urging their family to "conspire against the enemy, kill them, destroy them, and be aware of strife."[15]

In Anbar, U.S. Marine intelligence reports expressed shock at the rapid growth of the insurgency. By mid-August 2006 the average number of attacks exceeded fifty *per day* in Anbar Province alone, a stunning figure that represented a 57 percent increase since the I Marine Expeditionary Force had assumed responsibility for the province in February of that year. "Intensifying violence," one Marine report concluded, "is reflected in the preponderantly negative outlook of the Sunni population, in the continuing inability to develop adequate Iraqi security forces, and in the near complete failure of reconstruction and development projects across western Iraq."[16]

U.S. Army reports from the 1st Brigade of the 1st Armored Division in Ramadi were equally grim. "Al Qa'ida-related insurgents had almost complete freedom of movement throughout the city of Ramadi," army leaders complained. "They dominate nearly all of the city's key structures, including the city hospital, the largest in Anbar Province."[17] Their freedom of movement allowed them to place complex improvised subsurface explosive devices, which rendered much of the city impassable for U.S. and Iraqi forces. To make matters worse, al Qa'ida researchers were experimenting with chemical and biological weapons. Al Qa'ida had attempted to establish a mustard gas production facility in Mosul, had executed several chlorine gas attacks against U.S. forces, and was pursuing a low-level biological weapons capability.[18] At least one attack in Ramadi in 2006 involved chlorine gas.

The insurgency was precisely the opposite of what the United States intended. The presence of large numbers of American forces, combined with the gaping governance and security vacuum, had unexpectedly given a boost to its adversary and facilitated the second wave. Al Qa'ida, which had no foothold in Iraq before the U.S. invasion, was now the dominant power in a growing number of Iraqi cities. Yet al Qa'ida's tactics once it controlled an area were repulsive.

It engaged in appalling brutality and raw criminal activity—kidnapping, bank robbery, extortion, bribery, and smuggling. In 2004 and 2005 much of the criminal activity in Anbar was undertaken to support the insurgency—by financing bomb-making materiel and paying fighters, for instance. By 2006 al Qa'ida's greed had robbed and alienated the local population.[19]

Al Qa'ida was sowing the seeds of its own destruction.

The Return of the Tribes

One of the first indications that al Qa'ida was losing its grip on the Iraqi population came from the defection of the sheikhs in Anbar Province. Tribal leaders had grown weary of assassinations and corruption. Everyone had a lurid story to tell. One was Sheikh Abdul Rahman al-Janabi, a member of Albu Mahal tribe. He had served as a company-grade officer in Iraqi special forces during the Iran-Iraq war in the 1980s and had been wounded twice. After leaving military service in 1991, he was recalled to the army and served as a company commander from 2001 to 2003.

"When they kidnapped my uncle, Abdul Sattar Sijil—that was the eighteenth of October 2004—that's when my fight began with them officially," Janabi recalled. He helped free his uncle, but al Qa'ida fighters captured his brother and brutally tortured him, leaving him half dead. The images were seared into Janabi's memory. "After all of that was done to us," he explained, "Sheikh Jassim and I started gathering information relating to these terrorists and their places, their emplacements, and their arms."[20]

For Sheikh Sabah, the principal sheikh of the Albu Mahal tribe, the tipping point came in August 2004. Fighters associated with al Qa'ida in Iraq beheaded four members of a single family in the street. Family members came to pick up the mutilated bodies and bury them before nightfall, as is Islamic custom, but al Qa'ida turned them away. After a few days Sheikh Sabah then ordered workers from a nearby factory to bury the bodies, which were now decomposing, since their putrid smells filled the neighborhood. Al Qa'ida turned these workers back as well. Another week passed and the bodies were still out on the street. Al Qa'ida fighters then put TNT in each rotting body and finally asked their family members to pick them up. When the family came at dawn, al Qa'ida operatives exploded the bodies, killing another eight people and injuring many more.

Sheikh Sabah was beside himself. "I will ask a question," he said, shaking with rage. "If you are a Muslim, a Christian, Jewish, Buddhist, any religion, for what reason do you allow something like this to happen? This is what alienated people from the real resistance," he declared. "This is what I've seen with my own eyes. I've seen the bodies. And we tried to bury them, but we couldn't."[21]

Many in the province shared Sheikh Sabah's outrage. In Ramadi, Sheikh Ahmad Bezia Fteikhan al-Rishawi, Abdul Sattar's brother, took the initiative. "Look," he said to his fellow tribal sheikhs, "when are you going to have a normal life? When are you going to be able to get your dues from the government? When are you going to be able to send your children to school? When are you going to live a normal life, when these thugs are in charge?" During Saddam Hussein's reign, some of these sheikhs had enjoyed more autonomy. "These people are wearing masks," he said, referring to al Qa'ida. "They cannot build the country. People that can build government and sustain it are the police and the army. You cannot get your rights if you have no police and no army to protect you."[22]

For Anbar's sheikhs, this became a personal war. They weren't fighting for democracy, political freedom, or other philosophical ideals. And they certainly weren't fighting for the United States. They were fighting for their own survival, for their own people, and for power. As al Qa'ida in Iraq's brutality increased, the United States became the lesser of two evils. Earlier efforts to revolt against al Qa'ida had gone badly. In 2005, al Qa'ida in Iraq had engaged in skirmishes with members of the nationalist 1920 Revolution Brigade, affiliated with Muhammad Mahmoud Latif, as well as with groups loyal to Sheikh Nasser al-Fahadawi, leader of the Albu Fahad tribe. But al Qa'ida in Iraq unleashed a vicious campaign that killed Sheikh Nasser and nearly killed Latif, who was forced to flee from Iraq.[23] Others were decapitated or their bodies were dumped in the streets as a warning. Nine of the eleven sheikhs who were part of the original Anbar People's Council were killed.[24] Al Qa'ida leaders in Pakistan felt they had to intervene.

Crushed in the Shadows

In 2005, Ayman al-Zawahiri wrote a note to Abu Mus'ab al-Zarqawi that was extraordinary not just in its effusive candor but also in its subtle appreciation of the politics of the insurgency. Zawahiri's purpose, he explained, was to help Zarqawi, who was in Iraq, assess next steps. As bin Laden and Zawahiri saw it, local al Qa'ida affiliates could run day-to-day operations largely on their own. But it was central al Qa'ida's role to provide strategic guidance and to mandate changes when necessary. That time had come.

"The first stage," he reminded Zarqawi, was to "expel the Americans from Iraq." Only then could al Qa'ida establish a proper Islamic emirate in Iraq and extend the war to neighboring countries, including Jordan and Saudi Arabia. It was crucial, Zawahiri explained, to understand that success in removing U.S. forces hinged on support from the Muslim masses in Iraq. "In the absence of this popular support," he argued, "the Islamic mujahed movement would be crushed in the shadows."[25] The United States had the same idea. The evolving U.S. counterinsurgency approach in Iraq had identified winning local support as a key to success.[26] Zarqawi was failing in this area—and failing badly. One mistake had been to target Shi'ite communities. Zawahiri told Zarqawi to back off. While the Egyptian Zawahiri believed that Shi'a Islam was a religious school "based on excess and falsehood," targeting Shi'ites would cripple al Qa'ida's support among the broader Muslim community. "Is it something that is unavoidable?" he asked. "Or is it something that can be put off until the force of the mujahed movement in Iraq gets stronger?"

In addition, Zawahiri was concerned about the grisly violence committed by al Qa'ida in Iraq. "Among the things which the feelings of the Muslim populace who love and support you will never find palatable," he scolded, "are the scenes of slaughtering of the hostages."[27]

Like a father chiding his delinquent child, Zawahiri's letter mixed criticism and encouragement. But it also revealed internal squabbling within al Qa'ida. Just when al Qa'ida had begun to make progress in Iraq, the organization began to implode. Disregarding al Qa'ida's senior leaders in Pakistan, Zarqawi allowed al Qa'ida in Iraq's brutality to increase over the course of 2006. On February 22, al Qa'ida operatives bombed the Askariya Mosque in Samarra, one of the holiest sites in Shi'a Islam, and began terrorizing insurgent groups and tribes that refused to join it. The previous month, al Qa'ida had formed the Mujahidin Shura Council, merging with several smaller groups to form an umbrella organization. It lashed out at all obstructionists, warning Anbar's tribal leaders that if they did not join al Qa'ida, "our swords will be the only way of communications to bring justice and to make you an example to each and every one."[28]

Al Qa'ida's senior leaders in Pakistan were incensed. They sent a follow-up letter to Zarqawi. This time, Atiyah abd al-Rahman al-Libi, a trusted colleague of bin Laden and Zawahiri, wrote the message. He began by showering Zarqawi with praise for his "honorable characteristics," such as "fervor for the religion," "high aspirations to do what you see as right and true," and "strength and determination that many people lack." Atiyah then warned Zarqawi that "corruption and havoc," which God disproved of, were becoming pervasive. Then he dropped a bombshell: he suggested that Zarqawi relieve himself of command of al Qa'ida in Iraq if he could find someone who "is better and more suitable than you." The problem, Atiyah continued, was that Zarqawi's decision to wage war against the Shi'ites and conduct attacks in neighboring countries was gutting al Qa'ida's support in Iraq and across the region. Al Qa'ida leaders in Pakistan were particularly upset about Zarqawi's November 2005 triple suicide bombing in Amman, Jordan, which killed 60 people and injured 115 others. Most were Muslims. Television footage showed body parts and blood-splattered floors.

Atiyah's underlying message was that Zarqawi needed to get back in the box, show restraint, and consult with bin Laden and Zawahiri about next steps. It was urgent, he noted, to "mend your flaws in many things."[29] Though Zarqawi had formally joined al Qa'ida, he was badly out of touch with its senior leadership in Pakistan. This was unacceptable, Atiyah told him.

But his letter fell on deaf ears. Al Qa'ida in Iraq did try to rein in corruption. In one communiqué, its leaders admonished those who were involved in "illegal activities" and promised to exact revenge on anyone caught "looting and mugging the innocent."[30] But it was a halfhearted effort. The leader of al Qa'ida in Iraq had other things to worry about; he was being hunted by U.S. special operations forces. One of his wives begged him to leave Iraq, at least temporarily, to avoid danger. You can give orders to your deputies from outside the country, she insisted. "Me, me?" Zarqawi responded, incredulous. "I can't betray my religion and get out of Iraq."

The leader of al Qa'ida in Iraq would never renounce his struggle. "In the name of God," he proclaimed, "I will not leave Iraq until victory or martyrdom."[31]

Zarqawi was granted his wish, though perhaps a bit prematurely. U.S. and Iraqi forces killed him in June 2006, and al Qa'ida in Iraq simultaneously faced a growing revolt in Anbar.

An Unusual Choice

If given the choice, Americans and Iraqis might not have worked with Abdul Sattar in the Anbar Awakening. U.S. intelligence reports indicated that he was deeply involved in criminal activities. Abdul Sattar had apparently served in the Iraqi Army in 1991, deserted, and then served six months in prison. Although he had completed high school, he could barely read and write.[32] After the U.S. invasion in 2003, he smuggled weapons, vehicles, and even black oil—the residual oil that remains after the refining process, which can be further processed for other applications. U.S. intelligence officials also believed that Abdul Sattar was probably involved in the insurgency at one point, most likely smuggling foreign fighters into Iraq.[33] U.S. Army soldiers concluded that al Qa'ida may have been a customer of Sattar's at one time, buying black market fuel, arms, or supplies. But they assessed that Sattar was probably not aware of his direct support of al Qa'ida.[34] He was, in short, a typical leader in post-Saddam Iraq, working with all sides to survive and, when possible, to make a profit.

"People asked me how to prepare for coming to Anbar Province," said Lieutenant Colonel Jim Lechner from the U.S. Army's 1st Brigade of the 1st Armored Division, who worked closely with Abdul Sattar. "I would tell them to watch the HBO TV series *The Sopranos*."[35]

Abdul Sattar enjoyed women, partying, chain-smoking cigarettes, and drinking whiskey. When asked by a foreign journalist in 2006 about his vision for Iraq, his answer was unequivocal. "I want to have peace, democracy, justice, equality, and human rights," he said confidently. And then he turned to Lechner and whispered with a conspicuous grin, "And I want nightclubs too."[36]

The humor was quintessential Abdul Sattar. Unsurprisingly, his entrepreneurial activities made him unpopular with other tribal sheikhs. He was a "road gangster," said Sheikh Majed Abd al-Razzaq Ali al-Sulayman, proficient in "robbing in the streets."[37] Others agreed. "I tell you frankly," remarked Thamer Ibrahim Tahir al-Assafi, "we all disliked Sheikh Abdul Sattar Abu Risha" because "he was not a religious person."[38] But Sheikh Majed supported Abdul Sattar, in part because he believed that Abdul Sattar would be the guinea pig in a tribal revolt that was unlikely to succeed. "So we, the sheikhs, discussed among ourselves who will head the Awakening," he said. "So we chose the bad one, which was Abdul Sattar, because he was a troublemaker, and he had a bad record, so we chose Abdul Sattar. And, as you know, his tribe is a very small tribe."[39]

Still, Abdul Sattar had several qualities that distinguished him from other sheikhs. For one, he had stayed in Anbar, unlike those who had fled to Jordan and Syria to escape the violence. Thick ten-foot-high walls with observation towers ringed his compound. Relatives and other trusted tribesmen stood guard. Abdul Sattar's personal security detail comprised at least fifty men with rifles, machine guns, and a vast assortment of pickup trucks, sport utility vehicles, and sedans. The sheikh was charismatic and charming. Perhaps most important, he was, as Lechner described it, "mad as hell" at al Qa'ida.[40] The smallness of Abdul Sattar's tribe actually worked in his favor, since more prominent sheikhs did not want to risk their stature by taking on al Qa'ida.

Aided by Abdul Sattar's brother, Sheikh Ahmad Bezia Fteikhan al-Rishawi, the group began to work the phones over the summer of 2006, drumming up support. "We started thinking that we've got to get in touch with the tribal sheikhs and their cousins, the ones who were active, so we could incite them to fight al Qa'ida," said Ahmad. "Leave it to me," said Abdul Sattar. "I'll take care of it." "So he started moving," said Ahmad, "talking with the tribal sheikhs, one by one. He told them that he was ready to do something, and he gathered them for a conference."[41]

On September 9 they issued a communiqué consisting of eleven points, among them to bring the Iraqi Army back into Anbar, allow tribal forces into the police and army, and declare war on al Qa'ida. A security alliance between the sheikhs and Iraqi police was proposed and orchestrated by Lieutenant Colonel Deane, Lieutenant Colonel Lechner, and the CIA.[42] Unlike what had happened with previous tribal revolts in Anbar, the sheikhs agreed to ally with U.S. forces. Abdul Sattar began addressing the assembly, announcing the formation of the Awakening. He repeated the main points outlined in the document and then turned to American forces in the room. "We will consider you friendly forces if you will support us," Abdul Sattar said. "We're with whoever is against al Qa'ida."

But he went further, emphasizing that he would treat an attack on Americans as an attack on their own tribesmen. Abdul Sattar volunteered the allegiance of the men in the room. Most were second- and third-tier sheikhs. "I want you to have the same relation you have with me with all of these people here," he said to Colonel Sean MacFarland, the commander of the 1st Brigade of the 1st Armored Division, seated among the other sheikhs.[43] Servants then swept into the room, carrying large platters of roasted lamb and rice. The Awakening had begun.

"The war against al-Qaeda was waged first in Ramadi and then in every other tribal area," said Ahmad, Abdul Sattar's brother. "Whenever we cleared a tribal area of al Qa'ida, we set up a police station. We elected a representative company from every area. We took these people, and we went to the city of Ramadi, and we attacked in Ramadi. That's how we liberated Ramadi."[44]

American Support

Colonel MacFarland's 1st Brigade joined with the I and II Marine Expeditionary Force, the CIA, and U.S. special operations forces, seizing the moment in Anbar. U.S. Marines had already been working with Anbar sheikhs, including those who had fled to Jordan. From July to December 2005, the Marines conducted Operation Sayyad to drive al Qa'ida from the western Euphrates River Valley, with some success.[45] In the spring of 2006 the Marine Expeditionary Force held a tribal conference in Amman, Jordan. Several tribal leaders from Al-Qaim, in the western part of Anbar Province, explained to Abdul Sattar how they had revolted against al Qa'ida, but strongly advised him to get U.S. and Iraqi government support before attempting to confront the organization.

At the time of Abdul Sattar's decision to fight al Qa'ida, the 1st Brigade, the "Ready First Combat Team," was deployed to Ramadi. Colonel MacFarland, the brigade commander, built off a plan devised by the Marine staff to attack al Qa'ida's safe havens in Ramadi, establish a presence to challenge insurgent dominance of the city, and take back the city one block at a time. In the spring of 2006, Abdul Sattar met with Deane, Lechner, and MacFarland. "I've got the ability to provide three battalion-sized formations of tribal militia, right now," Abdul Sattar said, "if you'll help us out with some projects to try to make life better for our poor people."[46]

With the help of Ramadi's tribal leaders, U.S. forces established neighborhood watches. Screened members of tribal militias became auxiliary police and wore uniforms, carried weapons, and provided security within their defined tribal areas. Combat outposts manned by U.S. and Iraqi forces protected major routes and markets. In a few cases U.S. forces also provided direct security to key leaders' residences, including placing armored vehicles at checkpoints along the major access roads to their neighborhoods.[47]

Abdul Sattar's group organized twenty-five of the thirty-one tribes in Anbar. Their primary strategy was to persuade young men to join the police forces of Ramadi and other Anbar towns.[48] It took several months for the alliance to achieve critical strength. As promised, the sheiks persuaded tribal members to join the local police in large numbers. By December 2006 the Ramadi police force had doubled in size, from four thousand to eight thousand. In western Anbar, the number of police went from nearly zero to three thousand. The police force in the province grew to twenty-four thousand in mid-2007.[49] U.S. forces, whose policy was to place their officers within newly formed police units, could not staff up as quickly as the police units were growing. Perhaps the most significant change was that the new police, in contrast to their predecessors, were willing to fight. As recently as August 2006, half of the police officers in Fallujah had stayed home in the face of al Qa'ida's threats.[50] By January 2007 they were standing their ground.

Many of the new policemen were former members of insurgent groups. One sheik, Abu Azzam, said that the 2,300 men in his movement included members of fierce Sunni groups like the 1920 Revolution Brigade and the Mujahideen Army, which had previously fought U.S. forces.[51]

Other U.S. agencies pitched in. The CIA placed a number of sheikhs on its payroll, coordinating with U.S. Army and Marine forces, and helped target al Qa'ida leaders. In addition, special operations forces from Joint Special Operations Command (JSOC) and the Combined Joint Special Operations Task Force (CJSOTF) conducted a withering offensive against al Qa'ida leaders, killing a number of mid- and senior-level officials. They supported a group called Thawar al Anbar (Revolutionaries of al Anbar), which had emerged around the summer of 2006 and operated covertly, utilizing the same kind of informant networks and interrogation methods used by al Qa'ida in Iraq. Thawar al Anbar was so successful against al Qa'ida in the last few months of 2006, particularly in Ramadi, that al Qa'ida attempted—but failed—to negotiate a truce in December.

After Ramadi fell, other areas followed. Anbar's tribal sheikhs were impressed. "If you help me get rid of those who mean me harm, then you're obviously my friend," one sheikh remarked to U.S. Marine Major General Walter Gaskin. "If you fight along with me and shed your blood, you're my brother."[52]

Counterattack

Al Qa'ida leaders needed to counterattack quickly to stem their collapse. In October 2006 they created the Islamic State of Iraq, bringing in additional tribal and insurgent groups to oppose the alliance between the United States, Anbar tribes, and the Iraqi government. Al Qa'ida's goal remained expelling U.S. forces and establishing an Islamic caliphate in Iraq. The organization's decision to establish the Islamic State of Iraq was in part an attempt to increase its power by preventing the further fracturing of insurgent groups. By claiming to be a state, al Qa'ida also sought to gain legitimacy. Less publicized, but probably more important, was its attempt to unify Sunni Arabs by cracking down on corruption and assassinating recalcitrant sheiks. One al Qa'ida communiqué implored its foot soldiers to "avoid any awful act and replace it by nothing but a good deed."[53] Recognizing the importance of winning local support, al Qa'ida then began an intense propaganda campaign centered on Islamic motifs, which threatened defectors and attempted to shame them into rejoining its thinning ranks.

"To the people of Islam, the people of honor and generosity, have you become despicable and lost your honor?" the communiqué read. "Did it die inside you or have you lost it even though Allah has given you your heart, ears, and eyes?" Evoking Sayyid Qutb, Ayman al-Zawahiri, and other radicals, al Qa'ida leaders asked, "Why are you fleeing the jihad? . . . I say to the people of Islam," the message concluded, "you have accepted the beautifications of the devil who stopped you from jihad and your duties to fight our enemy, to the point that your words have become signs of blame and you have stopped jihad. What has happened to your wisdom?"[54]

The purpose of such propaganda was to win the ideological initiative. The problem, however, was that most Iraqis did not subscribe to al Qa'ida's radical version of Islam, especially when they saw its fighters engaging in criminal activities and slaughtering other Muslims. In an attempt to soften its image, al Qa'ida leaders tried to mend fences with some Anbar tribal leaders. In one document, al Qa'ida in Iraq's senior leaders outlined the need to "bite their wounds and suppress their rage and fury despite any provocations because God is watching them." Perhaps more important, al Qa'ida promised to create a special investigations unit that would "call to account anyone at fault according to the Sharia of God."[55] To several key tribal sheikhs, such as Abad Lufan al-Hadeb, al Qa'ida leaders sent a private letter apologizing profusely for targeting them and promising to "pay any compensation" if damage was done.[56] Abu

Hamza al-Muhajir, who took over al Qa'ida in Iraq after Zarqawi's death, sent a note to Abu Abdullah al-Shafi, the leader of Ansar al-Islam, a Sunni militant group that operated from northeast Iraq near the Iranian border, declaring that he would be "willing to hand over any person having committed a crime of blood or [who] took your money." If guilty, said Abu Hamza, Ansar al-Islam should feel free to assess whether the individual "deserves beheading"—and to do it.[57] Al Qa'ida was offering to sell out its more unruly members for the support of the respected sheikhs.

For those who refused the olive branch, it was all-out war. Al Qa'ida began a string of deadly attacks: 202 killed and 257 wounded in suicide bombings on November 23, 2006; 117 killed and 270 wounded on March 6, 2007; 152 killed and 347 wounded on March 27; 140 killed and 160 wounded on April 18; and 156 killed and 267 wounded on July 2. The casualty figures were unprecedented. Al Qa'ida targeted the public faces of the new alliance: key sheikhs and the police.[58] Harith Zaher al-Dhari, son of the leader of the Zobai tribe and head of the Association of Muslim Scholars, was assassinated, an act attributed to his organization's refusal to join the Islamic State of Iraq. Some thirty commanders of 1920 Revolution Brigade and Jaysh al-Islami, an Iraqi militant group that blended Salafism and Iraqi nationalism, were assassinated by al Qa'ida or killed in battles over arms caches in Anbar. In October, Sheikh abu Osama al-'Iraqi called on Osama bin Laden to denounce al Qa'ida in Iraq for killing Sunnis and targeting jihad fighters from other Sunni factions.

For several months Anbar's tribal sheikhs battled with al Qa'ida in Iraq. There were few set-piece battles or formal engagements; war was conducted through bombings, assassinations, and constant attrition. The police rounded up al Qa'ida members, and al Qa'ida responded by conducting an intimidation campaign against the police, their families, and the tribal sheiks who had turned against it. Prior to the Anbar Awakening, fewer than 3 percent of al Qa'ida in Iraq's attacks were targeted against Iraqi police. The rate rose to 15 percent by September and jumped to 30 percent by December 2006. And while 10 percent of al Qa'ida's attacks had targeted members of the Iraqi Army, this rate fell in March 2007 to 5 percent, where it remained for the rest of that year. Al Qa'ida quickly understood that the police force, not the army, was its most significant threat.[59]

By March 2007, al Qa'ida had largely been expelled from Ramadi, the city that had been the "heart of darkness," a danger zone for U.S. and Iraqi forces. The number of attacks in Anbar fell dramatically. U.S. deaths, which were running at roughly thirty a month in the province, fell to three in June 2007. Sheikh al-Dulami reported that Anbar had "been purged completely of AQI" and tribal and Iraq government forces were "encircling the organization's remnants in al-Tash area south of Ramadi."[60]

Americans sometimes had trouble believing that the addition of a few thousand police officers could have tipped the balance of power in Anbar Province so swiftly. These police were essentially untrained, inexperienced, and poorly equipped, especially in comparison to the 35,000 U.S. soldiers already in the province. Nevertheless, they had two critical advantages. First, the new police officers had joined the force at the urging of their tribal leaders in a society where tribal relationships were paramount. Second, they brought a flood of intelligence with them, since they were from the same neighborhoods—and the same demographic pool—as many of the al Qa'ida fighters. One U.S. Army lieutenant, Ed Clark, observed in May 2007 that "about 10 percent of our intelligence is actionable, while 90 percent of their intelligence is actionable."[61] In a conflict where intelligence is key, the defection of former insurgent members was a crucial force multiplier.

Al Qa'ida began to implode as its remaining factions turned on each other.[62] "Many of our fighters quit," one al Qa'ida operative wrote in his diary, "and some of them joined the deserters."[63] In a nod to Anbar's tribal leaders and their American and Iraqi backers, al Qa'ida leader Abu Hamza al-Muhajir recognized al Qa'ida's most serious obstacle. "They became united," he explained in a letter to

Ansar al-Sunnah leaders, "while we became divided, they achieved coalescence and embraced one another, they were united against everyone else, and we became united against ourselves."[64]

Baptized by Blood

On September 13, 2007, the first day of Ramadan, al Qa'ida assassinated Sheikh Abdul Sattar along with his nephew and two of his bodyguards. Abdul Sattar had climbed into his unarmored Land Cruiser to check on his horses, which were outside the secured perimeter of his compound but still on his property. Al Qa'ida operatives who had infiltrated his personal security detail packed between 60 and 80 pounds of homemade explosives into a roadside bomb and detonated it as Abdul Sattar crossed a small canal.[65] The funeral attracted some 1,500 mourners, including Iraq's national security adviser, interior minister, defense minister, and the second-in-command of U.S. forces in Iraq. It was an emotional ceremony. Many choked up, fighting back tears. Iraqi police and U.S. military vehicles lined the funeral procession route, which meandered from Abdul Sattar's home in Ramadi to the burial grounds nearby. He was laid next to his father and brothers, who had also been killed by al Qa'ida. Abdul Sattar's death was tragic. Yet his life—and now death—served as an inspiration for scores of Iraqis who had risen up against Qa'ida.

"This is the path of the mujahidin, the path of freedom, and the path conducive to the elimination of terrorism headed by al Qa'ida," defense minister Abdul Qadir Mohammed Jassim Obeidi said in his poignant eulogy. "This path cannot be baptized but by blood."[66]

Abdul Sattar served as an icon for the Awakening and the end of the second wave of al Qa'ida terrorism. He came from a small Anbar tribe and lacked the erudition and pedigree of Iraq's more prestigious tribal sheikhs, yet he was willing to shed his own blood. Abdul Sattar was only one of many Iraqis who fought al Qa'ida, reversing a situation so bleak that the Americans had nearly lost hope. Marine intelligence had assessed in August 2006 that "the social and political situation has deteriorated to a point that [U.S. and Iraqi forces] are no longer capable of militarily defeating the insurgency in al-Anbar."[67] Marine analysts were correct; U.S. and Iraqi forces could not militarily defeat al Qa'ida in Iraq by themselves.

The most effective method for reversing al Qa'ida's wave, it turned out, was not to place a large number of U.S. conventional forces on the ground to target the group. Rather, it was to engage in a covert war using U.S. Army and Marine soldiers to back up local forces, CIA case officers to bankroll tribal sheikhs and encourage fissures among insurgent groups, special operations forces to hunt down al Qa'ida fighters, and a robust, multiagency effort to collect and analyze human intelligence, cell phone intercepts, satellite imagery, and other types of intelligence. In addition, al Qa'ida's punishment strategy backfired as Iraq's population rose up in revolt.

An internal al Qa'ida analysis summarized the situation most succinctly. "Throughout the last four years," the author noted, the Americans "learned from their mistakes." They were successful in "creating ordeals within the mujahidin by tempting some factions to fight against the Islamic State with the direction of the Shiites." He also noted that al Qa'ida had brought problems on itself. By authorizing "the killings and random arrests" of civilians "and by demolishing their homes," al Qa'ida had stoked "Sunnis feeling that the Mujahidin were the biggest reason for their misfortunes and tribulations . . . The Islamic state of Iraq," the al Qa'ida assessment acknowledged, "is faced with an extraordinary crisis, especially in al-Anbar."[68]

The second wave was nearly over, though al Qa'ida in Iraq was not quite dead. Despite heavy losses in Anbar, its fighters attempted to consolidate control in several areas, including Ninawa Province, Salah ad-Din, Diyala, and Baghdad. But it had lost considerable power and prestige. As if al Qa'ida's heavy losses in Iraq weren't bad enough, it would now face its most serious test: sustained criticism from within Islam, attacking its very right to exist.

REVOLT FROM WITHIN

THE EGYPTIAN TOWN of Tura lies 8 miles south of Cairo, near the mouth of the Nile River Delta as it fans out into the Mediterranean Sea. Ancient Egyptians drew massive quantities of limestone out of quarries in the low, brooding hills east of the Nile and used the white, fine-grained, polished Tura limestone as facing stones for the great pyramids of Khufu and Khafre.[1] By 2007, however, Tura had been absorbed into greater Cairo and transformed into a gritty industrial hub distinguished by metalworks factories and Soviet-style apartment buildings.

On the northern edge of Tura, wedged between the east bank of the Nile and the Eastern Desert, sat one of the area's most infamous landmarks: the great Tura prison. The complex encompassed seven separate prisons, which housed some of Egypt's most renowned political prisoners.[2] It was ringed by twenty-five-foot-high concrete walls, parallel interior fencing, entry control points, and multiple guard towers. Thick layers of dust and grime clung to the buildings, and the grounds were a patchwork of dirt, sand, and parched grass. When Egyptian president Anwar Sadat came to power, one of his first acts was to take a pickax to the brick wall at Tura prison. When he had been in Tura prison, his cell contained "no bed, no small table, no chair, and no lamp," Sadat reported in his autobiography. "You simply can't imagine how filthy" it was, he wrote. In the winter "water oozed from the cell walls day and night, and in the summer huge armies of bugs marched up and down."[3]

It was here, at one of Tura's prisons, that al Qa'ida faced one of its most brazen attacks. The culprit was Sayyid Imam Abd al-Aziz al-Sharif, the former head of Egyptian Islamic Jihad and long-time colleague of Ayman al-Zawahiri. By 2007, Sharif had aged considerably. His beard had become almost pure white, though there were still some patches of dark hair in his eyebrows and beard. His eyesight had deteriorated and his skin had taken on a pale hue, thanks in part to being imprisoned for several years. He wore thick glasses that clung to his head and had rather large, protruding ears. But like that of an aging boxer, Sharif's frail body masked an energetic fighting spirit. After his break with Zawahiri and Egyptian Islamic Jihad in the early 1990s, Sharif had moved his family to Yemen, in 1994, and begun working as a doctor in the General Al-Thawrah Hospital. A month after the September 11 attacks he was arrested, and he was eventually extradited to Egypt, in February 2004. Egyptian authorities, who were concerned about his ties to al Qa'ida and other Islamic militant groups, threw him into Tura prison.

As the Anbar Awakening scattered the forces of Zarqawi, Sharif mounted a blistering attack against al Qa'ida.

"I say this to those who defend al Qa'ida's leaders," wrote Sharif. "Your friends bin Laden and al-Zawahiri and their followers are treacherous, backstabbing people. Anyone who admires their deeds is their partner in sin. They are now counted as people of weak faith because they committed the major sins of lying and treachery. Only a thin line separates them from being outright infidels."[4]

Sharif likened the September 11 attacks to a "trick of Lucifer," arguing that al Qa'ida succeeded only in creating "mountains of skulls, blood, torn body parts, devastation, captives, and humanitarian tragedies." But he saved his most withering criticism for his former friend Zawahiri, calling him "evil" and "impotent," the latter a particularly insidious insult for a proud Egyptian man.[5]

Sharif's attack, published in a book titled *Rationalization of*

Jihad in Egypt and the World, came at an inopportune time for al Qa'ida, just as it was facing a second reverse wave. Senior al Qa'ida leaders mustered a merciless and personal counterattack. Zawahiri led the charge, skewering Sharif in a 268-page rebuttal and calling him an apologist to "the Crusaders and Jews."[6] Sharif had been an icon for many radical Islamists, including al Qa'ida operatives, who had reverentially absorbed his works on jihad in their training camps. The verbal jousting quickly spread as a number of radical Islamists across the Muslim world jumped to Sharif's defense.

Indeed, the importance of Sharif's diatribe against al Qa'ida was less in the document itself, which was not particularly lucid or well written, than in the debates that ensued across the Muslim world, most of which occurred under the radar of Western audiences. As al Qa'ida engaged in violent conflict against the West in Afghanistan, Iraq, Pakistan, and other areas, it was drawn into a struggle across the treacherous landscape of the Arab press and the Internet. Al Qa'ida was now on the defensive as the second wave ebbed. And it was fighting a new kind of war.[7]

The First Volleys

Sharif's main target was al Qa'ida, though he was not an apologist for the West. He shared al Qa'ida's disgust with America's support for Israel and its wars in Iraq and Afghanistan, calling them an affront to humanity and Islam. Sharif was particularly hopeful that the Taliban would triumph in Afghanistan and establish sharia law, much as it had done in the 1990s. The Afghan war, he believed, was a defensive war in response to the American invasion. "Jihad in Afghanistan is the duty of its people and Muslim neighbors as needed," he explained.[8] His choice of words was important, indicating that jihad against the United States in Afghanistan was not just an option but a *duty*. Several years later he went even further, excoriating the West for conducting what he called an assault on

Muslims around the globe. "Following the 11 September events," he would write, "unprecedented discrimination against Muslims and Arabs in America and Europe took place and reached the point of killing them on the streets in reaction to the bombing, in addition to the infringement of their freedom and rights."[9]

This time, however, al Qa'ida, not the United States, was his main target. Sharif's goal in writing *Rationalization of Jihad in Egypt and the World* was to condemn the hijacking of Islam by what he considered to be an uneducated fringe group. Sharif had been contemplating writing such a book for several years. Starting in December 2006, he began to write, and his time in jail enabled him to reexamine his views. "One cannot write something, especially a lengthy research like the document, from memory without going back to any book unless it is of one's own ideas and old knowledge well-established in one's mind," he acknowledged.[10]

After completing a draft, he circulated it among Egyptian extremists in prison, asking for feedback. In February 2007, Egyptian prison authorities allowed him to host a small gathering of trusted colleagues, during which he carefully listened to their critiques. Sharif then revised the document and in April held a conference at the prison, where he presented *Rationalization of Jihad in Egypt and the World* to hundreds of jihadists. He also sent it for comment to the Islamic Research Council of Al-Azhar, the highest Islamic scholarly council in Egypt.[11]

Sharif opened several lines of attack against al Qa'ida. The first was a repudiation of civilian casualties. Al Qa'ida's perpetration of acts that resulted in civilian casualties, he argued, was a gross distortion of Islam. By 2007 terrorist attacks across the Muslim world had reached epidemic proportions, killing and maiming civilians in grotesque acts often captured on television and the Internet. That year there were 8,225 terrorist attacks and nearly 10,000 deaths from terrorism around the world, excluding Iraq—a 27 percent increase in deaths from 2006. In Iraq the numbers were staggering. Al Qa'ida in Iraq leaders committed gross human rights abuses, committing 6,210 terrorist attacks and 13,612 deaths. Even more alarming, 70 percent of the victims were civilians and, most discouraging for Sharif and others, over 50 percent of terrorist victims were Muslims.[12] In some countries, such as Iraq, Al Qa'ida in Iraq operatives proudly distributed videos of savage beheadings, which they performed by hand. Sharif was repulsed. "The Prophet, may the prayers and peace of God be upon him, forbade the indiscriminate killing of people and assured that those who do that do not belong to the Prophet, may the prayers and peace of God be upon him, for this method is a great sin," he wrote.[13] "There is nothing that invokes the anger of God and His wrath like spilling blood and wrecking property without justification."[14]

Sharif's decision to invoke the Prophet Muhammad and to castigate the indiscriminate violence as a "great sin" challenged al Qa'ida leaders. It was preposterous to accuse *all* Westerners of apostasy, Sharif argued; this went against the teachings and actions of the Prophet. He was particularly critical of Zawahiri, who had stated that since the population elects its leaders in a democracy, everyone could justifiably be targeted. "Cause the greatest damage and inflict the maximum casualties on the opponent, no matter how much time and effort these operations take," Zawahiri wrote in *Knights Under the Prophet's Banner*, referring especially to Jews and Christians, "because this is the language understood by the West."[15]

Adam Gadahn, the American-born al Qa'ida propagandist, agreed. "So after all the atrocities committed by America," he said, "why should we target their military only?" It was both permissible and scrupulous to "bomb their cities and civilians."[16]

This conclusion was absurd, Sharif retorted, and had no basis in Islam. For starters, there were countless theological minefields, not to mention moral ones, in such a cavalier approach to killing. Such violence would surely send the perpetrator to hell, not paradise. Were Muslims killed by the attacks? Were women and children wounded or killed? Had the individuals been invited to Muslim countries by Muslim hosts? If yes, then killing them was strictly prohibited under Islam, even if they were Christians or Jews. To support his point, Sharif cited the Prophet Muhammad's belief that war occurred on the battlefield between armies. "As far as we know," Sharif maintained, "they did not send any Muslim to undertake jihad operations inside the countries of Persia, the Romans, or Mecca before it was conquered."[17]

This argument also covered Jews and Christians, who had lived in communities throughout the Arab world for centuries and who had allowed Muslims to settle in their countries. Why kill them now? After all, the punishment for the *kafir*—one who does not believe in Islam—would be meted out in the next life.[18] "Let it be known to you, o Muslim," said Sharif, "that there is nothing in the sharia that calls for the killing of the Jews and the Christians, to whom some refer as the Crusaders." He continued that, "these people have been living in the Muslim countries since the distant past, and have been enjoying their rights as citizens of the country."[19] Sharif still condemned the United States and Israel for oppressing Muslims, but the real tragedy, he said, was that Muslims were dying in record numbers from terrorism.

The crux of this debate, it turned out, was over the definition of *takfir*, or nonbelief. *Takfir* can lead ultimately to the excommunication of a Muslim whose acts are in violation of Islam. Bin Laden and Zawahiri adopted a fairly liberal interpretation, condemning virtually all Muslims who didn't subscribe to their extreme interpretation of Islam as *takfiris*, potentially punishable by death. Sharif shuddered at this rationale, arguing that there were restraints on *takfir* to avoid unjustly accusing someone of nonbelief. Only those qualified in Islamic law could accuse someone of *takfir*. Sharif feared that an overly punitive interpretation of *takfir* would lead to mistakes, and consequently indiscriminate violence.

Why did al Qa'ida leaders adopt such a broad definition? Sharif maintained that ignorance drove them to such heresy. In his mind, al Qa'ida leaders did not have the religious qualifications to make *any* statements about Islam. Bin Laden and Zawahiri lacked proper

Islamic education, were not Islamic scholars, and therefore could not issue fatwas and religious edicts. "Regarding a sharia-based response," Sharif wrote, "al Qa'ida has no one who is qualified from a sharia perspective to make a response. All of them, bin Laden, al-Zawahiri, and others are not religious scholars on whose opinion you can count. They are ordinary persons."[20] As far as Sharif was concerned, bin Laden's and Zawahiri's pronouncements on *takfir* had no basis in Islam, which left al Qa'ida morally and religiously bankrupt. Quoting from the Qur'an, Sharif warned readers not to do "that of which thou hast no knowledge."[21] This error was particularly egregious, he noted, in the case of jihad because it involves human lives and property.

But bin Laden and Zawahiri were not the only guilty ones. The proliferation of social media—the Internet, Facebook, YouTube, Twitter, and other forums—meant that armies of charlatans and firebrands were preaching distorted versions of Islam to adolescents. Sharif feared that many impressionable young Muslims would fail to recognize that the vast majority of those preaching on Internet chat rooms were heretics, pure and simple. "Similar to the case of theology books," Sharif explained, "material posted on the international information network, the Internet, should not be accepted without scrutiny and without knowledge of the sharia qualifications of those who post them and their integrity, especially material containing incitement to Muslims to go on a collision course with others."[22]

Few people had attempted such bold criticism of al Qa'ida. Painting al Qa'ida as a fringe group put into words what had already been true: many of the young Muslims who plotted or executed attacks in the name of al Qa'ida had actually *abandoned* mosques and *shunned* established religious scholars, preferring the teachings of extremists who lacked Islamic credentials.

José Padilla, who was arrested by FBI officials in 2002 in Chicago, converted to Islam in Florida and linked up with a radical network of individuals with no Islamic pedigree. Several of the Madrid bombers, including Jamal Ahmidan, were heavily involved in drug trafficking, a major sin in Islam, and his accomplices had abandoned local mosques because the mosques weren't radical enough. The imams, they believed, did not support bin Laden's and Zawahiri's view that violent, offensive jihad was a duty of Muslims. Mohammad Sidique Khan and his accomplices involved in the July 2005 London attacks became radicalized outside the mosque and lambasted Muslim scholars for being out of touch with the extremist views of al Qa'ida. Abdulla Ahmed Ali, Tanvir Hussain, and their colleagues in the United Kingdom, who had planned to blow up airplanes on their way to the United States and Canada in 2006, became radicalized with the help of al Qa'ida operative Rashid Rauf, who had no serious Islamic credentials. Adam Gadahn came from a similar mold. After meeting Khalil al-Deek, Gadahn eschewed the mosque in Orange County, California, much to the dismay of mosque officials.

For Sharif, these uneducated al Qa'ida operatives were wolves in sheep's clothing. "O Muslim folks," Sharif warned, "jihad for Allah's sake is just, but do not allow those people and their likes to auctioneer with this noble cause. They push youths to extreme sacrifices, and they bring major catastrophes on the Muslims even though they are most careful about their personal safety and about reaping benefits without realizing the least benefit for Islam and the Muslims."[23]

Just as maddening to Sharif was the al Qa'ida leaders' skewed understanding of jihad. Sharif found the theory of the Egyptian scholar Sayyid Qutb that offensive jihad was a duty of all Muslims preposterous.[24] He wrote that "there must be some controls on the *fiqh* [theology] of jihad."[25] For starters, the Qur'an outlines several options for Muslims in response to a threat, not just violent jihad, including advocacy (*al-da'wa*), migration (*al-hijrah*), pardon (*al-afw*), forgiveness (*al-safh*), shunning (*al-i'rad*), and patience (*al-sabr*). "The Prophet, Allah's prayers and peace upon him, resorted to all of them," Sharif pointed out, "as did many of his disciples, Allah's favors on them."[26] War should be reserved for specific circumstances—for instance, when Muslim communities come under an imminent threat from outsiders.

Furthermore, Sharif argued that there were clear boundaries to jihad, especially when adolescents were involved. "Among the conditions for jihad becoming a duty is requiring the permission of the parents," he wrote.[27] Parents were an important barrier to prevent children from following false prophets. José Padilla, Mohammad Sidique Khan, Adam Gadahn, and many of al Qa'ida's younger foot soldiers had committed themselves to jihad without the permission—or, often, the awareness—of their parents. Most family members were devastated to learn of their involvement in terrorist acts.

Sharif left his most virulent attacks for Ayman al-Zawahiri, his old friend from Egypt and Pakistan. In an interview with the pan-Arab newspaper *Al-Hayat*, he accused Zawahiri of being motivated mostly by money, fame, and his own personal safety.[28] In addition, Sharif shamed Zawahiri and bin Laden for corrupting the minds of young Muslims, insisting that their punishment would be eternal damnation. Summoning the language of the holy book, he wrote that they "will go into the Fire, dwelling therein forever. Such is the reward of the wrongdoers."[29] It was a stunningly public and personal denunciation of al Qa'ida's leadership, especially Zawahiri, and caught much of the Arab world by surprise. Had Sharif not been in prison, his life would almost certainly have been in jeopardy.

Al Qa'ida Responds

For FBI leaders, Sharif's volley indicated that al Qa'ida's ideological support was beginning to weaken. "Their wave was cresting," suggested Philip Mudd. Perhaps the most important component of the struggle against al Qa'ida was to counter its ideology, what Philip Mudd called "al Qa'ida-ism." "In some ways," Mudd said, "the ideological fights are more important than the counterterrorist operations."[30]

But whose job was it within the U.S. government to develop and execute a counternarrative? Many agencies played a role. The

State Department was the lead for public diplomacy but had not developed a comprehensive interagency strategy to counteract al Qa'ida's ideology. In 1999 the State Department had disbanded the U.S. Information Agency, which had played a prominent role in countering Soviet ideology during the Cold War. The CIA was involved in some clandestine propaganda activity, but many senior officials did not view undermining al Qa'ida's ideology as a core mission. The Department of Defense was also involved in some efforts, but they were dispersed among U.S. Central Command, U.S. Special Operations Command, and other organizations. The FBI was not an ideal fit either. "I don't think the mission of the FBI is an ideological mission," explained Mudd. "Somebody else has to worry about ideas and how to prevent those ideas from spreading around the world."[31]

This conclusion produced an ad hoc and inadequate U.S. response. Nevertheless, al Qa'ida leaders—especially Ayman al-Zawahiri—understood the gravity of Sharif's exposé. To say that Zawahiri was angry about *Rationalization of Jihad in Egypt and the World* would be a gross understatement. He was apoplectic and deeply hurt by his old associate's accusations. He wrote that his long response was "one of the most difficult things that I have written in my life" and that he had agonized about whether to write it at all.[32] But the strategic dangers of remaining silent against someone with Sharif's credentials were simply too great. Quoting from the tenth-century Arab poet Abu al-Tayyib Ahmad ibn Husayn al-Mutanabbi, Zawahiri offered a glimpse into his inner struggles:

> Fate afflicted me with so many troubles that my heart was
> Wrapped in a membrane of arrows fired at me.
> Fresh volleys of arrows broke on those already in my heart.
> I no longer worry about them because it is fruitless to worry.[33]

It was one thing for his archenemy, President George W. Bush, to insult him. But it was quite another to be attacked by a once dear friend.

By this time Zawahiri had been on the run from the United States and virtually every Western and Middle Eastern government for over seven years. Many of his colleagues had been imprisoned or killed, some quite brutally; he was lucky to be alive. Still, he looked forlorn. His salt-and-pepper beard had grayed, and the circles under his eyes had darkened. Like Sharif, he wore thick glasses because of his dimming eyesight. The mark of constant prayer on his forehead, the *zebiba*, had become more pronounced. Even his teeth looked aged, with a conspicuous buildup of plaque on the bottom row.

Zawahiri called his manifesto *A Treatise on the Exoneration of the Nation of the Pen and Sword of the Denigrating Charge of Being Irresolute and Weak*. The majority of Sharif's document, he charged, criticized al Qa'ida but said virtually nothing about the Egyptian government, one of "the most corrupt regimes that Egypt has ever seen and has, as both its loyalists and opponents agree, perpetrated more torture and murders than any previous regime."[34] How could Sharif fail to criticize the Egyptian government? The only possibility, he mused, was that Egypt's security services must have assisted in writing, editing, and publishing the document. After all, Zawahiri pointed out, Sharif wrote from a prison cell in Egypt.

Zawahiri also accused Sharif of gross irresponsibility in failing to criticize the United States for its "barbarities." The indictment was a cheap shot. Sharif *had* criticized the United States and had supported jihad against the Americans in Afghanistan. In a rhetorical swipe, Zawahiri asked if the electrical current for the fax machine used to serialize Sharif's book also powered the Tura prison's electric chair. He also suggested that the Americans must have been involved in producing the document. "What is your opinion about the U.S. embassy and the FBI and CIA bureaus in Egypt?" he asked. "By the way, they are the bodies that supervise your revisions."[35]

It was a classic Zawahiri tactic. What better way of denigrating *Rationalization of Jihad in Egypt and the World* than to accuse Sharif of direct complicity with the infidels? But Sharif gave follow-up interviews with *Al-Hayat* to explain his arguments better, and his son, Isma'il, acknowledged that the book accurately reflected his father's views.

Even if the book was untainted by infidel views, Zawahiri insisted that it aided the enemies of Islam. "It served in the best possible way," he wrote, "the interests of the alliance that the crusaders and Jews have with our rulers, who act in contradiction of sharia . . . The United States is the first beneficiary from these revisions."[36]

Zawahiri then debated specific points. On civilian casualties, he conceded that al Qa'ida operatives had made mistakes in killing women and children, but pointed out that al Qa'ida was engaged in a war and "those who have made mistakes can be held accountable and those who suffered damage can be recompensed according to Sharia."[37] But jihad must continue, he protested. Even in the Prophet Muhammad's era, he pointed out, Muslim commanders made mistakes.

At the same time, Zawahiri maintained that it was legitimate to kill civilians, including Muslims, under some conditions. One was during night raids, in which al Qa'ida targeted specific individuals and killed women or children accidentally. "If they are not separated from the others," he wrote, "it is permitted to kill them including old people, women, young boys, sick persons, incapacitated persons, and unworldly monks."[38] A second condition involved killing those who supported infidels by providing money, information, or other aid. Although they were not engaged in actual fighting, abetting the enemy was just as condemnable. "It is permitted to kill women, young boys, and the old and infirm if they help their people," Zawahiri wrote.[39] A third condition was when civilians were used as human shields. "If they mix with others and one cannot avoid killing them along with the others," Zawahiri insisted, "then it is permitted to kill them."[40]

Logic was never Zawahiri's strong suit. His reasoning grew increasingly strained as the list of caveats for civilian casualties grew longer. He maintained, for example, that while the United States and its allies allowed women to join the armed forces, "those [women] who are not soldiers still behave like men" and "hence it is permitted to kill them."[41] The same applied to young boys and even infirm old men from the West. "We stated above that every Muslim in the world should now fight them and kill them wherever they are found, be they civilians or military men," he wrote. "We meant every word."[42]

As Zawahiri saw it, the Muslim world was engaged in a violent clash of civilizations with the West. It was the U.S.-led crusaders on one side and Islam on the other. Embellishing his political weight, Zawahiri did not refer to al Qa'ida in the document but rather to the "mujahideen." This rhetorical move presumptuously implied that he spoke for the entire *ummah*, or Islamic community. War was the only option in this struggle to the death. "This religion came through the sword, rose by the sword, will persist by the sword, and will be lost if the sword is lost," he claimed.[43] Zawahiri's argument was based not just on his understanding of Muslim actions since the apex of the caliphate but on his belief that the United States and its Arab allies, including Egypt, committed countless atrocities. Al Qa'ida's actions weren't terrorism, he said, but the United States' were.

Zawahiri also vigorously denied the charge that al Qa'ida failed to secure the support of the ulema, rattling off a list of individuals who supported al Qa'ida's views. They included the Afghan insurgent leader Jalaluddin Haqqani, Sayyid Qutb, Abdullah Azzam, and nearly two dozen others, some of whom, like Qutb, had been killed for their extreme convictions. Zawahiri also accused Sharif of hypocrisy. He lacked religious credentials, Zawahiri fumed, yet had the audacity to masquerade as an authority. "The author says he is neither a religious scholar nor a mufti but he still calls this action permitted, that action obligatory, and that one prohibited,"

Zawahiri wrote. "He passes Sharia judgments over momentous events that are rarely judged by one religious authority alone."[44]

Sharif's goal, Zawahiri charged, was to "stop the Muslim jihad" and prohibit protests against ruling regimes in the Middle East "whether by word of mouth or act of hand, or even peaceful protests in the form of demonstrations, strikes, sit-ins, conferences, and meetings."[45] Even worse, Sharif supported an appeasement strategy that placated the crusaders, Jews, and heretics in the Egyptian government. This was an unfair accusation. Sharif strongly supported jihad when Muslim nations were attacked but argued that jihad was only one of several options available to Muslims.

Still, a formidable army of extremists came to Zawahiri's defense, many of them Egyptians who had worked closely with Zawahiri and knew Sharif personally. Their goal was clear: to demean Sharif's name and disparage his credentials. One of the most vocal critics was Adil Abd al-Majeed Abd al-Bari, better known to his colleagues as Abbas or Abu Dia. In 1996, Zawahiri appointed Bari as head of Egyptian Islamic Jihad's cell in London, and he rented an apartment on Beethoven Street, a residential area within walking distance of Paddington train station.[46] Bari was an erudite, well-spoken lawyer who had defended numerous Islamists in Egyptian court, including the spiritual leader of al-Gama'a al-Islamiyya, Umar Abd al-Rahman, who was convicted in the United States for involvement in the 1993 World Trade Center bombing.[47] In the meantime Bari had become a wanted man. The United States indicted him for his alleged involvement in the 1998 terrorist attacks against its embassies in Nairobi and Dar es Salaam.[48] In 1999, Bari was imprisoned in the United Kingdom following Operation Challenge, a Scotland Yard and MI5 effort against Egyptian extremists.

Though he was stuck in jail, Bari could not stay on the sidelines. He leapt to Zawahiri's defense and labeled Sharif a failed leader who had been forced out of Egyptian Islamic Jihad because of his poor organizational skills. He was "dismissed as Amir [of Egyptian Islamic Jihad] because of his complacency about the group's concerns," Bari remarked. Sharif's book must have been inspired by revenge for his alienation from Egyptian Islamic Jihad a decade earlier. "His anger here is equal to his anger because of his dismissal from being the Amir of the group," Bari concluded.[49]

Muhammad Hasan Khalil al-Hakim, who used the nom de guerre Abu Jihad al-Masri, agreed. He was an al Qa'ida operational and propaganda leader who resided primarily in Iran. "This is not the first time we object to the opinions and fatwas by Shaykh Sayyid Imam," he said. "We were dumbfounded and amazed by how he ended his involvement with the jihad group which was for reasons inconsistent with Islamic law."[50] As al Qa'ida's senior leader for Egypt, he was not exactly objective. Hakim, who was later killed by a U.S. drone strike in Pakistan, had a boxer's muscular jaw, a tree trunk of a neck, and a receding hairline that gave him a wild, edgy aura. He also sported a thin layer of stubble and flashed a confident grin, like a Hollywood movie star. For Hakim, Sharif's *Rationalization of Jihad in Egypt and the World* was the pathetic last gasp of a failed leader. The document was motivated by revenge and vitriol, pure and simple.

Sharif had "lost his mind," remarked Hani al-Siba'i, an Egyptian lawyer and member of the Egyptian Islamic Jihad shura.[51] Siba'i, who was more colloquially referred to as "Doctor" or "Shaykh Doctor," had worked with both Zawahiri and Sharif. In 1999, Egyptian authorities convicted him in absentia, along with Zawahiri and Sharif, of planning to overthrow the Egyptian government and sentenced him to fifteen years in prison. But he had secured political asylum in the United Kingdom, where he established the Almaqreze Centre for Historical Studies in London. Over time he became an annoyance to the British, arguing on Al Jazeera that the July 2005 attacks were "a great victory" for al Qa'ida. Wearing a svelte navy blue blazer, button-down dress shirt, crisp white collar, and oval spectacles, he could have been mistaken for an investment banker had it not been for the scraggly beard and black Muslim prayer cap.

Speaking softly but confidently into the camera, he remarked that al Qa'ida had "rubbed the noses of the world's eight most powerful countries in the mud," a reference to the G-8 members, who were meeting in the United Kingdom at the time of the attack.[52]

Hakim, Saba'i, and others now considered Sharif a lackey of the West and its allies. "From the beginning of the memorandum to its end," wrote Siba'i, "he was in favor of the Americans and he poured out his anger against the two Shaykhs Usama bin Laden and Ayman al-Zawahiri."[53] For Hakim, Sharif's book was "the result of a strategic project for the Egyptian Intelligence."[54]

Many didn't believe that Sharif could criticize al Qa'ida and ignore the sins of the Egyptian government. "The question that presents itself and awaits a response from Shaykh Sayyid: Is the tyrant Hosni Mubarak to terrorize more than 70 million Egyptian Muslims" only to have Sharif ignore his actions? asked Abu-Basir al-Tartusi, a Syrian Salafi cleric also living in London, who posted his response to Sharif on jihadist websites.[55]

Perhaps the most powerful critique of Sharif, however, came from Hani al-Siba'i, who dug into Sharif's past writings and compared them to *Rationalization of Jihad in Egypt and the World.* His strategy was to use Sharif's past arguments to counter his current ones. Siba'i outlined how Sharif's past works had denounced Egyptian rulers as apostates and contended that "jihad against them is a must." In a document titled *Terrorism Is Part of Islam*, Sharif had written that "dividing people into civilians and military personnel is an invented way, and has no origin in the Islamic sharia."[56] For Saba'i and other detractors, Sharif had accomplished the antithesis of what his title promised.

"Shaykh Sayyid did not rationalize the work of jihad as he claims in his revisions titled 'Rationalization of Jihad,' but he canceled, abolished, and forbade jihad and incriminated those who are trying to revive it," remarked Abu-Basir al-Tartusi. "Therefore the correct title for his revisions should be 'Retraction of Jihad.'"[57]

The Debate Expands

Sharif had prepared for many of these criticisms. "I know how they think," he said, "and the suspicions they will cast. Therefore, I will reply to them before they present these suspicions."

To the charges of hypocrisy, he said that his early opinions on jihad, apparent in some of his writings like *The Essential Guide for Preparation*, had begun to change more than a decade before.

To the charges of bias by his jailers, the Egyptian government, he wrote, "What is significant is the evidence presented by the writing, and not where it took place."[58]

"Was I in an Egyptian jail in 1992 when I denounced Al-Jihad Organization's armed actions inside Egypt? I was in Pakistan at that time and I was in Sudan in 1994," he noted. "When I did this, was I in the hands of Egyptian intelligence?"[59] The real issue, he said, was the substance of his writing. "They know in advance that they cannot respond to the arguments in the document. This is because I do not speak without providing proof from the Qur'an and the prophet's Sunnah. They found that they had nothing left but to slander the author by alleging that it was written by the Egyptian intelligence service and the security services."[60]

Sharif also responded to the argument that his book was helping the Americans and other infidels. "This accusation was made against us when we joined the Afghan jihad against the communists," he remarked in an interview in *Al-Hayat*. "They said that we were U.S. agents and that our jihad served the United States against the Russians."[61] Neither Sharif nor most who supported him were zealots of the West. In their eyes, the United States, Israel, and Arab regimes were guilty of atrocities.

By late 2007 the debate had grown beyond either Sharif or Zawahiri and had moved into digital battlefields: jihadist websites, Internet chat rooms, e-mails, and newspapers and magazines spanning the Muslim world, though most Western officials were unaware of it. A growing throng began to attack Zawahiri and his defenders. Nabil Naim, an influential Egyptian Islamic Jihad member, described Hani al-Siba'i as one of the "jihadis of Scotland Yard."[62] Naim's voice carried a lot of influence, in part because of his long association with Zawahiri, Siba'i, and others. When Zawahiri left for Saudi Arabia and Pakistan in the 1980s, he turned over command of the Egyptian faction of Egyptian Islamic Jihad to Naim. By the mid-1990s, however, Naim began to have second thoughts about the effectiveness of the armed struggle against the Egyptian government and focused instead on Israel.[63] And he became extremely critical of Zawahiri's dangerous radicalization and push toward global jihad.

Others lamented that the continuing bloodshed was weakening Islam and causing Muslims to kill each other. "My brother Usama bin Laden, the image of Islam today is not at its best," wrote Salman al-Awdah, a Saudi cleric and Muslim scholar, in an open letter to bin Laden. "People all over the world say that Islam orders the killing of those who do not believe in it . . . Where is the mercy in killing people? Where is the mercy in turning many Muslim countries into regions of war and fighting? The Prophet, God's prayers and peace be upon him, conquered and subjugated the entire Peninsula without any massacres."[64]

Awdah, who was born in Al-Basr village in Saudi Arabia in 1956, was an antiestablishment Salafi cleric. Like Nabil Naim and others, he was deeply disturbed by al Qa'ida's atrocities. Much of the violence, he felt, was predicated on "misunderstood or misinterpreted arguments based on sharia."[65] Awdah used multiple media forums to convey his views. Extraordinarily photogenic, with his neatly trimmed black beard and white-and-red-checked kaffiyeh, he was a dynamic speaker and appeared regularly on Al Jazeera and other television programs. He also acted as the general supervisor for IslamToday.com, the website of the Saudi periodical *Al-Islam Al-Yawm*. Like many other critics of al Qa'ida, he was certainly not pro-American and had criticized the U.S. invasion of Iraq, cosigning an "open letter to the Iraqi people" that called for "defensive

Ayman al-Zawahiri played a key role as one of al Qa'ida's founders. But his support of civilian casualties and public feuds with Hamas, Muslim Brotherhood, and other organizations made him a controversial figure. *AP Photo/IntelCenter*

José Padilla, center, is escorted into a police vehicle by U.S. marshals. He was involved in an al Qa'ida plot to target apartment buildings in the United States before his arrest on March 8, 2002. *AP Photo/J. Pat Carter*

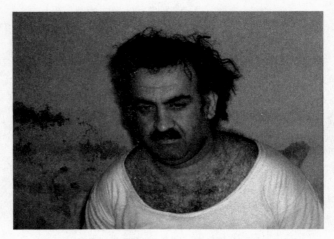

Khalid Sheikh Mohammed, one of the masterminds of the September 11 attacks, is shown shortly after his capture in Pakistan on March 1, 2003. His arrest came at the end of al Qa'ida's first wave of violent activity, thanks to Pakistan, the CIA, FBI, and other agencies. *AP Photo*

Abu Mus'ab al-Zarqawi, the head of al Qa'ida in Iraq, spearheaded al Qa'ida's second wave after the 2003 U.S. invasion of Iraq. The large U.S. and allied footprint contributed to al Qa'ida's resurgence and a rise in radicalization across the Muslim world. *AP Photo/U.S. Department of Defense*

On July 7, 2005, British terrorists attacked three Underground trains and this double-decker bus, killing 56 people and wounding more than 700 others. Al Qa'ida leaders in Pakistan planned the operation and trained the bombers. *AP Photo/Peter Macdiarmid*

Adam Gadahn was raised in southern California and recruited by an al Qa'ida facilitator while attending a mosque in Orange County. He later moved to Pakistan and became an active member of al Qa'ida's propaganda efforts. *Federal Bureau of Investigation*

Treason - 18 U.S.C. § 2381; Providing Material Support to Al
Qaeda - 18 U.S.C. § 2339B; Aiding and Abetting - 18 U.S.C. § 2

ADAM YAHIYE GADAHN

Aliases:
Abu Suhayb Al-Amriki, Abu Suhail Al-Amriki, Abu Suhayb, Yihya Majadin Adams, Adam Pearlman, Yayah, Azzam the American, Azzam Al-Amriki

DESCRIPTION

Date(s) of Birth Used:	September 1, 1978	Hair:	Brown
Place of Birth:	United States	Eyes:	Hazel
Height:	5'11"	Complexion:	Light
Weight:	210 pounds	Sex:	Male
Build:	Medium	Citizenship:	American
		Languages:	Arabic; English

Scars and Marks: Gadahn has scars on his chest and right forearm.
Remarks: None

CAUTION

Adam Yahiye Gadahn was indicted in the Central District of California for treason and material support to Al Qaeda. The charges are related to Gadahn's alleged involvement in a number of terrorist activities, including providing aid and comfort to Al Qaeda and services for Al Qaeda.

REWARD

The Rewards For Justice Program, United States Department of State, is offering a reward of up to $1 million for information leading to the arrest of Adam Yahiye Gadahn.

SHOULD BE CONSIDERED ARMED AND DANGEROUS

If you have any information concerning this person, please contact your local FBI office or the nearest American Embassy or Consulate.

Abdulla Ahmed Ali prepares his martyrdom video during a 2006 al Qa'ida plot to destroy airplanes on their way from London to the United States and Canada. But British police and intelligence foiled the plot, with help from U.S. agencies. *AP Photo/Metropolitan Police*

Sheikh Abdul Sattar Abu Risha (right) helped lead a revolt against al Qa'ida in Iraq, ending the second wave of violence. Al Qa'ida in Iraq's decision to kill large numbers of civilians alienated the local Iraqi population. *U.S. Department of Defense/Lance Corporal Julian Billmair*

Najibullah Zazi led an al Qa'ida plot to bomb New York City subways after training in Pakistan's tribal areas. But U.S. intelligence and law enforcement agencies discovered the plot and arrested Zazi in 2009, shortly before the attack. *AP Photo/Ed Andrieski*

After training with al Qa'ida in the Arabian Peninsula in Yemen, Umar Farouk Abdulmutallab attempted to blow up a Detroit-bound airliner in December 2009 as part of al Qa'ida's third wave. But the bomb partially malfunctioned and failed to take down the aircraft. *AP Photo/U.S. Marshals Service*

Anwar al-Awlaki, who was born in the United States, was instrumental in initiating a third wave of terrorism from his base in Yemen. He leveraged the Internet and other social media forums to distribute radical propaganda and recruit new members. *AP Photo/Site Intelligence Group*

On May 1, 2010, Faisal Shahzad tried to launch a terrorist attack in New York City, but the bomb failed to detonate. Shahzad had received his bomb-making training from the Tehreek-e Taliban Pakistan. *AP Photo/U.S. Marshals Service*

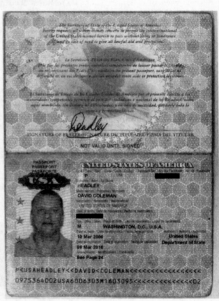

From his base in Chicago, David Headley presented a new model for terrorism during al Qa'ida's third wave. He worked simultaneously for several militant groups, including al Qa'ida and Lashkar-e-Taiba. *U.S. Department of Justice*

President Barack Obama talks with members of the national security team in the Situation Room of the White House on May 1, 2011, the day of the raid against Osama bin Laden. *White House/ Pete Souza*

Osama bin Laden's compound in Abbottabad, Pakistan. His capture signaled the end of the third wave and was a testament to the patient work of U.S. special operations forces, the CIA, the National Security Agency, and other secret agencies. *Central Intelligence Agency*

A U.S. MQ-1B Predator unmanned aerial vehicle prepares to take off. U.S. drone attacks increasingly targeted al Qa'ida leaders in Pakistan, Yemen, and other countries, contributing to the end of the third wave. *U.S. Air Force/Technical Sergeant Sabrina Johnson*

jihad" against U.S. military "occupation."[66] He believed the United States had come to the Middle East to start a Shi'a-Sunni war. "It will be good for Israel and the United States," Awdah argued. "They will support both sides, fan the fire of this war, and applaud it. People will kill each other."[67]

Another al Qa'ida critic was Shaykh Yusuf al-Qaradawi, an Egyptian Islamic theologian and affiliate of the Muslim Brotherhood, who condemned al Qa'ida and its tactics, arguing, "Islam says that unjustly killing human beings is a major crime that comes after polytheism and it has not been approved by divine scriptures."[68] Qaradawi was a heavyweight in many Muslim circles and had been banned from the United States and the United Kingdom for his extreme views, a testament to his credentials. He publicly supported suicide attacks against perceived foreign occupiers of Muslim lands—including those in Israel, Palestinian territory, and Iraq—but condemned al Qa'ida for attacking Muslims.

Qaradawi had impeccable religious credentials. In 1973 he earned a Ph.D. from Al-Azhar University, the Harvard of Sunni Islamic learning and Arab literature, writing his dissertation on "Zakah and Its Effect on Solving Social Problems." Yet he embraced modern technology and became a television icon, running a program called *Ash-Sharia wal-Hayat* (Sharia and Life) on Al Jazeera. He was an animated and charismatic speaker. On his show he could be histrionic, waving his hands and shouting at one moment, quiet and controlled the next, yet he was compelling and empathetic, and deftly used multiple media formats to reach young people all over the world. He could even be hip. He often wore a white prayer cap, fashionable glasses, and a button-down shalwar kameez. For IslamOnline.net, a popular website he helped found in 1997, he served as chief religious scholar. His anti-American and anti–al Qa'ida stance made him a paradox for U.S. intelligence agencies, who often disagreed about whether he was a moderate, mainstream, or extremist Sunni cleric. His criticism of Zawahiri showed that not all young Muslims were taken with al Qa'ida's appeals.

A number of other Egyptian Islamic Jihad members came to Sharif's defense. Ahmad Yusuf Hamdallah, an Egyptian Islamic Jihad leader, characterized Sharif's book as a "tsunami" that would affect current and future generations. He, too, scoffed at the idea that Sharif's new assertions were the result of pressure from Egypt's security agencies.[69] In 1981, Hamdallah had been convicted in connection with the assassination of Egyptian president Anwar Sadat, and he had spent years in and out of jail. Usamah Siddiq Ayyub, a prominent Egyptian Islamist living in Germany, described Sharif's writings as "a turning point," saying that "the revisions conducted by the Islamic Jihad derive their importance from the fact that they were drawn up by the first person to lay down the principles of jihadist ideology in the world."[70]

Equally significant, however, was the assault on al Qa'ida from two powerful Sunni organizations, Egypt's Muslim Brotherhood and Palestinian Hamas. In an article published on the Muslim Brotherhood's website, ikhwanweb.com, the group "welcomed the reviews carried out and declared by the Islamic Jihad group leaders."[71] After coming under withering criticism from Zawahiri for this modest support of Sharif, the group attacked Zawahiri himself. Dr. Isam al-Iryan, a member of the Muslim Brotherhood's Guidance Bureau and its chief spokesman, wrote that "al-Zawahiri's policy and preaching bore dangerous fruit and had a negative impact on Islam and Islamic movements across the world."[72] In addition, leaders of Hamas, which the U.S. government designated a terrorist organization, attacked Zawahiri.[73] Hamas's political leader, Khaled Meshaal, said that the group had "its own vision" and did not need al Qa'ida's advice.[74] "May God have mercy on our brother Ayman al-Zawahiri for making many mistakes," said Khalil Abu Layla, a senior Hamas leader.[75] Both were responding to Zawahiri's accusation that Hamas had flouted Islam and "fallen in the swamp of capitulation" by participating in Palestinian elections.[76]

The most devastating attacks against al Qa'ida came from a seemingly innocuous source. In 2008 al Qa'ida's media organization, As-Sahab, announced that Ayman al-Zawahiri was prepared to answer questions posted on jihadist websites. Hundreds of individuals responded, including supporters of al Qa'ida, media organizations, hostile critics, and presumably foreign intelligence agencies. At first blush it appeared to be a well-conceived propaganda and recruitment move. Al Qa'ida was leveraging some of the most advanced social media and encouraging a personable, one-on-one dialogue with the charismatic Zawahiri. This would perhaps be the public's only opportunity to engage directly with al Qa'ida's second-in-command. "I thank all who took an interest in As-Sahab's invitation to an open meeting with me," Zawahiri said, "and I thank in particular the unknown soldiers from those garrisoned on our front lines in jihadist media."[77] Yet Zawahiri's gamble backfired. In the manner of many town hall meetings, there were sycophants praising al Qa'ida, but also a sizable number who had come to express their grievances.

"Excuse me, Mr. Zawahiri," asked Mudarris Jughrafiya, who described himself as a geography teacher, "but who is it that is killing, with Your Excellency's blessing, the innocents in Baghdad, Morocco, and Algeria? Do you consider the killing of women and children to be jihad?"

Talib Jami'i Tib al-Jazaa'ir, a medical student from Algeria, similarly inquired, "Is killing women and children jihad in your view? I want al-Zawahiri to answer me about those who kill the people in Algeria. What is the legal evidence for killing the innocents?"

"And what is it that makes legitimate the spilling of the blood of even one Muslim?" asked another questioner, who identified himself as I'laamiyyah.

"Many people in the Islamic world," wrote another, "complain that al Qa'ida organization was behind many operations that targeted innocent civilians and Muslims within the Islamic nations and many Muslims and children died as a result of such operations. Do you not think that you are shedding prohibited and innocents' blood?"[78]

The exchange did not produce the propaganda victory Zawahiri had imagined. The decision to hold a virtual press conference suggested a desire to communicate and alleviate growing concerns among jihadists about the future of the movement. Instead, his responses, and particularly his failure to respond to some questions, revealed growing doubts about al Qa'ida.

Declining Support

In addition to growing discontent on the Internet and in the Arab press, public opinion polls showed that Zawahiri and al Qa'ida were losing the war for hearts and minds. Support for Osama bin Laden plummeted in much of the world: from 56 percent in 2003 to 20 percent in 2007 in Jordan; from 20 percent to 1 percent in Lebanon; from 15 percent to 5 percent in Turkey; from 59 percent to 41 percent in Indonesia; and from 46 percent to 38 percent in Pakistan.[79] Many had grown tired of the bloodshed. "Killing those civilians in civilian aircraft and trains and in buildings and hotels is not the legitimate form sanctioning the killing of an unbeliever," wrote Sharif. He warned Muslim youths, "O you young people, do not be deceived by the heroes of the Internet, the leaders of the microphones and the dealers of slogans who are themselves the largest suppliers of tombs and prisons."[80]

Through all of the criticism within Islam, however, there was no coordinated American response. Some officials, including the FBI's Philip Mudd, argued that this debate was an opportunity to support Islamic groups that opposed al Qa'ida, such as Egypt's Muslim Brotherhood. "The Brotherhood's role in our new decade-long campaign against al Qa'ida and its affiliates doesn't appear prominently in the U.S. debate," Mudd wrote. "It should, especially for those who accept the maxim that the enemy of an enemy is a friend."

But Mudd went further, arguing that the U.S. should reach out to the Brotherhood. "The rise of Muslim Brotherhood activists is an opportunity for the U.S. As we debate how to best respond to this Islamist wave, we should not lose sight of the fact that the Brotherhood could curb the spread of al Qa'ida's violent extremism."[81]

Yet Mudd's view was too radical for many U.S. government officials, who labeled the Brotherhood an extremist organization. Thus the reverse wave against al Qa'ida happened in the absence of a U.S. strategy to counter al Qa'ida's message. As U.S. officials dithered, it became clear that al Qa'ida had gone too far. Its leaders supported a nearly limitless war that had engulfed much of the Muslim world in bloodshed. Moreover, al Qa'ida had failed to establish a caliphate, a goal that many believed was naive and unrealistic to begin with. Instead, they had lost the one country where their version of sharia law was established, Afghanistan, after the overthrow of the Taliban. "There are those who say that jihad has conclusively failed as a method for removing the governing regimes in Muslim countries," a questioner remarked to Zawahiri during his virtual press conference. "They claim that this jihad has brought disasters upon our outreach and missionary work and [has not given us] a single good thing."[82]

Zawahiri had no response. The second wave had now ended. Al Qa'ida's punishment strategy, which involved targeting civilians, backfired. In several countries where al Qa'ida had established a foothold, such as Iraq, national security forces had improved and were able to establish order, undermining al Qa'ida's sanctuary. Stories about the decline of al Qa'ida began to appear in the media. Not only had the organization been losing support in its home region, it had repeatedly failed to hit the U.S. homeland. It was time to try again, thanks in part to the work of an upstart Yemeni-American named Anwar al-Awlaki.

PART III

THE THIRD WAVE

12

LEADERLESS JIHAD?

MAY 7, 2007, was a tepid spring evening in Cherry Hill, New Jersey. The setting sun painted a gilded layer within a band of clouds that slid across the sky. Only 5 miles east of Philadelphia in the Delaware Valley, Cherry Hill is an icon of American suburbia. *Money* magazine anointed it one of the most desirable places to live in the United States. It boasted one of the first large indoor shopping malls east of the Mississippi, with chic, upscale stores like Nordstrom and Abercrombie & Fitch, a median family income of $88,401, and a plethora of well-educated doctors, lawyers, and engineers.[1]

That evening, Dritan Duka and his brother Shain arrived at a split-level apartment on East Tampa Avenue. The Dukas were Albanians from Kosovo, whose family had entered the United States illegally through Mexico in 1984. They were in Cherry Hill to pick up three AK-47 Kalashnikov rifles, four M16 fully automatic assault rifles, and four handguns. But they were not alone. A team of FBI and other federal agents had tailed them. The FBI had clandestinely infiltrated the group and secured live video and sound of the meeting. Dritan Duka had ordered the weapons on April 6. He and several colleagues planned to mount a multipronged terrorist attack against U.S. soldiers and civilians at Fort Dix, a U.S. Army base about 30 miles away. The plan called for a quick strike and an equally rapid retreat—a hit-and-run. The group had completed training in the Pocono Mountains of Pennsylvania and at paintball complexes. In prior months they had also conducted surveillance of Fort Dix and other U.S. military bases.

In January 2007, a few months before, Dritan and Shain had explained to one of their colleagues, Besnik Bakalli, that they needed more weapons.

"We have four," said Shain.

"We have nine-millimeter handgun," added Dritan in a thick Albanian accent.

"We have one handgun," continued Shain. "We have shotgun."

"Yes," said Bakalli.

"We have an assault rifle, machine gun," Shain explained.

Bakalli stopped him. "It's a machine gun?"

"It's not a machine gun," chimed in Eljvir Duka, Dritan and Shain's twenty-three-year-old brother.

Dritan protested. "Yes, machine gun, it's not full Bam! Bam! Bam!" he said, trying to imitate the sound. "It goes by itself. Automatic. And we have that SKS," he continued.

Bakalli stopped him. "SKS?"

"Yes, SKS Yugoslavian," Shain answered, referring to the Yugoslav-made SKS automatic rifle, a poor man's version of the AK-47.[2]

These formidable weapons could certainly inflict damage, but the group needed assault rifles. The plan was to kill as many U.S. soldiers as possible. Two years later, Nidal Malik Hasan, a major in the U.S. Army, would use an FN Five-seveN semiautomatic weapon to shoot nearly four dozen people at Fort Hood, Texas, killing thirteen of them.[3] The Dukas didn't know this, of course, but they knew assault rifles would be necessary. In April 2007 they turned to a friend, Mahmoud Omar, to help procure the weapons.

"We need to talk." said Dritan. "The list, I need all the, the AKs. The M16s and all the handguns. AKs, the M16s and all the handguns. All of them I need," he repeated. "He has four right now. Each one. I want all of the AKs, all the M16s, I think there was four, no five AKs I think and four M16s. And I need all the handguns, one of each. Everything he had except that RPG and the M60."[4]

Omar agreed to buy the weapons from a contact in Baltimore; May 7 was the delivery day. As the FBI watched on hidden surveillance cameras, Omar, who was actually an FBI informant, handed over the weapons in the living room of his coffee-colored apartment on East Tampa Avenue.[5] Omar's haul included four Colt M16A1 machine guns, one Polytech AKS-762 semiautomatic rifle, and two Norinco AK-47 semiautomatic rifles.[6] Shortly after 9 p.m., a SWAT team and dozens of federal agents burst into the living room, which was sparsely decorated with a faded brown couch and low-end, off-white vertical blinds. Several other accomplices, including Mohamad Shnewer, Eljvir Duka, and Serdar Tatar were arrested at different locations that day.[7]

The disruption of the Fort Dix plot was a successful counterterrorist operation. The FBI had infiltrated an extremist cell preparing to conduct a combined-action operation against U.S. soldiers. They used signals intelligence and human assets to penetrate the cell, piece together the support network, and capture the plotters. While the cell members did not have a direct connection to al Qa'ida, they were nonetheless inspired by the message of Osama bin Laden, Ayman al-Zawahiri, and an up-and-coming radical preacher named Anwar al-Awlaki. It was the kind of strategy that some extremists, including the Syrian strategist Abu Mus'ab al-Suri, had embraced. Al-Suri, whose work was widely circulated on jihadist websites, encouraged Muslims to become involved in "individual jihad and small cell terrorism."[8]

Fort Dix also showed the limitations of an attack without the direct involvement of al Qa'ida or one of its affiliates. The cell was chronically short of weapons, deficient in the technological savvy to produce homemade explosives, and inept in countersurveillance techniques. While its members could have caused a limited number of casualties, they were unlikely to orchestrate a mass-casualty attack like those on New York and Washington in 2001, Madrid in 2004, and London in 2005. Still, the growing influence of Anwar al-Awlaki, based in Yemen, was the first indication that a third wave was imminent.

This Life Is Nothing

The Fort Dix plotters underwent a radicalization process fundamentally different from that of the September 11 hijackers, José Padilla, Adam Gadahn, and many other previous cases. The New Jersey group had never trained in an al Qa'ida camp, never been approached by an al Qa'ida recruiter, and never actually met an al Qa'ida operative. The core group—Mohamad Shnewer, Serdar Tatar, and the Duka brothers—came from different backgrounds.[9]

The Duka brothers—Dritan, Shain, and Eljvir—were from Debar, Macedonia, and spent time in Texas and Brooklyn before arriving in Cherry Hill. They had hopes of fame and fortune. Eljvir was in a rock-music video, Dritan was an extra in the television show *Law & Order*, and Shain was in a commercial for the World Wrestling Federation.[10] But these promising opportunities soon fizzled out. Dritan, whose friends often called him Anthony or Tony, was the oldest. At twenty-eight, he was stout and burly, played basketball, and hung out at the local Dunkin' Donuts. He and his wife, Jennifer Marino, an Italian-American convert to Islam, had five children. Eljvir, whose friends called him Sulayman or Elvis, and Shain were more rambunctious. High school classmates remember them as exuding "a gangster attitude" and as "incredibly disruptive" in school. Neither Eljvir nor Shain graduated from high school.[11] After they dropped out, they operated a roofing company, and then Dritan and Shain owned a pizza restaurant together in Turnersville, New Jersey. They sold the business in 2005 but made no money. This was not the America they had envisioned.

"We were lacking, our whole life lacking," Shain explained to Besnik Bakalli. "And our whole lives since we've been in America we have only gotten by," he continued. "There [were] times when it was very hard, and we would go into debt with the food suppliers that would bring us the supplies."

"Man, this life is nothing, man," replied Bakalli.

Shain's family had squeezed themselves into a small apartment. "We lived, Besnik, in an apartment, all of us. It was Dritoni with two kids. Look, my Dad, my Mom, Dritoni, his bride. He had two kids at the time, Dritoni, me, Sulayman," Shain lamented. There were ten people in total, crammed into a two-bedroom apartment.[12]

Mohamad Shnewer, a Palestinian from Jordan, moved to the United States when he was two years old. He was a chronic under-achiever, dropping out of Camden County College and living at his parents' house, with its unkempt yard and cluttered carport. After quitting his job at the family store following a dispute with his father, Shnewer began driving a taxi in Philadelphia. Over-weight, he struggled with low self-esteem and spent much of his free time watching Nickelodeon and playing video games, especially Madden NFL, the American football video game named after the sports commentator and Super Bowl–winning coach of the Oak-land Raiders. Shnewer knew the Duka brothers from high school, and Eljvir married one of his sisters, Hnan. They also attended the Al-Aqsa Islamic Society Mosque in Philadelphia and the Islamic Center of South Jersey in Palmyra.[13]

Serdar Tatar, the final key member of the plot, moved to the United States with his family in 1992 from Turkey. Although Tatar failed to graduate from Cherry Hill High School West, dropping out during his junior year, he earned a high school equivalency diploma and worked at his father's restaurant, Super-Mario's Pizza. As Tatar became more religious, his father, Muslim Tatar, grew increasingly perturbed. "I'm not a religious person," he said. "I don't want my son to be a religious person, but he was a religious person."[14] Serdar Tatar eventually left SuperMario's and took a job at a 7-Eleven convenience store on the Temple University campus. Yet he remained in contact with the Duka brothers and Mohamad Shnewer, whom he had met at Cherry Hill High School West.

The group shared a collective frustration with their lives. They often griped about the U.S. wars in Afghanistan and Iraq, the Russian war in Chechnya, and the plight of Palestinians. Yet these sentiments were not uncommon, especially among young Muslims, and it was unlikely that the men would have resorted to violence if an eloquent American preacher named Anwar al-Awlaki had not helped tip them in that direction.

The Rise of Awlaki

Anwar Nasser Abdulla al-Awlaki was born on April 22, 1971, in Las Cruces, New Mexico, where his father was studying on a Fulbright scholarship.[15] Awlaki spent much of his childhood in Yemen. His father served as minister of agriculture and fisheries there, and Awlaki studied in a secular high school in the capital, Sana'a. In 1991 he moved to the United States to attend Colorado State University. Awlaki was torn between Yemen's deeply conservative religious culture and freewheeling American ways.[16] He hesitated to shake hands with women on religious grounds, yet he was arrested twice for soliciting prostitutes. The first time, he pleaded guilty to a lesser charge by agreeing to enter an AIDS education program and pay $400 in fines and restitution. The second time, he pleaded guilty and was sentenced to three years' probation, fined $240, and ordered to perform twelve days of community service.[17]

Awlaki eventually became enthralled with jihad. After a summer visit to Afghanistan, he brought back an Afghan hat and wore it proudly around the Colorado State campus. In 1994 he married a cousin from Yemen, and he served as imam of the Denver

Islamic Society from 1994 to 1996, though he had no formal religious training. He was exactly the type of person that Sayyid Imam Abd al-Aziz al-Sharif and others had warned about—a charlatan posing as a trained Islamic scholar. Awlaki later served as imam of the Masjid Al-Ribat al-Islami mosque in San Diego, which was attended by two of the September 11 hijackers, Nawaf al-Hazmi and Khalid al-Midhar.[18] He relocated to northern Virginia in January 2001 and became imam of the Dar al-Hijrah mosque in Falls Church, which was attended by Hazmi and yet another September 11 hijacker, Hani Hanjour. Later he served as the Muslim chaplain at George Washington University.

Fluent in English, renowned for giving eloquent talks on Islam, and adept at attracting young non-Arabic speakers, Awlaki "was the magic bullet," according to the Dar al-Hijrah mosque's spokesman, Johari Abdul-Malik. "He had everything all in a box."[19] Indeed, Awlaki's charismatic, soft-spoken style and stirring lectures earned him a growing cadre of followers. He had a disarming aura and unnerving confidence, with an easy smile and a soothing, eloquent voice. He stood a lanky six feet, one inch tall, weighed 160 pounds, and had a thick black beard, an oversized nose, and wire-rimmed glasses. He spoke in a clear, almost hypnotic voice. "He had an allure," said Johari Abdul-Malik. "He was charming."[20]

When Awlaki spoke, he used his hands like an orchestra conductor, slicing them through the air and flicking his wrists. To emphasize points, he occasionally shrugged his shoulders or touched the tip of his index finger to his thumb, moving it downward in a sweeping motion, sometimes violently. For Awlaki, speaking was an art, not a duty.

He also understood the intricacies of the Internet and used it to broadcast his messages. His fluency in vernacular English, unabashed advocacy of jihad, and Web-savvy approach were a powerful combination. His lectures were available on the Internet and his CDs were sold in Islamic bookstores around the world. Awlaki operated his own blog and was active on several social networking sites. His supporters set up sites on Facebook and MySpace devoted to proselytizing his sermons and praising him. Awlaki envisioned himself as a vanguard figure among English-speaking Muslims. It was his mission to spread the word.

"Most of the Jihad literature is available only in Arabic and publishers are not willing to take the risk of translating it," Awlaki acknowledged. "The only ones who are spending the money and time translating Jihad literature are the Western intelligence services. And too bad, they would not be willing to share it with you."[21]

Most of Awlaki's on-line English lectures were nonviolent and centered on traditional religious themes, the FBI discovered, but some of his most stirring sermons blended Sayyid Qutb's rigid dogmatism with al Qa'ida's sweeping ambition to overthrow Arab regimes and weaken their Western backers. Qutb and several of his works, including his magnum opus, *In the Shade of the Qur'an*, had a profound impact on Awlaki, especially during his tenure in a Yemeni prison in 2006 and 2007.[22]

"Sayyid is a very prolific and eloquent writer. His style is unique," Awlaki confided. "I would be so immersed with the author I would feel that Sayyid was with me in my cell speaking to me directly. There was something about my reading in prison: I could feel the personality of the author through his words. I lived with *In the Shade of the Qur'an* for over a month."[23]

U.S. counterterrorism officials like Philip Mudd watched Awlaki as he developed his own firebrand style. His sermon "The Story of Ibn al-Aqwa" called for modern-day jihad and served as a source of radicalization and legitimacy for those seeking to fight the United States in Iraq or Afghanistan.[24] In 2006, in a departure from his earlier, more moderate lectures, Awlaki encouraged listeners to his lecture "Allah Is Preparing Us for Victory" to take part in jihad during what he called the "Golden Era." In the lecture, which was in English and available for download on several public websites, Awlaki strongly and openly supported violent jihad.[25]

For FBI and other intelligence officials, Awlaki's rise was disturbing, because he had a talent for connecting with impressionable Muslims. "He has credibility with young people," Mudd said.[26]

The Constants of Jihad

Awlaki's sermon "The Constants of Jihad" mesmerized the Fort Dix plotters. They obtained an audio recording of the lecture, in which Awlaki spoke in a relaxed, assured tone. He urged listeners, "Jihad will . . . carry on until the Day of Judgment since we are told to wipe out [non-Muslims] from the world."[27] Quoting from the Qur'an, he encouraged his followers to "fight those of the People of the Book who do not believe in God and the Last Day, who do not forbid what God and His Messenger have forbidden, who do not obey the rule of justice until they pay the tax and agree to submit."[28] Based on the writings of Yousef al-Ayyiri, the founder of al Qa'ida in Saudi Arabia, the sermon was posted on several websites commonly used by Muslim extremists, and Awlaki hit the mark.

"About Anwar al-Awlaki," Shain Duka exclaimed to his colleagues. "You gotta hear this lecture. You gotta hear it. The title? The title is 'Constants of Jihad.'"

His brother Dritan echoed this sentiment. "You gotta hear this lecture, this brother . . . him locked up in Yemen, Anwar al Awlaki the imam in Washington, D.C., they kicked him out of the U.S. and now they locked him up in Yemen. He was talking about jihad, the truth, no holds barred, straight how it is!"

Later, during the same conversation, which the FBI was clandestinely monitoring, the plotters listened to a recording of "Constants on the Path of Jihad."

"You gotta listen to this," Shain insisted. "He has a whole volume of this lecture."

Dritan added, with perceptible excitement, "You can't buy it nowhere . . . He's in jail, they arrest him, he's on house arrest . . . For stuff like this, in Yemen."

Shain agreed. "You can't find it," he said. "In his own country they locked him up for speaking like this . . . That's a good lecture, huh brother? . . . There's no lies with this guy."[29]

Awlaki had struck a chord with the Fort Dix plotters, interpreting Islam in a way they could understand and embrace. "This is the truth," said Eljvir Duka. "I don't give a damn what everybody says. This is Islam, this is the truth right here. So he doesn't sugarcoat, he doesn't have any boundaries to the truth in this, and it's very . . ." He paused.

"Why? Why am I stressing this point?" Eljvir asked rhetorically. "Because we're living in a time where confused Muslims themselves, they're confused . . . about our own brothers, you understand? So this lecture is very necessary for people today."[30]

For the Duka brothers and their colleagues, these were more than words. They were a clarion call to action.

"A lot of people are waking up, brother," remarked Serdar Tatar.

"They are waking up!" Dritan agreed, approvingly. "They're gonna wake up even more when, when they see the shining of the sword."

"Prepare as soldiers," declared Tatar.[31]

It was time to fight the infidels. Dritan told Bakalli that he was "going to start something," that "we have enough people," they could do jihad in the United States, and "Allah will keep [their families] safe."[32] In the minds of the plotters, Awlaki's lecture was a fatwa to attack the United States.

But Awlaki was not their only inspiration. They also watched jihadist videos, including the martyrdom videos of two September 11 hijackers.[33] On May 26, 2006, Mohamad Shnewer showed part of the group an al Qa'ida recruitment video that featured speeches by Osama bin Laden, as well as a video that glorified the September 11 terrorist attacks.[34] Dritan praised Osama bin Laden and prayed that Allah would protect him.[35] During a February 2007 trip to the Poconos, Shnewer played jihadist videos that featured the bombing of U.S. military vehicles. In one, a U.S. Marine's arm gets blown off.

When Shain Duka pointed this out, the group erupted in laughter.[36] Their self-indoctrination began to accelerate.

"I'm sad brother, sad, sad!" said Dritan Duka. "In Kosovo, Muslims are being shot. Bosnia because they are Muslim they are being shot. In Somalia because they are Muslim in Chechnya because they are Muslim. In Iraq, Afghanistan, and Palestine."

"Just because we are Muslim," repeated Bakalli.

Dritan nodded his head. "It's only because we are Muslim that we are being shot, don't think that it's because of any other reason! They don't like us brother. And if you aren't upset by it then you're not human anymore."[37]

For Dritan and his colleagues, the worst part was their own inaction.

"It gets me upset once in a while," said Shain. "When you see them fighting and we are—"

Bakalli cut him off. "We are in Dunkin' Donuts."

"Having a great time," Shain nodded.

"And us in Dunkin' Donuts," said Bakalli.[38]

An Unsung Hero

As the Duka brothers and their colleagues grew more agitated, Brian Morgenstern, an assistant manager at the Circuit City music store in Mount Laurel, New Jersey, saw something that frightened him. Morgenstern was a clean-shaven twenty-six-year-old with bright blue eyes, a sheepish grin, and long sideburns. In the first months of 2006, one of the Dukas' younger brothers, Burim, brought an 8-millimeter film to Circuit City and asked Morgenstern to convert it to a DVD format.

"I basically started the conversion process," Morgenstern said. "Everything was working out okay. I continued other projects that I had to do." He then glanced at the video. "I saw people firing handguns and rifles, and what it seemed to me as fully automatic weapons."[39] The tape showed approximately a dozen young men at a snow-covered, rustic firing range in Gouldsboro, Pennsylvania. Some could be heard shouting "Allahu Akbar!" ("God is great!") and "Jihad in the States."[40] The group included the Duka brothers, Serdar Tatar, Agron Abdullahu, and others firing at a range using a Beretta 92FS pistol, a Yugoslavian SKS semiautomatic rifle, a shotgun, and a Beretta CX4 Storm rifle.[41]

Morgenstern debated whether he should report the tape to the authorities. "I actually waited that night and weighed out my decisions," he said. "I went home. I talked to my family about it, thought their input would be very helpful on the situation."[42] He added, "I was considering whether or not this was really a threat, or something serious. I came to the conclusion that that's not my job or decision to make."[43]

The next day he called the Mount Laurel police. "They came over," he said, "and they looked at the video, and they stopped it at one point and said, 'Okay, this is serious, we need a copy.'"[44] Morgenstern made them a copy and subsequently handed the 8-millimeter film and the DVD back to the Fort Dix plotters.

The FBI and the Joint Terrorism Task Force out of Philadelphia immediately commenced an investigation.[45] The FBI opted to penetrate the cell using an informant, Mahmoud Omar, an Egyptian national, to record conversations with the men on the Circuit City video. Omar was a stout 180 pounds and had deep brown eyes, a shaved head, and a smooth, clean-shaven face.[46] But he had a deeply checkered past. He entered the United States illegally in 1995 through Mexico and had been convicted three times for bank fraud.[47] He had also illegally attempted to obtain a driver's license from the Virginia Department of Motor Vehicles.[48] When confronted with the last of his bank fraud charges, he was given a tantalizing offer by the FBI. Would he agree to be a cooperating informant?[49] Omar said yes, and began receiving cash payments and other benefits from the government that eventually totaled approximately $240,000.[50]

Omar did not have to start from scratch in penetrating the cell. He had attended the same mosque as Serdar Tatar in Palmyra, New Jersey, and shared with him an interest in cars. Omar had been in the business of buying, repairing, and then shipping cars overseas for sale, and Tatar was in need of a vehicle because his wife had been involved in an accident.[51] Omar also knew Mohamad Shnewer and identified him from a photograph taken from the Poconos firing range videotape.[52] He told the FBI that Shnewer was "tight with the religion," implying that he was a devout Muslim, and worked at his family-owned food market. Shnewer had previously delivered food to Omar's apartment, and Omar had repaired Shnewer's car. Omar had sometimes talked about the wars in Iraq and Afghanistan with Shnewer.[53]

Omar's participation was a pivotal break for the FBI. It allowed them to get close to the plotters without triggering suspicion. Omar gained access to the cell in March 2006, first by visiting Plaza Food Market & Halal Meats, the New Jersey grocery store owned by Mohamad Shnewer's father. Over the next several months he developed a relationship with Shnewer, accompanying the Dukas and Shnewer on a fishing trip in July 2006. During the trip Shnewer showed videos on his laptop of Iraqi insurgents attacking U.S. soldiers, as well as propaganda videos of Osama Bin Laden.[54]

Between August 11 and 14, Shnewer and Omar traveled to the U.S. Army base at Fort Dix, the U.S. Army base at Fort Monmouth, McGuire Air Force Base, Dover Air Force Base, and Lakehurst Naval Air Station to conduct surveillance for a potential terrorist attack.[55] Omar was hooked up with a body wire and had a closed-circuit television camera hidden in the dashboard of his vehicle. Shnewer took his laptop with him on the trips and played videos while Omar drove.[56] As they approached Fort Dix, Shnewer said that he was scouting the watchtowers from which officials could see who was entering and exiting the base. He bragged that it would be easy to infiltrate the checkpoints and get inside.[57]

As they drove into Fort Dix, Shnewer remarked, "This is

exactly what we are looking for. You hit 4, 5, or 6 humvees and light the whole place and retreat completely without any losses."[58]

Shnewer told Omar that he would think about the next surveillance target, discuss it with Eljvir Duka, and let Omar know. That night Shnewer conducted surveillance of Fort Monmouth on his own, though an FBI surveillance team was on his tail. After passing Fort Monmouth, Shnewer continued in the same direction for approximately 100 yards, then made a U-turn and drove slowly past the fort's main gate.[59]

After Shnewer and Omar returned to the Philadelphia area, they discussed targeting the U.S. Coast Guard facility in Philadelphia.[60] Around November 28, Serdar Tatar acquired a map of the U.S. Army base at Fort Dix, labeled "Cantonment Area Fort Dix, NJ," and provided it to Omar to help plan and coordinate an attack.[61] Tatar had obtained the map from his family's restaurant, which needed maps to deliver pizzas on the base. Omar gave the map to Shnewer, who placed it in a secret location.[62] By this time, however, Tatar had begun to suspect that Omar was a federal agent.[63]

Fortunately, the FBI had introduced a second informant, Besnik Bakalli, into the terrorist cell. Bakalli, who spoke Albanian, befriended the three Duka brothers and began recording their conversations. From July 2006 to January 2007 they met at a Dunkin' Donuts after attending mosque on Fridays.[64] On January 19, 2007, Dritan, Eljvir, Shain, and Bakalli went paintballing.[65] Bakalli also accompanied them on their second trip to the Poconos, in February 2007, where they discussed jihad and went to buy guns.[66] During that trip he recorded several conversations using a body wire and a surveillance video in the cabin occupied by the plotters.

On February 1, as they drove to Gouldsboro, Pennsylvania, Dritan Duka, Shain Duka, and Bakalli discussed their belief that the United States was waging an unjust war against Muslims.[67] Dritan and Shain opined that as Muslims, they had a duty to fight on behalf of other, oppressed Muslims. Shain and Dritan also discussed the benefits of dying as a martyr.[68] As Dritan Duka noted, several members of the group, including Serdar Tatar, wanted to kill Americans. "He wanted to join the American military," Dritan explained.

"What do you mean he wants to go?" asked Bakalli.

Dritan quickly responded, "And he's wanted to kill them from inside."

"Oh, he wants to go and join the army?" asked Bakalli again.

"Yeah!" said Dritan.

Bakalli was incredulous. "Are you serious?"

Dritan looked at him. "And he was very serious, just to get in and kill them," he said. "He's a maniac, he sees like we aren't human by watching Muslims get killed every day."[69]

They eventually arrived at 2717 Eagleview Drive, Gouldsboro, the same house the Duka brothers had rented the previous year. Prior to the group's arrival, the FBI had rented the house for a short period to install surveillance equipment. Beginning on February 2, law enforcement officials conducted video surveillance at Pennsylvania State Game Land 127, the same firearms range shown on the DVD from January 2006. They observed the group firing an SKS semiautomatic rifle, a Beretta Storm semiautomatic rifle, a Mossberg 12-gauge pump shotgun, and a 9-millimeter Beretta handgun.[70] The men blew through 1,000 rifle rounds, 1,000 handgun rounds, and 500 shotgun shells.[71] On the evening of February 4, Shnewer, who had brought his laptop, played an assortment of jihadist videos for the others.[72] The FBI had audio and photo surveillance. On the evening of February 5, the group discussed Islam.

"But what I am saying," said Dritan, "my point is, in order to spread your way you have to fight. So Islam, Islam is not going to war, just to take over the world . . . you are going to war to put Allah's laws on the earth . . . which is true justice."

Eljvir Duka agreed. He said that the fighting would end when "the Muslims have the . . . authority, true power in the world . . . Yeah," said Eljvir, "then it's gonna end."[73] Eljvir stated that it was their religious duty to join in the jihad because their Muslim brothers were being shot in Chechnya and elsewhere.

When they returned to Cherry Hill, the Duka brothers continued to conduct tactical training for an assault on U.S. soldiers.[74] Perhaps unsurprisingly, the group exaggerated the number of U.S. soldiers killed by Iraqi insurgents.

"When Zarqawi was alive," boasted Eljvir, "he tallied and gave estimated total—"

Dritan cut him off. "Thirty thousand" killed, he said.

"Forty thousand," replied Eljvir.

"Almost forty thousand," Dritan agreed.

"Forty thousand," repeated Eljvir.

"We've killed," affirmed Dritan. "American soldiers."[75]

By March, cell members were mentally preparing themselves for an attack.

"Do not fear, 'Oh I'm afraid, I don't know if I should do it,'" mimicked Dritan in a sarcastic voice. "Do it!" he shouted. "Be a man, do it!"

Bakalli responded, "No but Shaheen, it's—"

Dritan quickly interrupted him. "Because if it's your time, you're gonna die anyway!"

"Yeah but Shaheen," said Bakalli, "it's killing us man, you can't, you can't do it, we can't do it, we can't do it, we got no ass to do it. I mean—"

Dritan cut him off again. "I will do it Insh'allah."

"I mean, just because we don't know and for example we talk and talk," said Bakalli.

"We just haven't found out how to do it," remarked Dritan.

"With what to do it," Bakalli clarified, implying that they still lacked sufficient weapons.

"That's the problem," Dritan agreed, "because I'm ready! Where would we find them? It's hard to find when you don't know people. For now," he continued, "seven are a lot, you can do a lot with seven people."

"Yeah," said Bakalli.

"Eh," Dritan repeated confidently. "You can do a lot of damage man, seven people."[76]

Mahmoud Omar, who was still viewed with some skepticism as a possible informant, volunteered to help purchase firearms from a contact in Baltimore. During a March 28, 2007, telephone conversation between Dritan and Omar, which the FBI tapped, Omar explained that his Baltimore contact had provided a list of available weapons.[77] That evening Dritan Duka picked up the list from Omar and placed the order on April 6.[78] By this point the core cell members were Serdar Tatar, Mohamad Shnewer, and the three Duka brothers. It was not entirely clear that Fort Dix was the only target, or even the preeminent target. But their objective was clear: to kill U.S. military personnel.

On May 7, Omar delivered the weapons, and Dritan and Shain Duka were arrested at Omar's apartment. Mohamad Shnewer, Eljvir Duka, and Serdar Tatar, who were not present at the transaction, were detained at different locations that day.[79] All five were convicted of conspiracy to harm U.S. military personnel. Dritan and Shain Duka received life sentences, with an additional thirty years for weapons charges. Eljvir Duka and Mohamad Shnewer were given life sentences, and Serdar Tatar was sentenced to thirty-three years in prison.

JFK Plot

The Fort Dix plot was not the only terrorist threat from individuals inspired by al Qa'ida. In 2007, FBI agents arrested Russell Defreitas for plotting to blow up jet fuel supply tanks and pipelines at John F. Kennedy (JFK) International Airport in New York. Three of Defreitas's associates—Kareem Ibrahim, Abdul Kadir, and Abdel Nur—were also arrested. The cell had conducted physical surveillance of JFK Airport, made video recordings of its buildings and facilities, analyzed satellite photographs of the airport on the Internet, and sought additional expert advice, financing, and explosives.

There were several similarities between the JFK and Fort Dix plots. The JFK plotters did not have a direct relationship with al Qa'ida and had never spent time at a terrorist training camp, which made it more difficult for them to execute the plan they had concocted. In fact, they were an unimpressive lot. Russell Defreitas, the leader, was a naturalized U.S. citizen from Guyana who was sixty-three at the time of his arrest. He had a weathered face, pronounced wrinkles under his eyes, and a graying beard. Beneath a calm exterior, however, was an uncontrollable rage. Defreitas lived in a shabby apartment at 740 Euclid Avenue in Brooklyn, part of a row of dilapidated brick high-rise buildings. He had worked as a cargo handler for Evergreen Company at JFK Airport but was laid off in 2001 and cycled through an assortment of odd jobs. At one point he sold incense on the street.[80]

Defreitas's coterie of plotters was fairly innocuous. Kareem Ibrahim was sixty-two at the time of his arrest. He had retired after working at various accounting jobs and had played as a musician in a steel drum band that toured the United States. A citizen of Trinidad born as Winston Kingston, he had converted to Shi'a Islam around the age of twenty-one. Abdul Kadir, fifty-five, who had served as a member of the Guyanese Parliament, had the most nefarious connections of the group. He converted to Shi'a Islam around 1972 and developed a relationship with some Iranian government officials, unsuccessfully soliciting help from them and several terrorists to execute the plot.[81] Abdel Nur was fifty-seven at the time of his arrest and had been deported from the United States on drug-trafficking charges in the 1980s.

Yet despite their lack of terrorist training, the cell members displayed an uncanny desire to attack the United States. As with the Fort Dix plot, the FBI recruited an informant to penetrate Russell Defreitas's network. The informant's name was Steve Francis Taveras, and he went by several aliases, including Terry DeSouza and

Anas Knaddert.[82] Taveras had a sordid past that FBI officials lever-aged. He was convicted of federal drug trafficking and racketeering charges in the Southern District of New York in 1996 and was again convicted of drug trafficking in 2003. But the government offered to reduce his sentence if he agreed to be an informant, and dangled a salary that Taveras accepted. He had originally met Def-reitas at the Al-Khoei Mosque in Queens, New York.[83]

On July 13, 2006, an intermediary formally introduced Tav-eras to Defreitas at the Gertz Plaza Mall in Queens. Defreitas and Taveras met again on July 28 and August 1. Taveras's first objec-tive was to build trust with Defreitas, and he played on Defreitas's hatred of Israel and concern with the plight of Muslims. During a discussion of the 2006 Israeli war in Lebanon, Defreitas and Tav-eras agreed that Muslims always incurred the wrath of the world while Jews received a pass. Defreitas, who was beginning to warm up to Taveras, said he envisioned an attack that would make the World Trade Center strike seem small. On August 7, Defreitas asked Taveras whether he could speak to him about something confidential. Taveras nodded. Defreitas confided that there were "brothers" who wanted to do something bigger than the World Trade Center attacks. He said the "brothers" were not Arabs but were from Trinidad and Guyana. Defreitas said the operation involved a "cell" of "six or seven" people and inquired whether Tav-eras was interested in participating.[84]

This was textbook intelligence work: Defreitas had actually recruited the FBI's informant to join the terrorist plot!

"Can I ask you a question?" one of Defreitas's contacts asked Taveras in a phone call on September 10, which was recorded by the FBI. "Would you like to die as a martyr?"

Taveras was caught off guard. Yes, he replied, struggling to compose himself. Dying as a martyr was the greatest way to die in Islam.[85] Taveras thought he had hesitated too long, but his answer satisfied the cell member.

As the plan developed, Defreitas traveled to Guyana to meet

other members of the cell and discuss the plot. Recognizing that they had no terrorist training, Abdul Kadir and other members tried to enlist support from various sources: the Iranian government, the Trinidad militant group Jamaat al Muslimeen, and, most strikingly, al Qa'ida operative Adnan el-Shukrijumah.[86] U.S. officials failed to uncover any further links with Shukrijumah, indicating that the group had failed to connect with al Qa'ida.

Still, Defreitas pushed forward. On January 3, 4, 10, and 11 in 2007, he and Taveras conducted surveillance of JFK Airport. During each trip they traveled in Taveras's car, which the Joint Terrorism Task Force had fitted with audio and video equipment. In addition, law enforcement officers conducted their own surveillance of Defreitas and Taveras. Defreitas's goal was to attack the fuel tanks at the airport, which were linked to the Buckeye Pipeline, which distributed fuel and other petroleum products to sites in Pennsylvania, New Jersey, and New York. The pipeline was also the primary transporter of jet fuel to JFK and other New York area airports.[87]

Defreitas was growing impatient. On January 3 he announced that one of his contacts in the Caribbean "really wants to get this thing going. He's very sincere about it . . . So he really want[s] to get it done but he want[s] to get it done the right way," Defreitas told Taveras. "That way we don't want to regret starting something that we can't finish."

Later that evening Defreitas and Taveras called one of their contacts in Guyana to report on the day's surveillance. The FBI was again listening.

"Mission accomplished today," said Defreitas, clearly proud of himself.

"All right," came the response. "That's good, that's good, that's good."

Defreitas then responded that he had seen the American television evangelist Pat Robertson predicting that a disaster would hit America and a tsunami would hit several states. "So he's probably not too far off, huh?" Defreitas commented. His contact chuckled.

Defreitas and Taveras returned to JFK the next day, January 4. "I got to show you all the escape routes," explained Defreitas, "how to get in, and how to get out."[88]

Defreitas directed Taveras to the back side of the airport and then to another roadway inside the airport. They arrived at the fuel tanks, which were adjacent to a small body of water, and discussed blowing them up. Defreitas explained that security there was virtually non-existent. During the return drive from JFK, Defreitas discussed how much damage they could cause. He predicted that the plot would result in the destruction of the "whole of Kennedy," that only a few people would escape, and that part of Queens would explode because some of the pipes were underground. They would "get our blessings and our rewards" and "a place in paradise," Defreitas said confidently. It would also be a huge blow to the United States.

"Anytime you hit Kennedy, it is the most hurtful thing to the United States," Defreitas explained, struggling to control his excitement. "To hit John F. Kennedy, wow. They love John F. Kennedy like he's the man. If you hit that, this whole country will be in mourning. It's like you can kill the man twice."

During the conversation, Defreitas described how he had been waiting several years for the right opportunity to execute his plans. "These things used to come into my brain—well, I could blow this place up," he told Taveras. But he was afraid to act on it back then. "So I would just wipe it out of my head. And then I would go someplace again, and I would see the same thing. And I would sit and see a plane taxiing up the runway. And I would say, if I could get a rocket, then I could do a hit. By myself, I am thinking these things. But I had no connections with no Arabs or nobody—I'm a Muslim working in the airport for so many years."[89] He was now prepared to accomplish what he had only fantasized about.

After traveling to Guyana in late January 2007, Defreitas and Taveras returned to New York. The flight landed at JFK on February 28, and United States Customs and Border Patrol officers searched Defreitas and his belongings. They questioned him and copied his phone book, which contained the names and telephone numbers of Kadir and others involved in the plot. It is unclear whether this detainment was coordinated with the FBI, since it nearly compromised the case. Defreitas became increasingly suspicious that he was being watched, as did the other plotters.

"Right now in Trinidad," Abdul Kadir explained to Taveras in a phone call recorded by the FBI, it "is hot, with respect to national security, and the international security." Kadir, who was clearly frazzled, offered some advice: "When you're traveling, do not walk with anything that can implicate you. Remember the copies that you had?" he inquired, possibly referring to the downloaded Google Earth images of JFK Airport. "It will be advisable not to walk with that, just in case they decide to search you in Trinidad. Because if they search you and they find that, you have to explain to them what you're doing with that."[90]

By June 1 the plot had developed far enough for a likely prosecution. The FBI arrested Defreitas as he sat with Taveras at the Lindenwood Diner, a popular establishment in Brooklyn that served both New York City police officers and mob bosses. Taveras was sipping a coffee and downing a cheesecake and Defreitas had barely touched his salmon dinner when the FBI took Defreitas into custody.

"I didn't feel anything was wrong," said Sharon Fitzmaurice, the waitress who served them. "They didn't act suspicious."[91]

The same day Abdul Kadir was arrested at Piarco International Airport in Trinidad and Tobago aboard a plane headed to Venezuela and eventually to Iran.[92] Kareem Ibrahim and Abdel Nur were arrested shortly thereafter in Trinidad.[93] Ibrahim, Nur, and Kadir were later extradited to the United States, where they faced trial. Defreitas and Abdul Kadir were sentenced to life in prison.[94] Abdel Nur was sentenced to fifteen years in prison.[95]

By the time of the arrests, an attack was not yet imminent. Defreitas and his group had conspired to use explosives to attack JFK Airport, especially the fuel tanks and pipeline. They certainly hoped to cause devastation along the heavily populated areas transited by the pipeline and inflict economic and psychological damage on the U.S. economy. But the attack was probably not feasible, at least as envisioned by the plotters. Without closer links to al Qa'ida or another terrorist group, Defreitas and his band were severely hamstrung.

Still, the FBI's success in penetrating the cell illustrated an effective use of clandestine tactics. Defreitas was certainly impressed. "You guys are the best," he remarked to FBI agents after his arrest on June 1, when he was presented with bugged conversations implicating him in the plot.[96]

Amateur Hour

For senior FBI officials like Philip Mudd, these homegrown plots were a cause for concern. "As we sat around in meetings," he said, "a lot of us would go back to Oklahoma City. If one of those guys got lucky—for example, got the right mix of fertilizer—it could have been serious."[97]

Mudd referred to these types of terrorists as the "like-mindeds." Unlike the terrorists linked to core al Qa'ida in Pakistan or one of its affiliated groups, the like-mindeds represented the spread of al Qa'ida's ideology to "new recruits who are inspired but not trained by the group."[98] Al Qa'ida was struggling in Iraq and coming under withering criticism in the Arab world, and it had failed to develop a serious plot against the U.S. homeland for several years, thanks in part to improved U.S. counterterrorism efforts. CIA drones had killed several al Qa'ida external operations chiefs, such as Hamza Rabi'a, which had further disrupted the group's ability to plot an attack. Abu Ubaydah al-Masri, who was involved in the 2005 London attacks and the 2006 transatlantic plot, had died of tuberculosis.

All that was left, for the moment, were a handful of plots from the like-minded groups Mudd referred to. In December 2006, FBI agents arrested U.S. citizen Derrick Shareef when he attempted to purchase grenades and weapons for a self-planned terrorist attack in a Chicago shopping mall. Shareef was inspired by al Qa'ida's global ideology yet received no direction or assistance from a foreign terrorist group. In June 2006 the FBI arrested members of a Miami terrorist cell that planned to attack the Sears Tower in Chicago and the FBI field office in Miami. The group members were U.S. citizens who conspired to conduct attacks consistent with al Qa'ida's goals, although none of them had actual contact with an al Qa'ida member. While these groups could be dangerous, the absence of a direct connection to al Qa'ida or one of its affiliates made them dilettantes.

"You wouldn't believe how much cannon fodder I had," Abu Zubaydah had remarked after he was captured. For every competent operative Zubaydah had identified, there were dozens more who were mostly useless.[99] A select few homegrown terrorists like Timothy McVeigh, who bombed the Alfred P. Murrah Building in Oklahoma City in May 1995, had the military training to perpetrate a significant attack. At best, the 2006 and 2007 plots would have killed a handful of Americans and scared many more—no small feats, to be sure. But they were never going to be the spectacular, mass-casualty attacks al Qa'ida was hoping for.

More distressing for the FBI was the rise of charismatic individuals linked to al Qa'ida, especially Anwar al-Awlaki, who kept gaining followers.

One of the Fort Dix plotters, Eljvir Duka, who had been inspired by Awlaki, wrote a note to one of his cellmates. "May Allah shower you with his mercies and may Allah be the second one with you in your cell," he said. "Now you see why we were going to sacrifice all for the sake of Allah in jihad. The Prophet said 'fight in the way of Allah first with the mouth then with the sword.' We weren't able to finish," he continued.[100] But others would try again. This time, however, it wasn't an inspired network of like-mindeds that planned the attack. Core al Qa'ida was back, and the third wave was gaining momentum.

13

AL QA'IDA STRIKES BACK

THE QATAR AIRWAYS flight landed in Peshawar, Pakistan, the Pashtun city that Osama bin Laden, Ayman al-Zawahiri, and other Arab fighters had used as a base during the anti-Soviet jihad. It was August 28, 2008. As the plane taxied down the runway, Najibullah Zazi and his two colleagues, Adis Medunjanin and Zarein Ahmedzay, strained to peer through the plane's oval windows. From the runway they could see the airport's main terminal, a squat, rectangular building with grimy windows and a hulking crystal-blue sign outside that read PESHAWAR INTERNATIONAL AIRPORT. At one end of the airport a railroad line cut diagonally across the runway, a relic of the Khyber Pass Railway, the colonial-era route that zigzagged through the rugged snowcapped mountains along the Afghanistan-Pakistan border.

The three men had departed the day before from Newark International Airport on Qatar Airlines Flight 84.[1] "Our plan," said Zazi, "was to go to Afghanistan and fight with the Taliban."[2]

Zazi, who sometimes went by Najib, was a handsome twenty-four-year old immigrant from Afghanistan living in the United States. He had thick, neatly trimmed black hair, a wiry 2-inch-long beard, and a noticeable mole under his left eye. In the United States he dressed smartly, preferring button-down, collared shirts. He used several credit cards and he loved basketball. Such consumerism was a marked contrast to the values of his upbringing in Afghanistan. Born on August 10, 1985, in a small village in Paktia Province, he came from the Zazi (or Jaji) Pashtun tribe, as his last name indicated, which lives on both sides of the Afghanistan-Pakistan border. In 1992 his family moved to Peshawar as Afghanistan descended into civil war following the withdrawal of Soviet forces. Zazi's father, Mohammed Wali Zazi, did not stay long in Pakistan but moved to New York, where he scraped by as a cab-driver working twelve-hour shifts. Zazi and the rest of the family joined him in 1999 and settled into a two-bedroom apartment at 33-24 Parsons Boulevard, Apartment 6F, in Flushing, a cramped blue-collar neighborhood in Queens.[3]

Zazi was a devout Muslim as a teenager, though by no means radical. His family attended the Masjid Hazrati Abu Bakr Siddique, a large white mosque with a turquoise minaret located around the corner from their house. Some members of the mosque were extremists, such as Saifur Rahman Halimi, who had links with the radical Afghan jihadist Gulbuddin Hekmatyar.[4] Zazi struggled as a student at Flushing High School and eventually dropped out. Beginning in 2004, he became a fixture on Stone Street in Lower Manhattan's financial district, not far from Ground Zero, where he operated a coffee and pastries vending cart. Patrons remembered him as the affable, beaming man who wore a tunic and had a GOD BLESS AMERICA sign on his cart.[5] In 2006, Zazi married his cousin, who remained in Pakistan.

When he disembarked from the Qatar Airways plane at Peshawar International Airport, it was the start of a reunion for Zazi. He had come home. He brought two colleagues from New York: Medunjanin, a Bosnian immigrant who became a naturalized U.S. citizen in 2002 and had earned a master's degree in economics, and Ahmedzay, a New York City cabdriver and a high school friend of Zazi.

The trip to Pakistan, however, wasn't merely a homecoming. The men had come to fight for the Taliban. They met with senior al Qa'ida operatives, including former Florida resident Adnan el-Shukrijumah, and soon agreed to execute one of al Qa'ida's boldest plots since September 11, 2001: a suicide attack on the New York City subway system modeled in part on the successful 2005 attacks in London. Zazi's operation was an order of magnitude larger than the handful of amateur plots from "like-minded" networks. This one had the potential to kill scores of Americans and spread fear across the country. The plot involved some of al Qa'ida's most experienced operatives and focused on America's largest city.

It was up to U.S. intelligence and law enforcement agencies to uncover the plot, which was conceived and supported in Pakistan, and then track down Zazi and his terrorist cell before they could execute the attack. U.S. officials would have two desperate weeks in which to put the pieces together during an extraordinarily tense and terrifying hunt.

Onward to Waziristan

In January 2008, FBI director Robert Mueller appointed Art Cummings as the executive assistant director for the FBI's National Security Branch, putting him in charge of all counterterrorism and counterintelligence at the Bureau. Cummings had methodically moved up the FBI's ladder. "At every level, from street agent to field supervisor to headquarters executive, Art's career has concentrated on investigating and managing counterterrorism and counterintelligence operations," Mueller said in praise.[6] Cummings lived on a 23-foot sailboat near Annapolis, Maryland, not far from the U.S. Naval Academy, during the week. On many evenings he stopped at a deli near the Chesapeake Bay Bridge and picked up a sandwich, a bag of SunChips, and a cold drink. On the weekend he drove two hours south on Interstate 95 to Richmond, Virginia, where his wife, Ellen, and their three children lived.[7]

As he settled into his new job, intelligence reports coming into FBI Headquarters suggested that al Qa'ida might be shifting its strategy. "They began to focus more on taking advantage of walk-ins, people who found al Qa'ida and volunteered to conduct an attack on the U.S. homeland," observed Cummings. "This was very different from many of their previous operations, where they had been patiently involved in long, complex plans."

Al Qa'ida's shift in strategy was unsettling for some in the FBI. "What I am particularly concerned about," remarked Cummings, "is the day that al Qa'ida decides they *don't* want to do a 9/11-style attack and focuses on smaller, easier operations."[8] In October 2002, John Allen Muhammad and Lee Boyd Malvo had wreaked havoc in Washington, D.C., with only a Bushmaster XM-15 semiautomatic .223-caliber rifle. Two men with guns and a van can do a lot of damage, Cummings thought, and they might be hard to catch. Al Qa'ida was not quite there yet. But Cummings correctly foresaw that al Qa'ida's core leadership in Pakistan had begun to move toward more opportunistic plots.

In November 2008 an American citizen, Bryant Neal Vinas, was arrested for plotting to attack trains outside New York City. He had become radicalized with a small group of extremists, traveled to Pakistan to attend al Qa'ida training camps, developed a relationship with senior al Qa'ida leader Younis al-Mauritani, and planned attacks in the United States.[9] Vinas's contact with a volatile social network was exactly the kind of development that concerned Philip Mudd.

For Mudd, this network did not constitute a formal cell but rather an informal "cluster." It was an important distinction. Vinas had embedded in a nebulous community of like-minded individuals. They helped radicalize him through informal discussions, emotional support, and an opportunity to train overseas. For Mudd, the key moment in the radicalization process was when individuals like Vinas began asking a simple question: Why isn't anyone else defending Muslims against injustice? Here was the moment when vague discontent could boil over into specific and dangerous acts.[10]

Now Najibullah Zazi provided an ideal opportunity for al Qa'ida. When Zazi and his colleagues arrived in Peshawar, they stayed at the home of Zazi's uncle, Lal Mohammed.[11] Their goal was to fight the United States.

"I took this offer from Allah," explained Medunjanin, "and planned to go to Afghanistan to join the Taliban and wage jihad against the U.S. occupation and the corrupt and imposter Karzai government, to help overthrow it, and establish the perfect justice of Allah. This meant that we were presented to kill the occupying forces, including the United States military."[12]

They jumped in a taxi and directed the driver to take them to the Afghanistan border but were turned back by Pakistani security officials. They began inquiring around Peshawar about joining the Taliban. Soon word of their arrival reached Ahmad Bangash, an al Qa'ida external operations facilitator who sometimes went by Zahid. At the beginning of September, Bangash interviewed Zazi, Ahmedzay, and Medunjanin and decided that they should meet with senior al Qa'ida officials in Waziristan and potentially attend a training camp. Bangash was apparently impressed by their willingness to come so far and leave so much behind, without any intention of returning to the United States. He had likely checked into their backgrounds, which would have been easy because some of Zazi's family, including his wife, still lived in Peshawar.[13]

Bangash rented a Toyota Corolla and took them to North Waziristan in Pakistan's tribal areas to meet several al Qa'ida leaders, including external operations chief Saleh al-Somali. As his nom de guerre indicated, he originally hailed from Somalia, and he had advanced in al Qa'ida's propaganda outfit to head operational planning.[14] He was killed by a U.S. drone strike in Pakistan in December 2009. As a token of his dedication, Zazi gave Bangash a camera, a laptop, and cash for Somali.[15]

Zazi, Ahmedzay, and Medunjanin were then transported to an al Qa'ida training camp in South Waziristan. Unlike the expansive training camps in Afghanistan before the September 11 attacks, such as Derunta and al-Farouq, the al Qa'ida camps in Pakistan around this time tended to be small and were not well populated. They were also easier to abandon quickly if there was advance notice of a Pakistani raid or U.S. drone strike. After several days of weapons training, the three men left South Waziristan. For Zazi, the interaction with al Qa'ida operatives and visits to North and South Waziristan had a profound impact, bordering on a religious revelation.

"During the training, al Qa'ida leaders asked us to return to the United States and conduct martyrdom operations," Zazi acknowledged. "We agreed to this plan. I did so because of my feelings about what the United States was doing in Afghanistan."[16] Zazi had gone into Pakistan to join the Taliban but came out as a suicide bomber.

It is uncertain when Zazi began to radicalize, though his Queens mosque had experienced a major split after the September 11 attacks. When the imam, Mohammed Sherzad, spoke out against the Taliban and Osama bin Laden, pro-Taliban members of the mosque revolted, praying separately in the basement and the parking lot. They eventually ousted the imam. It is unclear where the Zazis fell, though Mohammed Sherzad said that he saw several members of the Zazi family, including Najibullah, praying in the parking lot with those who opposed him.[17] Over time, Zazi became more radical and began to seek out more radical voices. For example, he listened to Anwar al-Awlaki's lectures on-line.[18]

The plan was for Ahmedzay and Zazi to return to South Waziristan a month later to receive explosives training from al Qa'ida. Ahmedzay, who was beginning to have second thoughts about participating in the attack, decided not to go, and Zazi attended by himself.[19] Zazi's training in South Waziristan was critical for several reasons. It gave him the technical experience necessary to put together a bomb, which would have been more difficult if he had used only Internet instructions. Zazi was trained in peroxide-based detonators and explosives by two former students of the deceased senior bomb maker Abu Khabab al-Masri, who had pioneered peroxide-based mixtures, poisons, and chemical mixtures for al Qa'ida. Masri had been killed in a U.S. drone strike in South Waziristan in July 2008. Zazi received just under a week of training in South Waziristan. He also received two or three days of classroom training on firearms, followed by hands-on training that involved weapons assembly, cleaning, and firing with handguns, rifles, and other weapons.

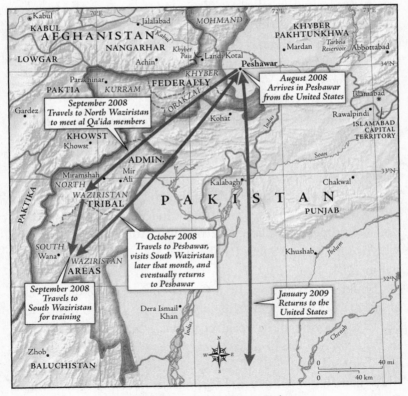

Figure 13: Map of Zazi's Trip to Pakistan

But the most intensive work was the explosives training. Zazi was instructed to prepare explosives in a room with the doors closed but with exhaust fans that could clear the fumes. Al Qa'ida bomb makers taught him to use the explosives HMTD and TATP, which had been used in the 2005 London attacks and Richard Reid's failed 2001 shoe bomb attack. After preparing the explosives, Zazi learned to prepare detonators using several combinations of ingredients: ghee (which is clarified butter) and flour, hydrogen peroxide and flour, and ammonium nitrate. He and his handlers discussed placing homemade bombs in suicide vests, which could be packed with ball bearings, nuts, or nails to maximize fragmentation and kill or maim a greater number of people.[20]

Al Qa'ida's plan called for Zazi, Medunjanin, and Ahmedzay to detonate a homemade explosive in a New York City target such as a bus, a movie theater, or a subway train crowded with people. Zazi was meticulous in planning for the operation. "I took notes on the training and later e-mailed a summary of the notes to myself, so that I could access them in the U.S.," he said.[21]

Zazi agreed to target New York City. Pre-attack casing, surveillance, and reconnaissance would be virtually unnecessary, because he was already familiar with the place. Several other al Qa'ida operatives besides Saleh al-Somali and Ahmad Bangash participated in the plot. One was Rashid Rauf, the British Pakistani who had been involved in the 2006 transatlantic plot foiled by MI5 and the London's Metropolitan Police. A second was Adnan el-Shukrijumah, who had trained with José Padilla at an al Qa'ida camp in Kandahar in 2001.[22]

Shukrijumah was one of al Qa'ida's most evasive operatives, a ghostly James Bond figure. Intelligence reports placed him at various locations around the world, occasionally at the same time, often in Pakistan but also in more exotic places such as Brazil, Guyana, and Trinidad. The 2007 JFK Airport plotters had tried to contact Shukrijumah but had failed. He spoke several languages—Arabic, English, Urdu, Spanish, and French—and was believed to carry passports from Saudi Arabia, Canada, Trinidad, and Guyana. He also used an impressive list of cover names, such as Jafar al-Tayyar, Hamad, and Abu Arif.[23] Shukrijumah possessed an affable personality that enabled him to blend into new environments quickly and remain amicable and composed under stress.

Shukrijumah stood five feet, six inches tall, had a medium build, and weighed something north of 130 pounds. He occasionally wore a beard, though sometimes he preferred a mustache and goatee. His pronounced nose bent slightly to the left, and he had a discernible scar on the left side of his face, approximately 1 inch down and 1 inch forward from his left earlobe, near his eye. He had thinning black hair, dark eyes, and an olive complexion that revealed his Saudi heritage.[24] Shukrijumah was born in Saudi Arabia on August 4, 1975, to Gulshair Muhammad el-Shukrijumah and Zuhrah Ahmed. His father was an Islamic scholar with the Saudi government. In 1983 he was transferred to New York City to lead a mosque in Brooklyn, but Shukrijumah and his family, including his sisters and brother, remained in Saudi Arabia. After he graduated from high school in Saudi Arabia, the family moved to New York City, around late 1995, to reunite with Gulshair, who moved them to Miramar, Florida, the following year.[25]

Miramar, a city with a subtropical climate located between Miami and Fort Lauderdale and flanked by the Everglades, must have been an abrupt change for the family compared with the seasonal harshness of the American Northeast. Shukrijumah attended classes at Broward Community College in Fort Lauderdale from the summer of 1996 to 1998, using the name Jumah A. El-Chukri. He majored in chemistry, but he never graduated.[26] In an extraordinary video, which the FBI released to the public to help identify Shukrijumah, he gave a presentation on jumpstarting a car to a Broward Community College class. It illustrated why he was so treasured by al Qa'ida: he had a knack for chemistry, computers, and technology, which made him useful for everything from bomb making to propaganda. And he was eminently likable, even funny.

"My name is Adnan," he said, with a discernible Saudi accent, standing in front of a blackboard smeared with white eraser marks. He wore a striped, button-down shirt that hung loosely over his pants and sported a thin beard. He occasionally consulted index cards cradled in his hands.

"First thing, I'm going to show, when we are jumpstarting a car we have two things. We have the good battery in your car, which is smiling here; and the dead battery in the dead car, which is angry here." He pointed to the blackboard, where he had sketched two three-dimensional boxes that represented the batteries.

"Then we have two cables, which is like this," he said, holding up a pair of gangly jumper cables resting on a chair at the front of the room. "One with two red sides and the other with two black sides."

Shukrijumah's presentation was simple and lucid. The students appeared to be interested; some took notes. Shukrijumah also explained the dangers of accidentally mixing the cables. "You can blow the fuse inside of the engine, inside of the car, under the hood," he explained, drawing a rudimentary hood on the chalkboard. "A second thing could happen that you could burn the PC, the computer in your car. All new cars now have computers to run the fuel injection system in the car.

"So whenever you see a man, don't be scared, or a woman, waiting for you to help them, stop and help them," he urged in conclusion. "But help them the right way."[27] When he finished the presentation, the students clapped approvingly as he placed the jumper cables on the chair. His message sounded like a Good Samaritan sermon.

However, not long after enrolling at Broward Community College, Shukrijumah had begun to show signs of violence. According to Broward County Central Courthouse records, Miramar police arrested him in October 1997 for felony charges of child abuse and battery.[28] He was twenty-two years old at the time and apparently hit one of his sisters in the face and bit another on the arm on

October 12. This episode seemed anomalous—a would-be al Qa'ida operative picking on girls.

He also began to show signs of radicalization around this time. He frequented the Darul Uloom Islamic Institute in Pembroke Pines, where he apparently met José Padilla, and by 1999 made his way to al Qa'ida camps in Afghanistan. He quickly became a proficient operator. He completed al Qa'ida's security course, which lasted nearly two months and covered such topics as target surveillance and secure communications techniques. Late in that year, Shukrijumah attended a basic weapons and explosives course at the al-Farouq camp in Kandahar.[29] The first part involved basic instruction on explosive materials and assembly. The second part was an advanced course that taught Shukrijumah how to construct an improvised device from commonly available materials like fertilizer and household chemicals, as well as how to build switches, circuits, and timers for homemade bombs. While in Kandahar he developed a close relationship with Khalid Sheikh Mohammed, who handpicked him for operations in the United States and Europe.[30]

Over the next several years, Shukrijumah was involved in a number of plots, most of which failed. Around 2001 he conducted surveillance of various targets in the United States, including the White House and areas frequented by former U.S. president Jimmy Carter. In September 2001 he reportedly sent a threatening e-mail to President Bush, apparently from an Internet café in Pakistan, saying that a day was coming "he would never forget." He was tasked by Khalid Sheikh Mohammed to attack the Panama Canal using vessels laden with explosives and to detonate them as they passed through the canal. The operation was never executed. He may also have been involved in al Qa'ida's chemical and biological programs beginning around 2002. Shukrijumah's understanding of the United States and his operational experience made him a key asset—and recruiter—for Najibullah Zazi.[31]

Final Preparations

The opportunity to mix with Adnan el-Shukrijumah, Saleh al-Somali, Rashid Rauf, and Ahmad Bangash must have been exhilarating for Zazi. The "martyrdom operation" began to take on a new significance. "To me," said Zazi, "it meant that I would sacrifice myself to bring attention to what the United States military was doing to civilians in Afghanistan by sacrificing my soul for the sake of saving other souls."[32]

How had Zazi and his colleagues been recruited so quickly? They had arrived in Peshawar, soldiered through an al Qa'ida training camp, and been sent to conduct a terrorist attack in the United States all within four months. What began as an exhilarating adventure to join the Taliban—perhaps in part to escape the doldrums of running a coffee and pastries cart in Lower Manhattan—became a well-planned, significant al Qa'ida terrorist plot. Zazi may have been surprised to make contact so effortlessly, especially since al Qa'ida was undoubtedly jittery about infiltration by Western spy agencies. Nevertheless, the speed of his conversion illustrated a striking vulnerability for al Qa'ida. It would be a herculean task to transform Zazi and his colleagues overnight into competent bomb makers and operators, especially since they had no background in weapons and explosives. Al Qa'ida's decision also suggested that its leaders were desperate for Americans with legitimate passports to conduct U.S.-based attacks.

In order to remind himself of the techniques he'd learned, Zazi sent handwritten notes to two of his e-mail accounts while in Pakistan, so he could later download them onto his laptop in the United States. The notes contained directions for making TATP by using hydrogen peroxide, acetone, and hydrochloric acid. They mentioned that acetone was found in nail polish remover and that hydrogen peroxide could be found in "Hair Salon—20–30%." The notes discussed formulations for mixing hydrogen peroxide with flour and listed ghee as a fuel that could be used to help initiate the explosive device.[33]

Armed with his recipe, Zazi flew from Peshawar to JFK Airport on January 15, 2009, aboard Qatar Airways Flight 83. Al Qa'ida operatives staggered the return dates for Zazi and his colleagues, almost certainly to minimize suspicion. Medunjanin departed at the end of September 2008 and Ahmedzay left Pakistan on January 22, 2009.[34] Zazi had given Ahmad Bangash his Hotmail and Yahoo! e-mail addresses for future communication. One was registered to a Kado Khan and the other to a Kado Gul in Peshawar, Pakistan. Yet since he'd been given little countersurveillance training, Zazi used nearly identical passwords for his e-mail accounts, making them easier for intelligence agencies to hack later on.[35]

Back in the United States, Zazi, Medunjanin, and Ahmedzay began operational planning for an attack. They agreed that Zazi would prepare the explosives, Zazi and Ahmedzay would assemble the devices in New York, and all three would conduct suicide attacks.[36] "Beginning around June 2009," said Zazi, "I accessed my bomb-making notes and began researching where to find the ingredients for the explosives. I also took trips to New York, and met with others to discuss the plan, including the timing of the attack, and where to make the explosives."

It was time for final preparations.

"I then used the bomb-making notes," he continued, "to construct explosives for the detonators in Denver. The explosive was hydrogen peroxide."[37]

By this time Zazi had moved from New York to Colorado, perhaps to elude the clandestine network of police and FBI informants swarming across New York City. But he had also run into serious financial troubles. According to court documents, Zazi filed for bankruptcy in United States Bankruptcy Court, Eastern District of New York, in March 2009.[38] His financial records show debt steadily rising from creditors typically used by his age group: Best

Buy, Bank of America, Chase Manhattan, Macy's, and T-Mobile.[39] He had virtually no money except for $500 in cash at his apartment, a $500 security deposit, $1,400 worth of household appliances, and the clothing he owned. He had nothing in checking or savings accounts.[40] He later completed an Internet course on personal financial management run by GreenPath, Inc., but he remained in a near-permanent state of debt.[41]

Zazi moved in with his aunt and uncle on East Ontario Drive in Aurora, Colorado, an upscale neighborhood surrounded by manicured golf courses. Aurora is located 8 miles east of Denver on the city's prairie fringe. It boasts a population of more than 300,000, and its modest collection of flourishing business parks and Fortune 500 companies follow a suburban cadence. Zazi worked as a driver for a ground transportation company named Big Sky, and then for ABC Airport Shuttle, driving a fifteen-person shuttle van between Denver International Airport and downtown Denver. In July 2009 his uncle kicked him out and he moved in with his parents, who had just relocated to an apartment complex on East Smoky Hill Road in Aurora.[42]

Zazi did, however, visit New York on at least two occasions before the impending attack. Early in 2009 he met with Ahmedzay and Medunjanin in Queens. They agreed to conduct the attacks during the month of Ramadan, which began on August 22 and ended on September 20. Zazi traveled a second time to New York and discussed further details with Ahmedzay. They decided to conduct suicide attacks on subway trains rather than target a large structure such as a building.[43] Zazi began to construct the bombs, using his notes as a reference. He conducted several Internet searches for hydrochloric acid and bookmarked websites on two different browsers for "Lab Safety for Hydrochloric Acid." He also searched a beauty salon website for hydrocide and peroxide. During July and August, Zazi purchased unusually large quantities of hydrogen peroxide and acetone products from beauty supply stores in the Denver metropolitan area. On July 25 he purchased six bottles of Liquid Developer Clairoxide, which contained high concentrations of hydrogen peroxide, at a beauty supply store in Aurora. On August 28 he purchased twelve 32-ounce bottles of Ms. K's Liquid 40 Volume, another hydrogen peroxide–based product, from the same store.[44]

Zazi preserved his sense of humor as he was preparing to kill innocent civilians. When an employee at the Beauty Supply Warehouse inquired about the volume of materials he was buying, he deadpanned, "I have a lot of girlfriends."[45]

Medunjanin and Ahmedzay helped.[46] They purchased a 1-gallon container of a product containing 20 percent hydrogen peroxide as well as an 8-ounce bottle of acetone. They procured an acetone product in the first week of September, as well as 32-ounce bottles of Ion Sensitive Scalp Developer, a product containing high levels of hydrogen peroxide, on three occasions during the summer of 2009.[47] Ahmedzay also evaluated potential bombing targets in New York, which was easy for him.[48] "I was familiar with the city," he had explained to Adnan el-Shukrijumah and other al Qa'ida operatives. "I was a New York City taxi driver, and knew the city very well."[49]

Now it was time to build the bombs. Zazi boiled some of the ingredients on the stove at his uncle's house in Aurora, but that posed too many security risks.[50] He searched for a suitable location. The July 2005 London bombers and the 2006 UK transatlantic plotters had rented apartments specifically to construct the bombs. Zazi, however, chose a nearby hotel in Aurora, where he checked into a suite that included a stove on August 28. On September 6 and 7 he rented the identical suite at the same hotel. His bomb-making notes suggested that in order to make TATP, it was necessary to heat the ingredients and make them highly concentrated. He used a pot to concentrate hydrogen peroxide by boiling it down, running the exhaust fans over the stove to vent the fumes. But he soon encountered problems, perhaps because he had spent so little time training in South Waziristan. On September 6 and 7, Zazi sent e-mails to Bangash asking about the correct mixture of ingredients to make explosives. Each message appeared to be more urgent in tone than the last. He mostly wanted to know how to incorporate the flour and ghee, two ingredients listed in the bomb-making instructions. Zazi emphasized in the e-mails that he needed answers quickly.[51]

On September 8, Zazi searched the Internet for a home improvement store in zip code 11354—Flushing, New York, his old neighborhood. He then searched the home improvement store's website for muriatic acid, a diluted version of hydrochloric acid that could be used as the third component of TATP. Zazi viewed four different types of muriatic acid, including one brand—Klean-Strip Green Safer Muriatic Acid—several times.[52]

In his conversations with Ahmad Bangash, Zazi had agreed to use the terms *wedding* and *marriage* to indicate that the operation was ready and the targets had been selected. The attack would involve the three suicide bombers—Zazi, Ahmedzay, and Medunjanin—detonating bombs on three separate subway cars in New York City. In a video teleconference involving FBI and New York Police Department officials, FBI experts pointed out that Zazi's notes, which had been seized through an intercept, indicated that his bombs were nearly identical to those manufactured by Mohammed Siddique Khan and the other London bombers. The method had become al Qa'ida's new trademark.

In early September, Zazi sent a message to Bangash. "The marriage is ready," he wrote.[53]

A Race Against the Clock

Zazi was less than two weeks away from an attack and had miraculously escaped detection. But U.S. and British intelligence agencies suddenly stumbled on an extraordinary lead, which came from a terrorist investigation in the United Kingdom earlier that year.

On April 8, 2009, UK police had arrested Pakistani national Abid Naseer and ten associates in Liverpool and Manchester, England, for involvement in an al Qa'ida–linked terrorist plot. The counterterrorist effort was code-named Operation Pathway and was led by MI5.[54] Like Zazi, Naseer had sent an e-mail in April to Ahmad Bangash, which was intercepted by intelligence officials, indicating that his group was prepared to carry out an imminent attack. Bangash had introduced Najibullah Zazi to senior al Qa'ida leaders in Pakistan. Abid Naseer, it turned out, had been in Peshawar in November 2008, around the same time as Zazi. In the e-mails, Naseer used coded language to refer to different types of explosives. In early April, again using coded language, he told Bangash that he was planning a large wedding for numerous guests between April 15 and 20 and that Bangash should be ready. UK authorities conducted searches of the plotters' homes, where they found large quantities of flour and oil as well as surveillance photographs of public areas in Manchester and maps of Manchester's city center posted on the wall.[55]

U.S. and British intelligence agencies continued to monitor Bangash's e-mail account. In early September they intercepted Zazi's message that the marriage was ready. This indicated that the attack was imminent, and the FBI and U.S. law enforcement officials immediately kicked into overdrive. By that time Zazi and his cell had decided to conduct the attacks on Manhattan subway lines on September 14, 15, or 16.[56] The clock was ticking. "I had a tingle in my stomach," said one senior New York Police Department official involved in the case. "I had never faced anything quite like this before."[57]

After being briefed on the intelligence, FBI director Mueller called together his closest advisers around 7 a.m. The mood was serious. The FBI would conduct a thorough investigation of Zazi and his network. But there were numerous questions: How many people were involved? Where were they? What was the plot? How advanced was it? For Philip Mudd, one of the first objectives was understanding the "spiderweb," which included more than just the plotters. It also meant uncovering the trainers and facilitators (some of whom were in Pakistan), the money trail, the bomb components (including where the plotters were purchasing the ingredients), individuals who had helped radicalize them, and possible targets.

It would be a challenging intelligence hunt, and Mudd's experience in the CIA came in handy. He believed the plot was manageable. "Now that we had them in our sights," he commented, "we needed to throw everything at the plotters."[58] The FBI, led by the Joint Terrorism Task Forces in Denver and New York, began tapping phones, contacting human sources who might have information, and collecting intelligence with the help of the CIA, National Security Agency, and other U.S. intelligence agencies. Still, the existence of a major domestic al Qa'ida plot was frustrating, since it raised questions about other plots the government had missed. "Damn," remarked Mudd. "We've been at this for almost ten years. Who else is out there?"[59]

With Zazi firmly in their sights, the Denver Joint Terrorism Task Force, led by the FBI, began conducting twenty-four-hour surveillance in Colorado, with assistance from the New York Joint Terrorism Task Force. On September 9, agents clandestinely followed Zazi as he left his residence in Aurora, rented a car, and began driving across the United States to New York.[60] "I am going to Chicago," he told his family. He would be going "for Tabligh," he said, meaning Islamic education.[61]

Zazi took a laptop computer that contained the bomb-making instructions and loaded up his car with the TATP mixture, wires, muriatic acid, and light bulbs.[62] Surveillance teams followed him during the entire 1,700-mile drive. Outside Denver he was pulled over by a police officer who looked inside the car but, after seeing nothing suspicious, let him go. Zazi was stopped again on the New Jersey side of the George Washington Bridge by Port Authority police, not New York Police Department officers. New York police commissioner Raymond Kelly apparently did not want to be responsible for allowing a bomb to enter New York City, just in case something went awry during the operation. So Port Authority pulled Zazi over as a part of a "random" stop, though bomb-sniffing dogs found nothing after circling the outside of his car.[63]

If the Joint Terrorism Task Force's goal was to keep the operation covert, it clearly didn't work. Zazi became spooked, believing that he was being followed—which he was.[64] He arrived in New York City on the afternoon of September 10 and traveled to Flushing. The FBI intercepted a call from Zazi's cell phone that day in which he expressed panic that law enforcement officers were tracking his movements.[65] He entered a mosque in Queens and dumped the items from his trunk—the muriatic acid, light bulbs, and wires—in the trash cans at the rear of the facility.[66] Agents from the Joint Terrorism Task Forces were not yet aware that Zazi had discarded the materials. They had partly lost track of him.

Ups and Downs

Detective Dan Sarkovsky from the New York City Police Department's Intelligence Division then contacted Ahmad Wais Afzali, a popular imam in Queens, for assistance. This would prove to be one of the most controversial moments in the investigation. Born into a wealthy family in Kabul, Afzali had fled Afghanistan with his parents and two brothers after the 1979 Soviet invasion. They moved to Queens, where his father opened two restaurants and the children graduated from high school. Afzali played handball and became passionate about cars. When he was a teenager, a former girlfriend accused him of rape and he pleaded guilty to attempted sexual abuse. Because of the felony conviction, he was the only member of his family to be denied U.S. citizenship. He began a career as an imam, first at a local mosque and later as the director of a funeral home that served the Muslim community. Afzali eventually became a respected imam, renowned for his passionate sermons, which, according to his wife, could "inspire tears" among attendants.[67]

He also began to act as a liaison between the police and the immigrant Afghan and Pakistani communities in Queens. Afzali had a reputation for respecting and supporting the United States, even opening his funeral home to a Muslim soldier from Queens who was killed in Iraq. The New York Police Department's intelligence unit sometimes contacted him when they had questions. After September 11, law enforcement agencies in several major U.S. cities, including New York, ramped up their outreach programs with Muslim communities.[68] Afzali had worked with the police on and off since September 11 without pay, acknowledging that he "was upset because the people involved claimed to follow my faith."[69]

Detective Sarkovsky asked Afzali whether he was familiar with four individuals, including Najibullah Zazi. Afzali responded that he knew three of the four.[70] Sarkovsky, accompanied by a lieutenant from the New York Police Department, then went to Afzali's house and showed him four photographs. Afzali identified three of the individuals, including Zazi, who had worshipped at a mosque where Afzali had led prayers. Unbeknown to the FBI, Sarkovsky asked Afzali to obtain information for the police about Zazi's whereabouts, intentions, and associates.[71] "Find out as much as possible about them," he pleaded.[72]

Sarkovsky did not share with Afzali the reason for the police interest in Zazi, nor did he tell the imam what he should or should not do to collect information.[73] In addition, FBI officials insist that the New York Police Department did not inform them of its decision to show the photos to Afzali, despite the fact that the Joint Terrorism Task Force, which answered to the FBI, was running the case.[74] Afzali quickly began to inquire within the community about Zazi, and on September 11 he received an angry call from Zazi's father, which lasted about twenty minutes.

"Who are you? And what do you want?" Mohammed Zazi demanded, clearly perturbed. FBI officials, who had tapped Mohammed Zazi's phone, were listening.[75]

"Don't worry, I am from the mosque," Afzali replied. Mohammed Zazi calmed down and took a deep breath.

"Where's your son?" began Afzali. "I want to talk to him."

"Why?" Mohammed Zazi shot back.

Afzali said he just wanted to talk to him.

"Is everything okay?" Mohammed Zazi asked.

"Yes," replied Afzali.[76]

Mohammed Zazi explained that his son was on a business trip to New York and gave Afzali his phone number. After hanging up, he dialed his son. "Afzali is going to call you," he explained, in a conversation the FBI was also listening to. "Afzali, the one in New York," he continued. Mohammed Zazi elaborated that he was referring to "the imam."

"So before anything else," he advised his son, "speak with Afzali. See if you need to go to Afzali or to make, make yourself aware, hire an attorney. What has happened? What have you guys done?"[77]

During the conversation, Zazi received a call from Afzali. He clicked over.

"How are you?" asked Zazi politely.

"What's going on?" asked Afzali. "I just want to say hello. Where have you been?"

Zazi responded, somewhat defensively, that he had moved to Colorado with his family and was working full-time.[78] Then Afzali got to the point.

"I want to speak with you about something," he told Zazi. "I want a meeting with you. You probably know why I'm calling you for this meeting. I was exposed to something yesterday from the authorities. And they came to ask me about your character. They asked me about you guys. I'm not sure if somebody complained about you. I'm not sure what happened. And I don't want to know." Referring to the New York Police Department, he relayed Detective Sarkovsky's request: "Please, we need to know who they are, what they're all about."[79]

Afzali inquired when Zazi had last traveled to Pakistan.

Eight months ago, Zazi replied.

"You went to visit your wife, right?" Afzali asked.

"Yeah," replied Zazi, somewhat curtly.

Afzali then explained that the police "came to the masjid to ask for help. That is a good sign. Trust me, that is a good sign. The bad sign is for them coming to you guys and picking you up automatically. Don't get involved in Afghanistan garbage, Iraq garbage," Afzali advised. He then added, "Listen, our phone call is being monitored."[80]

Later that day, FBI agents intercepted another phone call between Afzali and Zazi. Zazi told the imam that his rental car had been stolen and that he feared he was being watched. He also said that the people watching him took his car.

"Is there any evidence in the car?" Afzali inquired.[81]

"No," said Zazi, who explained that the people who took his car were probably the "same ones who had been following him all day."[82] Zazi ended the conversation, and Afzali didn't hear from him again.

FBI agents, who had been conducting extensive covert surveillance of Zazi and his colleagues, were unaware that Afzali had been brought into the case until they heard his voice on wiretaps. Furious that the investigation may have been compromised, the FBI took control of all matters related to the investigation, and tension between the FBI and the New York Police Department exploded.[83]

"Sometimes sources go bad," said Philip Mudd. "It happens."[84]

Zazi's suspicions about his car were accurate. The Joint Terrorism Task Force had towed his rental car, which was parked in Queens. During the search they found a laptop computer containing a JPEG document with nine pages of handwritten notes with formulations and instructions regarding the manufacture and handling of initiating explosives, main explosives charges, explosives detonators, and components of a fusing system.[85] They also raided the Queens residence where Zazi had spent the night and found an electronic weight scale in the closet. The scale and batteries both contained Zazi's fingerprints. FBI explosives experts concluded that the scale was suitable for performing several of the procedures outlined in the instructions, such as weighing the hydrogen peroxide and other precursor chemicals to determine proper concentrations and ratios.[86]

Rental records show that Zazi was supposed to return his car in New York on September 14, 2009. But on September 12, fearing that he had been compromised, he flew from La Guardia Airport to Denver.[87] After he returned to Colorado, agents executed a search warrant at his apartment complex on East Smoky Hill Road in Aurora.[88] On September 16 members of the Denver Joint Terrorism Task Force interviewed Zazi about the handwritten notes found on his computer. Zazi replied that he had never seen the document before. He claimed that if the handwritten notes were on his computer, he must have unintentionally received them as part of a religious book he had downloaded in August.[89] On September 17 and 18, FBI agents again interviewed Zazi in Denver. He admitted that during his 2008 trip to Pakistan he had attended courses and received instruction on weapons and explosives at an al Qa'ida facility in the tribal areas of Pakistan.[90]

Zazi was now desperate and told his uncle that he might kill himself.[91] Before anything else happened, however, he was arrested, on September 19. Five months later he pleaded guilty to conspiring to use weapons of mass destruction, conspiring to commit murder in a foreign country, and providing material support to a terrorist organization. In November, Ahmad Bangash, the al Qa'ida operative who had maintained contact with him, was arrested by Pakistani authorities. And on January 10, 2010, the FBI arrested Adis Medunjanin and Zarein Ahmedzay.[92]

Bring Him to Justice

The United States had escaped another terrorist attack, but a third wave of al Qa'ida activity was building. The plot had been thwarted in part because of a global counterterrorist hunt involving clandestine U.S. government agencies. Many of these agencies were not publically recognized, including the National Security Agency, whose communications intercepts were essential to understand the network. Still, the Najibullah Zazi case was unsettling for Art Cummings and Philip Mudd. There appeared to be a growing danger from radicalized Americans who were prepared to use violence in the United States. If this was to be the future of counterterrorism, better communication between the FBI and local law enforcement agencies would be necessary.

"Despite rising threats from groups outside al Qa'ida's core leadership, the risk from al Qa'ida central persists," wrote Mudd several months after the Zazi arrest. The plot, he concluded, illustrated that "al Qa'ida's core leadership, despite substantial losses, remains intent on striking critical infrastructure—especially transportation—in U.S. population centers."[93]

Based on Zazi's operation and similar plots, Mudd realized that al Qa'ida was not planning attacks as sophisticated as the September 11 events. Even when individuals had direct ties to al Qa'ida's leadership, he concluded that they were not "not typically directed out from the center of action (Pakistan/Afghanistan), but [were] instead drawn into it."[94] This development indicated the spread of al Qa'ida's revolutionary ideology. For several years Zazi had stewed over what he perceived as a U.S.-led global struggle against Islam. Much like the Fort Dix plotters, he had turned to on-line Islamic preachers. One was Anwar al-Awlaki. Another was Shaykh Abdallah Ibrahim al-Faisal, a radical Muslim cleric in Jamaica who had influenced Germaine Lindsay, one of the four suicide bombers in the 2005 London attacks. Zazi and his colleagues listened to Internet lectures, watched dozens of videos of the wars in Iraq and other countries, and turned their anger over the suffering of Muslims into rage and their rage into violence.

In a hushed New York City courtroom after his arrest, Zarein Ahmedzay quoted from the Qur'an and explained why he had prepared to kill himself and scores of innocent civilians on a New York City subway. "Verily, Allah has purchased of the believers their lives and their wealth for the price of Paradise, to fight in the way of Allah, to kill and get killed. It is a promise binding on the truth in the Torah, the Gospel and the Qur'an," he said.

Ahmedzay cited the Afghanistan and Iraq wars, condemning them as struggles "against Islam." He also mentioned the Israeli occupation of Palestinian territory and warned that the "Zionist Jews" were an acute threat to the United States. These realities, he argued, made violence unfortunate but inevitable. "I personally believed that conducting an operation in the United States would be the best way to end the wars," he said.[95]

Ahmedzay's logic ignored the fact that the United States had launched wars in both countries *because of* the attacks in New York and Washington. Ahmedzay may have believed that his own attack would produce in the United States something similar to the Spanish response to the 2004 Madrid attacks, which led to a withdrawal of Spanish forces from Iraq. In any event, his argument revealed a warped sense of reality. It also left many family members dismayed.

"If the guy was involved in all this stuff," said Habib Rasooli, a businessman in Queens and a relative of Najibullah Zazi, "I say, 'O.K., bring him to justice.' I'd bring him myself."[96]

Zazi's target was the United States. But it wasn't just America's largest cities that had to be concerned. Zazi had built his bombs in suburban Denver, nearly 2,000 miles away from his target. The plot included three individuals who lived in the United States, traveled freely with legitimate passports and driver's licenses, and understood the nuances and rhythms of American life. Zazi had even passed an airport security background check in 2009, only a few months before his planned attack. It all seemed too easy.

What could be next? American officials were about to find out.

14

THE RISE OF YEMEN

Art Cummings received an urgent message on his BlackBerry. It was Christmas Day 2009, and he was relaxing with his wife and children in Richmond. The temperature outside had climbed above freezing, and a cold rain had begun to fall. The week before, a huge storm that meteorologists referred to as the "I-95 Special" moved up Interstate 95 from Richmond to Washington, Baltimore, New York, and Boston, burying the region in snow and crippling public transportation.[1]

Someone from the FBI command center was now on the line. "Call back on your secure phone," he told Cummings.

When Cummings returned the call, he learned that a twenty-three-year-old Nigerian named Umar Farouk Abdulmutallab, who had worked with al Qa'ida operative Anwar al-Awlaki, had attempted to detonate an improvised explosive device on a North-west Airlines flight headed to Detroit. The bomb had been sown into his underwear but had failed to explode. Cummings jumped into his Dodge Charger and arrived at FBI Headquarters in the afternoon.[2] Washington's streets were deserted, and huge snow-drifts blocked the sidewalks outside FBI Headquarters on Pennsylvania Avenue. Cummings joined a secret video teleconference to discuss the plot with other senior officials, including White House counterterrorism chief John Brennan, National Counterterrorism Center director Michael Leiter, deputy secretary of the Department of Homeland Security Jane Lute, and several others.

The attack, they quickly discovered, had been planned in Yemen and perpetrated by the al Qa'ida fugitive Anwar al-Awlaki. A month before, a U.S. Army major, Nidal Malik Hasan, had gunned down thirteen people and wounded forty-three others at Fort Hood, Texas, partly because of Awlaki's instigation. In June 2009, Abdulhakim Mujahid Muhammad, who had changed his name from Carlos Bledsoe, opened fire with a semiautomatic rifle on a military recruiting center in Little Rock, Arkansas, killing one soldier and wounding another. He had listened to Awlaki's sermons and spent time in Yemen.[3] Awlaki had now become a dangerous enemy.

"The fact that fighting against the U.S. army is an Islamic duty today cannot be disputed," Awlaki announced in an essay defending the gunman. "No scholar with a grain of Islamic knowledge can defy the clear cut proofs that Muslims today have the right—rather than duty—to fight against American tyranny."[4]

While central al Qa'ida, based in Pakistan, had tried and failed to attack the U.S. homeland in recent years, its Yemeni affiliate proved more successful. A cadre of U.S. intelligence, military, diplomatic, and law enforcement officials, including Cummings, were now scrambling to identify Awlaki-inspired plots and disrupt them. In both the Abdulmutallab and Hasan cases, however, U.S. agencies had some information on the terrorists but failed to take adequate action. Looking back on the events, the White House admitted that the "U.S. government had sufficient information to have uncovered and potentially disrupted the December 25 attack." But intelligence analysts "failed to connect the dots that could have identified and warned of the specific threat."[5]

The third wave was triggered by several factors. One was al Qa'ida's ability to take advantage of weak governments in Yemen,

Somalia, and North Africa. In Yemen, President Ali Abdullah Saleh's regime began to collapse in the wake of widespread unhappiness with social, economic, and political conditions in the country. In nearby Somalia, al Shabaab, an Islamic militant organization dedicated to overthrowing the Somali government, made inroads into the southern part of the country in 2008 and 2009. Al Qa'ida initially adopted a selective strategy that involved targeting police, military, and other government officials instead of civilians. Much as in Afghanistan before September 11, there was little counterterrorism response from the United States in North Africa and the Arabian Peninsula, since U.S. policymakers were focused on Afghanistan, Pakistan, and Iraq. Lives had been lost in the Hasan attack and nerves had been frayed in both, but even more worrying, a new enemy had emerged: Anwar al-Awlaki. Yemen was now the center of al Qa'ida's third wave.

Inspire the Believers

The Shabwah region of Yemen lies southeast of the capital city, Sana'a, and borders the Gulf of Aden in the Arabian Sea. The weather is stifling and the land is lifeless. Soft tones of khaki and magenta color the sun-baked earth and crescent-shaped sand dunes. A series of rugged peaks climb to 7,000 feet, sprinkled with sparse vegetation and connected by parched riverbeds. When rain comes, which it rarely does, the water sprints down the thin, rocky valleys, washes out the topsoil, evaporates quickly, and leaves the land dry and thirsty. Apart from a few patches of farmed land, the rest is desert. Here, local tribesmen exist in perpetual poverty and violence. Bedouin encampments appear occasionally, populated by desert-dwelling Arab nomads. Shabwah was a resting point on the ancient caravan routes from North Africa to Asia, on which camels lugged incense and other commodities.

Figure 14: Map of Shabwah Governorate

This remote landscape attracted Anwar al-Awlaki, who had been a driving force in the rebirth of al Qa'ida's affiliate in the Arabian Peninsula. Its predecessor group had been decimated by Saudi intelligence, with some help from the United States, after its involvement in attacks such as that on the USS *Cole* in 2000. Abu Ali al-Harithi, its leader, was killed in a missile strike in 2002 along with Kamal Derwish, a U.S. citizen who helped radicalize the Lackawanna, New York, cell. The Arabian Peninsula had largely operated as a facilitation and support hub for foreign fighters in the years that followed, but it produced few major plots focused on the United States.[6]

In January 2009, al Qa'ida publicly announced that Saudi and Yemeni operatives had unified under the banner of a single group, which they named al Qa'ida in the Arabian Peninsula.[7] Awlaki pledged *bayat* to Nasir al-Wahishi, the group's amir, a thin, olive-skinned Yemeni with dark hair and crooked teeth.[8] Wahishi had attended al-Farouq training camp in Afghanistan in the late 1990s and had developed a close relationship with Osama bin Laden, handling some of his finances and guesthouses. In 2002, Wahishi fled to Iran along with some al Qa'ida leaders, but he was apparently arrested by the Iranian government and handed over to Yemeni authorities. He escaped from a Yemeni prison in 2006.[9]

Wahishi then spent several years building a network in Yemen dedicated to overthrowing the government of Ali Abdullah Saleh and establishing an Islamic emirate. U.S. intelligence agencies, which had been carefully monitoring the group's activities, were familiar with the new group's leaders. Wahishi's deputy, Said al-Shihri, was a Saudi national who had spent time in the U.S. prison in Guantánamo Bay. Al Qa'ida in the Arabian Peninsula included a combination of Yemeni jihadists, alumni from al Qa'ida in Iraq and the Saudi branch of al Qa'ida, and several other factions that were reunified under Wahishi. In his zeal to create an Islamic emirate, Wahishi also established an army to seize control of territory in southern Yemen.

The creation of an al Qa'ida affiliate in Yemen heralded the organization's reemergence in the land of the Prophet. Awlaki's decision to join the newly formed al Qa'ida in the Arabian Peninsula in 2009 was a coup for Wahishi. Al Qa'ida had a stale message before he arrived. Awlaki settled in the Shabwah Governorate, and he had several wives—a Yemeni, an American, and a Croatian national—and children.[10] From his Yemeni base, he ran his global jihadist enterprise, serving as a senior external operations chief. Awlaki continued to develop his blog (www.anwar-alawlaki.com), which was later shut down. He also improved his Facebook and MySpace pages and posted on YouTube and other social media forums to proselytize his jihadist message.

"The Internet has become a great medium for spreading the call of Jihad and following the news of the mujahideen," Awlaki wrote.[11] He encouraged supporters to become "Internet mujahideen" by establishing discussion forums, sending out e-mail blasts, posting or e-mailing jihadist literature and news, and setting up websites dedicated to distributing information. He mixed his impressive communication skills with an ability to simplify complex religious and political issues for mass consumption. He was not an Islamic scholar, had never studied at a credentialed Islamic university, and was unfit to issue religious guidance, but he was an impeccable salesman. His willingness to stand up to the United States made him a potent enemy.

Perhaps his most innovative contribution was to help create *Inspire* magazine. Published by al Qa'ida in the Arabian Peninsula, it took its name from a verse in the Qur'an describing the Battle of Badr, fought between Muslims and their opponents near Medina in Saudi Arabia. "And inspire the believers to fight," it encouraged readers.[12] An editorial in *Inspire's* introductory issue explained the magazine's raison d'être. "This Islamic Magazine," it proclaimed, "is geared towards making the Muslim a mujahid in Allah's path."[13]

The magazine presented a Salafi version of Islam in English and focused on issues of interest to al Qa'ida's Yemeni members. But its target audience was the broader English-speaking Muslim readership. The hope was that individuals would be "inspired" to conduct attacks against the West and its allies. *Inspire* magazine was modern in appearance and suited for a young, impressionable audience. The first issue included colorful computerized graphics; essays from al Qa'ida's top leaders, such as Osama bin Laden and Ayman al-Zawahiri; poems; helpful sections on how to send and receive encrypted messages; and suggestions about what to take (and not to take) when going on violent jihad. The editors also had a sense of humor, quoting part of a monologue by American comedian David Letterman on George W. Bush's memoir: "In the book, 'Decision Points,' he will reveal all the bad decisions and mistakes that George Bush made as President . . . this is *volume one*."[14]

The magazine also had a macabre side. In an essay titled "Make a Bomb in the Kitchen of Your Mom," there were step-by-step instructions in English on how to build a bomb with readily available household ingredients, complete with photographs and diagrams. Britain's external spy agency, MI6, and its signals intelligence agency, Government Communications Headquarters, mounted a cyber attack dubbed Operation Cupcake: when *Inspire* followers tried to download the sixty-seven-page magazine, they received recipes for "The Best Cupcakes in America" from the Ellen DeGeneres show.

Awlaki wrote the lead article for the first issue. "So what is the proper solution to this growing campaign of defamation?" he asked rhetorically, referring to a perceived war against Islam by Western governments. "The medicine prescribed by the Messenger of Allah is the execution of those involved," he answered. "Their proper abode is Hellfire."[15]

Many of al Qa'ida in the Arabian Peninsula's top leaders respected Awlaki's infectious confidence, willingness to be involved in terrorist operations, and contacts elsewhere in the movement. In January 2009 he released an article titled "44 Ways to Support Jihad," which outlined the many ways in which a person could participate. Some were extreme, like conducting suicide operations and sponsoring the family of a suicide bomber. Others were more innocuous, like fundraising.[16] He also recorded a sermon titled "The Story of Ibn al-Aqwa," which called for modern-day violent jihad and served as a source of radicalization and legitimacy for impressionable Muslims. Unlike the U.S.-born al Qa'ida official Adam Gadahn, who struggled to gain listeners despite thousands of YouTube posts, Awlaki soon built a significant following. His actions had an impact on Muslims around the world. This raised major civil liberties questions for social media companies.

Awlaki's blog and Facebook pages were shut down in November 2009. The video-sharing website YouTube removed hundreds of Awlaki videos. The company, owned by Google, explained that it would not remove videos containing purely religious content, but it would remove any that contained "dangerous or illegal activities such as bomb-making, hate speech and incitement to commit violence" or came from accounts "registered by a member of a designated foreign terrorist organization."[17] But there was a murky gray area between purely religious messages and violent messages. Awlaki moved effortlessly along that rhetorical frontier. In the end, the debate was moot. YouTube users continued to upload new Awlaki videos, and YouTube couldn't keep up with the numerous identical copies. The number of new websites and other forums hosting Awlaki proliferated.

U.S. intelligence agencies were particularly concerned because Awlaki was both a strategist *and an operator*. U.S. intelligence analysts believed that he was involved in a March 2009 suicide bombing against South Korean tourists in Yemen and an August 2009 attempt to assassinate Saudi prince Muhammad bin Nayif.[18] Awlaki's connection to Americans, especially those plotting attacks in the United States, concerned the FBI and CIA most of all.

U.S. citizen Barry Bujol, a resident of Hempstead, Texas, sought Awlaki's advice in joining al Qa'ida. Bujol had e-mailed Awlaki many times, requesting assistance in helping the mujahideen, and Awlaki had sent him "44 Ways to Support Jihad."[19] The FBI arrested Bujol for attempting to provide material support to al Qa'ida in the Arabian Peninsula. Paul Rockwood, who had converted to Islam in Virginia, became a strict adherent of Awlaki's after listening to "The Constants of Jihad" and "44 Ways to Support Jihad." He later planned a series of violent jihad-inspired assassinations and bombings.[20] In a case investigated by the FBI's Washington field office, U.S. citizen Zachary Chesser e-mailed Awlaki for spiritual guidance and asked for help in joining al Shabaab in Somalia. Chesser had watched online videos and listened to digitized lectures "almost obsessively," especially those by Awlaki.[21]

Awlaki responded several times, and Chesser started his own You-Tube home page under the username LearnTeachFightDie, where he posted videos and hosted discussions.[22] "Awlaki inspires people to pursue jihad," Chesser explained.[23]

Countless others, including Farooque Ahmed, who was arrested for planning bombings at Metrorail stations in Washington, D.C., listened to Awlaki's propaganda.[24] Senior FBI officials worried about terrorist use of the Internet. But it was more than the Internet, insisted Philip Mudd. "People radicalize via other people," he noted. "The Internet is an accelerator."[25]

Mudd saw the terrorist threat to the United States growing more diffuse now, with individuals who had never met an al Qa'ida member carrying on the al Qa'ida "revolution" in the United States. Al Qa'ida was not primarily interested in conducting its own attacks, he contended, but tried to inspire others. "The key to this twenty-first century revolution," Mudd believed, "is the Internet, which provides an avenue for the transmission of images (Abu Ghraib), preachers (Anwar Awlaki), publications (*Inspire*), and chat rooms in which future jihadists meet virtually to discuss what they see and hear. And to radicalize each other."[26]

One problem, he concluded, was that traditional intelligence methods—human and technical penetration of a clearly defined collection target—were not well suited to identifying these individuals, because they did not have identifiable links with terrorist groups. Most were watching videos and reading magazines. They were not directly in touch with known terrorists by phone or e-mail, which made it more difficult for probing U.S. intelligence agencies to find them. Anwar al-Awlaki had mastered the art of reaching out to these individuals. Essentially he had cast a wide net in the sea of potential operatives. Rather than recruit in traditional, risky ways, he could let people come to him. He had something special in store for one such recruit—Umar Farouk Abdulmutallab. Just as with Bujol, Rockwood, Chesser, and Ahmed, Awlaki didn't make the first move. Abdulmutallab came to him.

Alone and Afraid

Umar Farouk Abdulmutallab was born on December 22, 1986, in Lagos, Nigeria.[27] His father, Alhaji Umaru Mutallab, was chairman of the First Bank of Nigeria and the former Nigerian federal commissioner for economic development. Abdulmutallab, who was called Farouk by his family, enjoyed a privileged childhood.[28] His father owned a mansion in Abuja and houses in the Nigerian cities of Kaduna, Lagos, Katsina, and Funtua, as well as in London, and he spent a considerable part of his childhood in Kaduna, in an affluent neighborhood of the northern city. The area was an industrial hub, with an extensive rail and road network that transported textiles, machinery, steel, aluminum, and petroleum products to overseas markets.

Abdulmutallab held generally positive memories of his childhood, but they were mixed with some bad ones. "We live in terror throughout our lives," he wrote in an on-line chat room session in 2005, "that highway robbers don't stop us on the street at broad daylight, and sometimes we have sleepless nights fearing armed robbers will break into our houses. The police are apparently the robbers and the enemy," he noted with some dismay over the corruption in his home country.[29]

Abdulmutallab lived abroad for much of his childhood, attending various boarding schools and universities. When he was twelve, his parents sent him to the British School of Lomé in the West African country of Togo. He developed an early love of Islam, though he was by no means radical, and became increasingly involved in Islamic activities. When he was fifteen, the school's Muslim chaplain asked him to help run the *salat*, the obligatory prayer five times a day, and to encourage students to attend Qur'an classes. "The position instilled in me an added responsibility to be a good ambassador of Islam and a caller towards Allah," he recalled.[30]

In September 2005, Abdulmutallab enrolled at University College London to study mechanical engineering. He had a medium build, dark skin, and discolorations on his forehead. His full red-dish lips, flat nose, and boyish face made him look even younger than he was. Abdulmutallab's peers in London remembered him as a modest and affable student, sometimes excessively polite, who loved soccer and exhibited tenderness toward others.[31] In one session on the website Islamic Forum, a chat room for young Muslims at gawaher.com, a participant explained that her parents were having marital problems. "Stay strong sister, May Allah help you through this," Abdulmutallab wrote compassionately. "All i can do for you for now is pray. May Allah out of his Mercy help you. His is the Best disposer of all affairs."[32]

Abdulmutallab also had an infectious sense of humor, which was often self-deprecating. In one post on Islamic Forum, he expounded on the joys of sleeping. "During some holidays i use to sleep for about 10-12 hours," he wrote, "trying to imitate deep sleepers, i just loved the idea of someone being a heavy, deep sleeper, plus i believed in the more sleep, the taller one gets :laugh."[33] He ended his entry, as he often did, with "biggrin," a written version of the smiley-face icon that many others used in social media forums.

This outwardly charming young man also wrote on-line that he wrestled with bouts of loneliness, exposing a painful inner struggle. He was torn between his fastidious devotion to Islam and the realities of living in the West. "First of all, i have no friend," he wrote in one Islamic Forum posting. "Not because i do not socialise, etc. but because either people do not want to get too close to me as they go partying and stuff while i dont, or they are bad people who befriend me and influence me to do bad things. Hence i am in a situation where i do not have a friend. i have no one to speak to, no one to consult, no one to support me and i feel depressed and lonely. i do not know what to do."

Abdulmutallab was clearly not alone, at least in a physical sense. As a student, he had a daily schedule crammed with studying for classes, socializing with friends, praying, and playing soccer. Still, he felt isolated and torn between what he called "liberalism" and "extremism." "The Prophet said religion is easy and anyone who tries to overburden themselves will find it hard and will not be able to continue," he wrote. "So anytime i relax, i deviate sometimes and then when i strive hard, i get tired of what i am doing i.e. memorising the quran." The two competing lifestyles vexed him. "How should one put the balance right?" he asked.[34]

The on-line forum was generally supportive of struggling Muslims, but Abdulmutallab received some negative responses. "Hmmm," said one individual, whose chatroom name was D-ZiNeR, "this kinda was me some time ago . . . but now, im waaaay past it."[35]

A few others were more constructive. "You do have a friend always there!" said another, identifying herself as Batoota. "Never feel that you are alone . . . for Allah is the light of the heavens and the earth, He is the cure where there is an illness, He is the guide when all is lost, and He is the Merciful with his servants."[36]

Batoota's message was exactly what the struggling Abdulmutallab needed. "My God, you made me almost cry sister," he responded, the weight temporarily alleviated. "Thanks for the lovely words."[37]

During his time at University College London, he was a member of the university's Islamic Society, serving as its president during his second year, from 2006 to 2007. A fellow Muslim student frequently saw Abdulmutallab praying in the quiet room. Another recalled that he always wore traditional Nigerian dress for prayers on Friday. Muslim students in the Department of Mechanical Engineering occasionally sought religious advice from him, because they regarded him as knowledgeable.[38]

During his time at university, Abdulmutallab appeared to become more religiously conservative. In an on-line discussion of the morality of high school proms, his views were straightforward. "I think it's haram," he said, indicating that it was prohibited in Islam. "There's also the extravagance in spending for the prom, drinking usually takes place, music that excites the evil desires. For alcohol, it is even haram to sit on the table where it is served. In proms this will usually inevitably happen."[39]

Abdulmutallab had also become critical of the U.S. wars in Afghanistan and Iraq. He played a role in putting together a "War on Terror Week" at the university. The program brought together a variety of individuals, such as former Guantánamo Bay detainee Moazzam Beg, to examine the "death of thousands of innocent lives and thousands more detained illegally without trial or judgment."[40]

Struggling to find camaraderie in London, Abdulmutallab increasingly found company on chat rooms like the Islamic Forum and YouTube, but also on jihadist websites. It was his decision to seek companionship on-line that led him to Anwar al-Awlaki. Within a year of his graduation from University College London, he had become radical and decided to join al Qa'ida. What pushed Abdulmutallab over the edge? The answer lies in part in his relationship with Awlaki.

Training in Yemen

In 2005, Abdulmutallab had traveled to Yemen to study at the Sana'a Institute for the Arabic Language.[41] His goal was to improve his Arabic skills so he could read the Qur'an in its original language—pure and unadulterated.[42] But he also went as a tourist, meandering through the shops and markets of the picturesque Old City, tasting local delicacies (along with the food in Pizza Hut and Kentucky Fried Chicken), and visiting amusement parks.[43] Sana'a had been inhabited for more than 2,500 years. The grandeur of the architecture reinforced the faith of the impressionable young Abdulmutallab. Many of the tightly crammed houses were decorated with ornate stucco friezes, intricately carved frames, aesthetic coping that decorated the walls, and exquisite stained glass windows. One of the most popular attractions was the Suq al-Milh (Salt Market), where the Sana'a institute's students sampled warm bread, spices, raisins, and other local dishes.

For Abdulmutallab, Sana'a was a labyrinth; its oppressively high walls, narrow corridors, and strange noises frightened and tantalized him. Nevertheless, he wrote in an on-line post, "I find the city beautiful and the weather cool as the city is about 2000m above sea level," adding that the weather was so moderate that "even the Brits aren't complaining about the heat."[44]

Before he left London, Abdulmutallab had been listening to Awlaki's on-line sermons, including "44 Ways to Support Jihad." It was thus a shock to encounter this star of radical Islam in the flesh. The two first met at the Sana'a institute when Awlaki was introduced to the students. It was a surreal moment for Abdulmutallab and had a profound impact on his radicalization.

In "44 Ways," Awlaki complained that "the kuffar today are conspiring against us like never before." This onslaught, he argued, required a violent response in which "jihad becomes obligatory on every Muslim."

Awlaki's reasoning hearkened back to the extremist arguments of the Egyptian scholar Sayyid Qutb, who had been so influential for Osama bin Laden and Ayman al-Zawahiri. Qutb had argued that violent jihad was a duty for Muslims, on par with the five pillars of Islam: *zakat* (almsgiving), hajj (the pilgrimage to Mecca), *salat* (daily prayers), *sawm* (fasting during Ramada), and the *shahada* (accepting Muhammad as God's messenger).[45] A particularly important form of jihad, Awlaki continued, was to become a suicide bomber. "Asking Allah to die as a shaheed pleases Allah because it shows him that you are willing to give your life for him," he said.

For many al Qa'ida leaders, encouraging suicide operations was sufficient. But not for Awlaki. He went further, arguing that a failure to commit suicide could be disastrous for Islam. "44 Ways" included the following passage: "The reason why the enemies of Allah succeeded in defeating some Muslims and taking over their land is because they have lost their love for martyrdom."

Never mind that Awlaki hadn't volunteered to give up his own life—his words had a profound impact on Abdulmutallab. Back in London, Abdulmutallab downloaded such sermons as "Battle for the Hearts and Minds," "Lessons from the Companions Living as a Minority," and "The Dust Will Never Settle Down."[46] These lectures were mesmerizing. Awlaki spoke in a soothing, lucid tone, his voice rising and falling symphonically. He was a skilled orator and obsessively quoted U.S. newspapers and magazines, think-tank studies, and government reports to emphasize key points. In a particularly invidious lecture, "Battle for the Hearts and Minds," he cited articles from *U.S. News & World Report*, a study by the U.S.-based RAND Corporation, and the U.S. Department of Defense's *Quadrennial Defense Review* to support his claim that the United States was engaged in a clandestine effort to destroy Islam.

Abdulmutallab graduated from University College London in August 2008 as a satisfactory, though not academically outstanding, student.[47] Several months later he enrolled at the University of Wollongong in Dubai, United Arab Emirates, for a master's degree in international business. His religious views had gradually become more radical, but it wasn't until he went to Dubai that he made a final decision to conduct violent jihad. He decided to attack the United States, he later acknowledged, "in retaliation for U.S. support of Israel" and "in retaliation for the killing of innocent and civilian Muslims populations in Yemen, Iraq, Somalia, Afghanistan and beyond."[48] Around June 2009, Abdulmutallab told his parents that he was discontinuing his studies and would focus on sharia and Arabic in Yemen. His parents begged him to rethink his decision, pleading with him via text messages and phone calls, pointing out that he was doing well in school and would graduate later that year. Some of Abdulmutallab's replies were chilling. "I wish you could see the truth that I see," he explained. "I am now doing the right thing."[49]

Early in August 2009, Abdulmutallab returned to Yemen under the pretext of taking a refresher course in Arabic at the Sana'a institute. In truth he went to find Anwar al-Awlaki. This turned out to be more complicated than he had anticipated. Abdulmutallab initially tried calling, texting, and even e-mailing Awlaki, but with little success. After making inquiries at Al-Iman University, he contacted Sheikh Abdul Majeed al-Zindani, the founder of the university. In 2004 the U.S. Treasury Department had designated Zindani a terrorist because of his connections to Osama bin Laden and financial support of al Qa'ida.[50] Zindani had also founded the Charitable Society for Social Welfare, an organization that Awlaki worked for while living in San Diego. It is unclear whether Abdulmutallab ever spoke to Zindani, but he apparently talked to his son, Dr. Abdallah Zindani. Abdulmutallab then wrote a letter to Awlaki outlining his background and his motivation to conduct violent jihad. He saved the information on a flash drive and passed it to a third individual for Awlaki.[51]

He didn't have to wait long for an answer. He was soon contacted by an al Qa'ida operative, and a meeting was arranged.[52] The leaders of al Qa'ida in the Arabian Peninsula were extremely cautious, aware that Western intelligence agencies were tracking them. When Awlaki's men picked him up, they removed the battery and SIM card from Abdulmutallab's phone and made sure he left behind his laptop, clothes, camera, and books. En route, they repeatedly changed vehicles and drivers, took Abdulmutallab to various houses, and requested that he use several aliases—as did everyone else.[53]

Over the next few months, Abdulmutallab met with Awlaki several times. Initially they discussed basic issues, such as how Abdulmutallab had arrived in Yemen and his background and religious views. He had conviction and desire, but he badly needed training. In October he attended a training camp in the Shabwah region, where over two dozen fighters dug trenches, crawled through barbed wire, and practiced tactical movements such as clearing buildings. The daily routine at the training camp consisted of rising early, praying, reading the Qur'an, completing warm-up drills, and undergoing tactical training. After lunch the students completed additional tactical training drills, and at night they stayed in tents.[54]

While Abdulmutallab was at the camp, al Qa'ida leaders asked him whether he would be interested in participating in a suicide mission. He responded that he was interested and would consider it. He was particularly useful for al Qa'ida leaders because he had a Nigerian passport and a valid U.S. visa, so he could travel to the United States. In addition, he would probably not be known to Western intelligence agencies, since he was such a new recruit. In November, Abdulmutallab swore *bayat* to Nasir al-Wahishi and Osama bin Laden. Later that month, he returned to training camp. He improved his shooting skills, practiced battlefield maneuvers, underwent physical training, and listened to religious lectures by his instructors. Not all of it would be relevant to his suicide mission, but it provided an opportunity to bond with other fighters.

Around this time Abdulmutallab sent a text message to several family members saying that he would no longer be reachable and called his mother to say farewell, reportedly telling her that he was leaving for jihad.[55] "This is the last you'll hear from me," he explained. "This phone number will be destroyed. When you get this text I have already been gone for three weeks."[56]

In either late November or early December, Abdulmutallab was told that his mission would involve blowing up an airplane. He again met with Awlaki. The cleric asked if the young Nigerian agreed to conduct a suicide mission. "Yes," replied Abdulmutallab. Awlaki revealed that the mission would take place in the United States and provided some basic guidance. He requested that Abdulmutallab conduct the attack on a U.S. airline, carry out the attack only when he was ready, travel through an African country to avoid suspicion, and detonate the bomb over U.S. airspace.[57]

Early in December, Abdulmutallab prepared a *wasia*, or last will and testament, in a handwritten letter addressed to his parents. A video later released by al Qa'ida in the Arabian Peninsula's media arm, Al Malahim Media Foundation, showed him training in the Yemeni desert, armed with an AK-47 assault rifle. He and several dozen fighters fired assault rifles and rocket-propelled grenades and vaulted through obstacle courses. They used British, Israeli, and United Nations flags for target practice. Echoing Awlaki's propaganda pitch, Abdulmutallab explained that it was not just an obligation but a duty to fight. "The enemy is in your lands with their armies, the Jews and the Christians and their agents," he calmly explained, clad in a white robe and prayer cap, with an aging AK-47 and a black-and-white al Qa'ida flag in the background. "God said if you do not fight back, He will punish you and replace you."[58]

Abdulmutallab was now ready for the operation. He just had to execute it.

We Heard a Bang

Al Qa'ida leaders had apparently advised Abdulmutallab to wear Western clothes and to avoid looking "too Muslim" but not to appear to be concealing his faith.[59] On December 6, 2009, Abdulmutallab flew from Yemen to Addis Ababa, Ethiopia, on an Ethiopian Airlines flight. On December 9 he flew to Ghana, where he stayed for several days. Around December 16 he bought tickets for flights that would take him through Ethiopia, Ghana, Nigeria, and Amsterdam before arriving in Detroit—a circuitous route, as Awlaki had directed. He paid for the $2,831 tickets in cash, which is not unusual in Africa. On December 24 he boarded Northwest Airlines Flight 253 in Amsterdam, which was scheduled to arrive in Detroit on December 25. The flight carried 279 passengers and 11 crew members.[60]

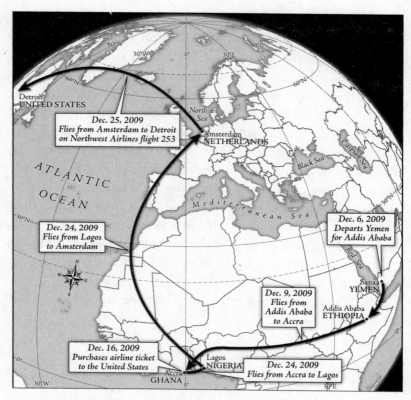

Figure 15: Abdulmutallab's Journey from Yemen to the United States

Abdulmutallab's bomb maker in Yemen, who used the name Ibrahim as-Siri, among other aliases, had an ingenious solution to the problem of airport security. Since the September 11 attacks and the failed 2006 transatlantic airlines plot, airport security had significantly improved. Airports around the world had banned a growing list of items, from box cutters to liquids, aerosols, and gels. In the United States, the Transportation Security Administration established a 3-1-1 rule that permitted each passenger to carry one 3.4 ounce (100 ml) bottle of liquid or less; one quart-sized, clear, ziplock bag; and one carry-on bag to be placed in a screening bin.[61]

Al Qa'ida's challenge, then, was to circumvent these improved security measures. As-Siri's solution was to build a bomb that could be placed in Abdulmutallab's underwear. The main explosive charge consisted of 76 grams of Pentaerythritol (also known as PETN).[62] The initiator consisted of a plastic syringe filled with ethylene glycol, which was supposed to be inserted into a chemical mixture of potassium permanganate stored in a cloth pouch in the underwear.[63] The flame produced by the reaction was designed to be sufficient to initiate the TATP a few seconds later, which in turn would initiate the PETN main charge. The explosion, al Qa'ida leaders hoped, would bring down the airplane. Part of the device was wrapped in cellophane tape to prevent bomb-sniffing dogs from detecting the vapors. Most important, the bomb did not include large pieces of metal, such as wires and batteries, making it difficult for airport screeners to identify.[64] As-Siri's design was successful: the bomb went undetected in Addis Ababa, Accra, Lagos, and Amsterdam.

But would it explode? As Northwest Airlines Flight 253 approached Detroit, Abdulmutallab went to the bathroom to make final preparations for death. He "purified" himself by praying, washing his body, brushing his teeth, and putting on perfume.[65] When he returned to his seat, 19A, he complained that his stomach was upset and draped a blanket over his body.

Jasper Schuringa, a soft-spoken Dutch filmmaker who was sitting in the same row as Abdulmutallab, described the scene. "We heard a bang, sounded like a firecracker going off, or a big balloon," he said. "Everybody reacted to the bang, but could not locate where it was coming from."[66]

Abdulmutallab had injected the syringe into the chemical mixture in his underwear, as As-Siri had instructed.[67] A few seconds later, smoke began billowing from the seat and down the aisle. But the main charge, the PETN, did not explode. "I jumped over passengers between me and smoke," said Schuringa. "I saw a guy sitting and shaking. He was holding something like a pillow. On the floor there was a pillow on fire."[68]

Passengers and crew then subdued Abdulmutallab and used blankets and fire extinguishers to put out the flames. One flight attendant, Dionne Ransom-Monroe, asked Abdulmutallab what he had in his pocket. "Explosive device," said Abdulmutallab placidly.[69]

He was holding a partially melted syringe, which was smoking. One alert passenger took the syringe from Abdulmutallab, shook it violently, and threw it to the floor of the aircraft.[70] Schuringa began moving quickly. "I took off his clothes and put the fire out with water," he said. "I took him out of his seat and took him to first class area and stripped him completely of his clothes. He was shaking and didn't say anything. The crew gave me plastic cuffs and I cuffed him with the crew's help."[71]

When Schuringa rose to leave the jet, his fellow passengers broke out in applause.

As-Siri's bomb had failed to explode, but it had ignited, injuring Abdulmutallab and two other passengers. The airplane landed shortly after the incident at Detroit Metropolitan Airport. Abdulmutallab was initially taken into custody by Customs and Border Protection and held at the international arrivals holding cell A-1.[72] He was later transported to the University of Michigan Medical Center. According to the Emergency Medical Services report, he had second-degree burns on his right inner thigh and genitals, first-degree burns on the palm of his left hand, and second-degree burns on the back of his left hand and right thumb. The bomb had partially exploded in his lap.[73]

The FBI then questioned Abdulmutallab. He described his radicalization process, visits to Yemen, meetings with Awlaki, and preparations for the attack.[74]

Despite the failure of the main charge to go off, al Qa'ida trumpeted the attack. "He infiltrated all the advanced, new machines and technologies and the security boundaries in the world's airports," a December communiqué gloated several days later.[75]

The attack was unsuccessful, though largely because of misfortune and a faulty bomb. Abdulmutallab's plot reminded many observers of Richard Reid's attempt to bring down American Airlines Flight 63 in December 2001. As in that case, fearless passengers such as Jasper Schuringa responded to the threat and detained the bomber. "I basically reacted directly," said Schuringa. "I didn't think."[76]

But U.S. intelligence agencies had failed to detect the plot. There had been some indications that Abdulmutallab was a possible threat. After receiving his message in October 2009 that "this is the last you'll hear from me," Abdulmutallab's father contacted Nigeria's intelligence agency, which put him in contact with U.S. officials. On November 18, Abdulmutallab's father met with officials at the U.S. embassy in Abuja, Nigeria, to discuss his son's radicalization and disappearance in Yemen. U.S. government officials recorded Abdulmutallab's name in the Terrorist Identities Datamart Environment (TIDE), which included approximately 550,000 names. They also recommended that Abdulmutallab be placed on the No Fly List, which would have prevented him from boarding the flight in Amsterdam.[77]

But CIA Headquarters and the National Counterterrorism Center's Watchlisting Office determined that there was insufficient information to place him on any of the watchlists.[78] While it would have been impossible to predict Abdulmutallab's eventual involvement in the attempted December 25 attack, the White House concluded in its review of the incident that the U.S. intelligence community should have been able to "link information on him with earlier intelligence reports that contained fragmentary information."[79] Indeed, separate reviews by the White House and the Senate Select Committee on Intelligence were explicit, castigating the intelligence community for having collected enough information between mid-October and late December to identify Abdulmutallab as a likely al Qa'ida operative. The intelligence community's focus, they argued, was on attacks by al Qa'ida in the Arabian Peninsula on Americans and American interests in Yemen, as well as on supporting counterterrorist efforts in Yemen.

But it was not focused on attacks from Yemen directed against the U.S. homeland.[80]

The U.S. intelligence community was fortunate that the bomb malfunctioned. Their inattention had almost cost American lives. Most galling to the FBI and the CIA was that this was the second such attack in a month. Again, Anwar al-Awlaki's fingerprints were everywhere.

A Ticking Time Bomb

Born in Arlington, Virginia, in 1970 to Palestinian parents, Nidal Malik Hasan graduated from Virginia Tech with an engineering degree in 1992 and joined the U.S. Army in 1995.[81] Hasan was not a typical soldier. He was noticeably overweight, with a receding hairline and fleshy olive-colored cheeks. His program director at Walter Reed Army Medical Center, where he was a resident in the psychiatric program from 2003 to 2007, described him as "very lazy," unfit to graduate, in the bottom 25 percent of students, and regularly failing fitness requirements. Hasan was placed on probation and often failed to show up for work.[82] He was deeply troubled by the fact that he was a devout Muslim serving in an army fighting several wars in Muslim lands.

In a June 2007 PowerPoint briefing titled "The Koranic World View as It Relates to Muslims in the U.S. Military," Hasan explained that he wanted to help "identify Muslim soldiers that may be having religious conflicts with the current wars in Iraq and Afghanistan." "It's getting harder and harder for Muslims in the service to morally justify being in a military that seems constantly engaged against fellow Muslims," he wrote, adding that several Islamic scholars had issued fatwas saying that Muslims could not serve in the U.S. military. He then explained that Islam was explicit about Muslims who murdered other Muslims. "And whoever kills a believer intentionally," he quoted from the Qur'an, "his punishment is hell; he shall abide in it, and Allah will send His wrath on him and curse him and prepare for him a painful chastisement."[83]

Hasan's briefing looked like it was designed to help soldiers who struggled to practice Islam while serving in the U.S. military. There had been a history of unfortunate events stemming from such conflicts. One of those cited in the briefing involved Hasan Akbar, who deployed with the U.S. Army's 101st Airborne Division. He tossed four hand grenades into several tents at a U.S. base in Kuwait in March 2003 and then fired his rifle during the ensuing chaos, killing two officers and wounding fourteen people. Another involved Marine Corporal Wassef Ali Hassoun, who deserted the military in Iraq after citing disapproval of the war as a Muslim.

Hasan's briefing offered straightforward recommendations. The "Department of Defense," he wrote, "should allow Muslim Soldiers the option of being released as 'Conscientious objectors' to increase troop morale and decrease adverse events."[84]

The briefing reflected Hasan's inner struggle, especially his warning of "adverse events" if Muslim soldiers were asked to deploy to Muslim countries. His reaction was symptomatic of the United States' difficulties in communicating its intentions in Iraq and Afghanistan to Muslims at home and abroad. The U.S. military was fighting *on behalf of* Muslim governments in the cases he referenced. Take Afghanistan: by 2007, U.S. forces were supporting a government in which 82 percent of Afghans had confidence in President Hamid Karzai, only 5 percent supported Taliban forces, and a striking 71 percent supported U.S. military forces in the country.[85] Iraq was more controversial because of the U.S. invasion, though by 2007 Nouri al-Maliki had taken over as prime minister and was fighting an increasingly unpopular al Qa'ida in Iraq. Still, the perception that the wars were "against Muslims" persisted.

During Hasan's medical residency and postresidency fellowship, his superiors and colleagues observed his views becoming increasingly radical. Witnesses reported that Hasan openly supported many of the principles of violent Islamist extremism in class and in written academic papers.[86] In the last month of his residency at Walter Reed, he fulfilled an academic requirement for graduation to make a scholarly presentation on psychiatric issues by giving an off-topic lecture on violent Islamic extremism. Hasan's draft consisted almost entirely of references to the Qur'an, without a single mention of a medical or psychiatric term. It also presented extremist interpretations of the Qur'an and suggested that revenge might be a defense for the terrorist attacks of September 11, 2001. Hasan's superiors warned him that he needed to revise the presentation if he wanted to graduate and concluded that it was "not scientific," "not scholarly," and a mere "recitation" of the Qur'an that "might be perceived as proselytizing." Both the draft and the final presentation warned that Muslim soldiers might kill other service members because of the conflict between God and the military.[87]

In December 2008, Hasan, like Umar Farouk Abdulmutallab, reached out to Anwar al-Awlaki. Hasan had met Awlaki in 2001 at the Dar al-Hijrah mosque in Falls Church, Virginia, where Awlaki was the imam. "Brother Nidal," Awlaki later explained, using Hasan's first name, "used to pray in my mosque."

Over the next six months, Hasan and Awlaki exchanged at least eighteen e-mails that discussed the afterlife, the appropriate time for jihad, and how to transfer funds abroad without being noticed by law enforcement.[88] "The first letter from Nidal was on December seventeenth, 2008," Awlaki said in a December 2009 interview. "He contacted me first." Like Abdulmutallab, Hasan had reached out to Awlaki, not the other way around.

"His first message," noted Awlaki, "was about the ruling of a Muslim soldier serving the American Army, killing his colleagues." Hasan had apparently inquired whether it was legitimate for a Muslim in the U.S. military to assassinate other soldiers.

"And, via a group of letters," Awlaki went on, "Nidal explained his point of view about killing Israeli civilians and he supported that, and through these letters he mentioned sharia-based and realistic excuses for targeting the Jews with rockets. Also, there were some messages through which he asked about a method of transferring some money to us in contributions for charity works."[89]

As his correspondence with Awlaki continued, Hasan became increasingly agitated. He found a dent in his car and a dirty diaper on the windshield after work one day, offenses that he believed were perpetrated by someone who objected to his religious views. He did not agree with the wars in Iraq and Afghanistan and told his commanding officer that he wanted out of the army, offering to repay what he owed for medical school. Hasan apparently went to the judge advocate general's office at Walter Reed to request that he be considered a conscientious objector and released from the army. But the officer informed him that he could not choose his wars. During this time, Hasan had a dream that he was in a "burning hellfire."

After he moved to Fort Hood, Texas, in July 2009, Hasan's inner struggles worsened. John William Van De Walker, who lived in the same apartment complex, used a key to scratch Hasan's gray Honda Civic LX after seeing the bumper sticker on his car, which read "Allah is our protector."[90]

Hasan was in a vicious circle. He was concerned about going to war and being captured. He was antagonizing his fellow soldiers to the point that they began harassing him. And now the army informed him that he would deploy to Afghanistan in the fall of 2009.[91] That was the last straw. At approximately 1:30 p.m. on November 19, Hasan walked into the Soldier Readiness Center at Fort Hood, a facility where soldiers were processed before and after deployment. He bowed his head for several seconds and then stood up and opened fire, screaming "Allahu Akbar!" It was all over in a few minutes. Hasan calmly and methodically killed thirteen people, mostly soldiers, and wounded forty-three others before he was shot, disarmed, and captured.[92]

One of the greatest tragedies of the attack, however, was that it could probably have been prevented.

That's Our Boy

Major Hasan had initially come to the attention of the FBI in December 2008 as part of an unrelated investigation by the San Diego Joint Terrorism Task Force (JTTF). His first e-mail to Awlaki had sparked concern within the San Diego JTTF because Hasan was affiliated with the U.S. military. It was troubling that a military employee had sought Awlaki's opinion. Department of Defense officials checked a military personnel database. They mistakenly concluded that Hasan was a communications officer, not a physician, by misreading "comm. officer" in Hasan's military file as referring to a communications officer rather than a commissioned officer.

Investigators assessed that the content of the e-mails was consistent with research being conducted by Hasan as a psychiatrist at Walter Reed. Consequently, the JTTF concluded that Hasan was not involved in terrorist activities or planning.[93] The task force decided not to disseminate Hasan's communications through normal intelligence channels. In the meantime, the San Diego JTTF learned of another e-mail from Hasan to Awlaki, which should have raised concerns.[94]

Much later, Awlaki would say, "I wonder where the American security forces" were. He was amazed that they had not uncovered his e-mail communication with Hasan, since they "claimed they can read the numbers of any license plate, anywhere in the world, from space."[95] The problem, it turned out, was not an inability to intercept e-mail communications but blatant bureaucratic failure.

In lieu of sending a normal intelligence communication, the San Diego JTTF sent a detailed memorandum to the Washington, D.C., JTTF on January 7, 2009. Hasan was stationed at Walter Reed at the time and therefore was in the jurisdiction of the Washington JTTF. Copies of that memorandum were also sent by the FBI to relevant agents in its Counterterrorism Division. The memorandum surveyed Awlaki's significance, included the content of Hasan's initial e-mail communications, and requested an inquiry into Hasan. On February 25, more than six weeks after the January 7 memorandum, the Washington JTTF assigned the lead to an individual from the Defense Criminal Investigative Service (DCIS), the law enforcement arm of the Department of Defense's Office of the Inspector General.[96]

The Washington JTTF's job was to figure out whether Hasan was engaged in terrorist activities, not whether he was becoming more radical. The DCIS agent in Washington queried the department's personnel database and cleared up the confusion over Hasan's status in the army. He also queried the FBI's investigative databases to determine whether Hasan had surfaced in any prior FBI counterterrorism or other investigations—and found nothing. Finally, the agent did a routine check of personnel files from a Department of Defense manpower center, which included Hasan's annual Officer Evaluation Reports from 2004 to 2008. The record here was somewhat confusing. The reports for 2007 and 2008 covered the years in which Hasan's public displays of radicalization to violent Islamist extremism were most pronounced, but they also praised his research concerning violent Islamist extremism as having some applicability to counterterrorism and recommended promotion to major.[97]

The DCIS agent saw that Hasan had not tried to hide his identity in his communications with Awlaki, which he believed implied that the e-mails were part of legitimate research efforts. The agent considered interviewing Hasan, his superiors, and his colleagues but decided against it, for two reasons. First, he believed that since Hasan's e-mails came from the San Diego JTTF's investigation of Awlaki, the Washington JTTF needed to tread carefully. Interviewing Hasan's superiors and colleagues might expose the investigation. Second, interviews might jeopardize Hasan's career. This would violate the requirement that FBI investigations use the "least intrusive means" possible.[98]

In addition, it wasn't entirely clear to the FBI that Hasan was doing anything illegal—at least not yet. The DCIS agent concluded that Hasan's communications posed no threat. The agent discussed his methodology, his rationale for not conducting interviews, and his conclusions with his FBI supervisor, who approved. Neither the DCIS agent nor the FBI supervisor contacted the San Diego JTTF to discuss and validate the findings. Eventually the FBI's interest in Hasan waned. Hasan communicated with Awlaki during the summer of 2009, but the San Diego JTTF did not link any of the subsequent communications to Hasan's first e-mail. Nor was the Washington JTTF provided with the additional communications.[99]

Shortly after the media began reporting on Hasan's attack at Fort Hood, one FBI agent told his DCIS colleague in San Diego, "You know who that is? That's our boy!"[100]

Jihadist websites were buzzing with excitement. "We ask God that his intention was to support Islam and Muslims, so that he may be rewarded well," remarked someone whose on-line name was Qannas al-Jazira on the Al-Fallujah Islamic Forums website.

"If the intention was to support the religion of God, or if it was for the sake of Muslims and their spilled blood, or their violated honors," said a Sayf al-Ma'rakah on the same website, "then he is a hero by all means. We ask God to accept him as one of the martyrs."[101]

An individual calling himself Jihadiste posted a congratulatory note on Muhajidin Electronic Network: "The hero who was martyred is Major Malik Nidal Hasan. May God have mercy on him and grant him eternal paradise . . . The Crusader Americas are now weeping for their dead and injured."[102]

"May God bring forth many more of your kind Nidal," remarked an individual who used the name Abu Harun al-Kuwaiti on Ana al-Muslim website. He cautioned, "I bear witness that you are a predator. The only thing you were missing was an explosive belt. What I mean is, that after you had taken out seven or eight with your Klash, you would have ended it with the push of a button that would have destroyed the building and everything in it."[103]

Al Qa'ida's media arm, Al Malahim Media Foundation, posted a forty-five-minute video of an interview with Awlaki. He praised Hasan and justified the killing of U.S. civilians, including children.[104] "Nidal Hassan is a hero," said Awlaki. "He is a man of conscience who could not bear living the contradiction of being a Muslim and serving in an army that is fighting against his own people. Nidal opened fire on soldiers who were on their way to be deployed to Iraq and Afghanistan. How can there be any dispute about the virtue of what he has done?"[105]

Approximately one month later, Umar Farouk Abdulmutallab tried to blow himself up above Detroit.

Giving Islam a Bad Name

For some FBI officials, like Art Cummings, Hasan's intentions were somewhat unclear. "His contacts with al-Awlaki to ask him for certain advice appeared to anyone looking at it to be research consistent with the paper he was writing on behalf of, and funded by, the U.S. military," Cummings pointed out. "His questions were probing: 'Well what about this, and how do you justify that?' So where was the snapping point?"[106]

For Philip Mudd, another problem was the enormous amount of raw information on terrorist activity generated by the U.S. intelligence community. "Maybe we could have identified Nidal Hasan," he said, "maybe not. But the volume of intelligence we were looking at was enormous. There are a lot of false positives." There were also legitimate civil liberty questions, Mudd continued, since "Americans have every right to visit websites and download Awlaki lectures."[107] Monitoring the Internet to find potential terrorists, Mudd believed, raised serious questions about how intelligence services can protect the public by preventing acts of violence *and* ensure that citizens have their free speech protected.[108]

Nevertheless, the fact remains that the United States had intelligence on both Abdulmutallab and Hassan as possible threats and failed to prevent the attacks. The Hasan case was particularly egregious, since the San Diego JTTF had intercepted e-mails between Hasan and Anwar al-Awlaki, a known terrorist. Whether Hasan was conducting official business was immaterial, since it should have raised suspicions that a U.S. government official was in regular contact with a terrorist. Hasan wasn't doing it covertly but was open about his work for the Department of Defense. It should have been caught. There was poor coordination between the FBI and the Department of Defense's Criminal Investigative Service, and between FBI field offices and headquarters. The congressional inquiry led by Senator Joseph Lieberman concluded that there were "specific and systemic failures in the government's handling of the Hasan case."[109]

Law enforcement aside, one thing was indisputable: Anwar al-Awlaki had now become one of America's most dangerous enemies, along with Osama bin Laden and Ayman al-Zawahiri. He spearheaded the third wave from his base in Yemen, as al Qa'ida in the Arabian Peninsula secured a foothold in a country with a financially, organizationally, and politically weak central government. Awlaki had direct involvement in two serious terrorist attacks and plots that matured within six weeks of each other. His media activities were radicalizing individuals around the world and preparing them for violent jihad. And Yemen, one of the poorest countries in the world, with a gross domestic product of $2,700 per capita, was catching up to the Afghanistan-Pakistan border region as terrorism's most dangerous breeding ground.[110]

Yet for all of the apparent gains made by al Qa'ida in the Arabian Peninsula, it paid a heavy price in the worldwide Islamic community. Many Muslims couldn't comprehend the violence. Abdulmutallab's fellow participants on the Islamic Forum were distraught. "If indeed that brother is trying to blow up a plane full of civilians with women and children on board," said one on-line participant, "that would be a criminal act and he deserved to be punished for it."[111]

Yet another, who went by the on-line name Dot, was even more frank, saying,"It's a shame that any Muslim would turn into a terrorist, trying to kill innocent civilians. Such people give Islam a bad name. I can't believe that someone who stayed in our friendly online community, for over 2 years, has failed terribly to learn anything from all the articles and posts that fill this forum, about the true spirit of Islam, being a message of peace and total submission to The All-Merciful, Allah, who forbade the killing of civilians even at times of war, and our beloved prophet Muhammad who taught us that if someone killed a single person, it would be as if he killed all humans, and if he saved a single person, it would be as if he saved all humans.

"We must not lose hope, insha'Allah," Dot concluded. "We will continue our mission, to call for Islam with peace and courtesy, and to teach young Muslims that all acts of terrorism against civilians are totally prohibited in Islam."[112]

15

A DIFFERENT BREED

O N OCTOBER 3, 2009, FBI agents from the Chicago Joint Terrorism Task Force watched David Coleman Headley leave his apartment, a whitewashed, four-story brick building on the north side of Chicago. They were conducting twenty-four-hour surveillance on him, posting agents outside his apartment, monitoring his e-mail accounts, and listening to his phone conversations. Headley was a tier-one terrorist target for the FBI, worthy of their best agents. He was on his way to O'Hare International Airport to catch a flight to Philadelphia and then to meet with terrorists in Pakistan, including a senior al Qa'ida external operations leader.

A light rain fell on the city, blown by stiff southwest winds, as the temperature crept above 50 degrees. Chicago was still reeling from the failure earlier that week of its bid to host the 2016 Olympic Games, which eventually went to the Brazilian city of Rio de Janeiro. President Barack Obama, basketball superstar Michael Jordan, and television mogul Oprah Winfrey had led an intense lobbying push, but the effort had fallen just short. Headley would have seen the headlines, but he was consumed by far more pressing issues.

He was born Daood Sayed Gilani in Washington, D.C., on June 30, 1960. What impressed FBI agents most about him were his many clandestine identities. A handsome man, he could blend into different environments with ease. "Headley was a very different case for us," said Art Cummings, "and he was more of an entrepreneur than Najibullah Zazi, Umar Farouk Abdulmutallab, and some of the more recent al Qa'ida attackers."[1] Philip Mudd agreed: "The case of David Coleman Headley, a Pakistani-American, reveals an 'A-level' plotter who operated in the United States."[2]

Headley was full of contradictions. His mother, Serrill Headley, was an American born in Maryland, and his father, Sayed Salim Gilani, was a Pakistani diplomat born in India. When traveling in the United States, he was David Headley, a debonair businessman with slicked-back hair, a clean-shaven face, and a neatly pressed Armani suit. He told acquaintances that he was a consultant for First World Immigration Services, a company that offered immigration services to clients, though this was just a cover for his terrorist operations. Headley, who had two wives, also had a wandering eye. In a January 2009 e-mail to Tahawwur Rana, a colleague, he commented on the "sites" in Denmark during his travels: "Girls here are really hot. Just the both of us should come here minus our girlfriends to have a good time."[3]

When he arrived in Pakistan, Headley became Daood Gilani. He slipped into a shalwar kameez, grew a beard, grasped a leatherbound copy of the Qur'an, and supported a Salafist interpretation of Islam. He even had different-colored eyes, one ice blue, the other deep brown. "He was a chameleon," said his uncle, William Headley. "He could slide smoothly between worlds."[4]

Earlier in 2009 an individual named Sajid Mir, a retired major in the Pakistan Army, sent an e-mail to Headley. Sajid was now a member of the Pakistani terrorist group Lashkar-e-Taiba, which had developed close relations with al Qa'ida. "I need to see you for some new investment plans," Sajid wrote on July 3. American intelligence agencies believed this referred to a terrorist plot.[5]

In the decade after September 11, 2001, al Qa'ida and other major terrorist operatives had become more proficient at using coded language in their communications. Their counterintelligence capabilities had also improved, though not enough to prevent the FBI from monitoring Headley's e-mail exchanges and phone conversations.

Headley responded by e-mail on July 8: "What do you want me to do. Where are you interested in making investments."[6] He sent another e-mail the same day: "I think when we get a chance we should revisit our last location again."[7]

U.S. intelligence agencies assumed the two were discussing another terrorist attack in India. Headley had conducted much of the preoperational reconnaissance for the grisly November 2008 terrorist attack in Mumbai, taking photographs and video footage of most of the target sites, such as the grandiose Taj Mahal Palace hotel. Ten operatives trained by Lashkar-e-Taiba assaulted targets with firearms, grenades, and improvised explosive devices, killing more than 170 people and wounding hundreds more. The attack captivated the world's largest media conglomerates, like CNN and Al Jazeera, who gave it twenty-four-hour coverage for several days.

Sajid e-mailed back on July 8 saying that Lashkar-e-Taiba had "some work for you over there too," a likely reference to India. "Matters are good enough to move forward."[8]

The next day Headley answered: "When you say 'move forward' do you mean in the North direction or towards [India]. Also in the future if we need to meet to discuss anything, do i have to come all the way over there or can we meet somewhere in the middle like Africa or middle east."[9]

Sajid, who was based in Pakistan, responded on July 9 that he meant toward India.[10] U.S. intelligence officials believed the "North" referred to yet another terrorist plot, this one targeting the Copenhagen, Denmark, offices of the newspaper *Morgenavisen Jyllands-Posten*. In 2005 the newspaper had published a series of controversial cartoons of the Prophet Muhammad, the most notorious of which showed the Prophet with a bomb in his turban. The cartoons triggered large-scale protests across the Muslim world and death threats against the cartoonists and several newspaper executives.

On July 10, Headley sent an e-mail back to Sajid asking for clarification. "I would like to know a few things if you can tell me," said Headley. "What is the status with the Northern project, is it still postponed indefinitely?" As for India, Headley asked whether it was "for checking out real estate property like before, or something different and if so tell me what you can please." Headley also inquired about the timeline. "Will i have to stay there continuously for a while, or back and forth like before."[11]

"There are some investment plans with me," Sajid responded later on July 10, indicating that he meant in India.[12]

Headley sent back an e-mail on July 18: "One very important thing I need to know please is that how long do you need me for, meaning how long should it take me to finish my work, in your opinion. And is it really urgent? Before it seemed that the Northern Project was really urgent."[13]

Sajid responded on July 18 that the India project "may take somewhere between 2 to 4 weeks."[14]

Headley replied on July 19 that "I think i can manage it." He would be available in October.[15]

Art Cummings and others at the FBI worked frantically to piece together the various operations. The Copenhagen plot involved Ilyas Kashmiri, a senior al Qa'ida leader who was operations chief for the militant group Harakat ul-Jihad al-Islami (HUJI) and a good example of how some Pakistani militants floated between groups. A second plot looked like it would be another Lashkar-e-Taiba attack in India, only a year after the Mumbai attack. What disturbed U.S. agents most, however, was that Headley seemed to be freelancing for several international terrorist organizations and governments. Over the rest of the summer the FBI continued to track his movements, listen to his phone calls, monitor his e-mail accounts, and collect intelligence from human sources close to Headley and his colleagues.

Sensing the urgency of the situation and concerned that an attack might be imminent, the FBI arrested Headley on October

3 at O'Hare International Airport. The agents found a number of items in his checked luggage, including a photocopy of the front page of an August 2009 issue of the *Morgenavisen Jyllands-Posten*, a street guide for Copenhagen, a list of phone numbers that included those of known terrorists, and a book entitled *How to Pray Like a Jew*. Also contained in the luggage was a memory stick with approximately ten short videos of potential attack sites.[16]

Headley was part of a new breed in the third wave. He worked simultaneously for several groups with connections to al Qa'ida, although each group was generally unaware of his involvement with the others. In addition he had worked as an informant for the U.S. Drug Enforcement Administration until 2002, and several years later he had begun working for Pakistan's spy agency, the Directorate for Inter-Services Intelligence. He was a suave, swashbuckling figure, and capturing him required an extensive hunt by the FBI and other U.S. intelligence agencies. They used a combination of human sources and technical collection methods in locations around the globe, from the gritty ethnic neighborhoods of north Chicago to India, Denmark, and the tribal areas of Pakistan.

Finding a Niche

In 1960, just a few months after Headley was born, his parents moved from Washington, D.C., to Pakistan. In 1966 they divorced, and his father, a diplomat and a poet, raised him in Pakistan. Headley attended elementary school in Karachi and moved on to high school at the Cadet College Hasan Abdal in Punjab Province, which prepared boys for Pakistan's armed forces. He developed a love of Islam and an abhorrence of India at a young age. "I disliked them," he acknowledged, referring to Indians, because they "dismembered Pakistan." Headley was eleven years old at the height of the Indo-Pakistani war, which led to Bangladesh's independence from Pakistan. During the hostilities, India's air force conducted a bombing raid that hit his school.[17]

He may not have minded that his classes were canceled. Headley acknowledged that he was a "very bad" student. His relationship with his stepmother also had begun to deteriorate.[18] At age seventeen he moved back to the United States to join his biological mother, who ran a bar called the Khyber Pass in Philadelphia. In 1985, Headley's mother put him in charge of the bar, an odd place for a Muslim to work. Perhaps unsurprisingly, Headley began to drink. He chased women and eventually started to smuggle heroin from Pakistan to the United States to make money. In 1988 he was arrested in Germany by DEA agents for heroin possession and distribution, and was sent to U.S. federal prison.[19] After his release he moved to New York City and opened a video rental business in 1996, but in 1997 he was arrested again for heroin possession and distribution.[20] This was a pivotal moment for Headley as a Muslim.

"He became devout when he got arrested for drugs," said his uncle, William Headley. "He made a commitment to Allah that if he got cleared of this, he would follow the life, and that he did."[21]

After his release from prison, Headley agreed to become a paid informant for the DEA, providing information on drug-trafficking activities.[22] He also began to strengthen his ties with extremist groups in Pakistan. In 2000 he briefly returned to Pakistan and began attending Lashkar-e-Taiba meetings, while still working for the DEA.

Initially formed in the 1980s in Pakistan by Hafiz Saeed, a former professor and anti-Soviet fighter educated in Saudi Arabia and Pakistan, Lashkar-e-Taiba is an Islamic fundamentalist organization devoted to liberating India-controlled Kashmir through violent means and placing all of Kashmir in Pakistan. After September 11, Lashkar-e-Taiba developed a more robust global presence that focused on fundraising overseas, proselytizing, and occasionally conducting operations. Its members subscribed to the Ahle Hadith school of Islamic thought, a strict Sunni sect with views similar to the Salafist views of al Qa'ida leaders.

Some Lashkar-e-Taiba and al Qa'ida officials had a strong bond dating back to the anti-Soviet war in Afghanistan. After the U.S.-backed overthrow of the Taliban regime, some Lashkar-e-Taiba officials aided al Qa'ida operatives fleeing into Pakistan. In March 2002, for instance, U.S. and Pakistani security forces captured al Qa'ida operative Abu Zubaydah at a Lashkar-e-Taiba safe house in Faisalabad.[23]

Headley found speeches by Hafiz Saeed particularly stirring. In 2000 he attended a speech by Saeed along with two hundred other supporters at a house in the Model Town section of Lahore. "One second spent conducting jihad," Saeed told the packed audience, is "superior to 100 years of worship."[24]

According to several people who knew him, including his uncle William, Headley began to radicalize around this time.[25] He was searching for an anchor in life and increasingly found it in a network of Pakistani militants. Headley supported Lashkar-e-Taiba's ideology and commitment to fight India and volunteered to join the organization. In December 2001 he returned to Pakistan, and Lashkar-e-Taiba put him through a series of five training courses. The first, which lasted for three weeks, focused on indoctrinating operatives with Lashkar-e-Taiba's ideology. Subsequent courses covered Qur'anic studies, weapons training, intelligence skills (such as setting up safe houses and surveillance), and antiterrorist training.[26] By 2004, Headley had completed his training, and he begged to be deployed to Kashmir to fight Indians. But Zakir Lakhvi, who was responsible for Lashkar-e-Taiba's military operations and was generally known as Zaki, had a different idea.[27]

"There was something better," Zaki explained, "to do in the future."

But Headley kept pushing. He was an American citizen, he told Zaki, and had spent considerable time there. He suggested that he could obtain a new passport "to make it easy to enter India undetected."

Zaki was intrigued. "There were a lot of Pakistanis who had U.S. passports," he responded, "but what was the place of birth, was it Pakistan or America?"

Headley's answer left Zaki breathless. "It was Washington," Headley affirmed.[28]

Headley suddenly became a critical recruit for Lashkar-e-Taiba. His name, Daood Sayed Gilani, sounded too Pakistani and would raise suspicions by Indian intelligence agents. He had to get it changed. In August 2005, with Lashkar-e-Taiba's support, he traveled to the United States to begin the process of changing his name, using a lawyer in Philadelphia. In October he returned to Pakistan to work with Lashkar-e-Taiba.

Several months later, Pakistan's tribal police arrested Headley near Landi Kotal in Khyber Agency, not far from the Afghanistan border, on his way to a meeting. The police were skeptical that he was Pakistani and believed he had disobeyed the posted signs saying that foreigners were not allowed in the tribal areas. After a few days of questioning, and after learning of Headley's association with Lashkar-e-Taiba, the police transferred Headley to the Directorate for Inter-Services Intelligence.

"My name is Major Ali," his ISI interrogator said. He asked what Headley was doing in the area.

"I was planning to go into India," Headley explained, noting that he was working with Lashkar-e-Taiba and "had applied to change my name" in the United States.

Just as Zaki had done, Major Ali calculated that Headley could be a potentially useful asset. He asked for Headley's cell phone number and inquired whether he would consider working for the ISI.

"I would not mind," said Headley.[29]

ISI officials then apparently performed a background check on Headley, and an ISI operative who identified himself as Major Iqbal phoned a few days later and said he wanted to talk. They met in a safe house in Lahore early in 2006, and Major Iqbal fired off a series of questions. What Lashkar-e-Taiba courses had Headley taken? What assignments had Lashkar-e-Taiba wanted him to perform?

Headley again explained that Lashkar-e-Taiba had sent him through several training courses and wanted to use him as an operative in India. Major Iqbal approved and asked Headley to contact him when he returned from the United States. Headley agreed. In February 2006 his name was formally changed to David Coleman Headley. He returned to Pakistan a few months later.[30]

At their first meeting following Headley's return, Major Iqbal explained that he wanted Headley to conduct intelligence work for the ISI in India. Headley agreed. He was an inexperienced operative, and Major Iqbal was skeptical about the training he had received from Lashkar-e-Taiba. "It wasn't very good," Major Iqbal later remarked.[31]

He instructed Headley to open an office in India using an immigration company as a front. Headley responded that he had a childhood friend, Tahawwur Rana, who worked in an office in Chicago for First World Immigration Services and could potentially be leveraged.

It sounded like a good idea, Major Iqbal said. "Acting as an immigration consultant," he noted, would "help the work" that he wanted Headley to perform.[32]

Headley set up an office in Mumbai and the ISI chipped in $25,000.[33] On his application for a business visa in India, which the Indian government approved, his Chicago-based friend Rana helped craft a formal letter explaining that "Mr. David C. Headley is our regional manager supervising and coordinating our operations in the Asian region and will be officially representing us there."[34] Headley now had a verifiable cover. He began taking ISI training courses in spotting and assessing potential recruits, recognizing Indian military insignia and movements, performing covert dead drops and pickups, and taking clandestine photography.[35] He kept in regular contact with Lashkar-e-Taiba officials but was primarily operating for ISI.

The Mumbai Attacks

In September 2006, Headley set up his office in the southern part of Mumbai, a thirty-minute car ride from most of his clandestine surveillance targets. More than twenty million people make their home in Mumbai, India's financial and entertainment hub. Headley conducted video surveillance of multiple sites, most notably the Taj Mahal Palace.[36] A gaudy five-star hotel situated on the Mumbai harbor, the Taj was a landmark of Indian prestige and consequently a target for Lashkar-e-Taiba.

In December 2006, Headley returned to Pakistan and met with both ISI and Lashkar-e-Taiba officials.[37] He briefed his ISI handler, Major Iqbal, on the contacts he had made in India and, most important, provided copies of his video surveillance. He did the same with his Lashkar-e-Taiba handlers. ISI and Lashkar-e-Taiba appeared to be in close collaboration on a plot to conduct terrorist attacks in Mumbai. Headley met with his ISI handler alone, the Lashkar-e-Taiba officials alone, and both together. He quickly realized, however, that the plot's "instruction emanated from Major Iqbal" of the ISI, who closely monitored what Headley was doing and provided general guidance. Many of the tactical details, however, were left to Lashkar-e-Taiba to work out.[38] This arrangement ensured that Lashkar-e-Taiba actually executed the operation, giving the ISI plausible deniability once the attack occurred.

Headley received instructions from ISI to return to Mumbai, which he did in February 2007.[39] Major Iqbal had asked him to take additional video footage of the second-floor meeting areas of the Taj hotel, where defense contractors held conferences, as well as other potential targets.

Headley returned to Pakistan in May and provided the additional video footage to his handlers. As the plans developed, Major Iqbal instructed him to return to India in the summer to "carry out further surveillance of the Taj hotel" and to "get the schedules for the conference halls at that hotel."[40] Headley arrived in Mumbai around September but returned to Pakistan later that month. He provided the ISI with additional videos of target sites. By then the attack plan had begun to firm up. It would involve nearly a dozen Lashkar-e-Taiba operatives, who would storm several locations in Mumbai, take and kill hostages, and, it was hoped, upset the entire country. Lashkar-e-Taiba officials may also have hoped that the attack would exacerbate frictions between India's Hindu and Muslim communities, perhaps even provoking an Indian military response, which would divide the country and facilitate Lashkar-e-Taiba recruitment.

But there were still questions about the operation. In March 2008, for example, Headley participated in a discussion of the attack with Lashkar-e-Taiba and Pakistani government officials in the city of Muzaffarabad, located in Pakistan-controlled Kashmir and barely 15 miles from the disputed border with India. The group carefully examined sea charts and debated possible entry points for the attack team, since most had agreed that the Lashkar-e-Taiba operatives would travel from Pakistan to India by sea. They went back and forth.

Zaki, an operational commander for Lashkar-e-Taiba, argued that the team should "land in front of the Gateway of India." Located on the waterfront in south Mumbai, the stately Gateway of India is a basalt arch that towers 85 feet high over the harbor and was used as a landing place for British governors and other distinguished individuals arriving in Mumbai by boat.

Headley disagreed. He had seen armed coast guard boats there and contended that it would be too dangerous to land. "To get to that point," Headley said, "the boat would have to circle around the southernmost point, which was a naval facility, naval base there, and it would be unsafe for a small boat to take that turn coming into the Gateway of India."

A Pakistani navy official agreed with Headley.

Someone suggested that the operatives land 40 miles away and covertly make their way to Mumbai, but a senior Lashkar-e-Taiba official dismissed this option. "These boys would not be very sophisticated," he explained, referring to the operatives, "and it would be hard for them to visit a country—a foreign location and then try to get a taxi or some kind of transportation back for such a long distance."[41]

Unable to resolve the disagreement, ISI and Lashkar-e-Taiba officials ordered Headley back to Mumbai to examine potential landing sites. They also asked him to take more video footage of the Chhatrapati Shivaji Terminus (the main railway station), several bus stations, and the Taj hotel. So Headley returned to Mumbai in April 2008 and took several boat rides around the city, scouting different landing sites. He saved the locations in a Global Positioning System device that Lashkar-e-Taiba officials had provided him. He also took video footage of a site populated by fishermen on the west side of Mumbai, which Lashkar-e-Taiba ultimately decided would be the landing site. He took surveillance of the Nuclear Research Center in Mumbai and more footage of the Taj hotel, the railway station, and other sites.[42]

Later in April, Headley returned to Pakistan, where he briefed his ISI and Lashkar-e-Taiba handlers. He then returned to the United States, staying in New York and Philadelphia. On April 23 he sent an e-mail to Major Iqbal. "I have some preliminary information and I am forwarding it to you," he wrote. "As I get more info, I will send it to you."[43] Major Iqbal had asked him to investigate several commercially available espionage devices, such as a wireless spy camera pen and a tiny, real-time digital camcorder, while he was in the United States.[44]

In June, Headley went back to Pakistan to meet with ISI and Lashkar-e-Taiba officials. ISI asked him to add at least one target, the Chabad House in Mumbai, to his list of surveillance targets. Chabad Houses exist in major cities around the world and serve as Jewish community centers, providing education and outreach for local Jews. But Pakistani officials believed that they had a more clandestine purpose. "That was a front office of Mossad," explained Major Iqbal, referring to Israel's external spy agency.

Headley nodded.

"Check the landing sites again," Major Iqbal continued, as well as the target list that he would eventually be given.[45]

Headley understood Major Iqbal to mean that Lashkar-e-Taiba officials would give him a list of targets that were being finalized. Indeed, Lashkar-e-Taiba shortly provided him with an updated list of targets for surveillance—the Taj hotel, Chabad House, Maharashtra State Police headquarters, Naval Air Station, central train station, and several other sites—and wanted him to recheck the landing site. Headley went back to Major Iqbal before heading to India.

"Do a detailed surveillance," Major Iqbal said.[46] He then instructed Headley to shut down the office since Headley wouldn't be able to return to India after the attack.

Meanwhile, Lashkar-e-Taiba was training a dozen operatives at a facility outside Muzaffarabad, though only ten would be deployed for the actual operation. By this time Lashkar-e-Taiba had decided that the attackers would travel to Mumbai by sea and use the fishermen's landing site recommended by Headley. They would also fight to the death rather than attempt to escape following the attacks. The plan called for them to utilize a GPS device to facilitate coordination of the attack and remain in phone contact with other Lashkar-e-Taiba members during the operation.[47]

Headley returned to Mumbai one last time in July 2008. He took his final video footage of target sites, including the Chabad House, and added two potential locations that weren't on the list—the Oberoi Hotel, which was near the landing point, and the Leopold Café, around the corner from the Taj hotel. He then returned to Pakistan, around August, and waited.

On November 26, Headley received a text message from Sajid. "Turn on the television," Sajid had typed.[48]

Headley was mesmerized by what he saw. His careful, patient reconnaissance had paid off. Ten operatives trained by Lashkar-e-Taiba were now carrying out assaults at the sites he had videotaped, with firearms, grenades, and improvised explosive devices. Al Qa'ida–affiliated websites were swamped with messages from revelers celebrating the Mumbai attacks as a battlefield victory against India, which they viewed as an infidel Hindu state that oppressed Muslims.

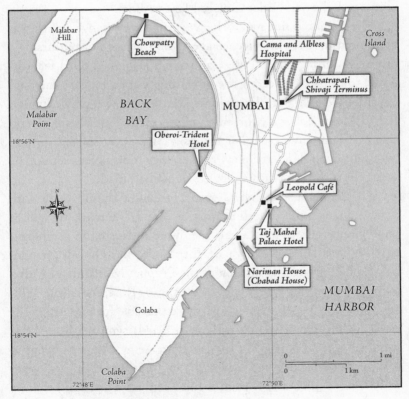

Figure 16: Map of 2008 Mumbai Terrorist Attacks

To perpetrate the Mumbai attacks, Headley had worked with Lashkar-e-Taiba and Pakistan's spy agency. Soon he would soon make his talents available to al Qa'ida leaders.

The Mickey Mouse Project

In November 2008, the same month as the Mumbai attacks, Lashkar-e-Taiba members discussed a new operation with Headley: targeting the *Morgenavisen Jyllands-Posten*. Headley cryptically hinted at his intention in a 2008 posting on an on-line forum called "abdalians7479," which mostly included friends from Headley's high school in Pakistan, Cadet College Hasan Abdal.[49]

"Everything is not a joke," he wrote in the exchange, which was monitored by U.S. intelligence agencies. "We are not rehearsing a skit on Saturday Night Live. Call me old-fashioned but I feel disposed towards violence for the offending parties, be they cartoonists from Denmark or Sherry Jones (Author of Jewel of Medina) or Irshad Manji (Liberal Muslim trying to make Lesbianism acceptable in Islam, amongst other things). They never started debates with folks who slandered our Prophet, they took violent action," he said, referring to the early followers of Muhammad.[50]

Lashkar-e-Taiba members gave Headley a thumb drive with basic economic and other information about Denmark, as well as photographs of two individuals they were interested in assassinating. One was Kurt Westergaard, the flamboyant Danish cartoonist who had drawn the cartoon of the Prophet Muhammad with a bomb in his turban. The other was Flemming Rose, the cultural editor of the newspaper, who was partly responsible for publishing the cartoons. Headley also met with an al Qa'ida sympathizer, Abdur Rehman, a retired major in the Pakistan Army whom he referred to as Pasha. Headley had met Pasha in a Lashkar-e-Taiba mosque in Lahore in 2003 and kept in regular contact. Pasha said that he approved of what Headley was doing, but urged him not to have lofty expectations.

"Lashkar guys had a habit of making plans and then backing off all the time," Pasha said. "But if they did" decide not to move forward, he continued, he "knew somebody who would—who would take care of this." That person, he hinted ominously, was "in the tribal area" and "had connections with al Qa'ida."[51]

Pasha later divulged that his colleague was in regular contact with Shaykh Sa'id al-Masri, al Qa'ida's general manager. Shaykh Sa'id was born in Egypt in December 1955 and had an impressive jihadist résumé. He was involved in the 1981 assassination of Egyptian president Anwar al-Sadat, spent three years in prison for his involvement, and left for Afghanistan in 1988 to join fellow jihadists. He apparently accompanied bin Laden from Afghanistan to Sudan in 1991 and served as the accountant for bin Laden's Sudan-based businesses, including his company Wadi al-Aqiq.[52] Shaykh Sa'id wasn't just "connected" to al Qa'ida; he was at its very heart.

In early December 2008, Headley returned to Chicago to make final preparations for his surveillance trip to Denmark. He chose the cover name Mickey Mouse Project, because the popular Disney icon was a cartoon character, an easy way to remember that the terrorist operation's goal was to attack the newspaper responsible for publishing the cartoons of the Prophet. He saved notes on his e-mail account so that he didn't have to take them on the airplane, just in case he was stopped by U.S. law enforcement officials.[53]

Around this time the FBI began to notice Headley. Its agents now had intelligence suggesting that he might have been involved in the Mumbai attack, based in part on their cooperation with Indian intelligence. FBI agents visited the house of one of his cousins in Philadelphia and asked him a series of questions. The cousin said that Headley was in Pakistan.[54] Headley's second wife had contacted U.S. officials in Pakistan and said that she suspected Headley was involved in terrorism.[55] FBI officials were concerned enough to continue monitoring his calls, e-mails, and movements. But they still struggled to grasp the extent of his operations.

In December 2008, Pasha sent an e-mail to Headley that was intercepted by U.S. intelligence agencies, commenting that al Qa'ida was still interested in supporting the Denmark attack. "First u visit MMP," Pasha said, a reference to the Mickey Mouse Project in Denmark, and then "we will discuss and c the concerned person if needed."[56]

Headley understood that the "other person" was Ilyas Kashmiri. Born in 1964, Kashmiri was a veteran of the anti-Soviet war in Afghanistan, during which he had lost an eye and an index finger. He eventually became the leader of Harakat ul-Jihad al-Islami and established his own unit, known as the 313 Brigade. "At that time," wrote a colleague of Kashmiri, "he was the apple of the eye of the Pakistani establishment and he was running a big jihadi camp in the area of Kotli, Azad Kashmir."[57] Kashmiri spent most of his career running training camps and conducting operations against India. Around 2005, however, he apparently swore *bayat* to Osama bin Laden, relocated to Pakistan's Federally Administered Tribal Areas, and leveraged his close relationship with al Qa'ida leaders such as Shaykh Sa'id al-Masri.[58] Kashmiri hated India and the United States and was a deadly operator. He had been involved in dozens of terrorist attacks and plots across South Asia and Europe. He later became a senior al Qa'ida external operations official, and he sat on al Qa'ida's military shura council until he was killed by a CIA drone in June 2011.

While Headley was impressed with Kashmiri's accomplishments, he poked fun at the al Qa'ida operator's lisp—Kashmiri had a habit of saying *shishtem* when he tried to say *system*.[59]

Pasha again reminded Headley that "if your friends decline"—a reference to Lashkar-e-Taiba—"we'll do that."[60]

In a subsequent e-mail, Headley asked Pasha how long he

should conduct surveillance in Copenhagen: "How much time should i spend there? a week, 10 days or 2 weeks?"[61]

Pasha responded the next day: "i think a week or tens [sic] days r ok initially."[62]

From the FBI's and CIA's perspective, Headley was involved in a startlingly complex range of clandestine activities. He was participating in terrorist plotting with al Qa'ida supporters, he remained in contact with Lashkar-e-Taiba operatives, and he was still nominally in touch with the ISI. He was his own boss, a free agent, which frustrated many of the people he worked with. "Futile are my advices," said one of his Lashkar-e-Taiba handlers in an e-mail, "coz you do what you feel like."[63]

In January 2009, Headley landed in Frankfurt, Germany, and drove to Copenhagen to conduct surveillance of *Morgenavisen Jyllands-Posten*. "It had five or six floors, and it was on King's Square," he jotted down.[64] He tried walking into the building, but the front door was secured. As cover for his visit, he told newspaper executives that he was visiting on behalf of an immigration business that was considering opening up offices in Denmark and that he was interested in advertising the business in the *Morgenavisen Jyllands-Posten*.[65] It was sufficient cover to fool newspaper representatives. He made an appointment with someone from the advertising office and conducted initial surveillance on his way into and out of the meeting. Headley then traveled to the *Morgenavisen Jyllands-Posten*'s office in Aarhus, Denmark's largest port city, to conduct surveillance, making an appointment with a woman from the advertising department.

"I checked out business opportunities here," Headley wrote to his friend Tahawwur Rana in Chicago, using coded language. "They seem quite promising. I am going right now to see if I can put an ad for our company and also check the feasibility to open up an office here."[66]

Later that month, Headley traveled to Pakistan to discuss the plot with both Lashkar-e-Taiba and al Qa'ida supporters. The FBI and other U.S. agencies continued to track his movements. Records of his e-mail use show that between late January and early March 2009, he sent e-mail messages from various locations in Pakistan.[67] He gave Pasha a copy of the surveillance video from the trip, which Pasha watched with interest.[68] Pasha affirmed his willingness to help with the attack and explained that Lashkar-e-Taiba was unlikely to support it "because of the—the situation after the Mumbai attacks. People were getting arrested," Pasha explained, "and there was tension generally for—for all these guys in Lashkar."

Following the international uproar over the Mumbai attacks, Pakistani government officials began nominally to crack down on Lashkar-e-Taiba members, arresting a number of them. But the actions were generally for show; most were released shortly thereafter.

Pasha also had some broader advice. Lashkar-e-Taiba, he explained, was fighting "the ISI's jihad." But Headley should join Ilyas Kashmiri and his group because they were fighting "God's jihad."[69]

On to Waziristan

So Pasha asked Headley to take a trip to Waziristan to visit Kashmiri. Headley agreed. Around February 2009, Pasha, Headley, and two others traveled to Waziristan to talk to Kashmiri. It was a major turning point for Headley: he was now visiting one of al Qa'ida's senior military officials.[70]

Headley explained to Kashmiri that he had conducted surveillance in Denmark for a terrorist attack against *Morgenavisen Jyllands-Posten.*

Kashmiri smiled and said that it was "very important that this—this attack be carried out as soon as possible." Like many Muslims worldwide, he was still livid about the cartoons, which he considered "disgraceful and humiliating." From a terrorist's perspective, no one had punished the newspaper in the four years that had passed.

Kashmiri said that he had seen Headley's video footage but had some suggestions on executing the attack. "Drive a truck of explosives inside—inside of that building," he advised.

But Headley politely disagreed, saying that it was "not feasible," since there were "blocks on the road that would not permit that."

Kashmiri then offered more specific help. He knew several terrorists in England who might help in the attack, and suggested that Headley talk to them. He also asked Headley to return to India to conduct additional surveillance of several Chabad Houses there, as well as the National Defence College. "If we were able to conduct an attack on it," said Kashmiri, "we would be able to kill more brigadiers in the Indian Army than had been killed in the four wars that Pakistan and India had fought previously."[71]

Kashmiri provided Headley with 80,000 Pakistan rupees in cash—approximately U.S. $1,000—for tickets and travel expenses.[72] In March, Headley went to India and conducted video surveillance in several cities, including Delhi, Pushkar, and Goa. In late March he returned to Pakistan and met with Lashkar-e-Taiba leaders, who informed him that the Denmark plot was "indefinitely postponed."[73] The ISI was also under enormous pressure after the Mumbai attack.

"Remove any stuff" from your house, Major Iqbal warned him, "pertaining to Lashkar and maybe move away for a little while."[74] Major Iqbal also ordered Headley not to contact him for the foreseeable future.

Undeterred, Headley arranged a meeting two months later with Ilyas Kashmiri in the tribal areas of Pakistan. Kashmiri explained that he had "spoken to the people that would carry out the operation from England" and had given them money for operational expenses. He also remarked that he wanted the assault to be a "stronghold option," much like the Mumbai attacks. It would probably involve several operatives armed with grenades and machine guns, who would storm into the *Morgenavisen Jyllands-Posten* office to kill some employees and take others hostage. Kashmiri wanted to punish the paper and send an unambiguous message to anyone who might think about desecrating the Prophet Muhammad.

Kashmiri knew that pulling off a terrorist attack in Denmark would be strikingly different from committing one in India. "The Danish response forces would not be as incompetent and timid as the Indians, and, therefore, we should expect that the siege won't last very long," he reflected. "The attackers should throw out the heads of the hostages from the window . . . to rush the Danes into assaulting the building. Shoot them first," he argued, "and then behead them later, so there wouldn't be a struggle." Kashmiri also advised Headley to "make a video of the attackers prior to the attack with some kind of message."[75]

In July, Headley traveled to England to meet with the two men identified by Kashmiri and inform them about the Denmark plot. "He expected [you] to give us the manpower and the funds, as well as the weapons for that project," said Headley.[76] But their response was lukewarm. According to Kashmiri, they were supposed to provide £10,000 (about U.S. $16,000), but they gave Headley only £2,000 (about $3,000). The men also said that they couldn't provide the manpower or the weapons, though they promised to travel to Pakistan and talk with Kashmiri. Still, Headley pushed on and traveled back to Copenhagen to conduct more surveillance. After pondering the logistical challenges, he made a phone call to Pasha, which was intercepted by U.S. intelligence.

Speaking in coded language, Headley noted, "If they are not fulfilling on it . . ." He paused. "Then B, B, they should, they should something as a B, option B."

"Okay," said Pasha.

Headley replied, "Yeah."

"On the contrary, on the contrary," Pasha interjected, "not B, but there should be B and C as well."

"Yeah," Headley responded, "there should be B and C as well."[77]

As Headley later explained, he was suggesting that in addition to the stronghold strategy advocated by Kashmiri, which they referred to as Option A, they should have alternatives, what they called Options B and C. These might include assassinating Kurt Westergaard or Fleming Rose, or perhaps both of them.[78]

After leaving Copenhagen, Headley flew to Atlanta around August 2009. The FBI had put out a warning on him, and customs officers stopped him at Atlanta International Airport and asked him to explain the purpose of his travel to Copenhagen. Headley replied that he had been there as a consultant for his immigration business. They eventually let him go, and he went on to Chicago.[79]

On September 21, Headley and Pasha talked on the phone, which again was bugged by U.S. intelligence agencies. Based on press reports he had seen, Headley believed that Kashmiri had been assassinated. But Pasha said the reports weren't true. "Buddy," said Pasha, "the reports that are coming in . . . by the grace of God, he is doing well."

"God willing," said Headley, referring to Kashmiri, "uh . . . who—you mean the Doctor?"

"Yes, yes," said Pasha.

"If this is true, I will say 100 prayers, 100 prayers. And also keep the fast, because—"

Pasha cut him off. "I don't know," he said, "but the matter over there has [sic] complicated. It is confirmed. Yesterday I had two . . . I received two confirmations yesterday that he is all right."[80]

On October 3 the Denmark plot was back on. In fact, Pasha told Headley that Kashmiri was asking about him.[81] Based on intercepted conversations with family members and other third parties, FBI officials thought that Headley intended to travel to Pakistan early that month. Before doing so, he planned to go to Philadelphia. On September 8 he had received an e-mail confirmation from Orbitz, an online travel agency, reflecting the purchase of a plane ticket from Chicago to Philadelphia on October 3. His plan was to meet with Pasha, Lashkar-e-Taiba officials, and Kashmiri in Pakistan and then to execute the Copenhagen attack.[82]

But the planning had gone far enough for U.S. government officials. Headley was arrested by FBI agents as he prepared to board the flight from Chicago to Philadelphia.

Business Must Go On

In characteristic fashion, Headley volunteered to work for the U.S. government after he was captured, telling FBI agents that he would implant a chip in or near Ilyas Kashmiri so that a CIA drone could target the al Qa'ida operative.[83] It was a predictable tactic. Headley was willing to continue playing for all sides. At one point, after being erroneously informed that Ilyas Kashmiri was dead, he told a family member that "the main thing is the business must go on." He wasn't particular about which "company" he worked for, he continued, as long as he was involved in the game.[84] This time, however, Headley's game was over. The FBI had won, and it wasn't about to let him go.

For FBI officials like Art Cummings, Headley came from a very different mold than Najibullah Zazi, Umar Farouk Abdulmutallab, and most other terrorists since September 11. He was unwilling to blow himself up on a subway, let alone conduct a terrorist attack. Rather, he preferred to remain in the shadows, collecting intelligence for various terrorist organizations and governments, including al Qa'ida. Headley was much more sophisticated than his predecessors. He used several methods of communication, including in-person meetings, telephone conversations, and e-mails from several accounts to throw off intelligence agencies. The account for one of his cell phones was registered to a dead man. So was his apartment in Chicago. And he relied on coded language in virtually all of his conversations. He referred to his Copenhagen plot as the "Mickey Mouse Project," "mmp," and "the northern project."

Instead of terrorism, he discussed "investments," "projects," "business," and "action."

In the end, though, Headley wasn't as good as he thought he was. Despite his best efforts, FBI and U.S. intelligence agencies tracked his movements, listened to his phone calls, monitored his e-mail accounts, and collected intelligence from many human sources on his activities.

His uncle, William, was stoic about his fate. "If he is absolutely guilty," he concluded, "then whatever punishment is doled out to him, he has to accept that."[85]

If Headley symbolized a more diffuse and decentralized al Qa'ida that could reach out to individuals from allied organizations such as Lashkar-e-Taiba, then the third wave was about to get even more intriguing. This time, however, the threat did not come from Lashkar-e-Taiba or even al Qa'ida's affiliate in Yemen. Instead it came from another group in Pakistan with ties to al Qa'ida: the Tehreek-e Taliban Pakistan.

16

A NEAR MISS

THE DARK GREEN 1993 Nissan Pathfinder crept west on Forty-fifth Street in New York City, the silhouette of its driver barely visible behind the car's tinted windows. It was a balmy eighty-degree Saturday evening in Times Square, just after 6 p.m. on May 1, 2010. The ebbing sun glinted off nearby skyscrapers as the area's famous pulsating neon lights began to gather strength in the dusk, transforming the ganglion of streets and alleyways into an electrifying commercial carnival. The cylindrical eight-story NASDAQ sign at 4 Times Square stood watch, with a palette of over sixteen million colors splashed across eight thousand panels displaying lavish advertisements and stock information. Times Square is an iconic landmark—a metaphor for everything American, from over-indulgence to technological innovation and celebration. Dubbed "the Crossroads of the World," it is an agora, in the words of writer James Traub, "a simulacrum of a place, an ingenious marketing device fostered by global entertainment firms."[1]

Gangs of tourists eddy through Times Square each day, enticed by Broadway shows and the mesmerizing lights. On New Year's Eve over one million giddy revelers pack into the streets to watch the Waterford crystal, energy-efficient LED ball drop at the stroke of midnight. Yet Times Square's swelling crowds and allure also make it a tempting target.

In May 2010, Faisal Shahzad, a thirty-year-old Pakistani who had recently become a naturalized U.S. citizen, pulled his Nissan Pathfinder to the curb at the southwest corner of Forty-fifth Street and Seventh Avenue with its hazard lights flashing.[2] He parked near the Minskoff Theatre, which had a hulking yellow billboard advertising the Broadway play *The Lion King*. Shahzad was about five feet, nine inches tall and had wavy black hair parted carefully in the middle and a thin layer of unshaven stubble. He had recently purchased the Pathfinder. He had not come to Times Square to soak in the atmosphere, however. After pulling over, he ignited a fuse in the backseat of his sport utility vehicle, waited for a few moments, and stepped onto the street. The car held an explosive device that he had assembled at his Connecticut home. Now he was preparing to detonate it. The bomb consisted of two analog battery-powered alarm clocks with electrical wire. They were routed to a canister filled with M88 fireworks, two red 5-gallon cans of gasoline, 250 pounds of urea-based fertilizer placed in white plastic bags, a pressure pot with more M88s, and three 20-gallon propane tanks.[3]

"It was in three sections," Shahzad later remembered. The first "was the fertilizer bomb. That was in the trunk. It was in a cabinet, a gun cabinet. The second was—if that plan didn't work—then the second would be the cylinder, the gas cylinders I had. And the third I had was a petrol, a gas to make fire in the car."[4]

Shahzad stepped out of the car and left the keys in the ignition, the motor still running. He was hoping to maim and kill scores of people, destroy portions of the surrounding buildings, and cause severe economic disruption. Times Square, teeming on a warm spring Saturday night, was ideal. He was going to teach the United States a lesson for daring to "attack" Muslim countries. "Until the hour the U.S. pulls its forces from Iraq and Afghanistan and stops the drone strikes in Somalia and Yemen and in Pakistan," he explained, "and stops the occupation of Muslim lands and stops killing the Muslims and stops reporting the Muslims to its government, we will be attacking U.S."[5]

He then started walking, at first briskly, toward Grand Central Station, listening for the explosion. It didn't come. He continued walking. Shahzad had designed the bomb to detonate between two and a half minutes and five minutes after he lit the fuse. But something malfunctioned. He didn't know what or how.

Around 6:30 p.m., a street vendor named Lance Orton stooped down to tie his shoes. "Wow," Orton said. "That looks like smoke's coming out of that thing."[6] He looked around to see if anyone else had noticed. No one had, at least at first. But the smoke continued to pour out of the car from all sides. Wayne Robinson, a vendor who worked with Orton, then alerted police officer Wayne Rhatigan, who was sitting atop a horse in Times Square.

"I saw the ignition running and the hazard lights on. It was kind of parked haphazardly," said Rhatigan, who smelled what he thought was gunpowder.[7] He circled the vehicle on his horse and radioed for assistance, sparking an evacuation of the surrounding area. Members of the New York Police Department's bomb squad and fire department came to the scene and began working furiously to identify the source of the smoke from inside the Pathfinder. If it was a bomb, they would have only seconds, or perhaps minutes, to diffuse it. Fire department officials used thermal imaging cameras to detect the heat source and sent in a robot, which smashed the back window and showed images of the bomb materiel.[8]

Shahzad was confused. What had happened to his bomb? Disappointed, he disappeared into the night.

Advance at America's Heart

The third wave continued. Barely four months after Umar Farouk Abdulmutallab's bombing on Northwest Airlines Flight 253, Faisal Shahzad had tried to launch a terrorist attack in the United States. Miraculously—again—the bomb failed to go off. Shahzad had received his bomb-making training in Pakistan, but unlike most serious plots after September 11, 2001, al Qa'ida was not directly involved. Instead, this attack stemmed from a shadowy group that called itself Tehreek-e Taliban Pakistan—the Pakistan Taliban.

Tehreek-e Taliban Pakistan was actually an umbrella organization under which various Islamist militant groups united in December 2007. The leader was Baitullah Mehsud, who hailed from the Mehsud tribe in South Waziristan.[9] The charismatic Mehsud was praised by fellow fighters for his "faithfulness, devotion and love for Jihad."[10] He was killed by a U.S. drone strike in August 2009. Tehreek-e Taliban Pakistan's primary goals were to establish an extreme interpretation of sharia law in areas they controlled along the Afghanistan-Pakistan border, unite against U.S. and other coalition forces in Afghanistan, and perform defensive jihad against the Pakistan Army. Many of their leaders were deeply anti-Western and in particular anti-American. "My desire is to advance at America's heart and strike it, and to destroy Americans' pride and self-conceit," Baitullah Mehsud told senior al Qa'ida leader Shaykh Sa'id al-Masri.[11]

From its inception, Tehreek-e Taliban Pakistan had developed links with al Qa'ida. By 2010 key Tehreek-e Taliban Pakistan leaders such as Hakimullah Mehsud and Qari Hussein had established a working relationship with al Qa'ida's chief operating officer, Atiyah abd al-Rahman al-Libi, religious leader Abu Yahya al-Libi, and military operational leader Ilyas Kashmiri, who had worked with David Headley. A U.S. intelligence assessment acknowledged that some Tehreek-e Taliban Pakistan leaders "are receptive to this message and increasingly are adopting al Qa'ida's anti-Western rhetoric and agenda."[12] Al Qa'ida leaders benefited from Tehreek-e Taliban Pakistan's safe haven in Mehsud tribal areas of Pakistan, and Tehreek-e Taliban Pakistan in turn benefited from al Qa'ida's training and explosives expertise to build bombs and execute attacks, as well as from its global terrorist links to raise funds. In a few cases the two groups cooperated in conducting terrorist attacks in Pakistani cities.[13]

Faisal Shazad's father, Bahar ul-Haq, was a senior official in the Pakistan Air Force who ascended to air vice marshal before retiring in 1992. An opponent of extremism, he spoke British-accented English and drank alcohol socially, but he was stern with his children and sometimes quick to anger. When Shahzad, who was born in Karachi on June 30, 1979, was twelve, his father was transferred from Jedda, Saudi Arabia, to Quetta, Pakistan.[14] Chauffeurs, servants, and armed guards tended to the family in an insular world made up almost exclusively of military families. When Shahzad entered high school in the mid-1990s, his family had settled in Karachi. Around 1998, Shahzad left Pakistan and landed at Southeastern University in Washington, D.C.[15]

Southeastern was a long way from Karachi. The now defunct university was situated at the intersection of Sixth and I streets in southwestern Washington, in an up-and-coming area nestled between the bustling restaurants of Washington's waterfront district and a series of low-income housing projects less than a mile from the U.S. Capitol. Shahzad studied there for five semesters, taking mostly business classes and maintaining a grade-point average of 2.78.[16] In 2000 he transferred to the University of Bridgeport, in Connecticut, whose well-groomed campus overlooks a tranquil section of Long Island Sound. Friends and acquaintances recalled that he strolled around campus with an air of confidence and often wore tight T-shirts that highlighted his well-defined muscles. On the weekends he sometimes hit New York City's Bengali-themed nightclubs, and he "could drink anyone under the table," recalled a former classmate.[17]

In many ways Faisal Shahzad was a successful immigrant. While not a stellar student, he received a bachelor of science degree in computer applications and information systems from the University of Bridgeport in 2001, and returned to earn a master's degree in business administration.[18] While working on his master's, he landed a job as an accountant at Elizabeth Arden, Inc. in nearby Stamford, Connecticut.[19] The company sponsored his H-1 working visa, which enables U.S. companies to employ foreign workers temporarily in specialty occupations.

The story of Shahzad's radicalization mirrors that of many terrorists, from José Padilla to Najibullah Zazi. Several factors contributed to his journey to terrorism: a growing obsession with easily available extremist information on the Internet, a network of radical colleagues to sympathize with, and—importantly—training and indoctrination by a terrorist group in Pakistan.

Around 2001, Shahzad began to visit tanzime.org and other websites to listen to religious lectures. Over the next several years he was drawn to the charismatic Anwar al-Awlaki because of the cleric's frankness and perceived elegance. Shahzad also listened to Shaykh Abdallah Ibrahim al-Faisal, who had helped radicalize London suicide bomber Germaine Lindsay. Much like Awlaki, Faisal preached across a range of media, including sermons in mosques, informal meetings, and religious courses. He also spread extremist propaganda through e-mail, fiery Internet preaching, and on-line chat rooms.[20] Faisal was arrested in the UK in February 2002 and was eventually convicted of encouraging the murder of Jews, Hindus, Americans, and other non-Muslims, telling his followers that the way forward was "the bullet, not the ballot."[21] In 2007, Shaykh Abdallah Ibrahim al-Faisal was deported to Jamaica, where he continued to influence individuals like Shahzad and support Islamic extremism.

While he was at the University of Bridgeport, Shahzad also met Muhammad Shahid Hussain, a young Pakistani who would eventually become a Tehreek-e Taliban Pakistan associate and would play a crucial role in transforming Shahzad into a terrorist. They briefly lived together, partied together, read the Qur'an, and talked about Islam and the plight of Muslims. By 2007, Shahzad had become increasingly disturbed at what he perceived as widespread aggression against Muslims in Iraq, Afghanistan, and Palestine.

Like Adam Gadahn and the young Muslims in Lackawanna, Shahzad withdrew from local mosques because most individuals did not share his beliefs. He attempted to convince some of his Connecticut- and New York–based friends that jihad—including violent jihad—was required for all Muslims, but he didn't find much support. Some in his immediate family were aware of his radicalization, but they, too, were mostly opposed to violent jihad.

Around 2007, Shahzad's friend Muhammad Shahid Hussain informed him that a Pakistani named Muhammad Shoaib could assist him with jihad training. Shoaib was a computer expert who had militant contacts. Hussain began including Shahzad and Shoaib on the same e-mail distributions in early 2008. They discussed articles and sermons related to Islam, as well as videos of mujahidin conducting successful attacks in countries like Iraq.[22] Shahzad's father noticed a change in his son, who had become more religious-minded, prayed regularly, fasted every Thursday, and grew a beard.[23]

Philip Mudd later commented that Shahzad's radicalization illustrated the continuing spread of al Qa'ida's revolutionary zeal. "The proven presence of plotters from affiliated groups during the past two years is perhaps the most significant evolution of the threat faced during this period," he wrote. "The Detroit airliner and Times Square attempts represent a rare and significant step by an ideological affiliate of al Qa'ida to show intent and capability to reach into the United States, the first time an affiliate has succeeded since 9/11."[24]

Shahzad had come to an important revelation: it was his *duty* to conduct violent jihad. Around this time he explained his epiphany to a friend in an e-mail, contending that Islam was under attack. "And today our beloved Prophet," he explained, "has been disrespected and disgraced in the whole world and we just sit and watch with shame and sorrow and most of us don't even care." He fumed about the arrogance of the United States and its allies. "Everyone knows how the Muslim country bows down to pressure from west," he wrote. "Everyone knows the kind of humiliation we are faced with around the globe."

Shahzad was equally disparaging about the Muslim world, which had strayed far from the "straight path." Echoing Sayyid Qutb and Ayman al-Zawahiri, he characterized most contemporary Muslims as infidels, accusing them of being "ignorant of Islam and illiterate of Quran and Sunnah."[25] The only course of action, he concluded, was to "fight them until there is no more tumult or oppression, and there prevail justice and faith in Allah altogether and everywhere."[26]

He concluded his e-mail by implying that he would now sacrifice everything—including his family—for jihad. His day of judgment was coming. But he was not yet ready to fight. First he needed training.

A Crash Course in Bomb Making

Shahzad's radicalization occurred just as he was developing into a successful businessman. After a stint at Elizabeth Arden, he secured a job in 2006 as a financial analyst for Affinion Group, a marketing and consulting business in Norwalk, Connecticut. He enjoyed steady work, became a naturalized U.S. citizen on April 17, 2009, and bought a home at 119 Long Hill Avenue in nearby Shelton. The 1,356-square-foot, three-bedroom Colonial was in a cozy neighborhood, within walking distance of an ice cream parlor and a handful of local restaurants, like Billy D's Full Belly Deli. He had also married Huma Asif Mian, a U.S. citizen who had graduated from the University of Colorado in Boulder, and had two children with her. Mian's Facebook page joked that she spent her time "Changing Diapers, Feeding Milk, Wiping Drools, Being Sleep Deprived." She also praised Shahzad.

"What can I say," she wrote, "he's my everything."[27] In their house Shahzad showed off birthday and greeting cards from admirers. One, which was addressed to "Sweetest Faisal," read like a poem:

And I'm really eager to know
how things are going at
your end, I'm thinking about
you, because you're one of
those special people, who matter
to me, and I would really
like for us, to keep in touch[28]

But this life was coming to an end. After quitting his job, Shahzad stopped making payments on his house and defaulted on the mortgage. His bank, Chase Home Finance, foreclosed on his home in September 2009 and then auctioned it off the following year.[29]Around July 2, 2009, Shahzad traveled to Pakistan and stayed with his family in Peshawar for six months. His wife and children stopped in Saudi Arabia to see her family and then joined him in Peshawar.[30] During this time Shahzad prepared to undertake terrorist training, but he told his wife that he would be traveling to Lahore to participate in the Muslim missionary fundamentalist movement Tablighi Jamaat.

Shahzad's immediate goal was to learn how to build a bomb. He had an American passport and could come into the United States legally without raising suspicion. His citizenship status would be valuable for Tehreek-e Taliban Pakistan and its al Qa'ida allies. In the fall of 2009, Shahzad met with Hakimullah Mehsud, who had replaced Baitullah Mehsud as head of Tehreek-e Taliban Pakistan, which had temporarily relocated to North Waziristan because of Pakistani military operations in South Waziristan. After patiently listening to Shahzad volunteer to attack the United States, Hakimullah advised him to attend a training camp in North Waziristan. Over the next several months, Shahzad met Hakimullah Mehsud several more times in preparation for the attack.[31]

The next forty-day period would be critical for the success of Shahzad's terrorist mission. From December 9, 2009, through January 2010 he lived with members and associates of Tehreek-e Taliban

Pakistan in North Waziristan and underwent training. Five of those days involved building and detonating different types of bombs, under the tutelage of an experienced bomb trainer who used several pseudonyms, including Angar. Each day of the training was conducted at a different site. Shahzad's trainers gave him a bomb-making manual to study, which he did for about two weeks. He practiced building and detonating bombs, using ammonium nitrate and other substances.[32] It was a crash course in bomb making, Shahzad later explained. "How to make a bomb," he said, "how to detonate a bomb, how to put a fuse, how many different types of bombs you can make."[33]

As FBI officials like Art Cummings later recognized, Tehreek-e Taliban Pakistan leaders took precautions with Shahzad. They isolated him from other operatives for at least two reasons. One was to prevent him from obtaining information about other plots, just in case he was captured and interrogated in the future. A second was to ensure that others didn't find out about his operation. The decision to isolate him was similar to what al Qa'ida leaders had done with Najibullah Zazi and al Qa'ida in the Arabian Peninsula officials had done with Umar Farouk Abdulmutallab.[34]

Shahzad also met with Qari Hussein, a senior Tehreek-e Taliban Pakistan leader, who provided him with $15,000 before he returned to the United States. During this period he discussed with Tehreek-e Taliban leaders—including Muhammad Shoaib, who would become his day-to-day handler—his plan to detonate a bomb in the United States. They also discussed potential targets. Shahzad recorded a suicide video titled "A Brave Effort by Faisal Shahzad to Attack the United States in Its Own Land," in which he declared that the impending attack was revenge for the U.S. war in Afghanistan. In the video, Shahzad praised Baitullah Mehsud and Abu Mus'ab al-Zarqawi as "martyrs." The video was produced by Umar Media, the public relations arm of Tehreek-e Taliban Pakistan, and was approximately forty minutes long. It began with footage of Shahzad holding and then firing a machine gun in what appeared to be the mountains of Pakistan. After approximately four and a half minutes, he spoke directly into the camera while holding the Qur'an.

"We have decided that we are going to raise an attack inside America," he said defiantly. One of the objectives, he explained, was to "incite the Muslims to get up and fight against the enemy of Islam . . . Jihad is one of the pillars upon which Islam stands. Jews and Christians have to accept Islam as a religion and if you don't do that, then you are bound to go in hellfire."[35]

Fully radicalized and committed to his mission, Shahzad now posed a serious threat to the United States. He had a strong desire to attack the U.S. homeland, an American passport to get into the country without raising suspicion, and some training to build a bomb. Earlier that year, he had explained his intentions in an e-mail to a friend. He criticized the views of so-called "moderate" Muslims. "I bet when it comes to defending the lands," said Shahzad, "his opinion"—referring to one Pakistani moderate—"would be we should do dialogue." He had "bought into the Western jargon" of calling the mujahideen "extremist," Shahzad wrote. "My sheikhs are in the field," he explained. "If you don't have the right teacher, then Satan should become your sheikh."[36]

Following in the footsteps of his heroes, Shahzad returned to the United States in February 2010 on an Emirates Airlines flight into New York's John F. Kennedy International Airport. It was time to execute the operation.

The Final Stage

Shahzad returned to Connecticut, less than an hour's drive from New York, but his family remained in Pakistan. He stayed in a hotel for a few weeks while he looked for housing.[37] He then rented a second-floor apartment at 202–204 Sheridan Street in Bridgeport, a three-story beige building in a drab neighborhood with cracked sidewalks and closely set houses. Shahzad had few indulgences. He slept on an air mattress in a spartan bedroom with a bare desk and a black folding chair. He drank instant coffee, lifted free weights, and watched a handful of DVDs, including the romance *Up in the Air*, starring George Clooney and Vera Farmiga. In many ways, Shahzad was an ordinary thirty-year-old American. He nibbled on Oreo cookies, barbecue potato chips, and Subway sandwiches washed down with milk, AriZona iced tea, or Gatorade. Only a few items in his apartment, such as the green, leather-bound Qur'an and prayer beads, hinted that he was a Muslim.[38]

Shahzad had been pondering an attack in New York City for some time. In April or May 2009 he had sent a PowerPoint presentation to Muhammad Shoaib with photographs of possible targets, including the World Financial Center, Grand Central Station, and the Federal Reserve Bank. He had also shown the presentation to several Tehreek-e Taliban Pakistan leaders, including explosives trainer Qari Hussein.[39]

When he left Pakistan, he had little money. So he turned to Tehreek-e Taliban Pakistan for help. "I asked them for some cash," he said. "My cash was like $4,500 that I had with me when I was leaving, and I asked for some more cash because I had to do the whole operation here, so they gave me initially $4,900 something."[40]

With over $9,000 in cash, a bomb-making manual in Urdu that he could barely read, his notes in English, and blind determination, Shahzad began to put together the bomb.[41] But unlike Najibullah Zazi, the 2005 London bombers, and the 2006 UK transatlantic plotters, he did not rent or purchase a separate location to build the bomb. He made it in his Bridgeport apartment, alone. Surprisingly, none of the neighbors became suspicious enough to call police. "Nothing alarmed me about him, because he was just a person in the neighborhood fixing his house. He didn't talk much to people," said Bill Jackson, a contractor working on the house next door.[42]

Shahzad's family did not contact authorities in the United States or Pakistan, despite their concern that Shahzad was becoming radical. In 2008, for example, Shahzad had asked his father for permission to fight in Afghanistan, but his father said no. Beginning in February 2010, he bought fertilizer, propane, gasoline, and other ingredients from stores across Connecticut.[43] They were legal purchases and consequently did not arouse suspicion. He generally paid in cash to avoid a paper trail, as he had been taught in counter-surveillance training. In March he drove to Matamoras, Pennsylvania, and went shopping at Phantom Fireworks Showroom. Video surveillance showed Shahzad clad in loose-fitting jeans and a jacket, strolling along the vacant aisles of the 20,000-square-foot store, calmly examining various types of fireworks and declining an offer of help from an assistant manager. He was particularly interested in M88 Silver Salute fireworks, a Phantom Fireworks brand that sold for $10.99 for a thirty-six-count box. The M88s were about an inch and a half long and an inch in diameter. Each contained roughly 50 milligrams of explosives, about the size of a quarter of an aspirin. If Shahzad hoped that M88 fireworks would ignite one another, however, he miscalculated. The M88s were about 98 percent paper, and each fuse had to be ignited individually.[44] The crash course in bomb making hadn't been enough.

Much like Najibullah Zazi, Shahzad had trouble making the bomb. He considered using ammonium nitrate but concluded that it would arouse too much suspicion. So he turned to urea-based fertilizer. Yet he could not find the right type of fertilizer and queried Muhammad Shoaib in Pakistan, who checked with Tehreek-e Taliban Pakistan explosives experts. The fertilizer he had was good enough, they replied.

Shahzad used the Internet to access websites that provided real-time video feeds of Times Square. These websites enabled him to determine which areas of Times Square drew the largest crowds and the times when those areas would be most populated. Shahzad also maintained regular contact with Tehreek-e Taliban Pakistan associates, especially Muhammad Shoaib, who acted as his liaison in Pakistan when he had questions. Using software programs that were installed on his laptop while he was in Pakistan, Shahzad and Shoaib were able to exchange information about the bomb he was building and other topics.[45] They communicated several times a week through social networking and file-sharing services, Voice Over Internet Protocol (VOIP), Virtual Private Networks (VPNs), and an occasional e-mail or telephone call—partly to conceal their identities. To evade intelligence and law enforcement agencies, they created new Gmail accounts to communicate with each other. Their last communication before the May 1 attack was only three or four hours earlier.[46]

In order to conduct the attack, Shahzad also needed somewhere to place the bomb. He settled on a sport utility vehicle, since it would be spacious enough to hold the materials. Around mid-April he found an advertisement for a Nissan Pathfinder on craigslist.org. Shahzad called the owner, a nineteen-year-old college student named Peggy Colas. They met in the parking lot of Price Rite grocery store in Bridgeport. Shahzad arrived in a black Isuzu Rodeo and paid with cash, handing Colas thirteen $100 bills. After buying the Pathfinder, he installed black window tinting to make it more difficult to see into the vehicle, presumably to hide the bombs.

Shahzad also purchased a semiautomatic rifle, which he planned to use in the event he was captured in connection with the bomb plot. To ensure that he was fully prepared if confronted by law enforcement authorities, he went to a firing range in Connecticut to practice shooting the gun.[47]

One of the benefits of his training in Pakistan was improved counterintelligence—what operators sometimes call tradecraft. Shahzad removed the license plates from the Pathfinder and bolted on plates he had picked up at a nearby junkyard. He used a prepaid cellular telephone, which he activated around April 16 and deactivated around April 28, to contact Colas. He spoke to her about a dozen times during this period.[48] And he continued to pay for almost everything with cash.

But he began to run short of money. While training in Pakistan, Shahzad had estimated that he could conduct the attack for

$9,000. Upon returning to Connecticut, however, he realized that the cost of rent, vehicles, Internet, and daily sustenance, combined with the cost of building the bomb, would exceed his available funding. So he begged Muhammad Shoaib for more money.

In mid-February 2010, Shoaib took around $5,000 to an Islamabad *hawala* owner. A *hawala* is an informal money-transfer system that operates outside of normal banking channels and relies on brokers, known as *hawaladars*, to transfer money from one location to another. *Hawalas* are a quick and cost-effective way to transfer money and are often used throughout the Middle East, North Africa, and South Asia. A customer approaches a *hawala* broker in one city and gives a sum of money to be transferred to a recipient in another city. The *hawala* broker calls another broker in the recipient's city and gives disposition instructions about the funds, usually minus a small commission. On February 25, Shahzad received the $5,000 in cash from a *hawala* broker in Massachusetts. But he soon realized that he needed more money and went back to Shoaib, who was beginning to get impatient. Still, Shoaib came through. On April 6, Shahzad picked up another $7,000 in cash from a *hawala* broker in Ronkonkoma, New York, which was sent at Shoaib's direction.[49]

As May 1 approached, Shahzad assembled the bomb at his home in Connecticut. During the late afternoon of May 1 he loaded the bomb into the back of the Pathfinder and folded his semiautomatic rifle into a laptop computer bag. He carefully wiped the inside of the vehicle with a towel to remove any fingerprints. He then drove for approximately an hour until he arrived in Times Square and parked the Pathfinder.[50] When the bomb didn't go off, he walked to Grand Central Station, carrying the 9-millimeter Kel-Tec rifle in his bag. "I was waiting to hear a sound but I couldn't hear any sound," he concluded, "so I thought it probably didn't go off."[51]

On his way home, Shahzad placed a call to his landlord saying that he was on the train home from New York and needed to be let into his apartment. When he got there, he sent a message, presumably to Muhammad Shoaib in Pakistan, explaining his failed attempt. He also began to follow media coverage of the attempted bombing.[52] FBI and other members of the New York Joint Terrorism Task Force immediately responded, evacuating the area around the bomb. New York police chief Raymond Kelly was in Washington, D.C., for the annual White House Correspondents Dinner when his cell phone rang, alerting him of the attempted bombing. He quickly informed mayor Michael Bloomberg, who was also at the dinner. At 10:55 p.m. the two men left the event, drove to the airport, and returned on the mayor's private jet, touching down just after midnight at La Guardia Airport.

The hunt for Shahzad had begun. Investigators quickly discovered that the vehicle had stolen Connecticut license plates and that the dashboard vehicle identification number (VIN) had been removed. Not knowing who was responsible, they were now racing to find the bomber before he conducted another attack—or fled the country. Fortunately, they had some clues. After they towed the Pathfinder to a Queens forensic garage, an Auto Crime Unit detective crawled underneath the vehicle and discovered that the VIN number on the Pathfinder's engine block was still intact.[53] The Nissan manufacturer had stamped the VIN on the firewall separating the engine from the cabin, and had included a different serial number system used to track inventory and identify stolen parts on the engine, chassis, and transmission.

Police then frantically began conducting interviews—with the Pathfinder's previous owner, Peggy Colas; with the owner of the license plates, who had sent them to a nearby junkyard; and with street vendors and pedestrians who may have glimpsed Shahzad getting out of the vehicle. Colas described Shahzad as a Middle Eastern or Hispanic male, possibly twenty-five to thirty-five years old, with short black hair, brown eyes, and a dark complexion. Connecticut State Police brought in a sketch artist to work with her on a portrait of Shahzad.[54]

Colas was horrified. "I'm soooo happy I got a new car :)," she had written on her Facebook page after selling the Pathfinder to

Shahzad a few weeks earlier. But her euphoria didn't last long. "OMG!" she wrote on May 4, "I HAD A CRAZY DAY . . . IT'S OFFICIAL. I HAVE BAD LUCK. SMH I HOPE THEY FIND THAT BASTARD."[55]

Joint Terrorism Task Force members also began combing through hundreds of hours of closed-circuit television video covering the time and place of the attempted bombing. This was much easier in theory than in practice. Times Square is covered by a maze of cameras, creating reams of video footage. Sifting through this proved to be an enormous, labor-intensive effort. They also traced Shahzad's Verizon cell phone records, since he had called Peggy Colas a dozen times to purchase the Pathfinder. The phone records helped break the case. Shahzad had received four calls from a Pakistani number and had placed a call to Phantom Fireworks in Pennsylvania—the source of the M88s in the car. More clues began to surface. Investigators began to trace other evidence left in the unexploded vehicle—the keys to Shahzad's black Isuzu Rodeo, two cans of gasoline, fertilizer, and three propane tanks. On May 3, Shahzad's landlord saw him enter the garage and noticed two bags of fertilizer there, which FBI agents later recovered, along with more fireworks.[56] It was now only a matter of time before law enforcement agencies arrested Shahzad.

"I was watching the news and then after a day or two I had realized they're getting close," he said, "so I decided to go to JFK and take a plane and try to go back, if I can."[57]

Using IP-to-IP chat, Shahzad contacted Shoaib several times between May 1 and May 3 to devise his escape. Shoaib planned to pick up Shahzad at the airport in Pakistan.[58] On May 3, Shahzad bought a ticket on Emirates Air Flight 202 to Dubai, with an apparent plan to continue to Pakistan, and drove to JFK Airport.[59] Around noon that day he was placed on the No Fly List, but he still managed to board the flight. Only minutes before it departed, law enforcement officials rushed onto the plane and arrested him; he had been identified by an alert U.S. Customs and Border Protection agent.[60] It was a dramatic end to a tense two-day manhunt.

After his arrest, Shahzad waved his *Miranda* rights and admitted his guilt. He acknowledged that he had purchased all of the components of the bomb found in his car in Times Square. He had loaded the car with the bomb, driven it to Times Square, and parked it. He had attempted to begin the detonation process before he had abandoned the car. And he believed that the bomb would kill about forty people.[61]

Tehreek-e Taliban Pakistan released a short video claiming responsibility for the attempted attack in revenge for the death of Baitullah Mehsud and the slaying of al Qa'ida in Iraq leaders Abu Omar al-Baghdadi and Abu Ayyub al-Masri.

"We Tehreek-e Taliban with all the Pride and Bravery," they announced, "take full responsibility for the recent attack in the USA."[62]

Behind the scenes, however, Tehreek-e Taliban Pakistan leaders were furious. Shahzad's failure to carry out the attack had not itself been a disaster, but the fact that Shahzad had divulged some of the group's plans, procedures, and tactical details was a serious concern.[63] Pakistani officials, working with the CIA and the FBI, arrested Muhammad Shoaib and several other accomplices, including Muhammad Shahid Hussain. Despite withering criticism over the years by U.S. government officials for supporting militant groups, Pakistani law enforcement and intelligence agencies illustrated on this occasion that they could be helpful.

Two Lovely Children

It might be tempting to dismiss Shahzad as an incompetent nitwit.[64] He was certainly clumsy and amateurish. But it was not all his fault. The bomb's problems—no way to initiate an explosive detonation, use of nonexplosive materials, difficulties with the urea-based fertilizer—indicated that his training was insufficient. Indeed, he had received less than a week of explosives-related training. Still, his car bomb nearly succeeded. In late June 2010 the New York Joint Terrorism Task Force conducted a controlled detonation of a bomb that was nearly identical to the one Shahzad used, except that the bomb technicians ensured that it would detonate. The technicians also placed other vehicles nearby to measure the explosive effects of the bomb. While it was impossible to calculate precisely the impact Shahzad's bomb would have had, the controlled detonation suggested that it would have been devastating to the surrounding area. It would have killed and maimed pedestrians in the blast zone and torn apart buildings in the vicinity.[65]

Shahzad remained remorseless.

"I take it there's no question that you intended that the bomb go off, that it explode on the street next to a building?" asked judge Miriam Goldman Cedarbaum during his trial in June 2010. "What building was going to be blown up by the bomb?"

"Well, I didn't choose a specific building," Shahzad responded, "but I chose the center of Times Square."

"Were there a lot of people in the street?" Judge Cedarbaum inquired.

"Yes," he said. "And obviously the time, it was evening, and obviously it was a Saturday, so that's the time I chose."

"That is," Judge Cedarbaum tried to clarify, "you wanted to injure a lot of people?"

"Yes," Shahzad replied coldly. "Damage to the building and to injure people or kill people. But again, I would point out one thing in connection to the attack, that one has to understand where I'm coming from, because this is—I consider myself a mujahid, a Muslim soldier. The U.S. and the NATO forces, along with 40, 50 countries has attacked the Muslim lands. We—"

"But not the people who were walking in Times Square that night," Judge Cedarbaum said, perplexed. "Did you look around to see who they were?"

"Well, the people select the government," Shahzad responded. "We consider them all the same. The drones, when they hit—"

"Including the children?" she interrupted, pressing him.

"Well," said Shahzad, "the drone hits in Afghanistan and Iraq, they don't see children, they don't see anybody. They kill women, children, they kill everybody. It's a war, and in war, they kill people. They're killing all Muslims."

"Now we're not talking about them," Judge Cedarbaum clarified, "we're talking about you."

"Well, I am part of that," he responded, starting to get annoyed. "I am part of the answer to the U.S. terrorizing the Muslim nations and the Muslim people, and on behalf of that, I'm avenging the attacks, because only—like living in U.S., the Americans only care about their people, but they don't care about the people elsewhere in the world when they die. Similarly, in Gaza Strip, somebody has to go and live with the family whose house is bulldozed by the Israeli bulldozer. There's a lot of aggression."[66]

Several months later Judge Cedarbaum sentenced Shahzad, who had become an American citizen the year before, to life in prison. "There is really no basis here for me to believe that somebody who falsely swore allegiance to this country, who swore to defend this country, who took oath a year ago to defend this country and to be loyal to it, has now announced and by his conduct has evidenced that his desire is not to defend the United States or Americans, but to kill them," she said.[67]

Shahzad responded, "I did swear, but I did not mean it."[68]

Osama bin Laden, who was holed up in his Abbottabad house in Pakistan and monitoring news of the attack, was perturbed. In a late 2010 letter to al Qa'ida's general operations manager, Atiyah Abd al-Rahman al-Libi, bin Laden expressed indignation. "Of course you know that this is not permissible to tell such a lie to the enemies and is considered perfidy," bin Laden explained. "Perhaps the brother was not aware of this," he said, referring to Shahzad, "but it has raised questions about him. Please ask our brothers in the Taliban in Pakistan to clarify the position and make clear that such perfidy is forbidden, and their position toward it and toward the brother is that perhaps he was unaware that what he was doing was considered perfidy."

But bin Laden wasn't done. He had recently seen a photo of Shahzad with Hakimullah Mehsud. "Please get clarification as to whether or not Mehsud was aware that the oath of American citizenship includes a pledge by the person taking the oath not to harm the United States," bin Laden told Libi. "You of course know the negative effects that can result from not minding this matter, and there is still the suspicion of the Mujahidin that they renege on oaths and commit perfidy."[69]

In an e-mail to a friend several years before, Shahzad had explained that the time was drawing near for violent jihad. Hearkening to the day of resurrection, he quoted from the Qur'an.

That Day shall a man flee from his brother,
And from his mother and his father,
And from his wife and his children.
Everyman, that Day, will have enough to make him careless
    of others.[70]

The verse was more apt than he knew. His own family—his father, wife, and in-laws—were among the most distraught. His father, Bahar ul-Haq, was stunned and humiliated about his son's activities, which cast a shadow over his stellar professional career and his family's reputation. Shahzad's father-in-law, M. A. Mian, offered these words: "We all know these things, what the geopolitical problems are," he said. "Every day we sit in our living rooms with our friends and we discuss these issues. But to go to this extreme, this is unbelievable. He has lovely children. Two really lovely children. As a father I would not be able to afford to lose my children."[71]

End of an Era

The Shahzad plot signaled the end of an era. Both Art Cummings and Philip Mudd retired from the U.S. government. For Mudd, the end was bittersweet. He had joined the CIA in 1985 and devoted most of his career to counterterrorism, moving to the FBI in 2005 and eventually becoming its senior intelligence adviser. President Obama nominated him to become undersecretary for intelligence and analysis in the Department of Homeland Security, with the support of Secretary Janet Napolitano. But Mudd quickly ran into problems. Democrats on Capitol Hill announced that they would probe Mudd's knowledge of and role in coercive interrogation techniques while he was at the CIA, including his time as deputy director of the Counterterrorism Center. Rather than risk a confirmation fight, he withdrew his name and retired early in 2010.

"The President believes that Phil Mudd would have been an excellent Undersecretary of Intelligence and Analysis but understands his personal decision and the choice he has made," remarked White House spokesman Nick Shapiro.[72] It was a halfhearted, if not disingenuous, defense of Mudd. The White House did not have the stomach for a major confrontation with congressional Democrats over the legacy of coercive techniques.

For Art Cummings, the end was sweeter. In his twenty-three-year career with the FBI he had worked virtually every type of case as an agent. He had systematically risen up the FBI's hierarchy to head counterterrorism and counterintelligence, thanks in part to his extraordinary competence, hard work, and blunt approach. It was fitting, then, for Cummings to retire on May 1, 2010, the day of Shahzad's attempted attack. The timing couldn't have been better.

"We're winning," Cummings said to himself. "Even Timothy McVeigh could put a serious bomb together. But al Qa'ida was clearly on the wane. Shahzad's bomb was a piece of crap."[73]

WE GOT HIM

B Y LATE 2010, Ayman al-Zawahiri was under excruciating stress. Life as a fugitive in Pakistan had taken a heavy toll on his health and psychological well-being. His moods swung between cagey optimism about the war and morbid fatalism. Perhaps his biggest albatross, however, was the CIA's drone program. For the past several years, Hellfire missiles from CIA drones had harassed al Qa'ida and allied leaders across Pakistan's tribal areas. For Zawahiri, the list of fallen comrades was haunting. Tehreek-e Taliban leader Baitullah Mehsud was killed in August 2009, external operations chief Saleh al-Somali in December 2009, general manager Shaykh Sa'id al-Masri in May 2010, senior al Qa'ida operations officer Abu 'Abd al-Rahman al-Najdi in September 2010. In nearby Iraq, al Qa'ida leader Abu Hamza al-Muhajir was killed in April 2010. The list went on.

In December 2010, Zawahiri sent an urgent message to Osama bin Laden. "The subject is that of security and precaution," Zawahiri wrote. "A lot, if not most, of the injuries resulting from the spy planes are a result of the negligence of the brothers who don't want to change their lifestyle and abandon simple things that every sane person would try to avoid."[1]

The pace of drone strikes had increased under CIA director Leon Panetta. With the support of the White House and Pentagon leadership, CIA officials believed that drone strikes were having a dramatic impact on al Qa'ida. As with most of America's successful efforts against al Qa'ida since September 11, the drone campaign involved several U.S. intelligence agencies, which recruited human assets in villages, intercepted electronic communications, and analyzed satellite and other imagery. The difference now was that they had improved the ability to pull it all together quickly and fire a missile when an opportunity arose. But the drone strikes were controversial; one Western public opinion poll found that 76 percent of respondents in the Federally Administered Tribal Areas opposed the U.S. drones and only 22 percent supported them.[2]

Zawahiri probably realized that if central al Qa'ida operatives in Pakistan failed to improve their security and change their procedures, the organization would be eliminated. Six months later al Qa'ida leaders warned their adherents in a public communiqué that the movement's survival hinged on "taking precautions, working in total secrecy, and making use of all means to do damage to the enemy."[3] Al Qa'ida was not dead. But it had been weakened and was now more decentralized than ever, with affiliated groups from Yemen to Iraq, allied groups like Lashkar-e-Taiba, and informal networks scattered across the globe.

In addition, several factors had limited Osama bin Laden's role in plotting attacks against the U.S. homeland, including communications obstacles and disagreements among the group's senior leaders. While al Qa'ida's leaders wanted to target the United States and other Western countries, some suggested focusing on Afghanistan and local wars elsewhere. In a May 2010 letter to bin Laden, Zawahiri indicated that the struggle with the United States and the West would be settled on the battlefields of Iraq and Afghanistan rather than "in [America's] backyard." A few months before, Shaykh Sa'id al-Masri had written to bin Laden and argued that al Qa'ida could not expand operations in the United States for the moment because of financial constraints, a limited number of operatives, and improved U.S. security procedures. And in a January 2010 letter to bin Laden, he and Atiyah abd al-Rahman al-Libi had warned that attempts to attack the United States might "not succeed."[4]

For Zawahiri and bin Laden, the more difficult struggle, and perhaps the most important one, was still being waged across the Internet and in social media forums. But even the battle of ideas for the hearts and minds of Muslims was not going well. Al Qa'ida had lost popular support because of its resort to violence, failure to achieve any of its strategic objectives, and promulgation of a fringe ideology.

The third wave was coming to an end. For the moment, Zawahiri was safe. His longtime colleague, however, was not. The end had come for Osama bin Laden.

Where Have You Been?

Around August 2010 the National Security Agency intercepted a cell phone call. Abu Ahmed al-Kuwaiti, who was suspected by U.S. intelligence agencies of being a courier to Osama bin Laden, received a call from an old friend. "Where have you been?" Kuwaiti's friend asked. "We've missed you. What's going on in your life? And what are you doing now?" It seemed like an innocent question.

"I'm back with the people I was with before," Kuwaiti responded, somewhat vaguely.

For eavesdropping intelligence analysts, it was a chilling moment. As Kuwaiti's friend undoubtedly realized, the answer suggested that he had returned to the inner circle of Osama bin Laden, the world's most wanted man. Understanding the heavy burden on Kuwaiti's shoulders, his friend paused for a moment. "May God facilitate," he solemnly replied.[5]

As with the intercept that initiated the hunt for Najibullah Zazi in October 2009, the National Security Agency had played a key role in picking up bin Laden's trail, which had mostly gone cold since the al Qa'ida leader had escaped from the mountains of Tora

Bora in December 2001. Now it was time for other U.S agencies to lend their skills: the Central Intelligence Agency, with its network of spies and special activities capabilities; the National Reconnaissance Office, with its range of clandestine satellites; the National Geospatial-Intelligence Agency, with its geospatial analysis; U.S. special operations forces, with their ability to conduct clandestine strikes; and the White House, trying to direct the show.

A few years earlier, Khalid Sheikh Mohammed and Abu Faraj al-Libi, who were still detained at the U.S. prison in Guantánamo Bay, had helped confirm that Kuwaiti was a trusted confidant and courier of bin Laden. Now U.S. intelligence agencies had a phone number to monitor. The CIA's Counterterrorism Center came alive. Agents quickly got a lock on Kuwaiti, who drove a white SUV with the image of a white rhino emblazoned on the spare-tire cover. They began tracking the vehicle.[6] In August 2010 an analyst tapped out a memo on "Closing in on Bin Laden Courier," saying that her team believed Kuwaiti was somewhere on the outskirts of Islamabad. A revised memo, titled "Anatomy of a Lead," was finished in September and e-mailed to a small group on a need-to-know basis.[7] U.S. intelligence agencies had tracked Kuwaiti to a walled compound in Abbottabad.

If bin Laden was hiding there, in a busy suburb not far from Pakistan's military academy, the news would challenge much of what the CIA had assumed about his hideout. His three-story compound was situated about a mile from the intersection of Karakoram Highway and Kokul Street, down a dirt road where cars kicked up chocolate clouds of dust. It was located in an area known as Bilal Town. In a small dwelling nearby, the CIA established a safe house to monitor Kuwaiti, his family, and others who came and went. U.S. agencies watched and waited, putting together a "pattern of life" for everyone at the compound.

U.S. analysts marveled at the counterintelligence practices used at the compound. When Kuwaiti or others left, they waited up to ninety minutes before even placing a battery in their mobile phones, let alone making a call.[8] The compound was about 2 miles northeast of downtown Abbottabad and was shaped like a scalene triangle with one of the corners shaved off. Its whitewashed exterior walls rose 18 feet above the ground and were topped with barbed wire. Built around 2005, it had a 7-foot-high privacy wall on a third-floor terrace, which enabled bin Laden to meander outside without being seen. In fact, privacy screens on the balconies blocked all sight lines. The house had no phone or Internet connections, which meant that it gave off no "electronic signature"—intelligence lingo for phone calls or e-mail traffic that can be monitored by prying agencies. Bin Laden had been excruciatingly careful in other ways, too: "They had not thrown the house waste or garbage to the street," said Asghar Marwat, one of his erstwhile neighbors, "but instead disposed of it inside the house."[9]

Access to the compound was possible only through a green metal gate that led down a gritty passageway with 12-foot-high walls on either side. It dead-ended at yet another security gate, which opened to an inner compound where bin Laden lived. Abu Ahmed al-Kuwaiti lived with his family in the guesthouse, separated from the main house by a 12-foot-high wall. The family of Kuwaiti's brother, who was co-owner of the complex, lived on the first floor of the main house with other women and children. Bin Laden lived on the second and third floors, behind translucent windows. The main house was spartan. Each bedroom had an attached bathroom and its own kitchen, which enabled its occupants to live independently. One of the first-floor rooms was used as a classroom, with a whiteboard, piles of paper, and stacks of children's textbooks. Neighbors said that none of the children living at the house went to local schools; they were home-schooled. Bin Laden and his coterie were mostly self-sufficient. Residents grew most of their vegetables within the compound and lived on a simple diet consisting of dates, olive oil, walnuts, onions, tomatoes, okra, carrots, and dried meat. In addition, two buffaloes provided milk and two hundred hens supplied eggs, a key source of protein.

Osama Bin Laden had been living as a prisoner in his own home, starved for information but unable to leave because of the suffocating security precautions. He had aged considerably since September 11. Standing a sinewy six feet, four inches, he had a haggard face that showed the toll of a life spent evading intelligence agencies from virtually every major country in the world. His deep, penetrating eyes looked fatigued and forlorn. His fist-length, wiry beard had turned gray, and dark weathered circles were now visible just beneath his eyesockets. Still, bin Laden kept a box of Just for Men hair coloring to die his beard.[10] One of his few pleasures was surfing through Al Jazeera and other satellite stations in a drab, cream-colored room; a blanket covered the window, and a single light bulb sent shadows dancing along the walls. The room was furnished with an antiquated television set perched on a cheap ply-wood desk and connected to a satellite by a jumbled mass of wires. Dusty books cluttered the room.[11]

On March 14, 2011, after seven months of intelligence-gathering, President Obama held a National Security Council meeting to discuss potential courses of action against the Abbottabad compound.[12] The connections with Kuwaiti, abnormally conspicuous security measures, and bin Laden's own history of frugal living were telling. What were their options in capturing or killing bin Laden?

Tough Choices

Over a decade of experience against al Qa'ida provided a wealth of information, both positive and negative, about those options. Each carried risks. CIA officials settled on five possibilities, which they pushed to decision-makers at the White House.[13]

The first two options involved working closely with Pakistan. One was to give the intelligence to Pakistan and let its agents conduct the raid. A second, slightly more plausible option was to work closely with Pakistan's ISI and other security agencies to capture or kill bin Laden. The U.S.-Pakistan relationship had worked fairly well after the September 11 attacks, when scores of al Qa'ida operatives, such as Khalid Sheikh Mohammed, Abu Zubaydah, Ramzi bin al-Shibh, and Abu Faraj al-Libi, were captured. During those years the CIA's chief of station had a good relationship with President Musharraf and the heads of ISI and the military.

The problem with both options, however, was that those days of trust and close collaboration were gone. By 2011 their relationship had deteriorated to the point that the CIA chief of station had a difficult time getting meetings with anyone higher than the head of the ISI's Counterterrorism Wing. To make matters worse, a senior Pakistan government official had publically identified at least one chief of station, compromising his covert position and forcing him to leave the country. Skirmishes had damaged the relationship: Pakistan's capture of CIA contractor Raymond Davis; hostilities along the Afghanistan-Pakistan border between U.S. and Pakistani forces; Pakistani government support of the Taliban and other Afghan insurgent groups; and attacks against supply trucks in Pakistan, which were loaded with fuel and supplies for U.S. and NATO forces in Afghanistan.

Could the United States trust Pakistan to cooperate and ensure that such a sensitive operation wasn't leaked? No, President Obama decided.

"There was a real lack of confidence that the Pakistanis could keep this secret for more than a nanosecond," said one of Obama's advisers involved in the National Security Council debates.[14]

A third option was a Predator strike. While drones had been effective in killing al Qa'ida leaders, as Zawahiri had acknowledged, a strike against bin Laden was bound to attract unprecedented public attention. With women and children from the bin Laden and Kuwaiti families in the compound, there would undoubtedly be a public backlash because of civilian casualties. The drone program was already unpopular in Pakistan. As far back as December 2005,

CIA and other U.S. officials had weighed the risks of drone strikes in Pakistan—especially compared to other military options—when they targeted al Qa'ida's external operations leader, Hamza Rabi'a. At that time senior Department of Defense officials had decided against sending in a team of U.S. special operations forces to capture Rabi'a and had killed him with a drone. In that case and over the next several years, the Department of Defense generally preferred CIA drone strikes to military boots on the ground, because drones didn't risk American lives. Yet a high-profile Predator strike against bin Laden might be different, especially if the Pakistani government was not involved in the operation. U.S. officials worried that the Pakistani government might react with a public relations campaign that highlighted the killing of women and children at the compound, which would exacerbate anti-Americanism in Pakistan.

The fourth option was an assault by a paramilitary CIA ground unit, which would minimize the number of casualties. In the late 1990s, U.S. officials considered various CIA ground options to capture or kill bin Laden while he was in Afghanistan, but they eventually rejected them as too risky.[15] Another problem was that this mission would be anything but covert. If bin Laden was indeed inside the compound, there would be a media circus. Was it too risky to open up America's most secretive intelligence units to an international microscope? And, regardless, were they the best military organization for this mission?

A variant of this option, which had been strongly considered in targeting bin Laden in the late 1990s, was the use of a surrogate force. By the fall of 1997, the CIA's bin Laden unit had sketched out a plan for utilizing Afghan "tribals" to capture bin Laden in Afghanistan and hand him over for trial either in the United States or in an Arab country. In February 1998, for example, CIA director George Tenet walked National Security Adviser Sandy Berger through a plan in which Afghan surrogates would subdue the guards, enter Tarnak Farms (bin Laden's residence at the time), and grab their target. CIA operative Gary Schroen, who was involved in the planning efforts, estimated that the probability of capturing or killing bin Laden was about 40 percent. In a May 6, 1998, cable to CIA Headquarters, Schroen also noted that there were risks. There would come a point, he wrote, when "we step back and keep our fingers crossed that the [tribals] prove as good (and as lucky) as they think they will be."[16] CIA and U.S. special operations forces had learned the hard way in Tora Bora in 2001 that relying on locals could be risky. They were not always reliable, would not be as proficient as as American forces, and might trigger questions from the public and Congress about why the world's only superpower had outsourced the most important raid in American history to someone else.

This left a final option: to utilize elite U.S. special operations forces to conduct a raid in close cooperation with the CIA. There were risks, of course. The failed attempt in April 1980 to rescue American hostages in Iran, code-named Operation Eagle Claw and led by the U.S. Army's Delta Force, had been a political nightmare for Jimmy Carter after several helicopters crashed and the operation was aborted. In the late 1990s, Clinton administration officials were also wary of using special operations forces to capture bin Laden because of the risks of American military casualties and concerns about the quality of intelligence. But as Lieutenant General William Boykin, a founding member of Delta Force and deputy undersecretary of defense for intelligence, bluntly summarized, "Opportunities were missed because of an unwillingness to take risks and a lack of vision and understanding."[17]

The fifth option was the most plausible, in part because special operations forces had conducted thousands of missions over the past decade in Afghanistan, Iraq, and other countries. They had plenty of practice. Perhaps more important, the CIA and SEAL Team Six, officially known as the Naval Special Warfare Development Group (DEVGRU), had developed a productive, close relationship, thanks in large part to the efforts of Vice Admiral William McRaven, the head of Joint Special Operations Command (JSOC), and Admiral

Eric Olson, the head of U.S. Special Operations Command. So President Obama turned to JSOC to execute the raid in collaboration with the CIA. Because of the sensitive nature of the operation, however, it would be considered a covert action and come under Title 50 of the United States Code. In practical terms, this meant that the bin Laden raid would technically be a CIA operation, not a Department of Defense one, though it would utilize SEALs during the execution phase.

In a National Security Council meeting on March 29, 2011, President Obama asked McRaven a series of tough questions: How much time will they need to get the strike going? How quickly can they move? What will they do if the compound has a safe room? What if bin Laden isn't there? How would you get bin Laden out?[18]

On April 29 the president met with his national security team in the Diplomatic Room of the White House before heading to Alabama to survey tornado damage. Not everyone on his team supported military action, including Michael Leiter, director of the National Counterterrorism Center. The intelligence that bin Laden was in the compound wasn't definitive, the operation was risky, and it could ignite a political firestorm in Pakistan. Most of these concerns had a familiar ring for those involved in the 1990s debates about targeting bin Laden. Yet the longer the administration waited to secure more intelligence, the greater the risk that bin Laden might leave, the more likely that he would realize he was being watched, and the higher the probability that U.S. planning efforts would leak. Almost exactly a year before, WikiLeaks had begun releasing classified material on the Internet. In October 2010 it had released the "Iraq War Logs" and that April it had begun releasing files related to Guantánamo.

On Saturday, April 30, the president said he wanted to talk to Vice Admiral McRaven. In a twelve-minute phone call, according to an aide who took notes of their conversation, the president told McRaven that he supported the mission. "I couldn't have any more confidence in you than the confidence I have in you and your force,"

Obama said. "Godspeed to you and your forces. Please pass on to them my personal thanks for their service and the message that I personally will be following this mission very closely."[19]

That was it. The decision had been made. By this time the CIA had "red-teamed to death" a broader series of questions. What if, for example, Abu Ahmed al-Kuwaiti and his family were drug dealers? This could explain some of the security precautions, though probably not the extent of them. But it still left unanswered the question of why the individual who lived on the second and third floors never left the building. And Kuwaiti's long-standing relationship with bin Laden and the intercepted phone calls suggested that a senior al Qa'ida leader was probably there. The intelligence was far from perfect, but CIA officials assessed that it was "likely" that bin Laden was the individual.[20]

The Raid

April 30, 2011, was a moonless night in the city of Abbottabad. The temperature had dipped from a comfortable 82 degrees in midafternoon to a brisk 57 degrees by midnight. A few scattered clouds lazily wisped across the sky, pushed by a gentle northeast breeze. The sounds of the day—the grating of plows and the shrill bleating of sheep—had given way to the placid tranquillity of evening.

Abbottabad sits on a plateau at the southwestern cusp of Rash Plain and is bounded on all sides by the Sarban Hills, which offer breathtaking views. The area is rich in minerals, with generous deposits of biotite, granite, limestone, schist, soapstone, and quartz. Once a vast lake, Rash Plain is still marshy in the center, though most of the area has been drained. Farmers grow maize and potatoes. Subsistence agriculture reigns supreme here. The Karakoram Highway slices through the city, heading south to the Indus Plain and north to the Indian border.

On Sunday, May 1, several members of the president's National

Security Council and a handful of others huddled around a large conference table in the Situation Room at the White House. They ordered sandwich platters from Costco. President Obama was there, along with National Security Adviser Tom Donilon, Vice President Biden, Secretary of State Hillary Clinton, Secretary of Defense Robert Gates, Chairman of the Joint Chiefs of Staff Admiral Michael Mullen, Assistant to the President for Homeland Security and Counterterrorism John Brennan, and Director of National Intelligence James Clapper. CIA director Leon Panetta participated by video teleconference from CIA Headquarters and sent one of his senior counterterrorism officials to attend in person.

"It was probably one of the most anxiety-filled periods of time, I think, in the lives of the people who were assembled," said Brennan. "The minutes passed like days."[21]

That evening bin Laden paced back and forth in the house. This seemed to calm him down. Around midnight on the night of April 30, nearly two dozen SEALs, a Pakistani-American translator, and a Belgian Malinois dog named Cairo lifted off from a base in Jalalabad, Afghanistan, 160 miles to the west of Abbottabad, aboard two MH-60 Black Hawk helicopters modified to mask heat, noise, and movement. Three large Chinook helicopters carrying a backup team of twenty-four SEALs put down near the Indus River, a ten-minute flight from the compound.[22] The helicopters closed in on the compound around one o'clock in the morning on May 1.

Neighbors were among the first to notice. "Helicopter hovering above Abbottabad at 1AM (is a rare event)," Sohaib Athar wrote on his Twitter account. "Go away helicopter, before I take out my giant swatter :-/"[23]

Athar was an information technology consultant working remotely in Abbottabad. His house was a mile and a half from bin Laden's compound. A night owl, he was typing on his laptop when he heard the helicopter blades.[24]

"A huge window shaking bang here in Abbottabad Cantt," he

tweeted a few minutes later. "I hope it's not the start of something nasty :-/"[25]

The SEALs first saw bin Laden as they advanced up to the third floor and he retreated to his bedroom. After entering the bedroom and pushing aside bin Laden's wives, who were trying to shield him, one of the SEALs focused the infrared laser of his M4 carbine on bin Laden's chest and squeezed the trigger. Bin Laden, who was wearing a tan shalwar kameez and a prayer cap, fell backward. The SEAL fired a second round into his head, just above his left eye, and spoke into his radio.

"Geronimo EKIA," he announced, using the acronym for "enemy killed in sction."[26]

Geronimo was the execution checklist word for the operation, which indicated that bin Laden had been killed. Several others were also killed: Abu Ahmed al-Kuwaiti, his thirty-three-year-old brother Abrar, Osama bin Laden's son Khalid, and Abrar's wife Bushra. Word quickly began to spread.

Someone shot a tweet back to Sohaib Athar from an account with the name ISuckBigTime. "Osama Bin Laden killed in Abbottabad, Pakistan.: ISI has confirmed it."

"Uh oh, there goes the neighborhood :-/" lamented Athar. "I need to sleep," he continued, "but Osama had to pick this day to die :-/"

Athar was now famous—or, perhaps more appropriately, infamous. "Uh oh," he later tweeted, "now I'm the guy who liveblogged the Osama raid without knowing it."[27]

Bin Laden's British step-grandson found out about the killing through a text message which read, "Your grand-dad is dead. Watch the news."[28]

Social media had now captured the most significant and ostensibly clandestine counterterrorism raid in U.S. government history—live. It took about forty minutes to land the helicopters, kill bin Laden, and scoop his archives into garbage bags.

The explosive global reaction to bin Laden's death began immediately, illustrating how far his ideas had spread—and how much he was reviled. An unprecedented wave of messages overwhelmed Twitter, surpassing a frenzied five thousand "tweets-per-second" rate on the night of May 1.[29] Western media outlets chimed in. The *New York Post* trumpeted, "We Got Him!" And the *New York Daily News* wrote "ROT IN HELL" in oversized print across a glossy photo of bin Laden.

Back at the White House, President Obama was visibly relieved. "We got him," he said solemnly.[30]

Bin Laden was now dead. But was it definitely him? U.S. agencies scrambled to confirm his identity. First, one of bin Laden's wives identified him to the SEAL team. Second, using facial recognition methods, CIA specialists compared photos of the body to known photos of bin Laden and were able to determine with 95 percent certainty that it was him. The process analyzed his facial features, including the shape and size of his eyes, ears, and nose. Third, DNA analysis conducted separately by Defense Department and CIA labs positively identified bin Laden. DNA samples collected from his body were compared to a comprehensive DNA profile derived from his extended family. Based on that analysis, U.S. officials concluded that the DNA was unquestionably his. The possibility of a mistaken identity was approximately one in 11.8 quadrillion. Fourth, based on an initial review of the captured documents from the compound, the SEALs assessed that much of this information, including personal correspondence between Osama bin Laden and others, would only have been in his possession. Finally, al Qa'ida released its own statement acknowledging the death of bin Laden.[31]

Still, the SEALs weren't done. They lugged out bags of hard drives, thumb drives, cell phones, DVDs, computers, and manuals in English and Arabic. The helicopters landed back in Jalalabad around 3 a.m. and were met by Vice Admiral McRaven and the CIA chief of station from Afghanistan. At dawn, bin Laden's body was loaded into a V-22 Osprey that flew to the USS *Carl Vinson*, a nuclear-powered aircraft carrier stationed in the Arabian Sea. The body was wrapped in a white burial shroud and washed following traditional Muslim burial customs. It was then placed in a weighted bag and a military officer read prepared remarks, which were translated into Arabic. Afterward, bin Laden's body was placed on a flat board, which was elevated on one side, and the body slid off into the sea.[32]

Full Circle

Like the organization he founded, the terrorist leader had come full circle. Al Qa'ida was born in August 1988 at his house in Peshawar, Pakistan. And he died at his compound in Abbottabad, only a hundred miles northwest. His firebrand version of Islam was in decline but not dead—at least, not yet. The past several years had been challenging for him as a fugitive. Bin Laden's most significant obsession remained al Qa'ida's struggle against the United States and its allies across South Asia and the Arab world. It had not been going as well as he had hoped.

Before going to Abbottabad, bin Laden had moved around like a vagabond. He had trekked through the Afghan mountains near Tora Bora and entered Pakistan in December 2001, briefly returned to Afghanistan around Konar Province sometime later, and lived for about two years in the city of Haripur, 20 miles southwest of Abbottabad along the Karakoram Highway. In 2005 he moved to Abbottabad. For an avowed militant, it was an ironic place to land. Founded in 1853, the city was named after Major James Abbott, the first British deputy commissioner of the region, who served from 1849 to 1853 under the British colonial administration of India. The city also was home to the Pakistan Military Academy, a four-year coeducational institution that trained Pakistan Army officers. Two thousand guests each year, from more than thirty-four countries, also received training there. Before leaving Abbottabad, Major Abbott wrote a poem about his experience in the city:

Oh Abbottabad we are leaving you now
To your natural beauty do I bow
Perhaps your winds [sic] sound will never reach my ear
My gift for you is a few sad tears
I bid you farewell with a heavy heart
Never from my mind will your memories thwart.[33]

The pursuit of al Qa'ida did not end with bin Laden's death. In June 2011, al Qa'ida's external operations chief, Ilyas Kashmiri, who had advised David Headley, was killed in a drone strike in South Waziristan. In August another drone strike killed Atiyah abd al-Rahman al-Libi, al Qa'ida's general manager, who served as a conduit between al Qa'ida's affiliated groups and its leadership. In September 2011 the United States killed Anwar al-Awlaki in northern Yemen. And later in 2011 a drone strike in Pakistan killed Jude Kenan Mohammad, an American who was part of the North Carolina jihad cell that planned attacks against the U.S. Marine base in Quantico, Virginia, but who had fled to Pakistan in late 2008.[34]

The third wave was over, thanks to several factors. First, the United States had developed a light-footprint approach, where it effectively targeted al Qa'ida leaders like Awlaki. In Pakistan the U.S. increased drone strikes that severely disrupted al Qa'ida's command and control, hampered communications, decreased morale, limited freedom of movement, and delayed the planning cycle of terrorist operations. In addition, the United States withdrew its conventional military forces from Iraq by December 2011 and began to decrease the number of forces in Afghanistan. Second, al Qa'ida had resurrected a punishment strategy in Pakistan, Iraq, and across Africa. On August 14, 2011, for example, al Qa'ida in Iraq helped coordinate forty-two attacks against civilians and Iraqi security forces, making it the most violent day of the year. Third, the United States increased support to countries across the Horn of Africa, the Arabian Peninsula, and North Africa. In several of these countries, such as Somalia, government forces effectively cracked down on al Qa'ida and its affiliates. A growing number of al Shabaab militants in that country began to defect to the government. Sheikh Ali Hassan Gheddi, a defector who had previously served as a deputy commander-in-chief of al Shabaab, indicated that "al Shabaab's cruelty against the people is what forced me to defect to the government side. They extort money from the people and deal with them against the teaching of Islam."[35]

Though the third wave had ended, al Qa'ida was not dead. The key challenge for U.S. and other Western policymakers was now straightforward: to prevent a fourth wave.

PART IV

THE FOURTH WAVE?

18

PREVENTION

FOR MANY OFFICIALS who had served at the center of America's counterterrorist efforts, including Art Cummings and Philip Mudd, Osama bin Laden's death was long overdue. There was an enormous sense of relief and satisfaction. Cummings, who had joined a global investment firm in Connecticut, praised the decision to order the raid. "It was a courageous step, a gutsy move," he thought. "If the U.S. had failed, it would have emboldened al Qa'ida and it would have been all over the news."

Cummings believed that the death of bin Laden dealt al Qa'ida a severe blow. "There was no charismatic leader left. Who is the face of al Qa'ida now? It doesn't have a single face."[1]

Philip Mudd's reaction was similar, though perhaps more reserved about the future. After retiring from the FBI, he took on projects for the New America Foundation, Oxford Analytica, and George Washington University. Mudd was in Washington when the news broke about bin Laden's raid. "I wouldn't say I was happy," he said. "That's not the right word. Maybe relieved."

As he turned on the television, Mudd was uncomfortable with the celebratory, almost giddy reaction in the United States, as hundreds gathered near the White House and Ground Zero in New York City, chanting "USA" and singing the national anthem and "God Bless America." "You don't celebrate killing someone like that," he emphasized. Not like a Super Bowl victory or a frat party. "War is never a good thing."

There was also nothing final about bin Laden's death, thought Mudd. The war wasn't over by a long shot. "Another chapter is written in a long book," he reflected.

It was a measured response. Mudd believed that while al Qa'ida's central leadership had weakened, the threat from its affiliates would probably grow more pronounced.[2]

A few years earlier, Director of National Intelligence John Negroponte had come to a similar realization. "Osama bin Laden, and al Qa'ida more broadly, had a mergers and acquisition strategy," Negroponte noted. Al Qa'ida leaders in Pakistan spent a considerable amount of time negotiating to "acquire" groups like Algeria's Salafist Group for Preaching and Combat, he pointed out, which became al Qa'ida in the Islamic Maghreb in 2006. "Al Qa'ida began to gradually behave more like a conglomerate with a loose corporate headquarters," Negroponte observed, "and delegated authority to its affiliates."[3]

An Evolving Threat

Negroponte's assessment was accurate. But some government officials appeared to mistake the end of the third wave for the end of al Qa'ida. Leon Panetta, who became secretary of defense in July 2011, remarked that the United States was "within reach of strategically defeating al Qa'ida."[4] President Obama repeated this claim, noting that "we have put al Qa'ida on a path to defeat" because of the death of bin Laden and other senior operatives.[5] But was this decline permanent?

The evidence is far from clear. As we have seen, there have been three major al Qa'ida waves over the past two and a half decades, characterized by a surge in terrorist plots and attacks, which have been followed by reverse waves. Based on al Qa'ida's ability to regenerate, America's counterterrorism priority should be preventing a fourth wave of al Qa'ida–inspired terrorism, a possible outcome if policymakers fail to understand past lessons.

Since its establishment, al Qa'ida has evolved from a somewhat hierarchical organization to a much more diffuse one comprising five tiers: central al Qa'ida, affiliated groups, allied groups, allied networks, and inspired networks.[6]

Central al Qa'ida included the organization's leaders, who were based in Pakistan. Despite the death of key figures like bin Laden, several top leaders remained. Al Qa'ida's goals continued to include overthrowing regimes in the Middle East (the near enemy) and fighting the United States and its allies (the far enemy) who supported them. Some senior officials, including Saif al-Adel and Yasin al-Suri, played key roles from Iran. Yasin al-Suri was a senior al Qa'ida facilitator who helped raise money through his connections to Gulf-based fundraisers, and he was also involved in al Qa'ida's external plotting. Several individuals, including Umar Abd al-Rahman (also known as Sayfullah), a son of the "blind sheikh," Umar Abd al-Rahman, plotted attacks against the United States. Still others had ties to the United States, including Adnan el-Shukrijumah and Adam Gadahn.

The second tier included a range of affiliated groups that became formal branches of al Qa'ida. They benefited from central al Qa'ida's financial assistance and received at least some guidance, training, arms, money, or other support. They often added *al Qa'ida* to their name to identify themselves as affiliates, such as al Qa'ida in Iraq, al Qa'ida in the Arabian Peninsula, al Qa'ida in the Islamic Maghreb, and al Qa'ida East Africa. In addition, al Shabaab operated in Somalia and enjoyed a relationship with diaspora communities elsewhere, including in the United States. In July 2010 the FBI arrested several individuals in the United States—Zachary Adam Chesser, Carlos Eduardo Almonte, and Mohamed Mahmood Alessa—because of their relationship with al Shabaab.[7] In October 2011 a Minnesota jury convicted Amina Farah Ali and Hawo

Mohamed Hassan, both naturalized U.S. citizens from Somalia, of conspiracy to provide material support to al Shabaab.[8]

The third tier involved allied groups that established a direct relationship with al Qa'ida but did not become formal members. This arrangement enabled the groups to remain independent and pursue their own goals but to work with al Qa'ida for specific operations or training purposes when their interests converged. One example was Tehreek-e Taliban Pakistan, whose interests remained largely parochial, though the group was involved in terrorist plots overseas—including Faisal Shahzad's failed attack in Times Square. In May 2011 the FBI arrested a group in Miami led by Hafiz Muhammad Sher Ali Khan for terrorist support to Tehreek-e Taliban Pakistan.[9] Another allied group was Lashkar-e-Taiba, which David Headley had worked with while living in Chicago. Lashkar posed a growing threat to the United States, and its close ties to Pakistan's spy agency further complicated America's relationship with Pakistan. In September 2011 the FBI arrested Jubair Ahmad in Woodbridge, Virginia, for providing material support to Lashkar-e-Taiba.[10] By 2012, a Salafist group in Nigeria named Boko Haram developed relations with al Qa'ida and conducted a range of attacks in the country.

The fourth tier involved allied networks, small, dispersed groups of adherents who enjoyed some direct connection with al Qa'ida. These groups were not large insurgent organizations but often self-organized networks that congregated, radicalized, and planned attacks. In June 2010 five young men from Alexandria, Virginia—Ahmed Abdullah Minni, Aman Hassan Yemer, Waqar Khan, Khalid Farooq, and Ramy Zamzam—were sentenced to ten years in a Pakistani prison for conspiring to commit terrorist attacks. They had developed a close relationship with al Qa'ida operatives, including Jude Kenan Mohammad.

Finally, the inspired networks were those who had no direct contact to al Qa'ida central but who were motivated by the al Qa'ida cause and outraged by perceived oppression in Iraq, Afghanistan,

Chechnya, and Palestinian territory. They tended to be motivated by a hatred of the West and its allied regimes in the Muslim world. Without direct support, these networks tended to be amateurish, though they could occasionally be lethal. In February 2011, Khalid Aldawsari was arrested in Lubbock, Texas, for planning terrorist attacks after purchasing sulfuric acid, nitric acid, wiring, and other bomb-making material.[11] In September 2011, Rezwan Ferdaus, who lived outside Boston, was arrested for plotting to attack the Pentagon and the U.S. Capitol with remote-controlled aircraft filled with C-4 plastic explosives.[12] Both had planned attacks without the aid of central al Qa'ida or its affiliated groups.

Wave Patterns

Al Qa'ida's ability to launch attacks has not been linear but has ebbed and flowed over time. Yet the West's record of learning from past successes and failures has been mixed, and policymakers have tended to be unsystematic in their analysis and shortsighted in their strategies. Preventing a fourth wave requires identifying the causes of each of the past al Qa'ida waves—and the reverse waves—and understanding their policy implications.

As explained in the introduction of this book, the first wave began with the attacks against the U.S. embassies in Tanzania and Kenya in 1998, followed by the bombing of the USS *Cole* in 2000. It crested with the September 11 attacks and was followed by a reversal as al Qa'ida leaders and operatives were captured or killed in Afghanistan, Pakistan, the United States, and elsewhere. A second wave began in 2003 after the U.S. invasion of Iraq. This was followed by a reverse wave in 2006, as al Qa'ida in Iraq was severely weakened, plots were foiled, and senior al Qa'ida operatives were killed or captured in Pakistan and other countries. A third wave took place between 2007 and 2009, fueled by Anwar al-Awlaki and the rise of al Qa'ida in the Arabian Peninsula. This was followed by a reverse wave that crested with the death of bin Laden and other senior al Qa'ida leaders.

The historical evidence suggests that three factors help explain the pattern of waves and reverse waves. One is variation in America's counterterrorism strategy. When the United States and its allies have used overwhelming force and deployed large numbers of conventional soldiers, al Qa'ida has benefited through increased radicalization and additional recruits. A light-footprint approach that relies on clandestine law enforcement, intelligence, and special operations forces to support foreign governments and conduct precision targeting has been more effective. Another factor is variation in al Qa'ida's strategy. When al Qa'ida killed large numbers of civilians by adopting a punishment strategy, it generally lost support from local populations. A third factor is the ability of local governments to establish basic law and order in their territory when faced with an al Qa'ida presence.

The struggle against al Qa'ida depends in part on the precise use of violence—what the Nobel Prize–winning economist Thomas Schelling referred to as the "diplomacy of violence."[13] It is a war in which the side that kills the most civilians loses. A decision to deploy a large number of military forces in the Muslim world could trigger a fourth wave, as might an unprovoked, preemptive attack against a Muslim country such as Iran. In addition, if al Qa'ida were to adopt a more careful, selective strategy and minimize civilian casualties, it could make inroads in areas like North Africa and the Arabian Peninsula, where some governments remain weak and unpopular. Finally, if the Arab Spring significantly erodes the strength of governments across the Arab world, as in Yemen, al Qa'ida may be able to retain a foothold.

Preventing a Fourth Wave

The evolution of al Qa'ida suggests that counterterrorism efforts must be adapted to changing conditions. Al Qa'ida's leadership and strategies have varied over time across different countries. Its affiliated and allied groups in countries like Yemen, Somalia, and Iraq have diverse leaders, approaches, and sometimes even goals—which may change as operatives are captured or killed. Despite these differences, preventing a fourth wave will doubtless hinge on several steps.

The first is implementing a light-footprint strategy that focuses on covert intelligence, law enforcement, and the use of special operations forces to conduct precision targeting of al Qa'ida and its financial and logistical support networks. The United States should withdraw most conventional forces from Afghanistan and rely primarily on clandestine operatives, as it has done in Colombia, the Philippines, and other countries experiencing counterinsurgencies. Most of the terrorists involved in homeland plots after September 11—from José Padilla's plan to blow up apartment buildings in the United States to Najibullah Zazi's and Faisal Shahzad's attempts to conduct terrorist attacks in New York City—were partly motivated by the large U.S. and allied conventional deployments overseas and by a conviction, however erroneous, that Muslims were their helpless victims. Such a strategy means refraining from sending large numbers of U.S. forces to Muslim countries. The bulk of the U.S. military should focus on such tasks as preparing for conventional wars in the Korean Peninsula, the Taiwan Straits, and other theaters.

There was an initial tendency after September 2001 to conceive of counterterrorism as a *military* campaign, especially among U.S. policymakers, who coined the term "war on terror" to describe the effort. Yet some officials had serious reservations about using the term; Secretary of Defense Rumsfeld, for example, noted that he was "concerned that the word 'war' led people to overemphasize the importance of the military instrument in this multi-dimensional conflict."[14] The decision to deploy large numbers of forces contributed to radicalization and facilitated al Qa'ida's recruitment and propaganda efforts. Perhaps more important, the capture or elimination of virtually every major al Qa'ida terrorist who was captured or killed—from Khalid Sheikh Mohammed in 2003 to Najibullah Zazi in 2009 and Osama bin Laden and Anwar al-Awlaki in 2011—was accomplished by clandestine agencies.

Local police and intelligence agencies have a permanent presence in cities and towns, a superior understanding of local groups, and better human sources than the military. As Bruce Hoffman argued in his book *Inside Terrorism*, a critical step in countering terrorist groups is for law enforcement officials to "develop strong confidence-building ties with the communities from which terrorists are most likely to come or hide in . . . The most effective and useful intelligence comes from places where terrorists conceal themselves and seek to establish and hide their infrastructure."[15] Although al Qa'ida is different from many other terrorist organizations because of its global reach, its modus operandi is not atypical. Like other groups, its members need to communicate with each other, raise funds, build a support network, plan and execute attacks, and establish a base (or bases) of operations. Most of its nodes are vulnerable to infiltration by intelligence agencies.

The second step is helping local governments establish basic law and order as a bulwark against al Qa'ida and other extremists. The countries most in danger of becoming an al Qa'ida safe haven lie in an arc that extends from North Africa to the Middle East and South Asia, an area that made up the Umayyad Caliphate from A.D. 661 to 750. It is no coincidence that al Qa'ida has attempted to set up its affiliates in this area: al Qa'ida in the Islamic Maghreb in North Africa, al Shabaab in the Horn of Africa, al Qa'ida in the Arabian Peninsula, al Qa'ida in Iraq, and al Qa'ida central in Pakistan. Of course, there is no formula for improving governance and counterterrorism capabilities overseas, which suggests that the United States and its allies need to adapt to local conditions.

Contrary to conventional wisdom, the Arab Spring has the potential to undermine stability and erode the strength of governments across this arc, which might provide an opportunity for al

Qa'ida's fourth wave to develop. Several countries in this region, such as Yemen, are in serious jeopardy of again providing al Qa'ida with a sanctuary, particularly in the Abyan and Shabwah Governorates along the Gulf of Aden. The U.S. and allied goal should be to establish effective central governments with security agencies capable of undermining al Qa'ida. Spreading democracy is important, but policymakers must be realistic. It is unclear whether the Arab Spring will increase the number of democratic states in the Arab world. State collapse could severely undermine counterterrorism efforts.

The third step is to aggressively exploit instances when al Qa'ida or its affiliates adopt a punishment strategy. Killing large numbers of civilians has generally backfired, undermining al Qa'ida's support and pushing even conservative Sunni religious and political figures to denounce al Qa'ida as un-Islamic. The U.S. government has done a poor job of publicly highlighting al Qa'ida's unpopularity in the Muslim world, even among conservative Muslims. Today no U.S. government agency has the lead role in countering al Qa'ida's ideology, a task that is shared by the State Department, Defense Department, CIA, and other organizations. Ultimately, it is the National Security Council's responsibility to appoint a lead agency and hold it responsible.

These three steps—utilizing a light-footprint strategy, improving the effectiveness of regimes in countries threatened by al Qa'ida, and exploiting al Qa'ida's tendency to kill civilians—would help ensure that no fourth wave occurs. One of the most important battlefields will be on the Internet, since the struggle against al Qa'ida and its allies remains in part a battle of ideas. Over the past decade, radicalization has become much less formal than it used to be. "Extremists are moving away from mosques to conduct their activities in private homes and premises," a British intelligence report concluded. "We assess that radicalization increasingly occurs in private meeting places, be they closed prayer groups at mosques, self-defense classes at gyms or training camps in the UK or overseas."[16]

The rise of the Internet and social media fundamentally changed terrorist activities. Individuals such as Anwar al-Awlaki, Adam Gadahn, and Shaykh Abdallah Ibrahim al-Faisal utilized YouTube, Facebook, Twitter, Internet chat rooms, and other forums to distribute propaganda, recruit new supporters, and seek financial aid. Some, like Awlaki, were successful in motivating individuals to conduct terrorist attacks. Others, like Gadahn, largely failed. As one al Qa'ida communiqué blithely noted in 2011, "In today's world, there's a place for the underground mujahideen who support the religion of Allah, men and women and youths in their cities and villages, and from their homes, and with their individual creativity and what is possible for them, as long as they are parallel with the general plans of the mujahideen[:] . . . the arena of electronic warfare."[17]

Yet as much as it has accomplished, al Qa'ida has often stumbled here. Parents, siblings, wives, and other family members of operatives were often devastated, even embarrassed by their relatives' terrorist activity. The wife of Mohammad Sidique Khan, the lead London bomber in 2005, said she was "ashamed" of her husband's activities. One of Najibullah Zazi's relatives remarked that "I'd bring him myself" to justice for his actions. Umar Farouk Abdulmutallab's parents were troubled by their son's attempt to blow up a Northwest Airlines flight and warned U.S. and Nigerian authorities that he was radicalizing. Abdulmutallab's Internet colleagues were also shocked, and one harshly reprimanded him for giving "Islam a bad name." And Faisal Shahzad's father-in-law was incredulous that he would "go to this extreme" with a wife and "two really lovely children."

Many al Qa'ida operatives have also failed to practice what they preach. Anwar al-Awlaki was arrested twice in San Diego for soliciting prostitutes. Adnan el-Shukrijumah was arrested in Broward County, Florida, for child abuse and battery. Adam Gadahn was arrested in Orange County, California, for assault and battery. Many al Qa'ida leaders have been attracted to pornography. The

Madrid bombers were involved in drug trafficking. These are the activities of criminals and gangsters, not hallowed religious leaders. Al Qa'ida leaders have come under withering criticism from Muslims worldwide, including deeply conservative Sunni leaders. Ayman al-Zawahiri faced criticism for slaughtering Muslims in his 2008 Internet question-and-answer session. Senior officials from Palestinian Hamas, Egypt's Muslim Brotherhood, and Egyptian Islamic Jihad dismissed al Qa'ida's leaders—and their ideology—as un-Islamic and a fringe phenomenon. "Islam is not bin Laden," said Mahmud Ezzat, the number-two official in the Muslim Brotherhood. "After September 11, there had been a lot of confusion. Terrorism was mixed up with Islam."[18]

A Long War

By the time of bin Laden's death, opinion polls already showed that he had been discredited among Muslims around the world. His support levels plummeted in Palestinian territory, Indonesia, Pakistan, Turkey, Lebanon, Egypt, and Jordan. The figures spoke for themselves. Al Qa'ida suffered as well, with support severely declining across the Muslim world, especially in the midst of the Arab Spring. Only 2 percent of Muslims in Lebanon and 5 percent in Turkey expressed favorable views of al Qa'ida in 2011. In Jordan, 15 percent had a positive opinion of al Qa'ida, while 22 percent in Indonesia and 21 percent in Egypt shared this few.[19] The trend was unmistakable.

The struggle against al Qa'ida and its ideology will be a long one. It will be measured in decades, not months or years. This is a concept that doesn't come easily to most Westerners. And the battlefield remains a global one, stretching from the great shores of America and the United Kingdom to the rugged peaks of Yemen and Pakistan. Preventing a fourth wave will require patience and fortitude. Shakespeare put it best in *Julius Caesar*, as Brutus and

Cassius discuss their struggle with the forces of Octavian and Marcus Antonius:

> There is a tide in the affairs of men.
> Which, taken at the flood, leads on to fortune;
> Omitted, all the voyage of their life
> Is bound in shallows and in miseries.
> On such a full sea are we now afloat,
> And we must take the current when it serves,
> Or lose our ventures.[20]

Brutus and Cassius did not fare well in their struggle with Caesar. Perhaps the United States and its allies will better adjust and adapt to the shifts in today's current.

ACKNOWLEDGMENTS

WRITING A BOOK is more an art than a science, much like a sculptor struggling to create a polished statue from a roughly hewn marble block. From the beginning, the goal of *Hunting in the Shadows* was to outline broad trends in the struggle against al Qa'ida using newly released court records from terrorism trials, declassified government documents, my own experience working in the Department of Defense, and the insights of those involved on the ground from South Asia to the Horn of Africa. Though I was trained as a political scientist at the University of Chicago, where I received my Ph.D., the book is deliberately more a history of al Qa'ida than a work of political science. Whatever the weaknesses of this book, they would have been far greater without the help of a talented group of colleagues who helped support, mold, and refine it.

An army of colleagues was critical in shaping the book and correcting mistakes. Several read portions of the manuscript or were willing to discuss chapters in detail. They included Bruce Hoffman, Bruce Riedel, Brian Jenkins, Philip Mudd, Art Cummings, John Negroponte, Fernando Reinares, Jim Dobbins, Paul Smith, Peter Clarke, Jim Lechner, Ben Connable, Dave Phillips, Jimmie Youngblood, Dan Darling, Michael Freeman, and Jeremy Pressman. Others offered support from the beginning, including Frankie

Shroyer, Brian Keeth, and Carlos Perez. I tested some of the early chapters for readability on several friends and colleagues, including Clark Johnson, Diane Johnson, Jack Newton, Alice Newton, and Suzanne Jones. Many other experts provided useful insights on al Qa'ida, including Peter Bergen, Steve Coll, Kim Cragin, Arturo Muñoz, and Robert Pape.

I would also like to thank U.S. government officials from the White House, Defense Department, State Department, Federal Bureau of Investigation, Department of Homeland Security, and intelligence community for their insights and tireless counterterrorism work. Government officials from Pakistan, Afghanistan, the United Kingdom, France, Spain, Italy, and Germany, among others, provided helpful information on the hunt for al Qa'ida and its affiliated groups. Most government officials did not want to be identified by name because of the sensitivity of their work, but the book could not have been written without their insights.

The team at W. W. Norton, led by Tom Mayer, was instrumental in all aspects of the book. Tom served as a friend and colleague during the conceptualization, writing, and editing stages and constantly encouraged me to shape the book into something readable yet substantive. I owe a heartfelt thanks to many others at Norton, including assistant editor Denise Scarfi, publicist Rachel Salzman, sales director Bill Rusin, and a host of talented individuals from the production and design departments, including Nancy Palmquist, Don Rifkin, Anna Oler, Ingsu Liu, and Chin-Yee Lai. Liz Duvall did a masterful job of copy editing and corrected errors in the manuscript. My agent, Eric Lupfer, was patiently willing to discuss ideas at every stage of the book and helped shape the direction of the book from the beginning. My assistant, Meagan Smith, was instrumental throughout the entire process, and I owe her an extraordinary debt of gratitude. Kathleen Cutsforth and Gina Frost helped get the manuscript across the finish line. Several individuals from RAND's Office of External Affairs, especially Jeff Hiday, Joe Dougherty, and Monica Banken, were particularly helpful on the publicity side. I also thank RAND president Michael Rich and National Security Research Division vice president Jack Riley for their assistance over the years.

Finally, my parents and three brothers have always been staunch supporters. And my wife and two daughters have been a constant source of inspiration—and joy—during the research and writing process. I dedicate this book to them.

NOTES

Author's Note: My interviews with several government officials were confidential, and the names of these interviewees have been withheld by mutual agreement. In addition, some documents cited in the notes may not yet be widely available, even though they have been declassified or are unclassified. I have nonetheless provided as complete bibliographic information as possible.

CHAPTER 1: A MODEL INVESTIGATION

1 Trial of Mr. Abdulla Ahmed Ali et al., Woolwich Crown Court, May 6, 2008.
2 Department for Communities and Local Government, *The Pakistani Muslim Community in England: Understanding Muslim Ethnic Communities* (London, 2009), p. 6.
3 E-mail from unnamed individual in Pakistan (possibly Rashid Rauf) to Abdulla Ahmed Ali, July 31, 2006. The author received copies of this e-mail and others cited in this chapter from British and American officials.
4 E-mail from Abdulla Ahmed Ali to unnamed individual in Pakistan (possibly Rashid Rauf), August 3, 2006.
5 E-mail from unnamed individual in Pakistan (possibly Rashid Rauf) to Abdulla Ahmed Ali, August 4, 2006.
6 E-mail from Abdulla Ahmed Ali to unnamed individual in Pakistan (possibly Rashid Rauf), August 6, 2006.
7 Mark Hough, interview, "Terror in the Skies," *BBC Panorama*, September 9, 2008.
8 Hanif Qadir, interview, ibid.
9 Trial of Mr. Abdulla Ahmed Ali et al., September 8, 2008.
10 Martyrdom video produced by Abdulla Ahmed Ali in Walthamstow, July 27, 2009.
11 Martyrdom video produced by Tanvir Hussain in Walthamstow, July 27, 2009.
12 Trial of Mr. Abdulla Ahmed Ali et al., May 6, 2008.
13 Andy Hayman, "Why I Suspect Jittery Americans Nearly Ruined Efforts to Foil Plot," *Times* (London), September 8, 2009.

14 E-mail from unnamed individual in Pakistan (possibly Rashid Rauf) to Abdulla Ahmed Ali, July 20, 2006.

15 Philip Mudd, interview with author, August 8, 2011. On Mohammed Gulzar and Mohammed al-Ghabra (below), also see, for example, Bruce Hoffman, "Radicalization and Subversion: Al Qaeda and the 7 July 2005 Bombings and the 2006 Airline Bombing Plot," *Studies in Conflict and Terrorism* 32 (2009): 1100–16.

16 U.S. Department of Treasury, *Treasury Designates Individual Supporting Al Qaida, Other Terrorist Organizations*, HP-206 (Washington, D.C., December 19, 2006).

17 Federal Bureau of Investigation, *Possible Hijacking Tactic for Using Aircraft as Weapons* (Washington, D.C., 2003), p. 1.

18 John Negroponte, interview with author, August 11, 2011.

19 Mudd interview, August 8, 2011.

20 Art Cummings, interview with author, September 2, 2011.

21 Ronald Kessler, *The Terrorist Watch: Inside the Desperate Race to Stop the Next Attack* (New York: Crown Forum, 2007), p. 2.

22 Quoted in Ronald Kessler, *The Secrets of the FBI* (New York: Crown, 2011), p. 203.

23 On Bojinka, see, for example, George Tenet, *At the Center of the Storm: My Years at the CIA*, with Bill Harlow (New York: HarperCollins, 2007), pp. 250–51.

24 Andy Hayman, *The Terrorist Hunters: The Ultimate Inside Story of Britain's Fight Against Terror*, with Margaret Gilmore (London: Bantam, 2009), pp. 247, 271, 280.

25 Trial of Mr. Abdulla Ahmed Ali et al., May 5, 2008.

26 Transcript of UK wiretap of Abdulla Ahmed Ali et al., August 3, 2006.

27 Trial of Mr. Abdulla Ahmed Ali et al., May 6, 2008.

28 E-mail from unnamed individual in Pakistan (possibly Rashid Rauf) to Abdulla Ahmed Ali, July 31, 2006; e-mail from Abdulla Ahmed Ali to unnamed individual in Pakistan (possibly Rashid Rauf), August 3, 2006; e-mail from unnamed individual in Pakistan (possibly Rashid Rauf) to Abdulla Ahmed Ali, July 13, 2006.

29 Hayman, *The Terrorist Hunters*, p. 267.

30 E-mail from unnamed individual in Pakistan (possibly Rashid Rauf) to Abdulla Ahmed Ali, July 13, 2006.

31 Kessler, *The Terrorist Watch*, p. 5.

32 Trial of Mr. Abdulla Ahmed Ali et al., May 5, 2008.

33 Martyrdom video produced by Abdulla Ahmed Ali.

34 Martyrdom video produced by Tanvir Hussain.

35 Douglas Alexander, interview, "Terror in the Skies," *BBC Panorama*, September 9, 2008.

36 Christopher Andrew, *Defend the Realm: The Authorized History of MI5* (New York: Knopf, 2009), p. 815.

37 John Reid, interview, "Terror in the Skies," *BBC Panorama*, September 9, 2008.

38 Martyrdom video produced by Umar Islam in Walthamstow, August 9, 2009.

39 Transcript from court proceedings, United Kingdom, May 2008. British government official, interview with author, August 23, 2011.

40 Transcript from court proceedings, United Kingdom, May 2008.

41 Michael Chertoff, interview, "Terror in the Skies," *BBC Panorama*, September 9, 2008.

42 Mudd interview, August 8, 2011.

43 Art Cummings interview, September 2, 2011.

44 Hayman, "Why I Suspect Jittery Americans Nearly Ruined Efforts to Foil Plot."

45 Reid interview, September 9, 2008.

46 Crown Prosecution Service, *"Aircraft Bomb" Plotters Guilty of Conspiracy to Murder* (London, July 2009).

47 Trial of Mr. Abdulla Ahmed Ali et al., May 5, 2008.

48 Hayman, "Why I Suspect Jittery Americans Nearly Ruined Efforts to Foil Plot."

49 Ibid.

50 House of Commons, Home Affairs Committee, *The Home Office's Response to Terrorist Attacks: Sixth Report of Session 2009–10, Vol. II* (London: Her Majesty's Stationery Office, February 2010).

51 David Blakey, *A Need to Know: HMIC Thematic Inspection of Special Branch and Ports Policing* (London: Her Majesty's Inspectorate of Constabulary, January 2003); Intelligence and Security Committee, *Report into the London Terrorist Attacks on 7 July 2005*, Cm 6785 (London: Her Majesty's Stationery Office, May 2006), pp. 36–37.

52 Peter Clarke, "Learning from Experience: Counter Terrorism in the UK since 9/11," speech, Colin Cramphorn Memorial Lecture, April 24, 2007.

53 Her Majesty's Government, *Contest, The United Kingdom's Strategy for Countering Terrorism*, Cm 8123 (London: Her Majesty's Stationery Office, 2011).

54 House of Commons, Home Affairs Committee, *The Government's Counter-Terrorism Proposals: First Report of Session 2007–08* (London: Her Majesty's Stationery Office, December 2007).

55 Bank of England, *Financial Sanctions: Terrorist Financing* (London, August 11, 2006).

56 Metropolitan Police, *Three Men Convicted of Conspiracy to Murder: Khan, Savant, and Zaman Were Found Guilty of Conspiracy to Murder Today* (London, July 2010).

57 Department of Homeland Security, "Remarks by Homeland Security Secretary Michael Chertoff, United States Attorney General Alberto Gonzales, FBI Director Robert Mueller and Assistant Secretary for TSA Kip Hawley" (Washington, D.C., August 10, 2006).

58 Mudd interview, August 8, 2011.

59 David C. Rapoport, "The Four Waves of Modern Terrorism," in Audrey Kurth Cronin and James M. Ludes, ed., *Attacking Terrorism: Elements of a Grand Strategy* (Washington: Georgetown University Press, 2004), p. 47.

60 Samuel P. Huntington, *The Third Wave: Democratization in the Late Twentieth Century* (Norman: University of Oklahoma Press, 1991).

61 Ayman al-Zawahiri, *Knights Under the Prophet's Banner*, trans. Laura Mansfield (Old Tappan, N.J.: TLG, 2002).

62 The data on al Qa'ida fatalities from 1998 to 2010 are from the Global Terror-

ism Database at the University of Maryland's National Consortium for the Study of Terrorism and Responses to Terrorism (START), www.start.umd.edu/start/; accessed December 15, 2011. The data include fatalities from attacks by al Qa'ida central and its affiliates in South Asia (Afghanistan and Pakistan), the Middle East (Iraq, Palestinian Territory, Saudi Arabia, Turkey, and Yemen), East Africa (Ethiopia, Kenya, Somalia, and Tanzania), North Africa (Algeria, Mali, Mauritania, Niger, and Tunisia), the Philippines, Europe, and the United States.

63 Audrey Kurth Cronin, *How Terrorism Ends: Understanding the Decline and Demise of Terrorist Campaigns* (Princeton, N.J.: Princeton University Press, 2009).

64 Thomas C. Schelling, *Arms and Influence* (New Haven, Conn.: Yale University Press, 1966).

65 On offshore balancing and counterterrorism, see Robert A. Pape and James K. Feldman, *Cutting the Fuse: The Explosion of Global Suicide Terrorism and How to Stop It* (Chicago: University of Chicago Press, 2010), pp. 12–13, 333–35.

CHAPTER 2: THE ORIGINS OF DISSENT

1 Perhaps the most comprehensive analysis of Egyptian militants prior to the September 11, 2001, attacks is Lawrence Wright, *The Looming Tower: Al-Qa'ida and the Road to 9/11* (New York: Knopf, 2006).

2 Ibid.

3 Al-Sayyid Imam Abd-al-Aziz al-Sharif, interview with Muhammad Salah, *Al-Hayat* (UK), December 8, 2007, part 1.

4 Ibid., part 3.

5 Muhammad Hasan Khalil al-Hakim, "Jihad Revisions: Truths and Presuppositions," Open Source Center (GMP20070721660002), June 11, 2007.

6 Ayman al-Zawahiri, *A Treatise on the Exoneration of the Nation of the Pen and Sword of the Denigrating Charge of Being Irresolute and Weak*, March 2008.

7 Ayman al-Zawahiri to Abu Mus'ab al-Zarqawi, July 9, 2005.

8 Sharif interview, part 1.

9 "Brief Biography of Ayman al-Zawahiri," 2RAD-2004-600457, a document written by one of Zawahiri's associates. Released by the Harmony Project, Combating Terrorism Center, West Point.

10 Samir W. Raafat, *Maadi 1904–1962: Society and History in a Cairo Suburb* (Cairo: Palm, 1994).

11 Gilles Kepel and Jean-Pierre Milelli, eds., *Al Qaeda in Its Own Words* (Cambridge, Mass.: Harvard University Press, 2008), p. 149.

12 Montasser al-Zayyat, *The Road to Al-Qaeda: The Story of Bin Laden's Right-Hand Man* (Ann Arbor, Mich.: Pluto, 2004), p. 16.

13 Ibid., p. 35.

14 Ibid., p. 43.

15 Ibid.

16 Sharif interview, part 1.

17 Zayyat, *The Road to Al-Qaeda*, p. 44.

18 "Al-Jihad Leader's Son on Father's Links to Al-Qa'ida," *Al-Hayat*, April 4, 2004.

19 Ayman al-Zawahiri, *Knights Under the Prophet's Banner*, trans. Laura Mansfield (Old Tappan, N.J.: TLG, 2002), p. 77.

20 Zayyat, *The Road to Al-Qaeda*, p. 41.

21 Ayman al-Zawahiri, *Al-Kitab al-Aswad* (The Black Book), 1992. At one point the book was available on the website www.tawhed.ws.

22 For footage of the speech, see www.pbs.org/wgbh/pages/frontline/shows/terrorism/etc/video.html. Also see Kepel and Milelli, *Al Qaeda in Its Own Words*, p. 153.

23 Richard Reeves, *Passage to Peshawar: Pakistan Between the Hindu Kush and the Arabian Sea* (New York: Simon & Schuster, 1984), p. 78.

24 There is some question about when Zawahiri returned to Peshawar. In his autobiography, he notes that "I was unable to return to the arena until mid-1986"; Zawahiri, *Knights Under the Prophet's Banner*, p. 35.

25 Ibid., p. 37.

26 Sharif interview, part 1.

27 Ibid.

28 Camille Tawil, *Brothers in Arms: The Story of Al-Qa'ida and the Arab Jihadists*, trans. Robin Bray (London: SAQI, 2010), pp. 100–3.

29 Zayyat, *The Road to Al-Qaeda*, p. 28.

30 Sayyid Imam Abd al-Aziz al-Sharif, *Al-Umdah fi 'Idad al-'Uddah* (The Primer in Preparing for Jihad) (Amman: Dar al-Bayariq, 1988).

31 Osama Rushdi, "How Did the Ideology of the 'Jihad Group' Evolve?" *Al-Hayat* (UK), January 30, 2002.

32 On the differences between defensive and offensive jihad, see Alfred Morabia, *Le gihad dans l'islam medieval: La combat sacré des origenes au douzième siècle* (Paris: Albin Michel, 1993); Rudolf Peters, *Islam and Colonialism: The Doctrine of Jihad in Modern History* (The Hague: Mouton, 1979); Ramadan al-Bouti, *Le jihad en islam: Comment le comprende? Comment le pratiquer?* (Damascus: Dar el-Fikr, 1996).

33 Mariam Abou Zahab and Olivier Roy, *Islamist Networks: The Afghan-Pakistan Connection*, trans. John King (New York: Columbia University Press, 2004), pp. 14–15.

34 Basil Mohammed, *Al-Ansar al-Arab fi Afghanistan* (The Arab Volunteers in Afghanistan) (Jeddah: House of Learning, 1991), p. 241.

35 Peter Bergen, *The Osama bin Laden I Know: An Oral History of Al Qa'ida's Leader* (New York: Free Press, 2006); Wright, *The Looming Tower*, p. 133.

36 The quotes are from the exhibit by "Tareekh Osama" (Osama's history), a document presented in *United States of America v. Enaam M. Arnaout*, United States District Court, Northern District of Illinois, Eastern Division, No. 02 CR 892, January 6, 2003.

37 Ibid.

38 Sharif interview, part 1.

39 Gilles Kepel, *Jihad: The Trail of Political Islam* (Cambridge, Mass.: Harvard University Press, 2002), pp. 159–84, 237–75.

40 Central Intelligence Agency, *Usama bin Ladin: Islamic Extremist Financier*, 1996. Released by the National Security Archive.

41 Najwa bin Laden, Omar bin Laden, and Jean Sasson, *Growing Up Bin Laden: Osama's Wife and Son Take Us Inside Their Secret World* (New York: St. Martin's, 2009), pp. 94, 115.

42 Sharif interview, part 1.

43 Ibid., part 3.

44 Adil Abd-al-Majid Abd-al-Bari, open letter, part 1, *Al-Hayat* (UK), August 28, 2008.

45 Ibid.

46 Qur'an, The Story (Al-Qasas): 28:50; Sharif interview, part 1.

47 Zawahiri, *Knights Under the Prophet's Banner*, pp. 110–11.

48 See, for example, Kepel and Milelli, *Al Qaeda in Its Own Words*, pp. 158–60.

49 Ayman al-Zawahiri, *Al-Hisad Al-Murr* (Bitter Harvest: Sixty Years of the Muslim Brotherhood), 1991. Also see Kepel and Milelli, *Al Qaeda in Its Own Words*, p. 171.

50 Sharif interview, part 1.

51 Bari, open letter, part 1.

52 Zayyat, *The Road to Al-Qaeda*, p. 68.

53 Bin Laden, bin Laden, and Sasson, *Growing Up Bin Laden*, p. 213.

54 Sayyid Qutb, *Milestones*, repr. ed. (New Delhi: Islamic Book Service, 2007), pp. 7–11.

55 Qur'an, The Feast (Al-Ma'ida), 5:50.

56 On Qutb's work, see Gilles Kepel, *The Prophet and Pharaoh: Muslim Extremism in Egypt* (Berkeley: University of California Press, 1985); Olivier Carré, *Mystique et politique* (Paris: Presses de la FNSP et Cerf, 1984); Ibrahim M. Abu Rabi, *Intellectual Origins of Islamic Resurgence in the Muslim Arab World* (Albany: SUNY Press, 1996).

57 See, for example, Kepel, *Jihad*, pp. 25–27.

58 Qutb, *Milestones*, p. 36.

59 Steve Coll, *Ghost Wars: The Secret History of the CIA, Afghanistan, and Bin Laden, from the Soviet Invasion to September 10, 2001* (New York: Penguin, 2004), p. 113.

60 Qutb, *Milestones*, p. 9.

61 Zawahiri, *Knights Under the Prophet's Banner*, p. 61.

62 Fawaz A. Gerges, *The Far Enemy: Why Jihad Went Global* (New York: Cambridge University Press, 2005), p. 101.

63 On the establishment of a caliphate, see, for example, Abu Bakr Naji, *The Management of Savagery: The Most Critical Stage Through Which the Ummah Will Pass* (Cambridge, Mass.: John M. Olin Institute for Strategic Studies at Harvard University, May 23, 2006).

64 Zawahiri, *Knights Under the Prophet's Banner*, p. 201.

65 Ibid., p. 47.

66 Sayyid Qutb to Tewfig al-Hakeem, undated, in Salah Abdel Fatah al-Khaledi, *Amerika min al-dakhil bi minzar Sayyid Qutb* (America from the Inside Through the

Eyes of Sayyid Qutb), 2nd ed., trans. Nidal Daraiseh (Damascus: Dar al-Qalam, 1986), p. 39.

67 Zahawiri argued that "Jerusalem will not be liberated unless the battle for Egypt and Algeria is won and unless Egypt is liberated." See, for example, Zayyat, *The Road to Al-Qaeda*.

68 Zawahiri, *Knights Under the Prophet's Banner*, p. 111.

69 Ibid.

70 Ayman al-Zawahiri, *Al Walaa wa al Baraa* (Loyalty and Enmity), obtained by *Al Hayat* (UK), January 14, 2003.

71 Zawahiri, *Knights Under the Prophet's Banner*, p. 113.

72 Ibid., p. 111.

73 The text is the second fatwa originally published on February 23, 1998, to declare a holy war against the West and Israel. It was signed by Osama bin Laden, head of al Qa'ida; Ayman al-Zawahiri, head of al-Jihad; Rifai Taha, leader of the Islamic Group; Sheikh Mir Hamzah, secretary of the Jamiat-ul-Ulema of Pakistan; and Fazlul Rehman, leader of the Jihad Movement in Bangladesh.

74 Robin Wright, "In from the Cold and Able to Take the Heat," *Washington Post*, September 12, 2005.

75 Ibid.

76 Philip Mudd, "The War on Terror: How We Do What We're Doing," speech, Miller Center, University of Virginia, April 3, 2007.

77 Federal Bureau of Investigation, *Bombings of the Embassies of the United States of America at Nairobi, Kenya, and Dar Es Salaam, Tanzania* (Washington, D.C., November 18, 1998); U.S. Department of State, *Report of the Accountability Review Boards: Bombings of the US Embassies in Nairobi, Kenya and Dar es Salaam, Tanzania on August 7, 1998* (Washington, D.C., 1999).

78 National Security Council e-mail, Richard Clarke to Sandy Berger, August 8, 1999; Central Intelligence Agency memo, "Khowst and the Meeting of Islamic Extremist Leaders on 20 Aug.," August 17, 1998. Released by the 9/11 Commission.

79 Bin Laden, bin Laden, and Sasson, *Growing Up Bin Laden*, p. 240.

80 See, for example, Dr. Gary W. Richter, *Osama bin Laden: A Case Study*, Sandia National Laboratories, U.S. Department of Energy, December 6, 1999. Released by the National Security Archives.

81 U.S. Embassy (Islamabad), cable, "TFXX01: Afghanistan: Reaction to U.S. Strikes Follows Predictable Lines: Taliban Angry, Their Opponents Support U.S.," August 21, 1998. Released by the National Security Archives.

82 U.S. Embassy (Islamabad), cable, "Afghanistan: Reported Activities of Extremist Arabs and Pakistanis Since August 20 U.S. Strike on Khost Terrorist Camps," September 9, 1998. Released by the National Security Archives.

83 National Security Council, *Strategy for Eliminating the Threat from the Jihadist Networks of al Qida: Status and Prospects*, December 2000. Released by the National Security Archives.

84 U.S. State Department, report, "U.S. Engagement with the Taliban on Usama Bin Laden," ca. July 16, 2001. Released by the National Security Archives.

85 Karl F. Inderfurth to Madeleine Albright, memo, "Subject: Your Meeting on Usama Bin Laden, Date: November 24, 1998." Released by the National Security Archives.

86 Presidential Daily Brief to President William Jefferson Clinton, "Subject: Bin Ladin Preparing to Hijack US Aircraft and Other Attacks, December 4, 1998." Released by the 9/11 Commission.

87 Executive Order 13129, "Blocking Property and Prohibiting Transactions with the Taliban," July 4, 1999.

88 National Security Council, "Strategy for Eliminating the Threat."

89 Gary Schroen to Michael Scheuer, e-mail, "Capture Op," May 5, 1998. Also see CIA, cable, "Comments on Planning for UBL Rendition," May 6, 1998. Released by the 9/11 Commission.

90 National Security Council, memo, "Political Military Plan DELENDA," September 1998 (attached to NSC memo, Richard Clarke to Condoleezza Rice, January 25, 2001). Released by the 9/11 Commission.

91 Handwritten note from James Steinberg on National Security Council memo, Richard Clarke to Sandy Berger, April 14, 2000. Released by the 9/11 Commission.

92 The 9/11 Commission, *The 9/11 Commission Report: Final Report of the National Commission on Terrorist Attacks Upon the United States* (New York: W. W. Norton, 2004), p. 138.

93 Gary C. Schroen, interview, *Frontline*, PBS, January 20, 2006.

94 CIA Briefing Materials, "Background Information: Evaluating the Quality of Intelligence on Bin Ladin (UBL) in Qandahar, 13–20 May 1999," ca. May 25, 1999. Compiled by the 9/11 Commission.

95 Michael Scheuer to Gary Schroen, e-mail, "Re: Your Note," May 17, 1999. Released by the 9/11 Commission.

96 U.S. State Department, report, "U.S. Engagement with the Taliban on Usama Bin Laden," ca. July 16, 2001. Released by the National Security Archives.

97 See, for example, Inderfurth to Albright, "Subject: Your Meeting on Usama Bin Laden"; U.S. State Department, cable, "Subject: Afghanistan: Taliban Agree to Visits of Militant Training Camps, Admit Bin Ladin Is Their Guest," January 9, 1997; U.S. State Department, cable, "Subject: Osama Bin Laden: Taliban Spokesman Seeks New Proposal for Resolving Bin Laden Problem," November 28, 1998; U.S. State Department, cable, "Subject: Usama Bin Ladin: Coordinating Our Efforts and Sharpening Our Message on Bin Ladin," October 19, 1998. Released by the National Security Archives.

98 National Security Council, "Strategy for Eliminating the Threat."

99 9/11 Commission, *The 9/11 Commission Report*, pp. 66–67.

100 Richard Clarke to Condoleezza Rice, memo, "Subject: Presidential Policy Initiative/Review—The Al Qida Network," January 25, 2001. Released by the National Security Archive.

101 "Egyptian Al-Jihad Leader's Son on Father's Link to Al-Qa'ida," *Al-Hayat* (UK), April 4, 2004.

CHAPTER 3: HUNTING IN THE HINDU KUSH

1 Agency Group 09, "U.S. Troops Describe Clearing Afghan Caves, Bunkers," U.S. Department of Defense, Federal Document Clearing House (FDCH) Regulatory Intelligence Database, March 28, 2002.

2 Mark Thompson, "The Soldier: Sudden Warrior," *Time*, September 9, 2002.

3 Agency Group 09, "U.S. Troops Describe Clearing Afghan Caves, Bunkers."

4 Captain U.S. Air Force, "Interview with Maj (U)," 74th Air Expeditionary Group, May 6, 2002. Released by the U.S. Air Force.

5 National Security Council, "Strategy for Eliminating the Threat from the Jihadist Networks of al Qida: Status and Prospects," December 2000. Released by the National Security Archives.

6 Captain U.S. Air Force, "Interview with Maj (U)."

7 Six A-10s attacked the al Qa'ida formation. The account of the A-10 attacks is in the Mission Reports (MISREPs) for Cherry 7, Cherry 3, and Cherry 1 for March 5, 2002. Released by the U.S. Air Force.

8 Agency Group 09, "U.S. Troops Describe Clearing Afghan Caves, Bunkers."

9 Al Qa'ida Manual, *The Black Book of Mountainous Operations and Training*, undated.

10 U.S. Air Force, *Operation Anaconda: An Airpower Perspective* (Washington, D.C., February 5, 2005), p. 15.

11 Ground Force Operations, January 1, 2002, found in Task Force Enduring Look Repository (TFELR hereafter). Released by the U.S. Air Force.

12 "Dossiers of Rebel Field Commanders," date unknown. Released by the Cold War International History Project and available at www.wilsoncenter.org/program/cold-war-international-history-project.

13 Major General Franklin L. Hagenbeck, interview, *Field Artillery*, September-October 2002, p. 5.

14 Dave Fiore, "Buster Hagenbeck Commands the Ground War Against the Terrorists in Afghanistan," *Florida State Times* 8, no. 1 (August 2002): 5.

15 Combined Joint Force Land Component Commander (CJFLCC) Ground Force Operations, January 1, 2002, TFELR. Also see "Point Paper, Operation Anaconda, Coalition Forces Land Component Command (CFLCC) Perspective," March 16, 2002, TFELR. Released by the U.S. Air Force.

16 Commander Joint Task Force (COMJTF) Mountain, Operation Order (OPORD) 02-001, 231630Z February 2002. Released by the U.S. Air Force.

17 Anaconda Concept of Operations (CONOPS) Briefing, February 20, 2002. Released by the U.S. Air Force.

18 Briefing, USCENTCOM/J2, February 28, 2002, TFELR. Released by the U.S. Air Force.

19 Chronology of United States Central Command Air Forces (Forward) for Operation Enduring Freedom, 1–28 February 2002. Released by the U.S. Air Force.

20 General Tommy Franks, *American Soldier* (New York: Regan, 2004), p. 379.

21 U.S. Army, *The United States Army in Afghanistan: Operation Enduring Freedom*, CMH Pub 70-83-1 (Washington, D.C.: Center for Military History, 2004), p. 34.

22 Message, Combined Joint Task Force (CJTF) Mountain to CFLCC, 072100Z March 2002. Released by the U.S. Air Force.

23 After Action Report, 19th ASOS. Released by the U.S. Air Force.

24 Message, CJTF MTN to CFLCC, 22100Z March 2002. Released by the U.S. Air Force.

25 Quoted in Adam Geibel, "Operation Anaconda, Shah-i-Kot Valley, Afghanistan, 2–10 March 2002," *Military Review* 82, no. 3 (May–June 2002).

26 Immediate Close Air Support (CAS) database, division fire support coordination element (DFSCOORD) data sheet. Released by the U.S. Air Force.

27 Air strike impact quoted in CJTF Mountain to CFLCC, 032100Z March 2002. Released by the U.S. Air Force.

28 Henry A. Crumpton, "Intelligence and War: Afghanistan, 2001–2002," in Jennifer E. Sims and Burton Gerber, eds., *Transforming U.S. Intelligence* (Washington, D.C.: Georgetown University Press, 2005), p. 175.

29 U.S. Air Force, *Operation Anaconda*, pp. 5–6.

30 Agency Group 09, "The Battle of Takur Ghar," U.S. Department of Defense, FDCH Regulatory Intelligence Database, May 24, 2002.

31 Report, CJTF Mountain to CFLCC, 052100Z March 02. Released by the U.S. Air Force.

32 Enemy casualty numbers are cited in Anaconda daily situation reports (sitreps). Released by the U.S. Air Force.

33 CJTF Mountain to CFLCC, 042100Z March 2002. Released by the U.S. Air Force.

34 GFAC Report, "Operation Anaconda After Action Report," March 15, 2002. Released by the U.S. Air Force.

35 Report CJTF Mountain to CFLCC, 072100Z March 2002. Released by the U.S. Air Force.

36 CJTF Mountain to CFLCC, March 16, 2002. Released by the U.S. Air Force.

37 Federal Bureau of Investigation, *FBI Director Names Arthur Cummings Executive Assistant Director for National Security Branch* (Washington, D.C., January 11, 2008).

38 Robin Wright, "In from the Cold and Able to Take the Heat," *Washington Post*, September 12, 2005.

39 Crumpton, "Intelligence and War," p. 164.

40 Bob Woodward, *Bush at War* (New York: Simon & Schuster, 2002), p. 51.

41 George Tenet, *At the Center of the Storm: My Years at the CIA*, with Bill Harlow (New York: HarperCollins, 2007), p. 207.

42 Douglas J. Feith, *War and Decision: Inside the Pentagon at the Dawn of the War on Terrorism* (New York: HarperCollins, 2008), pp. 75–76.

43 Gary C. Schroen, *An Insider's Account of How the CIA Spearheaded the War on Terror in Afghanistan* (New York: Ballantine, 2005), p. 28.

44 U.S. Department of Defense, "Abd al-Hadi al-Iraqi," undated.

45 Andrew J. Birtle, *Afghan War Chronology*, U.S. Army Center of Military History Information Paper (Washington, D.C.: March 22, 2002), pp. 2–3.

46 Stephen Biddle, *Afghanistan and the Future of Warfare: Implications for Army and Defense Policy* (Carlisle, Pa.: Strategic Studies Institute, U.S. Army War College, November 2002), pp. 8–10.

47 U.S. Army Military History Institute Tape 032602p, CPT M. int.; Tape 032802p, CPT D. int.; U.S. Army Military History Institute Archive, Carlisle Barracks, Pa. See also Dale Andrade, *The Battle for Mazar-e-Sharif, October-November 2001*, U.S. Army Center of Military History Information Paper (Washington, D.C.: March 1, 2002), pp. 2–3.

48 Biddle, *Afghanistan and the Future of Warfare*, p. 10.

49 See, for example, Combating Terrorism Center, *Abu Hafs Al Masri* (West Point, undated).

50 Peter Bergen, *The Osama Bin Laden I Know: An Oral History of Al Qaeda's Leader* (New York: Free Press, 2006), p. 14; Combating Terrorism Center, *Abu Hafs Al Masri*.

51 Najwa bin Laden, Omar bin Laden, and Jean Sasson, *Growing Up Bin Laden: Osama's Wife and Son Take Us Inside Their Secret World* (New York: St. Martin's, 2009), p. 208.

52 Ayman al-Zawahiri to Muhammad Atef, e-mail, April 15, 1999. The document was one of many in a laptop computer discovered in Kabul after the overthrow of the Taliban regime by *Wall Street Journal* reporter Alan Cullison; see Alan Cullison, "Inside Al-Qaeda's Hard Drive: Budget Squabbles, Baby Pictures, Office Rivalries—and the Path to 9/11," *Atlantic*, September 2004.

53 Bin Laden, bin Laden, and Sasson, *Growing Up Bin Laden*, p. 162.

54 Ahmed Rashid, *Descent into Chaos: The United States and the Failure of Nation-Building in Pakistan, Afghanistan, and Central Asia* (New York: Viking, 2008), pp. 3–6.

55 U.S. Army Military History Institute Tape 032802a, MAJ D. int.; Tape 032802p, MAJ C. int.; Tape 032602a, CPT H. et al. int.; U.S. Army Military History Institute Archive, Carlisle Barracks, Pa. Also see John Carland, *The Campaign Against Kandahar*, U.S. Army Center of Military History Information Paper (Washington, D.C., March 4, 2002), pp. 2–5.

56 U.S. Army Military History Institute Tape 032602p, CPT M. int.

57 James Dobbins, interview with author, September 19, 2011.

58 The United Nations Security Council endorsed the Bonn Agreement with a resolution, 1383, S/RES/1383 (2001), on December 6, 2001.

59 "Attacks Draw Mixed Response in Mideast," CNN, September 12, 2001.

60 Ibid.

61 See, for example, Fawaz A. Gerges, *The Far Enemy: Why Jihad Went Global* (New York: Cambridge University Press, 2005), pp. 185–250.

62 Al-Sayyid Imam Abd-al-Aziz al-Sharif, interview with Muhammad Salah, *Al-Hayat* (UK), December 8, 2007, part 2.

63 Muhammad ibn al-Hasan Shaybani, *The Islamic Law of Nations: Shaybani's Siyar*, trans. Majid Khadduri (Baltimore: Johns Hopkins University Press, 1966).

64 Ibid.

65 Ibid.

66 Human Rights Watch, *The Black Hole: The Fate of Islamists Rendered to Egypt* (New York, May 2005), p. 48.

67 Osama bin Laden, "Open Letter to Shaykh Bin Baz on the Invalidity of His Fatwa on Peace with the Jews," December 29, 1994.

68 Shaykh Salman Bin-Fahd al-Awdah, "Letter to Osama bin Laden," *Islam Today*, September 17, 2007.

69 Ali H. Soufan, *The Black Banners: The Inside Story of 9/11 and the War Against al-Qaeda* (New York: W. W. Norton, 2011). pp. 78–79.

70 Muhammad Hasan Ghulam Rabbani (aka Abu Badr), interview with ISI, undated. Document provided to author by a senior Pakistani official.

71 "Fundamentalists Correct U.S. Intelligence About Personalities of Sayf-al-Adl, Al Qa'ida's Military Commander and Colonel Makkawi," *Asharq al-Awsat*, April 1, 2002, p. 5.

72 *United States of America v. Zacarias Moussaoui*, Cr. No. 01-455-A, Substitution for the Testimony of Khalid Sheikh Mohammed, Defendant's Exhibit 941, July 31, 2006, p. 51. During court proceedings involving Zacarias Moussaoui, the U.S. government submitted a 58-page "Substitution for the Testimony of Khalid Sheikh Mohammed," which contained a summary of key revelations Khalid Sheikh Mohammed made during interrogations. Adel was apparently not informed of plans for the September 11 attacks until April 2001.

73 Saif al-Adel to Mukhtar [Khalid Sheikh Mohammed], letter, June 13, 2002. Released by the Harmony Project, Combating Terrorism Center, West Point.

74 Brynjar Lia, *Architect of Global Jihad: The Life of Al-Qaida Strategist Abu Mus'ab al-Suri* (New York: Columbia University Press, 2008).

75 Abu Mus'ab al-Suri, "The Jihadi Experiences: The Military Theory of Open Fronts," *Inspire* 1431 (Winter 2010): 31.

76 Saif al-Adel's book *Chatter on the World's Rooftop*, which he wrote at the al-Farouq camp in Khowst in 1994, was published in *Asharq al-Awsat*, October 24–30, 2006.

77 Shaykh Abu al Walid al-Masri, "The Story of the Afghan Arabs . . . ," was serially published in *Asharq al-Awsat*, December 8–14, 2004.

78 Combating Terrorism Center, *Cracks in the Foundation: Leadership Schisms in Al-Qa'ida 1989–2006* (West Point, September 2007), p. 19.

79 Muhammad al-Shafi'i, "Al-Qa'ida's Leader Sayf-al-Adl Criticizes Al-Qa'ida Ele-

ments Security Indiscipline and Accuses Taliban of Betrayal," *Asharq al-Awsat*, October 29, 2003, p. 5.

80 Tenet, *At the Center of the Storm*, p. 187.

81 Crumpton, "Intelligence and War," p. 162.

CHAPTER 4: AL QA'IDA IN PAKISTAN

1 George Tenet, *At the Center of the Storm: My Years at the CIA*, with Bill Harlow (New York: HarperCollins, 2007), p. 179.

2 Verbatim transcript of Combatant Status Review Tribunal Hearing for ISN 10024, Khalid Sheikh Mohammed, March 10, 2007, p. 18.

3 Central Intelligence Agency, "Khalid Shaykh Muhammad: Preeminent Source on Al-Qa'ida" (Washington, D.C., July 2004), p. 1. Document declassified by CIA.

4 Tenet, *At the Center of the Storm*, p. 251.

5 Scott Shane, "Inside a 9/11 Mastermind's Interrogation," *New York Times*, June 22, 2008.

6 Pervez Musharraf, *In the Line of Fire: A Memoir* (New York: Free Press, 2006), p. 240.

7 Tenet, *At the Center of the Storm*, p. 251.

8 Henry A. Crumpton, "Intelligence and War: Afghanistan, 2001–2002," in Jennifer E. Sims and Burton Gerber, eds., *Transforming U.S. Intelligence* (Washington, D.C.: Georgetown University Press, 2005), p. 176.

9 Shane, "Inside a 9/11 Mastermind's Interrogation."

10 Tenet, *At the Center of the Storm*, p. 251.

11 Robert Grenier, interview with author, November 6, 2007.

12 Tenet, *At the Center of the Storm*, p. 183.

13 Wendy Chamberlin, interview with author, August 27, 2008.

14 Ibid.

15 On a firsthand account of the crisis negotiations, see Bruce Riedel, *American Diplomacy and the 1999 Kargil Summit at Blair House* (Philadelphia: Center for the Advanced Study of India, University of Pennsylvania, 2002).

16 Chamberlin interview, August 27, 2008.

17 See, for example, the negotiations as outlined in Bob Woodward, *Bush at War* (New York: Simon & Schuster, 2002), p. 59. Also see Musharraf, *In the Line of Fire*, pp. 201–7.

18 Chamberlin interview, August 27, 2008.

19 K. Alan Kronstadt, *Pakistan-U.S. Anti-Terrorism Cooperation* (Washington, D.C.: Congressional Research Service, March 2003), p. 12.

20 Former Defense Intelligence Agency analyst, interview with author, January 2010.

21 Grenier interview, November 6, 2007.

22 FBI official, interview with author, July 8, 2011.

23 Saif al-Adel, "Al-Zarqawi: The Second Generation of Al-Qa'ida," 2006. While this

document was not published in a formal book format, Adel nonetheless detailed Zarqawi's life after he was killed by U.S. forces in Iraq.

24 Combating Terrorism Center, *Profile of Saif al-Adel* (West Point, N.Y.: United States Military Academy, undated), p. 7.

25 "Detained al-Qa'ida Leader Sayf al-Adl Chronicles Al-Zarqawi's Rise in Organization," *Al-Quds al-'Arabi*, May 21–22, 2005.

26 Najwa bin Laden, Omar bin Laden, and Jean Sasson, *Growing Up Bin Laden: Osama's Wife and Son Take Us Inside Their Secret World* (New York: St. Martin's, 2009), pp. 63, 294–95.

27 Philip Mudd, interview with author, August 8, 2011.

28 Quoted by Andrew Nagorski, *The Greatest Battle* (New York: Simon & Schuster, 2007), pp. 150–51.

29 Gary Berntsen and Ralph Pezzullo, *Jawbreaker: The Attack on Bin Laden and Al-Qaeda: A Personal Account by the CIA's Key Field Commander* (New York: Crown, 2005), p. 305. Berntsen commanded the CIA team in Afghanistan in late 2001, taking over from Gary Schroen.

30 Rahimullah Yusufzai, "Fall of the Last Frontier?" *Newsline* (Pakistan), June 2002.

31 Grenier interview, November 6, 2007; International Crisis Group, *Pakistan's Tribal Areas: Appeasing the Militants* (Brussels: December 2006), p. 14.

32 Zaffar Abbas, "Operation Eyewash," *Herald* (Pakistan), August 2005, p. 64.

33 Chamberlin interview, August 27, 2008.

34 Pervez Musharraf, interview, *Frontline*, PBS, September 23, 2002. *Frontline* provided the author with a copy of the transcript.

35 Memorandum for John A. Rizzo, Senior Deputy General Counsel, Central Intelligence Agency, from the U.S. Department of Justice Office of Legal Counsel, "Re: Application of United States Obligations Under Article 16 of the Convention Against Torture to Certain Techniques That May Be Used in the Interrogation of High Value al Qaeda Detainees," May 30, 2005, p. 6. Document declassified by the U.S. Department of Justice.

36 Diary of Abu Zubaydah, undated.

37 Ibid.

38 Verbatim transcript of Combatant Status Review Tribunal Hearing for ISN 10016, Zayn al Abidin Muhammad Husayn [Abu Zubaydah], March 19, 2007.

39 Ibid.

40 U.S. Department of Defense, Office for the Administrative Review of the Detention of Enemy Combatants at the U.S. Naval Base Guantánamo Bay, Cuba, "Subject: Summary of Evidence for Combatant Status Review Tribunal—Husayn, Zayn al Abidin Muhammad [Abu Zubaydah]," March 19, 2007.

41 Verbatim transcript of Combatant Status Review Tribunal Hearing for ISN 10016.

42 Tenet, *At the Center of the Storm*, pp. 145–46.

43 Presidential Daily Briefing, "Bin Laden Determined to Strike in U.S," August 6, 2001. The document was declassified, with redacted portions, in 2004.

44 Grenier interview, November 6, 2007. On the role of the CIA, also see Musharraf, *In the Line of Fire*, p. 237.

45 Ali H. Soufan, *The Black Banners: The Inside Story of 9/11 and the War Against al-Qaeda* (New York: W. W. Norton, 2011), p. 374; Shane, "Inside a 9/11 Mastermind's Interrogation."

46 Ronald Kessler, *The Terrorist Watch: Inside the Desperate Race to Stop the Next Attack* (New York: Crown Forum, 2007), p. 46.

47 Ibid.

48 Tenet, *At the Center of the Storm*, p. 240.

49 Verbatim transcript of Combatant Status Review Tribunal Hearing for ISN 10016.

50 Ibid.; U.S. Department of Defense, "Subject: Summary of Evidence for Combatant Status Review Tribunal—Husayn."

51 Verbatim transcript of Combatant Status Review Tribunal Hearing for ISN 10016.

52 Soufan, *The Black Banners*.

53 Central Intelligence Agency, *Detainee Reporting Pivotal for the War Against Al-Qa'ida* (Washington, D.C., June 2005), p. ii. The document was declassified by the CIA.

54 Memorandum from REDACTED, DCI Counterterrorist Center to Steven B. Bradbury, Principal Deputy Assistant Attorney General, Office of Legal Counsel, "Re: Effectiveness of the CIA Counterintelligence Interrogation Techniques," March 2, 2005. Also see Memorandum for John A. Rizzo from the U.S. Department of Justice Office of Legal Counsel, May 30, 2005, p. 9.

55 Art Cummings, interview with author, September 2, 2011.

56 Kessler, *The Terrorist Watch*, pp. 96–97.

57 Human Rights Watch to President George W. Bush, letter, December 26, 2002.

58 Human Rights Watch, *The United States' "Disappeared": The CIA's Long-Term "Ghost Detainees"* (New York, October 2004).

59 Memorandum for John A. Rizzo from the U.S. Department of Justice Office of Legal Counsel, May 30, 2005.

60 Soufan, *The Black Banners*.

61 Central Intelligence Agency, *Detainee Reporting Pivotal for the War Against Al-Qa'ida*, p. 1.

62 Memorandum from REDACTED, DCI Counterterrorist Center to Steven B. Bradbury. Also see Memorandum for John A. Rizzo from the U.S. Department of Justice Office of Legal Counsel, p. 8.

63 Central Intelligence Agency, *Detainee Reporting Pivotal for the War Against Al-Qa'ida*, Appendix B: "Detainee Reporting on al-Qa'ida."

64 U.S. Department of Defense, "Biography of Ramzi Bin al-Shibh," undated.

65 The 9/11 Commission, *The 9/11 Commission Report: Final Report of the National Commission on Terrorist Attacks Upon the United States* (New York: W. W. Norton, 2004), p. 161.

66 Verbatim transcript of Combatant Status Review Tribunal Hearing for ISN 10013, Ramzi bin al-Shibh, March 9, 2007.

67 Ibid.

68 Yosri Fouda, "Masterminds of a Massacre—9/11—One Year On," *Australian*, September 9, 2002.

69 U.S. Department of Defense, "Biography of Ramzi Bin al-Shibh."

70 Those who pledged *bayat* to bin Laden frequently used this phrasing. See, for example, *United States of America v. Zacarias Moussaoui*, Cr. No. 01-455-A, Substitution for the Testimony of Khalid Sheikh Mohammed, Defendant's Exhibit 941, July 31, 2006, p. 54.

71 Verbatim transcript of Combatant Status Review Tribunal Hearing for ISN 10013.

72 Bin Laden, bin Laden, and Sasson, *Growing Up Bin Laden*, p. 253.

73 U.S. Department of Defense, "Biography of Ramzi Bin al-Shibh."

74 U.S. Department of Defense, "Subject: Summary of Evidence for Combatant Status Review Tribunal—Al-Shib, Ramzi bin," February 8, 2007.

75 U.S. Department of Defense, "Biography of Ramzi Bin al-Shibh."

76 U.S. Department of Defense, "Subject: Summary of Evidence for Combatant Status Review Tribunal—Al-Shib"; Tenet, *At the Center of the Storm*, p. 243.

77 Central Intelligence Agency, "Khalid Shaykh Muhammad: Preeminent Source on Al-Qa'ida" (Washington, D.C., July 2004), p. 2. Document declassified by the CIA.

78 Fouda, "Masterminds of a Massacre."

79 U.S. Department of Defense, "Biography of Ramzi Bin al-Shibh."

80 Ramzi bin al-Shibh, "The Truth About the New Crusade: A Ruling on the Killing of Women and Children of Non-Believers," draft document, late 2001; see Alan Cullison, "Inside Al-Qaeda's Hard Drive: Budget Squabbles, Baby Pictures, Office Rivalries—and the Path to 9/11," *Atlantic*, September 2004.

81 "Covering Al-Qa'ida, Covering Saddam."

82 Central Intelligence Agency, *Detainee Reporting Pivotal for the War Against Al-Qa'ida*.

83 Hasan Mansoor, "Operation Against Al-Qaeda Activists to Be Intensified in Cities," *Friday Times* (Lahore), April 1, 2003, p. 6.

84 U.S. Department of Defense, "Subject: Summary of Evidence for Combatant Status Review Tribunal—Al-Shib."

85 FBI agent, interview with author, August 2010. Also see Department of Defense, Office for the Administrative Review of the Detention of Enemy Combatants at the U.S. Naval Base Guantánamo Bay, Cuba, "Subject: Summary of Evidence for Combatant Status Review Tribunal—Mudwani, Musab Omar Ali," February 8, 2007; *Musab Omar Ali al Mudwani, et al. v. George W. Bush, President of the United States, et al.*, United States District Court for the District of Columbia, Civil Action No. 04-CV-1194 (HHK), October 6, 2004.

86 "FBIistan," *Rawalpindi Jang*, March 3, 2003, p. 3.

87 Tenet, *At the Center of the Storm*, p. 252.

88 Ibid.

89 Verbatim transcript of Combatant States Review Tribunal Hearing for ISN 10024, Khalid Sheikh Mohammed, March 10, 2007.

90 Central Intelligence Agency, *Detainee Reporting Pivotal for the War Against Al-Qa'ida*, p. i; Central Intelligence Agency, "Khalid Shaykh Muhammad," p. 1.

91 U.S. Department of Defense, "Biography of Majid Khan," undated.

92 Fax from REDACTED, DCI Counterterrorist Center, "Briefing Notes on the Value of Detainee Reporting," April 15, 2005. See Memorandum for John A. Rizzo from the U.S. Department of Justice Office of Legal Counsel, May 30, 2005, p. 10. Document declassified by the U.S. Department of Justice.

93 On Zubair, see U.S. Department of Defense, "Biography of Mohd Farik bin Amin," undated.

94 On the "building block" process involving Khalid Sheikh Mohammed, see Central Intelligence Agency, "Khalid Shaykh Muhammad," p. 3.

95 U.S. Department of Defense, "Biography of Hambali," undated.

96 Statement of Philip Mudd, deputy director, Counterterrorist Center, Central Intelligence Agency, at hearing on assessing America's counterterrorism capabilities, August 3, 2004, Senate Committee on Governmental Affairs, 108th Cong.

97 Saif al-Adel to Mukhtar [Khalid Sheikh Mohammed], letter, June 13, 2002. Released by the Harmony Project, Combating Terrorism Center, West Point.

98 Osama bin Laden to Mullah Omar, e-mail, October 3, 2001; see Cullison, "Inside Al-Qaeda's Hard Drive."

99 Saif al-Adel to Mukhtar [Khalid Sheikh Mohammed], letter, June 13, 2002.

CHAPTER 5: COMING TO AMERICA

1 Mujahideen Data Form, New Comers Form, filled out by Abu Abdallah al Muhajik (aka José Padilla), July 24, 2000; José Padilla Criminal Record, State of Florida.

2 Osama bin Laden videotape, released December 13, 2001.

3 Central Intelligence Agency, *Al-Qa'ida: Railways a High Priority Target* (Washington, D.C., April 2004). Document declassified by the CIA.

4 Central Intelligence Agency, *Khalid Shaykh Muhammad: Preeminent Source on Al-Qa'ida* (Washington, D.C., July 2004), p. 1. Document declassified by the CIA.

5 *United States of America v. Zacarias Moussaoui*, Cr. No. 01-455-A, Substitution for the Testimony of Khalid Sheikh Mohammed, Defendant's Exhibit 941, July 31, 2006, p. 38.

6 Central Intelligence Agency, *Al-Qa'ida Remains Intent on Defeating US Immigration Inspections* (Washington, D.C., May 30, 2003). Document declassified by the CIA.

7 Al Qa'ida operative Shari al-Masri, among others, was involved in the plot.

8 Several FBI officials, interview with author, July 2011.

9 Deborah Sontag, "In Padilla Wiretaps, Murky View of 'Jihad' Case," *New York Times*, January 4, 2007.

10 Amanda Ripley, "The Case of the Dirty Bomber," *Time*, June 16, 2002.

11 "José Padilla's Past," *Chicago Sun-Times*, June 12, 2002, p. 6.

12 José Padilla Criminal Record.

13 Wanda J. DeMarzo, Beth Reinhard, and Martin Merzer, "Suspect's Years in South Florida Were Troubled," *Miami Herald*, June 11, 2002, p. 1.

14 Declaration of Michael H. Mobbs, special adviser to the undersecretary of defense for policy, August 27, 2002, reproduced in Respondents' Response to, and Motion to Dismiss, the Amended Petition for a Writ of Habeas Corpus, *José Padilla v. George W. Bush*, United States District Court, Southern District of New York, No. 02 Civ. 4445, at Exhibit A.

15 Ripley, "The Case of the Dirty Bomber."

16 See statement of FBI special agent John T. Kavanaugh, Jr., in *United States of America v. Kifah Wael Jayyousi, Kassem Daher*, United States District Court, Southern District of Florida, Case Number 04-3565(RID), December 1, 2004.

17 *United States of America v. Adham Amin Hassoun, Kifah Jayyousi, and José Padilla, et al.* United States District Court, Southern District of Florida, Case No. 04-60001-CR-COOKE/Brown, November 29, 2007.

18 Marc Sagemen, *Understanding Terror Networks* (Philadelphia: University of Pennsylvania Press, 2004), p. 135.

19 Statement of John T. Kavanaugh, Jr.

20 *United States of America v. Adham Amin Hassoun, Mohamed Hesham Youssef, Kifah Wael Jayyousi, Kassem Daher, and José Padilla*, United States District Court, Southern District of Florida, Case No. 04-60001-CR-COOKE, November 17, 2005.

21 Ibid.

22 Ibid.

23 Ibid.

24 Declaration of Mr. Jeffrey N. Rapp, director, Joint Intelligence Task Force for Combating Terrorism, submitted for the court's consideration in the matter of *José Padilla v. Commander C.T. Hanft, USN, Commander, Consolidated Naval Brig*, Case Number 04-CV-2221-26AJ.

25 *U.S. v. Hassoun, Youssef, Jayyousi, Daher, and Padilla.*

26 U.S. Department of Justice, *Remarks of Deputy Attorney General James Comey Regarding José Padilla* (Washington, D.C., June 1, 2004).

27 Mujahideen Data Form, New Comers Form, filled out by Abu Abdallah al Muhajik.

28 Deputy Secretary of Defense Paul Wolfowitz to the Honorable James B. Comey, letter, "Summary of José Padilla's Activities with Al Qaeda," May 28, 2004.

29 *U.S. v. Hassoun, Youssef, Jayyousi, Daher, and Padilla.*

30 Ibid.

31 Wolfowitz to Comey.

32 Declaration of Mr. Jeffrey N. Rapp.

33 Wolfowitz to Comey.

34 See, for example, Sagemen, *Understanding Terror Networks*, pp. 120–21.

35 Declaration of Mr. Jeffrey N. Rapp.

36 Ibid.

37 Wolfowitz to Comey.

38 Declaration of Mr. Jeffrey N. Rapp.

39 *United States of America v. Binyam Ahmed Muhammad*, Charge: Conspiracy, Official Department of Defense Charge Sheet, 2005.

40 Wolfowitz to Comey.

41 Ibid.

42 U.S. government officials, interview with author, June 2011. The information came from the U.S. government interview with Abu Zubaydah, June 10–14, 2002.

43 U.S. government officials interview, June 2011. The information came from the U.S. government interview with Abu Zubaydah, December 21, 2002.

44 Wolfowitz to Comey.

45 U.S. Department of Defense, "Ammar al-Baluchi," undated.

46 Wolfowitz to Comey.

47 One of al Qa'ida's top explosives trainers, Sufiyan Barhoumi, also provided Padilla with some training on improvised explosive devices. Barhoumi was captured in a raid by Pakistani forces, along with Abu Zubaydah and other militants, at Zubaydah's guesthouse on March 28, 2002.

48 *U.S. v. Binyam Ahmed Muhammad*, Charge: Conspiracy.

49 Central Intelligence Agency, *Khalid Shaykh Muhammad*, p. i.

50 Central Intelligence Agency, *Detainee Reporting Pivotal for the War Against Al-Qa'ida* (Washington, D.C., June 2005), pp. i–ii. Document declassified by the CIA. Also see Ali H. Soufan, *The Black Banners: The Inside Story of 9/11 and the War Against al-Qaeda* (New York: W. W. Norton, 2011), p. 354.

51 Philip Mudd, interview with author, August 8, 2011.

52 *U.S. v. Binyam Ahmed Muhammad*, Charge: Conspiracy.

53 Ibid.

54 Wolfowitz to Comey.

55 *United States of America v. José Padilla*, United States District Court, Southern District of Florida, Miami Division, Case No. 04-60001-CR-COOKE.

56 U.S. Department of Justice, *José Padilla and Co-Defendants Convicted of Conspiracy to Murder Individuals Overseas, Providing Material Support to Terrorists* (Washington, D.C., August 16, 2007).

57 Art Cummings, interview with author, September 2, 2011.

58 Ibid.

59 *Republic of France v. Rama*, Magistrates' Court of Paris, File number 0413839059, Judgment, June 16, 2005.

60 U.S. government official, interview with author, June 2011.

61 Some media reports have suggested that individuals from the Finsbury Park Mosque promoted his interest in jihad and facilitated his travel to Afghanistan. But Reid has refuted this argument, noting that he principally attended the Brixton Mosque because it was only five minutes away from his aunt's house, where he lived. U.S. government official interview, June 2011.

62 *United States of America v. Moussaoui* (E.D. VA.), CR-No 01-455A, Stipulation Regarding Richard Reid, filed April 20, 2006.

63 *Republic of France v. Rama.*

64 U.S. government official, interview with author, July 2011.

65 *Republic of France v. Rama.*

66 *United States of America v. Richard Colvin Reid, et al.*, United States District Court, District of Massachusetts, 02-CR-10013-WGY, Government's Sentencing Memorandum, January 17, 2003.

67 U.S. Department of Defense, "Ammar al-Baluchi."

68 Alan Cullison and Andrew Higgins, "Account of Spy Trip on Kabul PC Matches Travels of Richard Reid," *Wall Street Journal*, January 16, 2002.

69 *U.S. v. Reid*, Government's Sentencing Memorandum.

70 Ibid.

71 *Republic of France v. Rama.*

72 *U.S. v. Reid*, Affidavit of Margaret G. Cronin, FBI special agent.

73 Ibid., Government's State of Relevant Facts Provided at Defendant's October 4, 2002, Rule 11 Hearing.

74 U.S. Department of Justice, *British National Indicted for Conspiring with "Shoe Bomber" Richard Reid* (Washington, D.C., October 4, 2004).

75 *U.S. v. Reid*, Government's State of Relevant Facts.

76 Ibid.

77 Cathy Booth Thomas, "Courage in the Air," *Time*, September 1, 2002.

78 *U.S. v. Reid*, Affidavit of Margaret G. Cronin.

79 Ibid, Government's Sentencing Memorandum.

80 Ibid.

81 Transcript of January 20, 2003, court hearing in which Richard Reid was sentenced to life in prison for his confessed plan to try and blow up a jetliner with explosives he had hidden in his shoes. *U.S. v. Reid*, Sentencing Transcript, January 30, 2003.

82 Thomas, "Courage in the Air."

83 Sahim Alwan, interview, *Frontline*, PBS, July 24, 2003.

84 *United States of America v. Yahya Goba, et al.*, United States District Court, Western District of New York, 02-CR-214-S, Affidavit of FBI Special Agent Edward J. Needham, September 2002.

85 Alwan interview.

86 Mitchell D. Silber and Arvin Bhatt, *Radicalization in the West: The Homegrown Threat* (New York: New York City Police Department, Intelligence Division, 2007), p. 59. Also see Mitchell D. Silber, *The Al Qaeda Factor: Plots Against the West* (Philadelphia: University of Pennsylvania Press, 2012).

87 Alwan interview.

88 Federal Bureau of Investigation, *Terrorist Training and Recruitment of CONUS Subjects: Lackawanna, Portland, and Northern Virginia* (Washington, D.C.: FBI Counterterrorism Division, October 30, 2006). Document unclassified.

89 New York State Office of Homeland Security, *Terrorist Recruitment: Where Do the Jihadis Come From?* (New York, 2005), p. 5. Document unclassified.

90 Silber and Bhatt, *Radicalization in the West*, p. 61.

91 *U.S. v. Goba, et al.*, Affidavit of FBI Special Agent Edward J. Needham.

92 U.S. Department of Justice, *Yasein Taher Pleads Guilty to Providing Material Support to Al Qaeda* (Washington, D.C., May 12, 2003).

93 U.S. Department of Justice, *Mukhtar al-Bakri Sentenced for Providing Material Support to al Qaeda* (Washington, D.C., December 3, 2003).

94 *U.S. v. Goba, et al.*, Affidavit of FBI Special Agent Edward J. Needham.

95 U.S. Department of Justice, *Yasein Taher Pleads Guilty*.

96 Silber and Bhatt, *Radicalization in the West*, p. 62.

97 Federal Bureau of Investigation, *Terrorist Training and Recruitment of CONUS Subjects*.

98 *U.S. v. Goba, et al.*, Affidavit of FBI Special Agent Edward J. Needham.

99 Ibid.; U.S. Department of Justice, *Mukhtar al-Bakri Sentenced*.

100 Central Intelligence Agency, *Al-Qa'ida Remains Intent on Defeating U.S. Immigration Inspections* (Washington, D.C., 2003). Declassified by the CIA.

101 FBI official, interview with author, August 20, 2011. The information comes from a March 2003 debriefing of Khalid Sheikh Mohammed.

102 U.S. Department of Defense, "Biography of Majid Khan," undated.

103 Ibid.

104 Ibid.

105 Central Intelligence Agency, *Detainee Reporting Pivotal for the War Against Al-Qa'ida*.

106 Art Cummings interview, September 2, 2011.

107 Senior FBI officials interview, June 2011.

CHAPTER 6: AL QA'IDA IN IRAQ

1 "Al-Iraqiyah Carries Confessions by Perpetrators of Blasts in Baghdad," Baghdad Al-Iraqiyah television, January 25, 2010.

2 "Al Zarqawi's Group Publishes Fourth Part of 'Biographies of Eminent Martyrs' Series," Open Source Center (GMP20051128371002), November 22, 2005; "Al-Iraqiyah Carries Confessions."

3 "The Secrets of History: Zarqawi As I Knew Him," a treatise written by Shaykh Maysarat al-Gharib, December 2007.

4 Senior FBI official, interview with author, December 18, 2010.

5 "Al-Iraqiyah Carries Confessions."

6 Ibid. On the suicide bomber, whose name appeared to be Abu Faridah, see "'Biographies of Eminent Martyrs' Series Profiles 5 of Al Qa'ida's 'Martyrs' in Iraq," Open Source Center (GMP20070413668001), April 9, 2007.

7 "I Can't Find My Colleagues," BBC, August 19, 2003.

8 The Coalition Provisional Authority (CPA) administrator, L. Paul Bremer, was

briefed on the bombing by the FBI office head, Tom Fuentes. See Ambassador L. Paul Bremer III, *My Year in Iraq: The Struggle to Build a Future of Hope*, with Malcolm McConnell (New York: Simon & Schuster, 2006), p. 141.

9 George Packer, *The Assassins' Gate: America in Iraq* (New York: Farrar, Straus and Giroux, 2005), p. 217.

10 Bremer, *My Year in Iraq*, p. 141.

11 L. Paul Bremer III, Administrator of the Coalition Provisional Authority, to Mrs. de Mello, letter, August 21, 2003.

12 "Baghdad UN Bomb Blast 'Hindered the UK's Work,'" BBC, December 17, 2009.

13 Jean-Charles Brisard, *Zarqawi: The New Face of Al-Qaeda* (New York: Other Press, 2005).

14 U.S. Department of Defense, "Biography of Zayn al-'Abidin Abu Zubaydah," undated.

15 Joseph Felter and Brian Fishman, *Al Qa'ida's Foreign Fighters in Iraq: A First Look at the Sinjar Records* (West Point, N.Y.: Harmony Project, Combating Terrorism Center, 2007), p. 4.

16 U.S. Department of Defense, "Biography of Zayn al-'Abidin Abu Zubaydah."

17 Abu Mus'ab al-Zarqawi to al Qa'ida leaders, letter, January 2004. Released by the Harmony Project, Combating Terrorism Center, West Point.

18 John Negroponte, interview with author, August 11, 2011.

19 Coalition Provisional Authority, "CPA Fusion Cell Threat Warning," June 4, 2003.

20 Paul Bremer to Jaymie Durnan, e-mail, "Subject: Message for SecDef," June 30, 2003.

21 Coalition Provisional Authority, "Summary: Bomb-Making Tips, Mukhabarat Habits, Views from the Street," July 15, 2003.

22 Bremer to Durnan.

23 Coalition Provisional Authority, "Presidential Update," May 29, 2003.

24 L. Paul Bremer, interview with author, November 15, 2007.

25 Ibid.; Clayton McManaway, interview with author, December 12, 2007.

26 Ministerial Committee for National Security, "Curtailing Syrian Assistance to Iraqi Extremists: Draft Analysis of Options," May 2004.

27 Fred Smith to the Administrator, info memo, "Subject: Update on May 20th Meeting of Ministerial Committee for National Security," May 19, 2004; Fred Smith to the Administrator, info memo, "Subject: Materials for May 29th Meeting of Ministerial Committee for National Security," May 27, 2004; Frank Miller, interview with author, June 6, 2008; Ministerial Committee for National Security, "Security Situation—Updates and Analysis," May 6, 2004.

28 Ronald E. Neumann to the Administrator, info memo, "Subject: Highlights of the June 24th MCNS Meeting," June 24, 2004.

29 Coalition Provisional Authority, "Briefing Materials for the New Iraqi Leadership: Key Issues," May 2004.

30 Coalition Provisional Authority, Working Group on Threat from Saddamists,

"The Evolving Security Threat/Check List, Conclusions and Actions," May 10, 2004.

31 U.S. Department of State, Bureau of Intelligence and Research, Office of Research, "Iraqis Offer Dim Evaluation of Reconstruction Effort Thus Far," August 22, 2003.

32 "Iraqi Impressions of Coalition Forces and the Security Situation in Iraq: Office of Research Survey Results from 7 Cities in Iraq & Preliminary Results from Gallup Baghdad Survey," September 30, 2003.

33 Office of Policy Planning for the Authority, info memo, "Subject: 30 Day Review of the CPA '60-Day Plan,'" September 17, 2003.

34 Meghan O'Sullivan through Scott Carpenter to the Administrator, info memo, "Re: Readahead for August 23 Meeting with the GC," August 21, 2003.

35 Darrell Trent to the Administrator, info memo, "Subject: Ministry of Transportation Issues Update," December 15, 2003.

36 United States Central Command to Secretary of Defense, memo, "Subject: Energy Systems Stability and Security in Iraq," August 28, 2003.

37 Brief on Iraq Security and Military Issues, NSC Meeting, July 1, 2003.

38 McManaway interview, December 12, 2007.

39 Bremer interview, November 15, 2007.

40 Art Cummings, interview with author, September 2, 2011.

41 Eliza Manningham-Buller, "The International Terrorist Threat to the UK," speech, Queen Mary's College, London, November 9, 2006.

42 Cummings interview, September 2, 2011.

43 Saif al-Adel, "Jihadist Biography of the Slaughtering Leader Abu Mus'ab al-Zarqawi," Open Source Center (GMP20090817342001), June 20, 2009.

44 Zarqawi to al Qa'ida leaders.

45 Abu Bark Naji, *The Management of Savagery: The Most Critical Stage Through Which the Umma Will Pass*, trans. William McCants (Cambridge, Mass.: John M. Olin Institute for Strategic Studies, Harvard University, 2006), p. 24.

46 Bremer interview, November 15, 2007.

47 Pew Global Attitudes Project, *The Great Divide: How Westerners and Muslims View Each Other* (Washington, D.C., June 2006), p. 61.

48 Zarqawi to al Qa'ida leaders.

49 "The Secrets of History: Zarqawi As I Knew Him."

50 Zarqawi to al Qa'ida leaders.

51 Statement from Osama bin Laden, December 27, 2004. Bin Laden's endorsement read, "It should be known that Mujahid brother Abu-Mus'ab al-Zarqawi is the Amir of the Tanzim Qa'idat al-Jihad fi Bilad al-Rafidayn. The brothers in the group there should heed his orders and obey him in all that which is good."

52 Felter and Fishman, *Al Qa'ida's Foreign Fighters in Iraq.*

53 Brian Fishman, ed., *Bombers, Bank Accounts, and Bleedout: Al Qa'ida's Road In and Out of Iraq* (West Point, N.Y.: Harmony Project, Combating Terrorism Center, 2008), pp. 50, 70.

54 Ibid., p. 34.

55 See, for example, International Crisis Group, *In Their Own Words: Reading the Iraqi Insurgency*, Middle East Report 50 (Brussels, February 2006).

56 Negroponte interview, August 11, 2011.

57 Sayyid Imam Abd al-Aziz al-Sharif, "Rationalization of Jihad," part 15, December 26, 2007.

58 "Fatwa by 26 Saudi Ulema Urges 'Resistance' Against 'Occupation' Forces in Iraq," Al Jazeera, November 6, 2004.

59 Shaykh Bin-Fahd Salman al-Awdah, interview with Salim al-Shatti, Kuwaiti Al-Ra'i, March 1, 2007.

60 Bremer, *My Year in Iraq*, pp. 280–81.

61 L. Paul Bremer III to Commanding General, Combined Joint Task Force Seven, memo, "Subject: Detainee Policy Reform," April 15, 2004.

62 Donald Rumsfeld to Jerry Bremer and General John Abizaid, memo, "Subject: Detainee Operations in Iraq," April 30, 2004.

63 Muhyi K. Al Kateeb, Secretary General of the Governing Council, to Ambassador Paul Bremer, letter, May 13, 2004.

64 Lydia Khalil to the Administrator, memo, "Subject Readahead for May 12 GC-CPA Meeting," May 12, 2004.

65 Condoleezza Rice to POTUS, memo, "Subject: Telephone Call with Shaykh Ghazi Al-Yawr of Iraq," May 17, 2004.

66 Edward C. Schmults to the Deputy Administrator/Chief Policy Adviser, memo, "Subject: Compensation for Abu Ghraib Abuse Victims," May 8, 2004.

67 Edward C. Schmults to the Administrator, info memo, "Subject: Abu Ghraib Destruction Bullet-Point Timeline," May 23, 2004; Edward C. Schmults to the Administrator, action memo, "Subject: Abu Ghraib Draw-Down and Destruction Plan," May 26, 2004.

68 Jessica LeCroy to the Administrator, memo, "Subject: Your Question on Suicide-Bomber in Arbil," March 6, 2004. Attached to the memo was a draft cable written by Kris Keele, CPA Baghdad to SECDEF WASHDC SECSTATE WASHDC NSC WASHDC CJCS CDR USCENTCOM AMEMBASSY ROME USDA WASH DC, "Subject: CPA 0703: March 4 Meeting with KRG Minister of Interior Karim Sinjari," March 6, 2004.

69 Robert A. Pape and James K. Feldman, *Cutting the Fuse: The Explosion of Global Suicide Terrorism and How to Stop It* (Chicago: University of Chicago Press, 2010).

70 The data include attacks against all types of targets (civil and military). Data derived from Department of Defense, Coalition Provisional Authority, Daily Threat Updates (unclassified).

71 U.S. Department of Justice, *Federal Bureau of Investigation: Legal Attaché Program, Audit Report 04-18* (Washington, D.C.: Office of the Inspector General, Audit Division, March 2004), p. i.

72 Art Cummings, interview, *Frontline*, PBS, June 5, 2006.

73 National Intelligence Council, *The Terrorist Threat to the U.S. Homeland,*

National Intelligence Estimate (Washington, D.C., July 2007), p. 6. Document declassified.

74 See, for example, Peter Bergen and Paul Cruikshank, "The Iraq Effect: The War in Iraq and Its Impact on the War on Terrorism," *Mother Jones*, March/April 2007.

75 Ibid.

76 Pew Global Attitudes Project, *U.S. Image Up Slightly, But Still Negative* (Washington, D.C., June 2005), p. 41.

CHAPTER 7: THE MADRID ATTACKS

1 The Spanish text is "En homenaje y agradecimiento a todos las victimas del terrorismo cuya memoria permanece viva en nuestra convivencia y la enriquece constantemente. Los ciudadanos de Madrid, 11 de marzo de 2005." Author's translation.

2 The Spanish text is "A todos los que supieron cumplir con su deber en el auxilio a las victimas de los atentados del 11 de marzo de 2004 y a todos los ciudadanos anónimos que las ayudaron. Que el recuerdo de las víctimas y el ejemplar comportamiento del pueblo de Madrid permanezcan siempre."

3 Outside of continental Europe, the largest recent terrorist attack in European history had been the bombing of Pan Am Flight 103 over Lockerbie, Scotland, which killed 259 passengers and crew on board and 11 people on the ground.

4 Furgoneta Renault Kangoo, 0576 BRX, in Juzgado Central de Instrucción No. 6, Audiencia Nacional, Madrid, Sumario No. 20/2004, pp. 86–92. Also see Inspección técnico policial in Juzgado Central de Instrucción No. 6, Audiencia Nacional, Madrid, Sumario No. 20/2004, pp. 149–50.

5 Juzgado Central de Instrucción No. 6, Audiencia Nacional, Madrid, Sumario No. 20/2004, p. 1.

6 Funcionamiento del artefacto in Juzgado Central de Instrucción No. 6, Audiencia Nacional, Madrid, Sumario No. 20/2004, pp. 88–90.

7 Juzgado Central de Instrucción No. 97, Audiencia Nacional, Madrid, Sumario No. 20/2004, p. 31,840.

8 Informe técnico policial 112-IT-04, realizado por la sección de actuaciones especiales, in Juzgado Central de Instrucción No. 6, Audiencia Nacional, Madrid, Sumario No. 20/2004, p. 226.

9 Andrea Elliott, "Where Boys Grow Up to Be Jihadis," *New York Times*, November 25, 2007.

10 J.A.R., "14 identidades de un terrorista El Chino tenía una tarjeta de residencia autentica perteneciente a una partida de 300 robada en la Fabrica de Moneda y Timbre," *El País*, November 22, 2004.

11 Elliott, "Where Boys Grow Up to Be Jihadis."

12 Jorge A. Rodriguez, "Tres 'celulas' terroristas participaron en el 11-M, que fue financiado con droga," *El País*, April 15, 2004; Jorge A. Rodriguez, "El Tunecino declaré a España enemiga del islam por acudir a la guerra de Irak," *El País*, December 4, 2004.

13 Lawrence Wright, "The Terror Web," *The New Yorker*, August 2, 2004.

14 Testigo protegido, S 20-04-W-18 (17 de marzo de 2005) in Juzgado Central de Instrucción No. 6, Audiencia Nacional, Madrid, Sumario No. 20/2004, p. 1219.

15 Mitchell D. Silber and Arvin Bhatt, *Radicalization in the West: The Homegrown Threat* (New York: New York City Police Department, Intelligence Division, 2007), p. 39.

16 José María Irujo, *El agujero: España invadida por la yihad* (Madrid: Aguilar, 2005), p. 266.

17 Rodriguez, "El Tunecino declaré a España enemiga del islam por acudir a la guerra de Irak."

18 Europol, *Terrorist Activity in the European Union: Situation and Trends Report* (The Hague: Interpol, December 2003), p. 37.

19 Silber and Bhatt, *Radicalization in the West*, p. 39.

20 *'Iraq al-Jihad: Amal wa Akhtar: Tahlil al-Waqi' wa Istishraf li-l-Mustaqbal wa Khatawat 'Amaliyyah 'ala Tariq al-Jihad al-Mubarak* (Iraq the Jihad: Hopes and Dangers—Analysis of Facts and View of the Future and Operational Steps Toward the Blessed Jihad), 2003.

21 Silber and Bhatt, *Radicalization in the West*, p. 24.

22 Rodríguez, "Tres 'células' terroristas participaron en el 11-M, que fue financiado con droga."

23 "Suspect's Tapped Phone Calls Only Translated After Spain Bombings," *El País*, May 10, 2004.

24 José Maria Irujo, "Los hombres de Abu Dahdah y el 11-M," *El País*, June 20, 2004.

25 Fernando Reinares and Rogelio Alonso, "Maghreb Immigrants Becoming Suicide Terrorists: A Case Study on Religious Radicalization Processes in Spain," in Ami Pedahzur, ed., *Root Causes of Suicide Terrorism: The Globalization of Martyrdom* (London: Routledge, 2006), p. 183.

26 Much of this material was discovered after Jamal Zougam was arrested on March 13, 2004. His hard drive was seized; he was in possession of material on SIM cards, service message blocks, and other ways to secure phone and computer use.

27 R.M.R.: Maquinista-conduct del tren de la Calle Téllez (13 de Julio de 2005), in Juzgado Central de Instrucción No. 6, Audiencia Nacional, Madrid, Sumario No. 20/2004, pp. 3–4.

28 Mar Roman, "190 Killed in Madrid Trains 'Massacre,'" *Independent* (UK), March 11, 2004.

29 Tim Brown, Lindsay McGarvie, Steve McKenzie, and Russell Findlay, "Madrid Death Toll 200: We Have Buried Our Son," *Sunday Mail* (UK), March 14, 2004.

30 "The Day My Wife Was Snatched Away," BBC, March 13, 2004.

31 U.S. Department of State, *Spain: March Bombings Cast Shadow Over Parliamentary Vote and Relations with U.S.* (Washington, D.C.: Office of Research, July 22, 2004), p. 1.

32 Ministerio del Interior, *Víctimas de ETA* (Madrid: Oficina de Communicación, 2010).

33 Silber and Bhatt, *Radicalization in the West*, p. 24.

34 José María Irujo, *El agujero: España invadida por la yihad* (Madrid: Aguilar, 2005); Fernando Reinares, "After the Madrid Bombings: Internal Security Reforms and Prevention of Global Terrorism in Spain," *Studies in Conflict and Terrorism* 32, no. 5 (May 2009): 367–88.

35 Quoted in Reinares, "After the Madrid Bombings," p. 368.

36 See, for example, Artefacto desactivado en el parquet Azorín, in Juzgado Central de Instrucción No. 6, Audiencia Nacional, Madrid, Sumario No. 20/2004, pp. 87–90.

37 See various sections of Juzgado Central de Instrucción No. 6, Audiencia Nacional, Madrid, Sumario No. 20/2004.

38 Ibid., pp. 93–97, 190–203.

39 Funcionario del C.N.P. con carné in Juzgado Central de Instrucción No. 6, Audiencia Nacional, Madrid, Sumario No. 20/2004, p. 201.

40 Informe pericial 2005D0456 in Juzgado Central de Instrucción No. 6, Audiencia Nacional, Madrid, Sumario No. 20/2004, p. 284.

41 Décimo: Actuación policial con relación a la vivienda sita en la calle Carmen Martín Gaite de Leganés el 3 de abril de 2004, in Juzgado Central de Instrucción No. 6, Audiencia Nacional, Madrid, Sumario No. 20/2004, p. 197; Reinares and Alonso, "Maghreb Immigrants Becoming Suicide Terrorists," pp. 193–94.

42 Wright, "The Terror Web," p. 46.

43 See various sections of Juzgado Central de Instrucción No. 6, Audiencia Nacional, Madrid, Sumario No. 20/2004, such as pp. 93–97, 190–203.

44 Wright, "The Terror Web," p. 47.

45 Philip Mudd, interview with author, August 8, 2011.

46 Philip Mudd, "Rethinking Objectives in Afghanistan," *Foreign Policy*, November 17, 2010.

47 Osama bin Laden audiotape, "A Message to the Americans," Al Jazeera, October 18, 2003. On Spain and radical Islamic groups, see Manuel R. Torres Sorriano, "Spain as an Object of Jihadist Propaganda," *Studies in Conflict and Terrorism* 32, no. 11 (November 2009): 933–52.

48 Osama bin Laden audiotape, "Message to Europeans," Al Jazeera, April 15, 2004.

49 Bernard Lewis, *The Crisis of Islam: Holy War and Unholy Terror* (New York: Random House, 2004), pp. 34–35, 51.

50 Quoted in Fernando Reinares, "The Madrid Bombings and Global Jihadism," *Survival* 52, no. 2 (April-May 2010): 96.

51 "Islamist Website Confirm Death of Key Player in Spanish Train Bombing," *El País*, May 8, 2010.

52 Testigo protegido, S 20-04-W-18 (17 de marzo de 2005), in Juzgado Central de Instrucción No. 6, Audiencia Nacional, Madrid, Sumario No. 20/2004, p. 1218.

53 Spanish government officials, interview with author, November 2010.

54 Juzgado Central de Instrucción No. 17, Audiencia Nacional, Madrid, Sumario No. 20/2004, p. 4414.

55 See, for example, Reinares, "The Madrid Bombings and Global Jihadism," pp. 83–104.

56 George Tenet, *At the Center of the Storm: My Years at the CIA*, with Bill Harlow (New York: HarperCollins, 2007), p. 245.

57 Senior FBI official, interview with author, December 18, 2010. Also see "Remarks by President George W. Bush," commencement address, United States Coast Guard Academy, New London, Connecticut, May 23, 2007.

58 Tenet, *At the Center of the Storm*, p. 240.

59 Senior FBI official interview, December 18, 2010. Also see "Remarks by President George W. Bush."

60 Senior FBI official interview, December 18, 2010.

61 Department of Defense, Office for the Administrative Review of the Detention of Enemy Combatants at the U.S. Naval Base Guantánamo Bay, Cuba, "Subject: Summary of Evidence for Combatant Status Review Tribunal—al Libi, Abu Faraj," February 8, 2007.

62 Federal Bureau of Investigation and Department of Homeland Security, "Capture of Al-Qa'ida Leader Highlights Trends in International Jihadist Movement and Implications for U.S. Counterterrorism Efforts," June 30, 2005. Unclassified document.

63 U.S. Department of Defense, "Biography of Abu Faraj al-Libi," undated.

64 Department of Defense, "Subject: Summary of Evidence for Combatant Status Review Tribunal—al Libi."

65 On Pakistani operations in South Waziristan, see Seth G. Jones and C. Christine Fair, *Counterinsurgency in Pakistan* (Santa Monica, Calif.: RAND, 2010), pp. 46–56.

66 Pervez Musharraf, *In the Line of Fire: A Memoir* (New York: Free Press, 2006), p. 256.

67 Ibid., p. 253.

68 Ibid., p. 260.

69 Ibid.

70 Rahimullah Yusufzai, "How al-Libbi Was Nabbed," *News* (Pakistan), May 6, 2005.

71 Musharraf, *In the Line of Fire*, pp. 260–61.

72 Yusufzai, "How al-Libbi Was Nabbed." Also see, for example, Ismail Khan, "Al Libbi Held in Mardan," *Dawn* (Pakistan), May 5, 2005.

73 "Burqa Trap Set for Terror Suspect," BBC, May 5, 2005.

74 Musharraf, *In the Line of Fire*, p. 258.

75 Transcript of Open Session Combatant Status Review Tribunal Hearing for ISN 10017, Abu Faraj al-Libi, March 9, 2007; Department of Defense, "Subject: Summary of Evidence for Combatant Status Review Tribunal—Al Libi."

76 "Spanish Muslim Group Declares Osama bin Laden Has Forsaken Islam," *National Post*, March 12, 2005.

77 Dominic Bailey, "Prayers and Fears of Madrid's Muslims," BBC, March 16, 2004.

78 Reinares, "After the Madrid Bombings," p. 371.

79 Senior FBI official, interview with author, January 10, 2011.

80 Intelligence and Security Committee, *Could 7/7 Have Been Prevented? Review of the Intelligence on the London Terrorist Attacks on 7 July 2005*, Cm 7617 (London: Her Majesty's Stationery Office, May 2009), p. 28.

81 Intelligence and Security Committee, *Report into the London Terrorist Attacks on 7 July 2005*, Cm 6785 (London: Her Majesty's Stationery Office, 2006), p. 31.

CHAPTER 8: THE LONDON ATTACKS

1 "Full Text of July 7 Widow's Interview," *Sky News*, July 27, 2007.

2 Ibid.

3 Intelligence and Security Committee, *Report into the London Terrorist Attacks on 7 July 2005*, Cm 6785 (London: Her Majesty's Stationery Office, 2006), p. 9.

4 Ibid., p. 45.

5 Martyrdom video produced by Mohammad Sidique Khan, 2005.

6 See, for example, Office for National Statistics, *Census 2001: Leeds—the Big Picture* (London: Her Majesty's Stationery Office, 2002).

7 "Full Text of July 7 Widow's Interview."

8 David McNab, "Where the New Kid Is Old Hat," *Times Educational Supplement*, April 26, 2002.

9 "Full Text of July 7 Widow's Interview."

10 Mitchell D. Silber and Arvin Bhatt, *Radicalization in the West: The Homegrown Threat* (New York: New York City Police Department, Intelligence Division, 2007), pp. 33–34.

11 Shiv Malik, "My Brother the Bomber," *Prospect* (UK), no. 135, June 30, 2007.

12 Intelligence and Security Committee, *Could 7/7 Have Been Prevented? Review of the Intelligence on the London Terrorist Attacks on 7 July 2005*, Cm 7617 (London: Her Majesty's Stationery Office, May 2009), p. 17.

13 Silber and Bhatt, *Radicalization in the West*, pp. 40–41.

14 "Full Text of July 7 Widow's Interview."

15 *BBC News*, "Profile: Shehzad Tanweer" (London, 2005).

16 Ibid.

17 Intelligence and Security Committee, *Could 7/7 Have Been Prevented?*, p. 17.

18 House of Commons, *Report of the Official Account of the Bombings in London on 7th July 2005*, HC 1087 (London: Her Majesty's Stationery Office, May 2006), p. 2.

19 *BBC News*, "Profile: Germaine Lindsay" (London, 2005).

20 Intelligence and Security Committee, *Could 7/7 Have Been Prevented?*, p. 17.

21 Jamie Pyatt, "From an Angel to the Devil," *Sun*, September 24, 2005.

22 Silber and Bhatt, *Radicalization in the West*, pp. 40–41; Amy Waldman, "Seething Unease Shaped British Bombers' Newfound Zeal," *New York Times*, July 31, 2005.

23 Court transcript, Nighttime recording of occupants in Flat 4, 56 Hencroft Street, Slough, March 23, 2004.

24 Intelligence and Security Committee, *Could 7/7 Have Been Prevented?*, p. 7.

25 Ibid., p. 9.

26 Court transcript, Nighttime recording of occupants in Flat 4, 56 Hencroft Street, Slough, February 21, 2004.

27 Intelligence and Security Committee, *Could 7/7 Have Been Prevented?*, p. 9.

28 Court transcript, Nighttime recording of occupants in Flat 4, 56 Hencroft Street, Slough, March 23, 2004.

29 Intelligence and Security Committee, *Could 7/7 Have Been Prevented?*, p. 11.

30 Ibid., p. 12.

31 Intelligence and Security Committee, *Report into the London Terrorist Attacks on 7 July 2005*, p. 26.

32 See, for example, Central Intelligence Agency, *Al-Qa'ida: Railways a High Priority Target* (Washington, D.C., April 2004). Document declassified by the CIA.

33 Intelligence and Security Committee, *Report into the London Terrorist Attacks on 7 July 2005*, p. 23.

34 Ibid., p. 9.

35 Intelligence and Security Committee, *Could 7/7 Have Been Prevented?* p. 41.

36 Intelligence and Security Committee, *Report into the London Terrorist Attacks on 7 July 2005*, pp. 8, 33.

37 Intelligence and Security Committee, *Could 7/7 Have Been Prevented?*, p. 51.

38 Ronald Kessler, *The Terrorist Watch: Inside the Desperate Race to Stop the Next Attack* (New York: Crown Forum, 2007), p. 198.

39 Winston S. Churchill, *The Story of the Malakand Field Force: An Episode of Frontier War* (London: Leo Cooper, 1989), p. 3.

40 Senior FBI official, interview with author, February 4, 2011.

41 Daniel McGrory et al., "Meeting of Murderous Minds on the Backstreets of Lahore," *Times* (London), May 1, 2007.

42 Mohammad Sidique Khan's 2001 trip to Afghanistan and Pakistan was detailed during court trials in 2008 at Kingston Crown Court. See, for example, "7/7 Accused Had Afghan Training," BBC, May 20, 2008.

43 Court transcript, Nighttime recording of occupants in automobile, February 21, 2004.

44 Court transcript, Nighttime recording of occupants in Flat 4, 56 Hencroft Street, Slough, February 21, 2004.

45 Court documents; photographs of Shehzad Tanweer's and Mohammad Siddique Khan's passports, visas, and filed documents.

46 Mobarik A. Virk, "London Bombers Came to Karachi," *News* (Pakistan), July 19, 2004.

47 House of Commons, *Report of the Official Account of the Bombings in London on 7th July 2005*, p. 2.

48 McGrory et al., "Meeting of Murderous Minds."

49 Maqbool Ahmed, "Intelligence Agencies Focusing on Hotels," *Daily Times* (Pakistan), July 19, 2005; Virk, "London Bombers Came to Karachi."

50 Martyrdom video produced by Mohammad Sidique Khan, 2005.

51 Martyrdom video produced by Shehzad Tanweer, 2005.

52 Andy Hayman, *The Terrorist Hunters: The Ultimate Inside Story of Britain's Fight Against Terror*, with Margaret Gilmore (London: Bantam, 2009), pp. 104–5.

53 For descriptions of 18 Alexandra Grove, see ibid., pp. 97–98.

54 House of Commons, *Report of the Official Account of the Bombings in London*, p. 2.

55 Hayman, *The Terrorist Hunters*, p. 98.

56 House of Commons, *Report of the Official Account of the Bombings in London*, p. 2.

57 Intelligence and Security Committee, *Report into the London Terrorist Attacks on 7 July 2005*, p. 11.

58 House of Commons, *Report of the Official Account of the Bombings in London*, p. 2.

59 Pyatt, "One Day I'll Have to Tell the Children."

60 House of Commons, *Report of the Official Account of the Bombings in London*, p. 2.

61 "Full Text of July 7 Widow's Interview."

62 The timeline of the bombers' actions comes from House of Commons, *Report of the Official Account of the Bombings in London*, pp. 2–6.

63 Ibid.

64 Court transcript, recording of Hasib Hussain's telephone messages, July 7, 2005.

65 House of Commons, *Report of the Official Account of the Bombings in London*, p. 2.

66 Liza Pulman, "Me and My Bad Karma," *Guardian*, July 11, 2005.

67 Video statement by Ayman al-Zawahiri, Al Jazeera, September 1, 2005.

68 Video statement by Ayman al-Zawahiri, Al Jazeera, September 19, 2005.

69 John Negroponte, interview with author, August 11, 2011.

70 Art Cummings, interview, *Frontline*, PBS, June 5, 2006.

71 Marie Woolf, "Sir Iqbal Sacranie: 'There Can Never Be Justification for Killing Civilians,'" *Independent* (UK), July 18, 2005.

72 Jamie Pyatt, "Poisoned at the Mosque," *Sun* (UK), September 23, 2005.

73 Pyatt, "One Day I'll Have to Tell the Children."

74 Statement released by family of Hasib Hussain, July 2005.

75 Statement released by Bashir Ahmed, July 2005.

76 Video produced by Mohammad Sidique Khan, 2005.

77 "Full Text of July 7 Widow's Interview."

78 Will from Mohammad Sidique Khan, 2005.

79 "Full Text of July 7 Widow's Interview."

CHAPTER 9: RESURGENCE IN PAKISTAN

1 The preceding quotes are from Ayman al-Zawahiri and Adam Yahiye Gadahn, "An Invitation to Islam," video, As-Sahab Media, September 2006.

2 Federal Bureau of Investigation, *Adam Yahiye Gadahn: Most Wanted Terrorist* (Washington, D.C., October 11, 2006).

3 Zawahiri and Gadahn, "An Invitation to Islam."

4 National Intelligence Council, *The Terrorist Threat to the Homeland* (Washington, D.C., July 2007), p. 1.

5 Yahiye Adam Gadahn, "Becoming Muslim," letter, website of the Muslim Student Association of the University of Southern California, ca. November 1995. The University of Southern California later removed the Gadahn letter from its website.

6 Karen Darby, interview with Patrick the Lama, "Subject: The Music Group 'Beat of the Earth,'" undated.

7 Raffi Khatchadourian, "Azzam the American," *The New Yorker*, January 22, 2007.

8 Spinoza Ray Prozak (aka Chris Blanc), "Adam Yahiye (Y.A.) Gadahn: An Appeal," undated. This note was an attempt to deter any additional interviews from U.S. government officials. As he explained, "Note to Feds: I have no idea where he is, and have had no contact with the man for nearly a decade. Further, I have no idea where to find him, or what he has been doing in this time. Not only that, but I don't know anyone else who knows him, or ever saw a picture of him until you posted yours. Also, at the time he knew me I was opposed to all religion, including Islam, so he never mentioned a word of this. In summary, all that I know about Y. A. Gadahn is included in this article."

9 Ibid.

10 Adam Gadahn, "Review of Autopsy, Acts of the Unspeakable (Vile)," *Xenocide*, issue 5, undated.

11 Adam Gadahn, "Review of Enraptured, 7 Song Demo '92 (Demo),"ibid.

12 Annette Stark, "Peace, Love, Death Metal," *LA City Beat/Valley Beat*, September 9, 2004.

13 Gadahn, "Becoming Muslim."

14 Ibid.

15 Amy Argetsinger, "Muslim Teen Made Conversion to Fury," *Washington Post*, December 2, 2004.

16 Ali H. Soufan, *The Black Banners: The Inside Story of 9/11 and the War Against al-Qaeda* (New York: W. W. Norton, 2011), pp. 132–35.

17 Ibid.

18 Stuart Pfeifer, Richard Winton, and Eric Malnic, "Suspect on FBI's List Has Ties to California," *Los Angeles Times*, May 27, 2004.

19 Superior Court of California, County of Orange, Case Number: 97WM05335, Violation Date: April 9, 1997.

20 Unpublished letter from Adam Yahiye Gadahn to *The New Yorker*, February 2006.

21 Mitchell D. Silber and Arvin Bhatt, *Radicalization in the West: The Homegrown Threat* (New York: New York Police Department, Intelligence Division, 2007), p. 30.

22 Canadian Security Intelligence Service, *From Radicalization to Jihadization* (Ottawa, 2006), p. 2.

23 Unpublished letter to *The New Yorker*.

24 Senior FBI official, interview with author, March 4, 2011.

25 Ibid.

26 Ibid.

27 Ibid.

28 Federal Bureau of Investigation, *Protecting America from Terrorist Attacks: Please BOLO for Us* (Washington, D.C., May 26, 2004).

29 *United States of America v. Adam Gadahn, a.k.a. Azzam al-Amriki*, United States District Court, Central District of California, SA CR 05-254(A), October 2006.

30 Video released September 2005.

31 Federal Bureau of Investigation, *Adam Yahiye Gadahn*; *U.S. v. Adam Gadahn*.

32 Transcript of Press Conference Announcing Indictment of U.S. Citizen for Treason and Material Support Charges for Providing Aid and Comfort to al Qaeda, Washington, D.C., October 11, 2006.

33 T. E. Lawrence to H. S. Ede, letter no. 362, dated May 30, 1928, in David Garnett, ed., *The Letters of T. E. Lawrence* (New York, Doubleday, Doran, 1939), p. 610.

34 Philip Mudd, interview with author, August 8, 2011.

35 U.S. government official, interview with author, July 5, 2011.

36 Christina Lamb, "Airstrike Misses Al-Qaeda Chief," *Times* (London), January 15, 2006.

37 Ayman al-Zawahiri, video message to Bush, American people, January 2006.

38 National Intelligence Council, *The Terrorist Threat to the Homeland*, p. 1.

39 See, for example, Murray Gell-Mann, *The Quark and the Jaguar* (New York: Holt, 1994); John Holland, *Hidden Order* (Reading, Mass.: Addison-Wesley, 1995); Kevin Dooley, "A Complex Adaptive Systems Model of Organization Change," *Nonlinear Dynamics, Psychology, and Life Science* 1, no. 1 (1997): 69–97.

40 Bruce Hoffman, *Inside Terrorism*, rev. ed. (New York: Columbia University Press, 2006), p. 285.

41 Canadian Security Intelligence Service, *Is Canada Next?* (Ottawa, 2006), p. 2.

42 Mudd interview, August 8, 2011.

43 Six months after September 11, al Qa'ida had lost sixteen of twenty-five key leaders on the Pentagon's "Most Wanted" list; Rohan Gunaratna, *Inside Al Qa'ida: Global Network of Terror* (New York: Berkley, 2002), p. 303.

44 Senior FBI official interview, December 18, 2010.

45 National Intelligence Council, *Trends in Global Terrorism: Implications for the United States* (Washington, D.C., April 2006), p. 3.

46 Lorenzo Vidino, "The Hofstad Group: The New Face of Terrorist Networks in Europe," *Studies in Conflict and Terrorism* 30, no. 7 (July 2007): 579–92; Algemene Inlichtingen en Veiligheidsdienst, *From Dawa to Jihad: The Various Threats from Radical Islam to the Democratic Legal Order* (The Hague, December 2004).

47 Amir Mohammad Khan, "Spiralling into Chaos," *Newsline* (Pakistan), March 2004, pp. 34–36.

48 M. Ilyas Khan, "Profile of Nek Mohammad," *Dawn* (Pakistan), June 19, 2004.

49 M. Ilyas Khan, "Who Are These People?" *Herald* (Pakistan), April 2004, pp. 60–68.

50 Amir Mohammad Khan, "Spiralling into Chaos."

51 M. Ilyas Khan, "Who Are These People?"

52 Sailab Mahsud, "Caught in the Crossfire," *Herald* (Pakistan), April 2004, pp. 66–67.

53 Locals denied the existence of the last clause and argued that they had not agreed to register all foreigners with the government.

54 Mariam Abou Zahab, "Changing Patterns of Social and Political Life Among the Tribal Pashtuns in Pakistan," draft paper, 2007.

55 Rahimullah Yusufzai, interview, *Frontline*, PBS, October 3, 2006.

56 See comments of Lieutenant General Safdar made during the peace accords in Shakai; "Return of the Taliban," *Frontline*, PBS, October 2006.

57 Iqbal Khattak, "I Did Not Surrender to the Military, Said Nek Mohammad," *Friday Times* (Pakistan), April 30–May 6, 2004.

58 Ismail Khan and Dilawar Khan Wazir, "Night Raid Kills Nek, Four Other Militants," *Dawn* (Pakistan), June 19, 2004; Khattak, "I Did Not Surrender to the Military."

59 Ismail Khan, "Why the Waziristan Deal Is a Hard Sell," *Dawn* (Pakistan), October 14, 2006.

60 "Accord in Bajaur to Curb Terrorists," *Dawn* (Pakistan), May 31, 2005; "The Bajaur Massacre," *Dawn* (Pakistan), November 1, 2006; Mohammad Ali, "Peace Deal in Bajaur Soon, Says Aurakzai," *Dawn* (Pakistan), February 24, 2007.

61 "The 2008 *Time* 100 Finalists," *Time*, 2008, available at www.time.com/time/specials/2007/article/0,28804,1725112_1723512_1723546,00.html.

62 U.S. government officials, interviews with author, August and September 2011.

63 Transcript of Pervez Musharraf interview with Martin Smith, June 8, 2006.

64 Lieutenant General Michael D. Maples, *Current and Projected National Security Threats to the United States, Statement for the Record, Senate Select Committee on Intelligence* (Washington, D.C.: Defense Intelligence Agency, January 2007), p. 12.

65 Pakistan Ministry of Interior, *The Talibanisation Problem* (Islamabad, 2007).

66 On-line discussion at Al-Qawl al-Fasl Net website (since shut down), March 2010.

67 Mudd interview, August 8, 2011.

68 Ben Fox, "U.S. Citizen Listed as Terror Suspect Had 1997 Arrest, 'Very Extreme' Ideas," Associated Press, May 27, 2004.

69 "U.S. Identifies Seven Wanted in Connection with al Qaeda," CNN, May 27, 2004.

70 Scott Shane and Lowell Bergman, "FBI Struggling to Reinvent Itself to Fight Terror," *New York Times*, October 10, 2006.

71 Philip Mudd, interview, *Frontline*, PBS, June 2, 2006.

CHAPTER 10: THE TIDE TURNS IN IRAQ

1 Sheikh Abd al-Ibrahim al-Hardan al-Aethawi, interview, in Colonel Gary W. Montgomery and Chief Warrant Officer-4 Timothy S. McWilliams, eds., *Al-Anbar Awakening*, Vol. II, *Iraqi Perspectives* (Quantico, Va.: Marine Corps University Press, 2009), pp. 54–55.

2 Lieutenant Colonel Jim Lechner, interview with author, August 17, 2011.

3 Abd al-Ibrahim al-Hardan al-Aethawi interview.
4 Mitchell B. Reiss, *Negotiating with Evil: When to Talk to Terrorists* (New York: Open Road, 2010), pp. 177–220.
5 National Intelligence Council, *The Terrorist Threat to the US Homeland* (Washington, D.C., July 2007).
6 Lechner interview, August 17, 2011; Major Ben Connable, interview with author, August 15, 2011.
7 John Negroponte, interview with author, August 11, 2011.
8 Connable interview, August 15, 2011.
9 "State of the Insurgency in al-Anbar," I Marine Expedietionary Force (MEF) G-2, August 17, 2006.
10 Threatening communiqué from al Qa'ida in the Land of the Two Rivers, Harmony Database, NMEC-2007-637951, February 18, 2005.
11 Oath of Allegiance to the Islamic State of Iraq, Harmony Database, NMEC-2007-637854, date unknown.
12 Chicago Project on Suicide Terrorism, University of Chicago, available at http://cpost.uchicago.edu; accessed in December 2011.
13 Partial Muhammad Bin-Sabbar Muhammad al-Khuwi Abu Yasir Martyrdom Pledge, Harmony Database, NMEC-2007-658034, date unkown.
14 See, for example, Khalaf Ahmad Nawfal al-Rashdan Martyrdom Pledge for AQI, Harmony Database, NMEC-2007-657968, date unknown.
15 Will and Testament of a Suicide Bomber, Harmony Database, NMEC-2007-637872, date unknown.
16 "State of the Insurgency in al-Anbar."
17 Major Niel Smith and Colonel Sean MacFarland, "Anbar Awakens: The Tipping Point," *Military Review*, March-April 2008, p. 66.
18 Senior Defense Intelligence Agency analyst, interview with author, August 22, 2011.
19 Connable interview, August 15, 2011.
20 Sheikh Jassim Muhammad Saleh al-Suwadawi and Sheikh Abdul Rahman al-Janabi, interview, in Montgomery and McWilliams, *Al-Anbar Awakening*, Vol. II, *Iraqi Perspectives*, pp. 71–72.
21 Sheikh Sabah al-Sattam Effan Fahran al-Shurji al-Aziz, interview, ibid., p. 144.
22 Sheikh Ahmad Bezia Fteikhan al-Rishawi, interview, ibid., pp. 50–51.
23 Connable interview, August 15, 2011.
24 Jim Michaels, *A Chance in Hell: The Men Who Triumphed over Iraq's Deadliest City and Turned the Tide of War* (New York: St. Martin's, 2010), p. 102.
25 Ayman al-Zawahiri to Abu Mus'ab al-Zarqawi, letter, July 9, 2005. Released by the Harmony Project, Combating Terrorism Center, West Point.
26 U.S. Army and Marine Corps, *Counterinsurgency Field Manual* (Chicago: University of Chicago Press, 2007).
27 Zawahiri to Zarqawi.
28 Threatening communiqué from al Qa'ida in the Land of the Two Rivers.

29 Atiyah abd al-Rahman to Abu Mus'ab al-Zarqawi, letter, 2005. Released by the Harmony Project, Combating Terrorism Center, West Point.

30 Looting and theft announcement from al Qa'ida in the Land of the Two Rivers, Harmony Database, NMEC-2007-637813, December 24, 2004.

31 Um Mohammed, "Al Zarqawi's Wife Says in Web Statement She Urged Him to Leave Iraq," Associated Press, July 6, 2006.

32 Sattar was detained by U.S. forces in Iraq on at least two occasions: October 28 and November 8, 2004. He was quickly released both times.

33 Senior Defense Intelligence Agency analyst interview, August 22, 2011.

34 Lieutenant Colonel Jim Lechner, correspondence with author, October 29, 2011.

35 Lechner interview, August 17, 2011.

36 Ibid.

37 Sheikh Majed Al-Razzaq Ali al-Sulayman, interview, in Montgomery and McWilliams, *Al-Anbar Awakening*, Vol. II, *Iraqi Perspectives*, p. 131.

38 Dr. Thamer Ibrahim Tahir al-Assafi and Sheikh Abdullah Jallal Mukhif al-Faraji, interview, ibid., pp. 35–36.

39 Majed Al-Razzaq Ali al-Sulayman interview, pp. 132–33.

40 Lechner interview, August 17, 2011.

41 Ahmad Bezia Fteikhan al-Rishawi interview, pp. 46–47.

42 Lechner correspondence, October 29, 2011.

43 Michaels, *A Chance in Hell*, pp. 104–5.

44 Ahmad Bezia Fteikhan al-Rishawi interview, pp. 47–48.

45 Major General Stephen T. Johnson, interview, in McWilliams and Wheeler, eds., *Al-Anbar Awakening*, Vol. I, *American Perspectives*, p. 105.

46 Major General John R. Allen, interview, ibid., p. 236.

47 Smith and MacFarland, "Anbar Awakens," p. 67.

48 Colonel Sean MacFarland, interview, in McWilliams and Wheeler, eds., *Al-Anbar Awakening*, Vol. I, *American Perspectives*, p. 181.

49 Seth G. Jones and Martin Libicki, *How Terrorist Groups End: Lessons for Countering Al Qa'ida* (Santa Monica, Calif.: RAND, 2008), pp. 83–101.

50 Solomon Moore and Louise Roug, "Deaths Across Iraq Show It Is a Nation of Many Wars, with U.S. in the Middle," *Los Angeles Times*, October 7, 2006.

51 Richard A. Oppel, "Mistrust as Iraqi Troops Encounter New U.S. Allies," *New York Times*, July 16, 2007.

52 Major General Walter E. Gaskin, Sr., interview, January 11, 2008, Marine Corps Historical Center, Quantico, Virginia.

53 Statement from the Army of Islam on bombings of Muslim targets, Harmony Database, NMEC-2007-639043, May 4, 2007.

54 Communiqué from al Qa'ida in the Land of the Two Rivers to inspire jihad, Harmony Database, NMEC-2007-638026, November 9, 2007.

55 Press release of an Islamic State of Iraq Amir in Reaction to Attacks in the Amireah Region, Harmony Database, NMEC-2007-639155, date unknown.

56 Apology from ISI to the Sheik Abad Lufan al Hadeb, Harmony Database, NMEC-2007-657736, date unknown.

57 Abu Hamza al-Mujahir to Abi Abdullah al-Shafi'ee, letter, Harmony Database, MNFT-636898, April 30, 2007.

58 Disavowals of Who Oppose ISI and Pledges of Allegiance to ISI, Harmony Database, NMEC-2007-636883, date unknown.

59 Jones and Libicki, *How Terrorist Groups End*, pp. 83–101.

60 *Al-Hayah* (London), Open Source Center (GMP20070411825007), April 11, 2007.

61 Chris Kraul, "In Ramadi, A Ragtag Solution with Real Results," *Los Angeles Times*, May 7, 2007.

62 Letter from the Leader of One Group to Another, Harmony Database, NMEC-2007-636968, date unknown.

63 Abu Tariq, al Qa'ida sector leader, daily diary, 2007. The diary was seized by U.S. troops south of Balad, Iraq, in late 2007 or early 2008.

64 Abu Hamzah to Ansar al-Sunnah, letter highlighting divisions in the jihadist movement, Harmony Database, NMEC-2007-636878, date unknown.

65 Major General Tariq Yusif Mohammad al-Thiyabi, interview, in Montgomery and McWilliams, *Al-Anbar Awakening*, Vol. II, *Iraqi Perspectives*, p. 193.

66 "Iraqi TV Reports on Funeral Ceremony of Tribal Chief, Reaction to Bush Speech," BBC, September 14, 2007.

67 "State of the Insurgency in al-Anbar."

68 Analysis of the state of ISI, Harmony Database, NMEC-2007-612449, date unknown.

CHAPTER 11: REVOLT FROM WITHIN

1 John Romer, *The Great Pyramid: Ancient Egypt Revisited* (New York: Cambridge University Press, 2007).

2 The seven were Reception prison, Tura Farm prison, Tura Farm annex, Tura prison, Al-Mahkum prison, Tura Hospital prison, and a high-security prison known as Al-Aqrab prison.

3 Anwar el-Sadat, *In Search of Identity: An Autobiography* (New York: Harper and Row, 1977), p. 68.

4 Al-Sayyid Imam Abd-al-Aziz al-Sharif, interview with Muhammad Salah, *Al-Hayat* (UK), part 4, December 8, 2007.

5 Ibid.

6 Ayman al-Zawahiri, *A Treatise on the Exoneration of the Nation of the Pen and Sword of the Denigrating Charge of Being Irresolute and Weak*, March 2008.

7 For one of the best reviews of the Sharif-Zawahiri debate, see Lawrence Wright, "The Rebellion Within: An Al Qaeda Mastermind Questions Terrorism," *The New Yorker*, June 2, 2008.

8 Sharif interview, part 6.

9 Al-Sayyid Imam Abd-al-Aziz al-Sharif, "Future of the War in Afghanistan," *Al-Sharq al-Awsat* (UK), 2009.

10 Sharif interview, part 2.

11 Ibid.

12 National Counterterrorism Center, *2009 Report on Terrorism* (Washington, D.C., April 2010), p. 28; National Counterterrorism Center, *2007 Report on Terrorism* (Washington, D.C., April 2008), pp. 11, 36.

13 Sharif, *Rationalizing Jihad in Egypt and the World*, part 8, *Al-Misri Al-Yawm* (Egypt), 2007.

14 Ibid., part 1.

15 Ayman al-Zawahiri, *Knights Under the Prophet's Banner*, trans. Laura Mansfield (Old Tappan, N.J.: TLG, 2002), pp. 200–201.

16 *United States of America v. Adam Gadahn, a.k.a. Azzam al-Amriki*, United States District Court, Central District of California, SA CR 05-254(A), October 2006.

17 Sharif, *Rationalizing Jihad in Egypt and the World*, part 7.

18 Ibid., part 6.

19 Ibid., part 10.

20 Sharif interview, part 3.

21 Qur'an, The Night Journey (Al-Qasas): 17:36; Sharif interview, part 2.

22 Sharif, *Rationalizing Jihad in Egypt and the World*, part 2.

23 Ibid., part 12.

24 Sayyid Qutb, *Milestones*, repr. ed. (New Delhi: Islamic Book Service, 2007), pp. 53–76.

25 Sharif, *Rationalizing Jihad in Egypt and the World*, part 1.

26 Ibid., part 5.

27 Ibid., part 4.

28 Sharif interview, part 4.

29 Qur'an, The Gathering [of Forces] (Al-Hashr): 59:16–17; Sharif interview, part 4.

30 Philip Mudd, interview with author, August 8, 2011.

31 Philip Mudd, interview, *Frontline*, PBS, June 2, 2006.

32 Zawahiri, *A Treatise on the Exoneration of the Nation of the Pen and Sword*, pp. 1–2.

33 Ibid., p. 4.

34 Ibid., p. 9.

35 Ibid., p. 18.

36 Ibid., pp. 1–2.

37 Ibid., p. 6.

38 Ibid., p. 34.

39 Ibid.

40 Ibid., p. 35.

41 Ibid., p. 25.

42 Ibid.

43 Ibid., p. 29.

44 Ibid., p. 13.

45 Ibid., p. 2.

46 *United States of America v. Usama bin Laden, et al.* (Kenyan Embassy Bombing), United States District Court, Southern District of New York, Indictment S(9) 98 Cr. 1023 (LBS).

47 Brynjar Lia, *Architect of Global Jihad: The Life of al-Qaida Strategist Abu Mus'ab al-Suri* (New York: Columbia University Press, 2008), p. 210.

48 *U.S. v. Usama bin Laden, et al.* (Kenyan Embassy Bombing), Indictment S(9) 98 Cr. 1023 (LBS); *U.S. v. Usama bin Laden, et al.* (Kenyan Embassy Bombing), Indictment S(7) 98 Cr. 1023, transcript of Day 59 of the trial, June 5, 2001.

49 Adil Abd al-Majid Abd al-Bari, "Egyptian Islamist Leading Member Imprisoned in Britain Since 1988 Replies to the 'Jihadist Theoretician' and His Criticism of Al Qa'ida," *Al-Hayat* (UK), August 28, 2008.

50 Muhammad Hasan Khalil al-Hakim, "Response to Sayyid Imam al-Sharif," www.alhanein.com (since shut down); accessed November 2007.

51 Hani al-Siba'i, "The Exposition in Response to the Exposure," Al-Shura Islamic Network (www.elshouraa.ws/vb/) (since shut down); accessed February 2009.

52 "Head of London Center for Islamic History Hani Siba'i: In Islam, There Are No Such Things as Civilians," Al Jazeera (Qatar); July 8, 2005, reproduced on the Middle East Media Research Institute (MEMRI) TV Monitor Project, accessed December 5, 2011, www.memritv.org/clip/en/748.htm.

53 Siba'i, "The Exposition in Response to the Exposure."

54 Muhammad Hasan Khalil al-Hakim, "Jihad Revisions—Truths and Presuppositions," published on various jihadist websites, June 2007.

55 Abu-Basir al-Tartusi, "Response to 'Rationalization of Jihad,'" www.abubaseer.bizland.com, November 2007; accessed February 2009.

56 Siba'i, "The Exposition in Response to the Exposure."

57 Tartusi, "Response to 'Rationalization of Jihad.'"

58 Sharif interview, part 2.

59 Ibid., part 4.

60 Ibid.

61 Ibid.

62 Hani al-Siba'i, "Statement in Response to Accusation of Being British 'Spy,'" published on various jihadist websites (including www.al-faloja.info/vb), February 26, 2009.

63 Ahmad al-Khatib, "Story of Islamic Jihad Revisions," *Al-Misri Al-Yawm* (Egypt), November 19, 2007; Muhammad al-Shafi'i, interview with Muntasir al-Zayyat, *Al-Sharq al-Awsat* (UK), August 15, 2006.

64 Shaykh Salman Bin-Fahd al-Awdah, "Letter to Osama bin Laden," *Islam Today* (Saudi Arabia), September 17, 2007.

65 Salman al-Awdah, "Need for Mature Islamic Discourse to Tackle Violence," *Islam Today* (Saudi Arabia), November 17, 2007.

66 "Saudi Muslim Scholars Urge 'Resistance' Against Coalition Forces in Iraq," Al Jazeera, November 6, 2004.

67 Shaykh Bin-Fahd Salman al-Awdah, interview with Salim al-Shatti, *Al-Ra'i* (Jordan), March 2007.

68 Dr. Yusuf al-Qaradawi, "Exploding the Danish Embassy Is Distortion of the Image of Islam," *Al-Arab Online* (Qatar), Open Source Center (GMP20080603061001), June 3, 2008.

69 "Interview with Shaykh Ahmad Yusuf Hamdallah," *Al-Misri Al-Yawm* (Egypt), November 25, 2007; Muhammad Salah, "Jihad Leader in Bani Suwayf Backs Peaceful Call to End Violence," *Al-Hayat* (UK), February 17, 2000.

70 "Interview with Usamah Ayyub," *Al-Sharq al-Awsat* (UK), November 19, 2007.

71 Mohammed Solaiman, "El Erian Welcomes Jihad Group Reviews," ikhwanweb .com, November 11, 2007.

72 Khalifah Jaballah, "Al-Zawahiri Calls on the Muslim Brotherhood Group Members to Clarify Their Stand on the Arab Peace Initiative, and the Group Members Say 'Our Stand Is Clear,'" *Al-Misri Al-Yawm* (Egypt), July 6, 2007.

73 U.S. Department of State, *Country Reports on Terrorism 2008* (Washington, D.C., April 2009), p. 296.

74 "Hamas Rejects al-Qaeda's Support," BBC, March 5, 2006.

75 "Palestinian Hamas Leader Criticizes Summit Meeting, Al-Zawahiri Statement," BBC, March 12, 2007. Also see "Hamas Member Nazzal Reacts to Al-Zawahiri's Criticism of Movement," Al-Arabiyah, December 20, 2006.

76 "Al-Zawahiri Criticizes Fatah-Hamas Mecca Agreement," Al Jazeera, March 11, 2007; "Excerpt of Al-Zawahiri Criticizing Hamas-Led Government," Al Jazeera, December 20, 2006.

77 As-Sahab Media, "The Open Meeting with Shaykh Ayman al-Zawahiri," 2008.

78 Ibid.

79 Pew Research Center for the People and the Press, *Confidence in Obama Lifts U.S. Image Around the World* (Washington, D.C.: Pew Global Attitudes Project, 2009), p. 84.

80 Sharif, *Rationalizing Jihad in Egypt and the World*, part 6.

81 Philip Mudd, "Why the U.S. Should Engage the Muslim Brotherhood," *Atlantic*, February 21, 2011.

82 As-Sahab Media, "The Open Meeting with Shaykh Ayman al-Zawahiri."

CHAPTER 12: LEADERLESS JIHAD?

1 "Best Places to Live," *Money*, 2006, www.money.cnn.com/magazines/moneymag/ bplive/2006/snapshots/CS3412280.html; accessed December 3, 2011.

2 *United States of America v. Mohamad Shnewer, et al.*, United States Court of Appeals for the Third Circuit, Case 09-2300, Document 003110268756, August 31, 2010.

3 U.S. Department of Defense, *Protecting the Force: Lessons from Fort Hood* (Washington, D.C., 2010).

4 *U.S. v. Mohamad Shnewer, et al.*, Court of Appeals for the Third Circuit, Case 09-2300, Document 003110268756.

5 *United States of America v. Mohamad Shnewer, et al.*, United States District Court, District of New Jersey, Criminal No. 07-459 (RBK), Government Exhibits 94-A and 94-D.

6 Ibid., Document 132, January 15, 2008.

7 *U.S. America v. Mohamad Shnewer, et al.*, Court of Appeals for the Third Circuit, Case 09-2300, Document 003110268756.

8 Abu Mus'ab al-Suri, "The Jihadi Experiences: The Schools of Jihad," *Inspire*, no. 1431 (Summer 2010): 49.

9 *U.S. v. Mohamad Shnewer, et al.*, Court of Appeals for the Third Circuit, Case 09-2300, Document 003110268756.

10 Amanda Ripley, "The Fort Dix Conspiracy," *Time*, December 17, 2007.

11 George Anastasia, "A Radical Shift in Reputation for Six Men," *Philadelphia Inquirer*, May 14, 2007; Jason Laughlin, "Suspects in Terror Case Fought Hard to Fit In," *Courier-Post*, May 14, 2007.

12 *U.S. v. Mohamad Shnewer, et al.*, District Court of New Jersey, Criminal No. 07-459 (RBK), Exhibit 854-D, August 23, 2008. The date of the conversation was March 10, 2007, at approximately 1 p.m.

13 According to a mosque spokesman, they "very rarely" attended services. See Anastasia, "A Radical Shift in Reputation for Six Men."

14 Kareem Fahim and Andre Elliott, "Religion Guided 3 Held in Fort Dix Plot," *New York Times*, May 10, 2007.

15 *Nasser al-Awlaki v. Barack H. Obama, et al.*, United States District Court, District of Columbia, Declaration of Dr. Nasser al-Awlaki, August 28, 2010.

16 Anwar al-Awlaki, "A Question from a Reader on My Islamic Education," www .anwar-alawlaki.com. August 12, 2008.

17 San Diego Police and FBI officials, including some from the San Diego Joint Terrorism Task Force, interview with author, September 2011.

18 The 9/11 Commission, *The 9/11 Commission Report: Final Report of the National Commission on Terrorist Attacks Upon the United States* (New York: W. W. Norton, 2004), p. 221.

19 Caryle Murphy, "Facing New Realities as Islamic Americans," *Washington Post*, September 12, 2004.

20 Lee Keath and Ahmed al-Haj, "Tribe in Yemen Protecting U.S. Cleric," *Associated Press*, January 19, 2010.

21 Anwar al-Awlaki, "44 Ways to Support Jihad," www.anwar-alawlaki.com, January 5, 2009.

22 U.S. Department of Treasury, *Treasury Designates Anwar Al-Awlaki, Key Leader of Al-Qa'ida in the Arabian Peninsula*, TG-779 (Washington, D.C., July 16, 2010).

23 Anwar al-Awlaki, "Book Review 3: In the Shade of the Quran by Sayyid Qutb," www.anwar-alawlaki.com, June 22 2008.

24 Anwar al-Awlaki, "The Story of Ibn al-Aqwa," undated.

25 Anwar al-Awlaki, "Allah Is Preparing Us for Victory," undated.

26 Mudd interview, August 8, 2011.

27 Anwar al-Awlaki, "The Constants of Jihad," undated.

28 Qur'an, Repentance (Al-Tawba): 9:29.

29 *U.S. v. Mohamad Shnewer, et al.*, District Court of New Jersey, Criminal No. 07-459 (RBK), FBI recording of March 9, 2007 conversation between the Duka brothers and Besnik Bakalli, Full Recording, approximately 7:20 p.m.

30 Ibid.

31 *U.S. v. Mohamad Shnewer, et al.*, District Court of New Jersey, Criminal No. 07-459 (RBK), Exhibit 853-B.

32 *U.S. v. Mohamad Shnewer, et al.*, Court of Appeals for the Third Circuit, Case 09-2300, Document 003110268756.

33 The superseding indictment identifies one of the extremists as Sheikh Omar Abdel Rahman, who served a life sentence for his role in the New York World Trade Center bombing plot. See *U.S. v. Mohamad Shnewer, et al.*, District Court of New Jersey, No. 1:07-CR-00459-RBK, Superseding Indictment, January 15, 2008.

34 Ibid., Document 132.

35 Ibid., Exhibit 761-B.

36 *United States of America v. Shain Duka*, United States District Court, District of New Jersey, Complaint, No. 1:07-CR-00459-RBK, May 7, 2007.

37 *U.S. v. Mohamad Shnewer, et al.*, District Court of New Jersey, Criminal No. 07-459 (RBK), Exhibit 854-B, August 23, 2008. The date of the conversation was March 10, 2007, at approximately 1 p.m.

38 Ibid.

39 Brian Morgenstern, interview with Sean Hannity and Alan Colmes, "Hannity & Colmes," *Fox News*, May 29, 2007.

40 *U.S. v. Mohamad Shnewer, et al.*, District Court of New Jersey, Criminal No. 07-459 (RBK), Exhibit 70.

41 *United States of America v. Agron Abdullahu*, United States District Court, District of New Jersey, Criminal No. 07-459 (RBK), Superseding Information, undated.

42 Ripley, "The Fort Dix Conspiracy."

43 "Fort Dix Tipster Agonized over Tape," *Washington Times*, May 30, 2007.

44 "Fort Dix Tipster Shrugs Off 'Hero' Title," CNN, May 29, 2007.

45 *U.S. v. Agron Abdullahu*, District Court of New Jersey, Case 1:07-cr-00459-RBK, May 16, 2007.

46 *U.S. v. Mohamad Shnewer, et al.*, Court of Appeals for the Third Circuit, Case 09-2300, Document 003110268756.

47 *U.S. v. Mohamad Shnewer, et al.*, District Court of New Jersey, Criminal No. 07-459 (RBK), Trial Transcript, October 27, 2008.

48 *U.S. v. Mohamad Shnewer, et al.*, Court of Appeals for the Third Circuit, Case 09-2300, Document 003110268756.

49 *U.S. v. Mohamad Shnewer, et al.*, District Court of New Jersey, Criminal No. 07-459 (RBK), Trial Transcript, October 27, 2008.

50 Ibid.

51 *U.S. v. Mohamad Shnewer, et al.,* Court of Appeals for the Third Circuit, Case 09-2300, Document 003110268756.

52 *U.S. v. Mohamad Shnewer, et al.,* District Court of New Jersey, Criminal No. 07-459 (RBK), Trial Transcript, October 27, 2008.

53 Ibid.

54 Ibid., December 1, 2008.

55 Ibid., Exhibit 608 A-D.

56 *U.S. v. Mohamad Shnewer, et al.,* Court of Appeals for the Third Circuit, Case 09-2300, Document 003110268756.

57 *U.S. v. Mohamad Shnewer, et al.,* District Court of New Jersey, Criminal No. 07-459 (RBK), Exhibit 608-B.

58 *U.S. v. Shain Duka,* Complaint.

59 *U.S. v. Mohamad Shnewer, et al.,* District Court of New Jersey, Criminal No. 07-459 (RBK), Trial Transcript, November 25, 2008.

60 Ibid., Exhibit 609-B.

61 Ibid., Document 132, January 15, 2008.

62 Ibid.

63 Ibid., Exhibit 626-B; ibid., Document 132, January 15, 2008.

64 Ibid., December 1, 2008.

65 Ibid., Exhibits 761-A, 761-B, 761-C, 761-D.

66 Ibid., December 1, 2008.

67 Ibid., Exhibits 804-A and 804-B.

68 Ibid., Exhibit 804-B.

69 Ibid., Exhibit 854-B, August 23, 2008.

70 *U.S. v. Agron Abdullahu.*

71 Ibid., Document 146, March 24, 2008.

72 *U.S. v. Mohamad Shnewer, et al.,* District Court of New Jersey, Criminal No. 07-459 (RBK), Exhibits 812-A and 812-B.

73 Ibid., Exhibit 818-B.

74 Ibid., Document 132, January 15, 2008.

75 *U.S. v. Agron Abdullahu,* Document 146, March 24, 2008.

76 *U.S. v. Mohamad Shnewer, et al.,* District Court of New Jersey, Criminal No. 07-459 (RBK), Exhibit 854-B, August 23, 2008.

77 Ibid., Exhibit 641-B.

78 Ibid., Exhibits 642-A, 642-B, 642-C, and 642-D.

79 *U.S. v. Mohamad Shnewer, et al.,* Court of Appeals for the Third Circuit, Case 09-2300, Document 003110268756.

80 *United States of America v. Russell DeFreitas, et al.,* United States District Court, Eastern District of New York, Case 1:07-cr-00543-DLI, Document 160-1, March 8, 2010.

81 United States Attorney's Office, Eastern District of New York, "American and Guyanese Citizens Convicted of Conspiracy to Launch Attack at JFK Airport," August 2, 2010.

82 *U.S. v. Russell Defreitas, et al.*, Document 126-1, October 2, 2009.

83 Ibid.

84 Ibid., KTC: JK/MM, F. #2006R00688, June 1, 2007.

85 Ibid.

86 United States Attorney's Office, Eastern District of New York, "Abdul Kadir Sentenced to Life in Prison for Conspiring to Commit Terrorist Attack at JFK Airport," December 15, 2010; *U.S. v. Russell Defreitas, et al.*, Document 185, April 2, 2010.

87 *U.S. v. Russell Defreitas, et al.*, Document 160-1, March 8, 2010.

88 Ibid., KTC: JK/MM, F. #2006R00688, June 1, 2007.

89 Ibid.

90 Ibid.

91 Austin Fenner, "No Finer Diner in New York," *New York Post*, November 26, 2007.

92 U.S. Attorney's Office, "Abdul Kadir Sentenced to Life in Prison."

93 *U.S. v. Russell Defreitas, et al.*, March 24, 2010.

94 U.S. Attorney's Office, "Abdul Kadir Sentenced to Life in Prison."

95 U.S. Attorney's Office, Eastern District of New York, "Abdel Nur Sentenced to 15 Years in Prison for Providing Material Support to the Conspiracy to Commit a Terrorist Attack at JFK Airport," January 13, 2011.

96 *U.S. v. Russell Defreitas, et al.*, Document 126-1, October 2, 2009.

97 Mudd interview, August 8, 2011.

98 Philip Mudd, "Evaluating the Al-Qa'ida Threat to the U.S. Homeland," *CTC Sentinel* 3, no. 8 (August 2010): 2.

99 Mudd interview, August 8, 2011.

100 *U.S. v. Mohamad Shnewer, et al.*, District Court of New Jersey, Document 107-2, December 11, 2007.

CHAPTER 13: AL QA'IDA STRIKES BACK

1 *United States of America v. Najibullah Zazi*, United States District Court, Eastern District of New York, 09-CR-663 (RJD), Memorandum of Law in Support of the Government's Motion for a Permanent Order of Detention, September 24, 2009.

2 *U.S. v. Najibullah Zazi*, District Court, Eastern District of New York, Docket No.: 09 CR 663 (S-1), Transcript of Criminal Cause for Pleading, February 22, 2010.

3 Zazi's address can be found on a range of documents, including those he filed for bankruptcy. See United States Bankruptcy Court, Eastern District of New York, Najibullah Zazi (Debtor), Discharge of Debtor(s) Order of Final Decree, Case 1-09-42297-ess, Document 20, August 19, 2009.

4 Samantha Gross, David Caruso, and Michael Rubinkam, "Radical Influences All Around NYC Terror Suspect," Associated Press, October 4, 2009.

5 Simon Akam, Alison Leigh Cowan, Michael Wilson, and Karen Zraick, "From Smiling Coffee Vendor to Terror Suspect," *New York Times*, September 25, 2009.

6 Federal Bureau of Investigation, *FBI Director Names Arthur Cummings Executive Assistant Director for National Security Branch* (Washington, D.C., January 11, 2008).

7 Ronald Kessler, *The Secrets of the FBI* (New York: Crown, 2011), pp. 160–61.

8 Art Cummings, interview with author, September 2, 2011.

9 *United States of America v. Bryant Neal Vinas*, United States District Court, Eastern District of New York, Case 1:08-cr-00823-NGG, January 28, 2009.

10 Philip Mudd, interview with author, August 8, 2011.

11 *United States of America v. Mohammed Wali Zazi*, United States District Court, Eastern District of New York, 10-CR-60 (JG), Testimony of Amanullah Zazi, July 18, 2011.

12 Zarein Ahmedzay, Statement before the United States District Court, Eastern District of New York, April 23, 2010.

13 *United States of America v. Ferid Imam, et al.*, United States District Court, Eastern District of New York, Case 1:10-cr-00019-RJD, Document 53, Superseding Indictment, July 7, 2010.

14 Ibid.

15 *U.S. v. Najibullah Zazi*, District Court, Eastern District of New York, Transcript of Criminal Cause for Pleading.

16 Ibid.

17 Akam et al., "From Smiling Coffee Vendor to Terror Suspect."

18 U.S. Department of Justice, *Charges Unsealed Against Five Alleged Members of Al-Qaeda Plot to Attack the United States and United Kingdom* (Washington, D.C., July 7, 2010).

19 U.S. Department of Justice, *Zarein Ahmedzay Pleads Guilty to Terror Violations in Connection with Al-Qaeda New York Subway Plot* (Washington, D.C., April 23, 2010).

20 U.S. Department of Justice, *Charges Unsealed Against Five Alleged Members of Al-Qaeda Plot*.

21 *U.S. v. Najibullah Zazi*, District Court, Eastern District of New York, Transcript of Criminal Cause for Pleading.

22 Declaration of Mr. Jeffrey N. Rapp, Director, Joint Intelligence Task Force for Combating Terrorism, submitted for the Court's consideration in the matter of *José Padilla v. Commander C. T. Hanft*, USN, Commander, Consolidated Naval Brig, Case Number 04-CV-2221-26AJ; *United States of America v. Russell Defreitas, et al.*, United States District Court, Eastern District of New York, Cr. No. 07-543 (DLI), Document 185, April 2, 2010.

23 Federal Bureau of Investigation, *Wanted for Questioning: Adnan G. El Shukrijumah* (Washington, D.C., undated); U.S. Department of Justice, *Charges Unsealed Against Five Alleged Members of Al-Qaeda Plot*.

24 Federal Bureau of Investigation, *Seeking Information: Adnan G. El Shukrijumah* (Washington, D.C., undated).

25 Federal Bureau of Investigation, *Adnan G. El Shukrijumah: Most Wanted Terrorists,*

undated, available at www.fbi.gov/wanted/wanted_terrorists/adnan-g.-el-shukri jumah; accessed December 3, 2011.

26 Broward College, *Setting the Record Straight About Broward College and Former Student Shukrijumah* (Fort Lauderdale, Fla., undated).

27 Federal Bureau of Investigation, *Transcript of Adnan G. El Shukrijumah's Video* (Washington, D.C., undated).

28 Broward County, Clerk of the Court, 17th Judicial Circuit of Florida, Broward County Case Number: 97020044CF10A, Filing Date: November 26, 1997. Court documents listed his name as Jumah Adnan el-Shukri.

29 Deputy Secretary of Defense Paul Wolfowitz to Honorable James B. Comey, letter, "Summary of José Padilla's Activities with Al Qaeda," May 28, 2004.

30 Declaration of Mr. Jeffrey N. Rapp, Case Number 04-CV-2221-26AJ.

31 U.S. Department of Justice, *Charges Unsealed Against Five Alleged Members of Al-Qaeda Plot.*

32 *U.S. v. Najibullah Zazi*, District Court, Eastern District of New York, Transcript of Criminal Cause for Pleading.

33 Ibid., Memorandum of Law in Support of the Government's Motion for a Permanent Order of Detention.

34 *U.S. v. Ferid Imam, et al.*, Superseding Indictment.

35 *United States of America v. Najibullah Zazi*, United States District Court, District of Colorado, Affidavit in Support of Complaint and Arrest Warrant, September 19, 2009.

36 U.S. Department of Justice, *Zarein Ahmedzay Pleads Guilty to Terror Violations.*

37 *U.S. v. Najibullah Zazi*, District Court, Eastern District of New York, Transcript of Criminal Cause for Pleading.

38 United States Bankruptcy Court, Eastern District of New York, Najibullah Zazi (Debtor), Statement Pursuant to Local Bankruptcy Rule 1073-2(b), Case 1-09-42297-ess, Document 1, March 26, 2009.

39 Ibid., Order of Final Decree; ibid., Summary of Schedules, Case 1-09-42297-ess, Document 1, March 26, 2009.

40 Ibid., Summary of Schedules, Document 1.

41 Certification of Debtor Education, Najibullah Zazi (Debtor), Certificate Number 01401-NYE-DE-008012187, Case 1-09-42297-ess, Document 18, August 14, 2009.

42 NEFA Foundation, *"Target: America," The September 2009 New York/Denver Terror Plot Arrests* (New York, October 2009).

43 U.S. Department of Justice, *Zarein Ahmedzay Pleads Guilty to Terror Violations.*

44 *U.S. v. Najibullah Zazi*, District Court, Eastern District of New York, Memorandum of Law in Support of the Government's Motion for a Permanent Order of Detention.

45 Akam et al., "From Smiling Coffee Vendor to Terror Suspect."

46 Zarein Ahmedzay, Statement before the United States District Court.

47 *U.S. v. Najibullah Zazi*, District Court, Eastern District of New York, Memoran-

dum of Law in Support of the Government's Motion for a Permanent Order of Detention.

48 U.S. Department of Justice, *Zarein Ahmedzay Pleads Guilty to Terror Violations.*

49 Zarein Ahmedzay, Statement before the United States District Court.

50 *U.S. v. Mohammed Wali Zazi,* District Court, Eastern District of New York, Testimony of Amanullah Zazi.

51 *U.S. v. Najibullah Zazi,* District Court, Eastern District of New York, Memorandum of Law in Support of the Government's Motion for a Permanent Order of Detention.

52 Ibid.

53 U.S. Department of Justice, *Charges Unsealed Against Five Alleged Members of Al-Qaeda Plot.*

54 See, for example, Metropolitan Police, *Briefing Note: Operation Pathway* (London, April 2009).

55 U.S. Department of Justice, *Charges Unsealed Against Five Alleged Members of Al-Qaeda Plot.*

56 U.S. Department of Justice, *Zarein Ahmedzay Pleads Guilty to Terror Violations.*

57 Senior New York Police Department official, interview with author, March 29, 2011.

58 Mudd interview, August 8, 2011.

59 Ibid.

60 *United States of America v. Ahmad Wais Afzali,* United States District Court, Eastern District of New York, Complaint & Affidavit in Support of Arrest Warrant, September 19, 2009.

61 *U.S. v. Mohammed Wali Zazi,* District Court, Eastern District of New York, Testimony of Amanullah Zazi.

62 *U.S. v. Najibullah Zazi,* District Court, Eastern District of New York, Memorandum of Law in Support of the Government's Motion for a Permanent Order of Detention.

63 Senior New York Police Department officials, interviews with author, March 29, 2011, and September 1, 2011.

64 Zarein Ahmedzay, Statement before the United States District Court.

65 *U.S. v. Najibullah Zazi,* District Court, Eastern District of New York, Memorandum of Law in Support of the Government's Motion for a Permanent Order of Detention.

66 Ibid., Transcript of Criminal Cause for Pleading.

67 A. G. Sulzberger, "Imam and Informant Tells Why He Lied," *New York Times,* April 15, 2010; Al Baker and Karen Zraick, "Lawyer Defends Queens Imam Arrested in Terror Inquiry," *New York Times,* September 21, 2009.

68 Ronald L. Kuby (Attorney for Defendant Afzali) to the Honorable Frederic Block, letter, "Subject: United States v. Afzali, 09-716 (FB)," December 11, 2009.

69 Sulzberger, "Imam and Informant Tells Why He Lied."

70 Kuby to Block.

71 *U.S. v. Najibullah Zazi,* District Court, District of Colorado, Affidavit in Support of Complaint and Arrest Warrant.

72 Kuby to Block.

73 Ibid.

74 Cummings interview, September 2, 2011.

75 *U.S. v. Najibullah Zazi*, District Court, District of Colorado, Affidavit in Support of Complaint and Arrest Warrant.

76 *U.S. v. Ahmad Wais Afzali*, District Court, Eastern District of New York, Complaint & Affidavit in Support of Arrest Warrant.

77 *U.S. v. Najibullah Zazi*, District Court, District of Colorado, Affidavit in Support of Complaint and Arrest Warrant.

78 *U.S. v. Ahmad Wais Afzali*, District Court, Eastern District of New York, Complaint & Affidavit in Support of Arrest Warrant.

79 *U.S. v. Najibullah Zazi*, District Court, District of Colorado, Affidavit in Support of Complaint and Arrest Warrant.

80 Ibid.

81 Ibid.

82 Kuby to Block.

83 Ibid.

84 Mudd interview, August 8, 2011.

85 *U.S. v. Najibullah Zazi*, District Court, District of Colorado, Affidavit in Support of Complaint and Arrest Warrant.

86 *U.S. v. Najibullah Zazi*, District Court, Eastern District of New York, Memorandum of Law in Support of the Government's Motion for a Permanent Order of Detention.

87 Ibid.

88 Ibid.

89 *U.S. v. Najibullah Zazi*, District Court, District of Colorado, Affidavit in Support of Complaint and Arrest Warrant.

90 U.S. Department of Justice, *Three Arrested in Ongoing Terror Investigation* (Washington, D.C., September 20, 2009).

91 *U.S. v. Mohammed Wali Zazi*, District Court, Eastern District of New York, Testimony of Amanullah Zazi.

92 *U.S. v. Ferid Imam, et al.*, Superseding Indictment.

93 Philip Mudd, "Evaluating the Al-Qa'ida Threat to the U.S. Homeland," *CTC Sentinel* 3, no. 8 (August 2010): 2.

94 Ibid.

95 Zarein Ahmedzay, Statement before the United States District Court.

96 Akam et al., "From Smiling Coffee Vendor to Terror Suspect."

CHAPTER 14: THE RISE OF YEMEN

1 For references to the "I-95 special" snowstorm, see Carol Morello and Ashley Halsey III, "Massive Storm Sets December Record, Cripples Transit," *Washington Post*, December 20, 2009.

2 Ronald Kessler, *The Secrets of the FBI* (New York: Crown, 2011), pp. 1–4, 240.

3 Detective Tommy Hudson, Officer's Report, Arrest of Abdulhakim Mujahid Muhammad, June 1, 2009; Federal Bureau of Investigation, *Arrest of Abdulhakim Mujahid Muhammed* (Little Rock, Ark., June 2, 2009).

4 Anwar al-Awlaki, "Nidal Hassan Did the Right Thing," November 9, 2009.

5 White House, *Summary of the White House Review of the December 29, 2009, Attempted Terrorist Attack* (Washington, D.C., January 2010).

6 See, for example, Bruce Riedel and Bilal Y. Saab, "Al Qaeda's Third Front: Saudi Arabia," *Washington Quarterly* 31, no. 2 (Spring 1998): 33–46.

7 Video by Al Malahim Media Foundation, "Al Qa'ida in the Arabian Peninsula," January 2009.

8 Statement of James R. Clapper, Director of National Intelligence, in Support of Formal Claim of State Secrets Privilege, Response to *Nasser al-Awlaki v. Barack H. Obama, et al.*, Case 1:10-cv-01469-JDB, Document 15-2, August 25, 2010.

9 Senior U.S. government official, interview with author, June 25, 2011.

10 New York Police Department, *Special Analysis: Anwar al-Awlaki* (New York: Counterterrorism Bureau, December 2009).

11 Anwar al-Awlaki, "44 Ways to Support Jihad," February 2009.

12 Qur'an, Battle Gains (Al-Anfal): 8:65.

13 "Letter from the editor," *Inspire*, no. 1431 (Summer 2010): 2.

14 "Hear the World: A Collection of Quotes from Friend and Foe," ibid., p. 4.

15 Anwar al-Awlaki, "May Our Souls Be Sacrificed for You!" ibid., p. 27.

16 Awlaki, "44 Ways to Support Jihad."

17 E-mail from Victoria Grand, YouTube spokesman, to author, November 4, 2010.

18 Statement of James R. Clapper.

19 U.S. Department of Justice, *Texas Man Indicted for Attempting to Provide Material Support to al Qaeda in the Arabian Peninsula* (Washington, D.C., June 3, 2010); *United States of America v. Barry Walter Bujol, Jr.*, United States District Court, Southern District of Texas, Houston Division, Case 4:10-cr-00368, Document 5, Indictment, Filed on June 3, 2010.

20 *United States of America v. Paul Gene Rockwood, Jr.*, United States District Court, District of Alaska, Case 3:10-cr-00061-RRB, Document 4, July 21, 2010.

21 U.S. Senate Committee on Homeland Security and Governmental Affairs, *A Ticking Time Bomb: Counterterrorism Lessons from the U.S. Government's Failure to Prevent the Fort Hood Attack* (Washington, D.C., February 2011).

22 *United States of America v. Zachary Adam Chesser*, United States District Court, Eastern District of Virginia, Alexandria Division, Position of the United States with Respect to Sentencing Factors, Case 1:10-cr-00395-LO, Document 46, February 18, 2011.

23 *US. v. Zachary Adam Chesser*, Affidavit, July 21, 2010.

24 *United States of America v. Farooque Ahmed*, United States District Court, Eastern District of Virginia, Search and Seizure Warrant, October 26, 2010.

25 Philip Mudd, interview with author, August 8, 2011.

26 Hearing on *A Ticking Time Bomb: Counterterrorism Lessons From the U.S. Government's Failure to Prevent the Fort Hood Attack*, February 15, 2011, Before the Committee on Homeland Security and Governmental Affairs, 112th Congress (statement of Philip Mudd, senior global adviser, Oxford Analytica).

27 *United States of America v. Umar Farouk Abdulmutallab*, United States District Court, Eastern District of Michigan, Criminal Complaint, December 26, 2009.

28 University College London, *Umar Farouk Abdulmutallab: Report to UCL Council of Independent Inquiry Panel* (London, September 2010).

29 Farouk1986 (Umar Farouk Abdulmutallab), on-line post, Islamic Forum_Personal Announcements_I'm Off, March 25, 2005, 9:36 p.m.

30 Umar Farouk Abdulmutallab, Autobiography (on-line), 2007.

31 University College London, *Umar Farouk Abdulmutallab*.

32 Farouk1986 (Umar Farouk Abdulmutallab), on-line post, Islamic Forum_Coun selling Room_Problems In A Weak Family, February 19, 2005, 8:56 p.m.

33 Farouk1986 (Umar Farouk Abdulmutallab), on-line post, Islamic Forum_Polling Station_How Many Hours of Sleep Do, February 13, 2005, 12:22 p.m.

34 Farouk1986 (Umar Farouk Abdulmutallab), on-line post, Islamic Forum_Coun selling Room_I Think I Feel Lonely, January 28, 2005, 9:57 p.m.

35 D-ZiNeR, on-line post, Islamic Forum_Counselling Room_I Think I Feel Lonely, January 28, 2005, 11:22 p.m.

36 Batoota, on-line post, Islamic Forum_Counselling Room_I Think I Feel Lonely, February 8, 2005, 4:31 p.m.

37 Farouk1986 (Umar Farouk Abdulmutallab), on-line post, Islamic Forum_Coun selling Room_I Think I Feel Lonely, February 8, 2005, 4:47 p.m.

38 University College London, *Umar Farouk Abdulmutallab*.

39 Farouk1986 (Umar Farouk Abdulmutallab), on-line post, Islamic Forum_General Chat_Ball/prom, May 7, 2005, 12:00 p.m.

40 Farouk1986 (Umar Farouk Abdulmutallab), on-line post, Islamic Forum_UK_ War On Terror Week in Ucl, January 26, 2007, 4:28 p.m.

41 University College London, *Umar Farouk Abdulmutallab*.

42 Abdulmutallab, Autobiography.

43 Farouk1986 (Umar Farouk Abdulmutallab), on-line post, Islamic Forum_Per sonal Announcements_Want To Know Where I've Been? June 16, 2005, 6:29 p.m.; Farouk1986 (Umar Farouk Abdulmutallab), on-line post, Islamic Forum_Personal Announcements_Want To Know Where I've Been? June 23, 2005, 8:51 p.m.

44 Farouk1986 (Umar Farouk Abdulmutallab), on-line post, Islamic Forum_Personal Announcements_Want To Know Where I've Been? June 23, 2005, 8:51 p.m.

45 Sayyid Qutb, *Milestones*, repr. ed. (New Delhi: Islamic Book Service, 2007).

46 Anwar al-Awlaki, "Battle for the Hearts and Minds," undated; Awlaki, "Lessons from the Companions Living as a Minority," undated; Awlaki, "The Dust Will Never Settle Down," undated.

47 University College London, *Umar Farouk Abdulmutallab*.

48 *U.S. v. Umar Farouk Abdulmutallab*, District Court, Eastern District of Michigan, Southern Division, No. 10-CR-20005, Jury Trial, Vol. 5, October 12, 2011.

49 U.S. government official, interview with author, June 27, 2011.

50 United States Department of Treasury, *United States Designates bin Laden Loyalist*, JS-1190 (Washington, D.C., February 24, 2004).

51 U.S. government official, interview with author, July 5, 2011.

52 *U.S. v. Umar Farouk Abdulmutallab*, Jury Trial, Vol. 4, October 11, 2011.

53 U.S. government official, interview with author, June 27, 2011.

54 See, for example, "Umar Farouk Abdulmutallab Comments," training video of Abdulmutallab, Al Malahim Media Foundation (al Qa'ida in the Arabian Peninsula), 2010.

55 University College London, *Umar Farouk Abdulmutallab*.

56 U.S. government official interview, June 27, 2011.

57 Ibid.

58 "Umar Farouk Abdulmutallab Comments."

59 U.S. government official interview, June 27, 2011.

60 *U.S. v. Umar Farouk Abdulmutallab*, Criminal Complaint.

61 Transportation Security Administration, *3-1-1 for Carry-Ons Brochure* (Washington, D.C., undated).

62 U.S. Senate Select Committee on Intelligence, *Unclassified Executive Summary of the Committee Report on the Attempted Terrorist Attack on Northwest Airlines Flight 253* (Washington, D.C., May 18, 2010).

63 Wayne County EMS Report, Patient Name: Umar Farouk Abdulmutallab, December 25, 2009; *U.S. v. Umar Farouk Abdulmutallab*, District Court, Eastern District of Michigan, Criminal Complaint.

64 U.S. Department of Justice, *Umar Farouk Abdulmutallab Indicted for Attempted Bombing of Flight 253 on Christmas Day* (Washington, D.C., January 6, 2010).

65 *U.S. v. Umar Farouk Abdulmutallab*, Jury Trial, Vol. 4.

66 Wayne County Airport Police, Division of Airports, Summary of Statement for Jasper Schuringa, Case #12467, December 2009.

67 *U.S. v. Umar Farouk Abdulmutallab*, Jury Trial, Vol. 4.

68 Wayne County Airport Police, Summary of Statement for Jasper Schuringa.

69 U.S. Department of Justice, *Nigerian National Charged with Attempting to Destroy Norwest Airlines Aircraft* (Washington, D.C., December 26, 2009).

70 *U.S. v. Umar Farouk Abdulmutallab*, Criminal Complaint.

71 Wayne County Airport Police, Summary of Statement for Jasper Schuringa.

72 White House, *Summary of the White House Review of the December 29, 2009, Attempted Terrorist Attack*.

73 Wayne County EMS Report, Patient Name: Umar Farouk Abdulmutallab.

74 Attorney General Eric H. Holder, Jr., to the Honorable Mitchell McConnell, letter, February 3, 2010.

75 Communiqué from Al Qa'ida in the Arabian Peninsula, December 28, 2009.

76 Transcript of interview with Jasper Schuringa, CNN, December 26, 2009.

77 U.S. Senate Select Committee on Intelligence, *Unclassified Executive Summary of the Committee Report on the Attempted Terrorist Attack on Northwest Airlines Flight 253.*

78 Ibid.

79 White House, *Summary of the White House Review of the December 29, 2009 Attempted Terrorist Attack.*

80 U.S. Senate Select Committee on Intelligence, *Unclassified Executive Summary of the Committee Report on the Attempted Terrorist Attack on Northwest Airlines Flight 253;* White House, *Summary of the White House Review of the December 29, 2009 Attempted Terrorist Attack.*

81 U.S. Senate Committee on Homeland Security and Governmental Affairs, *A Ticking Time Bomb.*

82 Ibid., pp. 28, 33.

83 Major Hasan, "The Koranic World View as It Relates to Muslims in the U.S. Military," PowerPoint Briefing, June 2007.

84 Ibid.

85 BBC, ABC News, ARD, *Afghanistan: Where Things Stand* (Kabul, December 2007).

86 U.S. Senate Committee on Homeland Security and Governmental Affairs, *A Ticking Time Bomb.*

87 Ibid.

88 New York Police Department, *Special Analysis: Anwar al-Awlaki* (New York: Counterterrorism Bureau, Terrorism Threat Analysis Group, 2009).

89 Anwar al-Awlaki, interview, Al Jazeera, December 23, 2009.

90 Killeen Police Department, Incident/Investigation Report, TX0140400, August 16, 2009.

91 U.S. Senate Committee on Homeland Security and Governmental Affairs, *A Ticking Time Bomb.*

92 U.S. Department of Defense, *Protecting the Force: Lessons from Fort Hood,* U.S. Independent Review Related to Fort Hood (Washington, D.C., January 2010).

93 Federal Bureau of Investigation, *Investigation Continues into Fort Hood Shooting* (Washington, D.C., November 11, 2009.

94 U.S. Senate Committee on Homeland Security and Governmental Affairs, *A Ticking Time Bomb.*

95 Awlaki interview.

96 U.S. Senate Committee on Homeland Security and Governmental Affairs, *A Ticking Time Bomb.*

97 Ibid.

98 Ibid.

99 Ibid.

100 Ibid.

101 Postings by "Qannas al-Jazira" and "Sayf al-Ma'rakah," Al-Fallujah Islamic Forums website, http://202.71.102/68/~alfaloj/vb; accessed November 2009.

102 Posting by "Jihadiste," Mujahidin Electronic Network, http://majahden.com/vb/; accessed November 2009.

103 Posting by "Abu Harun al-Kuwaiti," Ana al-Muslim website, http://www.muslim .net; accessed November 2009.

104 Statement of James R. Clapper.

105 Anwar al Awlaki, "Nidal Hassan Did the Right Thing," November 9, 2009.

106 Kessler, *The Secrets of the FBI*, pp. 224–25.

107 Mudd interview, August 8, 2011.

108 Philip Mudd, Statement before the Committee on Homeland Security and Governmental Affairs, February 15, 2011.

109 U.S. Senate Committee on Homeland Security and Governmental Affairs, *A Ticking Time Bomb*, p. 7.

110 Central Intelligence Agency, *The World Factbook* (Washington, D.C., 2010).

111 RAHIMI, on-line post, Islamic Forum_General Chat_Terrorist Umar Farouk Abdulmutallab Has A Gawaher Account! December 30, 2009, 12:09 a.m.

112 Dot, on-line post, Islamic Forum_General Chat_Terrorist Umar Farouk Abdulmutallab Has A Gawaher Account! December 30, 2009, 1:08 a.m.

CHAPTER 15: A DIFFERENT BREED

1 Art Cummings, interview with author, September 2, 2011.

2 Philip Mudd, "Evaluating the Al-Qa'ida Threat to the U.S. Homeland," *CTC Sentinel* 3, no. 8 (August 2010): 2.

3 *United States of America v. Tahawwur Hussain Rana*, United States District Court, Northern District of Illinois, Eastern Division, Government Exhibit 09/11/09 SM/ DH, David Headley (ranger1david@yahoo.com) to Tahawwur Rana (tahawwur @yahoo.com), e-mail, "Subject: Copenhagen," January 20, 2009.

4 "Full Transcript of David Headley's Uncle's Interview," *NDTV*, May 3, 2010.

5 *U.S. v. Tahawwur Hussain Rana*, Government Exhibit 09/11/09 SM/DH, Sajid Mir (rare.layman@gmail.com) to David Headley (gulati22@hotmail.com), e-mail, "Subject: Re: ???," July 3, 2009 All e-mail communications between Headley and Mir cited below have the same subject line and are from this source.

6 David Headley (gulati22@hotmail.com) to Sajid Mir (rare.layman@gmail.com), e-mail, July 8, 2009.

7 Ibid.

8 Sajid Mir (rare.layman@gmail.com) to David Headley (gulati22@hotmail.com), e-mail, July 8, 2009.

9 David Headley (gulati22@hotmail.com) to Sajid Mir (rare.layman@gmail.com), e-mail, July 9, 2009.

10 Sajid Mir (rare.layman@gmail.com) to David Headley (gulati22@hotmail.com), e-mail, July 9, 2009.

11 David Headley (gulati22@hotmail.com) to Sajid Mir (rare.layman@gmail.com), e-mail, July 10, 2009.

12 Sajid Mir (rare.layman@gmail.com) to David Headley (gulati22@hotmail.com), e-mail, July 10, 2009.

13 David Headley (gulati22@hotmail.com) to Sajid Mir (rare.layman@gmail.com), e-mail, July 18, 2009.

14 Sajid Mir (rare.layman@gmail.com) to David Headley (gulati22@hotmail.com), e-mail, July 18, 2009.

15 David Headley (gulati22@hotmail.com) to Sajid Mir (rare.layman@gmail.com), e-mail, July 19, 2009.

16 *United States of America v. David C. Headley*, United States District Court, Northern District of Illinois, Eastern Division, Criminal Complaint, AO 91 (REV .5/85), October 2009.

17 *U.S. v. Tahawwur Hussain Rana*, Testimony of David Coleman Headley, Docket No. 09 CR 830, Vol. 1-A, May 23, 2011.

18 Ibid., Vol. 3-B, May 25, 2011.

19 Ibid., Vol. 5-A, May 31, 2011.

20 Ibid., Vol. 1-A.

21 "Full Transcript of David Headley's Uncle's Interview."

22 *U.S. v. Tahawwur Hussain Rana*, Cross-Examination of David Coleman Headley, Vol. 3-B, May 25, 2011.

23 Verbatim Transcript of Combatant Status Review Tribunal Hearing for ISN 10016, Zayn al Abidin Muhammad Husayn [Abu Zubaydah], March 19, 2007.

24 *U.S. v. Tahawwur Hussain Rana*, Testimony of Headley, Vol. 1-A.

25 "Full Transcript of David Headley's Uncle's Interview."

26 *U.S. v. Tahawwur Hussain Rana*, Cross-Examination of Headley, Vol. 3-B.

27 Ibid., Government's Santiago Proffer, April 11, 2011.

28 Ibid., Testimony of Headley, Vol. 1-A.

29 Ibid.

30 First Judicial District of Pennsylvania, Court of Common Pleas of Philadelphia County, Trial Division—Civil, Decree for Change of Name, Daood Gilani to David Coleman Headley, February 15, 2006.

31 *U.S. v. Tahawwur Hussain Rana*, Cross-Examination of Headley, Vol. 3-B.

32 Ibid., Testimony of Headley, Vol. 1-B, May 23, 2011.

33 Ibid., Cross-Examination of Headley, Vol. 3-B, May 25, 2011.

34 Raymond J. Sanders, Attorney-at-Law, Immigrant Law Center, to the Consulate General of India, 455 North Cityfront Plaza Drive, #850, Chicago, IL 60611, letter, "Re: Establishing a Branch Office in Mumbai, India," June 29, 2006. Government Exhibit DCH2.

35 *U.S. v. Tahawwur Hussain Rana*, Government's Santiago Proffer.

36 Ibid., Testimony of Headley, Vol. 1-B, May 23, 2011.

37 Ibid., Government's Santiago Proffer.

38 Ibid., Testimony of Headley, Vol. 1-B.

39 Ibid., Government's Santiago Proffer.

40 Ibid. Testimony of Headley, Vol. 1-B.

41 Ibid.

42 Ibid., Government's Santiago Proffer.

43 Ibid., Government Exhibit 04/23/08 DH/MI, David Headley (ranger1dave@ yahoo.com) to Major Iqbal (chaudherykhan@yahoo.com), e-mail, "Subject: Re: hi," April 23, 2008.

44 Ibid. Headley pasted four websites into his e-mail: www.4hiddenspycameras .com/wir24colpenc.html; www.spygadgets.com/merchant2/merchant.mvc?Screen =PROD&Product_Code=LSFX&Category_Code=;www.spygearco.com/PI-Spy CamStick-PE.htm#SpyCamStickSampleVideo; gizmodo.com/383172/yoto-t-i+ pen-spy-camera-has-built+in-memory-for-convenient-office-stakeouts.

45 Ibid., Testimony of Headley, Vol. 2-A, May 24, 2011.

46 Ibid.

47 Ibid., Government's Santiago Proffer.

48 Ibid., Testimony of Headley, Vol. 2-A.

49 Ibid., Volume 2-B, May 24, 2011.

50 Ibid., Government Exhibit 10/29/08 DH/Abdalians, David Headley (daoodgi lani@yahoo.com) to abdalians7479@yahoogroups.com, e-mail, "Subject: Re: [abdalians7479] The Protocols of Zion & Irreverent Fun," October 29, 2008.

51 Ibid., Testimony of Headley, Vol. 2-A.

52 *United States of America v. Usama bin Laden, et al.*, United States District Court, Southern District of New York, S(7) 98 Cr. 1023, February 9, 2001; Michael Scheuer, "Al-Qaeda's New Leader in Afghanistan: A Profile of Abu al-Yazid," *Terrorism Focus* 4, no. 21 (July 3, 2007).

53 *U.S. v. David C. Headley*, Criminal Complaint.

54 *U.S. v. Tahawwur Hussain Rana*, Government Exhibit 12/27/08 DH/ARS, David Headley (impervious2pain@yahoo.com) to Pasha (rawsal@hotmail.com), e-mail, "Subject: RE: pasha," December 24, 2008.

55 Ibid., Testimony of Headley, Vol. 2-B.

56 Pasha (rawsa1@hotmail.com) to David Headley (impervious2pain@yahoo.com), e-mail, "Subject: RE: pasha," December 25, 2008. Government Exhibit 12/27/08 DH/ARS.

57 Navid Masood Hashmi, "Ilyas Kashmiri Killed for Third Time?" *Ausaf* (Islamabad), June 9, 2011.

58 *United States v. Ilyas Kashmiri, et al.*, United States District Court, Northern District of Illinois, Eastern Division, No. 09 CR 830, Second Superseding Indictment, July 2010.

59 *U.S. v. Tahawwur Hussain Rana*, Testimony of Headley, Vol. 3-A.

60 Ibid., Government Exhibit 12/27/08 DH/ARS, Pasha (rawsa1@hotmail.com) to David Headley (impervious2pain@yahoo.com), e-mail, "Subject: RE: pasha," December 25, 2008.

61 Ibid., Government Exhibit 12/27/08 DH/ARS, David Headley (impervious 2pain@yahoo.com) to Pasha (rawsa1@hotmail.com), e-mail, "Subject: RE: Kullu Nafsin zaiqatul Mawt," December 27, 2008.

62 Ibid., Government Exhibit 12/28/08 ARS/DH, Pasha (rawsa1@hotmail.com) to David Headley (impervious2pain@yahoo.com), e-mail, "Subject: RE: Kullu Nafsin zaiqatul Mawt," December 28, 2008.

63 Ibid., Government Exhibit 09/11/09 SM/DH, Sajid Mir (rare.layman@gmail .com) to David Headley (gulati22@hotmail.com), e-mail, "Subject: Re: ???," August 11, 2009.

64 Ibid., Testimony of Headley, Vol. 2-B.

65 *U.S. v. David C. Headley*, Criminal Complaint.

66 *U.S. v. Tahawwur Hussain Rana*, Government Exhibit 01/19/09C DH/TR, David Headley (ranger1david@yahoo.com) to Tahawwur Rana (tahawwur@yahoo.com), e-mail, "Subject: Copenhagen, January 19, 2009."

67 *U.S. v. David C. Headley*, Criminal Complaint.

68 Ibid.

69 *U.S. v. Tahawwur Hussain Rana*, Testimony of Headley, Vol. 2-B.

70 *U.S. v. David C. Headley*, Criminal Complaint.

71 *U.S. v. Tahawwur Hussain Rana*, Testimony of Headley, Vol. 2-B.

72 Ibid., Vol. 5-A, May 31, 2011.

73 Headley had already been under the impression that the plot was postponed. See *U.S. v. Tahawwur Hussain Rana*, Government Exhibit 09/11/09 SM/DH, David Headley (gulati22@hotmail.com) to Sajid Mir (rare.layman@gmail.com), e-mail, "Subject: ???," July 8, 2009.

74 *U.S. v. Tahawwur Hussain Rana*, Testimony of Headley, Vol. 2-B.

75 Ibid.

76 Ibid., Vol. 3-A.

77 Ibid.

78 Ibid.

79 Ibid.

80 Ibid., Vol. 3-B.

81 *U.S. v. David C. Headley*, Criminal Complaint.

82 *U.S. v. Tahawwur Hussain Rana*, Testimony of Headley, Vol. 3-A.

83 Ibid., Vol. 5-A.

84 *U.S. v. David C. Headley*, Criminal Complaint.

85 "Full Transcript of David Headley's Uncle's Interview."

CHAPTER 16: A NEAR MISS

1 James Traub, *The Devil's Playground: A Century of Pleasure and Profit in Times Square* (New York: Random House, 2004), p. xiv.

2 *United States of America v. Faisal Shahzad*, United States District Court, Southern District of New York, Government's Memorandum in Connection with the Sentencing of Faisal Shahzad, Document 13, Case 1:10-cr-00541-MGC, September 29, 2010.

3 Ibid., Complaint, May 4, 2010.

4 Ibid., Guilty Plea, 10-CR-541 (MGC), June 21, 2010.

5 Ibid.

6 "Lance Orton Speaks About Alerting Police to Times Square Car Bomb," NBC News Transcripts, May 3, 2010.

7 Michael J. Feeney, Oren Yaniv, and Daniel Edward Rosen, "NYPD Officer Wayne Rhatigan a Dad Just Hours After Playing Hero During Times Square Bomb Crisis," New York Daily News, May 2, 2010.

8 Mayor Michael R. Bloomberg, Update to New Yorkers on Arrest and Investigation of Incident in Times Square (New York: City of New York, May 4, 2010); U.S. v. Faisal Shahzad, Complaint.

9 On a description of Baitullah Mehsud see, for example, U.S. Department of Justice, Wanted: Baitullah Mehsud (Washington, D.C.: Rewards for Justice, undated).

10 Statement of Waliur Rehman, "On the Subject of the Martyr Death of the Leader Baitullah Mehsud," Tehreek-e Taliban Pakistan, October 2009.

11 Shaykh Mustafa Abu al-Yazid, "Words of Condolences on the Martyrdom of Emir Baitullah Mehsud," As-Sahab Media, September 2009.

12 LTG Ronald L. Burgess, World Wide Threat Assessment (Washington, D.C.: Defense Intelligence Agency, March 10, 2011).

13 Michael E. Leiter, Director of the National Counterterrorism Center, "Understanding the Homeland Threat Landscape—Considerations for the 112th Congress," Hearing before the House Committee on Homeland Security, February 9, 2011; Leiter, "Nine Years after 9/11: Confronting the Terrorist Threat to the Homeland," Hearing before the U.S. Senate Homeland Security and Government Affairs Committee, September 22, 2010.

14 U.S. v. Faisal Shahzad, Guilty Plea.

15 U.S. Department of Justice, Certificate of Eligibility for Non-Immigrant Student Status for Faisal Shahzad, December 1998. The certificate was found at his Bridgeport, Connecticut, house in May 2010.

16 See, for example, Faisal Shahzad's academic transcript, Southeastern University, December 1998; found at his Bridgeport, Connecticut, house in May 2010.

17 Andrea Elliott, Sabrina Tavernise, and Anne Barnard, "For Times Square Suspect, Long Roots of Discontent," New York Times, May 15, 2010.

18 Statement from Michael Spitzer, Provost and Vice President for Academic Affairs, University of Bridgeport, May 4, 2010.

19 U.S. v. Faisal Shahzad, Guilty Plea.

20 On Shaykh Abdallah Ibrahim al-Faisal, see, for example, United States v. Attiqullah Sayed Ahmad, United States District Court, Southern District of California, Criminal Case No. 02cr0693-JM, December 8, 2003.

21 Hearing between Crown and el-Faisal (Appellant), Supreme Court of Judicature, Court of Appeal (Criminal Division), On Appeal from the Central Criminal Court (HHJ Beaumont QC), Royal Courts of Justice, London, Case No. 2003-01860-C2, February 17, 2004.

22 Senior FBI officials, interview with author, July 21, 2011.

23 Elliott, Tavernise, and Barnard, "For Times Square Suspect, Long Roots of Discontent."

24 Philip Mudd, "Evaluating the Al-Qa'ida Threat to the U.S. Homeland," *CTC Sentinel* 3, no. 8 (August 2010): 3.

25 Faisal Shahzad to [redacted]@hotmail.com, e-mail, "Subject: My Beloved and Peaceful Ummah," February 25, 2006.

26 Ibid. Shazad was quoting from Qur'an, Battle Gains (Al-Anfal), 8:39.

27 Huma Mian, May 2010.

28 Shezia, Chazi, and Tashfan to Faisal Shahzad, greeting card, May 1999; found at his Bridgeport, Connecticut, house in May 2010.

29 *Chase Home Finance v. Zhahzad* [sic], *Faisal, et al.*, State of Connecticut, Judicial Branch, Property Foreclosure, AAN-CV09-6001275-7, September 30, 2009; Chase Home Finance v. Zhahzad [sic], Faisal, et al., State of Connecticut, Judicial Branch, Notice of Public Auction, AAN-CV09-6001275-7, July 31, 2010.

30 *U.S. v. Faisal Shahzad*, Guilty Plea.

31 United States Attorney, Southern District of New York, "Faisal Shahzad Sentenced in Manhattan Federal Court to Life in Prison for Attempted Car Bombing in Times Square" (New York: U.S. Attorney's Office, October 5, 2010).

32 *U.S. v. Faisal Shahzad*, Government's Memorandum.

33 Ibid., Guilty Plea.

34 Art Cummings, interview with author, September 2, 2011.

35 *U.S. v. Faisal Shahzad*, Government's Memorandum.

36 Faisal Shahzad to [redacted], e-mail, April 2009.

37 There are some reports that Shahzad stayed in a Super 8 Motel in Milford, Connecticut, before moving into his Bridgeport house. See *U.S. v. Faisal Shahzad*, Guilty Plea.

38 The items are shown in photographs and on video footage taken inside Faisal Shahzad's apartment.

39 Senior FBI official interview, July 25, 2010.

40 *U.S. v. Faisal Shahzad*, Guilty Plea.

41 Ibid.

42 Amanda Raus, "Neighbors Recall Faisal Shahzad as Quiet, Normal," Associated Press, May 5, 2010.

43 *U.S. v. Faisal Shahzad*, Government's Memorandum.

44 Surveillance video of Faisal Shahzad, Phantom Fireworks, March 8, 2010; *U.S. v. Faisal Shahzad*, Complaint.

45 *U.S. v. Faisal Shahzad*, Government's Memorandum.

46 Ibid., Complaint.

47 Ibid., Government's Memorandum.

48 Ibid., Complaint.

49 Ibid., Indictment, June 17, 2010; United States Attorney, *Faisal Shahzad Sentenced in Manhattan Federal Court*; U.S. Department of Justice, *Faisal Shahzad Pleads*

Guilty in Manhattan Federal Court to 10 Federal Crimes Arising from Attempted Car Bombing in Times Square (Washington, D.C., June 21, 2010).

50 *U.S. v. Faisal Shahzad*, Guilty Plea.

51 Ibid.

52 Ibid., Government's Memorandum.

53 Raymond W. Kelly, press conference, Washington, D.C., May 4, 2010.

54 *U.S. v. Faisal Shahzad*, Complaint.

55 Peggy Colas, May 4, 2010.

56 United States Attorney, Southern District of New York, *Manhattan U.S. Attorney Charges Faisal Shahzad with Attempted Car Bombing in Times Square* (New York: U.S. Attorney's Office, May 4, 2010); *U.S. v. Faisal Shahzad*, Complaint. Also see, for example, William K. Rashbaum and Al Baker, "Smoking Car to an Arrest in 53 Hours," *New York Times*, May 4, 2010; Masood Haider, "Pakistan: Many Clues Said Available to Trace Times Square Bomb Plot Suspect," *Dawn* (Pakistan), May 6, 2010.

57 *U.S. v. Faisal Shahzad*, Guilty Plea.

58 Ibid., Complaint.

59 IntelCenter, *New York Times Square Vehicular Bombing* (Alexandria, Va., 2010); *U.S. v. Faisal Shahzad*, Government's Memorandum.

60 FBI Deputy Director John Pistole, *Prepared Remarks During Times Square Press Conference* (Washington, D.C.: Federal Bureau of Investigation, May 4, 2010); U.S. Department of Justice, *Statement of the U.S. Attorney's Office for the Southern District of New York, the Federal Bureau of Investigation, and the New York City Police Department on an Arrest in the Times Square Investigation* (New York, May 4, 2010); *U.S. v. Faisal Shahzad*, Complaint.

61 *U.S. v. Faisal Shahzad*, Government's Memorandum.

62 Statement from Qari Hussein, Tehreek-e Taliban Pakistan, May 2, 2010.

63 Senior FBI officials, interview with author, July 25, 2011.

64 Daniel Byman and Christine Fair, "The Case for Calling Them Nitwits," *Atlantic*, July/August 2010.

65 *U.S. v. Faisal Shahzad*, Government's Memorandum.

66 Ibid., Guilty Plea.

67 Ibid., Sentencing of Faisal Shahzad, Case 1:10-cr-00541-MGC, October 5, 2010.

68 Ibid.

69 Osama bin Laden to Atiyah 'Abd al-Rahman al-Libi, letter, October 17, 2010.

70 Faisal Shahzad to [redacted]@hotmail.com, e-mail, "Subject: My Beloved and Peaceful Ummah," February 25, 2006; Qur'an, He Frowned ('Abasa), 80:34–37.

71 Elliott, Tavernise, and Barnard, "For Times Square Suspect, Long Roots of Discontent."

72 White House, *Statement from Nick Shapiro* (Washington, D.C., June 2009).

73 Cummings interview, September 2, 2011.

CHAPTER 17: WE GOT HIM

1 Senior White House official, interview with author, October 22, 2011.

2 New America Foundation and Terror Free Tomorrow, *Public Opinion in Pakistan's Tribal Regions* (Washington, D.C., September 2010), p. 9.

3 As-Sahab Media, "You Are Held Responsible Only for Thyself—Part One," June 2011.

4 White House official, interview with author, December 3, 2011.

5 Senior U.S. government officials, interview with author, August 2011.

6 Nicholas Schmidle, "Getting Bin Laden," *The New Yorker*, August 8, 2011.

7 Adam Goldman and Matt Apuzzo, "The Man Who Hunted Osama Bin Laden," Associated Press, July 6, 2011.

8 Bob Woodward, "Death of Osama bin Laden: Phone Call Pointed to U.S. Compound—and to 'the Pacer,'" *Washington Post*, May 6, 2011.

9 Haq Nawaz Khan and Karin Brulliard, "Bin Laden's Hideout Better Known as a Tourism, Military Hub," *Washington Post*, May 2, 2011.

10 U.S. government officials, interview with author, September 3, 2011. These officials were involved in combing through the compound shortly after the May 1, 2011, raid.

11 Video footage of Osama bin Laden's compound provided by the U.S. Department of Defense, May 2011. The video was seized during the raid.

12 Jake Tapper, "President Obama to National Security Team: 'It's a Go,'" *ABC News*, May 2, 2011.

13 Senior U.S. government officials, interviews with author, August 1, 2011.

14 Schmidle, "Getting Bin Laden."

15 The 9/11 Commission, *The 9/11 Commission Report: Final Report of the National Commission on Terrorist Attacks Upon the United States* (New York: W. W. Norton, 2004), pp. 108–43.

16 Ibid., p. 112.

17 Ibid., p. 136.

18 Tapper, "President Obama to National Security Team."

19 Ibid.

20 Senior U.S. government officials interviews, August 1, 2011.

21 "Obama Tracked Bin Laden Raid in Real Time," UPI, May 2, 2001.

22 Adrian Brown, "Osama Bin Laden's Death: How It Happened," BBC, June 7, 2011.

23 Sohaib Athar, Twitter posting (@ReallyVirtual), May 1, 2011.

24 For an explanation of the account, see Sohaib Athar, @ReallyVirtual FAQ. As Athar explained, "I am writing this FAQ to save everyone's time (but especially mine), to clarify a few facts and to answer most of the (mostly redundant questions) that I am receiving via email and tweets."

25 Athar, Twitter posting.

26 Schmidle, "Getting Bin Laden."

27 Athar, Twitter posting.

28 "Death of Bin Laden: Live Report," *Sydney Morning Herald*, May 2, 2011.

29 "Osama bin Laden's Death Sets Twitter Record for 'Sustained Rate of Tweets,'" *Los Angeles Times*, May 2, 2011.

30 Schmidle, "Getting Bin Laden."

31 U.S. Department of Defense, *News Transcript on the Osama Bin Laden Raid* (Washington, D.C., May 7, 2011).

32 Jim Garamone, "Bin Laden Buried at Sea," American Forces Press Service, May 2, 2011.

33 Isobel Shaw, *Pakistan Handbook* (Hong Kong: Local Colour, 1990), p. 519.

34 *United States of America v. Daniel Patrick Boyd, et al.*, United States District Court, Eastern District of North Carolina, Superseding Indictment, No. 5:09-CR-216-1-FL, September 24, 2009.

35 Garowe Online, "Senior Al-Shabaab Commander Defects to Government," *Africa News*, December 2, 2009.

CHAPTER 18: PREVENTION

1 Art Cummings, interview with author, September 2, 2011.

2 Philip Mudd, interview with author, August 8, 2011.

3 John Negroponte, interview with author, August 11, 2011.

4 Elisabeth Bumiller, "Panetta Says Defeat of Al Qaeda Is 'Within Reach,'" *New York Times*, July 9, 2011.

5 President Barack Obama, "Remarks by the President on the Way Forward in Afghanistan," Washington D.C., June 22, 2011.

6 Bruce Hoffman, *Inside Terrorism*, rev. ed. (New York: Columbia University Press, 2006), p. 285.

7 *United States of America v. Mohamed Alessa and Carlos E. Almonte*, United States District Court, District of New Jersey, Criminal Complaint, Magistrate No.: 10-8109 (MCA), June 4, 2010; *United States of America v. Zachary Adam Chesser*, United States District Court, Eastern District of Virginia, Alexandria Division, Position of the United States with Respect to Sentencing Factors, Case 1:10-cr-00395-LO, Document 46, February 18, 2011.

8 *United States of America v. Ahmed Ali Omar, et al.*, United States District Court, District of Minnesota, Criminal No. 09-50 (JMR/SRN), July 20, 2010.

9 *United States of America v. Hafiz Muhammad Sher Ali Khan, et al.*, United States District Court, Southern District of Florida, Indictment, Case No.: 11-20331-cr-Jordan, May 12, 2011.

10 *United States of America v. Jubair Ahmad*, United States District Court, Eastern District of Virginia, Alexandria Division, Criminal No.: 1:11 MJ742, September 1, 2011.

11 *United States of America v. Khalid Ali-M Aldawsari*, United States District Court, Northern District of Texas, Criminal Complaint, Case No.: 5:11-MJ-017, February 23, 2011.

12 *United States of America v. Rezwan Ferdaus*, United States District Court, District

of Massachusetts, Document 6, Criminal Action Number: 11-cr-10331-RGS, September 29, 2011.

13 Thomas C. Schelling, *Arms and Influence* (New Haven, Conn.: Yale University Press, 1966).

14 Douglas J. Feith, *War and Decision: Inside the Pentagon at the Dawn of the War on Terror* (New York: HarperCollins, 2008), p. 87.

15 Bruce Hoffman, *Inside Terrorism*, 2nd ed. (New York: Columbia University Press, 2006), p. 169.

16 Quoted in Christopher Andrew, *Defend the Realm: The Authorized History of MI5* (New York: Knopf, 2009), p. 827.

17 As-Sahab Media, "You Are Held Responsible Only for Thyself—Part Two," June 2011.

18 "Egypt Muslim Brothers: Islam Is Not Bin Laden," *Egypt News*, May 2, 2011.

19 Pew Global Attitudes Project, *Osama Bin Laden Largely Discredited Among Muslim Publics in Recent Years* (Washington, D.C.: Pew Research Center, May 2, 2011).

20 William Shakespeare, *Julius Caesar*, Act 4, scene 3, 218–24.

INDEX

Page numbers in *italics* refer to maps and charts.